Welcome to Scotland's Highlands & Islands

The wild landscapes of Scotland's Highlands and islands offer the ultimate escape – one of the last corners of Europe where you can discover genuine solitude.

Lonely Landscapes

Since the 19th century – when the first tourists began to arrive, inspired by the Romantic movement's search for the sublime – the Scottish Highlands have been famed for their wild nature and majestic scenery. Today the region's biggest draw remains its magnificent landscape. At almost every turn is a vista that will stop you in your tracks, from the bluebell woods, gentle hills and warm autumn colours of Loch Lomond and the Trossachs to the primeval grandeur of Coigach and Assynt, where pillared peaks rear above desolate expanses of gnarled and ancient gneiss. Keep your camera close at hand.

Outdoor Adventures

Scotland's mountains, lochs and seaways offer some of the most rewarding outdoor adventures in Europe. As well as classic challenges such as the West Highland Way and the ascent of Ben Nevis, there are wilderness walks through the roadless wilds of Knoydart and Sutherland, and spectacular summits such as An Teallach, Stac Pollaidh and Suilven. Mountain bikers can enjoy a multitude of off-road routes, from easy trails through ancient pine forests to strenuous coast-to-coast rides, while the turbulent tidal waters around the Outer Hebrides, Orkney and Shetland provide the ultimate test of paddling mettle for sea-kayaking enthusiasts.

Legend & Tradition

Legend and tradition run deep in the Highlands. Crumbling forts and monastic cells were once home to Gaelic chieftains and Irish saints; lonely beaches and mountain passes once echoed to the clash of clan battles; and empty glens are still haunted by the ghosts of the Clearances. History is everywhere: in the tumbled stones of abandoned crofts preserved on a hillside like a fossil fragment; in the proud profile of broch and castle silhouetted against a Highland sunset; and in the Gaelic lilt of Hebridean speech and the Nordic twang of Shetland dialect.

A Taste of Scotland

Visitors will soon discover that Scotland's restaurants have shaken off their old reputation for deep-fried food and unsmiling service and can now compete with the best in Europe. A new-found respect for top-quality local produce means that you can feast on fresh seafood mere hours after it was caught, beef and venison that was raised just a few miles away from your table, and vegetables that were grown in your hotel's own organic garden. Top it all off with a dram of single malt whisky – rich, complex and evocative, the true taste of Scotland.

Scotland's
Highlands & Islands

**Orkney &
Shetland**
p229

**Northern Highlands
& Islands**
p173

**Inverness & the
Central Highlands**
p115

**Southern
Highlands &
Islands**
p46

Neil Wilson, Andy Symington

Contents

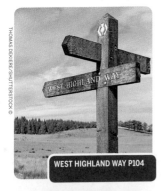

WEST HIGHLAND WAY P104

TRADITIONAL SCOTTISH
DRESS P280

Why I Love Scotland's Highlands & Islands

By Neil Wilson, Writer

It's the weather. Yes, seriously. We get four proper seasons here (sometimes all of them in one day) and that means that you get to enjoy the same landscapes over and over again in a range of different garbs – August hills clad in purple heather, native woodlands gilded with autumn colours, snow-patched winter mountains, and Hebridean machair sprinkled with a confetti of spring wildflowers. And the unpredictability of the weather means that even the wettest day can be suddenly transformed by parting clouds and slanting shafts of golden light. Sheer magic.

For more about our writers, see p320

Above: Tigh-na-sleubhaich (p113), West Highland Way

Scotland's Highlands & Islands

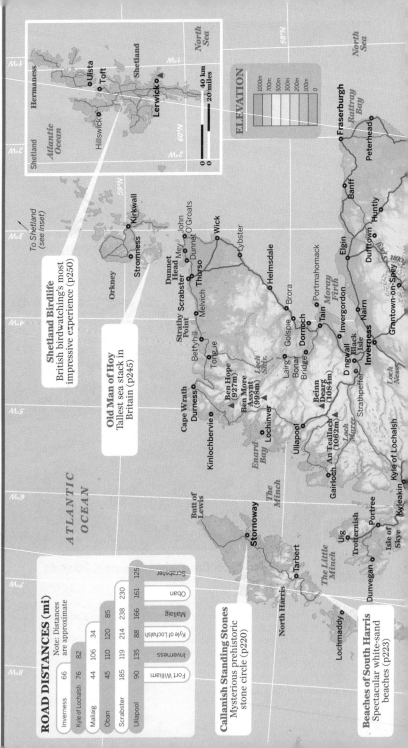

Shetland Birdlife
British birdwatching's most impressive experience (p250)

Old Man of Hoy
Tallest sea stack in Britain (p245)

ELEVATION

1000m
700m
500m
300m
200m
100m
0

ROAD DISTANCES (mi)
Note: Distances are approximate

	Fort William	Inverness	Kyle of Lochalsh	Mallaig	Oban	Scrabster
Inverness	66					
Kyle of Lochalsh	76	82				
Mallaig	44	106	34			
Oban	45	110	120	85		
Scrabster	185	119	214	238	230	
Ullapool	90	135	88	166	161	125

Callanish Standing Stones
Mysterious prehistoric stone circle (p220)

Beaches of South Harris
Spectacular white-sand beaches (p223)

Cairngorms
Playground for outdoor enthusiasts (p135)

Ben Nevis
Climb the highest Munro of them all (p164)

The West Highland Way
The best Highland hiking (p104)

Glen Coe
Dramatic scenery meets deep history (p155)

The Road to the Isles
Stunning scenery and Jacobite history (p165)

Picturesque Iona
Scotland's most sacred island (p98)

Cuillin Hills
Craggy peaks and inaccessible pinnacles (p211)

Scotland's Highlands & Islands'
Top 19

1

Whisky

1 Scotland's national drink – from the Gaelic *uisge bagh*, meaning 'water of life' – has been distilled here for more than 500 years. More than 100 distilleries are still in operation, producing hundreds of varieties of single malt, and learning to distinguish the smoky, peaty whiskies of Islay (p69), say, from the flowery, sherried malts of Speyside has become a hugely popular pastime. Many distilleries offer guided tours, rounded off with a tasting session, and ticking off the local varieties is a great way to explore the whisky-making regions. Lagavulin whisky (p70)

Walking the West Highland Way

2 The best way to appreciate the scale and grandeur of Scotland's landscapes is to walk them. Despite the wind and midges and drizzle, walking here is a pleasure, with numerous short- and long-distance trails, coastal paths and mountains begging to be trekked. Top of the wish list for many hikers is the 96-mile West Highland Way (p104) from Milngavie (near Glasgow) to Fort William, a challenging, weeklong walk through some of the country's finest scenery, finishing in the shadow of its highest peak, Ben Nevis.

SERGEBERTASIUSPHOTOGRAPHY/SHUTTERSTOCK ©

2

JURAJ KAMENICKY/SHUTTERSTOCK ©

Castles

3 Whether you're looking for grim, desolate stone fortresses looming in the mist, picture-postcard castles such as Eilean Donan (pictured; p203), or luxurious palaces built in expansive grounds by lairds more concerned with status and show than with military might, the Highlands sport the full range of castles, reflecting the region's turbulent history. Most castles have a story or 10 to tell of plots, intrigues, imprisonments and treachery, and a worryingly high percentage have a phantom rumoured to stalk their parapets.

Seafood

4 One of the great pleasures of a visit to Scotland is the opportunity to indulge in the rich harvest of the sea. The cold, clear waters around the Scottish coast provide some of the most sought-after seafood in Europe, with much of it being whisked straight from the quayside to waiting restaurant tables from London to Lisbon. Fortunately there are plenty of places to sample this bounty right here, with Oban (p86) topping the list of towns with more than their fair share of seafood restaurants. Oban Seafood Hut (p89)

Cuillin Hills

5 In a country famous for its stunning scenery, the Cuillin Hills (p211) take top prize. This range of craggy peaks is near-alpine in character, with knife-edge ridges, jagged pinnacles, scree-filled gullies and acres of naked rock. While they're a paradise for experienced mountaineers, the higher reaches of the Cuillin are off limits to the majority of walkers. Not to worry – there are easier trails through the glens and into the corries, where walkers can soak up the views and share the landscape with red deer and golden eagles.

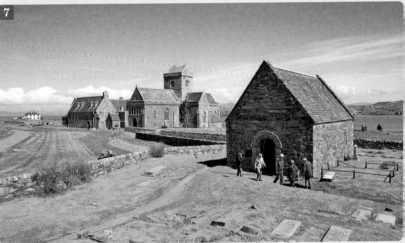

Whale Watching

6 Scotland is one of the best places in Europe for seeing marine wildlife (p37). In high season many west-coast cruise operators, notably on the Isle of Mull, can almost guarantee sightings of Minke whales (pictured) and porpoises, and the Moray Firth is famous for its resident population of bottlenose dolphins. Basking sharks – at up to 12m, the biggest fish to be found in British waters – are also commonly seen. And it's not just the wildlife that makes a boat trip a must – don't miss the chance to visit the Corryvreckan Whirlpool.

Picturesque Iona

7 Legend has it that when St Columba left Ireland in 563 to found a missionary outpost on Scotland's west coast, he kept sailing until he found a spot where he could no longer see his homeland on the southern horizon. That place was the little jewel of Iona (p98) – Scotland's most sacred island, and one of its most beautiful, with lush pastures bordered by granite rocks, white shell-sand beaches and shallow, turquoise waters. The Iona Community continues the island's spiritual calling in an abbey on the site of Columba's first chapel. Iona Abbey (p99)

Glen Coe

8 Scotland's most famous glen (p155) combines those two essential qualities of the Highland landscape – dramatic scenery and deep history. The peacefulness and beauty of this valley today belie the fact that it was the scene of a ruthless 17th-century massacre that saw the local MacDonalds murdered by soldiers of the Campbell clan. Some of the glen's finest walks – to the Lost Valley, for example – follow the routes used by clansmen and women trying to flee their attackers, where many perished in the snow.

Callanish Standing Stones

9 Few sights conjure up the mystery and romance of the Highlands and islands like the prehistoric monuments that punctuate the landscape from Orkney to the Western Isles. The 5000-year-old Callanish stones (p220) on the Isle of Lewis – contemporaries of the pyramids of Egypt – are the archetypal stone circle, with beautifully weathered slabs of banded gneiss arranged as if in worship around a central monolith. To experience the stones at dawn before the crowds arrive is to step back in time, and sense something deep and truly ancient.

The Road to the Isles

10 Immortalised in song and story, the Road to the Isles (p165) is the route from Fort William to Mallaig – jumping-off point for the Isle of Skye, the Small Isles and beyond to the Outer Hebrides. Steeped in Jacobite history – Bonnie Prince Charlie passed this way several times around 1745 – the route (followed by both road and railway) passes through some of Scotland's finest scenery, with views over dazzling white-sand beaches and emerald waters to a horizon pricked by the sharp peaks of Eigg, Rum and Skye.

Island Hopping

11 Much of the unique character of western and northern Scotland is down to the expansive vistas of sea and islands – there are around 790 islands off Scotland's coast, of which 94 are inhabited. A network of ferry services links these islands to the mainland and each other, and buying an Island Rover ticket provides a fascinating way to explore. It's possible to hop all the way from Arran or Bute to the Outer Hebrides (p217), touching the mainland only at Kintyre and Oban (pictured; p86).

Climbing Ben Nevis

12 The allure of Britain's highest peak is strong – around 100,000 people a year set off up the summit trail, though not all will make it to the top. Nevertheless, the highest Munro of them all is within the ability of anyone who's reasonably fit – treat Ben Nevis (pictured; p164) with respect and your reward (weather permitting) will be a truly magnificent view and a great sense of achievement. Real walking enthusiasts can warm up by hiking the 96-mile West Highland Way first.

The Old Man of Hoy

13 From the Mull of Kintyre to Duncansby Head, the patient craftsmanship of the sea has whittled the Scottish coastline into a profusion of sea stacks, chasms and natural arches. Many stacks are nicknamed 'old man', but none compare to the grandest old man of them all. At 137m tall (a third taller than London's Big Ben), the Old Man of Hoy (p245) is the tallest sea stack in Britain. Hike from Rackwick Bay for a spectacular view of the stack and, if you're lucky, rock climbers in action.

Shetland Birdlife

14 Sparsely populated, and with large areas of wild land, Scotland is an important sanctuary for all sorts of wildlife. Amazing birdwatching is on offer throughout the country, but the seabird cities of the Shetland Islands (p262) take first prize for spectacle. From their first arrival on the sea cliffs in late spring to the raucous feeding frenzies of high summer, the vast colonies of gannets (pictured), guillemots, puffins and kittiwakes at Hermaness, Noss and Sumburgh Head provide one of British birdwatching's most impressive experiences.

13

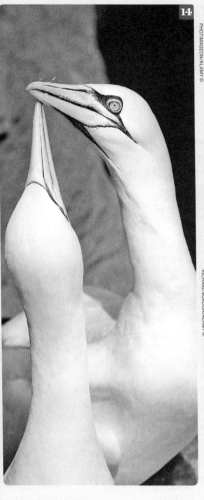

Sea Kayaking

15 The convoluted coastline and countless islands of Scotland's western seaboard are widely recognised as one of the finest sea-kayaking areas in the world (p40). Paddling your own canoe allows you to explore remote islands, inlets, creeks and beaches that are inaccessible on foot, and also provides an opportunity to get close to wildlife such as seals, otters, dolphins and seabirds. There are dozens of outfits offering guided kayaking tours for beginners, from a half day to a week, either camping on wild beaches or staying in comfortable B&Bs. Kylerhea (p207)

Beaches of South Harris

16 Scotland's Highlands and islands are never going to be famous for bucket-and-spade seaside holidays, but when it comes to scenically spectacular beaches, the region is up there with the best. And the vast stretches of blinding white shell-sand that line the west coast of South Harris (p223) in the Outer Hebrides are among the most beautiful in Europe – grass-covered dunes sprinkled with pink and yellow wildflowers, clear sparkling waters that range in hue from turquoise to emerald, and sunset views that take your breath away. Traigh Mor (p228)

North Coast 500

17 The Highlands abound in breathtaking views, but the far northwest truly stands apart. The North Coast 500 (p189) scenic drive, starting and finishing in Inverness, offers stunningly photogenic landscapes at every turn: mountain and sea are intimately entwined in a gloriously dramatic embrace, from the vertiginous sea cliffs of remote Cape Wrath to the distinctive pillared peaks and lonely lochs of Assynt, and the haunting, desolate beauty of Torridon. All of these, and the warm Scottish welcome found in classic Highland inns, make this an unforgettable corner of the country.

The Cairngorms

18 In the bare, boulder-strewn, 4000ft-high plateau of the Cairngorms (p135), Scotland harbours its own little haven of sub-Arctic tundra. The haunt of ptarmigan, dotterel and snow bunting, red deer (pictured), mountain hare and reindeer, these austerely beautiful granite hills provide a year-round playground for wildlife watchers and adventure sports enthusiasts. In summer you can enjoy hiking and mountain biking on trails that wind through the ancient Caledonian pine forests, while in winter there's skiing, snowboarding and full-on mountaineering on the snowy summits and icebound crags.

Ceilidhs

19 Evenings of traditional Scottish dancing (*ceilidh*, pronounced *kay*-li), with music provided by fiddles, *bodhrans* (handheld drums) and other instruments, have evolved into something of a tourist spectacle, but there are still plenty of places in the Highlands and islands, including Inverness, Ullapool and Knoydart (p169), where they're staged for locals rather than tourists – and visitors are always welcome. Don't worry if you don't know the steps; there's usually a 'caller' to lead the dancers, and no one cares if you get it wrong as long as you're enjoying yourself!

Need to Know

For more information, see Survival Guide (p297)

Currency
pounds sterling (£)

Languages
English, Gaelic, Lallans

Visas
Generally not needed for stays of up to six months. Not a member of the Schengen Zone.

Money
ATMs widely available. Credit cards widely accepted.

Mobile Phones
Uses the GSM 900/1800 network. Local SIM cards can be used in European and Australian phones. Patchy coverage in remote areas.

Time
UTC/GMT plus one hour during summer daylight saving time; UTC/GMT the rest of the year.

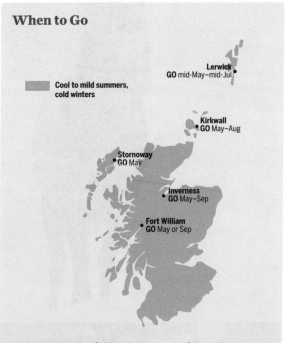

When to Go

Cool to mild summers, cold winters

Lerwick
GO mid-May–mid-Jul

Kirkwall
GO May–Aug

Stornoway
GO May

Inverness
GO May–Sep

Fort William
GO May or Sep

High Season
(Jul & Aug)

➡ Accommodation prices are 10% to 20% higher (book in advance if possible).

➡ Warmest time of the year, but often wet, too.

➡ Midges at their worst.

Shoulder
(May, Jun & Sep)

➡ Wildflowers and rhododendrons bloom in May and June.

➡ Best chance for dry weather; fewer midges.

➡ June evenings have daylight till 11pm.

Low Season
(Oct–Apr)

➡ Rural attractions and accommodation are often closed.

➡ Snow on hills from November to March.

➡ In December it gets dark at 4pm.

➡ Can be very cold and wet from November to March.

Useful Websites

Lonely Planet (www.lonely planet.com/scotland) Destination information, hotel bookings, traveller forum and more.

VisitScotland (www.visit scotland.com) Official tourism site; booking services.

Internet Guide to Scotland (www.scotland-info.co.uk) Best online tourist guide to Scotland.

Traveline (www.traveline scotland.com) Public transport timetables.

WalkHighlands (www.walk highlands.co.uk) Detailed walking guide with maps.

Important Numbers

Country code	☑44
International access code	☑00
Ambulance	☑112 or ☑999
Fire	☑112 or ☑999
Police	☑112 or ☑999

Exchange Rates

Australia	A$1	£0.57
Canada	C$1	£0.58
Euro	€1	£0.88
Japan	¥100	£0.68
NZ	NZ$1	£0.52
US	US$1	£0.75

For current exchange rates, see www.xe.com.

Daily Costs

Budget: Less than £40

➡ Dorm bed: £16–25
➡ Wild camping: free
➡ Food from supermarket: £5–10

Midrange: £40–130

➡ Double room at midrange B&B: £65–100
➡ Bar lunch: £12
➡ Dinner at midrange restaurant: £30
➡ Car hire: £38
➡ Petrol costs (per mile): around 15p

Top End: More than £130

➡ Double room at high-end hotel: £130–250
➡ Dinner at high-end restaurant: £40–60
➡ Flights to islands (each way): £65–130

Opening Hours

Hours may vary throughout the year; in rural areas many places have shorter hours from around October to April. In the Highlands and islands, Sunday opening is restricted. See Directory (p303) for more information.

Arriving in Scotland

Edinburgh Airport Bus 100 runs from the airport to Waverley Bridge (one way/return £4.50/7.50, 30 minutes), outside the main train station, via Haymarket and the West End every 10 minutes from 4am to midnight (every 30 minutes through the night). Trams run to the city centre (one way/return £6/8.50, 33 minutes, every six to eight minutes 6am to midnight). Taxis to the city centre cost around £20 and take about 25 minutes.

Glasgow Airport Bus 500 (24-hour service) runs every 10 or 15 minutes (half-hourly or hourly late at night) from the airport to Buchanan bus station via Central and Queen Street train stations (single/return £8/12, 25 minutes). You can include a day ticket on the bus network for £12 total or a four-day ticket for £18. Taxis are around £25.

Getting Around

Transport in Scotland can be expensive compared to the rest of Europe; bus and rail services are sparse in the more remote parts of the country. For timetables, check out Traveline Scotland (www.travelinescotland.com).

Car Useful for travelling at your own pace, or for visiting regions with minimal public transport. Cars can be hired in every town or city. Drive on the left.

Train Relatively expensive, with extensive coverage and frequent departures in central Scotland, but only a few lines in the northern Highlands and southern Scotland.

Bus Cheaper and slower than trains, but useful for more remote regions that aren't serviced by trains.

Boat A network of car ferries links the mainland to the islands of western and northern Scotland.

For much more on **getting around**, see p306

If You Like...

Outdoor Adventures

Fort William 'Outdoor Capital of the UK'; a centre for hiking, climbing, mountain biking and winter sports. (p159)

Shetland One of Scotland's top sea-kayaking coastlines, with an abundance of wildlife to observe. (p250)

Laggan Wolftrax Mountain biking for all abilities, from easy forest trails to black-diamond down-hilling. (p141)

Cairngorms Winter skiing and summer walking amid the epic beauty of this high, subarctic plateau. (p135)

Thurso An unlikely surfing mecca, but once you've got the drysuit on, the waves are world-class. (p183)

Scapa Flow The sunken remains of WWI German warships make this one of Europe's top diving sites. (p246)

Prehistoric Sites

Skara Brae Neolithic village where circular houses uncovered by eroding sand dunes preserve Stone Age furniture and fittings. (p242)

Maeshowe Enormous passage tomb with corbelled roof constructed from stone slabs; added intrigue of Viking graffiti. (p241)

Ring of Brodgar One of Scotland's most evocative sites, this circle of sandstone slabs impresses with sheer scale. (p242)

Callanish Standing Stones These gnarled fingers of gneiss shaggy with lichen are contemporaries of the pyramids of Egypt. (p220)

Kilmartin Glen Scotland's biggest concentration of prehistoric sites, with chambered cairns, standing stones and rock carvings. (p65)

Old Scatness This Shetland site is still being investigated, offering the chance to see archaeologists at work. (p258)

Rural Museums

Arnol Blackhouse Preserved in peat smoke since its last inhabitant departed; a genuine slice of 'living history'. (p220)

Highland Folk Museum Fascinating outdoor museum populated with real historic buildings reassembled here on site. (p141)

Scottish Crannog Centre Head back to the Bronze Age in this archaeological reconstruction of a fortified loch house. (p153)

Tain Through Time Very entertaining local museum with comprehensive display on Scottish history and Tain's silversmithing tradition. (p177)

Stromness Museum Exhibits on the Orkney fishing industry, the World Wars and local marine wildlife. (p243)

Coastal Scenery

Ardnamurchan The most westerly point on the British mainland, with superb views to Skye and Mull. (p164)

Achiltibuie This remote village enjoys a gorgeous coastal setting, looking out across the jewel-like Summer Isles. (p194)

Applecross Majestic views of the hills of Skye and magical sunset moments at this isolated village. (p200)

Tongue Wild sea lochs penetrate the rocky coast on this lonely stretch of the north coast. (p188)

Arisaig & Morar Long strands of silver sands and stunning panoramas to the isles of Eigg and Rum. (p166)

Unst The most northerly point of the British Isles boasts seabird cities ranged on ragged cliffs. (p260)

Classic Hikes

West Highland Way The grandaddy of Scottish long-distance walks, the one everyone wants to do. (p104)

Affric-Kintail Way A classic two-day cross-country hike, with a night in a remote hostel. (p128)

Great Glen Way The easiest of Scotland's long-distance paths, linking Fort William to Inverness.

Speyside Way Follows the River Spey through whisky country to the mountain resort of Aviemore. (p42)

Cape Wrath Trail From Fort William to Scotland's northwest corner through some of the country's remotest landscapes. (p193)

Hebridean Way A peaceful, leisurely path among the moors, lochs and wildflower-strewn dunes of the Outer Hebrides. (p226)

Remote Islands

Iona Beautiful, peaceful and of historic and cultural importance, Iona is the jewel of the Hebrides. (p98)

Eigg Most intriguing of the Small Isles, with its miniature mountain, massacre cave and singing sands. (p171)

Jura Wild, untamed, with more deer than people, and a dangerous whirlpool at its northern end. p74)

Handa Huge cliffs, raucous seabird colonies and a view of the Great Stack of Handa. (p192)

Westray & Papa Westray These magical islands at Orkney's northern end have great coastal scenery, birdwatching and historic sights. (p247)

PLAN YOUR TRIP IF YOU LIKE...

Top: Highland horse, Shetland (p250)

Bottom: View of Eigg (p171) and Rum (p170) from Arisaig (p166)

St Kilda Remote and spectacular, the soaring stacks of St Kilda are the ultimate island tick. (p227)

Natural Wonders

Old Man of Hoy Hoy is rugged and rocky, and its spectacular west coast includes Britain's tallest sea stack. (p245)

Corryvreckan Whirlpool One of the world's three most powerful tidal whirlpools, squeezed between Jura and Scarba. (p75)

Falls of Measach A trembling suspension bridge provides a scary viewpoint for one of Scotland's most impressive waterfalls. (p198)

Quiraing Skye has many impressive rock formations, but the weird Quiraing takes first place for strangeness. (p215)

Fingal's Cave Accessible only by boat, this columnar sea cave inspired Mendelssohn's *Hebrides Overture*. (p99)

Falls of Lora The narrow mouth of Loch Etive creates the country's most impressive tidal whitewater rapids. (p103)

Historic Castles

Dunvegan Castle The ancient seat of Clan Macleod, home to fascinating relics, including the legendary Fairy Flag. (p214)

Duart Castle This impressive Maclean stronghold is one of the oldest inhabited castles in Scotland. (p94)

Dunrobin Castle Country house offering a peek at the opulent lifestyle enjoyed by the Duke of Sutherland. (p179)

Kisimul Castle Seat of Clan MacNeil, this archetypal Highland castle is perched on a Hebridean islet. (p227)

Eilean Donan Castle Perfect lochside location makes this the Highlands' most photographed fortress. (p203)

Wild Beaches

Sandwood Bay A sea stack, a ghost story, a beautiful beach – who could ask for more? (p191)

Kiloran Bay A perfect curve of deep golden sand, the ideal vantage point for stunning sunsets. (p80)

Bosta A beautiful and remote cove filled with white sand beside an Iron Age house. (p220)

Durness A series of pristine sandy coves and duney headlands surround this northwestern village. (p190)

Scousburgh Sands Shetland's finest beach is a top spot for birdwatching, as well as a bracing walk. (p258)

Sanday This aptly named member of Orkney's North Isles is surrounded by spectacular white-sand beaches. (p249)

Month by Month

January

The nation shakes off its Hogmanay hangover and gets back to work, but only until Burns Night comes along. It's still cold and dark, but if there's snow on the hills, the skiing can be good.

Burns Night

Suppers all over Scotland (and the world, for that matter) are held on 25 January to celebrate the anniversary of national poet Robert Burns, with much eating of haggis, drinking of whisky and reciting of poetry.

Up Helly Aa

Half of Shetland dresses up with horned helmets and battleaxes in this spectacular re-enactment of a Viking fire festival (p253), with a torchlit procession leading the burning of a full-size replica of a Viking longship. Held in Lerwick on the last Tuesday in January.

February

The coldest month of the year is usually the best for winter hillwalking, ice-climbing and skiing. The days are getting noticeably longer now, and snowdrops begin to bloom.

Fort William Mountain Festival

(www.mountainfestival. co.uk) The UK's 'Outdoor Capital' celebrates the peak of the winter season with skiing and snowboarding workshops, talks by famous climbers, kids' events and a festival of mountaineering films.

April

The bluebell woods on the shores of Loch Lomond come into flower and ospreys arrive at their Loch Garten nest. Weather is improving, though heavy showers are still common.

Shetland Folk Festival

The end of April sees this engagingly eccentric music festival (p252), with performances of traditional music from around the world staged everywhere from Lerwick pubs to remote island village halls.

May

Wildflowers bloom on the Hebridean machair and puffins arrive at their Orkney and Shetland nesting colonies – May is when the Scottish weather is often at its best.

Scottish Series Yacht Races

(www.clyde.org/scottish -series) The scenic harbour at the West Highland fishing village of Tarbert fills with hundreds of visiting yachts for five days of racing, drinking and partying.

Fèis Ìle

B&Bs in Islay are booked out for this weeklong celebration (p69) of traditional Scottish music and whisky. Events include *ceilidhs,* pipe-band performances, distillery tours and whisky tastings.

June

Argyllshire is ablaze with pink rhododendron blooms. The long summer evenings (known in Orkney and Shetland as the simmer dim) stretch on till 11pm.

✈ UCI Mountain Bike World Cup

Around 20,000 mountain-biking fans gather at Nevis Range near Fort William for the spectacular World Cup (p160) downhill and 4X finals.

✲ St Magnus Festival

It barely gets dark at all at midsummer, making a magical setting for this celebration (p235) of music, poetry, literature and the visual arts. Held late June in Orkney.

July

School holidays begin at the start of July; the busiest time of year for campsites and B&Bs begins. It's high season for Shetland birdwatchers, with sea cliffs loud with nesting guillemots, razorbills and puffins.

☆ Mendelssohn on Mull

A weeklong festival (p93) of free classical music concerts at various venues in Mull, Iona and Oban (composer Mendelssohn was inspired by a visit to Mull in 1829).

☆ Hebridean Celtic Festival

The gardens of Lews Castle in Stornoway provide the scenic setting for this four-day extravaganza (p218) of folk, rock and Celtic music.

August

Highland games are taking place all over the region, but the midges are at their worst. On the west coast, this is the peak month for sighting minke whales and basking sharks.

✲ Groove Loch Ness

The best Scottish and international DJs play at this atmospheric festival (p131) in a spectacularly scenic setting beside Loch Ness.

✈ Plockton Regatta

Plockton Bay fills with sails as a fortnight of yacht and small-boat racing culminates in Regatta weekend (p201) with a street party, concert and *ceilidhs*.

☆ Argyllshire Gathering

Oban is the setting for one of the most important events (p87) on the Scottish Highland Games calendar, which includes a prestigious pipe-band competition.

September

School holidays are over, midges are dying off, wild brambles are ripe for picking in the hedgerows, and the weather is often dry and mild – an excellent time of year for outdoor pursuits.

☆ Braemar Gathering

The biggest and most famous Highland Games (p144) in the Scottish calendar, traditionally attended by members of the Royal Family, featuring Highland dancing, caber-tossing and bagpipe-playing. Held early September in Braemar, Royal Deeside.

October

Autumn brings a blaze of colour to the forests of Highland Perthshire and the Trossachs, as the tourist season winds down and thoughts turn to log fires and malt whiskies in country house hotels.

☆ Ullapool Guitar Festival

(www.ullapoolguitar festival.com) A lively weekend of concerts, *ceilidhs*, workshops and impromptu sessions devoted to the guitar, with performances from Scottish and international musicians.

✲ Cowalfest

(www.cowalfest.org) Dunoon and the lovely Cowal peninsula play host to this 10-day walking festival. As well as a huge range of guided walks, there are mountain-bike rides, horse rides, orienteering, exhibitions, art, theatre and concerts.

☆ Enchanted Forest

Crowds gather in the Explorers Garden at Pitlochry to experience this spectacular sound-and-light show. Three weeks of events occasionally spill into November. (p149)

Top: Braemar
Gathering (p144)

Bottom: Hebridean
Celtic Festival (p218)

Itineraries

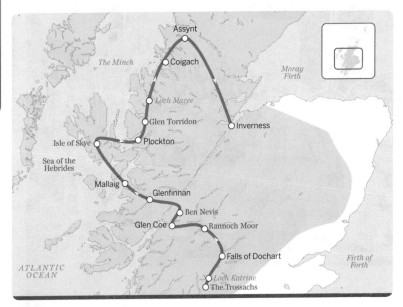

 2 WEEKS A Highland Fling

This tour takes in the scenic highlights of the Highlands, including the Isle of Skye.

Begin with a visit to the **Trossachs** for your first taste of Highland scenery; take a cruise on **Loch Katrine** and spend the night in Callander. Continue north via the **Falls of Dochart** at Killin and the fringes of **Rannoch Moor**.

The mountain scenery becomes more impressive, culminating in the grandeur of **Glen Coe**. Keen hill walkers will pause for a day at Fort William to climb **Ben Nevis** (plus another day to recover!) before taking the Road to the Isles past glorious **Glenfinnan** and the Silver Sands of Morar to **Mallaig**. Overnight here and dine at one of its seafood restaurants.

Take the ferry to the **Isle of Skye**, spending a day or two exploring Scotland's most famous island, before crossing the Skye Bridge back to the mainland, then head north via the pretty village of **Plockton** to the magnificent mountain scenery of **Glen Torridon**. Spend a day or two hiking here, then follow the A832 alongside lovely **Loch Maree** and continue north into the big-sky wilderness of **Coigach** and **Assynt**, before making your way back south with an overnight in **Inverness**.

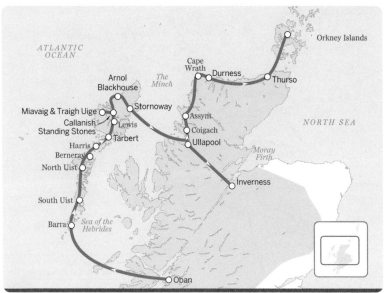

Island Hopscotch

This route is usually done by car, but the Oban–Barra–Stornoway–Ullapool–Inverness loop also makes a brilliant cycle tour (around 270 miles, including the 60 miles from Ullapool ferry terminal to Inverness train station, making both start and finish accessible by rail). CalMac's Island Hopscotch ticket No 8 includes all the ferries needed for the Outer Hebrides part of this route.

From **Oban** it's a five-hour ferry crossing to **Barra**; you'll arrive in the evening so plan to spend the night there (book ahead). In the morning, after a visit to romantic Kisimul Castle and a tour around the island, take the ferry to **South Uist**. Walk along the wild beaches of the west coast, sample the local seafood and, if you've brought your fishing rod, look forward to a bit of sport on the island's many trout lochs. There are good places to stay at Polochar, Lochboisdale and Lochmaddy (two nights should be enough).

Keep your binoculars handy as you follow the road north through Benbecula and **North Uist**, as this is prime birdwatching country. If you're camping or hostelling, a night at **Berneray** is a must before taking the ferry to **Harris**. Pray for sun, as the road along Harris' west coast has some of the most spectacular beaches in Scotland. The main road continues north from **Tarbert** (good hotels) through the rugged Harris hills to **Lewis**.

Don't go directly to Stornoway; instead head to the **Callanish Standing Stones** and **Arnol Blackhouse** museum – the highlights of the Western Isles. If you have time (two days is ideal), detour west to the beautiful beaches around **Miavaig** and **Traigh Uige**; there's plenty of wild and semiwild camping.

Spend your final night in the Hebrides in **Stornoway** (eating at Digby Chick), then take the ferry to **Ullapool**, where you have the choice of heading straight to **Inverness**, or continuing north around the mainland coast through the gorgeous wilderness of **Coigach** and **Assynt**, and on via **Cape Wrath** and **Durness** to **Thurso**, where the ferry to the **Orkney Islands** awaits.

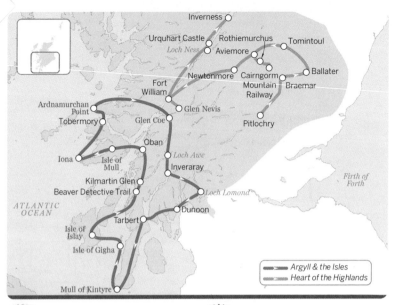

Argyll & the Isles
Heart of the Highlands

10 DAYS Argyll & the Isles

Argyll and its islands offer a varied taste of Highland scenery, wildlife and history, all within a few hours' drive of Glasgow.

Begin with a scenic drive from **Dunoon** to Portavadie via Benmore Botanic Garden, then take the ferry to the pretty fishing village of **Tarbert**. Devote a day to the Kintyre peninsula, taking in Campbeltown, the **Mull of Kintyre** and the **Isle of Gigha**. Then allow at least two days for touring **Islay** and its famous distilleries.

Back on the mainland, head north through Knapdale – visiting the **Beaver Detective Trail** – to the prehistoric sites of **Kilmartin Glen** and on to **Oban**.

Take the ferry to Craignure for a tour of the **Isle of Mull**, being sure to visit Duart Castle and **Iona**, before spending a night at **Tobermory**. From here you can cross to Kilchoan, allowing a trip to **Ardnamurchan Point,** the most westerly point of the British mainland, before the scenic drive along Loch Sunart to Corran Ferry.

Head back south via the scenic splendour of **Glen Coe** and the minor road through Glen Orchy to reach **Loch Awe**. From here you can return to your starting point by way of **Inveraray** and **Loch Lomond**.

1 WEEK Heart of the Highlands

The central and western Highlands are famous for mountain scenery, ancient pine forests and whisky distilleries.

Beginning in **Pitlochry**, abandon the main A9 road and enjoy a day's scenic drive east across the hills on the A924, and then north on the A93 through the ski area of Glenshee to the remote Highland outpost of **Braemar**. Spend a night here, and the following day either hike in the hills nearby or visit Balmoral Castle before spending your second night at **Ballater**.

From here the roller-coaster A939 takes you north to **Tomintoul** and Glenlivet, close to the heartland of Speyside whisky. Take your time visiting distilleries as you amble west along the Spey valley to **Aviemore**, in the Cairngorm National Park. Spend at least two nights here to explore the ancient pine forests of **Rothiemurchus** and take a trip on the **Cairngorm Mountain Railway**.

Head west, stopping at the Highland Folk Museum at **Newtonmore** before continuing to **Fort William**. Overnight here, then spend a morning exploring **Glen Nevis** and head north along the Great Glen to see **Urquhart Castle** and **Loch Ness** – leave time for a monster-spotting cruise – and finish up in **Inverness**.

Top: Urquhart
Castle (p131)

Bottom: Callanish
Standing Stones
(p220)

Mountains on Skye (p204)

Plan Your Trip
Activities

Scotland is a brilliant place for outdoor recreation. It caters to everyone, from those who enjoy a short stroll to full-on adrenaline junkies. Although hiking, biking, fishing and golf are the most popular activities, there is an astonishing variety of things to do.

JOHN FLEETWOOD/SHUTTERSTOCK ©

Need to Know

Best Time to Go

May, June and September are the best months for hiking and biking – best chance of dry weather and less chance of midges.

Best Outdoor Experiences

Hike the West Highland Way, climb Ben Nevis, cycle-tour the Outer Hebrides, mountain-bike a black trail at Laggan Wolftrax, sea kayak in Shetland.

Essential Hill Walking Gear

Good waterproofs, spare warm clothing, map and compass, mobile phone (but don't rely on it), first-aid kit, head torch, whistle (for emergencies), spare food and drink.

Safety Checklist

Check the weather forecast first; let someone know your plans; set pace and objective to suit slowest member of your party; don't be afraid to turn back if it's too difficult.

Walking

Scotland's wild, dramatic scenery and varied landscape has made walking a hugely popular pastime for locals and tourists alike, providing everything from after-breakfast strolls to the popular sport of Munro bagging (p33).

The best time of year for hill walking is usually May to September, although snow can fall on the highest summits even in midsummer. Winter walking on the higher hills of Scotland is for experienced mountaineers only, requiring the use of an ice axe and crampons.

What to Pack

Highland hikers should be properly equipped and cautious, as the weather can become vicious at any time of year. After rain, peaty soil can become boggy, so always wear stout shoes or boots and carry extra food and drink – many unsuspecting walkers have had to survive an unplanned night in the open. Don't depend on mobile phones (although carrying one with you is a good idea, and can be a life-saver if you can get a signal). If necessary, leave a note with your route and expected time of return in the windscreen of your car.

Maps

Britain's national mapping agency, the Ordnance Survey (OS), caters to walkers with a wide range of maps at different scales. The Landranger series at 1:50,000 (2cm to 1km, 1¼ inches to 1 mile; £8.99 per sheet) is the standard hiker's map. If you want more detail, the Explorer series at 1:25,000 (4cm to 1km, 2½ inches to 1 mile; £8.99 per sheet) shows features such as field boundaries and fences. Both series are also available as 'Active' versions (£14.99), which are completely waterproof. Tourist offices and bookshops usually stock a selection, or you can buy them online.

Alternatively, look out for the excellent, weatherproof walkers' maps published by Harveys at scales of 1:40,000 and 1:25,000. These are tailored to particular walking and climbing areas such as Ben Nevis or the Cairngorms, and there are also maps dedicated to long-distance footpaths.

Munro Bagging

At the end of the 19th century an eager hill walker, Sir Hugh Munro, published a list of Scottish mountains with summits of more than 3000ft (914m) above sea level. He couldn't have realised that in time his name would be used to describe any Scottish mountain over 3000ft. Many keen hill walkers now set themselves the target of reaching the summit of (or bagging all) of Scotland's 282 Munros.

To the uninitiated it may seem odd that Munro baggers see venturing into mist, cloud and driving rain as time well spent. However, for those who can add one or more ticks to their list, the vagaries of the weather are part of the enjoyment, at least in retrospect. Munro bagging is, of course, more than merely ticking off a list – it takes you to some of the wildest and most beautiful corners of Scotland.

Once you've bagged all the Munros you can move on to the Corbetts – hills over 2500ft (700m), with a drop of at least 500ft (150m) on all sides – and the Donalds, lowland hills over 2000ft (610m). And for connoisseurs of the diminutive, there are the McPhies: 'eminences in excess of 300ft (90m)' on the Isle of Colonsay.

Further Information

Every tourist office has leaflets (free or for a nominal charge) of suggested walks that take in local points of interest. For general advice, VisitScotland's Walking Scotland website (http://walking.visitscotland.com) describes numerous routes in various parts of the country, and also offers safety tips and useful information.

Other useful resources:

Mountaineering Council of Scotland (www.mountaineering.scot)

Ordnance Survey (www.ordnancesurvey.co.uk)

Ramblers' Association Scotland (www.ramblers.org.uk/scotland)

Scottish Mountaineering Club (www.smc.org.uk)

West Highland Way (p104)

Mountain Biking

A combination of challenging, rugged terrain, a network of old drove roads, military roads and stalkers' paths, and legislation that enshrines free access to the countryside has earned Scotland a reputation as one of the world's top mountain-biking destinations. Fort William has hosted the UCI Mountain Bike World Championships every year since 2007.

The Highlands and islands offer everything from custom-built forest trails with berms, jumps and skinnies to world-class downhill courses such as those at Laggan

Wolftrax and Nevis Range. But perhaps the region's greatest appeal is its almost unlimited potential for adventurous, off-road riding. Areas such as the Angus Glens, the Cairngorms, Lochaber, Skye and most of the Northwest Highlands have large roadless regions where you can explore to your heart's content.

Top trails include Glen Feshie, Glenlivet and Rothiemurchus Forest in the Cairngorms, Spean Bridge to Kinlochleven via the Lairig Leacach and Loch Eilde Mor, and the stretch of the West Highland Way between Bridge of Orchy and Kinlochleven. The 37-mile loop from Sligachan on Skye (south through Glen Sligachan to Camasunary, over to Kilmarie, and back north via Strath Mor) was voted by *Mountain Bike Rider* magazine as the best off-road trail in Britain.

OFFICIAL LONG-DISTANCE FOOTPATHS

WALK	DISTANCE	FEATURES	DURATION	DIFFICULTY
Great Glen Way	73 miles	Loch Ness, canal paths, forest tracks	4 days	easy
Speyside Way	66 miles	follows river, whisky distilleries	3-4 days	easy-medium
West Highland Way	96 miles	spectacular scenery, mountains & lochs	6-8 days	medium

Mountain bikers at Nevis Range (p163)

But the ultimate off-road experience is a coast-to-coast ride. There is no set route and no waymarking, so it's as much a planning and navigational challenge as a physical one. A coast-to-coast can be as short as the 36 miles from Ullapool to Bonar Bridge via Glen Achall and Glen Einig, or as long as the 250 miles from Aberdeen to Ardnamurchan (90% off-road).

The most popular route, though, is from Fort William to Montrose (starting and finishing at a railway station) via Fort Augustus, Aviemore, Tomintoul, Ballater and Edzell, taking in the Corrieyairack Pass, the Ryvoan Pass, Glen Builg, Glen Tanar and Glen Esk (195 miles). You can camp wild along the way or book accommodation at B&Bs and hostels, or join a guided expedition with an organisation such as Wilderness Scotland (p308).

Mountain Biking Trail Centres

Nevis Range (p163) Ski resort offering summer sport in the form of a world-championship down-hill course, and a 3.7-mile red-grade cross-country trail from the top station of the gondola.

Witch's Trails (p163) Has 22 miles of forest road and single-track in the shadow of Ben Nevis. Hosts the annual cross-country world championships and the annual 10 Under the Ben endurance event.

Laggan Wolftrax (p141) Forest centre near Newtonmore with everything from novice trails and a bike park to hard cross-country and a challenging black route with drop-offs, boulder fields and rock slabs.

Highland Wildcat (p179) The hills above Golspie harbour have the biggest single-track descent in the country (390m drop over 4 miles, from the top of Ben Bhraggie almost to sea level). Plenty for beginners and families, too.

Learnie Red Rocks (☑0300 067 6100; https://scotland.forestry.gov.uk/visit/learnie-red-rocks) **FREE** Just north of Rosemarkie; 10 miles of forest trails plus fun park, for all levels of skill and experience.

Kyle of Sutherland Trails (p178) Rocks and boardwalks add some technical challenges to 10.5 miles of blue-, red- and black-graded forest trails with great views.

Cycling

Cycling is an excellent way to explore Scotland's Highlands and islands. There are hundreds of miles of forest trails and quiet minor roads, and dedicated cycle routes along canal towpaths and disused railway tracks. Depending on your energy and enthusiasm, you can take a leisurely trip through idyllic glens, stopping at pubs along the way, or head off on a long and arduous road tour.

The network of signposted cycle routes maintained by Sustrans (www.sustrans.org.uk) makes a good introduction. Much of the network is on minor roads or cycle lanes, but there are long stretches of surfaced, traffic-free trails between Callander and Killin, between Oban and Ballachulish, and on Royal Deeside.

But it's the minor roads of the Northwest Highlands, the Outer Hebrides, Orkney and Shetland that are the real attraction for cycle tourers, offering hundreds of miles of peaceful pedalling through breathtaking landscapes. The classic Scottish cycle tour is a trip around the islands of the west coast, from Islay and Jura north via Mull, Coll and Tiree to Skye and the Outer Hebrides (bikes travel for free on Calmac car ferries).

Further Information

VisitScotland publishes a useful free brochure, *Active Scotland*, and has a website with more information (http://active.visitscotland.com). Many regional tourist offices have information on local cycling routes and places to hire bikes. They also stock cycling guides and books.

For up-to-date, detailed information on Scotland's cycle-route network contact Sustrans. Cycling UK (www.cyclinguk.org) is a membership organisation providing comprehensive information about cycling in Britain.

Birdwatching

Scotland is the best place in the British Isles (and in some cases, the only place) to spot bird species such as the golden eagle, white-tailed eagle, osprey, corncrake, capercaillie, crested tit, Scottish crossbill and ptarmigan, and the country's coast and islands are some of Europe's most important seabird nesting grounds.

There are more than 80 ornithologically important nature reserves managed by Scottish Natural Heritage (www.nnr.scot), the Royal Society for the Protection of Birds (www.rspb.org.uk) and the Scottish Wildlife Trust (www.swt.org.uk).

THE RIGHT TO ROAM

There is a tradition of relatively free access to open country in Scotland, a tradition that was enshrined in law in the 2003 Land Reform (Scotland) Bill, popularly known as 'the right to roam'. The Scottish Outdoor Access Code (www.outdooraccess-scotland.scot) states that everyone has the right to be on most land and inland waters, providing they act responsibly. You should avoid areas where you might disrupt or disturb wildlife, lambing (generally mid-April to the end of May), grouse shooting (from 12 August to the third week in October) or deer stalking (1 July to 15 February, but the peak period is August to October). You can get up-to-date information on deer stalking in various areas through the Heading for the Scottish Hills service (www.outdooraccess-scotland.scot/hftsh).

You are also free to pitch a tent almost anywhere that doesn't cause inconvenience to others or damage to property, as long as you stay no longer than two or three nights in any one spot, take all litter away with you, and keep well away from houses and roads. (Note that this right does not extend to the use of motorised vehicles.)

Local authorities aren't required to list and map rights of way, so they're not shown on Ordnance Survey (OS) maps of Scotland, as they are in England and Wales. However, the Scottish Rights of Way & Access Society (www.scotways.com) keeps records of these routes, provides and maintains signposting, and publicises them in its guidebook, *Scottish Hill Tracks*.

Minke whale near Lewis (p218)

Further information can be obtained from the Scottish Ornithologists Club (www.the-soc.org.uk).

Whale Watching

In contrast to Iceland and Norway, Scotland has cashed in on the abundance of minke whales off its coast by embracing whale watching rather than whaling. There are now dozens of operators around the coast offering whale-watching boat trips lasting from a couple of hours to all day; some have whale-sighting success rates of 95% in summer.

The best places to base yourself for whale watching include Oban, the Isle of Mull, Skye and the Outer Hebrides. Orkney and Shetland offer the best chance of spotting orcas (killer whales), while the Moray Firth has a resident population of bottlenosed dolphins. While seals, porpoises and dolphins can be seen year-round, minke whales are most commonly spotted from June to August, with August being the peak month for sightings.

The website of the Hebridean Whale & Dolphin Trust (https://hwdt.org) has lots of information on the species you are likely to see, and how to identify them. A booklet titled *Is It a Whale?* is available from tourist offices and bookshops, and provides tips on identifying the various species of marine mammal that you're likely to see.

Outfits operating whale-watching cruises include the following:

Sea Life Surveys (p95)

Seafari Adventures (p91)

Aquaxplore (p211)

Hebridean Adventures (p218)

Golf

Scotland is the home of golf. The game has been played here for centuries and there are more courses per head of population than in any other country. Most clubs are open to visitors; details can be found at www.scottishgolfcourses.com.

St Andrews is the headquarters of the game's governing body, the Royal and Ancient Golf Club, and the location of the world's most famous golf course, the Old Course. Although the major championship courses, including those at Carnoustie, Royal Troon and Turnberry, are in the south of the country, there are some superb courses in the Highlands, such as Royal Dornoch, Tain and Nairn. Many visiting golfers enjoy the challenge of the wild and some eccentric golf courses can be found dotted among the islands, such as Machrie on Islay, Askernish on South Uist and Whalsay in Shetland.

VisitScotland publishes *Golf in Scotland* (http://golf.visitscotland.com), a free annual brochure listing course details, costs and clubs, as well as information on where to stay.

Fishing

Fishing – coarse, sea and game – is enormously popular in Scotland; the lochs and rivers of the Highlands and islands are filled with salmon, sea trout, brown trout and Arctic char. Fly-fishing in particular is a joy – it's a tricky but rewarding form of angling, closer to an art form than a sport.

Fishing rights to most inland waters are privately owned and you must obtain a permit to fish in them – these are usually readily available from the local fishing tackle shop or hotel, which are also great sources of advice and local knowledge. Permits cost from around £5 to £20 per day but salmon fishing on some rivers – notably the Dee, Tay and Spey – can be much more expensive (up to £150 a day).

BEATING THE MIDGES

Forget Nessie. The Highlands have a real monster in their midst: a voracious, bloodsucking female fully 2mm long, known as *Culicoides impunctatus* – the Highland midge. (The male midge is an innocent vegetarian.) The bane of campers and as much a symbol of Scotland as the kilt or the thistle, they can drive some folk to distraction as they descend in swarms of biting misery. Though mostly vegetarian too, the female midge needs a dose of blood in order to lay her eggs. And like it or not, if you're in the Highlands in summer, you've just volunteered as a donor.

The midge season lasts from late May to early September, with June to August being the worst months. Climate change has seen warmer, damper springs and summers that seem to suit the midges just fine – in recent years they've increased both in numbers and in range. They're at their worst in the morning and evening, especially in calm, overcast weather; strong winds and strong sunshine help keep them away.

You can get an idea of how bad they are going to be in your area by checking the **midge forecast** (www.smidgeup.com/midge-forecast; only operates during midge season).

Be Prepared

Cover up by wearing long trousers and long-sleeved shirts, and (if the midges are really bad) a head net (available in most outdoor shops) worn over a brimmed hat. Also be sure to use a repellent.

Many kinds of repellents have been formulated over the decades, some based on natural ingredients such as citronella and bog myrtle, but until recently there was only one that worked reliably – DEET, which is a nasty, industrial chemical that smells bad, stings your eyes and seems to be capable of melting plastic. A repellent called Saltidin claims to be both effective and pleasant to use (marketed under the brand name Smidge).

However, there's another substance that has shot to prominence since 2005 despite not being marketed as an insect repellent. Avon's 'Skin So Soft' moisturiser spray is so effective that it is regularly used as a midge repellent by professionals including the Royal Marines, forestry workers and water engineers, as well as thousands of outdoor enthusiasts. You can find it in most outdoor stores in the west of Scotland. Not only does it keep the midges away, it leaves your skin feeling 'velvety soft'.

Top: Cyclist in the Highlands

Bottom: Fisher in Loch Ness (p130)

ILIAS KOUROUDIS/SHUTTERSTOCK ©

ILIAS KOUROUDIS/SHUTTERSTOCK ©

Canoeing on Loch Lubnaig (p59)

For wild brown trout the close season is early October to mid-March. The close season for salmon and sea trout varies between districts; it's generally from mid-October to mid-January.

FishPal (www.fishpal.com/scotland) provides a good introduction, with links for booking fishing on various rivers and lochs.

Canoeing & Kayaking

The sea lochs and indented coastline of Scotland's Highlands and islands provide some of the finest sea kayaking in the world. There are sheltered lochs and inlets ideal for beginners, long and exciting coastal and island tours, and gnarly tidal passages that will challenge even the most expert paddler, all amid spectacular scenery and wildlife – encounters with seals, dolphins and even whales are relatively common.

The inland lochs and rivers offer excellent Canadian and white-water canoeing. Lochs Lomond, Awe and Maree all have uninhabited islands where canoeists can set up camp, while a study of the map will suggest plenty of cross-country expeditions involving only minor portages. Classic routes include Fort William to Inverness along the Great Glen; Glen Affric; Loch Shiel; and Loch Veyatie–Fionn Loch–Loch Sionascaig in Assynt.

There are dozens of companies offering sea kayaking and canoeing courses and guided holidays, including the following:

Arran Adventure Company (p81)

NorWest Sea Kayaking (p192)

Rockhopper Sea Kayaking (p167)

Sea Kayak Shetland (p259)

Wilderness Scotland (p308)

Whitewave Outdoor Centre (p206)

Clearwater Paddling (☏01871-810443; www.clearwaterpaddling.com; Castlebay; per week all-inclusive from £785; ⊙May-Aug)

Further Information

➡ Scottish Canoe Association (www.canoescotland.org) Publishes coastal navigation sheets and organises tours, including introductory ones for beginners.

BRENDAN HOWARD/SHUTTERSTOCK ©

PLAN YOUR TRIP ACTIVITIES

Snowboarders at the Cairngorms (p139)

➡ *The Northern Isles* (by Tom Smith & Chris Jex) A detailed guide to sea kayaking the waters around Orkney and Shetland.

➡ *The Outer Hebrides* (by Mike Sullivan, Robert Emmott & Tim Pickering) A detailed guide to sea kayaking around the Western Isles.

➡ *Scottish Sea Kayak Trail* (www.scottishsea kayaktrail.com; by Simon Willis) Covers the Scottish west coast from the Isle of Gigha to the Summer Isles.

Snow Sports

There are five ski centres in Scotland, offering downhill skiing and snowboarding:

Cairngorm Mountain (p139) Has almost 30 runs spread over an extensive area (1097m).

Glencoe Mountain Resort (p155) Has only five tows and two chairlifts (1108m).

Glenshee Ski Resort (p145) Situated on the A93 road between Perth and Braemar; offers the largest network of lifts and the widest range of runs in all of Scotland (920m).

Lecht 2090 (p142) The smallest and most remote centre, on the A939 between Ballater and Grantown-on-Spey (793m).

Nevis Range (p163) Near Fort William; offers the highest ski runs, the grandest setting and some of the best off-piste potential in Scotland (1221m).

The high season is from January to April but it's sometimes possible to ski from as early as November to as late as May. It's easy to turn up at the slopes, hire some equipment, buy a day pass and head right off.

VisitScotland's *Ski Scotland* brochure is useful and includes a list of accommodation options. General information, and weather and snow reports, can be obtained from Ski Scotland (www.ski-scotland.com) and WinterHighland (www.winterhighland.info).

Rock Climbing

Scotland has a long history of rock climbing and mountaineering, with many of the classic routes on Ben Nevis and Glen Coe having been pioneered in the 19th century. The country's main rock-climbing areas

THE SPEYSIDE WAY

This long-distance footpath follows the course of the River Spey, one of Scotland's most famous salmon-fishing rivers. It starts at Buckie and first follows the coast to Spey Bay, east of Elgin, then runs inland along the river to Aviemore in the Cairngorms (with branches to Tomintoul and Dufftown). There are plans to extend the trail to Newtonmore.

The 66-mile route has been dubbed the 'Whisky Trail' as it passes near a number of distilleries, including Glenlivet and **Glenfiddich** (☑01340-820373; www.glenfiddich.co.uk; admission free, tours from £10; ☺9.30am-4.30pm; ℗), which are open to the public. If you stop at them all, the walk may take considerably longer than the usual three or four days! The first 11 miles from Buckie to Fochabers makes a good day hike (allow four to five hours).

The Speyside Way, a guidebook by Jacquetta Megarry and Jim Strachan, describes the trail in detail. Check out the route at www.speysideway.org.

include Ben Nevis (with routes up to 400m in length), Glen Coe, the Cairngorms, the Cuillin Hills of Skye, Arrochar and the Isle of Arran, but there are also hundreds of smaller crags situated all over the country. One unusual feature of Scotland's rock-climbing scene is the sea stacks found around the coastlines, the most famous of these being the 140m-high Old Man of Hoy (p245).

Rock Climbing in Scotland, by Kevin Howett, and the Scottish Mountaineering Club's regional Rock & Ice Climbs guides are excellent guidebooks that cover the whole country.

Further information:

Mountaineering Council of Scotland (www.mountaineering.scot)

Scottish Mountaineering Club (www.smc.org.uk)

Scuba Diving

It may lack coral reefs and warm waters but Scotland offers some of the most spectacular and challenging scuba diving in Europe. There are spectacular drop-offs, challenging drift dives (the Falls of Lora is a classic) and fascinating wildlife ranging from colourful jewel anemones and soft corals to giant conger eels, monkfish and inquisitive seals. There are also hundreds of fascinating shipwrecks.

Dive sites such as Scapa Flow in the Orkney Islands, where the seven remaining hulks of the WWI German High Seas Fleet, scuttled in 1919, lie on the sea bed, and the oceanic arches, tunnels and caves of St Kilda rank among the best in the world.

For more information on the country's diving options contact the Scottish Sub Aqua Club (www.scotsac.com).

Surfing

Even with a wetsuit on you definitely have to be hardy to enjoy surfing in Scottish waters. That said, the country does have some of the best surfing breaks in Europe.

The tidal range is large, which means there is often a completely different set of breaks at low and high tides. It's the north and west coasts, particularly around Thurso and in the Outer Hebrides, which have outstanding, world-class surf. Indeed, Lewis has the best and most consistent surf in Britain, with around 120 recorded breaks and waves up to 5m.

For more information contact Hebridean Surf (www.hebrideansurf.co.uk).

Regions at a Glance

Which parts of the Highlands and islands you choose to visit will naturally depend on how much time you have, and whether you've been here before. First-time visitors will want to squeeze in as many highlights as possible, so could try following the well-trodden route through the Trossachs, Pitlochry, Inverness, Loch Ness and Skye.

It takes considerably more time to explore the further-flung corners of the country, but the jaw-dropping scenery of the northwest Highlands and the gorgeous white-sand beaches of the Outer Hebrides are less crowded and ultimately more rewarding. The long journey to Orkney or Shetland means that you'll want to devote more than just a day or two to these regions.

Southern Highlands & Islands

Wildlife
Islands
Food & Drink

Whales & Eagles

This region is home to some of Scotland's most spectacular wildlife, including magnificent white-tailed sea eagles, majestic Minke whales and 12m-long basking sharks. It's also where the beaver – extinct in Britain for hundreds of years – has been reintroduced into the wild.

Island Hopping

Island hopping is one of the most enjoyable ways to explore Scotland's western seaboard. The cluster of islands within this region – Islay, with its whisky distilleries; wild and mountainous Jura; scenic Mull and the little jewel of Iona; and the gorgeous beaches of Colonsay, Coll and Tiree – provide a brilliant introduction.

The Harvest of the Sea

Whether you sit down to dine in one of Oban's or Tobermory's top restaurants or lounge by the harbourside and eat with your fingers, the rich harvest of the sea is one of the region's biggest drawcards.

p46

PLAN YOUR TRIP REGIONS AT A GLANCE

Inverness & the Central Highlands

Activities
Royalty
Legends

Hiking & Skiing

The Cairngorm towns of Aviemore and Fort William offer outdoor adventure galore, be it climbing Ben Nevis, walking the West Highland Way, biking the trails around Loch Morlich or skiing the slopes of Cairngorm.

Royal Deeside

The valley of the River Dee, often called Royal Deeside, has been associated with the royal family since Queen Victoria acquired a holiday home at Balmoral Castle in the 1850s. The nearby village of Ballater was once the terminus for the royal train and is filled with shops bearing the royal warrant.

Loch Ness Monster

Scotland's most iconic legend, the Loch Ness monster, lurks in the heart of this region. You might not spot Nessie, but the magnificent scenery of the Great Glen makes a visit worthwhile, as does Culloden battlefield, the undoing of another Scottish legend, Bonnie Prince Charlie.

p115

Northern Highlands & Islands

Scenery
Activities
History

Mountains & Lochs

From the peaks of Assynt and Torridon, to the jagged rock pinnacles of the Cuillin Hills, to the dazzling beaches of the Outer Hebrides, the big skies and lonely landscapes of the northern Highlands and islands are the very essence of Scotland, a wilderness of sea and mountains that remains one of Europe's most unspoilt regions.

Climbing & Kayaking

The northwest's vast spaces are one huge adventure playground for hikers, bikers, climbers and kayakers, and offer the chance to see some of the UK's most spectacular wildlife.

The Clearances

The abandoned rural communities of the north teach much about the Clearances, especially Arnol Blackhouse and Skye Museum of Island Life. The region is also rich in prehistoric remains, including the famous standing stones of Callanish.

p173

Orkney & Shetland

History
Wildlife
Music

Skara Brae

These treeless, cliff-bound islands have a fascinating Viking heritage and unique prehistoric villages, tombs and stone circles. Predating the pyramids of Egypt, Skara Brae is northern Europe's best-preserved prehistoric village, while Maeshowe is one of Britain's finest Neolithic tombs.

Birdwatching

Shetland is a birdwatcher's paradise, its cliffs teeming in summer with gannets, fulmars, kittiwakes, razorbills and puffins, and Europe's largest colony of Arctic terns. Several nature reserves include Hermaness on Unst, Scotland's northernmost inhabited island.

Folk Festivals

The pubs of Kirkwall, Stromness and Lerwick are fertile ground for exploring the traditional-music scene, with impromptu sessions of fiddle and guitar music. Both Orkney and Shetland host annual festivals of folk music.

p229

On the Road

Orkney &
Shetland
p229

Northern Highlands
& Islands
p173

Inverness & the
Central Highlands
p115

Southern
Highlands &
Islands
p46

Southern Highlands & Islands

Best Places to Eat

➜ Ninth Wave (p98)
➜ Café Fish (p96)
➜ Callander Meadows (p59)
➜ Starfish (p66)
➜ Ee-Usk (p89)

Best Places to Stay

➜ Monachyle Mhor (p59)
➜ Calgary Farmhouse (p97)
➜ Iona Hostel (p99)
➜ Highland Cottage (p95)
➜ Knap Guest House (p66)
➜ Glenartney (p82)

Why Go?

The impossibly complex coastline of Scotland's southwest harbours some of its most inspiring corners. Here, sea travel is key – dozens of ferries allow you to island-hop from the scenic splendour of Arran to majestic Mull or Tiree's lonely sands, via the whisky distilleries of Islay, the wild mountains of Jura, the scenic delights of diminutive Colonsay and Oban's sustainable seafood scene.

On fresh water too, passenger ferries, vintage steamboats, canoes and kayaks ply Loch Lomond and the Trossachs National Park, a memorable concentration of scenery that's very accessible but possessed of a wild beauty.

Wildlife experiences are a highlight here, from the rasping spout of a minke whale to the 'krek-krek' of a corncrake. Spot otters tumbling in the kelp, watch sea eagles snatch fish from a lonely loch and thrill to the sight of dolphins riding the bow-wave of your boat.

When to Go
Oban

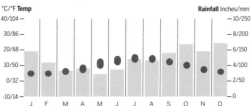

May Fèis Ìle (Islay Festival) celebrates traditional Scottish music and whisky.

Jun Roadsides and gardens become a blaze of colour with deep-pink rhododendron blooms.

Aug The best month of the year for whale watching off the west coast.

Southern Highlands & Islands Highlights

1 The Trossachs (p53) Exploring the lovely lochscapes and accessible walking and cycling routes.

2 Islay (p69) Visiting the smoky heavyweights of the whisky world on their peaty turf.

3 Arran (p81) Blowing away the cobwebs on this scenic, activity-packed island.

4 Corryvreckan Whirlpool (p75) Visiting the white waters of this maelstrom at the north end of lonely Jura.

5 Iona (p98) Journeying through wildlife-rich Mull to reach this holy emerald isle.

6 West Highland Way (p48) Hiking along the eastern shore of Loch Lomond.

7 Seafood Restaurants (p89) Tucking into a platter of fresh local langoustines at Ee-Usk or another one of Oban's eating establishments.

8 Machrihanish (p69) Teeing off on the great-value old and new golf courses down the Kintyre peninsula.

LOCH LOMOND & THE TROSSACHS

The 'bonnie banks' and 'bonnie braes' of Loch Lomond have long been Glasgow's rural retreat – a scenic region of hills, lochs and healthy fresh air within easy reach of Scotland's largest city. Today the loch's popularity shows no sign of decreasing. The scenic Trossachs have likewise long been popular for their wild Highland beauty, set so close to the southern population centres. With the region covered by a large national park, it makes a fine destination for outdoor activity, with some excellent walking and cycling on offer and lots of high-quality accommodation and eating choices.

Loch Lomond

Loch Lomond is mainland Britain's largest lake and, after Loch Ness, the most famous of Scotland's lochs. Its proximity to Glasgow (20 miles away) means that the tourist honey pots of Balloch and Luss get pretty crowded in summer. The eastern shore, which is followed by the West Highland Way long-distance footpath, is quieter and offers a better chance to appreciate the loch away from the busy main road.

Loch Lomond straddles the Highland border. The southern part is broad and island-studded, fringed by woods and Lowland meadows. However, north of Luss the loch narrows, occupying a deep trench gouged out by glaciers during the Ice Age, with 900m mountains crowding either side.

Activities

Walking

The West Highland Way (www.west-highland-way.org) runs along the loch's eastern shore, while the Rob Roy Way (www.robroyway.com) heads from Drymen to Pitlochry via the Trossachs. The Three Lochs Way (www.threelochsway.co.uk) loops west from Balloch through Helensburgh and Arrochar before returning to Loch Lomond at Inveruglas. The Great Trossachs Path (www.lochlomond-trossachs.org) links the loch with the Trossachs. There are numerous shorter walks around: get further information from tourist offices.

Rowardennan is the starting point for ascents of Ben Lomond (p53), a popular and relatively straightforward (if strenuous) climb.

Other Activities

The mostly traffic-free Clyde and Loch Lomond Cycle Way links Glasgow to Balloch (20 miles), where it joins the West Loch Lomond Cycle Path, which continues along the loch shore to Tarbet (10 miles). The park website (www.lochlomond-trossachs.org) details some other local routes.

Loch Lomond Leisure   WATER SPORTS

(☑ 0333 577 0715; www.lochlomond-scotland.com; Luss) From Luss pier, Loch Lomond Leisure runs speedboat tours of the loch (short trip £10/5 per adult/child) as well as waterskiing or wakeboarding (both £40/105 for one/three sets) and other splashy activities. Kayaks (£20/65 per hour/day) and various boats are also available for hire.

Balmaha Boatyard   BOATING

(☑ 01360-870214; www.balmahaboatyard.co.uk; Balmaha; ⊙ 9am-5pm Apr-Oct, to 4pm Nov-Mar) The operator runs an on-demand ferry to the island of Inchcailloch, just offshore (£5 return). It also rents out rowing boats (£40 per day) and motorboats (£60 per day).

Tours

Sweeney's Cruises   BOATING

(☑ 01389-752376; www.sweeneyscruiseco.com; Balloch Rd, Balloch) Offers a range of trips including a one-hour return cruise to Inchmurrin (adult/child £10.50/7, five times daily April to October, twice daily November to March) and a two-hour cruise around the islands (£19/10.50, twice daily May to September plus weekends April and October). The quay is directly opposite Balloch train station. It also runs summer trips from a dock at Loch Lomond Shores (p50).

Piped commentary is by Neil Oliver.

Cruise Loch Lomond   BOATING

(☑ 01301-702356; www.cruiselochlomond.co.uk; Tarbet; ⊙ 8.30am-5.30pm Easter-Oct) With departures from Tarbet and Luss, this operator runs short cruises and two-hour trips to Arklet Falls and Rob Roy's Cave (adult/child £15/8). There are several options. You can also be dropped off at Rowardennan to climb Ben Lomond (£15/9), getting picked up in the afternoon, or after a 7-mile hike along the West Highland Way (£15/9).

From its Tarbet office, it also rents out bikes (half-/full day £13/17).

Loch Lomond Seaplanes   SCENIC FLIGHTS

(☑ 01436-675030; www.lochlomondseaplanes.com; flights from £119) Loch Lomond Seaplanes

Loch Lomond & the Trossachs NP

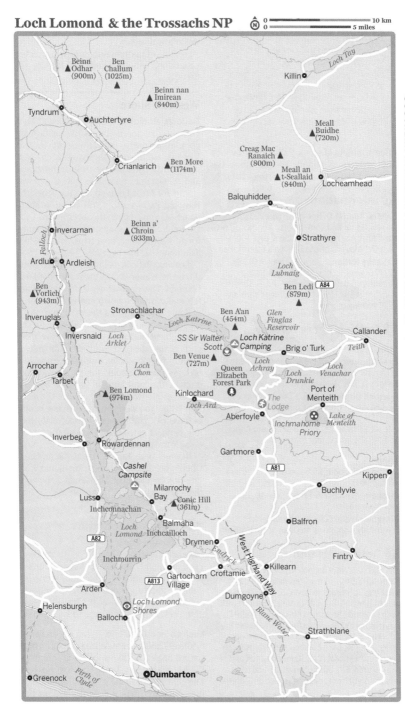

ℹ️ LOCH LOMOND WATER BUS

From mid-March to October a network of boats criss-crosses Loch Lomond, allowing you to explore the loch's hiking and biking trails using public transport. The Loch Lomond Water Bus timetable is available from tourist offices and on-line (www.lochlomond-trossachs.org).

offers a variety of scenic flights over the loch and western Scotland, leaving from the Cameron House Hotel just north of Balloch.

ℹ️ Information

Balloch Tourist Office (☑ 01389-753533; www.visitscotland.com; Balloch Rd; ☺ 9.30am-6pm Jul & Aug, to 5.30pm Jun & Sep, 10am-5pm Oct-May) Opposite Balloch's train station.

Balmaha National Park Centre (☑ 01389-722100; www.lochlomond-trossachs.org; Balmaha; ☺ 9.30am-4pm Apr-Oct, 9.30am-4pm Sat & Sun Nov-Mar) Has maps showing local walking routes.

ℹ️ Getting There & Away

BUS

First Glasgow (www.firstglasgow.com) Bus 1/1A runs from Argyle St in central Glasgow to Balloch (£5.30, 1½ hours, at least two per hour).

Scottish Citylink (☑ 0871 266 3333; www.citylink.co.uk) Coaches from Glasgow stop at Luss (£9.40, 55 minutes, 9 to 18 daily), Tarbet (£9.40, 65 minutes, 9 to 18 daily) and Ardlui (£16.90, 1½ hours, four to nine daily).

TRAIN

Glasgow–Balloch (£5.60, 45 minutes, every 30 minutes)

Glasgow–Arrochar & Tarbet (£12.40, 1¼ hours, four to seven daily)

Glasgow–Ardlui (£16.30, 1½ hours, four to seven daily, continuing to Oban or Fort William)

ℹ️ Getting Around

Bus 309 runs from Balloch to Drymen and Balmaha (£2.60, 20 minutes, nine to 10 daily), while bus 305 heads to Luss (£2.80, 20 minutes, nine to 10 daily). Bus 207 connects Balloch with Loch Lomond Shores and Alexandria. An **SPT Daytripper ticket** gives a family group unlimited travel for a day on most bus and train services in the Glasgow, Loch Lomond and Helensburgh area. Buy the ticket (£12.30 for one adult and two children, £21.80 for two adults and up to four children) from any train station or Glasgow bus station.

Tarbet and Ardlui are accessible by train and by Citylink buses between Glasgow and north-western destinations.

Local buses run from Helensburgh to Arrochar via Luss and Tarbet four times daily Monday to Friday.

Western Shore

Balloch, straddling the River Leven at Loch Lomond's southern end, is the loch's main population centre and transport hub. A Victorian resort once thronged by day trippers transferring between the train station and the steamer quay, it is now a 'gateway centre' for Loch Lomond and the Trossachs National Park. Visitors still arrive in abundance. On its edge, the overblown Loch Lomond Shores complex provides family-friendly attractions, boat trips, eating establishments and lots of retail.

Leaving Balloch behind, the road along the western shore offers great views of Loch Lomond. There's also busy traffic along what is a major route to north and west Scotland.

Some would say that the western shore of the loch serves a purpose: to take one for the team, accept the tour coaches and leave other parts of the lake comparatively traffic-free.

Head first for the picture-postcard village of **Luss**. Stroll among the pretty cottages, built by the local laird in the 19th century for his estate workers, and admire the loch-side vistas. You won't be alone: to live in one of these cute cottages must occasionally feel like being a celeb with paparazzi camped outside the door.

Beyond Luss, **Tarbet** sits at the junction where you choose between Argyll and Kintyre or Oban and the Highlands. Following the shore brings you to **Ardlui** and thence Crianlarich.

◎ Sights & Activities

Loch Lomond Shores   AREA
(www.lochlomondshores.com; ☺ 9.30am-6pm) Loch Lomond Shores, a major tourism development situated a half-mile north of Balloch, sports various visitor attractions, outdoor activities and boat trips. The heart of the development is a large shopping mall.

Loch Lomond Sea Life   AQUARIUM
(☑ 01389-721500; www.visitsealife.com; Loch Lomond Shores; £13.95, per person for 2 or more £12.30; ☺ 10am-5pm Mar-Oct, to 4pm Nov-Feb) The centrepiece of Loch Lomond Shores is this aquarium, which has displays on the

wildlife of Loch Lomond, an otter enclosure (housing short-clawed Asian otters, not Scottish ones), and a host of sea-life exhibits ranging from sharks to stingrays to sea turtles. It's a lot cheaper if you book online.

Maid of the Loch   SHIP
(www.maidoftheloch.com; ⊙11am-5pm school holidays & weekends Easter-Oct) **FREE** The vintage paddle steamer *Maid of the Loch,* built in 1953, is moored at Loch Lomond Shores while awaiting full restoration – you can nip aboard for a look around. With any luck, it might be operational for the 2019 summer.

🛏 Sleeping & Eating

Glenview   B&B **££**
(✆01389-528878; www.glenview-luss.co.uk; Luss; d £100-140; **P**⑦) In the centre of things on the road through Luss village, this white house offers a genuine welcome and three highly appealing suites. All are showroom-spotless: one comes with a full kitchen and dining area, the others with spacious lounge areas, with one also having a modish four-poster bed. Breakfast is continental, with a cooked option available in their cafe around the corner.

Loch Lomond Arms   INN **£££**
(✆01436-860420; www.lochlomondarmshotel. com; Main Rd, Luss; r £190-250; **P**⑦) Though you're paying quite a bit for the location, there's something very likeable about the modernised but still traditional rooms here, with their artful design, intriguing fabrics and creature comforts. There's a suite and self-catering options in nearby buildings. The bar and restaurant areas are attractive without pulling up any culinary trees.

Drover's Inn   PUB FOOD **££**
(✆01301-704234; www.thedroversinn.co.uk; Inverarnan; bar meals £9-14; ⊙11.30am-10pm Mon-Sat, to 9.30pm or 10pm Sun; **P**⑦) Don't miss this low-ceilinged howff (drinking den), just north of Ardlui, with its smoke-blackened stone, kilted bartenders, and walls festooned with moth-eaten stags' heads and stuffed birds. The convivial bar, where Rob Roy allegedly dropped by for pints, serves hearty hill-walking fuel and hosts live folk music on weekends.

Rooms could do with an upgrade but there are some newer ones in a separate building, the Stagger Inn.

Luss Seafood Bar   SEAFOOD **££**
(✆01436-860524; www.luss-seafoodbar.com; Church Rd, Luss; dishes £8-20; ⊙9am-6pm Feb-

Oct; ⑦) Curiously the eating establishments in Luss are tucked safely away from the lake; this place is no exception, set behind a shop on the main street. But it's a light, cheerful spot serving tasty fresh oysters, potted fish and smoked salmon. Prices are on the high side, but the produce is good. In winter it becomes a coffee shop.

Eastern Shore

Away from the busy western road, the loch's eastern shore is a quieter spot populated mostly by walkers and campers. Nevertheless, the narrow road gets busy. It runs from **Drymen** through attractive **Balmaha**, where you can hire boats.

There are several lochside picnic areas; **Milarrochy Bay** (1.5 miles north of Balmaha), has a nice gravel beach and superb views across the loch to the Luss hills.

The road ends at **Rowardennan**, where there's a hotel, hostels and boat hire, but the hiking trail West Highland Way (p48) continues north along the shore of the loch. It's 7 miles to **Inversnaid**, reachable by road from the Trossachs, and 15 miles to **Inveraran** at the loch's northern end. Rowardennan is also the launchpad for climbing Ben Lomond.

🛏 Sleeping & Eating

Book your accommodation ahead in the walking season, as it packs out. There are hostel, hotel and camping options as well as B&Bs along this stretch.

From March to September, wild camping is restricted on the eastern shore of Loch Lomond between Drymen and Ptarmigan Lodge (just north of the Rowardennan SYHA). There are campsites at Milarrochy, Cashel and Sallochy, and a hostel at Inversnaid.

Rowardennan SYHA   HOSTEL **£**
(✆01360-870259; www.syha.org.uk; Rowardennan; dm/tw/q £23.50/60/112; ⊙mid-Mar–mid-Oct; **P**⑦) Where the road ends on the eastern side of Loch Lomond, this is a postcard-quality retreat in an elegant ex-hunting lodge with lawns stretching right down to the water's edge. Whether you're walking the West Highland Way, climbing Ben Lomond or just putting your feet up, it's a great choice, with a huge lounge that has windows overlooking the loch.

Meals are available, including packed lunches for walkers, and there's a pub a short walk away. The wi-fi is a patchy satellite link.

Inversnaid Bunkhouse　　　　　HOSTEL £
(⏺ 01877-386249; www.inversnaid.com; Inversnaid; dm £20-23, d without bathroom £48-59, tent site per person £10; ⊙ Mar-Oct; 🅿 🛜 🐾) This former church is now a remote, welcoming hostel in a peaceful streamside location. It's popular with walkers and offers simple accommodation in crowded dorms, very pleasant doubles and grassy campsites (pre-pitched tents available). It's 15 miles from Aberfoyle by road, or by ferry from Loch Lomond's western side, or via an 8-mile walk north from Rowardennan on the West Highland Way.

A hot tub is great for aching muscles and the cafe serves simple meals (noon to 4pm and 6pm to 8pm), packed lunches and decent beers; you can also self-cater evening meals. It's a 15-minute uphill trudge from the lakeshore and trail, but they offer free transfers. A modern self-catering cabin is also available.

Cashel Campsite　　　　　CAMPSITE £
(⏺ 01360-870234; www.campingintheforest.co.uk; Rowardennan; site for 1/2 £18/25.45; ⊙ Mar-late Oct; 🅿 🐾) The most attractive campsite in this eastern shore area is 3 miles north of Balmaha, on the loch shore.

Oak Tree Inn　　　　　INN ££
(⏺ 01360-870357; www.theoaktreeinn.co.uk; Balmaha; s/d £80/100; 🅿 🛜) An attractive traditional inn built in slate and timber, this place offers bright, modern bedrooms for pampered hikers, plus super-spacious superior chambers, self-catering cottages and glamping pods with their own deck. The rustic restaurant brings locals, tourists and walkers together and dishes up hearty meals that cover lots of bases (mains £10 to £13; noon to 9pm). There's plenty of outdoor seating.

But it doesn't end there; the Oak Tree is an impressive set-up that brews its own beers, makes its own ice cream (and sells it in an adjacent cafe), and smokes its own fish. In fact, Balmaha basically is the Oak Tree these days.

Crianlarich & Tyndrum

POP 400

Surrounded by spectacular hillscapes at the northern edge of Loch Lomond and the Trossachs National Park, these villages are popular pit stops on the main A82 road for walkers on the West Highland Way and Munro-baggers. Crianlarich has a train station and more community atmosphere. Tyndrum (*tyne*-drum), 5 miles up the road, has two stations, a bus interchange, a petrol station and late-opening motorists' cafes, and is popular for the ascent of Munros **Cruach Ardrain** (1046m), **Ben More** (1174m) and magnificent **Ben Lui** (1130m).

🛏 Sleeping & Eating

Strathfillan Wigwams　　CAMPSITE, CABIN £
(⏺ 01838-400251;　　www.wigwamholidays.com; A82, Strathfillan; sites per adult/child £8/3, wigwam d small/large/en suite £40/50/75, lodge d £70-80; 🅿 📶 🛜 🐾) A working farm off the A82 between Crianlarich and Tyndrum, this place has heated 'wigwams': wooden A-frame cabins, with fridges and foam mattresses, that can sleep four at a pinch. More upmarket are the self-contained lodges with their own bathrooms and kitchen facilities. It also has camping and a shop. There's a two-night minimum on summer weekends. Wi-fi costs a small extra amount.

Crianlarich SYHA　　　　　HOSTEL £
(⏺ 01838-300260; www.syha.org.uk; Station Rd, Crianlarich; dm/tr/q £21/71/94; 🅿 📶 🛜) Well run and comfortable, with a spacious kitchen, dining area and lounge, this hostel is a real haven for walkers or anyone passing through. Dorms vary in size – there are some great en suite family rooms that should be booked in advance – but all are clean and roomy.

Ewich Guest House　　　　　B&B ££
(⏺ 01838-300536; www.ewich.co.uk; A82, Strathfillan; s £45, d £70-80; 🅿 🛜 🐾) This lovely Swiss-run stone farmhouse is just below the main road between Crianlarich and Tyndrum, but has a fabulous outlook over a valley, with uplifting views and a large garden. It's very handy for walking and cycling routes and boasts enticing rooms with cheerful fabrics and floorboards. Breakfast has home-laid eggs and there's a personable pooch.

Walker-friendly features like packed lunches, laundry and a drying room are also available.

Real Food Café　　　　　CAFE £
(⏺ 01838-400235; www.therealfoodcafe.com; A82, Tyndrum; mains £7-10; ⊙ 7.30am-8pm Nov-Mar, to 9pm Apr-Oct; 🛜 ♿) 🍴 Hungry hillwalkers throng the tables in this justifiably popular cafe. The menu looks familiar – fish and chips, soups, salads and burgers – but the owners make an effort to source sustainably and locally, and the quality shines through.

ⓘ Getting There & Away

BUS

Scottish Citylink (www.citylink.co.uk) runs several buses daily to Glasgow (£18.70, 1¾ hours), Fort William (£15.70, 1¼ hours) and Skye (£41.20, four to five hours) from both Crianlarich and Tyndrum. One bus a day goes to Oban in summer (£12.70, 1¼ hours).

TRAIN

Trains run to Tyndrum and Crianlarich from Fort William (£19.90, 1¾ hours, four daily Monday to Saturday, two on Sunday), Oban (£11.70, 1¼ hours, four or six daily) and Glasgow (£21.10, two hours, three to seven daily).

Arrochar

The village of Arrochar has a wonderful location, looking across the head of Loch Long to the jagged peaks of the Cobbler (Ben Arthur). The mountain takes its name from the shape of its north peak (the one on the right, seen from Arrochar), which looks like a cobbler hunched over his bench. The village makes a picturesque overnight stop.

Cobbler   HIKING
(Ben Arthur) To climb the Cobbler, an impressively handsome mountain of 884m, start from the roadside car park at Succoth near the head of Loch Long. A steep uphill hike through woods is followed by an easier section heading into the valley below the triple peaks. Then it's steeply uphill again to the saddle between the north and central peaks.

The central peak is higher, but awkward to get to – scramble through the hole and along the ledge to reach the airy summit. The north peak to the right is an easy walk. Allow five to six hours for the 5-mile round trip.

Village Inn   INN ££
(☑01301-702279;   www.villageinnarrochar.co.uk; Shore Rd; d £120-125; P🐾❄) The black-and-white 19th-century Village Inn is a gloriously convivial pub boasting a beer garden with a great view of the Cobbler. There are 14 en suite bedrooms, lovely renovated chambers, some with loch views and most with decent bathrooms. Meals (11am to 9pm) are bar standards supplemented by more ambitious blackboard specials – they're somewhat overpriced (mains £10 to £17) but tasty enough.

CLIMBING BEN LOMOND

Standing guard over the eastern shore of Loch Lomond is Ben Lomond (www.nts.org.uk; 974m), Scotland's most southerly Munro. It's a popular climb: most follow the Tourist Route up and down from Rowardennan car park. It's a straightforward route on a well-used and maintained path; allow five hours for the 7-mile round trip.

The Ptarmigan Route is less crowded and has better views, following a narrow but clearly defined path up the western flank, directly overlooking the loch, to a curving ridge leading to the summit. You can then descend via the Tourist Route, making this option a satisfying circuit.

To find the start of the Ptarmigan path, head north from Rowardennan car park 600m, past the SYHA hostel; cross the bridge after Ben Lomond Cottage and immediately turn right along a path through the trees. The route is then easy to follow.

The Trossachs

The Trossachs region has long been a favourite weekend getaway, offering outstanding natural beauty and excellent walking and cycling routes within easy reach of the country's southern population centres. With thickly forested hills, romantic lochs, national-park status and an interesting selection of places to stay and eat, its popularity is sure to continue.

The Trossachs first gained cachet in the early 19th century, when curious visitors came from across Britain, drawn by the romantic language of Walter Scott's poem 'Lady of the Lake', inspired by Loch Katrine and Rob Roy, about the derring-do of the region's most famous son.

In summer, the Trossachs can be overburdened with coach tours, but many of these are for day trippers – peaceful, long evenings gazing at the reflections in the nearest loch are still possible. If you can, it's worth timing your visit to avoid weekends.

Aberfoyle & Around

POP 700
Little Aberfoyle has lots to do close at hand and has great accommodation options nearby. It's also a stop on the Rob Roy Way

WORTH A TRIP

HILL HOUSE

Built in 1902 for Glasgow publisher Walter Blackie, Hill House (☑01436-673900; www.nts.org.uk; Upper Colquhoun St, Helensburgh; adult/child £10.50/7.50; ☉11.30am-5pm Mar-Oct) is perhaps architect Charles Rennie Mackintosh's finest creation – its timeless elegance still feels chic today. The interiors are stunning, with rose motifs and fabulous furniture. Water soaking through the rendered cement exterior means that you'll find the house enclosed in a giant covering structure. You can stay on the top floor here – check the Holidays section of the NTS website. It's near Upper Helensburgh station, though not all trains stop there.

The house also has a beautiful garden. Mackintosh was very protective of his creation: he once chided Mrs Blackie for putting the wrong-coloured flowers in a vase in the hall.

If you're arriving at Helensburgh Central station, it's about a 1-mile uphill walk to Hill House. Buses 302 and 306 can get you close.

(p48). However, it's crawling with visitors on most weekends and dominated by a huge car park, and is easily overwhelmed by day trippers. Callander or other Trossachs towns appeal more as a base.

◎ Sights & Activities

Inchmahome Priory RUINS
(☑01877-385294; www.historicenvironment.scot; Lake of Menteith; incl ferry adult/child £7.50/4.50; ☉10am-5pm Apr-Sep, to 4pm Oct, last ferry to island 45min before closing) From the **Lake of Menteith** (called 'lake' not 'loch' due to a mistranslation from Gaelic), 3 miles east of Aberfoyle, a ferry takes visitors to these substantial ruins. Mary, Queen of Scots was kept safe here as a child during Henry VIII's 'Rough Wooing'. Henry attacked Stirling, trying to force Mary to marry his son in order to unite the kingdoms.

★**Loch Katrine Circuit** CYCLING
An excellent 20-mile circular cycle route from Aberfoyle starts on the **Lochs & Glens Cycle Way** on the forest trail. Following the southern shore of Loch Achray, you reach the pier on Loch Katrine. The 10.30am boat (or afternoon sailings in summer) takes you to the western shore, from where you can follow the beautiful B829 via Loch Ard back to Aberfoyle.

Instead of getting the boat, you could bike it along the loch's northern shore, adding an extra 14 miles to the trip. An alternative to the forest trail from Aberfoyle is taking the A821 over Duke's Pass.

The Lodge OUTDOORS
(David Marshall Lodge; ☑0300 067 6615; www.forestry.gov.uk; A821; car park £1-3; ☉10am-4pm Oct-Dec & Mar-Apr, to 3pm Jan & Feb, to 5pm May-Jun & Sep, to 6pm Jul & Aug) Half a mile north of Aberfoyle, this nature centre has info about the many walks and cycle routes in and around the **Queen Elizabeth Forest Park**. There are live wildlife cameras offering a peek at osprey and barn-owl nests among others. The centre is worth visiting solely for the views.

Picturesque but busy waymarked trails start from here, ranging from a light 20-minute stroll to a nearby waterfall – with great interactive play options for kids – to a hilly 4-mile circuit. The centre has a popular cafe. Also here, **Go Ape!** (☑0333 920 4859; www.goape.co.uk; adult/child £33/25; ☉Sat & Sun Nov & Feb-Easter, Wed-Mon Easter-Oct) will bring out the monkey in you on its exhilarating adventure course of long ziplines, swings and rope bridges through the forest. Look out, too, for the spooky mirror sculptures by local artist Rob Mulholland.

🛏 Sleeping & Eating

Bield B&B ££
(☑01877-382351; www.thebield.net; Trossachs Rd, Aberfoyle; s/d £50/65; P 🐾) With a kind, genuine welcome, the Bield is exactly the sort of place you want after a long day's walking or cycling. This striking sandstone house has large, comfortable rooms, a sociable breakfast table and views from its hillside location just above Aberfoyle's centre. Prices are very reasonable.

★**Lake of Menteith Hotel** HOTEL £££
(☑01877-385258; www.lake-hotel.com; Port of Menteith; r £150-255; P 🐾🐾) Soothingly situated on a lake (yes, it's the only non-loch in Scotland) 3 miles east of Aberfoyle, this genteel retreat makes a great romantic getaway. Though all rooms are excellent, with a contemporary feel, it's worth an upgrade to the enormous 'lake heritage' ones with a view of the water: it really is a sensational outlook.

Even if you're not staying, head down to the waterside bar-restaurant (mains £10 to £17; open noon to 2.30pm and 5.30pm to 9pm, closed Monday and Tuesday from November to February). Check the website for packages.

★ **Aberfoyle Delicatessen & Trossachs Butcher** DELI £
(📞01877-382242; www.aberfoyledelibutcher.co.uk; 3 Dukes Ct, Aberfoyle; pies £2.20; ⊗8.30am-1.30pm & 2-5pm) This main-street shop is a cut above most of Aberfoyle's culinary offerings. There's good produce for self-caterers and excellent sandwiches, but the pies are a step beyond even those. Steak and black pudding? Venison? It's all delicious, and ingredients are specified for those with dietary needs.

ℹ️ Information

Aberfoyle Tourist Office (📞01877-381221; www.visitscotland.com; Main St; ⊗10am-5pm Apr-Oct, to 4pm Nov-Mar; 📶) A large office with a good selection of walking information.

ℹ️ Getting There & Away

First (www.firstgroup.com) has six daily buses (Monday to Saturday) from Stirling (£5.20, 55 minutes).

DRT operates in the Aberfoyle area.

Lochs Katrine & Achray

This rugged area, 7 miles north of Aberfoyle and 10 miles west of Callander, is the heart of the Trossachs. **Loch Katrine Cruises** (📞01877-376315; www.lochkatrine.com; 1hr cruise adult £12-14, child £6.50-7.50) run from Trossachs Pier at the eastern tip of beautiful Loch Katrine. One of these is the fabulous centenarian steamship *Sir Walter Scott;* check the website for departures, as it's worth taking a trip on this veteran if possible. There are various one-hour afternoon sailings, and at 10.30am (plus additional summer departures) there's a trip to Stronachlachar at the other end of the loch. From Stronachlachar (accessible by car via a 12-mile road from Aberfoyle), you can reach Loch Lomond's eastern shore at isolated Inversnaid. A tarmac path links Trossachs Pier with Stronachlachar, so you can take the boat out and walk/cycle back (14 miles). At Trossachs Pier, **Katrinewheelz** (📞01877-376366; www.katrinewheelz.co.uk; bike hire per half-/full day from £15/20; ⊗9am-5pm Apr-Oct, 11am-3pm Sat & Sun Nov-Dec & Feb-Mar) hires out good bikes. The cafe is mediocre so bring a picnic or eat at the other end of the loch.

Loch Achray Walks HIKING
The path to the rocky cone called **Ben A'an** (454m) begins at a car park just east of the Loch Katrine turn-off. It's easy to follow and the return trip is just under 4 miles. A tougher walk is up rugged **Ben Venue** (727m). Start walking from the signed car park just south of the Loch Katrine turn-off (7.5 miles return).

Loch Katrine Camping CABIN £
(📞01877-376317; www.lochkatrinecamping.com; Loch Katrine; pods £40-80; 🅿️ 📶 👶) Just beyond the ferry pier on Loch Katrine, this is a pleasing new place to stay, offering tent and motorhome pitches as well as cute camping pods with a little deck. They sleep two or four and come in two categories, one with underfloor heating and en suite bathroom. Book them well ahead. It's cheaper if you bring your own linen.

There's a two-night minimum stay for the en suite ones, one of which is adapted for wheelchair use.

Callander

POP 3100
Callander, the principal Trossachs town, has been pulling in tourists for over 150 years, and has a laid-back ambience along its main thoroughfare that quickly lulls visitors into lazy pottering. There's an excellent array of accommodation options here, and some intriguing places to eat. Good walking and cycling routes are close at hand.

◉ Sights & Activities

★ **Hamilton Toy Collection** MUSEUM
(📞01877-330004; www.thehamiltontoycollection.co.uk; 111 Main St; adult/child £3/1; ⊗10.30am-5pm Mon-Sat, noon-5pm Sun Apr-Oct; 👶) The Hamilton Toy Collection is a powerhouse of 20th-century juvenile memorabilia, chockfull of dolls houses, puppets and toy soldiers. It's an amazing collection and a guaranteed nostalgia trip. Phone ahead in winter as it opens some weekends.

> ℹ️ **TROSSACHS TRANSPORT**
>
> **DRT** (Demand Responsive Transport; 📞01786-404040; www.stirling.gov.uk) covers the Trossachs area. It sounds complex, but basically it means for the price of a bus you get a taxi to where you want to go. There are various zones. Taxis should preferably be booked 24 hours in advance by phone.

1

2

Scottish Castles

Scotland is home to more than one thousand castles, ranging from meagre 12th-century ruins to magnificent Victorian mansions. They all began with one purpose: to serve as fortified homes for the landowning aristocracy. But as society became more settled and peaceful, defensive features gave way to ostentatious displays of wealth and status.

Curtain Wall Castles

Norman castles of the 12th century were mainly of the 'motte-and-bailey' type, consisting of earthwork mounds and timber palisades. The first wave of stonebuilt castles emerged in the 13th century, characterised by massive curtain walls up to 3m thick and 30m tall to withstand sieges, well seen at Dunstaffnage Castle.

Tower Houses

The appearance of the tower house in the 14th century marks the beginning of the development of the castle as a residence. Clan feuds, cattle raiders and wars between Scotland and England meant that local lords built fortified stone towers in which to live.

1. Balmoral Castle (p143) 2. Dunvegan Castle (p214) 3. Dunstaffnage Castle (p103)

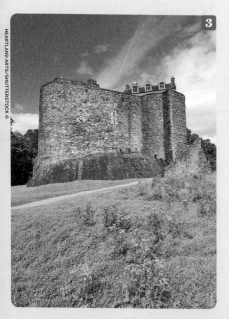

Artillery Castles

The arrival of gunpowder and cannon in the 15th century transformed castle design, with features such as gun loops, round towers, bulwarks and bastions making an appearance.

Status Symbols

The Scottish Baronial style of castle architecture, characterised by a profusion of pointy turrets, crenellations and stepped gables, had its origins in 16th- and 17th-century castles such as Craigievar and Castle Fraser, and reached its apotheosis in the royal residences of Glamis and Balmoral.

Bracklinn Falls & Callander Crags WALKING
Impressive Bracklinn Falls are reached by track and footpath from Bracklinn Rd (30 minutes each way from the car park). Also off Bracklinn Rd, a woodland trail leads up to Callander Crags, with great views over the surroundings; a return trip from the car park is about 4 miles.

Wheels Cycling Centre CYCLING
(☏01877-331100; www.scottish-cycling.com; bike per hour/day/week from £8/20/90; ☺10am-6pm Mar-Oct) The Trossachs is a lovely area to cycle around. On a cycle route, excellent Wheels Cycling Centre has a wide range of hire bikes. To get here from the centre of Callander, take Bridge St off Main St, turn right onto Invertrossachs Rd and continue for a mile.

🛌 Sleeping

★Callander Hostel HOSTEL £
(☏01877-331465; www.callanderhostel.co.uk; 6 Bridgend; dm/d £19.50/60; P@☎) ⏛ This hostel in a mock-Tudor building has been a major labour of love by a local youth project and is now a top-class facilty. Well-furnished dorms offer bunks with individual lights and USB charge ports, while en suite doubles have super views. Staff are lovely, and it has a spacious common area and share kitchen as well as a cafe and garden.

Abbotsford Lodge HOTEL ££
(☏01877-330066; www.abbotsfordlodge.com; Stirling Rd; d £75-85; ☺mid-Feb–early Nov; P☎) Offering excellent value for stylish contemporary rooms in a handsome Victorian house, this main-road choice has energetic owners who provide first-class hospitality and have a real eye for design. There are fabulous, spacious superiors (from £125) as well as cheaper top-floor rooms – with shared bathroom – that have lovably offbeat underroof shapes. It caters to cyclists and walkers with bike storage and packed lunches.

Room-only rates are available, but breakfast is top-notch. There are some appealing options for families, though no under-6s are allowed.

Arden House B&B ££
(☏01877-339405; www.ardenhouse.org.uk; Bracklinn Rd; d £100-125; ☺Mar-Oct; P☎) This elegant home has a fabulous hillside location with verdant garden and lovely vistas; close to Callander's centre but far from the crowds. The rooms are impeccable, with lots of natural light, and include large upstairs doubles with great views. Welcoming owners, noble architectural features – super bay windows – and a self-catering studio make this a top option.

There's a two-night minimum stay in summer.

Callander Meadows B&B ££
(☏01877-330181; www.callandermeadows.co.uk; 24 Main St; s £60, d £75-95; P☎☀) Upstairs at this recommended restaurant (p59) are some very appealing chambers, elegantly kitted out with solid furniture and good modern shower rooms. One, which can serve as a family room, has a four-poster bed. The owners are very welcoming and you are right in the heart of Callander. Breakfast is excellent.

★Roman Camp Hotel HOTEL £££
(☏01877-330003; www.romancamphotel.co.uk; off Main St; s/d/superior £135/160/260; P☎☀) Callander's best hotel is centrally located but feels rural, set by the river in beautiful grounds. Endearing features include a lounge with blazing fire and a library with a tiny secret chapel. It's an old-fashioned warren of a place with four grades of rooms; standards are certainly luxurious, but superiors are even more appealing, with period furniture, excellent bathrooms, armchairs and fireplace.

The upmarket restaurant is open to the public. Reassuringly, the name refers not to toga parties but to a ruin in the adjacent fields.

🍴 Eating

Mhor Bread CAFE, BAKERY £
(☏01877-339518; www.mhorbread.net; 8 Main St; light meals £2-6; ☺7am-5pm Mon-Sat, 8am-5pm Sun; ☎) ⏛ Great bread (sourdough, seeded, local) for picnics is baked at this high-street spot, which is also a good stop for decent coffee, pies and filled rolls. The steak and haggis pie is a treat.

★Venachar Lochside SCOTTISH ££
(☏01877-330011; www.venachar-lochside.com; Loch Venachar; mains £13-18; ☺noon-4pm Jan-Nov, plus 5.30-8.30pm Fri & Sat Jun-Sep; ☎♿) On lovely Loch Venachar, 4.5 miles west of Callander, this cafe-restaurant has a stunning waterside setting and does a nice line in carefully sourced produce (including delicious local trout) prepared in innovative ways. It opens from 10am for coffees, teas and baked goods. You can also hire boats and tackle to go fishing for trout on the loch.

Check its Facebook page for dinner openings.

★**Callander Meadows**　　　SCOTTISH **££**
(🖉01877-330181; www.callandermeadows.co.uk; 24 Main St; dinner mains £13-19; ⊙10am-2.30pm & 6-8.30pm Thu-Sun year-round, plus Mon May-Sep; 🛜) Informal and cosy, this well-loved restaurant in the centre of Callander occupies the front rooms of a Main St house. It's truly excellent; there's a contemporary flair for presentation and unusual flavour combinations, but a solidly British base underpins the cuisine. There's a great beer/coffee garden out the back, where you can also eat. Lighter lunches such as sandwiches are also available.

Poppy Seed　　　SCOTTISH **££**
(🖉01877-330329;www.poppyseedrestaurant.co.uk; Leny Rd; mains £12-18; ⊙noon-9pm Thu-Tue; 🛜) A revamp has seen this restaurant of a small main-road hotel invigorated by young owners. Start with an aperitif from the fine spirit selection of the handsome bar, then move through to dine on a short menu of quality ingredients prepared with imagination and deftly presented. In winter it's closed lunchtimes except on Sundays.

Mhor Fish　　　SEAFOOD **££**
(🖉01877-330213; www.mhorfish.net; 75 Main St; mains £9-18; ⊙noon-9pm Tue-Sun, closed Tue also Nov–mid-Feb; 🛜) 🥢 This simply decorated spot, with formica tables and a hodgepodge of chairs, sources brilliant sustainable seafood. Browse the fresh catch then eat it pan-seared in the dining area accompanied by a decent wine selection, or fried and wrapped in paper with chips to take away. It's all great, and calamari and oysters are wonderfully toothsome starters.

ℹ Getting There & Away

First (www.firstgroup.com) operates buses from Stirling (£5.80, 45 minutes, hourly Monday to Saturday, every two hours Sunday).

Kingshouse (🖉01877-384768; www.kingshousetravel.com) has buses between Callander and Killin (£5.30, 40 minutes, five to six Monday to Saturday).

For Aberfoyle, use DRT (p55) or get off a Stirling-bound bus at Blair Drummond safari park, cross the road and pick up an Aberfoyle-bound bus.

Balquhidder & Around

North of Callander, you'll skirt past the shores of gorgeous Loch Lubnaig. Not as famous as some of its cousins, it's still well worth a stop for its sublime views of forested hills. In the small village of Balquhidder (ball-whidder), 9 miles north of Callander off the A84, there's a churchyard with – perhaps – Rob Roy's grave. In the church itself is the 8th-century St Angus' stone, probably a marker to the original tomb of St Angus.

🛏 Sleeping

Mhor 84　　　INN **££**
(🖉01877-384646; www.mhor84.net; A84, Kingshouse; r without breakfast £90; 🅿🛜🐾) 🥢 At the A84 junction, this 18th-century inn has been given a modern-retro revamp and is an upbeat place with bags of facilities, simple, good-value rooms and a delicious menu of hearty, nourishing meals following the Mhor philosophy of local and sustainable. A great pit stop for drivers, walkers and cyclists. Some rooms are in a rear cottage; there's also a self-catering one.

There are three menus served: breakfast from 8am to noon, a daytime one from noon to 5pm and dinner to 9pm.

★**Monachyle Mhor**　　　HOTEL **£££**
(🖉01877-384622; www.monachylemhor.net; d £195-285, wagon £125; ⊙Feb-Dec; 🅿🛜🐾) 🥢 A luxury hideaway with a fantastically peaceful location overlooking two lochs, Monachyle Mhor is a great fusion of country Scotland and contemporary attitudes to design and food. Rooms are superb and feature quirkily original decor, particularly the fabulous 'feature rooms'. Otherwise, go glamping in a retro wagon or kip in a romantic…ferry waiting room. The restaurant is excellent.

It's an enchanting combination of top-class hospitality with a relaxed rural atmosphere: dogs and kids happily romp on the lawns, and no one looks askance if you come in flushed and muddy after a day's fishing or walking.

ℹ Getting There & Away

Local buses between Callander and Killin stop at the main-road turn-off to Balquhidder, as do daily buses with **Scottish Citylink** (www.citylink.co.uk) between Edinburgh and Oban/Fort William.

Balquhidder is part of the DRT scheme (p55), which you can use to get to Monachyle Mhor from the main road.

Killin

POP 800

A fine base for the Trossachs or Perthshire, this lovely village sits at the western end of Loch Tay and has a spread-out, relaxed feel, particularly around the scenic Falls of

Dochart, which tumble through the centre. On a sunny day people sprawl over the rocks by the bridge, with pint or picnic in hand. Killin offers fine walking around the town, and there are mighty mountains and glens close by.

🏃 Activities

Five miles northeast of Killin, Ben Lawers (1214m) rises above Loch Tay. Walking routes abound; one rewarding circular walk heads up into the Acharn forest south of town, emerging above the treeline to great views of Loch Tay and Ben Lawers. Killin Outdoor Centre (☑01567-820652; www.killinoutdoor. co.uk; Main St; bike per 24hr £25, kayak/canoe per 2hr £25; ☺8.45am-5.30pm) provides walking advice.

Glen Lochay runs westwards from Killin into the hills of Mamlorn. You can take a mountain bike up the glen; the scenery is impressive and the hills aren't too difficult. It's possible, on a nice summer day, to climb over the top of Ben Challum (1025m) and descend to Crianlarich, but it's hard work. A potholed road, not maintained and no longer suitable for cars, also connects Glen Lochay with Glen Lyon.

Killin is on the Lochs & Glens Cycle Way from Glasgow to Inverness. Hire bikes from helpful Killin Outdoor Centre (which also has canoes and kayaks and, in winter, crampons and snowshoes).

Loch Tay Fish 'n' Trips FISHING
(☑07967 567347; www.lochtayfishntrips.co.uk) Loch Tay is famous for its fishing – salmon, trout and pike are all caught here. Fish 'n' Trips can kit you out for a day's fishing with a boat, tackle and guide for £120 for two people, or rent you a boat for £60 a day.

🛏 Sleeping & Eating

High Creagan CAMPSITE £
(☑01567-820449;www.facebook.com/highcreagan caravanpark; Aberfeldy Rd; per person tent/caravan sites £7/9; ☺Apr-Oct; ℗) High Creagan is a long-established favourite with a good-humoured boss and a well-kept, sheltered campsite with plenty of grass set high on the slopes overlooking sparkling Loch Tay, 3 miles east of Killin. Under-15s aren't allowed in the tent area (for insurance reasons), as there's a stream running through it.

⭐ Courie Inn INN ££
(☑01567-831000; www.thecourieinn.com; Main St; d £99-140; ℗🛜) An excellent all-round choice, Courie Inn has quality, comfortable rooms decorated with restrained modern elegance; they come in a variety of sizes, including a sumptuous suite with views. It artfully blends the traditional and contemporary. Downstairs, the restaurant does smart bistro food (mains £11 to £15; daily 5pm to 8.30pm, plus noon to 3pm Friday to Sunday), and there's a bar.

Old Bank B&B ££
(☑01567 829317; www.theoldbankkillin.co.uk; Manse Rd; s/d £55/80; ℗🛜) This four-square building with a pretty garden stands proud above the main street in Killin. It's a genuinely welcoming place, with a host who does everything in her power to make you feel welcome. Breakfast is abundant and the rooms are super-comfortable, with contemporary colours, hill views and thoughtful extras.

ⓘ Getting There & Away

Kingshouse (www.kingshousetravel.com) runs five to six buses Monday to Saturday to Callander (£5.30, 40 minutes), where you can change for Stirling.

ROB ROY

Nicknamed Red ('ruadh' in Gaelic, anglicised to 'roy') for his ginger locks, Robert MacGregor (1671–1734) was the wild leader of the wildest of Scotland's clans, outlawed by powerful neighbours, hence their sobriquet, Children of the Mist. Incognito, Rob became a prosperous livestock trader, before a dodgy deal led to a warrant for his arrest.

A legendary swordsman, the fugitive from justice then became notorious for daring raids into the Lowlands to carry off cattle and sheep. Forever hiding from potential captors, he was twice imprisoned, but escaped dramatically on both occasions. He finally turned himself in and received his liberty and a pardon from the king. He lies buried – perhaps – in the churchyard at Balquhidder; his uncompromising later epitaph reads 'MacGregor despite them'. His life has been glorified over the years due to Walter Scott's novel and the 1995 film. Many Scots see his life as a symbol of the struggle of the common folk against the inequitable ownership of vast tracts of the country by landed aristocrats.

SOUTH ARGYLL

The impossibly tortuous coastline of the mainland and islands of South Argyll would confuse the most adept geographer. Sea lochs slice the rugged land into peninsulas that offer some of Scotland's most spectacular coastal scenery. The archipelago of islands includes the whisky Shangri La of Islay, the brooding hills of lonely Jura and the retro charms of Bute.

Cowal

The remote and picturesque Cowal Peninsula is cut off from the rest of the country by the lengthy fjords of Loch Long and Loch Fyne. It comprises rugged hills and narrow lochs, with only a few small villages and the old-fashioned, down-at-heel holiday resort of Dunoon. It makes for great, off-the-beaten-track exploration at a very accessible range from busier Glasgow and Loch Lomond.

The attractive Cowal Way (www.cowalway.co.uk) is a 57-mile walking path crossing the region.

From Arrochar, the A83 to Inveraray loops around the head of Loch Long and climbs into spectacular Glen Croe. The pass at the head of the glen is called the Rest and Be Thankful. As you descend Glen Kinglas on the far side, the A815 forks to the left just before Cairndow; this is the main overland route into Cowal.

There are ferries to Cowal from Gourock and Tarbert. Buses run from Glasgow to Dunoon via the ferry. Other buses run by West Coast Motors (☑ 01586-559135; www.westcoastmotors.co.uk) head overland into and around the peninsula.

Dunoon & Around

Like Rothesay on Bute, Dunoon is a Victorian seaside resort that owes its existence to the steamers that once carried thousands of Glaswegians on pleasure trips 'doon the watter' in the 19th and 20th centuries. Fortunes declined when cheap foreign holidays stole the market and Dunoon is still a bit down in the dumps. Bypass its ugly town centre and take in the magnificent perspectives along the long waterfront.

The town's main attraction is still, as it was in the 1950s, strolling along the promenade, licking an ice-cream cone and watching the yachts at play in the Firth of Clyde.

Benmore Botanic Garden   GARDENS
(☑01369-706261; www.rbge.org.uk; A815; adult/child £6.50/free; ⊙10am-6pm Apr-Sep, to 5pm Mar & Oct) This garden, 7 miles north of Dunoon, contains Scotland's finest collection of flowering trees and shrubs, including impressive displays of rhododendrons and azaleas, and is entered along a spectacular avenue of giant redwoods. A highlight is the Victorian fernery, nestled in an unlikely fold in the crags. The cafe here (which also opens through some of the winter) appeals for lunch or coffee. Buses run between here and Dunoon.

Cowal Highland
Gathering   CULTURAL, SPORTS
(www.cowalgathering.com; Hillfoot St, Dunoon; ⊙late Aug) One of the closest Highland Games to the southern cities, this Dunoon extravaganza is held in late August. The spectacular finale features more than 1000 bagpipers saluting the chieftain.

ⓘ Getting There & Away

BOAT

Dunoon is served by two competing ferry services from Gourock (near Greenock). Argyll Ferries is better if you are travelling on foot and want to arrive in the town centre.

Argyll Ferries (www.argyllferries.co.uk; adult/child £4.65/2.35, 25 minutes, half-hourly Monday to Saturday, hourly Sunday)

Western Ferries (www.western-ferries.co.uk; adult/child/car £4.60/2.30/17.60, 20 minutes, two to three hourly) Arrives at a pier just over a mile from the centre of Dunoon. Departs from McInroy's Point, 2 miles south of Gourock train station on the Irvine road; Scottish Citylink buses run to here.

BUS

McGill's Buses (☑ 08000 51 56 51; www.mcgillsbuses.co.uk) run from Glasgow to Dunoon (£9.80, two hours, five to seven daily) via the ferry. It's quicker between Gourock and Glasgow to jump on the train.

Buses around the Cowal Peninsula, to Inveraray (£3.90) and to Rothesay on Bute (£3.50), are operated by West Coast Motors.

Tighnabruaich

POP 200

Sleepy little seaside Tighnabruaich (tinna-*broo*-ah) is one of the most attractive villages on the Firth of Clyde and by far the most appealing place at which to overnight on the Cowal Peninsula.

★ **Botanica** BISTRO **££**
(☑ 01700-811186; www.botanicafood.co.uk; Main St; dinner mains £14-23; ☺ 8.30am-4pm Wed, Thu & Sun, to 11pm Fri & Sat, extended summer hours; 🛜🚗) In the centre of Tighnabruaich village, this place offers a touch of eclecticism focused on solid British ingredients, with simple classics like asparagus with Bearnaise sauce making a lovely lunchtime treat, and a changing dinner menu featuring locally landed fish. Understandably, it tends to pack out for dinner, so it's best to book. It also has four rooms available.

Bute

POP 6500

The scenic island of Bute lies pinched between the thumb and forefinger of the Cowal Peninsula, separated from the mainland by a narrow, picturesque strait. The Highland Boundary Fault cuts through the middle of the island so that, geologically speaking, the northern half is in the Highlands and the southern half is in the central Lowlands. The main town, Rothesay, is a Victorian resort with a long waterfront and noteworthy castle; south of here is the grand pile of Mount Stuart, one of Scotland's finest stately homes. The west side of the island features dreamy outlooks across to the hills of Arran.

ⓘ Information

Isle of Bute Discovery Centre (☑ 01700-507043; www.visitscotland.com; Victoria St; ☺ 9.30am-5.30pm Jul & Aug, to 5pm Apr-Jun & Sep, 10am-5pm Oct, 10am-4pm Mon-Sat & 11am-3pm Sun Nov-Mar; 🛜) There's a free audiovisual display here that provides an upbeat introduction to the island. It's in Rothesay's restored Winter Gardens building – once an entertainment venue and still serving as a cinema.

ⓘ Getting There & Away

Buses run by West Coast Motors cross to Bute from the Cowal Peninsula.

CalMac (☑ 0800 066 5000; www.calmac. co.uk) has ferries between Wemyss Bay and Rothesay (adult/car £3.15/11.30, 35 minutes, roughly hourly). Another crosses the short stretch of water between Rhubodach in the north of the island and Colintraive (adult/car £1.15/5.95, five minutes, half-hourly) in Cowal.

Rothesay

POP 4500

From the mid-19th century until the 1960s, Rothesay was one of Scotland's most popular holiday resorts, bustling with day trippers disembarking from numerous steamers crowded around the pier. Its hotels were filled with elderly holidaymakers and convalescents taking advantage of the famously mild climate.

Cheap foreign holidays saw Rothesay's fortunes decline, but a nostalgia-fuelled resurgence of interest has seen many Victorian buildings restored. The grassy, flowery waterfront and row of noble villas make it a lovely place to be once again.

⊙ Sights

Rothesay Castle CASTLE
(☑ 01700-502691; www.historicenvironment.scot; King St; adult/child £5/3; ☺ 9.30am-5.30pm Apr-Sep, 10am-4pm Sat-Wed Oct-Mar) The splendid, ruined 13th-century Rothesay Castle, with seagulls and jackdaws nesting in the walls, was once a favourite residence of the Stuart kings. It is unique in Scotland in having a circular plan, with four stocky round towers. The landscaped moat, with manicured turf, flower gardens and lazily cruising ducks, makes a picturesque setting.

Victorian Toilets HISTORIC BUILDING
(Rothesay Pier; adult/child 40p/free; ☺ 9am-3.45pm Mon-Thu, to 4.45pm Fri-Sun Oct-Apr, 8am-5.45pm Mon-Thu, to 7.30pm Fri-Sun May-Sep) Dating from 1899, these toilets are a monument to lavatorial luxury – a disinfectant-scented temple of green and black marbled stoneware, glistening white enamel, glass-sided cisterns and gleaming copper pipes. The attendant will escort you into the bathrooms of the opposite sex for a look around when unoccupied. You can shower here, too.

🛏 Sleeping

Bute Backpackers Hotel HOSTEL **£**
(☑ 01700-501876; www.butebackpackers.co.uk; 36 Argyle St; s/tw/d £25/45/50, s without bathroom £20; 🅿🛜🐾) An appealing budget option on Rothesay's main thoroughfare, this large, well-equipped place has private rooms of various sizes at bargain prices. Some are en suite, but the shared bathrooms are modern and spotless, with power showers. The kitchen is huge, and there's a barbecue as well.

★ **Boat House**　　　　　　　B&B **££**
(☑01700-502696; www.theboathouse-bute.co.uk;
15 Battery Pl; d £80-90; 🛜🐾) Boat House
brings a touch of class to Rothesay's guesthouse scene, with quality fabrics and furnishings and an eye for design that makes
it feel like a boutique hotel, without the
expensive prices. Rooms are very swish, with
a kitchenette and breakfast provided. Other
features include a garden, sea views, a central location and a ground-floor room kitted
out for wheelchair users.

There's a two-night minimum stay on
weekends.

Glendale Guest House　　　　B&B **££**
(☑01700-502329; www.glendale-guest-house.com;
20 Battery Pl; s £47, d £66-90, f £125; 🅿🛜) This
grand Victorian waterfront villa, complete
with turret, offers very generous rooms with
plush furniture and good family options.
Front-facing bedrooms have superb sea views
from large windows, as do the lavishly elegant
lounge and the breakfast room, where you'll
find homemade smoked haddock fishcakes
on the menu among other interesting options.
Genial hosts make for a pleasurable stay.

St Ebba　　　　　　　　　　B&B **££**
(☑01700-500059; www.rothesayaccommodation.
co.uk; 37 Mountstuart Rd; s/d £45/70; 🅿🛜) Turn
left from the ferry in Rothesay and follow
the shoreline to reach this typically noble
Victorian lodge, divided into two B&Bs. This
place, entered down the right, takes full advantage of the lovely views with its spacious
rooms with big windows. Sea-view rooms
cost an extra £10. Courteous hosts.

🍴 **Eating**

★ **Musicker**　　　　　　　　CAFE **£**
(☑01700-502287; www.musicker.co.uk; 11 High
St; mains £3-7; ⏱10am-5pm Mon-Sat; 🛜🖉)
This cool little cafe serves Bute's best coffee,
alongside a range of home baking, soups
and sandwiches with imaginative fillings. It
also sells CDs, books and guitars, and sports
an old-fashioned jukebox.

Harry Haw's　　　　　　　BISTRO **££**
(☑01700-505857; www.harryhawsbute.co.uk; 23
High St; mains £9-15; ⏱noon-9pm; 🛜🖉) There
are great scenes at this welcoming modern
bistro with an attractive interior and views
over Rothesay Castle. Its moderate prices
and pleasing range of deli-style fare plus
burgers, local roast meat and tasty pas-
tas make it a standout. The staff are very
friendly and so cheerful you'll wonder if
there's something in the water.

Around Rothesay

★ **Mount Stuart**　　　　HISTORIC BUILDING
(☑01700-503877; www.mountstuart.com; adult/
child £13/7.50; ⏱11am-4pm Apr, May & Oct, to
5pm Jun-Sep, see website for winter hours, grounds
10am-6pm Mar-Oct) The family seat of the
Stuart Earls of Bute is one of Britain's more
magnificent 19th-century stately homes, the
first to have a telephone, underfloor heating
and a heated pool. Its eclectic interior, with
an imposing central hall and chapel in Italian marble, is heavily influenced by the third
Marquess' interests in Greek mythology and
astrology. The drawing room has paintings
by Titian and Tintoretto among other masters. Mount Stuart is 5 miles south of Rothesay; bus 490 runs here hourly.

Buy tickets at the visitor centre (or book
online), from where it's a 15-minute stroll
(a courtesy bus is also available) through
lovely grounds to the house. Entry is either
by guided tour or free visit, depending on
the time. Private tours (£20 or £40) offer
glimpses of the pool and more bedrooms.

There's a cafe serving famously opulent
afternoon teas (book ahead).

Discounted ferry-plus-entrance tickets are
available from **CalMac** (www.calmac.co.uk).

Inveraray
POP 600

There's no fifty shades of grey around here:
this historic planned village is all black and
white – even logos of high-street chain shops
conform. Spectacularly set on the shores of
Loch Fyne, Inveraray was built by the Duke
of Argyll in Georgian style when he re-
vamped his nearby castle in the 18th century.

⊙ **Sights**

Inveraray Castle　　　　　　CASTLE
(☑01499-302203; www.inveraray-castle.com; adult/
child/family £11/8/32; ⏱10am-5.45pm Apr-Oct)
This visually stunning castle on the north
side of town has been the seat of the Dukes
of Argyll – chiefs of Clan Campbell – since
the 15th century. The 18th-century building,
with its fairy-tale turrets and fake battlements, houses an impressive armoury hall,
its walls patterned with more than 1000 pole
arms, dirks, muskets and Lochaber axes.
Entry is slightly cheaper if you book online.

FYNE FOOD & DRINK

Eight miles north of Inveraray, at the head of Loch Fyne, it pays to stop by two great local establishments:

Loch Fyne Oyster Bar (☑01499-600482; www.lochfyne.com; Clachan, Cairndow; mains £13-26; ☺9am-5pm; ☏) The success of this cooperative is such that it now lends its name to dozens of restaurants throughout the UK. But the original is still the best, with large, salty, creamy oysters straight out of the lake, and fabulous salmon dishes. The atmosphere and decor is simple, friendly and unpretentious; it also has a shop and deli where you can eat casually.

Fyne Ales (☑01499-600120; www.fyneales.com; Achadunan, Cairndow; tours £5; ☺10am-6pm) The friendly folk here do a great range of craft beers in this attractive modern brewery off the A83 9 miles northeast of Inveraray. There's a lovely bar-cafe (with outdoor seating) where you can taste them all: the light, citrussy Jarl is a standout. Call ahead to book tours, which run for about 45 minutes. A range of walks tackle the pretty glen from a car park nearby.

Inveraray Jail   MUSEUM
(☑01499-302381; www.inverarayjail.co.uk; Church Sq; adult/child £11.50/7; ☺9.30am-6pm Apr-Oct, 10am-5pm Nov-Mar; ☷) At this entertaining interactive tourist attraction you can sit in on a trial, try out a cell and discover the harsh tortures that were meted out to unfortunate prisoners. The attention to detail – including a life-sized model of an inmate squatting on a 19th-century toilet – is excellent, and actors enliven things during busy periods. Last admission is an hour before closing.

🛏 Sleeping & Eating

★George Hotel   INN ££
(☑01499-302111; www.thegeorgehotel.co.uk; Main St E; d £90-135; P☏☷) The George boasts a magnificent choice of opulent, individual rooms decorated with sumptuous period furniture. Some feature four-poster beds, Victorian roll-top baths and/or private jacuzzis (superior rooms and suites cost £145 to £180 per double; the library suite is quite a sight). Some rooms are in an annexe opposite and there are also self-catering options.

The cosy wood-panelled bar, with rough stone walls, flagstone floor and peat fires, is a delightful place for all-day bar meals, and has a beer garden.

Samphire   SEAFOOD ££
(☑01499-302321; www.samphireseafood.com; 6a Arkland; dinner mains £11-21; ☺noon-2.30pm & 5.30-9pm Wed-Fri, noon-2.30pm & 5-11pm Sat, noon-2.30pm & 5-9pm Sun; ☏) 🍴 There's lots to like about this compact restaurant that makes an effort to source sustainable local seafood. There's a fairly light touch from the kitchen, which tends to let the natural flavours shine through, with very pleasing results.

ⓘ Getting There & Away

Scottish Citylink (www.citylink.co.uk) has buses running from Glasgow to Inveraray (£13, 1¾ hours, up to nine daily). Some continue to Campbeltown (£14.20, 2¼ hours); others to Oban (£10.80, 1¼ hours). There are also buses to Dunoon (£3.90, 1¼ hours, three daily Monday to Saturday)

Crinan Canal

Completed in 1801, picturesque Crinan Canal runs for 9 miles from Ardrishaig to Crinan allowing seagoing vessels – mostly yachts, these days – to take a short cut from the Firth of Clyde and Loch Fyne to the west coast of Scotland, avoiding the long passage around the Mull of Kintyre. You can easily walk or cycle the canal towpath in an afternoon.

★Venture West   BOATING
(☑07789 071188; www.venture-west.co.uk; Crinan Harbour; 2½-hour trip adult/child £35/25; ☺Mar-Oct) Venture West has really enjoyable boat trips run from Crinan (other pick-up points are available) out to Jura, the Garvellach islands and the Corryvreckan Whirlpool. Highlights include sea eagles and (tide-dependent) landings on remote islands. Note that trips run from the old harbour, a little further west than the harbour at the end of the canal. Longer trips head to Iona and Staffa.

★Crinan Hotel   HOTEL £££
(☑01546-830261; www.crinanhotel.com; Crinan; s £155, d £230-290; ☺Mar-Dec; P☏☷) Romantic Crinan Hotel boasts one of the west coast's most spectacular views. All the bright, light rooms enjoy wonderful perspectives, and the somewhat faded old-world atmosphere is beguiling, with paintings throughout and a top-floor gallery. You're paying for the

ambience and view here: don't expect five-star luxury. It's run with welcoming good humour and offers various eating options.

The restaurant Westward (set dinner £45; ⊘7-8.30pm; 🐾) does posh set dinners, the cosy Crinan Seafood Bar (mains £13-19; ⊘noon-2.30pm & 6-8.30pm; 🐾) does great fresh food, including excellent local mussels with white wine and garlic, and the nearby Crinan Coffee Shop (snacks £3-7; ⊘9am-6pm Apr-Oct; 🐾) has great home baking. Upstairs, Lock 16 opens for seafood dinners with spectacular views on summer weekends.

ⓘ Getting There & Away

West Coast Motors (www.westcoastmotors.co.uk) has the 425/426 service from Lochgilphead that runs along the canal to Crinan once or twice Monday to Friday. This allows you to walk the canal one way and get the bus back the other.

Kilmartin Glen

This magical glen is the focus of one of the biggest concentrations of prehistoric sites in Scotland. Burial cairns, standing stones, stone circles, hill forts and cup-and-ring-marked rocks litter the countryside. Within a 6-mile radius of Kilmartin village there are 25 sites with standing stones and more than 100 rock carvings.

In the 6th century, Irish settlers arrived in this part of Argyll and founded the kingdom of Dál Riata (Dalriada), which eventually united with the Picts in 843 to create the first Scottish kingdom. Their capital was the hill fort of Dunadd, on the plain to the south of Kilmartin.

Kilmartin House Museum   MUSEUM
(🖉01546-510278; www.kilmartin.org; adult/child £6.50/2.50; ⊘10am-5.30pm Mar-Oct, 11am-4pm Nov-late Dec) This museum, in Kilmartin village, is a fascinating interpretive centre that provides a context for the ancient monuments you can go on to explore, alongside displays of artefacts recovered from various sites. Funding has nearly been achieved for a major redevelopment of the museum, so check the website for the latest details before visiting. It also has a cafe (mains £5-9; 🐾🖉) 🍴 and a good shop with handicrafts and books on Scotland.

Dunadd Fort   ARCHAEOLOGICAL SITE
(⊘24hr) FREE This hill fort, 3.5 miles south of Kilmartin village, was the seat of power of the first kings of Dál Riata, and may have been where the Stone of Destiny was originally located. Faint rock carvings of a boar and two footprints with an ogham inscription may have been used in inauguration ceremonies. The prominent little hill rises straight out of the boggy plain of Moine Mhor Nature Reserve.

A slippery path leads to the summit, where you can gaze out on much the same view that the kings of Dál Riata enjoyed 1300 years ago.

ⓘ Getting There & Away

Bus 423 between Oban and Ardrishaig (three to five Monday to Friday, two on Saturday) stops at Kilmartin (from Oban £5.60, one hour).

You can walk or cycle along the Crinan Canal from Ardrishaig, then turn north at Bellanoch on the minor B8025 road to reach Kilmartin (12 miles one way). It's a lovely journey.

Kintyre

The 40-mile long Kintyre peninsula is almost an island, with only a narrow isthmus at Tarbert connecting it to Knapdale. During the Norse occupation of the Western Isles, the Scottish king decreed that the Vikings could

---

RETURN OF THE BEAVER

Beavers had been extinct in Britain since the 16th century. But in 2009 they returned to Scotland, when a population of Norwegian beavers was released into the hill lochs of Knapdale, Argyll. After a broadly successful trial, the beavers are now here to stay; the first successful reintroduction of a previously extinct mammal to Britain.

If the beavers are still present, you can try to get a glimpse of them on the Beaver Detective Trail. This circular walk starts from the Barnluasgan forestry car park on the B8025 road to Tayvallich, about 1.5 miles south of the Crinan Canal. There's an information hut here. The trail is 3 miles, but you might glimpse them at pretty Dubh Loch just half a mile down the track.

Near here, the Heart of Argyll Wildlife Organisation (🖉01546-810218; www.heartofargyllwildlife.org; Barnluasgan; ⊘10am-5pm Apr-Oct) has a visitor centre and runs guided wildlife walks, including beaver-oriented ones.

claim as their own any island they circumnavigated in a longship. So in 1098 the wily Magnus Barefoot stood at the helm while his men dragged their boat across this neck of land, validating his claim to Kintyre.

The coastline is spectacular on both sides, with stirring views of Arran, Islay, Jura and Northern Ireland. On a sunny day the water shimmers beyond the stony shore. Hiking the Kintyre Way is a great means of experiencing the peninsula, which has a couple of cracking golf courses at Machrihanish near Campbeltown.

Tarbert

POP 1100

The attractive fishing village and yachting centre of Tarbert is the gateway to Kintyre, and is most scenic, with buildings strung around its excellent natural harbour. A crossroads for nearby ferry routes, it's a handy stepping stone to Arran or Islay, but is well worth a stopover on any itinerary.

The picturesque harbour is overlooked by the crumbling, ivy-covered ruins of **Tarbert Castle** (⊘24hr) FREE, rebuilt by Robert the Bruce in the 14th century. You can hike up via a signposted footpath beside **Loch Fyne Gallery** (☑01880-820390; www.lochfynegallery. com; Harbour St; ⊘10am-5pm Mon-Sat, 10.30am-5pm Sun), which showcases the work of local artists.

🎊 Festivals & Events

Tarbert Seafood Festival　　　FOOD & DRINK
(www.tarbertfestivals.co.uk; ⊘1st weekend Jul) Food stalls, cooking demonstrations, music and family entertainment.

Tarbert Music Festival　　　MUSIC
(www.tarbertfestivals.co.uk; ⊘3rd weekend Sep) A festival of live folk, blues, jazz, rock, beer, *ceilidhs* (evenings of traditional Scottish entertainment), more beer...

OFF THE BEATEN TRACK

WALK KINTYRE

Tarbert is the starting point for the 103-mile **Kintyre Way** (www.kintyreway. com), a walking route that meanders the length of the peninsula to Southend at the southern tip and around to Machrihanish. It's very scenic, with wonderful coastal views nearly the whole way.

🛏 Sleeping & Eating

Starfish Rooms　　　B&B **£**
(☑01880-820304; www.starfishtarbert.com; Castle St; s/d without breakfast £35/70; 🛜) Above the restaurant of the same name, but run separately, this corridor of compact, floor-boarded en suite rooms is a good deal, particularly for single travellers. Rooms 6 and 7 are doubles with attractive exposed stone walls. Breakfast isn't included, but there are cafes very close at hand.

★**Knap Guest House**　　　B&B **££**
(☑01880-820015;　www.knapguesthouse.co.uk; Campbeltown Rd; d £90-99; 🛜) This cosy upstairs spot at the bend in the main road offers faultless hospitality, luxurious furnishings and an attractive blend of Scottish and Far Eastern decor, with wooden elephants especially prominent. The welcome is warm, and there are great harbour views from the breakfast room, where the open kitchen allows you to admire the host at work. Prices drop in low season.

Rooms are plush, with the owner's years in hospitality paying dividends for guests. One is a suite (£135 to £180), which has an excellent, spacious lounge area with vistas.

Moorings　　　B&B **££**
(☑01880-820756; www.themooringsbb.co.uk; Pier Rd; s £50-60, d £80; P🛜) Follow the harbour just past Tarbert's centre to this spot, which is beautifully maintained and decorated by one man and his dogs. It has great views over the water and an eclectic menagerie of ceramic and wooden animals and offbeat artwork; you can't miss it from the street.

★**Starfish**　　　SEAFOOD **££**
(☑01880-820733;　www.starfishtarbert.com; Castle St; mains £12-23; ⊘6-9pm Sun-Thu, noon-2pm & 6-9pm Fri & Sat mid-Mar–Oct; 🛜) 🍴 This attractive, very welcoming restaurant does simple, stylish seafood of brilliant quality. A great variety of specials – anything from classic French fish dishes to Thai curries – are prepared with whatever's fresh off the Tarbert boats that day. There are options for vegetarians and meat-eaters too, and decent cocktails. Closed Sunday and Monday early and late in the season.

ℹ Getting There & Away

BOAT

CalMac (www.calmac.co.uk) operates a car ferry from Tarbert to Portavadie on the Cowal

SKIPNESS

Tiny Skipness, 13 miles south of Tarbert, is pleasant and quiet with great views of Arran. Beyond the village rise the substantial remains of 13th-century Skipness Castle (www.historicenvironment.scot; ⊘castle & chapel 24hr, tower 9.30am-5.30pm Apr-Sep, 10am-4pm Oct) FREE, a former possession of the Lords of the Isles.

Attached to Skipness House, near the castle, Skipness Seafood Cabin (☑01880-760207; www.skipnessseafoodcabin.co.uk; dishes £3-18; ⊘11am-7pm Sun-Fri late May-Sep) has a great summer scene on a fine day, serving no-frills but delicious local fish and shellfish dishes at outdoor picnic tables that have grand views over the grassy coast across to Arran. It's famous for its crab rolls, which are on the small side: add on a pot of mussels or plate of gravadlax.

The hot smoked salmon from Skipness Smokehouse (☑01880-760378; www.creelers.co.uk; ⊘noon-5pm Sun-Fri Mar-Dec) behind Skipness Castle was one of the highlights of a long-standing seafood restaurant on Arran. That's closed, but you can get hold of it at their new smokehouse here, along with other treats. There's usually somebody around even outside the official opening hours.

Peninsula (adult/car £2.70/8.40, 25 minutes, six to 12 daily). From late October to March there are also ferries to Lochranza on Arran (adult/car £2.90/9.70, 1¼ hours, one daily) that must be booked in advance.

Ferries to Islay and Colonsay depart from Kennacraig ferry terminal, 5 miles southwest.

BUS

Tarbert is served by four to five daily coaches with **Scottish Citylink** (www.citylink.co.uk), between Campbeltown (£8.40, one hour) and Glasgow (£17.70, 3¼ hours).

Gigha

POP 200

Gigha (*ghee*-ah; www.gigha.org.uk) is a low-lying island, 6 miles long by about 1 mile wide, famous for its sandy beaches, pristine turquoise water and mild climate – subtropical plants thrive in Achamore Gardens (☑01583-505275; www.gigha.org.uk; Achamore House; suggested donation adult/child £6/3; ⊘dawn-dusk). Other highlights include the ruined church at Kilchattan, the bible garden at the manse, and Gigha's picturesque northern end.

The island was famously purchased by its residents in 2002, though they have had some financial problems since. Local Gigha cheeses include goats cheese and oak-smoked cheddar.

Gigha Hotel   INN ££

(☑01583-505254; www.gighahotel.com; Ardminish; s £65, d £92-98; [P][⊛][⊛]) The island's quirky hotel, just south of the central junction, has a variety of cosy rooms, some with views. It also serves breakfasts, bar meals and restaurant dishes (mains £10 to £16).

★The Boathouse   SEAFOOD ££

(☑01583-505123; www.boathouseongigha.com; Ardminish; mains £10-20; ⊘11.30am-9pm mid-Mar-Oct; [⊛]) This picturesque stone cottage is right by the water near the ferry slip. It's *the* place to go for fresh seafood: local lobster, delicious oysters and sustainable, organic Gigha-farmed halibut are the highlights. Sit at the deck outside and admire the idyllic view. You can also camp here (£4/2 per adult/child), but space is limited so call in advance.

ⓘ Getting There & Away

CalMac (www.calmac.co.uk) runs from Tayinloan in Kintyre (adult/car £2.60/7.60, 20 minutes, roughly hourly). Stopping at the terminal are four to five daily buses with **Scottish Citylink** (www.citylink.co.uk), in each direction between Glasgow/Tarbert and Campbeltown

Campbeltown & Around

POP 4800

Blue-collar Campbeltown is set around a beautiful harbour. It still suffers from the decline of its fishing and whisky industries and the closure of the nearby air-force base, but is rebounding on the back of golf tourism, increased distillery action and a ferry link to Ayrshire. The spruced-up seafront backed by green hills lends the town a distinctly optimistic air.

WORTH A TRIP

MULL OF KINTYRE

A narrow winding road, 15 miles long, leads south from Campbeltown to the Mull of Kintyre, passing good sandy beaches near Southend. This remote headland was immortalised in the famous song by Paul McCartney and Wings; the former Beatle owns a farmhouse in the area. From the road's end, a 30-minute steep downhill walk leads to a clifftop lighthouse, with Northern Ireland, only 12 miles away, visible across the channel. Don't leave the road when the frequent mists roll in; it's easy to become disoriented.

◉ Sights & Activities

Springbank   DISTILLERY

(☑01586-551710; www.springbankwhisky.com; 85 Longrow; tours from £7; ⊙tours 10am, 11.30am, 1.30pm & 3pm Mon-Fri, 10am & 11.30am Sat) There were once no fewer than 32 distilleries around Campbeltown, but most closed in the 1920s. Today this is one of only three still in operation. It is also one of the few around that distills, matures and bottles all its whisky on the one site, making for an interesting tour. It produces a quality malt, one of Scotland's finest. Various premium tours take you deeper into the process.

Davaar Cave   CAVE

(⊙24hr) FREE A very unusual sight awaits in this cave on the southern side of Davaar island, at the mouth of Campbeltown Loch. On the wall of the cave is an eerie painting of the Crucifixion by local artist Archibald MacKinnon, dating from 1887. You can walk to the island at low tide: check tide times with the tourist office.

🛏 Sleeping & Eating

★**Campbeltown Backpackers**   HOSTEL £

(☑01586-551188; www.campbeltownbackpackers. co.uk; Big Kiln St; dm £20; P🖥) ✎ This beautiful hostel occupies a central former school building: it's great, with a modern kitchen, state-of-the-art wooden bunks and access for people with disabilities. Profits go to maintain the Heritage Centre (opposite) that runs it. Rates are £2 cheaper if you book ahead.

Argyll Hotel   INN ££

(☑01583-421212; www.argylehotelkintyre.co.uk; A83, Bellochantuy; s £45, d £80-90; P🖥🐾) Right on a fine stretch of beach with a magnificent outlook to Islay and Jura, this traditional inn 10 miles north of Campbeltown on the main road is run with cheery panache. Rooms are cosy and breakfast is a highlight, with creative egg dishes and a wealth of homemade jams, as you gaze over the water. The restaurant does some inventive fusion fare.

The water reaches the heady heights (for Scotland) of 11°C in summer if you fancy a dip. Don't confuse this place with the Argyll Arms Hotel in Campbeltown itself.

Royal Hotel   HOTEL £££

(☑01586-810000; www.machrihanishdunes.com; Main St; r £185-215; P🖥) Historically Campbeltown's best address, this reddish sandstone hotel opposite the harbour is looking swish again. It caters mostly to yachties and golfers. Although rack rates feel overpriced, there are often online specials and rooms are very spacious and attractive. There are some excellent midweek specials that include golf at Machrihanish Dunes and a couple of extras.

Food is served noon to 9pm Sunday to Thursday, and to 10pm Friday and Saturday.

🍷 Drinking & Nightlife

Ardshiel Hotel   BAR

(☑01586-552133; www.ardshiel.co.uk; Kilkerran Rd; ⊙noon-11pm Mon-Sat, from 12.30pm Sun; 🖥) This friendly hotel has one of Scotland's best whisky bars, the perfect place to learn more about the Campbeltown distilling tradition and to taste the local malts. With over 700 whiskies to choose from, it's not a place for the indecisive.

ℹ Getting There & Away

AIR

Loganair (www.loganair.co.uk) flies between Glasgow and Campbeltown's mighty runway at Machrihanish.

BOAT

Kintyre Express (☑01586-555895; www. kintyreexpress.com; ⊙Apr-Sep) operates a small, high-speed passenger ferry from Campbeltown to Ballycastle in Northern Ireland (£50/90 one way/return, 1½ hours, daily May to August, Friday to Sunday April and September). You must book in advance. From Ballycastle it heads on to Islay (£60/95 one way/return from Ballycastle) and back before the return trip to Campbeltown. It also runs charters.

CalMac (www.calmac.co.uk) runs thrice weekly May to September between Ardrossan in Ayrshire and Campbeltown (adult/car £7.90/41.70, 2¾ hours); the Saturday return service stops at Brodick on Arran.

BUS

Scottish Citylink (www.citylink.co.uk) runs from Campbeltown to Glasgow (£21.60, 4¼ hours, four to five daily) via Tarbert, Inveraray and Loch Lomond. Change at Inveraray for Oban.

Islay

POP 3200

The home of some of the world's greatest and peatiest whiskies, whose names reverberate on the tongue like a pantheon of Celtic deities, Islay (*eye*-lah) is a wonderfully friendly place whose welcoming inhabitants offset its lack of scenic splendour compared to Mull or Skye. The distilleries are well geared-up for visits, but even if you're not a fan of single malt, the birdlife, fine seafood, turquoise bays and basking seals are ample reasons to visit. Locals are among Britain's most genial: a wave or cheerio to passersby is mandatory, and you'll soon find yourself unwinding to relaxing island pace. The only drawback is that the waves of well-heeled whisky tourists have induced many sleeping options to raise prices to eye-watering levels.

Tours

Islay Sea Safaris   BOATING

(☑01496-840510; www.islayseasafari.co.uk; Port Ellen) Customised tours (£25 to £30 per person per hour) by sea from Port Ellen to spot some or all of Islay and Jura's distilleries in a single day, as well as birdwatching trips, coastal exploration, and trips to Jura's remote west coast and the Corryvreckan Whirlpool.

✱ Festivals & Events

Fèis Ìle   MUSIC, FOOD & DRINK

(Islay Festival; www.islayfestival.com; ⊘ late May) A weeklong celebration of traditional Scottish music and whisky. Events include *ceilidhs* (evenings of traditional Scottish entertainment), pipe-band performances, distillery tours, barbecues and whisky tastings. The island packs out; book accommodation well in advance.

Islay Jazz Festival   MUSIC

(www.islayjazzfestival.co.uk; ⊘ 2nd weekend Sep) This three-day festival features a varied line-up of international talent playing at various venues across the island.

ℹ Information

Bowmore Tourist Office (☑ 01496-305165; www.islayinfo.com; The Square; ⊘10am-5pm Mon-Sat, noon-3pm Sun Mar-Jun, 9.30am-5.30pm Mon-Sat, noon-3pm Sun Jul & Aug, 10am-5pm Mon-Sat Sep-Oct, 10am-3pm Mon-Fri Nov-Feb) One of the nation's best tourist offices. The staff will bend over backwards to find you accommodation if things look full up.

ℹ Getting There & Away

There are two ferry terminals: Port Askaig on the east coast, and Port Ellen in the south. Islay airport lies midway between Port Ellen and Bowmore.

AIR

Loganair (www.loganair.co.uk) flies up to three times daily from Glasgow to Islay, while **Hebridean Air Services** (☑ 0845 805 7465; www.hebrideanair.co.uk; Oban Airport, North Connel) operates twice daily on Tuesday and Thursday from Oban to Colonsay and Islay.

BOAT

CalMac (www.calmac.co.uk) runs ferries from Kennacraig to Port Ellen or Port Askaig (adult/car £6.70/33.45, two hours, three to five daily).

GOLF AT MACHRIHANISH

Machrihanish, 5 miles northwest of Campbeltown, is home to a couple of classic golf courses:

Machrihanish Golf Club (☑01586-810277; www.machgolf.com; Machrihanish; green fee £75) Machrihanish Golf Club is a classic links course, designed by Old Tom Morris. It's remarkably good value compared to courses of a similar standard elsewhere in Scotland. The famous first hole requires a very decent drive across the bay, or you'll literally end up on the beach. Nearby is an upmarket hotel and restaurant, as well as self-catering villas.

Machrihanish Dunes (☑01586-810000; www.machrihanishdunes.com; Machrihanish; green fee £75) Much newer than its venerable neighbour Machrihanish Golf Club, the Dunes is an impressive seaside experience and commendably light on snobbery: the clubhouse is a convivial little hut, kids play free and there are always website offers. Good packages including accommodation are available.

On Wednesday and Saturday in summer you can travel to Colonsay (adult/car £4.15/17.30, 1¼ hours, day trip possible) and Oban (adult/car £9.60/51.45, four hours).

Book car space on ferries several days in advance.

❶ Getting Around

BICYCLE

There are various places to hire bikes, including **Islay Cycles** (☑07760 196592; www.islaycycles. co.uk; 2 Corrsgeir Pl, Port Ellen; bikes per day/ week from £20/70) and **Port Charlotte Bicycle Hire** (☑01496-850488; Main St, Port Charlotte; 1/3 days £15/35; ☺9am-6pm).

BUS

A bus links Ardbeg, Port Ellen, Bowmore, Port Charlotte, Portnahaven and Port Askaig (Monday to Saturday only). You can get unlimited travel for 24 hours for £10, but fares are low anyway. Pick up a copy of the *Islay & Jura Public Transport Guide* from the Bowmore Tourist Office or on the ferry on the way over.

CAR

Islay Car Hire (☑01496-810544; www.islay carhire.com; Islay Airport) offers car hire from £35 a day and can meet ferries.

TAXI

There are various taxi services on Islay; **Carol's Cabs** (☑07775 782155, 01496-302155; www. carols-cabs.co.uk) is one that can take bikes.

Port Ellen & Around

Port Ellen is Islay's principal entry point. The coast stretching northeast is one of the loveliest parts of the island, where within 3 miles you'll find three of whisky's biggest names: Laphroaig, Lagavulin and Ardbeg.

The kelp-fringed skerries (small rocky islands or reefs) of the **Ardmore Islands**,

---

GONE FISHIN'

A lifetime's experience of exploring his native rivers, lochs and coastline means there isn't much that professional guide Duncan Pepper of **Fishinguide Scotland** (☑07714-598848; www.fishinguide.co.uk; daily per person from £150; ⏷) doesn't know about Scottish fishing. Though based in Argyll, he leads fishing trips all over Scotland for salmon, trout, pike, pollack and more. Packages include travel, instruction, permits, tackle and a lavish picnic lunch.

---

near Kildalton, are a wildlife haven and home to Europe's second-largest colony of common seals.

◉ Sights

The three southern distilleries of Laphroaig, Lagavulin and Ardbeg are arrayed in an easy succession east of town. The Port Ellen distillery itself, dismantled apart from its malting works in 1983, is due to reopen by 2021.

Ardbeg　　　　　　　　　　　DISTILLERY
(☑01496-302244; www.ardbeg.com; tours from £6; ☺9.30am-5pm Mon-Fri year-round, plus Sat & Sun Apr-Oct) Ardbeg's iconic peaty whiskies start with their magnificent 10-year-old. The basic tour is good, and it also offers longer tours involving walks, stories and extended tastings. It's 3 miles northeast of Port Ellen; there's a good cafe (p71) for lunch here, too.

Lagavulin　　　　　　　　　　DISTILLERY
(☑01496-302749; www.lagavulindistillery.com; tours from £6; ☺9am-6pm Mon-Fri, to 5pm Sat & Sun May-Sep, 9am-5pm daily Apr & Oct, 10am-4pm Mon-Sat Nov-Mar) Peaty and powerful, this is one of the triumvirate of southern distilleries near Port Ellen. The Core Range tour (£15) is a good option, cutting out much of the distillery mechanics that you might have already experienced elsewhere and replacing it with an extended tasting.

Laphroaig　　　　　　　　　　DISTILLERY
(☑01496-302418; www.laphroaig.com; tours from £10; ☺9.45am-5pm daily Mar-Oct, to 4.30pm daily Nov & Dec, to 4.30pm Mon-Fri Jan & Feb) Laphroaig produces famously peaty whiskies just outside Port Ellen. Of the various premium tastings that it offers, the 'Water to Whisky' tour (£100) is recommended – you see the water source, dig peat, have a picnic and try plenty of drams.

Kildalton Cross　　　　　　　MONUMENT
(Kildalton; ☺24hr) 𝗙𝗥𝗘𝗘 A pleasant drive or ride leads past the distilleries to ruined **Kildalton Chapel**, 8 miles from Port Ellen. In the kirkyard is the exceptional late 8th-century Kildalton Cross. There are carvings of biblical scenes on one side and animals on the other.

🛏 Sleeping & Eating

Kintra Farm　　　　　CAMPSITE, B&B £
(☑01496-302051; www.kintrafarm.co.uk; tent site £6-8, plus adult/child £4/2; ☺May-Sep; 🅿🐾) At the southern end of Laggan Bay, 3.5 miles northwest of Port Ellen, Kintra is a basic but beautiful campsite on buttercup-sprinkled

Islay, Jura & Colonsay

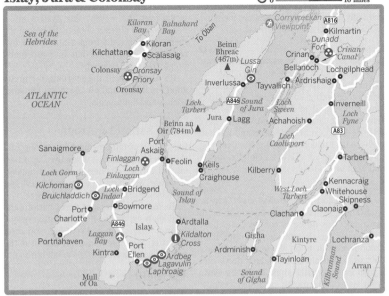

turf amid the dunes, with sunset views across the beach. There's also B&B and self-catering cottages at this working farm.

Askernish B&B
B&B **££**

(☑01496-302536; www.askernishbandb.co.uk; 49 Frederick Cres, Port Ellen; s £50, d £90-100; 🛜) Very handy for the Port Ellen ferry slip, this dark-stone Victorian house was once the local medical practice; indeed, one of the rooms is in the former surgery, while another is the waiting room. Rooms are generous, with old-style flowery decor but modern bathroom fittings. The owner takes real interest in her guests and is a delight.

Old Kiln Café
CAFE **£**

(☑01496-302244; www.ardbeg.com; Ardbeg; mains £8-13; ⊙10am-3.45pm Mon-Fri year-round, plus Sat & Sun Apr-Oct; 🛜) Housed in the former malting kiln at Ardbeg distillery, this cafe serves homemade soups, tasty light meals, heartier daily specials and a range of desserts, including traditional clootie dumpling (a rich steamed pudding filled with currants and raisins).

SeaSalt
BISTRO, PIZZA **££**

(☑01496-300300; www.seasalt-bistro.co.uk; 57 Frederick Cres, Port Ellen; mains £10-16; ⊙noon-2.30pm & 5-8.45pm) This buzzy modern place represents an unusual combination in Port Ellen: a takeaway doing kebabs, pizzas and bacon rolls, but also a bistro. High-backed dining chairs are comfortable for devouring local seafood off a menu of daily specials. The prawn and crayfish cocktail is a great place to start. It also opens from 10am to noon for coffee and breakfasty fare.

Bowmore

POP 700

Islay's attractive Georgian capital was built in 1768 to replace the village of Kilarrow, which just had to go – it was spoiling the view from the laird's house. Its centrepieces are the **Bowmore Distillery** (☑01496-810441; www.bowmore. com; School St; tours from £10; ⊙9.30am-5pm Mon-Sat, noon-4pm Sun Mar-Oct, 10am-5pm Mon-Sat Nov-Feb) and distinctive **Round Church** at the top of Main St, built in circular form to ensure that the devil had no corners to hide in. He was last seen in one of the island's distilleries.

🛏 Sleeping

★ Lambeth House
B&B **££**

(☑01496-810597; lambethguesthouse@tiscali.co.uk; Jamieson St; s/d £70/98; 🛜) Cheerily welcoming, and with smart modern rooms with top-notch en suite bathrooms, this is a sound option in the centre of town. The host is a long-time expert in making guests feel at home, and her breakfasts are reliably good. Rooms vary substantially in size but their prices are the same, so ask for a larger one when booking.

Dha Urlar   B&B ££
(☑07967505991;www.dha-urlar-bed-and-breakfast. co.uk; Cruach; r £125-150; 🅿🛜) Just a mile out of Bowmore, this place sits in an elevated position granting spectacular perspectives across moorland to Jura, the Mull of Kintyre and the coast of Ireland. Rooms have lots of space, comfortable beds and modern bathrooms. Breakfast is served from an open kitchen while your hosts helpfully supply you with lots of local information.

Island Bear   B&B ££
(☑01496-301462; www.islandbear.co.uk; Shore St; s/d £75/100; 🛜) As central as you can be in Bowmore, this house is compact and built very vertically, though some ground-floor accommodation is on the way. Rooms are cosy and inviting, with modern decor and stylish en suite bathrooms. There are views from two of the rooms, a kindly welcome and tasty breakfasts.

Bowmore House   B&B £££
(☑01496-810324; www.thebowmorehouse.co.uk; Shore St; s/d from £85/135; 🅿🛜) This stately former bank building has plenty of character and super water views. It's a top-level B&B, with coffee machines in the rooms, an honesty minibar with bottles of wine and local ales, and plush king-sized beds. Rooms are spacious, high-ceilinged and light. Further rooms are in adjacent cottages, also available on a self-catering basis.

 Eating

Peatzeria   ITALIAN ££
(☑01496-810810; www.peatzeria.com; 22 Shore St; mains £11-18; ⊙noon-10pm, closed Mon in winter; 🛜) This is one of those names that just had to be...nice work, punsters! An impressively realised church conversion has created a warmly welcoming Italian restaurant that specialises in toothsome stone-baked pizzas but also does a great line in antipasti, lasagne and other pasta dishes. The weatherproof conservatory seating area has special views over the bay.

Harbour Inn   BRITISH ££
(☑01496-810330; www.bowmore.com; The Square; mains £15-20; ⊙noon-2.30pm & 6-9.30pm; 🛜) Owned by the Bowmore Distillery, this restaurant at the **Harbour Inn** (s/d from £115/

145) is the classiest in town. The conservatory-style dining area offers wonderful sunset views over the water. Islay oysters are a delicious and obvious choice; the rest of the menu could benefit from a little more seasonal and local focus, but is competently prepared and presented.

It's also open in the morning for pretty good breakfasts and all afternoon for sandwiches and light meals.

Port Charlotte & Around

Eleven miles from Bowmore, on the opposite shore of Loch Indaal, is attractive Port Charlotte, a former distillery town that appeals as a base. Museums in town and distilleries close by mean there's plenty to do.

Six miles southwest of Port Charlotte the road ends at **Portnahaven**, a picturesque fishing village. For seal-spotting, you can't do better; there are frequently dozens of the portly beasts basking in the small harbour.

◉ Sights

★**Bruichladdich**   DISTILLERY
(☑01496-850190; www.bruichladdich.com; Bruichladdich; tours from £5; ⊙9am-6pm Mon-Fri, to 5pm Sat, 10am-4pm Sun Apr-Sep, reduced hours Oct-Mar) A couple of miles from Port Charlotte, Bruichladdich (brook-*lad*-dy) is an infectiously fun distillery to visit and produces a mind-boggling range of bottlings; there's always some new experiment cooking. The standard expression is lightly peated, but they turn out some phenolic monsters under the Port Charlotte and Octomore labels. They also make a gin here, the Botanist, infused with local herbs. A generous attitude to tastings makes for an uplifting visit.

Kilchoman   DISTILLERY
(☑01496-850011; www.kilchomandistillery.com; Rockfield Farm, Kilchoman; tours from £7; ⊙9.45am-5pm Apr-Oct, closed Sat & Sun Nov-Mar) 🌿 Likeable Kilchoman, set on a farm, is one of Scotland's smallest distilleries. It grows and malts some of its own barley here and does its own bottling by hand. It has a wide variety of attractively packaged expressions: the 100% Islay whiskies are the ones produced from the home-grown barley. The tour is informative and the tasting generous. There's also a good cafe.

Museum of Islay Life   MUSEUM
(☑01496-850358; www.islaymuseum.org; Port Charlotte; adult/child £4/1; ⊙10.30am-4.30pm Mon-Fri

Apr-Oct) Islay's long history is lovingly recorded in this museum, housed in the former Free Church. Prize exhibits include an illicit still, 19th-century crofters' furniture, and a set of leather boots once worn by the horse that pulled the lawnmower at Islay House (so it wouldn't leave hoof prints on the lawn!).

🛏 Sleeping & Eating

Islay SYHA
HOSTEL £

(☎01496-850385; www.syha.org.uk; Main St, Port Charlotte; dm/tw/q £20/48/90; ☺Apr-Oct; @�ऀ) This clean and modern brick hostel has spotless dorms with washbasins and a large kitchen and living room. It's housed in a former distillery building with views over the loch. The bus stops nearby. Breakfast and heatable dinners are available. Have a crack at Islay Monopoly, one of the board games on hand.

Distillery House
B&B ££

(☎01496-850495; mamak@sky.com; Main St, Port Charlotte; s £38, d £80, tw without bathroom £76; ☐ऀ) For genuine islander hospitality at a fair price, head to this homely B&B, on the right as you enter Port Charlotte from the north. Set in part of the former Lochindaal distillery, it's run by a kindly local couple who make their own delicious marmalade and oatcakes. Rooms are well kept and most comfortable. The cute single has sea views. Minimum two-night stay.

Port Charlotte Hotel
HOTEL £££

(☎01496-850360; www.portcharlottehotel.co.uk; Main St, Port Charlotte; s/d/f £175/240/290; ☐ऀ☻) This lovely old Victorian hotel has individually decorated bedrooms – modern but classic in style – with crisp white sheets, good toiletries and sea views. It's a friendly place with a plush lounge, cosy bar and quality restaurant.

Yan's Kitchen
BISTRO ££

(☎01496-850230; www.yanskitchen.co.uk; Main St, Port Charlotte; tapas £4-7, mains £13-22; ☺food noon-3pm & 5.30-9pm Tue-Sun Apr-Oct; ☝) On the left as you enter Port Charlotte from the north, this cabin-like restaurant offers confident bistro cuisine, using ingredients like duck breast and local scallops to create satisfying, well-presented plates, whether Spanish tapas or evening seafood specials. The appealing wooden-floored interior takes full advantage of the coastal views. It's also open from 10.30am to noon for coffee and scones.

DON'T MISS

ISLAY'S DISTILLERIES

Islay has nine working distilleries, with a tenth, the back-from-the-dead Port Ellen, on the way. All welcome visitors and run tours, which you should definitely book ahead by phone, as they have maximum numbers and can fill up days in advance. More expensive, specialised tours let you taste more malts and take you further behind the scenes. Pick up the invaluable pamphlet listing tour times from the Bowmore Tourist Office (p69). Five of the nine distilleries can be reached by the island's buses; a bit of walking, hitching or cabbing will easily get you to the others.

Port Askaig & Around

Port Askaig is set in a picturesque nook halfway along the Sound of Islay. It's little more than a hotel, shop (with ATM), petrol pump and ferry pier. There are three distilleries within reach and ferry connections to the mainland and Jura, just across the strait.

Three miles southwest, lush meadows swathed in buttercups and daisies slope down to reed-fringed Loch Finlaggan. This bucolic setting was once the most important settlement in the Hebrides, the central seat of power of the Lords of the Isles from the 12th to the 16th centuries.

⭐ Finlaggan
RUINS

(☎01496-840644; www.finlaggan.org; adult/child £4/2; ☺ruins 24hr, museum 10.30am-4.15pm Mon-Sat Apr-Oct) Three miles from Port Askaig, tumbledown ruins of houses and a chapel on an islet in a shallow loch mark what remains of the stronghold of the Lords of the Isles. A wooden walkway leads over the reeds and water lilies to the island, where information boards describe the remains. Start your exploration at the visitor centre, which has some good explanations of the site's history and archaeology and a video featuring Tony Robinson. The island itself is open at all times.

The setting is beautiful and the history fascinating. The MacDonald clan, descendants of the legendary warrior Somerled, administered their island territories from here from the 12th to the 15th centuries and entertained visiting chieftains in their great hall. A smaller island, Eilean na Comhairle, was reserved for solemn councils. Though this unassuming inland loch seems a strange place from which to wield serious political power, it had likely been an important place since prehistoric times. A crannog, fort and early Christian chapel were all located here, and the presence of ritual stones possibly aligned to the brooding Paps of Jura means the MacDonalds may have appropriated a place that already had strong ritual significance.

Buses between Bowmore and Port Askaig stop at the road junction, from where it's a 15-minute walk to the loch.

Ballygrant Inn PUB
(☑ 01496-840277; www.ballygrant-inn.co.uk; Ballygrant; ⊙ 11am-1am Mon-Sat, 12.30pm-midnight Sun; 🐾) If you're serious about whisky, you'll want to stop by this attractive bar to try one of its 700-plus malts. Though customer service can vary, the owners have a deep knowledge of local whisky and can guide your selection. There are also quality ales on tap and good food here, with outdoor tables to admire the view.

Jura
POP 200

Jura lies long, dark and low off the coast like a vast Viking longship, its billowing sail the distinctive triple peaks of the Paps of Jura. A magnificently wild and lonely island, it's the perfect place to get away from it all –

as George Orwell did in 1948. Orwell wrote his masterpiece *Nineteen Eighty-Four* while living at the remote farmhouse of Barnhill in the north of the island.

Jura takes its name from the Old Norse *dyr-a* (deer island) – an apt appellation, as the island supports a population of around 6000 red deer, outnumbering their human cohabitants by about 30 to one.

There's a shop but no ATM on Jura; you can get cash back with debit cards at the Jura Hotel.

◉ Sights

Isle of Jura Distillery DISTILLERY
(☑ 01496-820385; www.jurawhisky.com; Craighouse; tours from £6; ⊙ 10am-4.30pm Mon-Sat Apr-Oct, to 4pm Mon-Fri Nov-Mar) There aren't a whole lot of indoor attractions on the island of Jura apart from visiting the Isle of Jura Distillery. The standard tour runs twice a day, while specialist tours (£15 to £25) take you deeper into the production process and should be booked in advance.

Lussa Gin DISTILLERY
(☑ 01496-820323; www.lussagin.com; Ardlussa) At the northern end of Jura island, three local women have set up this distillery in the former stables of the Ardlussa estate. It produces gin that's flavoured with local botanicals. Phone ahead to book a tour (£6), which includes a taste of the refreshing lemony spirit.

THE SCOTTISH MAELSTROM

The Gulf of Corryvreckan – the channel (0.6 miles wide) between the northern end of Jura and the island of Scarba – is home to one of the most notorious tidal whirlpools in the world.

On Scotland's west coast, the rising tide – the flood tide – flows northwards. As it moves up the Sound of Jura, to the east of the island, it is forced into a narrowing bottleneck jammed with islands and builds up to a greater height than the open sea to the west of Jura. As a result, millions of tonnes of sea water pour westwards through the Gulf of Corryvreckan at speeds of up to 8 knots – an average sailing yacht is going fast at 6 knots.

The Corryvreckan Whirlpool forms where this mass of moving water hits an underwater pinnacle, which rises from the 200m-deep sea bed to within just 28m of the surface, and swirls over and around it. The turbulent waters create a magnificent spectacle, with white-capped breakers, standing waves, bulging boils and overfalls, and countless miniature maelstroms whirling around the main vortex.

Corryvreckan is at its most violent when a flooding spring tide, flowing west through the gulf, meets a westerly gale blowing in from the Atlantic. In these conditions, standing waves up to 5m high can form and dangerously rough seas extend more than 3 miles west of Corryvreckan, a phenomenon known as the Great Race.

You can see the whirlpool by making the long hike to the northern end of Jura (p75), or by taking a boat trip from Islay, Ardfern or the Isle of Seil.

For tide times, see www.whirlpool-scotland.co.uk.

🏃 Activities

There are few proper footpaths, and off-path exploration often involves rough going through giant bracken, knee-deep bogs and thigh-high tussocks. Hill access may be restricted during the deer-stalking season (July to February); the Jura Hotel can provide details. Look out for adders – the island is infested with them, but they're shy snakes and will move away as you approach.

Corryvreckan Viewpoint   HIKING

A good Jura walk is to a viewpoint for the Corryvreckan Whirlpool. From the northern end of the public road (a 16-mile return trip from here) hike past Barnhill to Kinuachdrachd Farm (6 miles). Just before the farm a footpath forks left and climbs before traversing rough and boggy ground, a natural grandstand for viewing the turbulent waters of the **Gulf of Corryvreckan**.

If you've timed it right (check tide times at the Jura Hotel), you will see the whirlpool as a writhing mass of white water.

Jura Island Tours   BUS

(☑ 01496-820314; www.juraislandtours.co.uk; short/long tours from Craighouse £15/25, from Feolin £25/35) Alex runs informative tours of the island in a modern minibus. Minimum numbers apply, but call regardless as he can put groups together.

🛏 Sleeping & Eating

Places to stay are very limited, so book ahead. As well as the Jura Hotel, there's a handful of B&Bs and several self-catering cottages let by the week (see www.juradevelopment.co.uk). One of these is remote Barnhill, where Orwell stayed.

You can camp (£5 per person) in the field below the Jura Hotel; there's a toilet and shower block that walkers, yachties and cyclists can also use. From July to February check on the deer-stalking situation before wild camping.

The Jura Hotel, a cafe and shop are basically the only places to get a bite to eat on the island. Some B&B providers offer evening meals.

Jura Hotel   HOTEL **££**

(☑ 01496-820243; www.jurahotel.co.uk; Craighouse; s £65, d £100-130; **P**🤶) The heart of Jura's community is this hotel, which is warmly welcoming and efficiently run. Rooms vary in size and shape, but all are renovated and inviting. The premier rooms, which all have sea views, are just lovely, with understated elegance and polished modern bathrooms. Eat in the restaurant or the convivial pub.

Barnhill   COTTAGE **££**

(☑ 01786 850274; www.escapetojura.com; per week from £1200; **P**🤶) The cottage where George Orwell stayed is in a gloriously remote location in Jura's north. It sleeps eight and is 7 miles from the main road on a rough 4WD track, and 25 miles from the pub. It's pretty basic but has a generator.

Ardlussa Estate   B&B **£££**

(☑ 01496-820323; www.ardlussaestate.com; Ardlussa; d £150; **P**🤶) This grand shooting lodge in Jura's north offers B&B accommodation in two plush rooms with beautiful vistas. Lavish four-course dinners made with estate produce cost £50 per head. There's also a substantial self-catering wing sleeping up to 10 people.

Antlers   CAFE **£**

(☑ 01496-820496; www.facebook.com/antlers.jura; Craighouse; light meals £4-9; ⏱ 10am-4pm Easter-Oct) 🍴 This community-owned cafe has a craft shop and displays on Jura heritage. It does tasty home baking, venison burgers, sandwiches and more. Sit out on the deck to enjoy the view. It does takeaway dinners on Fridays and sometimes opens for sit-ins. Not licensed – £3 corkage.

ℹ Getting There & Away

A **car ferry** (☑ 01496-840681; www.argyll-bute.gov.uk) shuttles between Port Askaig on Islay and Feolin on Jura (adult/car/bicycle £1.85/9.60/free, five minutes, hourly Monday to Saturday, every two hours Sunday). There is no direct car-ferry connection to the mainland.

From April to September, **Jura Passenger Ferry** (☑ 07768 450000; www.jurapassengerferry.com; one way £20; ⏱ Apr-Sep) runs from Tayvallich on the mainland to Craighouse on Jura (one hour, one or two daily except Wednesday). Booking is recommended (you can do this online).

ℹ Getting Around

The island's only **bus service** (☑ 01436-810200; www.garelochheadcoaches.co.uk) runs between the ferry slip at Feolin and Craighouse (20 minutes, six to seven Monday to Saturday), timed to coincide with ferry arrivals and departures. Some of the runs continue north as far as Inverlussa.

Hire bikes from **Jura Bike Hire** (☑ 07768 450000; Craighouse; bike hire per day £15) in Craighouse.

YVONNESTEWARTHENDERSON/SHUTTERSTOCK ©

1. Iona (p98)

Iona Abbey (p99) is the spiritual heart of the island.

2. Kilmartin Glen (p65)

This magical glen is the focus of one of the biggest concentrations of prehistoric sites in Scotland.

3. Islay (p69)

Islay's distilleries, such as Ardbeg (pictured; p70), produce some of the world's greatest and peatiest whiskies.

4. Jura (p74)

A magnificently wild and lonely island, Jura is the perfect place to get away from it all.

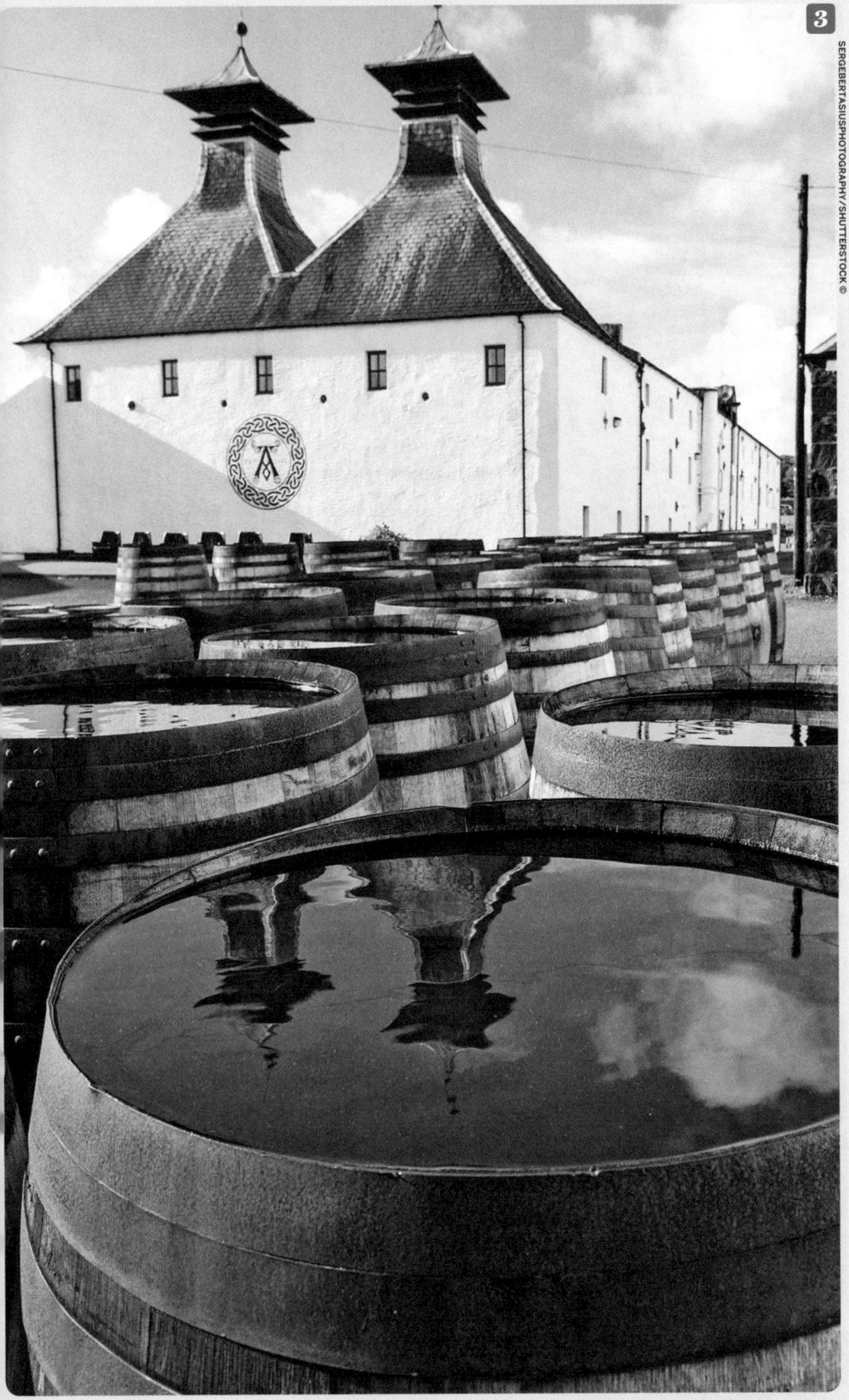

SERGEBERTASIUSPHOTOGRAPHY/SHUTTERSTOCK ©

1

2

4

VACLAV SEBEK/SHUTTERSTOCK ©

1. Oban seafood
Fresh seafood, such as from the famous Oban Seafood Hut (pictured, p89), is a real Oban highlight.

2. Mull wildlife (p92)
Mull's varied landscapes and habitats offer the chance to spot some of Scotland's rarest and most dramatic wildlife, including sea eagles (pictured).

3. Tarbert (p66)
This attractive fishing village and yachting centre, with its excellent natural harbour (pictured) is the gateway to Kintyre (p65).

4. West Highland Way (p104)
This famous long-distance walking route runs along the eastern shore of Loch Lomond (p112).

DMITRY NAUMOV/SHUTTERSTOCK ©

Colonsay

POP 100

Legend has it that when St Columba set out from Ireland in 563, his first landfall was Colonsay. But on climbing a hill he found he could still see the distant coast of his homeland, and pushed on north to Iona, leaving behind only his name (Colonsay means 'Columba's Isle').

Colonsay is a little jewel-box of varied delights, none exceptional but each exquisite – an ancient priory, a woodland garden, a golden beach – set amid a Highland landscape in miniature: rugged, rocky hills, cliffs and sandy strands, machair and birch woods, even a trout loch.

◎ Sights & Activities

There are several good sandy beaches, but **Kiloran Bay** in the northwest, a scimitar-shaped strand of dark golden sand, is outstanding.

★**Oronsay Priory** RUINS
(☻24hr) FREE If the tide is right, don't miss walking across the half-mile of cockleshell-strewn sand linking Colonsay to smaller Oronsay. Here you can explore the 14th-century ruins of one of Scotland's best-preserved medieval priories. There are two beautiful 15th-century stone crosses in the kirkyard, but the highlight is the collection of superb carved grave slabs in the Prior's House. The island is accessible on foot for about 1½ hours either side of low tide; there are tide tables at the ferry terminal and hotel.

Colonsay House Gardens GARDENS
(☑01951-200316; www.colonsayholidays.co.uk; Kiloran; ☻gardens dawn-dusk, walled garden noon-5pm Wed & Fri, 2-5pm Sat Easter-Sep, 2-4.30pm Wed Oct) FREE Situated at Colonsay House, 1.5 miles north of Scalasaig, these gardens are tucked in an unexpected fold of the landscape and are famous for their outstanding collection of hybrid rhododendrons and unusual trees. The formal walled garden around the mansion has a terrace cafe.

Colonsay Brewery BREWERY
(☑01951-200190; www.colonsaybrewery.co.uk; Scalasaig; ☻call for hours) The Colonsay Brewery gives you the chance to have a look at how it produces its hand-crafted ales – the Colonsay IPA is a grand pint.

Kevin Byrne WALKING
(☑01951-200320; byrne@colonsay.org.uk) Kevin Byrne offers customised guided tours on foot (£15) or in your own car (£40). There are also special tours focusing on Colonsay island's fern life.

⊨ Sleeping & Eating

Accommodation is limited and should be booked before coming to the island. Wild camping is allowed. See www.colonsay.org.uk for self-catering listings.

As well as the Colonsay Hotel, there are a couple of cafes on the island for food.

Backpackers Lodge HOSTEL £
(☑01951-200312; www.colonsayholidays.co.uk; Kiloran; dm/tw £22/56; P ♠) Set in a former gamekeeper's house, this lodge is a 30-minute walk from the ferry on Colonsay (you can arrange to be picked up). Smart refurbished twin rooms are a great deal and are set in the house, with bunk rooms in a smaller stone building alongside. There's a kitchen in another building.

★**Colonsay Hotel** HOTEL ££
(☑01951-200316; www.colonsayholidays.co.uk; Scalasaig; s/d from £85/115; ☻mid-Mar–Oct; P ♠ ♠) ❢ This wonderfully laid-back hotel is set in an atmospheric old inn dating from 1750, a short walk uphill from the ferry pier in Scalasaig. It's a plush 18th-century place with well-appointed rooms, some with lovely views and four-poster beds. The bar and restaurant are the island's main social centres.

❶ Information

General information is available at www.colonsay.org.uk and at the ferry waiting room (the ferry pier is at Scalasaig, the main village, which has a shop but no ATM).

Colonsay Bookshop (☑01951-200320; www.houseoflochar.com; Scalasaig; ☻3-5.30pm Mon-Sat Apr-Oct, or by appointment) This tiny bookshop near the ferry pier in Scalasaig has an excellent range of books on Hebridean history and culture.

❶ Getting There & Around

AIR

Hebridean Air Services (www.hebrideanair.co.uk) operates flights from Oban's airport (at North Connel) to Colonsay and Islay twice daily on Tuesday and Thursday.

BICYCLE

You can hire bikes from **Archie McConnell** (☑ 01951-200355; www.colonsaycottage.co.uk; Colnatarun Cottage, Kilchattan; per day £8-10) – book in advance and he'll deliver them to anywhere on the island.

BOAT

CalMac (www.calmac.co.uk) runs ferries from Oban to Colonsay (passenger/car £7.40/37.60, 2¼ hours, seven weekly in summer, three in winter). From April to October, on Wednesday and Saturday, the ferry from Kennacraig to Islay continues to Colonsay (adult/car £4.15/17.30, 1¼ hours) and on to Oban. A day trip from Islay allows you six to seven hours on the island.

BUS

Colonsay Minibus Tour (☑ 01951-200141; adult/child £10/5), a service aimed at day trippers, makes two circuits of the island on Wednesdays, to meet the arriving and departing ferries – you can be dropped off/picked up at any point on the circuit.

ARRAN

POP 4600

Enchanting Arran is a jewel in Scotland's scenic crown. The island is a visual feast, and boasts culinary delights, its own brewery and distillery, and stacks of accommodation options. The variations in Scotland's dramatic landscape can all be experienced on this one island, best explored by pulling on the hiking boots or jumping on a bicycle. Arran offers some challenging walks in the mountainous north, while the island's circular coastal road is very popular with cyclists.

ⓘ Information

The **tourist office** (☑ 01770-303774; www. visitscotland.com; ☺ 9am-5pm Mon-Sat Mar-Oct, plus 10am-5pm Sun Apr-Sep, 10am-4pm Mon-Sat Nov-Feb) is in Brodick. The ferry from Ardrossan also has some tourist information. Useful websites include www.visitarran.com.

ⓘ Getting There & Away

CalMac runs ferries between Ardrossan and Brodick (adult/car £3.90/15.55, 55 minutes, four to nine daily). From April to late October services also run between Claonaig on the Kintyre peninsula and Lochranza (adult/car £2.90/9.70, 30 minutes, seven to nine daily). In winter this service runs to Tarbert (1¼ hours) once daily and must be reserved.

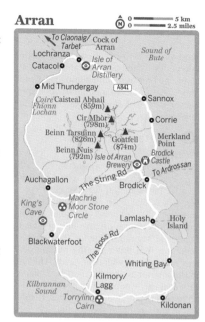

ⓘ Getting Around

BICYCLE

Several places hire out bicycles, including these in Brodick:

Arran Adventure Company (☑ 01770-303349; www.arranadventure.com; Auchrannie Rd) Has good mountain bikes.

Arran Bike Hire (☑ 07825-160668; www. arranbikehire.com; Shorehouse, Shore Rd; per half-day/full day/week £11/15/65; ☺ 10am-4pm Apr-Oct) On the waterfront in Brodick. Hires out trail bikes and hybrids and can offer advice on mountain-biking routes.

BUS

Four to seven buses daily go from Brodick pier to Lochranza (£3.15, 45 minutes), and many head the other way to Lamlash (£2) and Whiting Bay (£2.75, 30 minutes), then on to Kildonan and Blackwaterfoot. Pick up a timetable from the tourist office.

An Arran Dayrider costs £6.30 from the driver, giving a day's travel. Download a bus timetable from www.spt.co.uk.

CAR

Island of Arran Car Hire (☑ 01770-302839; www.arran-motors.co.uk; car part-day/24hr from £35/38; ☺ 8am-5.30pm Mon-Sat, 10am-5pm Sun) is at the service station by Brodick ferry pier.

Brodick & Around

POP 800

Most visitors arrive in Brodick, the beating heart of the island of Arran, and congregate along the coastal road to admire the town's long curving bay. On a clear day it's a spectacular vista, with Goatfell looming over the forested shore.

⊙ Sights & Activities

Brodick Castle   CASTLE

(NTS; ☎01770-302202; www.nts.org.uk; castle & park adult/child £14/10, park only £7.50/6.50; ⊙castle 11am-4pm May-Aug, 11am-3pm Apr & Sep, park 9.30am-sunset year-round) This elegant castle 2 miles north of Brodick evolved from 13th-century origins into a stately home and hunting lodge for the Dukes of Hamilton. You enter via the hunting gallery, wallpapered with deer heads. The rest of the interior is characterised by fabulous 19th-century wooden furniture and an array of horses 'n' hounds paintings. Helpful guides and laminated sheets – the kids' ones are more entertaining – add info. At last visit it was closed for renovations, due to reopen in spring 2019.

The extensive grounds, now a country park with various trails among the rhododendrons, justify the steep entry fee.

Isle of Arran Brewery   BREWERY

(☎01770-302353; www.arranbrewery.com; tours £5; ⊙10am-5pm Mon-Sat, 12.30-5pm Sun Apr-Sep, 10am-3.30pm Mon & Wed-Sat Oct-Mar) This brewery, 1.5 miles from Brodick off the Lochranza road, produces the excellent Arran beers, which include the addictive Arran Dark. Tours run daily: call for times as they vary by season. They last about 45 minutes and include a tasting of all the beers.

Isle of Arran Heritage Museum   MUSEUM

(☎01770-302636; www.arranmuseum.co.uk; Rosaburn; adult/child £4/2; ⊙10.30am-4.30pm Apr-Oct) This museum has a varied collection of historical and ethnographic items, from prehistoric stone tools to farming implements. There's quite a bit to see across several heritage buildings, with good background on the island and its people. Gardens and a cafe round out the experience. It's on the way to the castle from Brodick.

★Goatfell   HIKING

The walk up and down Goatfell (874m), the island's highest point, is 8 miles return (up

to eight hours), with trailheads at Brodick and Brodick Castle among others. In fine weather there are superb views to Ben Lomond and Northern Ireland. It can, however, be very cold and windy up here; take appropriate maps (available at the tourist office), waterproofing and a compass.

✿ Festivals & Events

Arran Mountain Festival   SPORTS

(☎01770-303347; www.arranmountainfestival. co.uk; ⊙mid-May) This four-day event offers a wide range of walking and climbing activities led by experienced mountain guides, with events for all abilities. Most cost between £15 and £25 and can be booked online.

Arran Folk Festival   MUSIC

(www.arranevents.com; ⊙Jun) A three-day festival with concerts and great atmosphere in Brodick. Free daytime sessions are usually in the Douglas hotel, with evening concerts (tickets around £20) in Brodick Hall.

⊨ Sleeping

Brodick Bunkhouse   HOSTEL £

(☎01770-302968; www.brodickbunkhouse.co.uk; Alma Rd; dm £25; ℗☎) A short stroll from the ferry, behind the Douglas hotel, this handy hostel has attractive, comfortable triple-decker bunks with individual plugs and USB ports. It's generally unstaffed, with keycode entry. It has a simple kitchen and access for people with disabilities. No under-18s are admitted.

★Glenartney   B&B ££

(☎01770-302220; www.glenartney-arran.co.uk; Mayish Rd; d £75-100; ⊙Easter-Oct; ℗☎☀) ⌀ Uplifting bay views and genuine, helpful hosts make this a cracking option. Airy, stylish rooms make the most of the natural light at the top of the town. Comfortable lounges, help-yourself home baking and pod coffee plus a sustainable ethos make for a very pleasurable stay. Top facilities for cyclists, plus drying rooms and trail advice for hikers are added bonuses.

Broomage   B&B ££

(☎01770-302115; www.facebook.com/the.broomage; r £80; ℗☎) Run by a young family, this luminous modern spot has two rooms with huge beds (they can become twins) and shiny modern bathrooms (one exterior to the room). There's a large lounge, amiable hospitality and breakfast featuring local produce. Downstairs is a self-catering apartment. It's fairly discreetly signposted; turn down the road by the Royal Bank of Scotland.

Belvedere Guest House B&B **££**
(☑01770-302397; www.belvedere-guesthouse.co.uk; Alma Rd; s £50, d £90-100; P 🤶) Overlooking town, bay and surrounding mountains, this place has very well-presented rooms with comfortable mattresses. Make sure you pay extra to grab room 1 or 2, each of which is spacious and has fabulous vistas over the water. Breakfast has plenty of choice; there's also a self-catering cottage. It's a likeable Brodick base with a laid-back and helpful host.

Douglas HOTEL **£££**
(☑01770-302968; www.thedouglashotel.co.uk; Shore Rd; r £160-200, ste £230; P 🤶🐾) Opposite the ferry, the Douglas is a smart, stylish haven of island hospitality. Views are magnificent and luxurious rooms with smart contemporary fabrics make the most of them. There are numerous thoughtful touches such as binoculars to admire the vistas, and bathrooms are great. The downstairs **bar and bistro** (bistro mains £13-20, bar meals £10-15; ⊙bistro 6-9.30pm, bar noon-9.30pm; 🤶🥢) are also recommended. Prices drop midweek and in winter.

🍴 Eating

Wineport CAFE **£**
(☑01770-302101; www.wineport.co.uk; Cladach Centre; light meals £4-11; ⊙11am-5pm Apr-Oct, Sat & Sun only Feb & Mar) Located 1.5 miles from Brodick, next to the Isle of Arran Brewery, whose ales are offered on tap, this summer-only cafe-bar has great outdoor tables for sunny days and does a nice line in pleasing pub-style fare, such as wings, wedges, pork burgers, local mussels and sharing platters. It opens for dinner some nights, but hours vary widely each year.

⭐**Brodick Bar & Brasserie** BRASSERIE **££**
(☑01770-302169; www.brodickbar.co.uk; Alma Rd; mains £13-22; ⊙noon-2.30pm & 5.30-9pm Mon-Sat; 🤶) This is one of Arran's most enjoyable eating experiences. The regularly changing blackboard menu brings modern French flair to a Brodick pub, with great presentation, efficient service and delicious flavour combinations. You'll have a hard time choosing, as it's all brilliant. It's very buzzy on weekend evenings. It was for sale at the time of research so things may change.

Fiddlers' Music Bar CAFE, BISTRO **££**
(☑01770-302579; www.fiddlersmusicbar.com; Shore Rd; mains £10-15; ⊙food 11am-9pm; 🤶🥢) A likeable little place with a really cheerful vibe, Fiddlers' is run by local musicians and does an all-round job as pub, venue, cafe and bistro. It hosts live folk music every evening and there's a range of tasty food with some decent vegetarian choices. Check out the appropriate toilet seats.

🛍 Shopping

Arran Art Trail ARTS & CRAFTS
(www.arranopenstudios.com) Arran is home to quite a few creatives making a wide variety of art and handicrafts. This trail maps out a couple of dozen studios that you can visit around the island; grab the brochure from the tourist office or see the website.

Corrie to Lochranza

The coast road heads north from Brodick to small, pretty Corrie, where there's a Goatfell trailhead. After **Sannox**, with a sandy beach and great mountain views, the road cuts inland. Heading to the very north, on the island's main road, visitors weave through lush glens flanked by Arran's towering mountain splendour. This is perhaps the most beautiful section of the whole Arran coastal circuit.

Lochranza

POP 200
The village of Lochranza has a stunning location in a small bay on Arran island's north coast. It's characterised by the ruined 13th-century **Lochranza Castle** (www.historic environment.scot; ⊙24hr) **FREE**, a ruin standing proud on a little promontory. The nearby **Isle of Arran Distillery** (☑01770-830264; www.arranwhisky.com; tours adult/child £8/free; ⊙10am-5pm Mar-Oct, 10.30am-4pm Nov-Feb) produces a light, aromatic single malt. The Lochranza area bristles with red deer, who wander insouciantly into the village to crop the grass.

⭐**Lochranza SYHA** HOSTEL **£**
(☑01770-830631; www.syha.org.uk; dm/d/q £24.50/64/108; ⊙mid-Mar–Oct, plus Sat & Sun year-round; P @ 🤶🐾) 🍃 An excellent hostel in a charming spot with lovely views. Rooms sport chunky wooden furniture, keycards and lockers. Rainwater toilets, energy-saving heating solutions and a wheelchair-accessible room show thoughtful design, while plush lounging areas, a kitchen you could run a restaurant out of, a laundry, a drying room, red deer in the garden and welcoming management combine for a top option.

★ **Butt Lodge**   B&B **££**
(☑ 01770-830333; www.buttlodge.co.uk; s from £72, d £85-95, ste £110-125; ☺ Mar–mid-Oct; **P** 🛜) Down a short potholed road, this Victorian hunting lodge has been adapted by keen young owners to offer contemporary comfort with relaxed style and genuine hospitality. Rooms give perspectives over hills, garden and the rustic village golf course, with its red deer greenkeepers. The Castle suite is a fabulous space with views three ways and a mezzanine seating area.

Treats include tea and cake in the afternoons, and a spacious lounge to stretch out in. Look out for yoga and other retreats in low season.

West Coast

Blackwaterfoot is the largest village on the west coast of Arran, with a shop and hotel. It's pleasant enough, though not the most scenic of the island's settlements. You can walk to **King's Cave** (☺ 24hr) **FREE** from here (6 miles), and this walk can easily be extended to **Machrie Moor Stone Circle** (☺ 24hr) **FREE**, the highlight of the area.

★ **Cafe Thyme**   CAFE **£**
(☑ 01770-840608; www.oldbyre.co.uk; Old Byre Visitor Centre, Machrie; dishes £8-12; ☺ 10am-5pm, reduced winter hours; 🛜🅿) At the Old Byre Visitor Centre, this is a very pleasant spot, with chunky wooden tables, outdoor seating and sweeping views from its elevated position. It has home baking, a wide tea selection and decent coffee. Less predictably, the food menu features great Turkish pizza, meze boards and smartly priced daily specials. Lunches are served from noon to 3pm.

South Coast

The landscape in the south of Arran is gentler than in the north; the road drops into little wooded valleys, and it's particularly lovely around **Kilmory** and **Lagg**, from where a 10-minute walk will take you to **Torrylinn Cairn**, a chambered tomb over 4000 years old. **Kildonan** has pleasant sandy beaches, a gorgeous water outlook, a hotel, a campsite and an ivy-clad ruined castle.

In genteel **Whiting Bay**, strung out along the water, you'll find small sandy beaches and easy one-hour walks through the forest to the **Giant's Graves** and **Glenashdale**

Falls – keep an eye out for golden eagles and other birds of prey.

Lagg Distillery   DISTILLERY
(☑ 01786-431900; www.laggwhisky.com; Lagg) Still under construction when we last passed by, this new malt-whisky distillery will open to visitors in 2019. Run by the same folk who operate the distillery in Lochranza, it will focus on a peatier style. There's also an orchard being planted, so look out for cider and apple brandy further down the track.

★ **Sealshore Campsite**   CAMPSITE **£**
(☑ 01770-820320; www.campingarran.com; Kildonan; 1-/2-person tents £9/16, pods for 2 people £35; ☺ Mar-Oct; **P** 🛜🅿) Living up to its name, this excellent small campsite is right by the sea (and the Kildonan Hotel) and has one of Arran's finest views from its grassy camping area. There are good facilities, including BBQs, power showers and a day room; the breeze keeps the midges away. Cosy camping pods or a fabulously refurbished Roma caravan offer non-tent choices.

Lamlash

POP 1000

Lamlash, just 3 miles south of Brodick, is in a dazzling setting strung along the beachfront. The bay was used as a safe anchorage by the navy during WWI and WWII.

Holy Island   ISLAND
Just off Lamlash, this island is owned by the Samye Ling Tibetan Centre and used as a retreat, but day visits are allowed. A tide-dependent **ferry** (☑ 01770-700463, 07970 771960; tomin10@btinternet.com; return adult/child £12/6; ☺ daily Apr-Oct; by arrangement Tue & Fri Nov-Mar) zips across from Lamlash. No dogs, bikes, alcohol or fires are allowed on Holy Island. A good walk to the top of the hill (314m), takes two or three hours return. You can stay at the **Holy Island Centre for World Peace & Health** (☑ 01770-601100; www.holyisle.org; dm/s/d £32/55/80; ☺ Apr-Oct). Prices include full (vegetarian) board.

★ **Glenisle Hotel**   HOTEL **£££**
(☑ 01770-600559; www.glenislehotel.com; Shore Rd; s/d/superior d £102/157/207; 🛜) This stylish hotel offers great service and high comfort levels. Rooms are decorated with contemporary fabrics; 'cosy' rooms under the sloping roof are a little cheaper. All feel fresh and include binoculars for scouring the seashore; upgrade to a 'superior' for the best

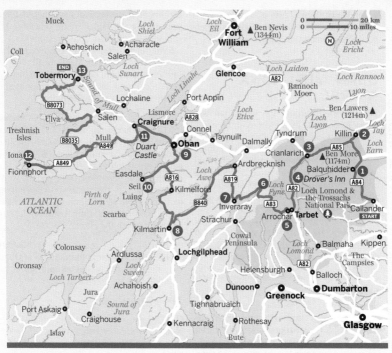

Driving Tour
The Trossachs to Mull

START CALLANDER
END TOBERMORY
LENGTH 240 MILES; TWO TO FOUR DAYS

Having explored the southern part of the Trossachs, head north out of Callander on the A84, following pretty Loch Lubnaig before optional detours of a few miles to see Rob Roy's grave at **1 Balquhidder** (p59) and the Falls of Dochart at pretty **2 Killin** (p59).

Continue on the A85 to **3 Crianlarich** (p52), surrounded by Highland majesty, then turn left on the A82 to follow the western shore of Loch Lomond. Stop for a look and/or pint at the quirky **4 Drover's Inn** (p51), then deviate right at Tarbet onto the A83 – shortly thereafter, **5 Arrochar** (p53) makes for a scenic lunch stop.

Head through scenic Glen Croe, over the pass and into Glen Kinglas, then follow the shore of Loch Fyne – stops at the **6 Fynes Ales brewery** (p64) and/or oyster bar obligatory! – to picturesque **7 Inveraray** (p63).

Go right through the arch here on the A819, then left onto the B840, a lonely road following stiletto-like Loch Awe. You'll eventually reach **8 Kilmartin** (p65), with its great museum and evocative prehistoric sights.

Follow the A816 north to **9 Oban** (p86), where good accommodation options, a handsome harbour and delicious seafood await. You may want to deviate to see the island of **10 Seil** (p91) en route: from here, great boat trips can take you out to the Corryvreckan Whirlpool. Catch a ferry from Oban to Mull and follow the A849 southwest via **11 Duart Castle** (p94) to the island's tip at Fionnphort, where you cross to the emerald jewel of **12 Iona** (p98) and can take a boat trip to the spectacular rock formations of Staffa.

Retrace your steps, then follow Mull's winding west coast on the B8035 and B8073 via spectacular coastline and the beach at Calgary to arrive at the colourful shorefront houses of the main town, **13 Tobermory** (p94).

water views. Downstairs is excellent **food** (mains £12-18; ⊘noon-8.45pm; 🐾📶) and lovely outdoor seating by the garden.

OBAN, MULL, IONA & TIREE

The Victorian harbour town of Oban is a pretty place in its own right, with an excellent seafood scene, and is also a major gateway to the Hebrides. The big island drawcard is Mull, whose majestic scenery, birdlife and pretty capital Tobermory are complemented by the enchanting holy island of Iona just offshore. But the attributes of other islands really merit exploration: the strange rock formations of uninhabited Staffa, the walking on Kerrera, the intriguing slate-quarrying communities of Seil, the peace of Coll and the glorious windswept beaches of Tiree.

Oban

POP 8600

Oban, the main gateway to many of the Hebridean islands, is a waterfront town on a delightful bay, with sweeping views to Kerrera and Mull. It's peaceful in winter, but in summer the town centre is jammed with traffic and crowded with holidaymakers and travellers headed for the archipelago. But the setting is still lovely, and Oban's brilliant seafood restaurants are marvellous places to be as the sun sets over the bay. There's a real magic to the location.

⊙ Sights

Oban Distillery   DISTILLERY
(📞01631-572004; www.malts.com; Stafford St; tours £10; ⊘noon or 12.30-4.30pm Dec-Feb, 9.30am-5pm Mar-Jun & Oct-Nov, 9.30am-7.30pm Mon-Fri & 9.30am-5pm Sat & Sun Jul-Sep) This handsome distillery has been in operation since 1794. The standard guided tour leaves regularly (worth booking) and includes a dram, a take-home glass and a taste straight from the cask. Specialist tours (£40) run once on Mondays to Fridays in summer. Even without a tour, it's still worth looking at the small exhibition in the foyer.

Dunollie Castle   CASTLE
(📞01631-570550; www.dunollie.org; Dunollie Rd; adult/child £6/3; ⊘10am-5pm Mon-Sat, noon-5pm Sun Apr-Oct) A pleasant 1-mile stroll north along the coast road leads to Dunollie Castle, built by the MacDougalls of Lorn in the 13th

century and unsuccessfully besieged for a year during the 1715 Jacobite rebellion. It's ruined, but ongoing conservation work is offering increasing access. The nearby 1745 House – seat of Clan MacDougall – is an intriguing museum of local and clan history, and there are pleasant wooded grounds and a cafe. Free tours run twice daily.

McCaig's Tower   HISTORIC BUILDING
(cnr Laurel & Duncraggan Rds; ⊘24hr) Crowning the hill above town is this Colosseum-like Victorian folly, commissioned in 1890 by local worthy John Stuart McCaig, with the philanthropic intention of providing work for unemployed stonemasons. To reach it on foot, make the steep climb up Jacob's Ladder (a flight of stairs) from Argyll St; the bay views are worth the effort.

Pulpit Hill   VIEWPOINT
An excellent viewpoint to the south of Oban Bay; the footpath to the summit starts by Maridon B&B on Dunuaran Rd.

🏃 Activities

Hire a bike – try **Oban Cycles** (📞01631-566033; www.obancyclescotland.com; 87 George St; per day/week £25/125; ⊘10am-5pm Tue-Sat Feb-Dec) – for the local bike rides listed in a leaflet at the tourist office, including a 16-mile route to Seil.

Various operators offer boat trips (adult/child £10/5) to spot seals and other marine wildlife, departing from North Pier.

Oban has lots of outdoor shops and is a good place to get kitted out for the Highland and island outdoors.

Sea Kayak Oban   KAYAKING
(National Kayak School; 📞01631-565310; www.seakayakoban.com; Argyll St; ⊘10am-5pm Mon-Fri, 9am-5pm Sat, 10am-4pm Sun, winter hours greatly reduced) Sea Kayak Oban has a well-stocked shop, great route advice and sea-kayaking courses, including an all-inclusive two-day intro for beginners (£170 per person). It also has full equipment rental for experienced paddlers – trolley your kayak from the shop to the ferry (kayaks carried free) to visit the islands. Three-hour excursions (adult/child £50/35) leave regularly in season.

Puffin Adventures   DIVING
(📞01631-566088; www.puffin.org.uk; Port Gallanach) If you fancy exploring the underwater world, Puffin Adventures offers a two-hour package (£90) for complete beginners, often with same-day availability, as well as four-

day diving courses. A serious professional set-up, it has training services and excursions for more experienced divers as well. It's located south of Oban near the Kerrera ferry.

⌖ Tours

★ **Basking Shark Scotland**   BOATING

(☏ 07975 723140; www.baskingsharkscotland. co.uk; ⊙Apr-Oct) Runs boat trips focused on finding and observing basking sharks – the world's second-largest fish – and other notable marine species. The one-day options leave from Coll, synchronised with the ferry from Oban, and cost £140, or £195 with swimming/snorkelling. Multiday trips are available, as are low-season research trips. It also offers excursions allowing you to swim or kayak with seals.

Coastal Connection   BOATING

(☏01631-565833; www.coastal-connection.co.uk) Runs wildlife-spotting trips (adult/child £30/20), fast day trips to Tobermory (£40/25) and custom excursions to many west coast islands in a speedy, comfortable boat.

⚜ Festivals & Events

Highlands & Islands Music & Dance Festival   MUSIC

(www.obanfestival.org; ⊙early May) An exuberant celebration of traditional Scottish music and dance, when Oban packs out.

West Highland Yachting Week   SAILING

(www.whyw.co.uk; ⊙late Jul or early Aug) Oban becomes the focus of one of Scotland's biggest yachting events, when hundreds of yachts cram into the harbour and the town's bars are jammed with thirsty sailors.

Oban Games   CULTURAL, SPORTS

(Argyllshire Gathering; www.obangames.com; adult/child £10/5; ⊙late Aug) A key event in the Highland games calendar, the Oban Games include a prestigious pipe-band competition.

⌗ Sleeping

Despite having lots of B&B accommodation, Oban can still fill up quickly in July and August, so try to book ahead. Avoid the substandard, tourist-trap B&Bs south of the roundabout on Dunollie Rd. If you can't find a bed in Oban, consider Connel, 4 miles north.

★ **Backpackers Plus**   HOSTEL £

(☏01631-567189; www.backpackersplus.com; Breadalbane St; dm/s/tw/d incl bathroom & breakfast £20/29/54/60; @ 🕾) This is a friendly

place in an old church with a good vibe and a large and attractive communal lounge with lots of sofas and armchairs. A buffet breakfast is included, plus there's free tea and coffee, a laundry service and powerful showers. Private rooms are available in adjacent buildings: they are a very good deal.

Brand-new en suite doubles are in the old church hall, while a former guesthouse has sweet shared-bathroom options with a good common kitchen.

Oban Backpackers   HOSTEL £

(☏01631-562107; www.obanbackpackers.com; Breadalbane St; dm £18.50-20.50; @ 🕾) Simple, colourful, relaxed and casual, this hostel has plenty of atmosphere. Dorms are basic, with high ceilings and plenty of space; prices vary according to size. Top bunks are wall-mounted. There's a sociable downstairs lounge with big windows and zebra-patterned couches, plus a sizeable kitchen. Breakfast is available for £3 and a safe is on hand (no lockers).

Oban SYHA   HOSTEL £

(☏01631-562025; www.syha.org.uk; Corran Esplanade; dm/tw £24/58, plus £3 per person for non-members; Ⓟ@🕾) Set in a grand Victorian villa on the Esplanade, 0.75 miles north of Oban's train station, this hostel is modernised to a high standard, with comfy wooden bunks, lockers, good showers and a lounge with great views across Oban Bay. All dorms are en suite; the neighbouring lodge has three- and four-bedded rooms. Breakfast is available. Dorm rates drop substantially in low season.

★ **Elderslie Guest House**   B&B ££

(☏01631-570651; www.obanbandb.com; Soroba Rd; s £50-56, d £75-88; ⊙Apr–mid-Oct; Ⓟ🕾) A B&B can be a difficult balancing act: making things modern without losing cosiness, being friendly and approachable without sacrificing privacy. At this spot a mile south of Oban the balance is absolutely right, with a variety of commodious rooms with big showers, large towels and lovely outlooks over greenery. Breakfast is great, there's outdoor lounging space and the hosts are excellent.

Old Manse Guest House   B&B ££

(☏01631-564886; www.obanguesthouse.co.uk; Dalriach Rd; s/d £80/98; ⊙Mar-Oct; Ⓟ🕾) Set on the hillside above town, this Oban B&B commands magnificent views over to Kerrera and Mull. It's run with genuine enthusiasm, and the owners are constantly adding thoughtful

SOUTHERN HIGHLANDS & ISLANDS OBAN

Oban

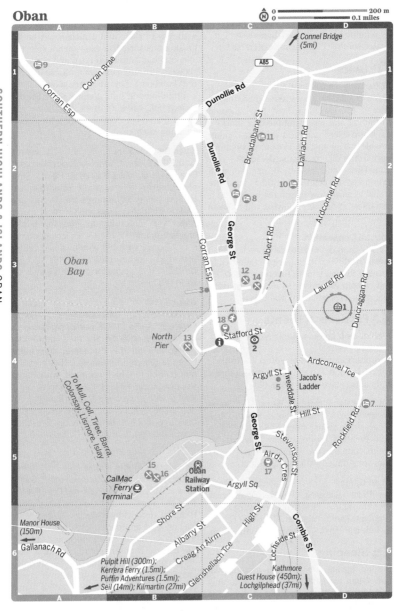

Oban Bay

North Pier

CalMac Ferry Terminal

Oban Railway Station

Manor House (150m)

Gallanach Rd

To Mull, Coll, Tiree, Barra, Colonsay, Lismore, Islay

Connel Bridge (5mi)

Corran Brae
Corran Esp
Dunollie Rd
Breadalbane St
Dalriach Rd
Ardconnel Rd
Dunollie Rd
George St
Albert Rd
Corran Esp
Laurel Rd
Duncraggan Rd
Stafford St
Ardconnel Tce
Argyll St
Jacob's Ladder
Tweeddale St
Hill St
Rockfield Rd
George St
Stevenson St
Airds Cres
Argyll Sq
Shore St
Albany St
Creag An Airm
Glenshellach Tce
High St
Lochside St
Combie St

Pulpit Hill (300m);
Kerrera Ferry (1.5mi);
Puffin Adventures (1.5mi);
Seil (14mi); Kilmartin (27mi)

Kathmore
Guest House (450m);
Lochgilphead (37mi)

new features to the bright, cheerful rooms, such as binoculars, DVDs, poetry, corkscrews and tartan hot-water bottles. There are breakfast menus, with special diets catered for.

It was for sale at the time of research so things may change.

Fàilte B&B **££**
(☏ 01631-570219; www.failtebedandbreakfastoban. co.uk; Rockfield Rd; s £50, d £80-90; ☺ Feb-Nov; ℗ ☎) Solicitous host Thomas knows a thing or two about guest comfort and the thoughtful extras here (powerpoints, disposable

Oban

razors, real milk in the mini-fridge) make for a very comfortable stay. Rooms are pleasingly contemporary with a white-and-blond Scandinavian feel and modern showers. The family's quality artworks decorate the building and breakfast features fresh fruit and homemade breads and jams.

Kathmore Guest House B&B ££
(☑ 01631-562104; www.kathmore.co.uk; Soroba Rd; s £50, d £65-75; ℗ 🛜) A 10-minute stroll from Oban's centre, this warmly welcoming place mixes traditional Highland hospitality and hearty breakfasts with a wee touch of boutique flair in its stylish bedspreads and colourful artwork. It's actually two adjacent houses combined. There's a comfortable lounge and outdoor garden deck where you can enjoy a glass of wine on long summer evenings.

Sandvilla Guesthouse B&B ££
(☑ 01631-564483; www.holidayoban.co.uk; Breadalbane St; d £75-90; ℗ 🛜) Upbeat, bright and modern, this well kept B&B is our favourite of several options on this street. Enthusiastic owners guarantee a personal welcome and service with a smile. No young children are allowed.

Manor House HOTEL £££
(☑ 01631-562087; www.manorhouseoban.com; Gallanach Rd; r £195-270; ℗ 🛜🐾) Built in 1780 for the Duke of Argyll, the old-fashioned Manor House is Oban's finest hotel. It has small but elegant Georgian-style rooms – the majority with lovely sea views – with antiques and period-style wallpaper, plus a classy restaurant serving Scottish/French cuisine (table d'hôte dinner £49). Rates include access to a local gym and golf course. No under-12s.

✖ Eating

Oban Seafood Hut SEAFOOD £
(☑ 07881418565; www.facebook.com/obanseafood.hut.9; Railway Pier; mains £3-13; ⊙10am-6pm mid-Mar–Oct) If you want to savour superb Scottish seafood without the expense of an upmarket restaurant, head for Oban's famous seafood stall – it's the green shack on the quayside near the ferry terminal. Here you can buy fresh and cooked seafood to take away, such as excellent prawn sandwiches, dressed crab and fresh oysters, for a pittance.

Little Potting Shed Cafe CAFE, VEGETARIAN £
(☑ 01631-358150; www.facebook.com/thelittlepottingshedcafeoban; 5 John St; light meals £4-9; ⊙9am-5pm daily, to 9pm Fri & Sat Jul & Aug; 🛜🐾🥗) Up a side alley off Oban's main street, this sweet spot has wooden tables and an excellent choice of vegetarian and vegan savoury and sweet bites. The vegan breakfast is also tasty, the coffee is good and strong, there's a wide selection of teas, and the non-dairy ice-cream is perfect for a summer's day. It's dog-friendly.

★ Ee-Usk SEAFOOD ££
(☑ 01631-565666; www.eeusk.com; North Pier; mains £14-24; ⊙noon-3pm & 5.45-9.30pm Apr-Oct, noon-2.30pm & 5.45-9pm Nov-Mar; 🛜) 🐾 Bright and modern Ee-Usk (how you pronounce *iasg*, Gaelic for fish) occupies a prime pier location. Floor-to-ceiling windows allow diners on two levels to enjoy sweeping views while sampling local sustainable seafood ranging from fragrant fish cakes to langoustines and succulent fresh fish. A bevy of serving staff make it swift and efficient, and they'll try to give you the best view available. Both the food and location are first-class.

Waterfront Fishouse Restaurant SEAFOOD ££
(☎01631-563110; www.waterfrontfishouse.co.uk; 1
Railway Pier; mains £13-20; ⊙noon-2pm & 5.30-
9pm, extended hours Jun-Aug; 🐾👪) Waterfront
is housed on the top floor of a converted
seamen's mission, and the stylish, unfussy
decor, bathed by the summer evening sun,
does little to distract from the seafood
freshly landed at the quay just a few metres
away. The menu ranges from classic haddock and chips to fresh oysters, scallops and
langoustines. It's best to book for dinner.

Coast SCOTTISH ££
(☎01631-569900; www.coastoban.co.uk; 104
George St; mains £17-20; ⊙noon-2pm & 5.30-9pm
Tue-Sat Feb-late Dec; 🐾) With a stylishly casual
contemporary interior, this place in a former bank offers well-integrated plates with
a focus on local game and seafood. Dishes
are presented with flair but don't stray into
pretension; the flavours are trusty and quality combinations that work very well.

🍸 Drinking & Nightlife

Oban Inn PUB
(☎01631-567441; www.facebook.com/theobaninn;
1 Stafford St; ⊙11am-1am; 🐾) It's a pleasure to
see this four-square 18th-century pub open
again after some years closed, with its solid
walls, flagstone floor and roof beams in the
cosy front bar. It has Fyne Ales on tap, making it a prime spot for a waterfront pint, with
a good mix of locals, visitors and yachties.

Aulay's Bar PUB
(☎01631-562596; www.aulaysbar.com; 8 Airds
Cres; ⊙11.30am-11pm; 🐾) An authentic Scottish pub, Aulay's is cosy and low-ceilinged,
its walls covered with old photographs of
Oban ferries and other ships. It pulls in a
mixed crowd of locals and visitors with its
warm atmosphere and wide range of malt
whiskies. There are two sides: the left door
leads to a quieter lounge bar.

ARGYLL SEA KAYAK TRAIL

This 96-mile **route** (www.paddleargyll.
org.uk) promoted by the local government runs from Oban to Helensburgh
via sea lochs and the Crinan canal. It's a
spectacular paddle; the only annoyance
is not being able to traverse the canal's
locks: bookable trolleys are provided for
easy portage. Paddlers are encouraged
to register online.

ℹ Information

Large areas of central Oban have free wi-fi. **Oban
Library** (☎01631-571444; www.argyll-bute.
co.uk; 77 Albany St; ⊙10am-1pm & 2-7pm Mon &
Wed, to 6pm Thu, to 5pm Fri, to 1pm Sat; 🐾) has
computer terminals and wi-fi.
Lorn & Islands District General Hospital
(☎01631-567500; www.obanhospital.com;
Glengallan Rd) At the southern end of town,
clearly signposted off the main road.
Oban Tourist Office (☎01631-563122; www.
oban.org.uk; 3 North Pier; ⊙10am-5pm Mon-
Sat, 11am-3pm Sun Nov-Mar, 9am-5.30pm
Mon-Sat, 10am-5pm Sun Apr-Oct) Helpful; on
the waterfront.

ℹ Getting There & Away

AIR
Hebridean Air Services (www.hebrideanair.
co.uk) Flies from North Connel airfield to the
islands of Coll, Tiree, Colonsay and Islay.

BOAT
Oban is a major gateway to the Hebrides. The
CalMac Ferry Terminal (☎01631-562244;
www.calmac.co.uk; Railway Pier) is in the centre,
close to the train station, with ferries running
from here to Mull, Islay, Colonsay, Coll, Tiree,
Barra and Lismore.

BUS
Scottish Citylink (www.citylink.co.uk) has two
to five buses connecting Glasgow (£20.50, three
hours) with Oban. Most of these travel via Tarbet
and Inveraray; in summer, one goes via Crianlarich. Two buses Monday to Saturday head north
to Fort William (£9.40, 1½ hours).

TRAIN
ScotRail trains run to Oban from Glasgow
(£25.30, three hours, three to six daily). Change
at Crianlarich for Fort William.

ℹ Getting Around
Hazelbank Motors (☎01631-566476; www.
obancarhire.co.uk; Lynn Rd; car hire per day/
week from £40/225; ⊙8.30am-5pm Mon-Sat)
Hires out cars. You might get a van cheaper
than a hatchback.
Lorn Taxis (☎01631-564744)

Around Oban

Kerrera
POP 50
Some of the area's best **walking** is on Ker-
rera, which faces Oban across the bay.
There's a 6-mile circuit (allow three hours),

which follows tracks or paths and offers the chance to spot wildlife such as Soay sheep, wild goats, otters, golden eagles, peregrine falcons, seals and porpoises. At the island's southern end, there's a **ruined castle**.

Kerrera Bunkhouse   HOSTEL **£**
(☑ 01631-566367; www.kerrerabunkhouse.co.uk; Lower Gylen; dm £16, tent £45; ☺ Easter-Sep; 🐾) This charming seven-bed bunkhouse in a converted 18th-century stable is near Gylen Castle, a 2-mile walk south from the ferry on Kerrera (keep left at the fork just past the telephone box). Booking ahead is recommended. There's also a spacious platform-pitched tent with a double bed and stove. You can get snacks and light meals at the neighbouring **Kerrera Tea Garden** (light meals £2-9; ☺ 10.30am-4.30pm) 🍴.

ⓘ Getting There & Away

CalMac run a daily passenger ferry to Kerrera from Gallanach, 2 miles southwest of the Oban town centre (adult single/return £3.10/4.65, 5 minutes, half-hourly in summer, eight to nine daily in winter).

Seil
POP 600

The small island of Seil, 10 miles southwest of Oban, is best known for its connection to the mainland – the graceful **Bridge over the Atlantic**, designed by Thomas Telford and opened in 1793.

On the west coast is the pretty conservation village of **Ellenabeich**, with whitewashed cottages and rainwater barrels backed by a wee harbour and rocky cliffs. It was built to house local slate workers, but the industry collapsed in 1881 when the sea broke into the main quarry – the flooded pit can still be seen. The **Scottish Slate Islands Heritage Trust** (☑ 01852-300449; www.slateislands.org.uk; ☺ 10.30am-4.30pm) displays fascinating old photographs illustrating life in the village in the 19th and early 20th centuries.

Just offshore is small **Easdale Island**, which has more old slate-workers' cottages and the interesting **Easdale Island Folk Museum** (☑ 01852-300370; www.easdalemuseum.org; suggested donation £3; ☺ 11am-4pm Apr–mid-Oct). The island once housed 450 people, but the population fell to just seven old-timers by 1950. It now has a healthier 50-odd after a program welcoming incomers.

OFF THE BEATEN TRACK

LUING
A ferry hop from Seil's southern end takes you to the neighbouring island of Luing, a quiet backwater that has no real sights but is appealing for wildlife walks and easy-going bike rides.

Confusingly Ellenabeich is also referred to as Easdale, so 'Easdale Harbour', for example, is on the Seil side.

🏃 Activities

★ **Sealife Adventures**   BOATING
(☑ 01631-571010; www.sealife-adventures.com; B844; 3/4/5hr trip £52/69/80) Sealife Adventures, based on the eastern side of Seil island near the bridge, has a large, comfortable boat offering wildlife cruises with knowledgable guides and trips to the Corryvreckan Whirlpool.

★ **Seafari Adventures**   BOATING
(☑ 01852-300003; www.seafari.co.uk; Ellenabeich; ☺ Apr-Oct) Runs a series of exciting boat trips in high-speed rigid inflatables to Corryvreckan Whirlpool (adult/child £42/32; call about dates for 'Whirlpool Specials', when the tide is strongest). There are also three-hour summer whale-watching trips (£53/40), day-long cruises to Iona and Staffa (£90/68) and private charters available to other islands. There's a minimum of six passengers required for low-season departures.

Sea Kayak Scotland   KAYAKING
(☑ 01852-300770; www.seakayakscotland.com; courses for 1/2/4 people per person £125/90/70) Year-round hire, instruction and guided sea-kayaking trips run by an experienced operator.

🎉 Festivals & Events

World Stone-Skimming Championships   SPORTS
(www.stoneskimming.com; ☺ Sep) Anyone who fancies their hand at ducks and drakes should try to attend a flooded slate quarry in Easdale on a Sunday in late September. There's no use boasting about the number of skips: once it's hit the water a minimum of three times it's all about the distance reached.

🛏 Sleeping & Eating

An Lionadh
RENTAL HOUSE **££**

(☎ 01688-400388; www.anlionadh.co.uk; Easdale; per week £1000; 🛜 🐾) Occupying a comparatively lofty position on the tranquil island of Easdale, this is a standout self-catering option with views both ways: over the village and out to the west, where a grassy lawn lets you contemplate the vistas at great leisure. There are four bedrooms, a lounge and a very attractive kitchen/dining area.

★ Puffer
CAFE **££**

(☎ 01852-300022; www.pufferbar.com; Easdale; mains £8-15; ⊙ food 11am-4pm & 6-8pm Mon-Sat, 11am-4pm Sun Easter-Oct, call for winter opening; 🛜 🐾) 🍴 Easdale Island is fed and watered by the Puffer, named after the boats that once served the community. It combines pub, tearoom and restaurant. There are front and back decks, both very pleasant, and all-day sandwiches, burgers, and deli platters (appropriately served on a slate). Evening meals step it up a notch, with quality dishes based on regional produce.

ℹ Getting There & Around

West Coast Motors (☎ 01586-555885; www.westcoastmotors.co.uk) Bus 418 runs four to five times a day, except Sunday, from Oban to Ellenabeich (£3, 45 minutes), and on to North Cuan (£3, 53 minutes) at Seil's southern tip for the ferry to Luing.

Easdale Ferry (☎ 01631-562125; www.argyll-bute.gov.uk) Has a daily passenger-only ferry service from Ellenabeich to Easdale Island (£2.10 return, bicycles free, five minutes, shuttle service at busy times, otherwise every 30 minutes).

Luing Ferry (www.argyll-bute.gov.uk; North Cuan; return per person/car £2.10/8.50) Departs every 30 minutes from Seil's southern tip for the three-minute trip to Luing.

Mull

POP 2800

From the rugged ridges of Ben More and the black basalt crags of Burg to the blinding white sand, rose-pink granite and emerald waters that fringe the Ross, Mull can lay claim to some of the finest and most varied scenery in the Inner Hebrides. Noble birds of prey soar over mountain and coast, while the western waters provide good whale watching. Add a lovely waterfront 'capital', an impressive castle, the sacred island of Iona and easy access from Oban, and you can see why it's sometimes impossible to find a spare bed on the island.

👉 Tours

Mull's varied landscapes and habitats offer the chance to spot some of Scotland's rarest and most dramatic wildlife, including sea eagles, golden eagles, otters, dolphins and whales. Numerous operators offer walking or road trips to see them; email mull@visitscotland.com for a full list.

Nature Scotland
WILDLIFE

(☎ 07743 956380; www.naturescotland.com) Young, enthusiastic guides offer a range of excellent wildlife tours, including afternoon trips that can link to ferries (adult/child £30/25, four hours), evening otter-spotting trips (£40/35, three to four hours), all-day walking trips (£60/50, seven hours) and winter stargazing excursions (£40/30, two to three hours).

Mull Eagle Watch
BIRDWATCHING

(☎ 01680-812556; www.mulleaglewatch.com; adult/child £8/4; ⊙ Apr-Sep) Britain's largest bird of prey, the white-tailed eagle, or sea eagle, has been successfully reintroduced to Mull, and the island is crowded with birdwatchers raptly observing the raptor. Two-hour tours to observe this bird are held in the mornings and afternoons, and must be booked in advance.

Turus Mara
BOATING

(☎ 01688-400242; www.turusmara.com; ⊙ Apr–mid-Oct) Offers trips from Ulva Ferry in central Mull to Staffa and the Treshnish Isles (adult/child £65/32.50, six hours), with an hour ashore on Staffa and two hours on Lunga, where you can see seals, puffins, kittiwakes, razorbills and many other species of seabird. There are also trips to Staffa alone (£32.50/18, 3¾ hours) and birdwatching-focused trips (£75/37.50, eight hours).

Transfer is also available from the Craignure ferry terminal, allowing you to visit as a day trip from Oban.

Staffa Tours
BOATING

(☎ 07831 885985; www.staffatours.com; ⊙ Apr–mid-Oct) Runs boat trips from Fionnphort and Iona to Staffa (adult/child £35/17.50, three hours), or Staffa plus the Treshnish Isles (also available from Tobermory and Ardnamurchan; £65/32.50, six hours). Before and after the seabird season, the trip is shorter (£50/30, five hours), not landing on Lunga. There are also connection-plus-tour options leaving from Oban.

Mull, Coll & Tiree

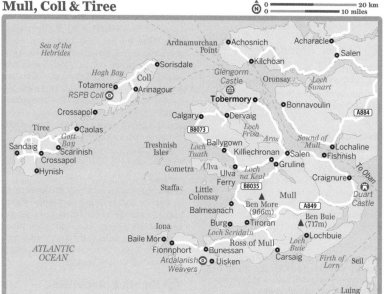

Mull Magic WALKING
(☑ 01688-301213; www.mullmagic.com) Offers guided walking tours in the Mull countryside to spot eagles, otters, butterflies and other wildlife. Customised tours are also available; check the website for the different itineraries.

Isle of Mull Wildlife Expeditions WILDLIFE
(☑ 01688-500121; www.torrbuan.com; adult/child £44.50/39.50) Six-hour Land Rover tours of the island with the chance of spotting red deer, golden eagles, peregrine falcons, white-tailed sea eagles, hen harriers, otters and perhaps dolphins and porpoises. The cost includes pick-up from your accommodation or the ferry, a picnic lunch and binoculars. It's possible as a day trip from Oban.

★⃰ Festivals & Events

Mull Music Festival MUSIC
(www.facebook.com/mullmusicfestival; ⊘ last weekend Apr) Four days of foot-stomping traditional Scottish and Irish folk music at Tobermory's pubs.

Mendelssohn on Mull MUSIC
(www.mendelssohnonmull.com; ⊘ early Jul) A weeklong festival of chamber music, with performances around Mull island.

❶ Information

There's a bank with an ATM in Tobermory; otherwise you can get cash back with a purchase from Co-op food stores.

Craignure Tourist Office (☑ 01680-812377; www.visitscotland.com; Craignure; ⊘ 9am-5pm Mon, 8.30am-5pm Tue-Sat, 10am-5pm Sun Sep-Jun, 9am-6.15pm Mon, 8.30am-6.15pm Tue-Sat, 10am-4.15pm Sun Jul & Aug) Opposite the ferry slip.

Explore Mull (☑ 01688-302875; www.isle-of-mull.net; Ledaig; ⊘ 9am-5pm Easter-Jun & Sep–mid-Oct, to 7pm Jul & Aug; ☎) In Tobermory car park. Has local information, can book all manner of island tours and hires out bikes.

Mull & Iona Community Hospital (☑ 01680-300392; www.nhshighland.scot.nhs.uk; Craignure) Has an A&E department.

❶ Getting There & Away

CalMac (www.calmac.co.uk) has three car ferries that link Mull with the mainland:

Oban to Craignure (adult/car £3.60/13.40, 40 minutes, every two hours) The busiest route – bookings are advised if you have a car.

Lochaline to Fishnish (adult/car £2.40/7.15, 15 minutes, at least hourly, except four daily on winter Sundays) On the east coast of Mull.

Tobermory to Kilchoan (adult/car £2.75/8.65, 35 minutes, seven daily Monday to Saturday, five Sunday April to October, three Monday to Saturday November to March) Links to the Ardnamurchan peninsula.

ℹ️ Getting Around

BICYCLE

You can hire bikes for around £20 per day from various places around the island, including Explore Mull (p93) in Tobermory.

BUS

West Coast Motors (☎01680-812313; www.westcoastmotors.co.uk) connects ferry ports and main villages. Its Discovery Day Pass (adult/child £15/7.50) is available from April to October and grants a day's unlimited bus travel.

The routes useful for visitors are bus 95/495 from Craignure to Tobermory, bus 96/496 from Craignure to Fionnphort, and bus 494 from Tobermory to Dervaig and Calgary.

CAR

Almost all of Mull's road network consists of single-track roads. There are petrol stations at Craignure, Fionnphort, Salen and Tobermory.

Mull Car Hire (☎07425 127900; www.mullcarhire.co.uk; car hire per day/week £50/280) Rents out small cars. Will bring cars to the ferry terminal.

Mull Taxi (☎07760 426351; www.mulltaxi.co.uk) Based in Tobermory.

Craignure & Around

POP 200

Located 3 miles south of Craignure, where the principal ferries from the mainland arrive, is Duart Castle, the ancestral seat of the Maclean clan, enjoying a spectacular position on a rocky outcrop overlooking the Sound of Mull. Otherwise there's not much to see at Craignure.

Duart Castle   CASTLE
(☎01680-812309; www.duartcastle.com; adult/child £7/3.50; ⊙10.30am-5pm daily May–mid-Oct, 11am-4pm Sun-Thu Apr) Originally built in the 13th century, it was abandoned for 160 years before a 1912 restoration. As well as dungeons, courtyard and battlements with memorable views, there's lots of clan history – none worse than the story of Lachlan Cattanach, who took his wife on an outing to an island in the strait, then left her there to drown when the tide came in.

A bus to the castle meets some of the incoming ferries at Craignure (£11 return including castle entrance), but it's a pretty walk to get here, too.

★ **Craignure Bunkhouse**   HOSTEL £
(☎01680-812043; www.craignure-bunkhouse.co.uk; Craignure; dm/q £24/90; 🅿🛜) An excellent hostel near the ferry slip, this purpose-built accommodation features top en suite dorms fetchingly decked out in wood. Bunks have lots of headroom and individual USB chargers, lamps and powerpoints. There are also double bunks for families. The ecologically minded design means sustainable sleeping, and the hostel has a great kitchen, sociable common area and enthusiastic staff.

Tobermory

POP 1000

Mull's main town is a very picturesque little fishing and yachting port with brightly painted houses arranged around a sheltered harbour. It's a great base, with good places to eat, inviting pubs and an array of quality accommodation both along the harbour-front and on the hill behind.

◎ Sights & Activities

The children's TV program *Balamory* was set here, and while the series stopped filming in 2004, regular repeats mean that the town still swarms in summer with toddlers (and nostalgic teenagers) towing parents around the locations (you can get a *Balamory* info sheet from tourist offices).

Whale-watching boat trips run out of Tobermory harbour. A range of tours can be booked at Explore Mull (p93) in the water-front car park.

Hebridean Whale & Dolphin Trust   MUSEUM
(☎01688-302620; www.whaledolphintrust.co.uk; 28 Main St; ⊙10.30am-4.30pm Mar-Nov) FREE This place has displays, videos and interactive exhibits on whale and dolphin biology and ecology, and is a great place for kids to learn about sea mammals. It also provides information about volunteering and reporting sightings of whales and dolphins. Opening times are rather variable.

Mull Aquarium   AQUARIUM
(☎01688-302876; www.mullaquarium.co.uk; Ledaig; adult/child £5/4; ⊙9.30am-5pm Easter-Oct; 👶) By the harbour car park, this aquarium has good information on the local marine environment, and little touch pools with crabs, starfish and the like for kids. All the creatures are returned to the sea after they've done a four-week shift here.

Mull Museum   MUSEUM

(📷 01688-301100; www.mullmuseum.org.uk; Main St; ⏱ 10am-4pm Mon-Sat Easter-Oct) **FREE** Mull Museum, which records the history of the island, is a good place to go on a rainy day. There are interesting exhibits on crofting, and on the *Tobermory Galleon,* a ship from the Spanish Armada that sank in Tobermory Bay in 1588 and has been the object of treasure seekers ever since. Donations are appreciated in this volunteer-run set-up.

Tobermory Distillery   DISTILLERY

(📷01688-302647; www.tobermorymalt.com; Ledaig; tours £8; ⏱ 10am-5pm) This bijou distillery was established in 1798. It doesn't always open on winter weekends; phone ahead to check or book. There are two whisky lines here: the standard Tobermory and the lightly peated Ledaig. The standard tour lets you taste one of them; for £10, you can try them both.

Sea Life Surveys   WILDLIFE

(📷01688-302916; www.sealifesurveys.com; Ledaig) Whale-watching trips head from Tobermory harbour to the waters north and west of Mull. An all-day whale-watch allows up to seven hours at sea (£80), and has a 95% success rate for sightings. The four-hour Whalewatch cruise (adult/child £60/30) is better for families. Shorter seal-spotting excursions are also available (£25/12.50, two hours).

🛌 Sleeping

Tobermory has dozens of B&Bs, but the place can still be booked solid any time from May through to August, especially at weekends. Most options close in winter.

Tobermory SYHA   HOSTEL £

(📷 01688-302481; www.syha.org.uk; Main St; dm/tw/q £20/60/112; ⏱ Mar-Oct; @ 🛜) This hostel has a great location in a Victorian house right on the waterfront. It's got an excellent kitchen and spotless if somewhat austere dorms, as well as good triples and quads for families. It books out fast in summer.

★Sonas House   B&B ££

(📷 01688-302304; www.sonashouse.co.uk; Fairways, Erray Rd; s/d £90/130, apt for 2 excl/incl breakfast £100/130; P 🛜 ❄) Here's a treat: a B&B with a heated, indoor 10m swimming pool! Sonas is a large, modern house (follow signs to the golf course) offering luxury in a beautiful setting with superb Tobermory Bay views. Both rooms are beautifully done out with blond wood and other colours; 'Blue Poppy' has its own balcony. There's

also a self-contained studio apartment. Hospitality is faultless.

Harbour Guesthouse   B&B ££

(📷 01688-302209; www.harbourguesthouse -tobermory.com; 59 Main St; s £65-70, d £90-110; ⏱ Easter–mid-Oct; 🛜) On the harbourfront, this is a cute Tobermory base that offers rooms varying in size and shape that have been refurbished and are most comfortable. Great harbour views and cordial hosts.

Cuidhe Leathain   B&B ££

(📷 01688-302504; www.cuidhe-leathain.co.uk; Breadalbane St; r £100; ⏱ Apr-Oct; 🛜) A handsome 19th-century house in Tobermory's 'upper town', Cuidhe Leathain (coo-lane), which means Maclean's Corner, exudes a cosily cluttered Victorian atmosphere. The rooms are beautifully plush, with plunger coffee and decent teas. Breakfasts will set you up for the rest of the day, and the owners are a fount of knowledge about Mull and its wildlife. Minimum two-night stay.

★Highland Cottage   BOUTIQUE HOTEL £££

(📷 01688-302030; www.highlandcottage.co.uk; Breadalbane St; d £160-175; ⏱ Apr–mid-Oct; P 🛜 ❄) Antique furniture, four-poster beds, embroidered bedspreads, fresh flowers and candlelight lend this small hotel (only six rooms) an appealingly old-fashioned cottage atmosphere, but with all mod cons, including cable TV, full-size baths and room service. There's also an excellent restaurant here (dinner £42.50), and the personable owners are experts in guest comfort.

🍴 Eating

Pier Café   CAFE £

(📷 07786 197377; www.facebook.com/thepiercafe tobermory; The Pier; light meals £7-10; ⏱ 9.30am-5pm Mon-Thu, to 7pm Fri & Sat, 10.30am-5pm Sun mid-Mar–Oct; 🛜 ♿) A cosy wee corner with local art on the walls, tucked beneath Café Fish at the north end of Tobermory village, the Pier serves great coffee and breakfast rolls, top baguettes that may feature local squat lobster or other seafood, plus tasty lunches such as haddock and chips, pasta and sandwiches.

Fish & Chip Van   FISH & CHIPS £

(📷 01688-301109; www.tobermoryfishandchipvan. co.uk; Main St; fish & chips £6-10; ⏱ 12.30-9pm Mon-Sat Apr-May, 12.30-9pm daily Jun-Sep, 12.30-7pm Mon-Thu, to 8pm Fri & Sat Oct-Mar) If it's takeaway you're after, you can tuck into some of Scotland's best gourmet fish and chips down on the Tobermory waterfront. And where else will you find a chip van selling freshly cooked scallops?

★ **Café Fish** SEAFOOD **££**
(☑01688-301253; www.thecafefish.com; The Pier; mains £15-26; ☺noon-3pm & 5.30-11pm mid-Mar–Oct; 🐾) 🍴 Seafood doesn't come much fresher than the stuff served at this warm and welcoming little restaurant overlooking Tobermory harbour. Crustaceans go straight from boat to kitchen to join rich seafood stew, fat scallops, fish pie and catch-of-the-day on the daily-changing menu, where confident use of Asian ingredients adds an extra dimension. Book ahead.

Hebridean Lodge SCOTTISH **££**
(☑01688-301207; www.hebrideanlodge.co.uk; Salen Rd, Baliscate; mains £17-21; ☺6.30-8.30pm Mon-Fri Easter-Dec) Above a gallery and shop, this mezzanine restaurant offers delicious local produce at chunky wooden tables. There's a warm welcome and fine, fresh seafood and lamb, with daily specials complementing the short menu of generous-spirited Scottish cuisine. Book ahead.

WHALE WATCHING ON MULL

The North Atlantic Drift – a swirling tendril of the Gulf Stream – carries warm water into the cold, nutrient-rich seas off the Scottish coast, resulting in huge plankton blooms. Small fish feed on the plankton, and bigger fish feed on the smaller fish; this huge seafood smorgasbord attracts large numbers of marine mammals, from harbour porpoises and dolphins to minke whales and even – though sightings are rare – humpback and sperm whales.

There are dozens of operators around the coast offering whale-watching boat trips lasting from a couple of hours to all day; some have sighting success rates of 95% in summer.

While seals, porpoises and dolphins can be seen year-round, minke whales are migratory. The best time to see them is from June to August, with August being the peak month for sightings. The website of the Hebridean Whale & Dolphin Trust (www.whaledolphintrust.co.uk) has lots of information on the species you are likely to see, and how to identify them.

🍷 Drinking & Entertainment

★ **Mishnish Hotel** PUB
(☑01688-302500; www.mishnish.co.uk; Main St; ☺11am-1am; 🐾) 'The Mish', near the pier on the harbourfront, is a favourite hang-out for visiting yachties and a great place for a pint, with a very convivial atmosphere. Wood-panelled and flag-draped, this is a good old traditional pub where you can listen to live folk music, toast your toes by the open fire or challenge locals to a game of pool.

★ **Comar** PERFORMING ARTS
(☑01688-302211; www.comar.co.uk) Mull's lively arts scene includes a famous theatre group, regular art exhibitions and concerts. This arts organisation puts on exhibitions, plays and concerts in Tobermory's An Tobar Arts Centre (☑01688-302211; www.comar.co.uk; Argyll Tce; ☺10am-5pm Mon-Sat May-Sep, 11am-4pm Tue-Sat Oct-Apr) FREE and elsewhere. Check its website for upcoming events.

North Mull

The road from Tobermory west to Calgary cuts inland, leaving most of Mull's north coast wild and inaccessible. It continues through the settlement of Dervaig to the glorious beach at Calgary. From here onwards you are treated to spectacular coastal views; it's worth doing the route in reverse from Gruline for the best vistas.

⊙ Sights

Calgary Beach BEACH
Mull's best (and busiest) silver-sand beach, flanked by cliffs and with views out to Coll and Tiree, is about 12 miles west of Tobermory. And yes – this is the place from which Canada's more famous Calgary takes its name.

Glengorm Castle GALLERY, PARK
(☑01688-302321; www.glengormcastle.co.uk; Glengorm; ☺buildings 10am-5pm Easter-Oct) FREE A long, single-track road leads north for 4 miles from Tobermory to majestic Glengorm Castle, with views across the sea to Ardnamurchan, Rum and the Outer Hebrides. The castle outbuildings house a nature centre, farm shop and the excellent Glengorm Coffee Shop (light meals £3-9; 🐾🍴) 🍴. The castle, which also has upmarket B&B acccommodation (p97), is not open to the public, but you're free to explore the beautiful grounds, where several good walks are signposted. Guided nature walks also run from here; check the website for times.

Calgary Art in Nature GALLERY
(☎01688-400256; www.calgary.co.uk; Calgary; entry by donation; ⊙10am-5pm Mar-Nov) 🅿 Run with enthusiasm and vision, this place just back from Calgary beach is an excellent art space, and also has great self-catering accommodation. On-site silversmiths and wood sculptors ply their trade in their workshops, while a luminous gallery exhibits high-quality work from local artists. Other pieces dot the woodland ramble on the hill behind. There's also the good Calgary Farmhouse Tearoom (light meals £5-9; ⊙10am-5pm Easter-Oct, to 2pm Mon-Fri Nov-Mar; 🛜) 🅿 here.

🛏 Sleeping & Eating

Dervaig Hostel HOSTEL £
(☎01688-400313; dervaigbunkrooms@gmail.com; Dervaig; dm/q £18/60; ⊙Apr-Oct; 🅿🛜) Comfortable bunkhouse accommodation in Dervaig's village hall, with self-catering kitchen and sitting room. The dorms have good en suite bathrooms and comfortable bunks.

★**Calgary Farmhouse** COTTAGE ££
(☎01688-400256; www.calgary.co.uk; Calgary; per week summer apt & cottages £500-2000, per 3 days studios & cabin £200-270; 🅿🛜🐾) 🅿 This brilliant complex near Calgary beach offers a number of fantastic apartments, cottages and houses, beautifully designed and fitted out with timber furniture and wood-burning stoves. The Hayloft is spectacular, with noble oak and local art, while the wood-clad longhall-like Beach House has luxury and dreamy views. Romantic Kittiwake, a beautiful wooden camping cabin among trees, has bay views and a boat ceiling.

There are options sleeping from two to 10. The larger ones go by the week in summer, but smaller ones are available for shorter stays. There's a good on-site cafe that sells some foodstuffs too. Bikes are available for hire.

Bellachroy INN ££
(☎01688-400314; www.thebellachroy.co.uk; Dervaig; s/d £85/125; ⊙Easter-Oct; 🅿🛜🐾) The Bellachroy is an atmospheric 17th-century droving inn with seven comfortable bedrooms with stripy carpets; they vary in size. The bar is a focus for local social life and serves decent food (noon to 2.30pm and 6pm to 8.30pm). Management are very helpful.

Glengorm Castle B&B £££
(☎01688-302321; www.glengormcastle.co.uk; r £135-290; 🅿🛜🐾) Bristling with turrets as a real castle should, this accommodation enjoys an unforgettable location, with huge windows framing green fields sloping down to the water. The attractive interior has 20th-century art instead of stags' heads. Bedrooms are all different, with lots of space and character. It's got lively, genuinely friendly owners, and kids will have a ball running around the grounds.

Rooms are £30 more expensive if you only stay one night. There are also various self-catering cottages available (£495 to £890 per week).

Am Birlinn SCOTTISH ££
(☎01688-400619; www.ambirlinn.com; Penmore, Dervaig; mains £14-24; ⊙noon-2.30pm & 5-9pm Wed-Sun mid-Mar–Oct; 🛜) 🅿 Occupying a spacious and modern wooden building between Dervaig and Calgary, this is an interesting dining option. Locally caught crustaceans and molluscs are the way to go here, though there are burgers, venison and other meat dishes available. Free pick-up and drop-off from Tobermory or other nearby spots is offered. There's also a bar.

South Mull

The road from Craignure to Fionnphort climbs through wild and desolate scenery before reaching the southwestern part of the island, which consists of a long peninsula called the Ross of Mull. The Ross has a spectacular south coast lined with black basalt cliffs that give way further west to white-sand beaches and pink granite crags. The cliffs are highest at Malcolm's Point, near the superb Carsaig Arches.

The village of Bunessan is home to a cottage museum; a minor road leads south from here to the beautiful white-sand bay of Uisken, with views of the Paps of Jura.

At the western end of the Ross, 35 miles from Craignure, is Fionnphort (*finn*-a-fort) and the Iona ferry. The coast here is a beautiful blend of pink granite rocks, white sandy beaches and vivid turquoise sea.

◉ Sights

Ardalanish Weavers WORKSHOP
(☎01681-700265; www.ardalanish.com; ⊙10am-5pm Apr-Oct, to 4pm Mon-Fri Nov-Mar) 🅿 Fleeces from the Hebridean sheep on this farm are woven into fine woollen products using venerable looms, which you can see at work in the old cowshed. Hot drinks and snacks are available at the shop, which sells weaving

and farm produce. You can also feed the Highland cattle here. It's on a remote rural backroad 2 miles south of Bunessan.

Ross of Mull Historical Centre MUSEUM
(Tigh na Rois; ☑ 01681-700659; www.romhc.org.uk; Bunessan; entry by donation; ⊙ 10am-4pm Mon-Fri Apr-Oct, other times by arrangement) The little village of Bunessan is home to the Ross of Mull Historical Centre, a cottage museum by a ruined mill that houses displays on local history, geology, archaeology, genealogy and wildlife.

🛏 Sleeping & Eating

Ross of Mull Bunkhouse HOSTEL £
(☑ 07759 615200; www.rossofmullbunkhouse. co.uk; Fionnphort; dm/s/tw £24/48/70; ℗ 🛜) Run by enthusiastic young owners, this excellent year-round bunkhouse about a mile from the Iona ferry offers a rural atmosphere, top-notch modern bathrooms and spacious, comfortable four-berth rooms with sturdy metal bunks, USB ports and bedside lights. There's an attractive common room with fireplace, guitars and loch views, plus a brilliant kitchen and a drying room.

Fidden Farm CAMPSITE £
(☑ 01681-700427; Fidden, Fionnphort; sites per adult/child £10/5; ⊙ Easter-Aug; ℗ 🛝) A basic but popular and beautifully situated campsite, with views over pink granite reefs to Iona and Erraid. It's just over a mile south of Fionnphort. It can be very blowy when the wind gets up. Opening months vary a little from year to year.

★ Seaview B&B ££
(☑ 01681-700235; www.iona-bed-breakfast-mull. com; Fionnphort; s £65, d £90-105; ⊙ mid-Mar–Oct; ℗ 🛜 🛝) 🍃 Just up from the ferry, Seaview has beautifully decorated bedrooms and a breakfast conservatory with grand views across to Iona. The rooms are compact and charming, with gleaming modern bathrooms. The owners are incredibly helpful and also offer tasty three-course dinners (not in summer), often based around local seafood, while breakfasts include locally sourced produce.

Achaban House B&B ££
(☑ 01681-700205; www.achabanhouse.co.uk; Fionnphort; s/d £46/75; ℗ 🛜) This super refurbished rural house has very pleasing contemporary rooms with modern fabrics and a light, uncluttered feel. Some rooms look over the loch below. It's casual and friendly;

the ideal base for visiting Iona with the ferry less than a mile away. Guests have use of an excellent kitchen and a lounge with wood-burning stove. Continental breakfasts feature homemade bread.

★ Ninth Wave SCOTTISH £££
(☑ 01681-700757; www.ninthwaverestaurant.co.uk; Bruach Mhor, Fionnphort; 3-/4-/5-course dinner £48/56/68; ⊙ sittings 7pm Wed-Sun May-Oct) 🍃 This excellent croft restaurant is owned and operated by a lobster fisherman and his Canadian wife. The daily menu makes use of locally landed shellfish and crustaceans, vegetables and salad grown in the garden, and quality local meats with a nose-to-tail ethos. It's all served in a stylishly converted bothy. Advance bookings (a couple of weeks at least) are essential. No under-12s.

It's worth going all-in and taking on the superb cheeseboard if you've got room. Don't miss the handmade chocolates infused with locally foraged flavours.

Iona

POP 200

Like an emerald teardrop off Mull's western shore, enchanting, idyllic Iona, holy island and burial ground of kings, is a magical place that lives up to its lofty reputation. From the moment you embark on the ferry towards its sandy shores and green fields, you'll notice something different about it. To appreciate its charms, spend the night: there are some excellent places to do it. Iona has declared itself a fair-trade island and actively promotes ecotourism.

History

St Columba sailed from Ireland and landed on Iona in 563, establishing a monastic community with the aim of Christianising Scotland. It was here that the *Book of Kells* – the prize attraction of Dublin's Trinity College – is believed to have been transcribed. It was taken to Ireland for safekeeping from 9th-century Viking raids.

The community was re-founded as a Benedictine monastery in the early 13th century and prospered until its destruction during the Reformation. The ruins were given to the Church of Scotland in 1899, and by 1910 a group of enthusiasts called the Iona Community Council had reconstructed the abbey. It's still a flourishing spiritual community offering regular courses and retreats.

WORTH A TRIP

STAFFA

Felix Mendelssohn, who visited the uninhabited island of Staffa, off Mull, in 1829, was inspired to compose his 'Hebrides Overture' after hearing waves echoing in the impressive and cathedral-like **Fingal's Cave**. The cave walls and surrounding cliffs are composed of vertical, hexagonal basalt columns that look like pillars (Staffa is Norse for 'Pillar Island'). You can land on the island and walk into the cave via a causeway. Nearby **Boat Cave** can be seen from the causeway, but you can't reach it on foot. Staffa also has a sizeable puffin colony, north of the landing place.

Northwest of Staffa lies a chain of uninhabited islands called the Treshnish Isles. The two main islands are the curiously shaped **Dutchman's Cap** and **Lunga**. You can land on Lunga, walk to the top of the hill, and visit the shag, puffin and guillemot colonies on the west coast at Harp Rock.

Unless you have your own boat, the only way to reach Staffa and the Treshnish Isles is on an organised boat trip from Fionnphort, Iona, Tobermory, Ardnamurchan, Seil or the Ulva ferry slip. Operators include Turus Mara (p92), Staffa Tours (p92), Staffa Trips and Seafari Adventures (p91).

Sights

Past the abbey, look for a footpath on the left signposted **Dun I** (dun-ee). An easy 15-minute walk leads to Iona's highest point, with fantastic 360-degree views.

★**Iona Abbey** HISTORIC BUILDING
(☎01681-700512; www.historicenvironment.scot; adult/child £7.50/4.50; ⏲9.30am-5.30pm Apr-Sep, 10am-4pm Oct-Mar) Iona's ancient but heavily reconstructed abbey is the spiritual heart of the island. The spectacular **nave**, dominated by Romanesque and early Gothic vaults and columns, is a powerful space; a door on the left leads to the beautiful **cloister**, where medieval grave slabs sit alongside modern religious sculptures. Out the back, the **museum** displays fabulous carved high crosses and other inscribed stones, along with lots of background information. A replica of the intricately carved St John's Cross stands outside the abbey.

Next to the abbey is an ancient **graveyard** where there's an evocative Romanesque chapel, as well as a mound that marks the burial place of 48 of Scotland's early kings, including Macbeth. Former Labour party leader John Smith is also buried in this cemetery. The ruined **nunnery** nearby was established at the same time as the Benedictine abbey. The museum is closed Sundays in winter.

Iona Heritage Centre MUSEUM
(☎01681-700576; www.ionaheritage.co.uk; entry by donation; ⏲10am-5.15pm Mon-Sat Easter-Oct) This place covers the history of Iona, crofting and lighthouses; there's also a craft shop and a cafe serving delicious home baking.

Tours

Alternative Boat Hire BOATING
(☎01681-700537; www.boattripsiona.com; ⏲Mon-Thu Apr–mid-Oct) Offers cruises in a traditional wooden sailing boat for fishing, birdwatching, picnicking or just admiring the scenery. Three-hour afternoon trips cost £30/10 per adult/child; on Wednesday there's a full-day cruise (£50/20; 10am to 5pm). Bookings are essential.

Staffa Trips BOATING
(☎01681-700358; www.staffatrips.co.uk; ⏲Apr–mid-Oct) Runs three-hour boat trips to Staffa (adult/child £35/17.50) on the MV *Iolaire,* departing Iona pier at 9.45am and 1.45pm, and from Fionnphort at 10am and 2pm, with one hour ashore on Staffa.

Sleeping & Eating

There are B&B options, camping, a hostel and a pair of hotels on the island. It's imperative to book accommodation well ahead in spring and summer. Very little is open in winter apart from the hostel.

There are a couple of hotel restaurants, and the abbey has a cafe, as does the heritage centre. There's also a supermarket and a mediocre fast-food place by the ferry.

★**Iona Hostel** HOSTEL £
(☎01681-700781; www.ionahostel.co.uk; dm adult/child £21/17.50, tw £42, bothy s/d £40/60; P 📶) This working ecological croft and environmentally sensitive hostel is one of Scotland's most rewarding and tranquil places to stay. Lovable black Hebridean sheep surround the building, which features pretty, practical

and comfy dorms and an excellent kitchen-lounge. There's a fabulous beach nearby, and a hill to climb for views. It's just over a mile from the ferry on Iona, past the abbey.

There's also a cute wheeled bothy nearby, perfect for a bit of solitude.

★ **Argyll Hotel**   HOTEL **££**
([✔]01681-700334;   www.argyllhoteliona.co.uk;   s £79, d £99-119;   ⊙mid-Mar–mid-Oct;   🛜📶) ⚘
This lovable, higgledy-piggledy warren of a hotel has great service and appealing snug rooms (those with sea views cost more – £174 for a double), including good-value family options. The rooms offers simple comfort and relaxation rather than luxury. Most look out to the rear, where a huge organic garden supplies the restaurant. This is a relaxing and amiably run Iona haven.

Iona Pods   CABIN **££**
([✔]01681-700233; www.ionapods.com; pods £80; 🅿📶) Sleeping up to four, these pods on a working croft have a simple kitchen. There's power, but washing and toilet facilities are separate.

ⓘ Getting There & Away

The ferry from Fionnphort to Iona (£3.40 adult return, five minutes, hourly) runs daily. Cars can only be taken with a permit. There are also various day trips available to Iona from Tobermory and Oban.

Tiree

POP 700

Low-lying Tiree (tye-*ree;* from the Gaelic *tiriodh,* meaning 'land of corn') is a fertile sward of lush, green machair liberally sprinkled with yellow buttercups, much of it so flat that, from a distance, the houses seem to rise out of the sea. It's one of the sunniest places in Scotland, but also one of the windiest – cyclists soon find that, although it's flat, heading west usually feels like going uphill. One major benefit – the constant breeze keeps away the midges.

The surf-lashed coastline here is scalloped with broad, sweeping beaches of white sand, hugely popular with windsurfers and kite-surfers. Most visitors, however, come for the birdwatching, beachcombing and lonely coastal walks.

In the 19th century Tiree had a population of 4500, but poverty, food shortages and overcrowding led the Duke of Argyll to introduce a policy of assisted emigration.

Between 1841 and 1881, more than 3600 left, many emigrating to Canada, the USA, Australia and New Zealand.

◎ Sights & Activities

Look out for the Tyree gin distillery, due to open on the island in around 2020. The gin is already produced on the mainland using local botanicals.

Skerryvore Lighthouse Museum   MUSEUM
([✔] 01879-220045; www.hebrideantrust.org; Hynish; ⊙9am-5pm May-Sep) [FREE] The picturesque harbour and hamlet of Hynish, near Tiree's southern tip, was built in the 19th century to house workers and supplies for the construction of lonely Skerryvore Lighthouse, 10 miles offshore. This museum occupies the old workshops by the sand-filled but flushable harbour; up the hill is the signal tower once used to communicate by semaphore with the lighthouse.

An Iodhlann   LIBRARY
([✔] 01879-220793; www.aniodhlann.org.uk; Scarinish; ⊙9am-1pm Mon & Wed-Thu Sep-Jun, 11am-5pm Mon-Fri Jul & Aug) [FREE] An Iodhlann is a historical and genealogical library and archive, where some of the tens of thousands of descendants of Tiree emigrants come to trace their ancestry. The centre stages summer exhibitions on island life and history. Check the website for winter opening times as it varies by volunteer availability.

Wild Diamond   WATER SPORTS
([✔] 07712 159205; www.wilddiamond.co.uk; Cornaig; ⊙Apr-Oct) Professional and friendly, this outfit runs courses in windsurfing (£35/100 per session/day), kitesurfing (£70/120 per half-/full day), surfing, sand-yachting and stand-up paddleboarding, and rents out equipment including surfboards.

Blackhouse Watersports   WATER SPORTS
([✔] 07711 807976; www.blackhouse-watersports. co.uk; Gott Bay; ⊙Mar-Nov) Operating out of a beach hut at the far end of Gott Bay, this welcoming set-up runs kitesurfing (£100) and surf (£35) lessons, hires kayaks (£25 for three hours, including wetsuit), lends out fishing tackle and rents bikes (£10 per day).

🎪 Festivals & Events

Tiree Music Festival   MUSIC
(www.tireemusicfestival.co.uk; ⊙mid-Jul) Held over a weekend in mid-July, this is a very likeable festival with a range of folksy, bluesy and rootsy music. They like to keep it small

so limit the capacity; book ahead. Campsites are set up around the festival area in Crossapol.

Tiree Wave Classic   SPORTS
(www.tireewaveclassic.co.uk; ⊘Oct) Reliable wind and big waves have made Tiree one of Scotland's top windsurfing venues. The annual Tiree Wave Classic competition has been held here since 1986, making it one of the world's longest-standing windsurfing championships.

🛏 Sleeping & Eating

Millhouse Hostel   HOSTEL £
(⊠01879-220802; www.tireemillhouse.co.uk; Cornaig; dm/s/tw £24/42/56; P🤶) Housed in a converted barn next to an old ruined water mill, this small but comfortable hostel is 5 miles west of the Tiree ferry pier. The dorms have beds rather than bunks, there's a common area and it's cheaper if you stay more than one night.

Balinoe Campsite   CAMPSITE £
(⊠07712 159205; www.tireecampsite.co.uk; Balinoe; tent sites adult/child £12/6, dm £23, pods £30; ⊘Apr-Oct; P🤶🏕) Balinoe is a sheltered campsite with full facilities in the southwest of Tiree island, near Balemartine, with great views of Mull. There are campsites with optional electric hook-up, pods and a very basic bothy. It's cheaper for multinight stays. A self-catering cottage is available year-round.

★Rockvale Guest House   B&B ££
(⊠01879-220675;   www.rockvaletiree.co.uk; Balephetrish; s £68, d £88-98; P🤶🏕) Smart, comfortable, modern accommodation and a genuine welcome make this easily Tiree's best midrange accommodation choice. It's situated in the north of the island and does things with real panache. Breakfast is way above average, and features smoothies, fruit skewers, poached egg with spinach and pesto or banana mash.

Ceàbhar   SCOTTISH ££
(⊠01879-220684;   www.ceabhar.com;   Sandaig; mains £8-15; ⊘7-8.30pm Wed-Sat Easter-Oct, plus Tue Jul & Aug; 🤶🏕) ◆ At Tiree's western end, this attractive restaurant looks out over the Atlantic towards the sunset. The cordial owners have the right attitude; they grow their own salads, eschew chips, and brew craft beer. The menu includes handmade pizzas, soups, fish of the day and local lamb, with lots of vegetarian options. Book ahead.

A snug cottage sleeps up to eight people in five bedrooms.

ℹ Information

There's a bank (without an ATM), post office and supermarket in Scarinish, the main village on Tiree, half a mile south of the ferry pier. You can get cash back with debit-card purchases at the Co-op.

Some tourist information is available at the ferry terminal. A useful website is www.isleof tiree.com.

ℹ Getting There & Away

AIR

Loganair flies from Glasgow to Tiree daily. **Hebridean Air Services** (www.hebrideanair.co.uk) operates from Oban to Tiree via Coll (one way from Oban/Coll £65/10, twice daily Monday and Wednesday).

BOAT

CalMac (www.calmac.co.uk) has a ferry from Oban to Tiree (adult/car £10.60/57.65, four hours, one daily) via Coll, except on Friday when the boat calls at Tiree first (three hours 20 minutes). The one-way fare from Coll to Tiree (one hour) is £3.45/15.60 per adult/car.

On Wednesdays, the ferry continues to Barra in the Outer Hebrides (from Tiree adult/car £9.05/46.85 one way, three hours), and stops again on the way back to Oban, allowing a long day trip to Tiree from the mainland. In high summer, a day trip is also possible on Saturdays.

ℹ Getting Around

Rent bicycles and cars from **MacLennan Motors** (⊠01879-220555; www.maclennanmotors. com; Pierhead, Scarinish; per day car £45, bicycle £10; ⊘9am-5pm Mon-Fri, to 1pm Sat) at the ferry pier. **Tiree Fitness** (⊠07867 304640; www.tireefitness.co.uk; Sandaig; per day/week from £15/65) has better bikes and will deliver them to the ferry (£5 extra).

There's a transport-on-demand service on Tiree; phone 01879-220419.

Coll

POP 200

Coll is more rugged and less populous than Tiree, its neighbour. The northern part of the island is a mix of bare rock, bog and lochans (small lochs), while the south is swathed in golden shell-sand beaches and machair dunes up to 30m high. It's a gloriously relaxing place.

The island's main attraction is the peace and quiet – empty beaches, bird-haunted coastlines, and long walks along the shore. The biggest and most beautiful sandy beaches are at Crossapol in the south, and Hogh Bay and Cliad on the west coast.

In summer the corncrake's 'krek-krek' is heard at the RSPB Coll (☑01879-230301; www. rspb.org.uk; ☺24hr) at Totronald in the southwest of the island. From Totronald a sandy 4WD track runs north past the dunes backing Hogh Bay to the road at Totamore, allowing walkers and cyclists to make a circuit back to Arinagour rather than backtracking.

🛏 Sleeping & Eating

There's a handful of places to stay, several of them excellent. You can wild camp for free on the hill above the Coll Hotel; ask at the hotel first.

★Coll Bunkhouse   HOSTEL £
(☑01879-230217; www.collbunkhouse.com; Arinagour; dm/tw £22/50; P 🐾 🛜 🎱) This gorgeous modern bunkhouse is in Coll's main settlement, just a 10- to 15-minute walk from the ferry pier. It's a great facility, with a kitchen, good showers and access for travellers with disabilities.

Island Café   CAFE ££
(☑01879-230262; www.visitcoll.co.uk; Arinagour; mains £6-13; ☺11am-2pm & 5-9pm Wed-Sat, noon-6pm Sun; 🛜) This cheerful spot serves hearty, homemade meals such as sausage and mash, haddock and chips, and vegetarian cottage pie, accompanied by organic beer, wine and cider. Sunday roasts are legendary on Coll island.

ⓘ Information

For information on Coll, visit www.visitcoll.co.uk. Arinagour, half a mile from the ferry pier, is Coll's only village, home to a shop, post office (with ATM), craft shops and aged petrol station. Pride of the island is the phone mast; there was virtually no signal until 2015.

ⓘ Getting There & Away

AIR

Hebridean Air Services (www.hebrideanair. co.uk) operates from Oban to Coll (one way £65, twice daily Monday and Wednesday) and on to Tiree (£10).

BOAT

Ferries with CalMac (www.calmac.co.uk) run from Oban to Coll (adult/car £10.60/57.65, 2¾ hours, one daily) and on to Tiree, except on Friday when the ferry calls at Tiree first. The one-way fare between Coll and Tiree (one hour) is £3.45/15.60 per adult/car.

On Wednesdays, the ferry continues to Barra in the Outer Hebrides (from Coll adult/car £9.05/46.85 one way, four hours), and stops again on the way back to Oban, allowing a long day trip to Coll from the mainland. In high summer, a day trip is also possible on Saturdays.

ⓘ Getting Around

There is no public transport. Mountain bikes can be hired from the post office (☑01879-230395; fionaangus233@btinternet.com; per day £20; ☺9am-1pm Mon-Sat) in Arinagour, while walking is another good option. Locals always offer lifts.

NORTH ARGYLL

The northern parts of Argyll harbour a diverse range of attractions, including two of Scotland's most photogenic castles and an island made for exploration by bike. Though it's often traversed rapidly by folk heading for the northern Highlands, it's worth slowing down to appreciate its many charms.

Loch Awe

Loch Awe is one of Scotland's most beautiful lochs, with rolling forested hills around its southern end and spectacular mountains in the north. It lies between Oban and Inveraray and is the longest loch in Scotland – about 24 miles – but is less than 1 mile wide for most of its length. At its northern end, it escapes to the sea through the narrow Pass of Brander, where Robert the Bruce defeated the MacDougalls in 1309.

★Kilchurn Castle   CASTLE
(www.historicenvironment.scot; Dalmally; ☺9.30am-5.30pm Apr-Sep, 10am-4pm Oct) FREE At the northern end of Loch Awe are the scenic ruins of the strategically situated and much-photographed Kilchurn Castle. Built in 1440, it enjoys one of Scotland's finest settings. Even when it's not open, it's worth visiting for the scenic stroll to it. It's a half-mile walk from an unmarked car park on the A85, just west of the Inveraray turnoff between Dalmally and Lochawe.

Cruachan Power Station   NOTABLE BUILDING
(☑01416-149105; www.visitcruachan.co.uk; A85; adult/child £7.50/2.50; ☺9.30am-4.45pm Apr-Oct, 10am-3.45pm Mon-Fri Nov-Dec & Feb-Mar) In the Pass of Brander, by the A85, you can visit this power station. Electric buses take you more than half a mile inside Ben Cruachan,

allowing you to see the pump-storage hydro-electric scheme, which occupies a vast cavern hollowed out of the mountain. The tour takes half an hour. Falls of Cruachan railway station (seasonal) is very close by.

ℹ Getting There & Away

Trains from Glasgow to Oban stop at Dalmally and Lochawe villages.

In summer three daily buses with **Scottish Citylink** (www.citylink.co.uk) from Glasgow to Oban go via Dalmally, Lochawe village and Cruachan Power Station.

Connel & Taynuilt

Hemmed in by dramatic mountain scenery, Loch Etive stretches 17 miles from Connel to Kinlochetive (accessible by road from Glencoe). Some very different but worthwhile sights complement the beautiful scenery around here.

★**Bonawe Iron Furnace**   HISTORIC SITE
(☎01866-822432; www.historicenvironment.scot; Taynuilt; adult/child £5/3; ⊙9.30am-5.30pm Apr-Sep) Bonawe Iron Furnace is one of the region's most unusual historical sights. Near Taynuilt (not Bonawe), and dating from 1753, it was built by an iron-smelting company from Cumbria because of the abundance of birch and oak in the area. The coppiced wood was made into the charcoal that was needed for smelting the iron. It's now a tranquil, beautiful place, with the old buildings picturesquely arranged around a green hillside, and there's great background information on the iron industry. Take a picnic!

Falls of Lora   WATERFALL
(Connel) At Connel Bridge, 5 miles north of Oban, the loch joins the sea via a narrow channel partly blocked by an underwater rock ledge. When the tide flows in and out, water pours through this bottleneck, creating spectacular white-water rapids known as the Falls of Lora. Park near the north end of the bridge and walk back into the middle to have a look.

Dunstaffnage Castle   CASTLE
(☎01631-562465; www.historicenvironment.scot; adult/child £6/3.60; ⊙9.30am-5.30pm Apr-Sep, 10am-4pm Oct, 10am-4pm Sat-Wed Nov-Mar)

WORTH A TRIP

CASTLE STALKER

One of Scotland's most spectacularly sited castles, Castle Stalker (☎01631-730354; www.castlestalker.com; Portnacroish; adult/child/family £20/10/50; ⊙tours Apr-Oct) perches on a tiny offshore island – Monty Python buffs will recognise it as the castle that appears in the final scenes of the film *Monty Python and the Holy Grail*. Visits are by two-hour guided tour by a family member (book by email or phone), and leave from a boat dock just off the A828. There's a maximum of one a day, so arrange your visit in advance.

Dunstaffnage, 2 miles west of Connel, looks like a child's drawing of what a castle should be – square and massive, with towers at the corners, and perched on top of a rocky outcrop. It was built around 1260 and was captured by Robert the Bruce during the Wars of Independence in 1309. The haunted ruins of the nearby 13th-century chapel contain lots of Campbell tombs decorated with skull-and-crossbone carvings.

Inverawe Smokehouse & Fishery   FOOD & DRINKS
(☎Easter-Dec 01866-822808, Jan-Easter 01866-822777; www.inverawe-fisheries.co.uk; Inverawe, near Taynuilt; ⊙9am-5pm mid-Mar–Oct; 🛜👶) Aficionados of smoked salmon should pay a visit to Inverawe Smokehouse and Fishery, 2 miles east of Taynuilt, where local salmon (and trout, herring and venison) is smoked over split oak logs. There's also an angling school and trout fishery where you can learn to fly-fish, lots of family-friendly features, and a tearoom where you can sample the smokery's mouthwatering produce.

ℹ Getting There & Away

Trains from Glasgow to Oban stop at Taynuilt and Connel.

In summer one daily bus with **Scottish Citylink** (www.citylink.co.uk) bus from Glasgow to Oban goes via Taynuilt and Connel. Citylink services between Oban and Fort William also stop in Connel.

Walking the West Highland Way

Best Viewpoints

➡ Conic Hill, p110

➡ Inversnaid, p110

➡ Above Crianlarich, p111

➡ Mam Carraigh, p112

➡ Devil's Staircase, p113

➡ Old military road above
Kinlochleven, p113

Best Wild Camping

➡ Garadhban, p110

➡ Inversnaid Boathouse, p110

➡ Doune Bothy, p111

➡ Inveroran, p112

Why Go?

From the outskirts of Glasgow, Scotland's biggest city, the West Highland Way leads through fertile, populous Lowland countryside to the shores of Loch Lomond, on the threshold of the Highlands. From there it carries you north, through rugged glens, beside fast-flowing streams and past wild moorland where magnificent mountains are never out of sight. The very names have an alluring ring: Rannoch Moor, Glen Coe, Devil's Staircase.

Not only is the West Highland Way a rich sensory experience, it's also steeped in history. The route follows long stretches of drove roads, along which cattle were once taken to market; the flat beds of old railway lines; roads along which coaches and horses once jolted; and the 18th-century military road built to subdue rebellious Highlanders.

This is the most popular long-distance path in Scotland (and Britain for that matter); something like 30,000 walkers go the full distance each year, so you'll rarely be short of like-minded company from around the world.

When to Go

Tyndrum

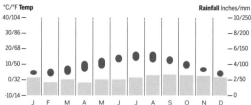

Feb Experienced walkers can have spectacular snow-covered scenery almost to themselves.

May The woods along Loch Lomond's shores are a purple blaze of Scottish bluebells.

Oct Not as busy as summer, the midges have gone and autumn colours start to appear.

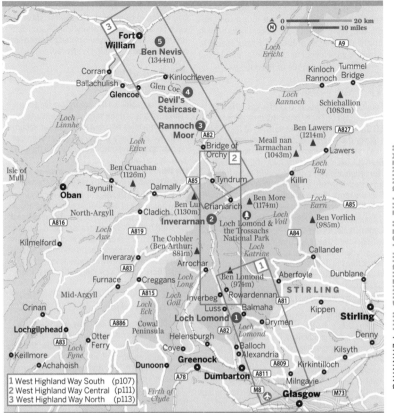

1 West Highland Way South (p107)
2 West Highland Way Central (p111)
3 West Highland Way North (p113)

West Highland Way Highlights

❶ Loch Lomond (p48)
Soaking up the gorgeous scenery along the bonnie banks of this lovely loch.

❷ Drover's Inn (p51)
Enjoying a well-earned pint of ale at this atmospheric pub at Inverarnan.

❸ Rannoch Moor (p151)
Revelling in the wild open spaces of bleak but beautiful Rannoch Moor.

❹ Devil's Staircase (p114)
Taking in the dramatic views from the highest point of the walk.

❺ Ben Nevis (p164)
Rounding off your achievement with an ascent of Ben Nevis, Britain's highest summit.

PLANNING

The walk begins at Milngavie, easing you into things with the two least strenuous days before you hit the harder stuff going north of Rowardennan. Spreading it over seven days means only one long day (between Tyndrum and Kings House) and a majority of comfortable days; don't overlook the fact that it's not only horizontal distance that matters – the Way involves a total of 3500m (11,500ft) of ascent.

Of course, you can take much longer, by doing shorter days, or by taking time out to knock off some of the nearby Munros – Ben Lomond and Ben Nevis are the two obvious candidates. Or you can do a one-day hike on a part of the way – recommended sections include Inversnaid to Inverarnan (7 miles), and Kings House to Glen Nevis (19 miles).

Navigation is generally straightforward: the route is clearly waymarked with the official thistle-and-hexagon logo, and there's a shelf-full of guidebooks and maps to enlighten and entertain you along the way. By the time you reach Fort William you might even be supremely fit and ready to climb Ben Nevis, or continue along the Great Glen Way (p130) to Inverness.

❶ Maps & Books

Four OS Landranger 1:50,000 maps – No 64 *Glasgow*, No 56 *Loch Lomond & Inveraray*, No 50 *Glen Orchy & Loch Etive* and No 41 *Ben Nevis* – cover the Way, although it's much easier to use a purpose-designed, all-in-one route map. Both the excellent Harvey 1:40,000 Route map *West Highland Way* and the superbly designed Rucksack Readers guide *The West Highland Way* are more than adequate, and include lots of practical information for walkers.

Trailblazer's *West Highland Way*, by Charlie Loram, is the most comprehensive guidebook, with detailed trail maps and information on accommodation, places to eat and tourist attractions in Glasgow, Fort William and all the villages along the way.

❶ Accommodation

If you're planning to rely on serviced accommodation (hotels, B&Bs and hostels) it's essential to book rooms in advance; the official website (www.westhighlandway.org) lists most of the accommodation along the route. Note that Kings House is an accommodation 'bottleneck' with just the one hotel (closed for renovations until 2019). Public transport here is limited to one bus every two hours (last bus westbound around 8.18pm) and taxis are expensive, so plan ahead and don't get caught out.

There are several fully serviced campsites along the way, as well as two official backpacker camping places (free, no facilities, one-night stay only) at Garadhban Forest and Inversnaid

---

❶ PRACTICALITIES
....

Duration seven days

Distance 96 miles (154km)

Difficulty moderate

Start Milngavie

Finish Fort William

Transport train, bus

Summary Scotland's most popular long-distance path, passing through some of the country's finest landscapes, from suburban Glasgow to the foot of the highest mountain in Britain.

Boathouse. From March to September local bylaws forbid camping on the eastern shore of Loch Lomond between Drymen and Rowardennan, except at recognised campsites; elsewhere, responsible wild camping is allowed.

❶ Guided Walk & Baggage Services

Rather than doing all the organising, you can take advantage of the services offered by a few small companies who can arrange your accommodation and carry your luggage between overnight stops. Some outfits go a step further and provide you with sheaves of information about the Way and the places through which you pass, or can provide a guide to lead you on the walk.

Easyways (☑ 01324-714132; www.easyways. com) has years of experience organising accommodation and baggage transfer; **Transcotland** (☑ 01887-820848; www.transcotland.com) also has a good track record and can provide reams of directions and background information. **Wilderness Scotland** (www.wildernessscotland. com) offers guided walks along the West Highland Way.

❶ Information

The official West Highland Way website (www. westhighlandway.org) is a useful resource, covering most things you need to know: from the route itself, equipment and planning to weather, accommodation, food and notices about temporary closures and diversions.

The *West Highland Way Pocket Companion*, a free booklet listing accommodation and facilities along the route (updated annually), can be picked up at most tourist offices in the region.

There are ATMs at Milngavie, Drymen, Crianlarich, Tyndrum, Kinlochleven and Fort William.

❶ Getting There & Away

The official start of the West Highland Way is a granite obelisk (unveiled in 1992) beside the bridge over the Allander Water on Douglas St, Milngavie, but for most people the journey begins at Milngavie train station. Buses stop here and there's a car park near the station, just off Station Rd. To reach the obelisk from the station, go through the underpass and up a flight of steps to the pedestrianised centre of Milngavie. Bear left at the underpass exit to join Douglas St, passing through a shopping precinct before reaching the Allander Water and the official start point.

Fort William, at the end of the walk, has frequent rail and bus connections to other parts of Scotland, including an overnight sleeper train to London.

If you plan to walk just a section of the Way, Crianlarich, Tyndrum and Bridge of Orchy are well served by trains; contact **ScotRail** (☎0344 811 0141; www.scotrail.co.uk) for details. **Scottish Citylink** (www.citylink.co.uk) buses on the Glasgow–Fort William route stop at Crianlarich, Tyndrum and Bridge of Orchy. **Traveline Scotland** (☎0871 200 22 33; www.travelinescotland.com) provides a journey planner and timetable information for all public transport in Scotland.

From April to October a network of passenger ferries criss-crosses Loch Lomond, linking the main A82 road on the western shore with various locations along the West Highland Way on the eastern shore. A Loch Lomond Water Bus (www.lochlomond-trossachs.org/waterbus) timetable is available from tourist offices and online.

THE WALK

Day One: Milngavie to Drymen

➤ **Duration** 4½ to 5½ hours

➤ **Distance** 12 miles (19km)

From the obelisk on Douglas St, descend the ramp beneath the huge West Highland Way sign, pass through a small car park and follow a path along a disused railway, then upstream beside the Allander Water, to Mugdock Wood. At the end of the wood, paths and a track take you past a couple of small lochs to the B821. Turn left and follow the road for about 300m to a stile giving onto a path to the right. As you skirt Dumgoyach Hill watch out for Bronze Age standing stones to your right, just before the hill. A mile past Dumgoyach Bridge you pass Glengoyne Distillery; 800m further on you reach the Beech Tree Inn (☎01360-550297; www.thebeech treeinn.co.uk; mains £10-15; ⏲kitchen 11am-9pm Mon-Fri, 10.30am-10pm Sat, to 9pm Sun Apr-Sep, shorter hrs Oct-Mar; 🛜🍽) at Dumgoyne. In the village of Killearn, 1.5 miles to the right, there's accommodation, shops, pubs and a post office.

Follow the old railway track to Gartness, from where you're on a road most of the way to the edge of Drymen. A mile beyond Gartness there's a basic campsite available at Drymen Camping, from where a view of Loch Lomond makes its first appearance.

West Highland Way (South)

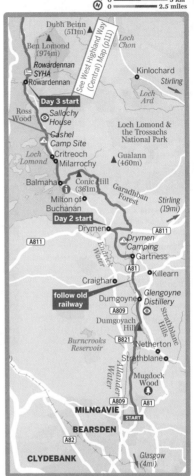

Pass a quarry and continue along the road; just past a sharp left bend, the Way leaves the road and follows a path to the right. If you're going to Drymen, continue along the road and cross the A811 to enter the village.

Drymen

Drymen is a pretty village with a central green and lots of character. There are plenty of accommodation and eating options, an excellent pub, several shops and a small supermarket.

TREASUREGALORE/SHUTTERSTOCK ©

1. Dumgoyne
On day one from Milngavie you'll pass the Glengoyne Distillery (p107).

2. Rannoch Moor (p112)
Revel in the wild open spaces of this bleak but beautiful landscape

3. Ben Nevis (p113)
Round off your achievement by enjoying the view (pictured) from Britain's highest summit.

4. Conic Hill (p110)
Detour here for the wonderful panorama over Loch Lomond.

DISCLAIMER

Although the authors and publisher have done their utmost to ensure the accuracy of all information in this guide, they cannot accept any responsibility for any loss, injury or inconvenience sustained by people using this book. They cannot guarantee that the paths and routes described here have not become impassable for any reason in the interval between research and publication. The fact that a walk is described in this guidebook does not mean that it is safe for you and your walking party. You are ultimately responsible for judging your own capabilities in the conditions you encounter.

Day Two: Drymen to Rowardennan

➠ **Duration** five to 6½ hours

➠ **Distance** 14 miles (22.5km)

From near the A811 just outside Drymen, a forest track gradually climbs to **Garadhban Forest** (backpacker campsite, no facilities). Just over an hour from Drymen, a side path runs left to the village of **Milton of Buchanan**; it's also the alternative route when Conic Hill is closed to dog walkers during the lambing season (late April to early May). There are a couple of B&Bs in the village but no pubs or shops.

The Way climbs then contours north of the summit of **Conic Hill** (358m), but it's worth the short detour to the top for the wonderful panorama over **Loch Lomond**. This viewpoint also has a special, even unique significance: from the summit you can make out the unmistakeable line of the Highland Boundary Fault, separating the Lowlands from the Highlands – so from this point on you really are in the Highlands.

Descend to **Balmaha**, a small lakeside village usually thronged with people messing about in boats. As well as the National Park Centre (p50), there's a small shop and the Oak Tree Inn (p52), which offers accommodation, food and a bar.

Continue along the shore of Loch Lomond, passing a marker commemorating the Way's opening in 1980, to **Milarrochy** (one hour from Balmaha; campsite available). From **Critreoch**, about 800m further on, the path dives into a dark forest and emerges to follow the road for about 1 mile. Just after you join the road is the Cashel Campsite (p52). A mile beyond Sallochy House, the Way climbs through **Ross Wood**, its magnificent oaks making it one of Scotland's finest natural woodlands, to Rowardennan.

Rowardennan

Rowardennan is little more than a hamlet, but it has a **hotel** (☎01360-870273; www. rowardennanhotel.co.uk; d £90-135; ☺Feb-Dec; ℙ☎☜☀) and a SYHA hostel (p51), and Rowchoish Bothy (free, no facilities) is 2.5 miles north. Rowardennan is also the starting point for the ascent of Ben Lomond (974m).

Day Three: Rowardennan to Inverarnan

➠ **Duration** six to 7½ hours

➠ **Distance** 14 miles (22.5km)

From Rowardennan follow the unsealed road that parallels the loch shore. Just past private Ptarmigan Lodge an alternative path branches left and follows the shoreline; it's more interesting, but much rougher going (not recommended with a heavy backpack) than the upper route, which follows a track higher up the hillside. The lower path leads past a natural rock cell in a crag about 1.5 miles north of Ptarmigan Lodge, which is known as **Rob Roy's prison**: the famous outlaw is said to have kept kidnap victims here. From both routes you can reach **Rowchoish Bothy**, a simple stone shelter.

Not far beyond the bothy the forestry track gives way to a path, which dives down to the loch for a stretch of difficult walking to **Cailness**. From here the going improves to **Inversnaid**, shortly before which the path crosses Snaid Burn just above the impressive **Inversnaid Falls**. The huge Inversnaid Hotel could be a good place to stop for refreshments before you tackle the next and toughest section of all.

For a couple of miles north from Inversnaid, the path twists and turns around large boulders and tree roots, a good test of balance and agility. A mile or so into this, the Way passes close to **Rob Roy's cave**, where he is alleged to have hidden from the authorities, although it's little more than a gap beneath fallen blocks of rock. Further on, **Doune Bothy** provides basic accommodation (no facilities). Almost 1 mile beyond the bothy, at **Ardleish**, there's a landing stage used by the ferry across to the **Ardlui Hotel** (☏ 01301-704243; www.ardlui.com; s/d £60/120, pod £35, camping per adult/child/car £7/4/4; P 🛜 🐾).

From Ardleish, you leave the loch and climb to a col below **Cnap Mór** (164m), where on a clear day there are good views north towards the Highlands and south over Loch Lomond. The path descends into **Glen Falloch**; a footbridge over **Ben Glas Burn** heralds your arrival at Inverarnan. Just upstream is the spectacular **Beinglas Falls**, a cascade of 300m (1000ft) – very impressive after heavy rain.

Inverarnan

There's a choice of B&B and camping accommodation in Inverarnan, as well as an excellent country pub, the Drover's Inn (p51), which also offers food and lodging.

Day Four: Inverarnan to Tyndrum

→ **Duration** 4½ to 5½ hours

→ **Distance** 13 miles (21km)

From Inverarnan the route follows the attractive River Falloch most of the way to **Crianlarich**, the approximate halfway point of the Way. About 4 miles along, it crosses the river and joins an old military road. This track climbs out of Glen Falloch, and then at a stile into the forest, a path leads down to the right towards Crianlarich. There's no real need to go to Crianlarich, though there are B&Bs, a youth hostel, a bar and restaurant and a small shop with an ATM.

The Way climbs to the west from the stile, offering good views east to **Ben More** (1174m), and continues through the trees for about 2 miles. Next, it crosses under the railway line, goes over the road and crosses a wooden bridge over the River Fillan. Pass the remains of **St Fillan's Priory**, turn left and go on to Strathfillan Wigwams (p52) at Auchtertyre Farm. The route crosses the A82 once more, and in less than an hour you make it to Tyndrum.

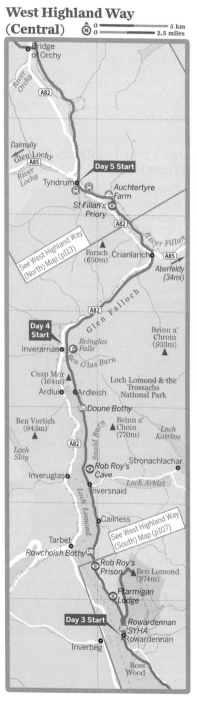

West Highland Way (Central)

WALKING THE WEST HIGHLAND WAY THE WALK

Tyndrum

Tyndrum, originally a lead-mining settlement and now a popular staging point between Glasgow and Fort William, is strung out along the A82. It has shops (including one selling outdoor equipment), hotels, B&Bs and campsites, and is well served by train and bus. Eating places include the Real Food Café (p52).

Day Five: Tyndrum to Kings House Hotel

→ **Duration** 6½ to eight hours

→ **Distance** 19 miles (30.5km)

From Tyndrum the route soon rejoins the old military road and crosses the railway line, affording easy walking with lovely views. Three miles from Tyndrum, you cross a burn at the foot of Beinn Dòrain (1074m), the hill that dominates this section of the path.

The path climbs gradually to pass the entrance to Glen Orchy, crossing the railway again, heralding the beginning of the really mountainous scenery. The hamlet of Bridge of Orchy is dominated by the Bridge of Orchy Hotel. Cross the old bridge (built in 1750) that gives the settlement its name and climb through the trees to the crest of Mam Carraigh, from where there are superb views across to Rannoch Moor. The path then winds down to the secluded Inveroran Hotel. It's possible to camp wild (no facilities) beside a stone bridge 400m west of the hotel (caution: this area is subject to flooding after heavy rains).

The Way follows the minor road, which soon becomes a track, climbing gently past some plantations and out onto Rannoch Moor. There's no shelter for about 7 miles, and Bà Bridge, about 3 miles beyond the plantations, is the only real marker point. It can be very wild and windy up here, and there's a real sense of isolation. A cairn marks the summit at 445m and from here there's a wonderful view down into Glen Coe. As the path descends from the moor to join the road again, you can see the chairlift of the Glencoe Mountain Resort (p155) to the left. There's a cafe at the base station, about 500m off the West Highland Way. Kings House Hotel is just over 1 mile ahead, across the A82.

Kings House Hotel

Dating from the 17th century, the Kings House Hotel (p155) was originally used as barracks for George III's troops. It's closed for renovations until January 2019, so you won't be able to get a bed here until then. In the meantime, however, you can catch a bus to Glencoe village, 11 miles west, where there's a wider selection of accommodation. It's possible to camp for free across the bridge behind the hotel.

Day Six: Kings House Hotel to Kinlochleven

→ **Duration** three to four hours

→ **Distance** 9 miles (14.5km)

From Kings House Hotel the route follows the old military road and then goes along-

---

LOCH LOMOND

Loch Lomond fills a trough that was gouged by a glacier flowing south from the ice sheet that covered Rannoch Moor during the last Ice Age, and straddles the boundary between the Highlands and the Lowlands, so that two distinct environments can be seen along its shores.

The southern part of the loch is broad, shallow and dotted with 38 islands, and bordered by relatively flat, low-lying arable land. This part of the loch freezes over during severe winters, and it has been possible to reach the islands on foot on several occasions over the last 50 years.

The northern end of the loch is deep and narrow (at its deepest, just south of Inversnaid, the water depth is 190m), generally less than 1 mile wide, and enclosed by steep mountains rising to 900m. The slopes at the loch shore are covered by Scotland's largest remnant of native oak woodland, mixed with newer conifer plantations. Botanical studies have found that 25% of all known British flowering plants and ferns can be found along the West Highland Way on the eastern shore, which is famous for its display of Scottish bluebells in spring.

side the A82 to a parking area at Altna-feadh. This is a wonderful vantage point from which to appreciate the mountainous scenery of Glen Coe. The conical peak to your left is Buachaille Etive Mor (1022m).

From here the Way turns right, leaving the road to begin a steep, zigzagging climb up the Devil's Staircase. The cairn at the top is at 548m and marks the highest point of the Way. The views are stunning, especially on a clear day, and you may even be able to see Ben Nevis (1345m). The path now winds gradually down towards Kinlochleven, hidden below in the glen. As you descend you join the Blackwater Reservoir access track, and meet the pipes that carry water from there down to the town's hydroelectric power station. It's not a particularly pretty sight but was essential for the now-defunct aluminium smelter, the original reason for the town's establishment in 1907; the electricity generated is now used to power Fort William's aluminium works.

Kinlochleven

Kinlochleven eases you back into 'civilisation' before you arrive at Fort William and experience the sensory onslaught that one feels after returning from the wilderness. There's plenty of B&B, hostel and camping accommodation, including the Blackwater Hostel & Campsite (p159), as well as a village store and small supermarket.

The Ice Factor (p159), housed in part of the the former smelting plant, has the world's largest indoor ice-climbing wall (plus a 'normal' climbing wall), so you can watch people performing amazing vertical feats while you tuck into a large pizza in the centre's cafe.

Day Seven: Kinlochleven to Fort William

➡ **Duration** six to 7½ hours

➡ **Distance** 15 miles (24km)

From Kinlochleven follow the road north out of town and turn off opposite the school. The path climbs through woodland to the old military road, from which you get a grand view along Loch Leven to the Pap of Glencoe (740m). Climb gradually to the crest, just beyond which are the ruins of several old farm buildings at Tigh-na-sleubhaich. From here the Way continues

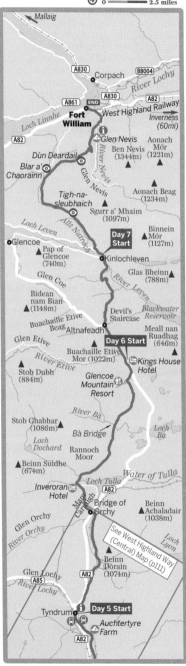

West Highland Way (North)

THE DEVIL'S STAIRCASE

The steep zigzags on the West Highland Way where it climbs out of Glen Coe were given the name 'Devil's Staircase' by the soldiers who built them back in 1750 as part of a military road linking Stirling Castle to Fort William. It was superseded by Thomas Telford's road through Glen Coe in the early 19th century (and by the modern A82 in 1933), but the name Devil's Staircase was again used during the building of the Blackwater Reservoir above Kinlochleven in 1905–09. At this time, navvies working on the dam used the route to go drinking at the Kings House Hotel – in harsh winter weather, many perished in the snow on the way back.

gently downhill and into conifer plantations 2 miles further on. You emerge at Blar a' Chaorainn, which is nothing more than a bench and an information board.

The Way leads on and up, through more plantations; occasional breaks in the trees provide fine views of Ben Nevis. After a few miles, a sign points to nearby Dùn Deardail, an Iron Age fort with walls that have been partly vitrified (turned to glass) by fire.

A little further on, cross another stile and follow the forest track down towards Glen Nevis. Across the valley the huge bulk of Ben Nevis fills the view. A side track leads down to Glen Nevis, which can make a good base for an ascent of 'the Ben'.

Continue along the path if you're heading for Fort William, passing a small graveyard just before you meet the road running through Glen Nevis. Turn left here; soon after, there's a large visitor centre (p162) on the right. Continue along the roadside into Fort William. The official end of the West Highland Way is in Gordon Sq, at the far end of Fort William's pedestrianised main street, marked by a bronze sculpture of a weary hiker rubbing his feet. After a rest on one of the benches thoughtfully provided here, you can look forward to an end-of-walk celebration in one of the town's several restaurants and bars.

Fort William

Fort William promotes itself as the 'Outdoor Capital of the UK' (www.outdoorcapital. co.uk), and has good rail and bus connections to the rest of the country. There's a wide range of hostel and B&B accommodation, including Fort William Backpackers (p160) and 6 Caberfeidh (p161), and lots of places to eat – the Grog & Gruel (☎ 01397-705078; www.grogandgruel.co.uk; 66 High St; mains £8-19; ☺ bar meals noon-9pm, restaurant 5-9pm; 🛜 📶 🐾) does great Mexican grub. If you're camping, be aware that the nearest campsite (p163) is back in Glen Nevis, 2.5 miles before you reach Fort William, as is the SYHA hostel (p163); both are signposted off the Way above Glen Nevis.

Inverness & the Central Highlands

Best Places to Eat

➡ Lime Tree (p161)

➡ Café 1 (p121)

➡ Restaurant at the Cross (p141)

➡ Lochleven Seafood Cafe (p159)

➡ Old Forge (p169)

Best Places to Stay

➡ Rocpool Reserve (p121)

➡ Grange (p161)

➡ Lovat (p134)

➡ Milton Eonan (p154)

➡ Trafford Bank (p120)

Why Go?

From the sub-Arctic plateau of the Cairngorms to the hills of Highland Perthshire and the rocky peaks of Glen Coe, the central mountain ranges of the Scottish Highlands are testimony to the sculpting power of ice and weather. Here the landscape is at its grandest, with soaring hills of rock and heather bounded by wooded glens and waterfalls.

Not surprisingly, this part of the country is an adventure playground for outdoor-sports enthusiasts. Aviemore, Glen Coe and Fort William draw hill walkers and climbers in summer, and skiers, snowboarders and ice climbers in winter. Inverness, the Highland capital, provides urban rest and relaxation, while nearby Loch Ness and its elusive monster add a hint of mystery.

From Fort William, base camp for climbing Ben Nevis, the Road to the Isles leads past the beaches of Arisaig and Morar to Mallaig, jumping-off point for the isles of Eigg, Rum, Muck and Canna.

When to Go

Inverness

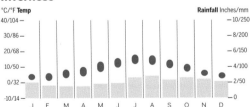

Apr–May Mountain scenery is at its most spectacular, with snow lingering on the higher peaks.

Jun Fort William hosts the UCI Mountain Bike World Cup, pulling huge crowds.

Sep Ideal for hiking and hill walking: midges are dying off, but weather is still reasonably good.

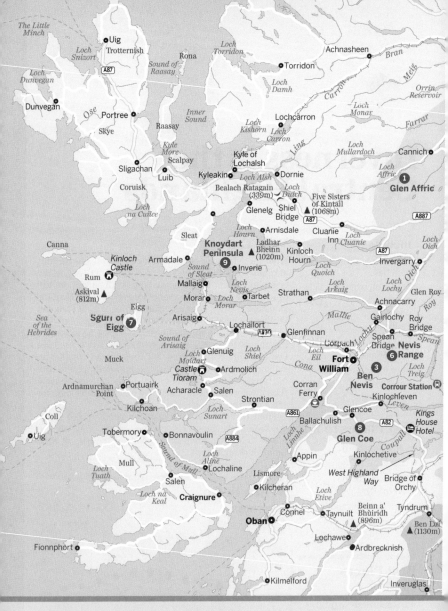

Central Highlights Highlights

1 Glen Affric (p128) Hiking among the hills, lochs and forests of Scotland's most beautiful glen.

2 Rothiemurchus Estate (p135) Wandering through ancient Caledonian forest in the heart of the Cairngorms.

3 Ben Nevis (p164) Making it to the summit of the UK's highest mountain – and being able to see the view.

4 Glen Lyon (p154) Exploring the woods and mountains around this gorgeous and romantic glen.

5 Rannoch Moor (p151) Keeping right on to the end

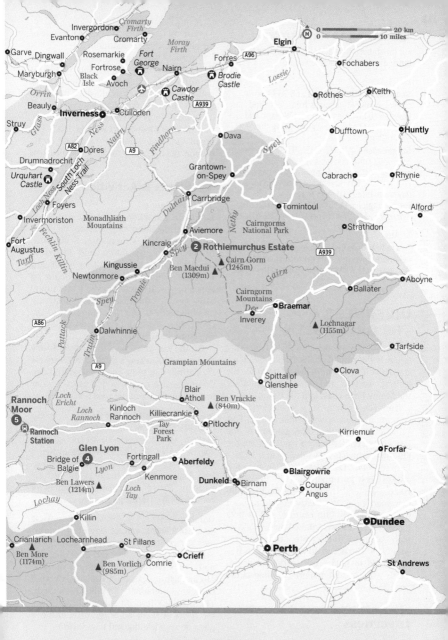

of the road at this bleak but
beautiful moor.

6 **Nevis Range** (p163)
Rattling your teeth loose on
this championship downhill
mountain-bike course.

7 **Sgurr of Eigg** (p171)
Taking in the stunning
panorama from the summit of
this dramatic island peak.

8 **Glen Coe** (p155) Soaking

up the moody but magnificent
scenery (when you can see it!).

9 **Knoydart Peninsula**
(p168) Venturing into the
country's most remote and
rugged wilderness.

❶ Getting There & Around

For timetable information, call **Traveline Scotland** (www.travelinescotland.com).

BUS

Scottish Citylink (☎ 0871 266 3333; www.citylink.co.uk) Runs buses from Perth and Glasgow to Inverness and Fort William, and links Inverness to Fort William along the Great Glen.

Stagecoach (☎ 01463-233371; www.stagecoachbus.com) The main regional bus company, with offices in Aviemore, Inverness and Fort William. Dayrider tickets are valid for a day's unlimited travel on Stagecoach buses in various regions, including Inverness (£6.80), Aviemore (£7.30) and Fort William (£9.10).

TRAIN

Two railway lines serve the region: the Perth–Aviemore–Inverness line in the east, and the Glasgow–Fort William–Mallaig line in the west.

INVERNESS & THE GREAT GLEN

Inverness, one of Britain's fastest growing cities, is the capital of the Highlands. It's a transport hub and jumping-off point for the central, western and northern Highlands, the Moray Firth coast and the Great Glen.

The Great Glen is a geological fault running in a line across Scotland from Fort William to Inverness. The glaciers of the last ice age eroded a deep trough along the fault line, which is now filled by four lochs – Linnhe, Lochy, Oich and Ness. The glen has always been an important communication route – General George Wade built a military road along the southern side of Loch Ness in the early 18th century, and in 1822 the various lochs were linked by the Caledonian Canal (p160) to create a cross-country waterway. The A82 road along the glen was completed in 1933 – a date that coincides neatly with the first modern sightings of the Loch Ness Monster.

Inverness

POP 61,235

Inverness has a great location astride the River Ness at the northern end of the Great Glen. In summer it overflows with visitors intent on monster hunting at nearby Loch Ness, but it's worth a visit in its own right for a stroll along the picturesque River Ness, a cruise on Loch Ness, and a meal in one of the city's excellent restaurants.

Inverness was probably founded by King David in the 12th century, but thanks to its often violent history few buildings of real age or historical significance have survived – much of the older part of the city dates from the period following the completion of the Caledonian Canal in 1822. The broad and shallow River Ness, famed for its salmon fishing, runs through the heart of the city.

◉ Sights & Activities

★ **Ness Islands**   PARK

The main attraction in Inverness is a leisurely stroll along the river to the Ness Islands. Planted with mature Scots pine, fir, beech and sycamore, and linked to the river banks and each other by elegant Victorian footbridges, the islands make an appealing picnic spot. They're a 20-minute walk south of the castle – head upstream on either side of the river (the start of the Great Glen Way), and return on the opposite bank.

On the way you'll pass the red sandstone towers of **St Andrew's Cathedral** (11 Ardross St), dating from 1869, and the modern Eden Court Theatre (p122), which hosts regular art exhibits, both on the west bank.

Inverness Museum & Art Gallery   MUSEUM
(☎ 01463-237114; www.inverness.highland.museum; Castle Wynd; ⊙10am-5pm Tue-Sat Apr-Oct, noon-4pm Thu-Sat Nov-Mar) **FREE** Inverness Museum & Art Gallery has wildlife dioramas, geological displays, period rooms with historic weapons, Pictish stones and exhibitions of contemporary Highland arts and crafts.

Dolphin Spirit   WILDLIFE WATCHING
(☎ 07544 800620; www.dolphinspirit.co.uk; Inverness Marina, Stadium Rd; adult/child £18.50/12; ⊙ Easter-Oct) Four times a day in season, this outfit runs cruises from Inverness into the Moray Firth to spot the UK's largest pod of bottlenose dolphins – around 130 animals. The dolphins feed on salmon heading for the rivers at the head of the firth, and can often be seen leaping and bow-surfing.

☞ Tours

Loch Ness by Jacobite   BOATING
(☎ 01463-233999; www.jacobite.co.uk; Glenurquhart Rd; adult/child £23/15; ⊙ Jun-Sep; 🐾) Boats depart from Tomnahurich Bridge twice daily for a three-hour cruise along

Inverness

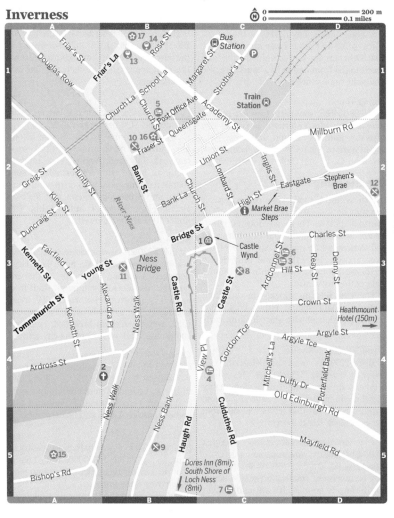

N 0 _____ 200 m
   0 _____ 0.1 miles

INVERNESS & THE CENTRAL HIGHLANDS INVERNESS

the Caledonian Canal to Loch Ness and back, with a live commentary on local history and wildlife. Buy tickets at the tourist office (p122) and catch a free minibus to the boat. Other cruises and combined cruise and coach tours, from one to 6½ hours, are also available, some year-round.

Happy Tours　　　　　　　　　　　BUS

(☑07828 154683; www.happy-tours.biz; per person £70) Provides entertaining guided day trips by minibus around Inverness, taking in various sights including Loch Ness, Urquhart Castle and Culloden.

🛏 Sleeping

Inverness has a good range of backpacker accommodation, and also some excellent boutique hotels. There are lots of guesthouses and B&Bs along Old Edinburgh Rd and Ardconnel St on the east side of the river, and on Kenneth St and Fairfield Rd on the west bank; all are within 10 minutes' walk of the city centre.

The city fills up quickly in July and August, so you should either book your accommodation or else start looking early in the day.

Black Isle Bar & Rooms　　　HOSTEL £

(☑01463-229920; www.blackislebar.com; 68 Church St; dm/s/d £25/55/100; 🛜) It's a beer drinker's dream come true – top-quality hostel accommodation in a central location, upstairs from a bar that serves real ales from the local Black Isle Brewery.

Bazpackers Backpackers Hotel　　HOSTEL £

(☑01463-717663; www.bazpackershostel.co.uk; 4 Culduthel Rd; dm/d £18/60; @🛜) 🌱 This may be Inverness' smallest hostel (34 beds), but it's hugely popular. It's a friendly, quiet place – the main building has a convivial lounge centred on a wood-burning stove, and a small garden and great views (some rooms are in a separate building with no garden). The dorms and kitchen can be a bit cramped, but the showers are great.

Inverness SYHA　　　　　　HOSTEL £

(SYHA; ☑01463-231771; www.syha.org.uk; Victoria Dr; dm/tr £19/77; P@🛜) Inverness' modern 166-bed hostel is 10 minutes' walk northeast of the city centre. Clean and well-equipped, with comfy beds and a flashy stainless-steel kitchen. Booking is essential, especially at Easter and in July and August.

Bught Caravan Park & Campsite　CAMPSITE £

(☑01463-236920; www.invernesscaravanpark.com; Bught Lane; tent sites per person £10, campervans £20; ☺Easter-Sep; 🛜) A mile southwest of the city centre near Tomnahurich Bridge, this camping ground is hugely popular with backpackers.

Ardconnel House　　　　　　B&B ££

(☑01463-240455; www.ardconnel-inverness.co.uk; 21 Ardconnel St; r per person £45-50; 🛜) The six-room Ardconnel is one of our favourites (advance booking is essential, especially in July and August) – a terraced Victorian house with comfortable en suite rooms, a dining room with crisp white table linen, and a breakfast menu that includes Vegemite for homesick Antipodeans. Kids under 10 years not allowed.

Ach Aluinn　　　　　　　　B&B ££

(☑01463-230127; www.achaluinn.com; 27 Fairfield Rd; r per person £40-45; P🛜) This large, detached Victorian house is bright and homely, and offers all you might want from a B&B – a private bathroom, TV, reading lights, comfy beds with two pillows each, and an excellent breakfast. Less than 10 minutes' walk west from the city centre.

Crown Hotel Guest House　　B&B ££

(☑01463-231135; www.crownhotel-inverness.co.uk; 19 Ardconnel St; s/d from £60/70; P@) Two of the six bedrooms here are family rooms, and there's a spacious lounge equipped with games consoles, DVDs and board games.

★ Trafford Bank　　　　　　B&B £££

(☑01463-241414; www.traffordbankguesthouse. co.uk; 96 Fairfield Rd; d £130-150; P🛜) Lots of rave reviews for this elegant Victorian villa, which was once home to a bishop, just a mitre's-toss from the Caledonian Canal and 10 minutes' walk west from the city centre. The luxurious rooms include fresh flowers and fruit, bathrobes and fluffy towels – ask for the Tartan Room, which has a wrought-iron king-size bed and Victorian roll-top bath.

★ Heathmount Hotel　　BOUTIQUE HOTEL £££

(☑01463-235877; www.heathmounthotel.com; Kingsmills Rd; r from £160; P🛜) Small and friendly, the Heathmount combines a popular local bar and restaurant with eight designer hotel rooms, each one different, ranging from a boldly coloured family room in purple and gold to a slinky black velvet four-poster double. Five minutes' walk east of the city centre.

★ **Rocpool Reserve** BOUTIQUE HOTEL £££
(☎01463-240089; www.rocpool.com; Culduthel
Rd; r from £270; [P]🔊) Boutique chic meets
the Highlands in this slick and sophisticated little hotel, where an elegant Georgian
exterior conceals an oasis of contemporary
cool. A gleaming white entrance hall lined
with red carpet and contemporary art leads
to designer rooms in shades of chocolate,
cream and gold; a restaurant by Albert Roux
completes the luxury package.

Expect lots of decadent extras in the
more expensive rooms, ranging from two-
person showers to balcony hot tubs with
aquavision TV.

✗ Eating

Velocity Cafe CAFE £
(☎01463-419956; www.velocitylove.co.uk; 1 Crown
Ave; mains £4-7; ⊙8am-5pm Mon-Wed & Fri, to
9pm Thu, 9am-5pm Sat, 10am-5pm Sun; 🔊🖉🚻)
✔ This cyclists cafe serves soups, sandwiches and salads prepared with organic,
locally sourced produce, as well as yummy
cakes and coffee. There's also a workshop
where you can repair your bike or book a
session with a mechanic.

★ **Café 1** BISTRO ££
(☎01463-226200; www.cafe1.net; 75 Castle St;
mains £12-28; ⊙noon-2.30pm & 5-9.30pm Mon-
Fri, 12.30-3pm & 6-9.30pm Sat; 🖉🚻) ✔ Café 1
is a friendly, appealing bistro with candlelit tables amid elegant blonde-wood and
wrought-iron decor. There is an international menu based on quality Scottish produce, from Aberdeen Angus steaks to crisp
pan-fried sea bass and meltingly tender pork
belly. There's a separate vegan menu.

Contrast Brasserie BRASSERIE ££
(☎01463-223777; www.glenmoristontownhouse.
com/restaurant; 20 Ness Bank; mains £16-24;
⊙noon-10pm) Book early for one of the
best-value restaurants in Inverness – a
dining room that drips designer style, with
smiling professional staff and truly delicious
food prepared using fresh Scottish produce.
The two-/three-course lunch menu (£13/16)
and three-course early bird menu (£18, 5pm
to 6.30pm) are bargains.

Mustard Seed BISTRO ££
(☎01463-220220; www.mustardseedrestaurant.
co.uk; 16 Fraser St; mains £13-23; ⊙noon-3pm &
5.30-10pm) ✔ The menu at this bright and
bustling bistro changes weekly, but focuses
on Scottish and French cuisine with a mod-

ern twist. Grab a table on the upstairs balcony if you can – it's the best outdoor lunch
spot in Inverness, with a great view across
the river. And a two-course lunch for £10 –
yes, that's right – is hard to beat.

Rocpool MEDITERRANEAN £££
(☎01463-717274; www.rocpoolrestaurant.com;
1 Ness Walk; mains £14-31; ⊙noon-2.30pm &
5.45-10pm Mon-Sat) ✔ Lots of polished wood,
crisp white linen and leather booths and
banquettes lend a sophisticated nautical air to this relaxed bistro, which offers
a Mediterranean-influenced menu that
makes the most of quality Scottish produce,
especially seafood. The two-course lunch
is £17.

🍺 Drinking & Nightlife

MacGregor's BAR
(www.macgregorsbars.com; 113 Academy St;
beer set menu for 2 from £21; ⊙11am-midnight
Mon-Thu, 11am-1am Fri & Sat, noon-midnight Sun)
Decked out in timber and tweed, this bar
strikes a distinctly modern chord. There's a
huge selection of Scottish craft beers on tap,
and even a beer 'set menu' described as 'a
journey through the basics of craft beer'. The
beer nerdiness extends to the gents' toilets,
where urinals and washbasins have been
fashioned out of beer kegs.

Clachnaharry Inn PUB
(☎01463-239806; www.clachnaharryinn.co.uk;
17-19 High St, Clachnaharry; ⊙11am-11pm Mon-
Thu, 11am-1am Fri & Sat, noon-11pm Sun; 🐕) Just
over a mile northwest of the city centre, on
the bank of the Caledonian Canal just off
the A862, this is a delightful old coaching
inn (with beer garden out the back) serving an excellent range of real ales and good
pub grub.

Phoenix PUB
(☎01463-233685; www.phoenixalehouse.co.uk; 108
Academy St; ⊙11am-1am Mon-Sat, noon-midnight
Sun) Beautifully refurbished, this is the most
traditional of the pubs in the city centre,
with a mahogany horseshoe bar and several real ales on tap, including beers from
the Cairngorm, Cromarty and Isle of Skye
breweries.

☆ Entertainment

Hootananny LIVE MUSIC
(☎01463-233651; www.hootanannyinverness.
co.uk; 67 Church St; ⊙noon-1am Mon-Thu, to 3am
Fri & Sat, 4pm-midnight Sun) Hootananny is the

city's best live-music venue, with traditional folk- and/or rock-music sessions nightly, including big-name bands from all over Scotland (and, indeed, the world). The bar is well stocked with a range of beers from the local Black Isle Brewery.

Ironworks LIVE MUSIC, COMEDY
(📞0871 789 4173; www.ironworksvenue.com; 122 Academy St) With live bands (rock, pop, tribute) and comedy shows two or three times a week, the Ironworks is the town's main venue for big-name acts.

Eden Court Theatre THEATRE
(📞01463-234234; www.eden-court.co.uk; Bishop's Rd; ⊙box office from 10am Mon-Sat, from 11am Sun, until show time; 🔊) The Highlands' main cultural venue – with theatre, art-house cinema and a conference centre – Eden Court stages a busy program of drama, dance, comedy, music, film and children's events, and has a good bar and restaurant. Pick up a program from the foyer or check the website.

ℹ Information

Inverness Tourist Office (📞01463-252401; www.visithighlands.com; 36 High St; ⊙9am-5pm Mon & Wed-Sat, from 10am Tue, 10am-3pm Sun, longer hours Mar-Oct; 🔊) Accommodation booking service; also sells tickets for tours and cruises.

ℹ Getting There & Away

AIR
Inverness Airport (INV; 📞01667-464000; www.invernessairport.co.uk) is at Dalcross, 10 miles east of the city, off the A96 towards Aberdeen. There are scheduled flights to Amsterdam, London, Manchester, Dublin, Orkney, Shetland and the Outer Hebrides, as well as other places in the UK.

Stagecoach (www.stagecoachbus.com) bus 11/11A runs from the airport to Inverness bus station (p122) (£4.40, 25 minutes, every 30 minutes).

BUS
Services depart from **Inverness bus station** (Margaret St). Most intercity routes are served by **Scottish Citylink** (www.citylink.co.uk) and **Stagecoach**. **National Express** (📞08717 818181; www.nationalexpress.com) has services to London (from £30, 13½ hours, one daily – more frequent services require changing at Glasgow).

Aberdeen (Stagecoach) £13.45, four hours, hourly
Aviemore £10.80, 45 minutes, eight daily
Edinburgh £32.20, 3½ to 4½ hours, seven daily
Fort William £12.20, two hours, six daily
Glasgow £32.20, 3½ to 4½ hours, hourly
Portree £26.40, 3¼ hours, two daily
Thurso (Stagecoach) £21, 3½ hours, three daily
Ullapool £14, 1½ hours, two daily except Sunday

If you book far enough in advance, **Megabus** (📞0141-352 4444; www.megabus.com) offers fares from as little as £1 for buses from Inverness to Glasgow and Edinburgh, and £10 to London.

TRAIN
Aberdeen £29.70, 2¼ hours, eight daily
Edinburgh £40, 3½ hours, eight daily
Glasgow £40, 3½ hours, eight daily
Kyle of Lochalsh £20, 2½ hours, four daily Monday to Saturday, two Sunday; one of Britain's great scenic train journeys
London £180, eight to nine hours, one daily direct; others require a change at Edinburgh
Wick £18, 4½ hours, four daily Monday to Saturday, one or two on Sunday; via Thurso

ℹ Getting Around

BICYCLE
Ticket to Ride (📞01463-419160; www. tickettoridehighlands.co.uk; Bellfield Park; per day from £30; ⊙9am-6pm Apr-Aug, Wed-Mon Sep & Oct) Hires out mountain bikes, hybrids and tandems; can be dropped off in Fort William. Will deliver bikes free to local hotels and B&Bs.

BUS
City services and buses to places around Inverness, including Nairn, Forres, the Culloden battlefield, Beauly, Dingwall and Lairg, are operated by **Stagecoach**. An Inverness Zone 2 Dayrider ticket costs £6.80 and gives unlimited travel for a day on buses as far afield as Culloden, Fortrose and Drumnadrochit.

CAR
Focus Vehicle Rental (📞01463-709517; www. focusvehiclerental.co.uk; 6 Harbour Rd) The big boys charge from around £55 to £75 per day, but Focus has cheaper rates starting at £45 per day.

TAXI
Inverness Taxis (📞01463-222222; www. inverness-taxis.com) There's a taxi rank outside the train station.

Around Inverness

Culloden Battlefield

The Battle of Culloden in 1746 – the last pitched battle ever fought on British soil – saw the defeat of Bonnie Prince Charlie and the end of the Jacobite dream when 1200 Highlanders were slaughtered by government forces in a 68-minute rout. The Duke of Cumberland, son of the reigning King George II and leader of the Hanoverian army, earned the nickname 'Butcher' for his brutal treatment of the defeated Jacobite forces. The battle sounded the death knell for the old clan system, and the horrors of the Clearances soon followed. The sombre moor where the conflict took place has scarcely changed in the ensuing 260 years.

Culloden Visitor Centre   MUSEUM
(NTS; www.nts.org.uk/culloden; adult/child £11/9.50; ⊙9am-7pm Jun-Aug, to 6pm Mar-May, Sep & Oct, 10am-4pm Nov-Feb; P) This impressive visitor centre has everything you need to know about the Battle of Culloden in 1746, including the lead-up and the aftermath, with perspectives from both sides. An innovative film puts you on the battlefield in the middle of the mayhem, and a wealth of other audio presentations must have kept Inverness' entire acting community in business for weeks. The admission fee includes an audio guide for a self-guided tour of the battlefield itself.

ⓘ Getting There & Away

Culloden is 6 miles east of Inverness. Bus 5 runs from Eastgate shopping centre in Inverness to Culloden battlefield (£3.15, 30 minutes, hourly except Sunday).

Fort George

The headland guarding the narrows in the Moray Firth opposite Fortrose is occupied by the magnificent and virtually unaltered 18th-century artillery fortification of Fort George.

Fort George   FORTRESS
(HES; ☑01667-462777; www.historicenvironment.scot; adult/child £9/5.40; ⊙9.30am-5.30pm Apr-Sep, 10am-4pm Oct-Mar; P) One of the finest artillery fortifications in Europe, Fort George was established in 1748 in the aftermath of the Battle of Culloden, as a base for George II's army of occupation in the Highlands. By the time of its completion in 1769 it had cost the equivalent of around £1 billion in today's money. It still functions as a military barracks; public areas have exhibitions on 18th-century soldiery, and the mile-plus walk around the ramparts offers fine views.

Given its size, you'll need at least two hours to do the place justice. The fort is off the A96 about 11 miles northeast of Inverness; there is no public transport.

Nairn

POP 9775

Nairn is a popular golfing and seaside resort with good sandy beaches. You can spend many pleasant hours wandering along the East Beach, one of the finest in Scotland.

The most interesting part of town is the old fishing village of Fishertown, down by the harbour, a maze of narrow streets lined with picturesque cottages.

The big events in the town's calendar are the Nairn Highland Games (www.nairn highlandgames.co.uk; ⊙mid-Aug) and the Nairn Book & Arts Festival (www.nairnfestival.co.uk; ⊙Sep).

Nairn Museum   MUSEUM
(☑01667-456791; www.nairnmuseum.co.uk; Viewfield House; adult/child £4/3; ⊙10am-4.30pm Mon-Fri, to 1pm Sat Apr-Oct) Nairn Museum, a few minutes' walk from the tourist office, has displays on the history of the harbour community of Fishertown, as well as on local archaeology, geology and natural history.

Sunny Brae Hotel   HOTEL ££
(☑01667-452309; www.sunnybraehotel.com; Marine Rd; s/d from £90/115; P🖰) Beautifully decked out with fresh flowers and potted plants, the Sunny Brae enjoys an enviable location with great views across the Moray Firth. The hotel restaurant specialises in Scottish produce cooked with Continental flair.

Boath House Hotel   HOTEL £££
(☑01667-454896; www.boath-house.com; Auldearn; s/d from £190/295; P🖰) This beautifully restored Regency mansion, set in private woodland gardens 2 miles east of Nairn on the A96, is one of Scotland's most luxurious country-house hotels. It includes a spa offering holistic treatments and a highly regarded restaurant (three-/six-course dinner £45/70).

KELSEYNY/SHUTTERSTOCK ©

1. Urquhart Castle (p131)
Commanding a superb location, Urquhart Castle is a popular Nessie-hunting hot spot.

2. Highland Perthshire (p146)
This land of mountains, forest and lochs – and Highland cows (pictured) – boasts some of the UK's finest scenery.

3. Glen Coe (p155)
Scotland's most famous glen is also one of its grandest.

4. The Cairngorms (p135)
The largest national park in the UK contains diverse landscapes, including one of Scotland's largest remnants of Caledonian forest in Rothiemurchus Estate (p135).

DGB IMAGES/ALAMY ©

CRAIG HASTINGS/S/SHUTTERSTOCK ©

IWETA0077/SHUTTERSTOCK ©

KILTEDARAB/SHUTTERSTOCK ©

NATALIA PAKLINA/SHUTTERSTOCK ©

1. Fort George (p123)
Situated outside Inverness, this is one of the finest artillery fortifications in Europe.

2. Royal Deeside (p142)
The upper valley of the River Dee, in the Cairngorms (p135), has long been associated with the monarchy.

3. Blair Castle (p150)
This is one of the most popular tourist attractions in Scotland.

4. Small Isles (p169)
These scattered jewels lie to the south of Skye. The most popular with visitors are Rum and Eigg (pictured, as seen from Muck).

Classroom　　　　GASTROPUB **££**

(☎01667-455999; www.theclassroombistro.com; 1 Cawdor St; mains £14-26; ⊙noon-4.30pm & 5-9pm; 🛜🍴) 🍷 Done up in an appealing mixture of modern and traditional styles – lots of richly glowing wood with designer detailing – Classroom doubles as cocktail bar and gastropub, with a tempting menu that ranges from Cullen skink (soup made with smoked haddock, potato, onion and milk) to Highland steak with peppercorn sauce.

❶ Getting There & Away

Buses run hourly (less frequently on Sunday) from Inverness to Nairn (£6.05, 30 minutes) and on to Aberdeen. The bus station is just west of the town centre.

The town also lies on the Inverness–Aberdeen railway line, with five to seven trains a day from Inverness (£6.30, 15 minutes).

Cawdor Castle

This castle (☎01667-404615; www.cawdorcastle. com; Cawdor; adult/child £11.50/7.20; ⊙10am-5.30pm May-Sep; P), 5 miles southwest of Nairn, was once the seat of the Thane of Cawdor, one of the titles bestowed on Shakespeare's *Macbeth*. The real Macbeth – an ancient Scottish king – couldn't have lived here though, since he died in 1057, 300 years before the castle was begun. Nevertheless the tour gives a fascinating insight into the lives of the Scottish aristocracy.

Cawdor Tavern (www.cawdortavern.co.uk; mains £12-25; ⊙food served noon-9pm Mon-Sat, 12.30-9pm Sun; P🛜🍴), in the village close to Cawdor Castle, is worth a visit, though it can be difficult deciding what to drink as it stocks more than 100 varieties of whisky. There's also excellent pub food, with tempting daily specials.

West of Inverness

Beauly

POP 1365

Mary, Queen of Scots is said to have given this village its name in 1564 when she visited, exclaiming: '*Quel beau lieu!*' (What a beautiful place!). Founded in 1230, the red-sandstone Beauly Priory is now an impressive ruin, haunted by the cries of rooks nesting in a magnificent centuries-old sycamore tree.

Priory Hotel　　　　HOTEL **££**

(☎01463-782309; www.priory-hotel.com; The Square; s/d from £58/89; P🛜) The Priory Hotel, on Beauly's central square, has bright, modern rooms and serves good bar meals.

★**Corner on the Square**　　　CAFE **£**

(☎01463-783000; www.corneronthesquare.co.uk; 1 High St; mains £7-13; ⊙8.30am-5.30pm Mon-Fri, 8.30am-5pm Sat, 9.30am-5pm Sun) Beauly's best lunch spot is this superb little delicatessen and cafe that serves breakfast (till 11.30am), daily lunch specials (11.30am to 4.30pm) and excellent coffee.

❶ Getting There & Away

Buses 28 and 28A from Inverness run to Beauly (£5.30, 30 to 45 minutes, hourly Monday to Saturday, five on Sunday), and the town lies on the Inverness–Thurso railway line.

Strathglass & Glen Affric

The broad valley of Strathglass extends about 18 miles inland from Beauly, followed by the A831 to Cannich (the only village in the area), where there's a grocery store and a post office.

Glen Affric (www.glenaffric.org), one of the most beautiful glens in Scotland, extends deep into the hills beyond Cannich. The upper reaches of the glen are designated as the Glen Affric National Nature Reserve (www.nnr.scot).

About 4 miles southwest of Cannich is Dog Falls, a scenic spot where the River Affric squeezes through a narrow, rocky gorge. A circular walking trail (red waymarks) leads from Dog Falls car park to a footbridge below the falls and back on the far side of the river (2 miles, allow one hour).

The road continues beyond Dog Falls to a parking area and picnic site at the eastern end of Loch Affric, where there are several short walks along the river and the loch shore. The circuit of Loch Affric (10 miles, allow five hours walking, two hours by mountain bike) follows good paths right around the loch and takes you deep into the heart of some very wild scenery.

It's possible to walk all the way from Cannich to Glen Shiel on the west coast (35 miles) in two days, spending the night at the remote Glen Affric SYHA (p129). The route is now part of the waymarked Affric-Kintail Way (www.affrickintailway.com), a 56-mile walking or mountain-biking trail leading from Drumnadrochit to Kintail via Cannich.

A minor road on the east side of the River Glass leads to the pretty little conservation village of Tomich, 3 miles southwest of Cannich, built in Victorian times as accommodation for estate workers. The road continues (unsurfaced for the last 2 miles) to a forestry car park, the starting point for a short (800m) walk to Plodda Falls.

🛏 Sleeping & Eating

Glen Affric SYHA   HOSTEL £
(SYHA; ☑ bookings 0845 293 7373; www.syha. org.uk; Allt Beithe; dm £24.50; ⊙ Apr–mid-Sep) This remote and rustic hostel is set amid magnificent scenery at the halfway point of the cross-country walk from Cannich to Glen Shiel, 8 miles from the nearest road. Facilities are basic and you'll need to take all supplies with you (and all litter away). Book in advance. There is no phone, internet or mobile phone signal at the hostel.

Cannich Caravan & Camping Park   CAMPSITE £
(☑ 01456-415364; www.highlandcamping.co.uk; sites per adult/child £9/5, pods s/d £26/36; 🐾) Good, sheltered spot, with on-site cafe and the option of wooden camping 'pods'. Mountain bikes for hire from £17 a day.

⭐**Kerrow House**   B&B ££
(☑ 01456-415243; www.kerrow-house.co.uk; Cannich; r per person £45-50; 🅿🐾) 🐾 This wonderful Georgian hunting lodge has bags of old-fashioned character – it was once the home of Highland author Neil M Gunn – and has spacious grounds with cosy self-catering cottages (from £510 per week) and 3.5 miles of private trout fishing. It's a mile south of Cannich on the minor road along the east side of the River Glass.

Tomich Hotel   HOTEL ££
(☑01456-415399; www.tomichhotel.co.uk; Tomich; s/d from £75/120; ⊙closed Dec & Jan; 🅿🐾🐾) About 3 miles southwest of Cannich on the southern side of the River Glass, this Victorian hunting lodge has a dog-friendly bar with blazing log fire that serves food from noon to 9pm; an intimate, candlelit restaurant, and eight comfortable en suite rooms. It can organise trout fishing on local waters.

⭐**Struy Inn**   SCOTTISH £££
(☑01463-761308; www.thestruy.co.uk; Struy Village; mains £18-27; ⊙5.30-9.30pm Wed-Sun Apr-Oct, Thu-Sat Nov-Mar; 🅿🐾) Set in the heart of lovely Strathglass, on the road between Cannich and Beauly, this fine Victorian inn is a haven of old-fashioned charm. It houses a top-quality restaurant serving the finest Scottish cuisine; with just 18 seats, booking is essential.

❶ Getting There & Away

Stagecoach (www.stagecoachbus.com) buses 17 and 117 run from Inverness to Cannich (£5.90, one hour, two daily Monday to Friday) via Drumnadrochit. D&E Coaches (www. decoaches.co.uk) runs a service from Inverness to Cannich that continues to Tomich (£6.50, 1¼ hours, three daily, weekdays only).

Black Isle

The Black Isle – a peninsula rather than an island – is linked to Inverness by the Kessock Bridge. Bypassed by the main A9 road, it's a peaceful backwater of wooded hills, picturesque villages and dramatic coastlines, with the added attraction of Scotland's best mainland dolphin-watching spot.

Black Isle Brewery   BREWERY
(☑01463-811871; www.blackislebrewery.com; Old Allangrange; ⊙10am-6pm Mon-Sat year-round, 11am-5pm Sun Easter-Sep) 🐾 FREE One of Britain's best artisan breweries, Black Isle Brewery has won many awards for its organically produced ales. Enjoy a free tour then try a glass of Yellowhammer, a light, hoppy and refreshing bitter, or the strong, flowery Heather Honey Beer. It's a few miles north of the Kessock Bridge.

Fortrose & Rosemarkie

At Fortrose Cathedral (HES; Cathedral Sq; ⊙9.30am-5.30pm Apr-Sep, to 4.30pm Oct-Mar) FREE you'll find the vaulted crypt of a 13th-century chapter house and sacristy, and the ruinous 14th-century south aisle and chapel. Chanonry Point, 1.5 miles to the east, is a favourite dolphin-spotting vantage point; there are one-hour dolphin-watching cruises (☑01381-622383; www. dolphintripsavoch.co.uk; adult/child £18/12) departing from the harbour at Avoch (pronounced 'auch'), 3 miles southwest.

In Rosemarkie, the Groam House Museum (☑01381-620961; www.groamhouse. org.uk; High St, Rosemarkie; ⊙11am-4.30pm Mon-Fri, 2-4.30pm Sat & Sun Apr-Oct) FREE has a superb collection of Pictish stones engraved with designs similar to those on Celtic Irish stones.

INVERNESS & THE CENTRAL HIGHLANDS BLACK ISLE

From the northern end of Rosemarkie's High St, a short but pleasant signposted walk leads you through the gorges and waterfalls of the Fairy Glen.

Once you've worked up a thirst, retire to the bar at the Anderson ($\square$ 01381-620236; www.theanderson.co.uk; Union St, Fortrose; ⊙4-11pm, closed Sun-Tue Nov-Mar) to sample its range of real ales (including Belgian beers and Somerset cider) and more than 200 single malt whiskies.

Cromarty

POP 725

The pretty village of Cromarty at the northeastern tip of the Black Isle has lots of 18th-century red-sandstone houses, and a lovely green park beside the sea for picnics and games. An excellent walk, known as the 100 Steps, leads from the north end of the village to the headland viewpoint of South Sutor (4 miles round trip).

Hugh Miller's Cottage
& Museum   MUSEUM

(NTS; www.nts.org.uk; Church St; adult/child £6.50/5.50; ⊙1-5pm Apr-Sep) This thatch-roofed cottage is the birthplace of Hugh Miller (1802–56), a local stonemason and amateur geologist who pioneered the study of fossil fishes in Scotland; he later moved to Edinburgh and became a famous journalist and newspaper editor. The Georgian villa next door is home to a museum celebrating his life and achievements.

Ecoventures   WILDLIFE WATCHING

($\square$ 01381-600323; www.ecoventures.co.uk; Cromarty Harbour; adult/child £30/23) Ecoventures runs two-hour boat trips from Cromarty harbour into the Moray Firth to see bottlenose dolphins and other wildlife.

Sutor Creek   CAFE ££

($\square$ 01381-600855; www.sutorcreek.co.uk; 21 Bank St; mains £13-18; ⊙noon-9pm May-Sep, Thu-Sun Oct-Apr; 🖷) 🖉 This excellent little cafe-restaurant serves wood-fired pizzas and fresh local seafood including Shetland scallops, Lewis mussels, and Cromarty langoustines with garlic and lemon butter.

Couper's Creek   CAFE £

($\square$ 01381-600729; www.couperscreek.co.uk; 20 Church St; mains £6-11; ⊙10am-5pm; 🖷) This lively cafe serves cake, coffee, ice-cream sundaes and superb, doorstep-size open sandwiches with salad.

🛈 Getting There & Away

Stagecoach (www.stagecoachbus.com) buses 26 and 26A run from Inverness to Cromarty (£5.30, one hour, hourly Monday to Saturday).

Loch Ness

Deep, dark and narrow, Loch Ness stretches for 23 miles between Inverness and Fort Augustus. Its bitterly cold waters have been extensively explored in search of Nessie, the elusive Loch Ness monster, but most visitors see her only in the form of a cardboard cut-out at Drumnadrochit's monster exhibitions. The busy A82 road runs along the northwestern shore, while the more tranquil and picturesque B862 follows the southeastern shore. A complete circuit of the loch is about 70 miles – travel anticlockwise for the better views.

🏃 Activities

The 79-mile Great Glen Way (www.highland.gov.uk/ggw) long-distance footpath stretches from Inverness to Fort William, where walkers can connect with the West Highland Way. It is described in detail in *The Great Glen Way,* a guide by Jacquetta Megarry and Sandra Bardwell.

The Great Glen Way can also be ridden (strenuous!) by mountain bike, while the Great Glen Mountain Bike Trails at Nevis Range and Abriachan Forest offer challenging cross-country and downhill trails. You can hire a mountain bike in Fort William (p162) and drop it off in Inverness (p122), and vice versa.

The South Loch Ness Trail (www.visitinvernesslochness.com) links a series of footpaths and minor roads along the less-frequented southern side of the loch. The 28 miles from Loch Tarff near Fort Augustus to Torbreck on the fringes of Inverness can be done on foot, by bike or on horseback.

The climb to the summit of Meallfuarvonie (699m), on the northwestern shore of Loch Ness, makes an excellent short hill walk: the views along the Great Glen from the top are superb. It's a 6-mile round trip, so allow about three hours. Start from the car park at the end of the minor road leading south from Drumnadrochit to Bunloit.

The Great Glen Canoe Trail (www.greatglencanoetrail.info), a series of access points, waymarks and informal campsites, allows you to travel the length of the glen by canoe or kayak.

DORES INN

While crowded tour coaches pour down the west side of Loch Ness to the hot spots of Drumnadrochit and Urquhart Castle, the narrow B862 road along the eastern shore is relatively peaceful. It leads to the village of Foyers, where you can enjoy a pleasant hike to the **Falls of Foyers**.

But it's worth making the trip just for the **Dores Inn** (☑01463-751203; www.thedoresinn. co.uk; Dores; mains £10-27; ⊘pub 10am-11pm, food served noon-2pm & 6-9pm; P🖡), a beautifully restored country pub furnished with recycled furniture, local landscape paintings and fresh flowers. The menu specialises in quality Scottish produce, from haggis, turnips and tatties (potatoes), and haddock and chips, to steaks, scallops and seafood platters.

The garden enjoys a stunning view along Loch Ness, and even has a dedicated monster-spotting vantage point. The nearby campervan, emblazoned with Nessie-Serry Independent Research, has been home to dedicated Nessie hunter Steve Feltham (www.nessie hunter.co.uk) since 1991; in 2015 he finally concluded that Nessie was in fact a giant catfish!

✦ Festivals & Events

Groove Loch Ness　　　　　MUSIC
(www.groovefestival.co.uk; ⊘Aug) A vast lochside field at the village of Dores hosts this successor to the now-defunct Rock Ness Festival, a one-day smorgasbord of the best in Scottish and international DJs.

Drumnadrochit

POP 1100

Seized by Loch Ness Monster madness, its gift shops bulging with Nessie cuddly toys, Drumnadrochit is a hotbed of beastie fever, with two monster exhibitions battling it out for the tourist dollar.

◉ Sights & Activities

Urquhart Castle　　　　　CASTLE
(HES; ☑01456-450551; adult/child £9/5.40; ⊘9.30am-8pm Jun-Aug, to 6pm Apr, May & Sep, to 5pm Oct, to 4.30pm Nov-Mar; P) Commanding a superb location 1.5 miles east of Drumnadrochit, with outstanding views (on a clear day), Urquhart Castle is a popular Nessie-hunting hot spot. A huge visitor centre (most of which is beneath ground level) includes a video theatre (with a dramatic 'reveal' of the castle at the end of the film) and displays of medieval items discovered in the castle. The site includes a huge gift shop and a restaurant, and is often very crowded in summer.

The castle was repeatedly sacked and rebuilt (and sacked and rebuilt) over the centuries; in 1692 it was blown up to prevent the Jacobites from using it. The five-storey tower house at the northern point is the most impressive remaining fragment and offers wonderful views across the water.

Loch Ness Centre & Exhibition　　MUSEUM
(☑01456-450573; www.lochness.com; adult/child £7.95/4.95; ⊘9.30am-6pm Jul & Aug, to 5pm Easter-Jun, Sep & Oct, 10am-4pm Nov-Easter; P🖡) This Nessie-themed attraction adopts a scientific approach that allows you to weigh the evidence for yourself. Exhibits include original equipment – sonar survey vessels, miniature submarines, cameras and sediment coring tools – used in various monster hunts, plus original photographs and film footage of sightings. You'll find out about hoaxes and optical illusions, as well as learning a lot about the ecology of Loch Ness – is there enough food in the loch to support even one 'monster', let alone a breeding population?

Nessie Hunter　　　　　BOATING
(☑01456-450395; www.lochness-cruises.com; adult/child £16/10; ⊘Easter-Oct) One-hour monster-hunting cruises, complete with sonar and underwater cameras. Cruises depart from Drumnadrochit hourly (except 1pm) from 10am to 6pm daily.

🛏 Sleeping

BCC Loch Ness Hostel　　　HOSTEL£
(☑07780 603045; www.bcclochnesshostel.co.uk; Glen Urquhart; tr/q from £60/75, tent sites per person £5, 2-person pods £70; P🖡) Clean, modern, high-quality budget accommodation located 6.5 miles west of Drumnadrochit, halfway between Cannich and Loch Ness; booking well in advance is recommended. There's also a good campsite with the option of luxury glamping pods.

Loch Ness Backpackers Lodge　　HOSTEL£
(☑01456-450807; www.lochness-backpackers. com; Coiltie Farmhouse, East Lewiston; dm/d from

£20/50; (P)(🛜)) This snug, friendly hostel housed in a cottage and barn has six-bed dorms, one double and a large barbecue area. It's almost a mile from Drumnadrochit, along the A82 towards Fort William; turn left where you see the sign for Loch Ness Inn, just before the bridge.

Borlum Farm Camping CAMPSITE £
(☑01456-450220; www.borlum.co.uk; sites per adult/child £10.50/5.50; ⊙Mar-Oct; 🛜) An attractive farm-based campsite with a mix of grass pitches and hard standings, beside the main road half a mile southeast of Drumnadrochit.

★**Loch Ness Inn** INN ££
(☑01456-450991; www.staylochness.co.uk; Lewiston; s/d/f £99/120/140; (P)🛜) Loch Ness Inn ticks all the weary traveller's boxes, with comfortable bedrooms (the family suite sleeps two adults and two children), a cosy bar pouring real ales from the Cairngorm and Isle of Skye breweries, and a rustic restaurant (mains £10 to £20) serving wholesome fare. It's conveniently located in the quiet hamlet of Lewiston, between Drumnadrochit and Urquhart Castle.

Drumbuie Farm B&B ££
(☑01456-450634; www.loch-ness-farm.co.uk; s/d from £54/68; (P)🛜) A B&B in a modern house on a working farm surrounded by fields full of sheep and highland cattle, with views over Urquhart Castle and Loch Ness. Walkers and cyclists are welcome.

✗ Eating & Drinking

Fiddler's Coffee Shop & Restaurant CAFE ££
(www.fiddledrum.co.uk; mains £12-20; ⊙11am-11pm; 🛜) The coffee shop here serves cappuccino and croissants, while the restaurant dishes up traditional Highland fare, such as venison and haggis, and a wide range of bottled Scottish beers. There's also a whisky bar with a huge range of single malts.

Benleva Hotel MICROBREWERY
(☑01456-450080; www.benleva.co.uk; Kilmore Rd; ⊙noon-midnight Mon-Thu, to 1am Fri, to 12.45am Sat, 12.30-11pm Sun; 🛜) Set in an 18th-century manse a half-mile east of the main road, the Benleva is a rough diamond of a pub – a bit frayed around the edges but with a heart of gold. The beer is the main event, with a selection of real ales from around the country, including those from their own Loch Ness Brewery, located nearby.

❶ Getting There & Away

Stagecoach (www.stagecoachbus.com) buses run from Inverness to Drumnadrochit (£3.70, 30 minutes, six to eight daily, five on Sunday) and Urquhart Castle car park (£4, 35 minutes).

Fort Augustus

POP 620

Fort Augustus, at the junction of four old military roads, was originally a government garrison and the headquarters of General George Wade's road-building operations in the early 18th century. Today it's a neat and picturesque little place bisected by the Caledonian Canal, and often overrun by coachtour crowds in summer.

◎ Sights & Activities

Caledonian Canal CANAL
(www.scottishcanals.co.uk) At Fort Augustus, boats using the Caledonian Canal are raised and lowered 13m by a 'ladder' of five consecutive locks. It's fun to watch, and the neatly landscaped canal banks are a great place to soak up the sun or compare accents with fellow tourists. The **Caledonian Canal Centre** (Ardchattan House, Canalside; ⊙9am-6pm) FREE, beside the lowest lock, has information on the history of the canal.

Clansman Centre MUSEUM
(www.scottish-swords.com; ⊙10am-6pm Apr-Oct) FREE This exhibition of 17th-century Highland life has live demonstrations of how to put on a plaid (the forerunner of the kilt) and how the claymore (Highland sword) was made and used. There is also a workshop where you can purchase handcrafted reproduction swords, dirks and shields.

Cruise Loch Ness BOATING
(☑01320-366277; www.cruiselochness.com; adult/child £14.50/8.50; ⊙hourly 10am-4pm Apr-Oct, 1pm & 2pm Nov-Mar) One-hour cruises on Loch Ness are accompanied by the latest high-tech sonar equipment so you can keep an underwater eye open for Nessie. There are also one-hour evening cruises, departing 8pm daily (except Friday) April to August, and 90-minute speedboat tours.

🛏 Sleeping & Eating

Morag's Lodge HOSTEL £
(☑01320-366289; www.moragslodge.com; Bunoich Brae; dm/tw from £24.50/62; (P)@🛜) This large, well-run hostel is based in a big Victorian house with great views of Fort

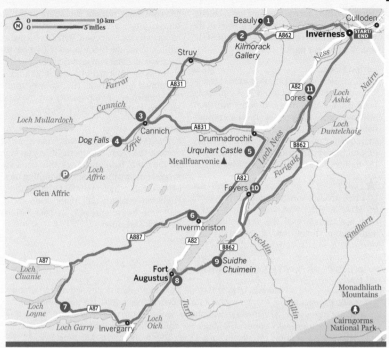

Driving Tour
A Loch Ness Circuit

START INVERNESS
END INVERNESS
LENGTH 130 MILES; SIX TO SEVEN HOURS

Head out of Inverness on the A862 to Beauly, arriving in time for breakfast at ❶ **Corner on the Square** (p128). Backtrack a mile and turn right on the A831 to Cannich, passing ❷ **Kilmorack Gallery**, which exhibits contemporary art in a converted church. The scenery gets wilder as you approach ❸ **Cannich**; turn right and follow the single-track road to the car park at ❹ **Dog Falls**. Take a stroll along the rushing river, or hike to the viewpoint (about one-hour round trip; 2.5 miles) for a glimpse of remote Glen Affric.

Return to Cannich and turn right on the A831 to Drumnadrochit, then right on the A82 past picturesque ❺ **Urquhart Castle** (p131) and along the shores of Loch Ness. At ❻ **Invermoriston**, pause to look at the old bridge, built by Telford in 1813, then head west on the A887 towards Kyle of Lochalsh; after 16 miles go left on the A87 towards

Invergarry. You are now among some of the finest mountain scenery in the Highlands; as the road turns east above Loch Garry, stop at the famous ❼ **viewpoint** (layby on right, signposted Glengarry Viewpoint). Through a quirk of perspective, the lochs to the west appear to form the map outline of Scotland.

At Invergarry, turn left on the A82 to reach ❽ **Fort Augustus** and a late lunch at the Lovat or Lock Inn. Take the B862 out of town, following the line of General Wade's 18th-century military road, to another viewpoint at ❾ **Suidhe Chuimein**. A short (800m) walk up the well-worn path to the summit affords an even better panorama.

Ahead, you can choose the low road via the impressive ❿ **Falls of Foyers**, or stay on the high road (B862) for more views; both converge on Loch Ness at the ⓫ **Dores Inn** (p131), where you can sip a pint with a view along Loch Ness, and even stay for dinner before returning to Inverness.

Augustus' hilly surrounds, and has a convivial bar with open fire. It's hidden away in the trees up the steep side road just north of the tourist office car park.

B&B **££**

(☏01320-366576; www.lorien-house.co.uk; Station Rd; s/d £70/80; P🛜) Lorien is a cut above your usual B&B – the bedrooms are spick and span, the house is set up to accommodate walkers and cyclists, the breakfasts include smoked salmon, and there's a library of walking, cycling and climbing guides in the lounge. No children under 10 years.

★Lovat HOTEL **£££**

(☏01456-459250; www.thelovat.com; Main Rd; d from £173; P🛜🐾) 🗭 A boutique-style makeover has transformed this former huntin'-and-shootin' hotel into a luxurious but eco-conscious retreat set apart from the tourist crush around the canal. The bedrooms are spacious and stylishly furnished, while the lounge is equipped with a log fire, comfy armchairs and grand piano.

It has an informal brasserie and a highly acclaimed restaurant (five-course dinner £55), which serves top-quality cuisine (open noon to 2.30pm and 6pm to 9pm).

Lock Inn PUB FOOD **££**

(☏01320-366302; Canal Side; mains £10-15; ⏱meals noon-8pm) A superb little pub right on the canal bank, the Lock Inn has a vast range of malt whiskies and a tempting menu of bar meals, which includes Orkney salmon, Highland venison and daily seafood specials; the house speciality is beer-battered haddock and chips.

MONSTERS, MYTHS & LOCH NESS

Highland folklore is filled with tales of strange creatures living in lochs and rivers, notably the kelpie (water horse) that lures unwary travellers to their doom. The use of the term 'monster', however, is a relatively recent phenomenon, whose origins lie in an article published in the *Inverness Courier* on 2 May 1933, entitled 'Strange Spectacle on Loch Ness'.

The article recounted the sighting of a disturbance in the loch by Mrs Aldie Mackay and her husband: 'There the creature disported itself, rolling and plunging for fully a minute, its body resembling that of a whale, and the water cascading and churning like a simmering cauldron.'

The story was taken up by the London press and sparked a flurry of sightings that year, including a notorious on-land encounter with London tourists Mr and Mrs Spicer on 22 July 1933, again reported in the *Inverness Courier:*

'It was horrible, an abomination. About 50 yards ahead, we saw an undulating sort of neck, and quickly followed by a large, ponderous body. I estimated the length to be 25ft to 30ft, its colour was dark elephant grey. It crossed the road in a series of jerks, but because of the slope we could not see its limbs. Although I accelerated quickly towards it, it had disappeared into the loch by the time I reached the spot. There was no sign of it in the water. I am a temperate man, but I am willing to take any oath that we saw this Loch Ness beast. I am certain that this creature was of a prehistoric species.'

The London newspapers couldn't resist. In December 1933 the *Daily Mail* sent Marmaduke Wetherell, a film director and big-game hunter, to Loch Ness to track down the beast. Within days he found 'reptilian' footprints in the shoreline mud (soon revealed to have been made with a stuffed hippopotamus foot). Then in April 1934 came the famous long-necked monster photograph taken by the seemingly reputable Harley St surgeon Robert Kenneth Wilson. The press went mad and the rest, as they say, is history.

In 1994, however, Christian Spurling – Wetherell's stepson, by then 90 years old – revealed that the most famous photo of Nessie ever taken was in fact a hoax, perpetrated by his stepfather with Wilson's help. Today, of course, there are those who claim that Spurling's confession is itself a hoax. And, ironically, the researcher who exposed the surgeon's photo as a fake still believes wholeheartedly in the monster's existence.

There have been regular sightings of the monster through the years (see www.lochnesssightings.com), with a peak in 1996–97 (the Hollywood movie *Loch Ness* was released in 1996), but reports have tailed off in recent years.

Hoax or not, the bizarre mini-industry that has grown up around Loch Ness and its mysterious monster since that eventful summer last century is a spectacle in itself.

ⓘ Getting There & Away

Scottish Citylink (www.citylink.co.uk) and **Stagecoach** (www.stagecoachbus.com) buses from Inverness to Fort William stop at Fort Augustus (£8 to £11.20, one hour, five to eight daily Monday to Saturday, five on Sunday).

THE CAIRNGORMS

The Cairngorms National Park (www.cairn gorms.co.uk) is the largest national park in the UK, more than twice the size of the Lake District. It stretches from Aviemore in the north to the Angus Glens in the south, and from Dalwhinnie in the west to Ballater and Royal Deeside in the east.

The park encompasses the highest land-mass in Britain – a broad mountain plateau, riven only by the deep valleys of the Lairig Ghru and Loch Avon, with an average alti-tude of more than 1000m and including five of the six highest summits in the UK. This wild mountain landscape of granite and heather has a sub-Arctic climate and supports rare alpine tundra vegetation and high-altitude bird species, such as snow bunting, ptarmigan and dotterel.

This is prime hill-walking territory, but even couch potatoes can enjoy a taste of the high life by riding the Cairngorm Mountain Railway (p138).

Aviemore

POP 3150

The gateway to the Cairngorms, Aviemore is the region's main centre for transport, accommodation, restaurants and shops. It's not the prettiest town in Scotland by a long stretch – the main attractions are in the surrounding area – but when bad weather puts the hills off-limits, Aviemore fills up with hikers, cyclists and climbers (plus skiers and snowboarders in winter) cruising the outdoor-equipment shops or recounting their latest adventures in the cafes and bars. Add in tourists and locals and the eclectic mix makes for a lively little town.

Aviemore is on a loop off the A9 Perth–Inverness road. Almost everything of note is to be found along the main drag, Gram-pian Rd; the train station and bus stop are towards its southern end.

The Cairngorm Mountain funicular rail-way and ski area lie 10 miles southeast of Aviemore along the B970 (Ski Rd) and its continuation, past Coylumbridge and Glenmore.

◉ Sights

★**Rothiemurchus Estate**　　　　　FOREST

(www.rothiemurchus.net) The Rothiemurchus Estate, which extends from the River Spey at Aviemore to the Cairngorm summit pla-teau, is famous for having one of Scotland's largest remnants of **Caledonian forest**, the ancient forest of Scots pine that once cov-ered most of the country. The forest is home to a large population of red squirrels, and is one of the last bastions of the capercaillie and the Scottish wildcat.

The **Rothiemurchus Centre** (☑01479-812345; www.rothiemurchus.net; Ski Rd, Inverdruie; ⊙9.30am-5.30pm; 🅿) **FREE**, a mile south-east of Aviemore along the B970, sells an *Explorer Map* detailing more than 50 miles of footpaths and cycling trails, including the wheelchair-accessible 4-mile trail around **Loch an Eilein**, with its ruined castle and peaceful pine woods.

Strathspey Steam Railway　　HERITAGE RAILWAY

(☑01479-810725;　　www.strathspeyrailway.co.uk; Station Sq; return ticket adult/child £15/11.80; 🅿) The Strathspey railway runs steam trains on a section of restored line between Aviemore and Broomhill, 10 miles to the northeast, via Boat of Garten. There are four or five trains daily from June to August, and a more limited service in April, May, Septem-ber, October and December, with the option of enjoying afternoon tea, Sunday lunch or a five-course dinner on board.

An extension to Grantown-on-Spey is under construction, but will not be complete for several years.

Craigellachie Nature Reserve　NATURE RESERVE

(www.nnr.scot; Grampian Rd) **FREE** This reserve is a great place for short hikes across steep hillsides covered in natural birch forest where you can spot wildlife such as the peregrine falcons that nest on the crags from April to July. A trail leads west from Aviemore SYHA (p136) and passes under the A9 into the reserve.

🕴 Activities

Bothy Bikes　　　　　　MOUNTAIN BIKING

(☑01479-810111; www.bothybikes.co.uk; 5 Granish Way, Dalfaber; per half-/full day from £16/20; ⊙9am-5.30pm) Located in northern Aviemore, this place rents out mountain bikes and can also advise on routes and trails; a good choice for beginners is the Old Logging Way, which runs from Aviemore to Glenmore, where you can make a circuit of Loch Morlich before returning. For experienced bikers, the whole of the Cairngorms is your playground. Booking recommended.

Rothiemurchus Fishery   FISHING

(🖉 01479-812915; www.rothiemurchus.net; Rothiemurchus Estate; ⊙ 9.30am-5pm Sep-May, to dusk Jun-Aug; ♿) Cast for rainbow trout at this loch at the southern end of the village; buy permits (from £10 for one hour, plus £7 for tackle hire) at the Fish Farm Shop. If you're new to fly-fishing, there's a beginner's package, including tackle hire, one hour's instruction and one hour's fishing, for £49 per person.

For experienced anglers, there's also salmon and sea-trout fishing on the River Spey – a day permit costs around £30. Numbers are limited, so it's best to book in advance.

Cairngorm Sled-Dog Centre   DOG SLEDDING

(🖉 07767-270526; www.sled-dogs.co.uk; Ski Rd; ♿) This outfit offers 45-minute dog-sledding training sessions (adult/child £60/40) on local forest trails with a team of huskies, or a three-hour sled-dog safari (£175 per person) into the hills (children must be at least 12 years old). The sleds have wheels, so snow's not necessary. The centre is 3 miles east of Aviemore, signposted off the road to Loch Morlich.

There are also one-hour guided tours of the kennels (adult/child £8/4) and sled-dog museum.

Cairngorm Brewery   BREWERY

(🖉 01479-813303; www.cairngormbrewery.com; Dalfaber Industrial Estate; tours per person £5; ⊙ 10am-5.30pm Mon-Sat year-round, 12.30-4pm Sun May-Sep) Creator of multi-award-winning Trade Winds ale; tours of the brewery begin at 11.30am and 2.30pm on weekdays.

🛏 Sleeping

Aviemore SYHA   HOSTEL £

(SYHA; 🖉 01479-810345; www.syha.org.uk; 25 Grampian Rd; dm £23; 🅿 @ 🛜) Upmarket hostelling in a spacious, well-equipped modern building, five minutes' walk south of the village centre. There are four- and six-bed rooms, and a comfortable lounge with views of the mountains.

Rothiemurchus Camp & Caravan Park   CAMPSITE £

(🖉 01479-812800; www.rothiemurchus.net; Coylumbridge; tent sites per adult/child £12/3) The nearest campsite to Aviemore is this year-round park, beautifully sited among Scots pines at Coylumbridge, 1.5 miles along the B970.

Aviemore Bunkhouse   HOSTEL £

(🖉 01479-811181; www.aviemore-bunkhouse.com; Dalfaber Rd; dm/d/f from £23/55/75; 🅿 @ 🛜) This independent hostel provides accommodation in bright, modern six- or eight-bed dorms, each with private bathroom, and one twin/family room. It has a drying room, secure bike storage and wheelchair-accessible dorms. From the train station, cross the pedestrian bridge over the tracks, turn right and walk south on Dalfaber Rd.

Cairngorm Hotel   HOTEL ££

(🖉 01479-810233; www.cairngorm.com; Grampian Rd; s/d from £84/118; 🅿 🛜) Better known as 'the Cairn', this long-established hotel is set in the fine old granite building with the pointy turret opposite the train station. It's a welcoming place with comfortable rooms and a determinedly Scottish atmosphere, with tartan carpets and stags' antlers. There's live music on weekends, so it can get a bit noisy – not for early-to-bedders.

Ardlogie Guest House   B&B ££

(🖉 01479-810747; www.ardlogie.co.uk; Dalfaber Rd; s/d £80/100, bothy per 3 nights £360; 🅿 🛜) Handy to the train station, the welcoming five-room Ardlogie has great views over the River Spey towards the Cairngorms, and the chance of spotting red squirrels from your bedroom window. There's also self-catering accommodation in the Bothy, a cosy, two-person timber cabin. Facilities include a boules pitch in the garden. Two-night minimum stay.

Ravenscraig Guest House   B&B ££

(🖉 01479-810278; www.aviemoreonline.com; Grampian Rd; s/d from £65/90; 🅿 🛜) Ravenscraig is a large, flower-bedecked Victorian villa with seven spacious en suite rooms, plus another six in a modern chalet at the back (one wheelchair accessible). It serves traditional and veggie breakfasts in an attractive conservatory dining room.

Old Minister's House   B&B £££

(🖉 01479-812181; www.theoldministershouse.co.uk; Ski Rd, Inverdruie; s/d £160/170; 🅿 🛜) This

The Cairngorms

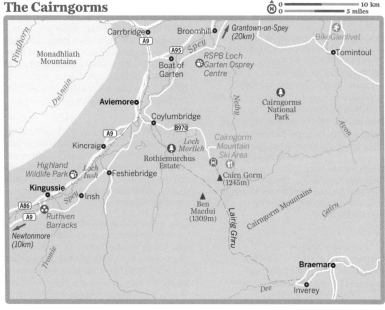

former manse dates from 1906 and has five rooms with a luxurious, country-house atmosphere. It's in a lovely setting amid Scots pines on the banks of the River Druie, southeast of Aviemore.

✖ Eating & Drinking

★ Route 7 Cafe   CAFE £
(☑01479-812433; http://highlandhomecentre.com/route-7-cafe.html; 18 Dalfaber Industrial Estate; mains £6-10; ⏲9am-4pm; 🅿🛜🚲) This place, named for the cycle route that passes the door, takes a bit of finding (at the end of the side road that passes Cairngorm Brewery), but is well worth seeking out for its hearty menu of burgers, grilled sandwiches and salads; also wood-fired pizzas (noon to 3pm weekends only). Cyclists can use the power washer and tools outside.

Mountain Cafe   CAFE ££
(www.mountaincafe-aviemore.co.uk; 111 Grampian Rd; mains £10-15; ⏲8.30am-5pm Mon-Fri, to 5.30pm Sat & Sun; 🅿🚲🚲) The Mountain Cafe offers freshly prepared local produce with a Kiwi twist (the owner is from New Zealand): healthy breakfasts of muesli, porridge and fresh fruit (till 11.30am); hearty lunches of seafood chowder, burgers and imaginative salads; and home-baked breads, cakes and biscuits. Caters for vegan, coeliac and nut-allergic diets.

Roo's Leap   AMERICAN ££
(☑01479-811161; www.roosleap.com; Station Sq; mains £8-15, steaks £22-25; ⏲noon-2.30pm & 5-9pm Mon-Fri, noon-9pm Sat & Sun; 🛜🚲) Friendly service, cold bottled beer and great barbecue contribute to the antipodean atmosphere at this lively restaurant set in the old railway station building. However, the menu is more like classic American and Tex Mex – sizzling steaks, juicy burgers, fajitas and nachos.

Winking Owl   PUB
(www.thewinkingowl.co; Grampian Rd; ⏲noon-11pm Mon-Thu, 11am-1am Fri & Sat, 12.30-11pm Sun; 🛜) Lively local pub that operates under the wing of the Cairngorm Brewery. It's popular with hikers and climbers, and serves a good range of real ales and malt whiskies.

ⓘ Information

There are ATMs outside the Tesco supermarket, and currency exchange at the post office and the **tourist office** (☑01479-810930; www.visitaviemore.com; The Mall, Grampian Rd; ⏲9am-5pm Mon-Sat, 10am-4pm Sun year-round, longer hours Jul & Aug), all located on Grampian Rd.

ℹ Getting There & Away

BUS

Buses stop on Grampian Rd opposite the train station; buy tickets at the tourist office (p137). Services include the following:

Edinburgh £28.50, four hours, five daily

Glasgow £28.50, 2¾ hours, five daily

Grantown-on-Spey £4, 35 minutes, five daily weekdays, two Saturday

Inverness £10.80, 45 minutes, eight daily

Perth £20.90, 2¼ hours, five daily

Bus 31 links Aviemore to Cairngorm Mountain car park (£2.90, 30 minutes, hourly) via Coylumbridge and Glenmore. A Strathspey Dayrider/ Megarider ticket (£7.30/18.40) gives one/seven days unlimited bus travel from Aviemore as far as Cairngorm, Carrbridge and Kingussie; buy it from the bus driver.

TRAIN

The train station is on Grampian Rd.

Edinburgh £41, three hours, six daily

Glasgow £41, three hours, six daily

Inverness £12.80, 40 minutes, 12 daily

ℹ Getting Around

Several places in Aviemore, Rothiemurchus Estate (p135) and Glenmore have mountain bikes for hire. Easy off-road cycle tracks link Aviemore with Glenmore and Loch Morlich to the east, and Boat of Garten to the north.

Bothy Bikes (p135) charges from £20 a day for a quality bike with front suspension and disc brakes.

Around Aviemore

Loch Morlich

Six miles east of Aviemore, Loch Morlich is surrounded by some 8 sq miles of pine and spruce forest that make up the Glenmore Forest Park. Its attractions include a sandy beach (at the east end) and a watersports centre.

The visitor centre at Glenmore has a small exhibition on the Caledonian forest and sells the *Glenmore Forest Park Map,* detailing local walks. The **circuit of Loch Morlich** (one hour) makes a pleasant outing; the trail is pram- and wheelchair-friendly.

🏃 Activities

★ **Glenmore Lodge**   ADVENTURE SPORTS
(☑ 01479-861256; www.glenmorelodge.org.uk; Glenmore; 1-day courses from £65) One of Brit-

ain's leading adventure-sports training centres, offering courses in hill walking, rock climbing, ice climbing, canoeing, mountain biking and mountaineering. The centre's comfortable **B&B accommodation** (☑ 01479-861256; www.glenmorelodge.org.uk; Glenmore; s/tw £60/83; 🅿🐕🏊) is available to all, even if you're not taking a course, as is the indoor climbing wall, gym and sauna.

Loch Morlich
Watersports Centre   WATER SPORTS
(☑ 01479-861221; www.lochmorlich.com; ⊙ 9am-5pm Easter-Oct) This popular outfit rents out Canadian canoes (£23 an hour), kayaks (£9), sailboards (£18), sailing dinghies (£25) and stand-up paddle boards (£15), and also offers instruction.

Cairngorm Reindeer Centre   TOURS
(www.cairngormreindeer.co.uk; Glenmore; adult/ child £15/9; ⊙ closed early Jan–mid-Feb; 🐕) The warden here leads guided walks to see and feed Britain's only herd of reindeer, which are very tame and will even eat out of your hand. Walks take place at 11am daily (weather-dependent), plus there's another at 2.30pm from May to September, and a third at 3.30pm Monday to Friday in July and August.

🛏 Sleeping

Glenmore Campsite   CAMPSITE £
(☑ 01479-861271; www.campingintheforest.co.uk; tent & campervan sites £18-27; ⊙ year-round; 🐕) Campers can set up base at this attractive lochside site with pitches amid the Scots pines; rates include up to four people per tent/campervan.

Cairngorm Lodge SYHA   HOSTEL £
(☑ 01479-861238; www.syha.org.uk; Glenmore; dm £19.50; ⊙ closed Nov & Dec; 🅿@🛜🐕) Set in a former shooting lodge that enjoys a great location at the east end of Loch Morlich; booking ahead is essential.

ℹ Getting There & Away

Bus 31 links Aviemore with Loch Morlich and Glenmore (£2.90, 20 minutes, hourly) .

Cairngorm Mountain

Cairngorm Mountain Railway   FUNICULAR
(☑ 01479-861261; www.cairngormmountain.org; adult/child return £13.90/9.30; ⊙ every 20min 10am-4pm May-Nov, 9am-4.30pm Dec-Apr; 🅿) The national park's most popular attrac-

tion is this funicular railway that will whisk you to the edge of the Cairngorm plateau (altitude 1085m) in just eight minutes. The bottom station is at the Coire Cas car park at the end of Ski Rd; at the top is an exhibition, a shop (of course) and a restaurant. Unfortunately, for environmental and safety reasons, you're not allowed out of the top station in summer unless you book a guided walk.

From May to October, a 90-minute guided walk to the summit of Cairn Gorm (£21.60 per person) departs twice a day, while a four-hour guided hill walk runs four days a week. Check the website for details.

Cairngorm Mountain Ski Area   SNOW SPORTS
(www.cairngormmountain.org; 1-day ski pass per adult/child £35/21) Aspen or Val d'Isère it ain't, but with 19 runs and 23 miles of piste, Cairngorm is Scotland's most popular ski area. When the snow is at its best and the sun is shining you can close your eyes and imagine you're in the Alps; sadly, low cloud, high winds and horizontal sleet are more likely.

Ski or snowboard hire is around £26/19 per adult/child per day; there are lots of hire outlets at Coire Cas, Glenmore and Aviemore.

The season usually runs from December until the snow melts, which may be as late as the end of April, but snowfall here is unpredictable – in some years the slopes can be open in November, but closed for lack of snow in February. During the season the tourist office (p137) in Aviemore displays snow conditions and avalanche warnings. You can check the latest snow conditions at www.cairngormmountain.org/lifts-pistes and www.winterhighland.info.

Kincraig & Glen Feshie

At Kincraig, 6 miles southwest of Aviemore, the Spey widens into Loch Insh, home of the **Loch Insh Outdoor Centre** (☑01540-651272; www.lochinsh.com; Kincraig; day ticket incl all activities adult/child £35/25; ◷8.30am-5.30pm; ⭗), which offers canoeing, windsurfing, sailing, mountain biking and fishing, as well as B&B accommodation.

Beautiful, tranquil Glen Feshie extends south from Kincraig, deep into the Cairngorms, with Scots pine woods in its upper reaches surrounded by big, heathery hills. The 4WD track to the head of the glen makes a great mountain-bike excursion (25-mile round trip).

★ **Highland Wildlife Park**   ZOO
(☑01540-651270; www.highlandwildlifepark.org; Kincraig; adult/child £17/9.95; ◷10am-6pm Jul & Aug, to 5pm Apr-Oct, to 4pm Nov-Mar; ⓟ) This place features a drive-through safari park as well as animal enclosures offering the chance to view rarely seen native wildlife, such as wildcats, capercaillies, pine martens, white-tailed sea eagles and red squirrels, as well as species that once roamed the Scottish hills but have long since disappeared, including wolf, lynx, wild boar, beaver and European bison.

There are also iconic species from around the world – snow leopard, red panda, Amur tiger and polar bear (a polar bear cub was born in 2018, the first to be born in the UK for 25 years).

Visitors without cars get driven around by staff (at no extra cost). Last entry is two hours before closing.

Carrbridge

POP 700

Carrbridge, 7 miles north of Aviemore, is a good alternative base for exploring the region. It takes its name from the graceful old bridge (spotlit at night), built in 1717, over the thundering rapids of the River Dulnain.

**Landmark Forest
Adventure Park**   AMUSEMENT PARK
(☑0800 731 3446; www.landmarkpark.co.uk; adult/child £20.70/18.60; ◷10am-7pm mid-Jul–mid-Aug, to 6pm early Jul & late Aug, to 5pm Sep-Jun; ⭗) Set in a forest of Scots pines, this is a theme park with a difference: the theme is timber. The main attractions are the Ropeworx high-wire adventure course, the Red Squirrel Nature Trail (a raised walkway through the forest canopy that allows you to view red squirrels, crossbills and crested tits), and the view from the Fire Lookout Tower.

ℹ Getting There & Away

Bus 34 runs from Inverness to Carrbridge (£5.35, 45 minutes, six daily Monday to Friday, three on Saturday) and onwards to Grantown-on-Spey (£2.90, 20 minutes). Bus 32 links with Aviemore (£2.90, 15 minutes, five daily except Sunday).

Boat of Garten

Boat of Garten is known as the Osprey Village because these rare and beautiful birds of prey nest nearby at the RSPB Loch Garten Osprey Centre (☑01479-831694; www.

INVERNESS & THE CENTRAL HIGHLANDS AROUND AVIEMORE

rspb.org.uk/lochgarten; Tulloch; osprey hide adult/child £5/2; ⊘osprey hide 10am-6pm Apr-Aug). The ospreys migrate here each spring from Africa and nest in a tall pine tree.

There is flexible, good-quality homestay accommodation at Fraoch Lodge (📞01479-831331; www.scotmountainholidays.com; Deshar Rd; per person £25-30; ⓟ📶), along with a wide range of outdoor activities, while the Boat Hotel (📞01479-831258; www.boathotel.co.uk; s/d from £75/95; ⓟ📶🐾) offers country-style accommodation.

ℹ Getting There & Away

Boat of Garten is 5 miles northeast of Aviemore. The most interesting way to get here is on the Strathspey Steam Railway (p135) from Aviemore, or you can ride or walk along National Cycle Network Route 7 (allow 30 to 40 minutes by bike, two hours on foot).

Grantown-on-Spey

POP 2430

Grantown (gran-ton) is an elegant Georgian town with a grid of streets and a broad, tree-lined main square. It is a fine example of a planned settlement, founded by Sir Ludovic Grant in 1766 as a centre for the linen industry, and later becoming a tourist town after Queen Victoria's visit in 1860.

THE SNOW ROADS

The Snow Roads (https://visitcairngorms.com/snowroads) is a 90-mile scenic driving route between Blairgowrie in Perthshire and Grantown-on-Spey, by way of Braemar and Ballater. It takes in two high mountain passes that are often snow-covered in winter – Glenshee and the Lecht (both are ski centres) – and is marked by a series of landscape artworks at particularly picturesque viewpoints:

Connecting Contours A gracefully sinuous bench beside the A93 on the southern approach to Glenshee.

The Watchers A series of eerie steel shapes reminiscent of standing stones, near Corgarff Castle.

Still A polished steel sculpture that frames the view near Tomintoul.

The route is not signposted, but described online and in a leaflet available from local tourist offices.

A favoured haunt of anglers and the tweed-cap-and-green-wellies brigade, Grantown is thronged with visitors in summer, but it reverts to a quiet backwater in winter. Most hotels can kit you out for a day of fly-fishing on the Spey, or put you in touch with someone who can.

Grantown Museum MUSEUM
(📞01479-872478; www.grantownmuseum.co.uk; Burnfield Ave; adult/child £4/free; ⊘10am-5pm Mon-Sat Apr-Oct; ⓟ🚻) A small museum that chronicles the history of the town and its relationship to Clan Grant; also houses a tourist information point (📞01479-870477; Burnfield Ave; ⊘10am-5pm Mon-Sat Apr-Oct).

Brooklynn B&B ££
(📞01479-873113; www.woodier.com; Grant Rd; s/d £48/96; ⓟ📶) 🍴 This beautiful Victorian villa features original stained glass and wood panelling, and seven spacious, luxurious rooms (all doubles have en suites). The food – dinner is available (£28 per person), as well as breakfast – is superb, too.

★**Muckrach Country House Hotel** HOTEL £££
(📞01479-851227; www.muckrach.com; Dulnain Bridge; r from £209; ⓟ📶🐾) Built as a Victorian shooting lodge in 1860, Muckrach has been tastefully converted into a luxurious country house hotel with a relaxed and informal atmosphere. The lounge, complete with grand piano, serves coffee, cake and snacks through the day, and the restaurant (mains £13 to £21) serves a brasserie-style menu at lunch and dinner weekdays, and all day Saturday.

ℹ Getting There & Away

Bus 34X runs from Inverness to Grantown-on-Spey (£6.70, 1¼ hours, six daily Monday to Friday, three Saturday) and on to Aviemore (£4, 35 minutes).

Kingussie & Newtonmore

The old Speyside towns of Kingussie (kin-yew-see) and Newtonmore sit at the foot of the great heather-clad humps known as the Monadhliath Mountains. Newtonmore is best known as the home of the excellent Highland Folk Museum, Kingussie for one of the Highlands' best restaurants.

The road west from Newtonmore to Spean Bridge passes Ardverikie Estate and Loch Laggan, famous as the setting for the BBC TV series *Monarch of the Glen*.

Sights & Activities

Ruthven Barracks RUINS
(HES; ⊙24hr; P) FREE Ruthven Barracks was one of four garrisons built by the British government after the first Jacobite rebellion of 1715, as part of a Hanoverian scheme to take control of the Highlands. Ironically the barracks were last occupied by Jacobite troops awaiting the return of Bonnie Prince Charlie after the Battle of Culloden. Perched dramatically on a river terrace and clearly visible from the main A9 road near Kingussie, the ruins are spectacularly floodlit at night.

Highland Folk Museum MUSEUM
(☏01540-673551; www.highlandfolk.museum; Kingussie Rd, Newtonmore; ⊙10.30am-5.30pm Apr-Aug, 11am-4.30pm Sep & Oct; P) FREE This open-air museum comprises a collection of historical buildings and artefacts revealing many aspects of Highland culture and lifestyle. Laid out like a farming township, it has a community of traditional thatch-roofed cottages, a sawmill, a schoolhouse, a shepherd's bothy (hut) and a rural post office. Actors in period costume give demonstrations of woodcarving, wool-spinning and peat-fire baking. You'll need at least two to three hours to make the most of a visit here.

Laggan Wolftrax MOUNTAIN BIKING
(http://scotland.forestry.gov.uk/visit/laggan-wolftrax; Strathmashie Forest; trails free, parking per day £3; ⊙10am-6pm Mon, 9.30am-5pm Tue, Thu & Fri, 9.30am-6pm Sat & Sun) Ten miles southwest of Newtonmore, on the A86 road towards Spean Bridge, this is one of Scotland's top mountain-biking centres with purpose-built trails ranging from open-country riding to black-diamond downhills with rock slabs and drop-offs. Includes bike hire outlet and a good cafe (open 10am to 5pm April to October).

Highland All Terrain ADVENTURE
(☏01528-544358; www.quadbiketours.co.uk; Old Filling Station, Kinloch Laggan; per person from £50) Join an off-road quad-bike tour of Ardverikie Estate, which appears as Glen Bogle in the TV series *Monarch of the Glen*. Tours range from one hour to 3½ hours, and take in many of the TV locations. Located 15 miles southwest of Newtonmore.

Sleeping & Eating

★ Eagleview Guest House B&B ££
(☏01540-673675; Perth Rd, Newtonmore; r £78-85; P🅿🌐🐾) Welcoming Eagleview is one of the most pleasant places to stay in the area, with beautifully decorated bedrooms, super-king-size beds, spacious bathrooms with power showers (except room 4, which has a Victorian slipper bath!), and nice little touches such as cafetières (coffee plungers) with real coffee – and fresh milk – on your hospitality tray.

★ Restaurant at the Cross SCOTTISH £££
(☏01540-661166; www.thecross.co.uk; Tweed Mill Brae, off Ardbroilach Rd, Kingussie; 3-course lunch/dinner £30/55; ⊙noon-2pm & 7-8.30pm; P🌐) 🐾 Housed in a converted watermill, the Cross is one of the finest restaurants in the Highlands. The intimate, low-raftered dining room has an open fire and a patio overlooking the stream, and serves a daily changing menu of fresh Scottish produce accompanied by a superb wine list (booking essential).

If you want to stay the night, there are eight stylish rooms (double or twin £110 to £200) to choose from.

Getting There & Away

BUS
Kingussie and Newtonmore are served by **Scottish Citylink** (www.citylink.co.uk) coaches on the main Perth-to-Inverness bus route, as well as local Stagecoach buses.

Aviemore £3.70, 20 minutes, hourly
Inverness £10.70, 1½ hours, three daily, change at Carrbridge
Perth £17.10, 1¾ hours, one daily

TRAIN
Kingussie and Newtonmore are on the Edinburgh/Glasgow-to-Inverness railway line.
Edinburgh £37.50, 2¾ hours, seven daily Monday to Saturday, two Sunday
Inverness £12.80, one hour, eight daily Monday to Saturday, four Sunday

Tomintoul & Around
POP 320
Tomintoul (tom-in-towel) is a pretty, stone-built village with a grassy, tree-lined main square. It was built by the Duke of Gordon in 1775 on the old military road that leads over the Lecht pass from Corgarff, a route now followed by the A939 (usually the first

road in Scotland to be blocked by snow when winter closes in). The duke hoped that settling the dispersed population of his estates in a proper village would help to stamp out cattle stealing and illegal distilling.

The Glenlivet Estate (now the property of the Crown) has lots of walking and cycling trails – the estate's **tourist office** (🖉 01479-870070; www.glenlivetestate.co.uk; Main St; ⏱ 9am-5pm Mon-Fri) distributes free maps of the area – and a spur of the Speyside Way long-distance footpath runs between Tomintoul and Ballindalloch, 15 miles to the north.

Accommodation for walkers includes the **Smugglers Hostel** (🖉 01807-580364; www.thesmugglershostel.co.uk; Main St; dm/tw £20/85; 🛜), housed in the old village school. The highly recommended **Argyle Guest House** (🖉 01807-580766; www.argyletomintoul.co.uk; 7 Main St; d/f from £70/120; 🛜🐾) is a more comfortable alternative (best porridge in the Cairngorms!).

For something to eat in town, try **Clockhouse Restaurant** (🖉 01807-580378; The Square; mains £10-21; ⏱ 11am-9pm Tue-Sun); the best food in the area is out of town at **Coffee Still** (🖉 07599 973845; www.coffeestillcafe.co.uk; BikeGlenlivet Trail Centre; mains £6-9; ⏱ 10am-5pm Thu-Mon; 🅿🐾).

Tomintoul & Glenlivet Discovery Centre   MUSEUM
(🖉 01807-580760; discovery@tgdt.org.uk; The Square; ⏱ 10am-5pm Apr-Oct) **FREE** This visitor centre and rural museum celebrates local history, with reconstructions of a crofter's kitchen and a blacksmith's forge.

BikeGlenlivet   MOUNTAIN BIKING
(www.glenlivetestate.co.uk; trails free, parking £3) There's excellent mountain-biking at this trail centre, 4.5 miles north of Tomintoul, off the B9136 road. Custom-built trails range from the 9km blue run for beginners to the 22km red route for more experienced riders. Cafe and bike hire on site.

Cockbridge to Tomintoul Road

The A939, known as the Cockbridge-Tomintoul road – a magnificent roller-coaster of a route much loved by motorcyclists – crosses the Lecht pass (637m), where there's a small skiing area with lots of short easy and intermediate runs.

Corgarff Castle   CASTLE
(HES; 🖉 01975-651460; www.historicenvironment.scot; adult/child £6/3.60; ⏱ 9.30am-5.30pm Apr-Sep; 🅿) In the wild hills of the eastern Cairngorms, near the A939 road from Cockbridge to Tomintoul, is the impressive fortress of Corgarff Castle. The tower house dates from the 16th century, but the star-shaped defensive curtain wall was added in 1748 when the castle was converted into a military barracks in the wake of the Jacobite rebellion.

Lecht 2090   SNOW SPORTS
(www.lecht.co.uk) The Lecht is Scotland's smallest snow-sports centre. In winter, you can hire skis, boots and poles for £22 a day; a one-day lift pass is £30. In summer (weekends only), the chairlift serves mountain-biking trails (day ticket £30); there are no bike-hire facilities, though, so you'll need to bring your own.

Royal Deeside

The upper valley of the River Dee stretches west from Aboyne and Ballater to Braemar, closely paralleled by the A93 road. Made famous by its long association with the monarchy – today's Royal Family still holiday at Balmoral Castle, built for Queen Victoria in 1855 – the region is often called Royal Deeside.

The River Dee, renowned world-over for its salmon fishing, has its source in the Cairngorm Mountains west of Braemar, the starting point for long walks into the hills. The FishDee website (www.fishdee.co.uk) has all you need to know about fishing on the river.

Ballater
POP 1530

The attractive little village of Ballater owes its 18th-century origins to the curative waters of nearby Pannanich Springs (now bottled commercially as Deeside Natural Mineral Water), and its prosperity to nearby Balmoral Castle.

The village received a double dose of misfortune when the Old Royal Station (its main tourist attraction) burned down in May 2015, followed by the worst flooding in living memory in January 2016. The restored station building reopened in 2018 with a museum, restaurant and tourist office.

Note the crests on the shop fronts along the main street proclaiming 'By Royal Appointment' – the village is a major supplier of provisions to Balmoral Castle.

Activities

As you approach Ballater from the east the hills start to close in, and there are many pleasant walks in the surrounding area. The steep woodland walk up **Craigendarroch** (400m) takes just over one hour. **Morven** (871m) is a more serious prospect, taking about six hours return, but offers good views from the top.

You can hire bikes from **CycleHighlands** (☑ 01339-755864; www.cyclehighlands.com; The Pavilion, Victoria Rd; bicycle hire per half-/full day £15/20; ⊙ 9am-6pm) and **Bike Station** (☑ 01339-754004; www.bikestationballater.co.uk; Station Sq; bicycle hire per 3hr/day £12/18; ⊙ 9am-6pm), which also offer guided bike rides and advice on local trails.

🛏 Sleeping & Eating

Ballater Hostel   HOSTEL £
(☑ 01339-753752; www.ballater-hostel.com; Bridge Sq; dm/tw from £22/50; 🛜) 𝄢 Tucked up a lane near the bridge over the River Dee, this is an attractive, ecofriendly hostel with six en suite private rooms (sleeping two to eight). Rooms have personal lockers and reading lamps, and there's a comfortable lounge with big, soft sofas and a wood-burning stove.

★ **Auld Kirk**   HOTEL ££
(☑ 01339-755762; www.theauldkirk.com; Braemar Rd; r from £85; 🅿🛜🐾) Here's something a little out of the ordinary – a seven-bedroom hotel housed in a converted 19th-century church. The interior blends original features with sleek modern decor – the pulpit now serves as the reception desk, while the lounge is bathed in light from leaded Gothic windows. Breakfast not included, but guests can buy it at the hotel's coffee shop.

Rock Salt & Snails   CAFE £
(☑ 07834 452583; www.facebook.com/rocksalt andsnailsballater; 2 Bridge St; mains £4-9; ⊙ 10am-5pm Mon-Fri, to 9pm Sat, to 6pm Sun May-Sep, 10am-5pm Mon-Sat, 11am-5pm Sun Oct-Apr; 🛜🚼🐾) A great little cafe serving excellent coffee and tempting lunch platters featuring locally sourced deli products

(cheese, ham, salads etc), including a kids' platter.

ℹ Getting There & Away

Bus 201 runs from Aberdeen to Ballater (£12.10, 1¾ hours, hourly Monday to Saturday, six on Sunday) via Crathes Castle, and continues to Braemar (£6.25, 35 minutes) every two hours.

Balmoral Castle

Built for Queen Victoria in 1855 as a private residence for the Royal Family, **Balmoral Castle** (☑ 01339-742534; www.balmoralcastle. com; Crathie; adult/child £11.50/6; ⊙ 10am-5pm Apr-Jul, last admission 4.30pm; 🅿) kicked off the revival of the Scottish Baronial style of architecture that characterises so many of Scotland's 19th-century country houses. The admission fee includes an interesting and well-thought-out audio guide, but the tour is very much an outdoor one through garden and grounds.

As for the castle itself, only the ballroom, which displays a collection of Landseer paintings and royal silver, is open to the public. Don't expect to see the Queen's private quarters! The main attraction is learning about Highland estate management, rather than royal revelations.

You can buy a booklet that details several waymarked walks within Balmoral Estate; the best is the climb to **Prince Albert's Cairn**, a huge granite pyramid that bears the inscription 'To the beloved memory of Albert the great and good, Prince Consort. Erected by his broken hearted widow Victoria R. 21st August 1862'.

The massive pointy-topped mountain that looms to the south of Balmoral is **Lochnagar** (1155m), immortalised in verse by Lord Byron, who spent his childhood years in Aberdeenshire:

England, thy beauties are tame and domestic

To one who has roamed o'er the mountains afar.

Oh! for the crags that are wild and majestic,

The steep frowning glories of dark Lochnagar.

     Lord Byron, Lochnagar

Balmoral is eight miles west of Ballater, and can be reached on the Aberdeen–Braemar bus.

Braemar

POP 450

Braemar is a pretty little village with a grand location on a broad plain ringed by mountains where the Dee valley and Glen Clunie meet. In winter this is one of the coldest places in the country – temperatures as low as -29°C have been recorded – and during spells of severe cold, hungry deer wander the streets looking for a bite to eat. Braemar is an excellent base for hill walking, and there's also skiing at nearby Glenshee.

◉ Sights & Activities

An easy walk from Braemar is up Creag Choinnich (538m), a hill to the east of the village above the A93. The 1-mile route is waymarked and takes about 1½ hours return. For a longer walk (4 miles; about three hours return) and superb views of the Cairngorms, head for the summit of Morrone (859m), southwest of Braemar. Ask at the tourist office (p145) for details of these and other walks.

Braemar Castle   CASTLE
(www.braemarcastle.co.uk; adult/child £8/4; ◷10am-5pm Jul & Aug, Wed-Sun Apr-Jun, Sep & Oct; P) Just north of Braemar village, turreted Braemar Castle dates from 1628 and served as a government garrison after the 1745 Jacobite rebellion. It was taken over by the local community in 2007, which now offers guided tours of the historic castle apartments. There's a short walk from the car park to the castle.

Braemar Mountain Sports   CYCLING
(☑01339-741242; www.braemarmountainsports.com; 5 Invercauld Rd; bike hire per 4hr/day £15/20; ◷9am-6pm) You can hire bikes from Braemar Mountain Sports. It also rents skiing and mountaineering equipment.

✦ Festivals & Events

Braemar Gathering   SPORTS
(☑01339-755377; www.braemargathering.org; adult/child from £12/2; ◷Sep) There are Highland games in many towns and villages throughout the summer, but the best known is the Braemar Gathering, which takes place on the first Saturday in September. It's a major occasion, organised every year since 1817 by the Braemar Royal Highland Society.

Events include Highland dancing, pipers, tug-of-war, a hill race up Morrone, tossing the caber, hammer- and stone-throwing and the long jump. International athletes are among those who take part.

These kinds of events took place informally in the Highlands for many centuries as tests of skill and strength, but they were formalised around 1820 as part of the rise of Highland romanticism initiated by Sir Walter Scott and King George IV. Queen Victoria attended the Braemar Gathering in 1848, starting a tradition of royal patronage that continues to this day.

🛏 Sleeping

Rucksacks Bunkhouse   HOSTEL £
(☑01339-741517; 15 Mar Rd; bothy £7, dm £12-15, tw £36; P) This appealing cottage has a comfy dorm, and cheaper beds in an alpine-style bothy (shared sleeping platform for 10 people; bring your own sleeping bag). Extras include a drying room (for wet-weather gear), a laundry and even a sauna (£10 an hour). The friendly owner is a fount of knowledge about the local area.

Braemar SYHA   HOSTEL £
(☑01339-741659; www.syha.org.uk; 21 Glenshee Rd; dm/tw £21/49; ◷Feb-Oct; P@🛜🐾) This hostel is housed in a grand former shooting lodge just south of Braemar village centre on the A93 to Perth. It has a comfy lounge with pool table, and a barbecue in the garden.

Braemar Caravan Park   CAMPSITE £
(☑01339-741373; www.braemarcaravanpark.co.uk; tent sites incl 2 people £22.50; ◷closed mid-Oct–mid-Dec; 🛜) There is good camping here, in a sheltered spot surrounded by mountains, with hot showers, a laundry and a small shop selling caravan and camping essentials.

Braemar Cabins   CABIN ££
(☑01339-741242; http://braemarcabins.com; 7-9 Invercauld Rd; 3 nights from £285; P🛜🐾) These attractive larch-clad cabins at the entrance to the village can sleep up to four people in two double or twin bedrooms (some wheelchair accessible). They have underfloor heating, well-equipped kitchens and outdoor decks. In high season the minimum stay is one week (£695).

Braemar Lodge Hotel   HOTEL ££
(☑01339-741627; www.braemarlodge.co.uk; Glenshee Rd; dm/s/d from £15/80/120; P🛜) This Victorian shooting lodge on the southern outskirts of Braemar has bags of character, not least in the wood-panelled Malt Room

145

bar, which is as well stocked with mounted deer heads as it is with single malt whiskies. There's a good restaurant with views of the hills, plus a 12-berth hikers' bunkhouse (book in advance) in the hotel grounds.

Craiglea B&B ££
(☑ 01339-741641; www.craigleabraemar.com; Hillside Rd; d/f from £72/107; P �) Craiglea is a homely B&B set in a pretty stone cottage with three en suite bedrooms. Vegetarian breakfasts are available and the owners can rent you a bike and give advice on local walks.

Eating

Bothy CAFE £
(Invercauld Rd; mains £4-7; ⊙9am-5.30pm Sun-Thu, to 6pm Fri & Sat;) An appealing little cafe tucked behind the Mountain Sports (p144) shop, with a sunny terrace out front and a balcony at the back overhanging the river.

Taste CAFE £
(☑ 01339-741425; www.taste-braemar.co.uk; Airlie House, Mar Rd; mains £5-9; ⊙10am-5pm Tue-Sat;) Taste is a relaxed little cafe which has armchairs in the window bays, and serves homemade soups, sandwiches, coffee and cakes.

Information

The **tourist office** (☑ 01399-741600; The Mews, Mar Rd; ⊙9am-6pm Aug, to 5pm Jun, Jul, Sep & Oct, shorter hours Nov-May), opposite the Fife Arms Hotel, has lots of useful info on walks in the area.

Getting There & Away

Bus 201 runs from Aberdeen to Braemar (£12.10, 2¼ hours, every two hours Monday to Saturday, five on Sunday). The 50-mile drive from Perth to Braemar is beautiful, but there's no public transport on this route.

The Angus Glens

Five scenic glens – Isla, Prosen, Clova, Lethnot and Esk – cut into the hills along the southern fringes of the Cairngorms National Park, accessible from Kirriemuir in Angus. All have attractive scenery, though each glen has its own distinct personality: Glen Clova and Glenesk are the most beautiful, while Glen Lethnot is the least frequented. You can get detailed information on walks

GLENSHEE

The route along the A93 from Braemar to Blairgowrie through the ski area of Glenshee is one of the most scenic drives in the country. It's fantastic **walking** country in summer, and has some of Scotland's best **skiing** in winter.

Although this is Scotland's biggest ski area, there's only a car park, ticket office, cafe and uplift – no services or accommodation.

With 22 lifts and 36 runs **Glenshee Ski Resort** (☑ 01339-741320; www.ski-glenshee.co.uk; 1-day ski pass per adult/child £30/20) is Scotland's largest skiing area. When the sun burns through the clouds after a good fall of snow, you'll be in a unique position to drink in the beauty of the country; the skiing isn't half bad either.

The chairlift, which also opens in July and August for walkers and mountain bikers, can whisk you up to 910m, near the top of the Cairnwell (933m).

in the Angus Glens from the **Gateway to the Glens Museum** (kirriemuirmuseum@angusalive.scot; 32 High St; ⊙10am-5pm Tue-Sat) **FREE** in Kirriemuir and from the Glen Clova Hotel (p146) in Glen Clova.

Getting There & Away

There is no public transport to the Angus Glens other than a limited school-bus service along Glen Clova; ask at the Gateway to the Glens Museum in Kirriemuir for details.

Glen Clova

The longest and loveliest of the Angus Glens stretches north from Kirriemuir for 20 miles, broad and pastoral in its lower reaches but growing narrower and craggier as the steep, heather-clad Highland hills close in around its head.

The minor road beyond the Glen Clova Hotel (p146) ends at a Forestry Commission car park at Glen Doll with a **ranger centre** (☑ 01575-550233; Glen Doll; parking £2; ⊙9am-6pm Apr-Sep, to 4.30pm Oct-Mar) and picnic area, which is the trailhead for a number of strenuous walks through the hills to the north.

Jock's Road is an ancient footpath that was much used by cattle drovers, soldiers, smugglers and shepherds in the 18th and 19th centuries; 700 Jacobite soldiers passed this way during their retreat in 1746, en route to defeat at Culloden. From the car park the path strikes west along Glen Doll, then north across a high plateau (900m) before descending steeply into Glen Callater and on to Braemar (15 miles; allow five to seven hours). The route is hard going and should not be attempted in winter; you'll need OS 1:50,000 maps numbers 43 and 44.

An easier walk leads from Glen Doll car park to **Corrie Fee**, a spectacular glacial hollow in the edge of the mountain plateau (4.5-mile round trip, waymarked).

Glen Clova Hotel   HOTEL **££**
(☑ 01575-550350; www.clova.com; s/d from £85/120; P ❅) The Glen Clova Hotel is a lovely old drover's inn near the head of the glen, and a great place to get away from it all. As well as 18 comfortable, country-style, en suite rooms (one with a four-poster bed), it has a rustic, stone-floored climbers' bar with a roaring log fire, and a **restaurant** (☑ 01575-550350; mains £9-25; ⊘ noon-7.45pm Sun-Thu, to 8.45pm Fri & Sat, shorter hours Nov-Mar; P ❅). No mobile phone reception.

Glenesk

The most easterly of the Angus Glens, Glenesk runs for 15 miles from Edzell to lovely **Loch Lee**, surrounded by beetling cliffs and waterfalls.

Fifteen miles up the glen from Edzell, the public road ends near **Invermark Castle**, an impressive ruined tower. From the car park, good hiking trails lead to a 17th-century kirkyard beside Loch Lee (1 mile), the monument at **Queen's Well** (a spring once visited by Queen Victoria; 2 miles), and the summit of **Mt Keen** (939m; 5 miles).

Glenesk Retreat & Folk Museum   MUSEUM
(www.gleneskretreat.scot; admission by donation; ⊘ 10am-5pm Mon-Fri, to 6pm Sat & Sun Apr-Oct; P ❅) ⏺ Ten miles up Glenesk from Edzell is a former shooting lodge that houses a fascinating collection of antiques and artefacts documenting everyday life in the glen from the 17th to the early 20th centuries – 860 people once lived here; today the population is less than 100.

There's also internet access, a gift shop and a restaurant (mains £5 to £10) serving superb fish and chips.

HIGHLAND PERTHSHIRE

The Highland border cuts diagonally across Scotland from Dumbarton to Stonehaven, dividing the county of Perthshire into two distinctive regions. Highland Perthshire, spreading north of a line from Comrie to Blairgowrie, is a land of mountains, forest and lochs, with some of the finest scenery in the UK. The ancient city of Dunkeld, on the main A9 road from Perth to Inverness, is the main gateway to the region.

❶ Getting There & Around

Citylink (p118) buses from Edinburgh or Glasgow to Inverness stop at Birnam and Pitlochry. There are regular buses from Perth to most of the towns in the area. Trains running between Perth and Inverness stop at Blair Atholl and Pitlochry.

Away from the main A9 Perth-to-Inverness road, public transport is thin on the ground, and often geared to the needs of local schools.

Dunkeld & Birnam

POP 1005
The Tay runs like a storybook river through the heart of Perthshire's Big Tree Country, where the twin towns of Dunkeld and Birnam are linked by Thomas Telford's graceful bridge of 1808. As well as Dunkeld's ancient cathedral, there's much walking to be done in this area of magnificent forested hills. These same walks were one of the inspirations for Beatrix Potter to create her children's tales.

There's less to see in Birnam, a name made famous by Macbeth. There's not much left of Birnam Wood, but a riverside path leads to the **Birnam Oak**, a venerable 500-year-old survivor from Shakespeare's time, its ageing boughs propped up with timber supports. Nearby is the 300-year-old Birnam Sycamore.

◉ Sights & Activities

Dunkeld Cathedral   CHURCH
(HS; www.dunkeldcathedral.org.uk; High St; ⊘ 9.30am-5.30pm Apr-Sep, 10am-4pm Oct-Mar) **FREE** Situated on the grassy banks of the River Tay, Dunkeld Cathedral is one of the most beautifully sited churches in Scotland; don't miss it on a sunny day, when there are few lovelier places to be. Half the cathedral is still in use as a church; the rest is a romantic ruin. It partly dates from the 14th century, having suffered damage during

the Reformation and the battle of Dunkeld (Jacobites versus the government) in 1689.

The Wolf of Badenoch, a fierce 14th-century noble who burned towns and abbeys to the ground in protest at his excommunication, is buried here – undeservedly – in a fine medieval tomb behind the wooden screen in the church.

Dunkeld House Grounds GARDENS
(⊙24hr) FREE Waymarked walks lead upstream from Dunkeld Cathedral through the gorgeous grounds of Dunkeld House Hotel, formerly a seat of the dukes of Atholl. In the 18th and early 19th centuries the 'planting dukes', as they became known, planted more than 27 million conifers on their estates 'for beauty and profit', introducing species such as larch, Douglas fir and sequoia, and sowing the seeds of Scottish forestry.

The abundance of vast, ancient trees here has given rise to the nickname Big Tree Country (www.perthshirebigtreecountry. co.uk). Just west of the cathedral is the 280-year-old '**parent larch**', the lone survivor of several planted in 1738, and said to have provided the seed stock for all Scottish larch trees. On the far side of the river is **Niel Gow's Oak**, another ancient tree, said to have provided inspiration for legendary local fiddler Niel Gow (1727–1807).

Loch of the Lowes
Wildlife Centre WILDLIFE RESERVE
(☑01350-727337; www.swt.org.uk; adult/child £4/50p; ⊙10am-5pm Mar-Oct, 10.30am-4pm Fri-Sun Nov-Feb; P) Loch of the Lowes, 2 miles east of Dunkeld off the A923, has a visitor centre devoted to red squirrels and the majestic osprey. There's a birdwatching hide (with binoculars provided), where you can see the birds nesting during breeding season (late April to August), complete with a live video link to the nest.

Beatrix Potter Exhibition & Garden MUSEUM
(www.birnaminstitute.com; Station Rd; £3; ⊙10am-4.30pm; P⛟) In the middle of Birnam village is the small, leafy Beatrix Potter Garden; the children's author, who wrote the evergreen story of *Peter Rabbit,* spent her childhood holidays in the area. Next to the park, in the Birnam Arts Centre, is a small exhibition on Potter and her characters.

Hermitage WALKING
One of the most popular walks near Dunkeld is the Hermitage, where a well-marked trail follows the River Braan to Ossian's Hall, a quaint folly built by the Duke of Atholl in 1758 overlooking the spectacular Falls of Braan (salmon can be seen leaping here, especially in September and October). It's signposted off the A9 just west of the village.

🍽 Sleeping & Eating

⭐ **Jessie Mac's** HOSTEL, B&B £
(☑01350-727324; www.jessiemacs.co.uk; Murthly Tce, Birnam; dm/d from £20/59; 🛜🐾) 🍴 Set in a Victorian manse complete with baronial turret, Jessie Mac's is a glorious cross between B&B and luxury hostel, with three gorgeous doubles and four shared or family rooms with bunks. Guests make good use of the country-style lounge, sunny dining room and well-equipped kitchen, and breakfasts are composed of local produce, from organic eggs to Dunkeld smoked salmon.

Erigmore Estate LODGE ££
(☑01350-727236; www.erigmore.co.uk; Birnam; d 3 nights from £273; P🐾) Scattered around the wooded, riverside grounds of Erigmore House, the former country retreat of a

---

FISHING & RAFTING ON THE TAY

The Tay is Scotland's longest river (117 miles) and the most powerful in Britain, with a flow rate greater than the Thames and the Severn combined. It's also Europe's most famous salmon river, attracting anglers from all over the world (the season runs from 15 January to 15 October). The British record rod-caught salmon, weighing in at a whopping 64lb (29kg) was hooked in the Tay near Dunkeld in 1922 by local woman Georgina Ballantine.

Salmon fishing has an air of exclusivity and can be expensive, but anyone – even complete beginners – can have a go. There's lots of information on the FishTay website (www.fishtay. co.uk), but novices would be best to hire a guide – check out Fishinguide Scotland (p70).

The Tay is also famous for its canoeing, kayaking and white-water rafting; the latter is best around Grandtully rapids near Aberfeldy, where Splash (p152) runs rafting trips.

wealthy clipper ship's captain, these luxury timber lodges provide cosseted comfort complete with outdoor deck and – at the more expensive end of the range – a private hot tub. The house itself contains shared facilities, including a bar, restaurant and swimming pool.

There's a three-night minimum stay.

★**Taybank** PUB FOOD **££**
(☑ 01350-727340; www.thetaybank.co.uk; Tay Tce, Dunkeld; mains £9-13; ⊙food served noon-9pm; **P**) 🢄 Top choice for a sun-kissed pub lunch by the river is the Taybank, a regular meeting place and performance space for folk musicians and a wonderfully welcoming bar serving ales from the local Strathbraan Brewery. There's live music several nights per week, and the menu features local produce with dishes such as smoked venison or grilled sea trout.

ℹ Information

Dunkeld Tourist Office (☑ 01350-727688; www.dunkeldandbirnam.org.uk; The Cross; ⊙10.30am-4.30pm Mon-Sat, 11am-4pm Sun Apr-Oct, longer hours Jul & Aug, Fri-Sun only Nov-Mar) Has information on local hiking and biking trails.

ℹ Getting There & Away

Citylink (p122) buses running between Glasgow/ Edinburgh and Inverness stop at the Birnam Hotel (£18.10, two hours, two or three daily). **Stagecoach** (www.stagecoachbus.com) runs hourly buses (only five on Sunday) between Perth and Dunkeld (£2.80, 45 minutes), continuing to Aberfeldy.

Pitlochry
POP 2780

Pitlochry, with the scent of the Highlands already in the air, is a popular stop on the way north. In summer the main street can be a conga line of tour groups, but linger a while and it can still charm – on a quiet spring evening it's a pretty place with salmon leaping in the Tummel and good things brewing at the Moulin Hotel.

◎ Sights & Activities

One of Pitlochry's attractions is its beautiful riverside; the River Tummel is dammed here, and if you're lucky you might see salmon swimming up the fish ladder to Loch Faskally above (May to November; best month is October).

★**Pitlochry Dam**
Visitor Centre VISITOR CENTRE
(www.pitlochrydam.com; Armoury Rd; ⊙9.30am-5.30pm; **P**) FREE Opened in 2017, this architecturally stunning visitor centre is perched above the dam on the River Tummel, and houses an exhibition that details the history of hydroelectricity in Scotland, alongside the life cycle of the Atlantic salmon (all hydro stations need a fish ladder to allow salmon to migrate upstream past the dams). Includes an excellent cafe.

★**Edradour Distillery** DISTILLERY
(☑ 01796-472095; www.edradour.co.uk; Moulin Rd; tour adult/child £10/5; ⊙10am-5pm Mon-Sat Apr-Oct, to 4.30pm Mon-Fri Nov-Mar; **P** 🦽) This is proudly Scotland's smallest and most picturesque distillery and one of the best to visit: you can see the whole process, easily explained, in one building. It's 2.5 miles east of Pitlochry by car, along the Moulin road, or a pleasant 1-mile walk.

Blair Athol Distillery DISTILLERY
(☑ 01796-482003; www.malts.com; Perth Rd; standard tour £8; ⊙10am-5pm Apr-Oct, to 4pm Nov-Mar) Tours here focus on whisky making and the blending of this well-known dram. More detailed private tours give you greater insights and superior tastings.

Explorers Garden GARDENS
(☑ 01796-484600; www.explorersgarden.com; Foss Rd; adult/child £4/1; ⊙10am-5pm Apr-Oct; **P**) This gem of a garden is based around plants brought to Scotland by 18th- and 19th-century Scottish botanists and explorers such as David Douglas (after whom the Douglas fir is named), and celebrates 300 years of collecting and the 'plant hunters' who tracked down these exotic species.

Pass of Killiecrankie HISTORIC SITE
(NTS; parking £2; ⊙24hr; **P** 🦽) FREE The beautiful, rugged Pass of Killiecrankie, 3.5 miles north of Pitlochry, where the River Garry tumbles through a narrow gorge, was the site of the 1689 Battle of Killiecrankie that ignited the Jacobite rebellion. The visitor centre (NTS; ☑ 01796-473233; www.nts.org.uk; ⊙10am-5pm Apr-Sep, 11am-4pm Oct; **P** 🦽) FREE has great interactive displays on Jacobite history and local flora and fauna. There's plenty to touch, pull and open – great for kids. There are some stunning walks along the wooded gorge, too; keep an eye out for red squirrels.

Highland Fling Bungee   ADVENTURE SPORTS
(☑0845 366 5844; www.bungeejumpscotland.
co.uk; per person £79, repeat jumps £30) Based
at Killiecrankie, 3.5 miles north of Pitlochry,
Highland Fling offers breathtaking 130ft
bungee jumps off the bridge over the River
Garry gorge on weekends year-round, plus
selected weekdays from March to October.

⚔ Festivals & Events

Enchanted Forest   LIGHT SHOW
(www.enchantedforest.org.uk; adult/child £20/10;
☺Oct) This spectacular three-week sound-
and-light show staged in Faskally Wood near
Pitlochry is a major family hit.

Winter Words   LITERATURE
(www.pitlochry.org/events; ☺Feb) A 10-day literary festival, with a packed program of talks
by authors, poets and broadcasters. Past
guests have ranged from novelist Louis de
Bernières to mountaineer and author Sir
Chris Bonington.

🛏 Sleeping

Pitlochry Backpackers Hotel   HOSTEL £
(☑01796-470044; www.scotlands-top-hostels.
com; 134 Atholl Rd; dm/tw £20/53; ☺Apr–mid-
Nov; P@🛜) Friendly, laid-back and very
comfortable, this is a cracking hostel smack
bang in the middle of town, with three- to
eight-bed dorms that are in mint condition.
There are also good-value en suite twins and
doubles, with beds, not bunks. Cheap breakfast and a pool table add to the convivial
party atmosphere. No extra charge for linen.

Ashleigh   B&B £
(☑01796-470316; www.ashleighbedandbreakfast.
com; 120 Atholl Rd; s/d £30/57; 🛜) Genuine
welcomes don't come much better than
Nancy's, and her place on the main street
makes a top Pitlochry pit stop. Two comfortable doubles share an excellent bathroom,
and there's an open kitchen stocked with
goodies where you make your own breakfast
in the morning. A home away from home
and a standout budget choice. Cash only;
no kids.

She also has a good self-catering apartment with great views, available by the night.

⭐**Craigatin House**   B&B ££
(☑01796-472478; www.craigatinhouse.co.uk; 165
Atholl Rd; d from £107, ste £134; P@🛜) Several
times more tasteful than the average Scottish B&B, this elegant house and garden is
set back from the main road. Chic contem-

porary fabrics covering expansive beds offer
a standard of comfort above and beyond the
reasonable price; the rooms in the converted
stable block are particularly inviting. A fabulous breakfast and lounge area gives views
over the lush garden.

Breakfast choices include whisky-laced
porridge, smoked-fish omelettes and apple
pancakes. No children under 13 years.

⭐**Fonab Castle Hotel**   HISTORIC HOTEL £££
(☑01796-470140; www.fonabcastlehotel.com; Foss
Rd; r from £225; P🛜) This Scottish Baronial
fantasy in red sandstone was built in 1892 as
the country house of Lt Col George Sande-
man, a scion of the famous port and sherry
merchants. Now a luxury hotel and spa, it
has a tasteful modern extension with commanding views over Loch Faskally, and a
superb restaurant serving the finest Scottish
venison, beef and seafood.

Knockendarroch House   HOTEL £££
(☑01796-473473; www.knockendarroch.co.uk;
Higher Oakfield Rd; d incl dinner from £245;
P🛜🐾) Top of the town and boasting the
best views, this genteel, well-run hotel has
a range of luxurious rooms with huge windows that take advantage of the Highland
light. The standard rooms have better views
than the larger, slightly pricier superior
ones; a couple have great little balconies,
perfect for a sundowner. Meals are highly
commended.

🍴 Eating & Drinking

⭐**Moulin Hotel**   PUB FOOD ££
(☑01796-472196; www.moulinhotel.co.uk; Kirk-
michael Rd; mains £9-16; ☺food served noon-
9.30pm; P🛜🐾) A mile away from town but
a world apart, this atmospheric inn has low
ceilings, ageing wood and snug booths. It's
a wonderfully romantic spot for a home-
brewed ale (there's a microbrewery out

back) and some Highland comfort food: try the mince and tatties, or game casserole. It's a pleasant uphill stroll from Pitlochry, and an easy roll down afterwards.

Port-na-Craig Inn BISTRO ££
(☑ 01796-472777; www.portnacraig.com; Port-na-Craig; mains £8-17; ⊙ 11am-8.30pm; P ⌕) Across the river from the town centre, this cute little cottage sits in what was once a separate hamlet. Top-quality main meals are prepared with confidence and panache; there are also simpler sandwiches, kids' meals and light lunches. Or you could just sit outdoors by the river with a pint and watch the salmon anglers.

🛍 Shopping

Melt Gallery ARTS & CRAFTS
(☑ 01796-472358; www.meltgallery.com; 14 Bonnethill Rd; ⊙ 10am-5pm Thu-Tue) This gallery is a treasure trove of quality Scottish arts and crafts, including polished aluminium jewellery that is handmade in the owner's workshop at the back. Potential purchases include paintings, photography, bronzes, ceramics and more unusual items – ever seen a Harris Tweed cafetière cosy? You have now...

ℹ Information

Pitlochry Tourist Office (☑ 01796-472215; www.perthshire.co.uk; 22 Atholl Rd; ⊙ 9.30am-5.30pm Mon-Sat, 10am-4pm Sun Mar-Oct, longer hours Jul & Aug, shorter hours Nov-Feb) Good information on local walks.

ℹ Getting There & Away

BUS
Scottish Citylink (www.citylink.co.uk) Buses run two to four times daily to Inverness (£18.10, 1¾ hours), Perth (£11.50, 50 minutes), Edinburgh (£18.10, two to 2½ hours) and Glasgow (£18.10, 2¼ hours).

Megabus (☑ 0871 266 3333; www.megabus.com) Offers discounted fares to Inverness, Perth, Edinburgh and Glasgow.

Stagecoach (www.stagecoachbus.com) Buses run to Aberfeldy (£3, 40 minutes, hourly Monday to Saturday, three Sunday), Dunkeld (£2.60, 40 minutes, hourly Monday to Saturday) and Perth (£4.10, 1¼ hours, hourly Monday to Saturday).

TRAIN
Pitlochry is on the main railway line from Perth (£14.40, 30 minutes, nine daily Monday to Saturday, five on Sunday) to Inverness (£23.40, 1¾ hours, same frequency).

ℹ Getting Around

Local buses between Pitlochry and Blair Atholl stop at Killiecrankie (£1.75, 10 minutes, three to seven daily).

Escape Route (☑ 01796-473859; www.escape-route.co.uk; 3 Atholl Rd; bike hire per half/full day from £16/24; ⊙ 9am-5.30pm Mon-Sat, 10am-5pm Sun) Rents out bikes and provides advice on local trails; it's worth booking ahead at weekends.

Blair Atholl

The village of Blair Atholl dates only from the early 19th century, springing up along the main road to the north after a new bridge was thrown across the River Tilt in 1822 (the original 16th-century Black Bridge, upgraded by General Wade in 1730, still stands just under a mile upstream at Old Bridge of Tilt).

Blair Castle is the main attraction here, but there's also the Atholl Country Life Museum, the old watermill, and many superb walks in the surrounding countryside, from short strolls through the castle grounds and longer walks to various viewpoints, to day-long hikes along Glen Tilt and up into the surrounding mountains (details from the information point in the museum).

★ Blair Castle CASTLE
(☑ 01796-481207; www.blair-castle.co.uk; adult/child £12/7.70; ⊙ 9.30am-5.30pm Easter-Oct, 10am-4pm Sat & Sun Nov-Mar; P ⌕) One of the most popular tourist attractions in Scotland, magnificent Blair Castle – and its surrounding estates – is the seat of the Duke of Atholl, head of the Murray clan. (The current duke visits every May to review the Atholl Highlanders, Britain's only private army.) It's an impressive white heap set beneath forested slopes above the River Garry. Thirty rooms are open to the public and they present a wonderful picture of upper-class Highland life from the 16th century on.

The original tower was built in 1269, but the castle underwent significant remodelling in the 18th and 19th centuries. Highlights include the 2nd-floor Drawing Room with its ornate Georgian plasterwork and Zoffany portrait of the fourth duke's family, complete with a pet lemur (yes, you read that correctly) called Tommy; and the Tapestry Room draped with 17th-century wall hangings created for Charles I. The **dining room** is sumptuous – check out the 9-pint wine glasses – and the **ballroom** is a vast oak-panelled chamber hung with hundreds of stag antlers.

Blair Atholl Watermill CAFE £
(☎ 01796-481321; www.facebook.com/blairatholl watermill; Ford Rd; mains £4-8; ☺ 9.30am-5pm late Mar-Oct; P 🤶 🐕) 🍴 This working watermill grinds its own flour and bakes its own bread, and serves it up in this atmospheric cafe as deliciously fresh sandwiches and toasties. You can watch the mill at work, and even sign up for bakery courses.

Lochs Tummel & Rannoch

The scenic route along Lochs Tummel and Rannoch (www.rannochandtummel.co.uk) is worth doing any way you can – by foot, bicycle or car. Hillsides shrouded with ancient birchwoods and forests of spruce, pine and larch make up the fabulous **Tay Forest Park**, whose wooded hills roll into the glittering waters of the lochs; a visit in autumn, when the birch leaves are at their finest, is recommended.

Eighteen miles west of Kinloch Rannoch the road ends at romantic and isolated **Rannoch Station**, which lies on the Glasgow–Fort William railway line. Beyond sprawls the desolate expanse of Rannoch Moor (p151). There's an excellent tearoom on the station platform, and a welcoming small hotel alongside. Be aware that Rannoch Station is a dead-end, and the nearest service station is at Aberfeldy.

The Queen's View at the eastern end of Loch Tummel is a magnificent viewpoint with a vista along the loch to the prominent mountain of Schiehallion. The nearby **visitor centre** (www.forestry.gov.uk; admission free, parking £2; ☺ 9am-6pm Apr-Oct, 10am-4pm Nov-Mar; P) provides parking and houses a cafe and gift shop.

Kinloch Rannoch is a great base for walks and cycle trips, or for fishing on Loch Rannoch for brown trout, Arctic char and pike; you can get permits (£8 per day) at the Country Store in the village. Walking trails lead into the wildlife-rich Black Wood of Rannoch, a remnant of Caledonian pine forest on the south shore of the loch.

Schiehallion (1083m), whose conical peak dominates views from Loch Rannoch, is a relatively straightforward climb from Braes of Foss car park (6.5 miles return), and is rewarded by spectacular views. See www.john muirtrust.org/trust-land/east-schiehallion for more information.

🛏 Sleeping & Eating

There are useful accommodation listings at www.rannochandtummel.co.uk.

Places to eat are widely scattered – think about bringing a picnic lunch just in case.

Kilvrecht Campsite CAMPSITE £
(☎ 01350-727284; https://scotland.forestry.gov.uk; Kilvrecht; tent sites with/without car £10/5; ☺ Apr-mid-Oct) This basic but beautiful campsite (toilet block, but no electricity or hot water) is 2 miles west of Kinloch Rannoch on the south shore of the loch. Hiking and mountain-biking trails begin from the site.

RANNOCH MOOR

Beyond Rannoch Station, civilisation fades away and Rannoch Moor begins. This is the largest area of moorland in Britain, stretching west for eight barren, bleak and uninhabited miles to the A82 Glasgow–Fort William road. A triangular plateau of blanket bog occupying more than 50 sq miles, the moor is ringed by high mountains and puddled with countless lochs, ponds and peat hags. Water covers 10% of the surface, and it has been canoed across, swum across, and even skated across in winter.

Despite the appearance of desolation, the moor is rich in wildlife, with curlew, golden plover and snipe darting among the tussocks, black-throated diver, goosander and merganser on the lochs, and – if you're lucky – osprey and golden eagle overhead. Herds of red deer forage alongside the railway, and otters patrol the loch shores. Keep an eye out for the sundew, a tiny, insect-eating plant with sticky-fingered leaves.

A couple of excellent (and challenging) walks start from Rannoch Station – north to Corrour Station (11 miles, four to five hours) from where you can return by train; and west along the northern edge of the moor to the Kings House Hotel (p158) at the eastern end of Glen Coe (11 miles, four hours).

Moor of Rannoch
Restaurant & Rooms   HOTEL £££
(📞 01882-633238; www.moorofrannoch.co.uk; Rannoch Station; s/d £125/180; ☺mid-Feb–Oct; 🅿🐾) At the end of the road beside Rannoch train station, this is one of Scotland's most isolated places (no internet, no TV, only fleeting mobile-phone reception), but luckily this beautifully renovated hotel is here to keep your spirits up – a magical getaway. It does excellent dinners (three courses £35, 6.30pm to 8pm), and can prepare a packed lunch.

Rannoch Station Tea Room   CAFE £
(📞 01882-633247; www.rannochstationtearoom.co.uk; Rannoch Station; mains £4-6; ☺8.30am-4.30pm Mon-Thu & Sat, 10am-4.30pm Sun; 🅿🐾) This superb little tearoom sits on the platform at remote Rannoch Station, serving coffee, sandwiches and cake to visiting hikers, mountain bikers and railway excursionists. Next door, in the former waiting room, is a fascinating exhibition on Rannoch Moor and the history of the railway.

❶ Getting There & Around

A demand-responsive minibus service (www.pkc.gov.uk) – ie you have to phone and book it at least 24 hours in advance – runs between Kinloch Rannoch and Rannoch Station (£3, 35 minutes).

Elizabeth Yule Coaches (📞 01796-472290; www.elizabethyulecoaches.co.uk) operates a bus service from Pitlochry to Kinloch Rannoch (£4.10, 50 minutes, three to five daily Monday to Saturday April to October) via Queen's View and the Inn at Loch Tummel.

There are two to four trains daily from Rannoch Station north to Fort William (£11.10, one hour) and Mallaig, and south to Glasgow (£25.30, 2¾ hours).

Aberfeldy

POP 1895

Aberfeldy is the gateway to Breadalbane (the historic region surrounding Loch Tay), and a good base: adventure sports, angling, art and castles all feature on the menu here. It's a peaceful, pretty place on the banks of the Tay, but if it's moody lochs and glens that steal your heart, you may want to push a little further west.

The B846 road towards Fortingall crosses the Tay via the elegant Wade's Bridge, built in 1733 as part of the network of military roads designed to tame the Highlands.

◉ Sights & Activities

The Birks of Aberfeldy, made famous by a Robert Burns poem, offer a great short walk from the centre of town, following a vigorous burn upstream past several picturesque cascades.

Aberfeldy Distillery   DISTILLERY
(www.dewarsaberfeldydistillery.com; tour per person from £10.50; ☺10am-6pm Mon-Sat, noon-4pm Sun Apr-Oct, 10am-4pm Mon-Sat Nov-Mar; 🅿) At the eastern end of Aberfeldy, the home of the famous Dewar's blend offers a good 90-minute tour. After the usual overblown film, there's a museum section with audio guide, and an entertaining interactive blending session, as well as the tour of the whisky-making process. More expensive tours allow you to try venerable Aberfeldy single malts and others.

Castle Menzies   CASTLE
(www.castlemenzies.org; adult/child £6.50/3; ☺10.30am-5pm Mon-Sat, 2-5pm Sun Easter-Oct; 🅿) Castle Menzies is the 16th-century seat of the chief of clan Menzies (*ming*-iss), magnificently set against a forest backdrop. Inside it reeks of authenticity, despite extensive restoration work. Check out the fireplace in the dungeon-like kitchens, and the gaudy Great Hall with windows revealing a ribbon of lush, green countryside extending into wooded hills beyond the estate. It's about 1.5 miles west of Aberfeldy, off the B846.

Watermill   GALLERY
(www.aberfeldywatermill.com; Mill St; ☺10am-5pm Mon-Sat, 11am-5pm Sun Oct-Apr, to 5.30pm May-Sep) FREE You could while away several hours at this converted watermill, which houses a cafe (📞 01887-822896; mains £5-8; 🍴) 🍷, bookshop and art gallery exhibiting contemporary works of art. The shop has the biggest range of titles in the Highlands, with a great selection of books on Scottish history, landscape and wildlife.

Splash   RAFTING
(📞 01887-829706; www.rafting.co.uk; Dunkeld Rd; ☺9am-9pm; 🍴) Splash offers family friendly white-water rafting on the River Tay (adult/child £40/30, Wednesday to Sunday year-round) and more advanced adult trips on the Tummel (Grade III/IV, June to September) and the Orchy (Grade III/V, October to March). It also offers pulse-racing descents on river bugs (£60), canyoning (£55) and mountain-bike hire (per half-/full day £15/20).

Highland Safaris   TOURS

(📞 01887-820071;www.highlandsafaris.net;⊙ 9am-5pm, closed Mon Nov-Feb; 🚹) This outfit offers an ideal way to spot some wildlife or simply enjoy Perthshire's magnificent countryside. Standard trips include the 2½-hour Mountain Safari (adult/child £40/25), which includes whisky and shortbread in a mountain bothy; and the four-hour Safari Trek (adult/child £75/45), culminating in a walk in the mountains and a picnic.

You may spot wildlife such as golden eagles, osprey and red deer. There's also gold panning for kids (£5) and mountain-bike hire (£20 per day).

🛏 Sleeping & Eating

Tigh'n Eilean Guest House   B&B **££**

(📞 01887-820109; www.tighneilean.co.uk; Taybridge Dr; s/d from £48/80; P 🛜 ❄) Everything about this property screams comfort. It's a gorgeous place overlooking the Tay, with individually designed rooms – one has a jacuzzi, while another is set on its own in a cheery yellow summer house in the garden, giving you a bit of privacy. The garden itself is fabulous, with hammocks for lazing in, and the riverbank setting is delightful.

Balnearn Guest House   B&B **££**

(📞01887-820431; www.balnearnhouse.com; Crieff Rd; s/d/f from £55/75/120; P 🛜❄) Balnearn is a sedate and luxurious mansion near the centre of town, with space to spare. Most rooms have great natural light, and there's a particularly good family room downstairs. Breakfast has been lavishly praised by guests, and the attentive, cordial hosts are helpful while respecting your privacy.

⭐**Inn on the Tay**   PUB FOOD **££**

(📞 01887-840760; www.theinnonthetay.co.uk; Grandtully; mains £10-22; ⊙food served noon-2.45pm & 5-8.45pm; P 🛜🚹) This convivial pub, with its modern bistro-style dining room, makes a great pit stop on the way west to Loch Tay. The menu is simple – salads, burgers, fish and chips – but top quality, and there's an outdoor deck above the river, where you can enjoy a drink while watching rafters and canoeists descend the Grandtully rapids.

❶ Getting There & Away

Stagecoach (www.stagecoachbus.com) bus 23 runs from Perth to Aberfeldy (£4.10, 1½ hours, hourly Monday to Saturday, fewer on Sunday)

via Dunkeld; from Pitlochry (£3.80, 40 minutes), you'll need to change buses at Ballinluig. There's no bus link west to Killin.

Local buses run a circular route from Aberfeldy through Kenmore, Fortingall and back to Aberfeldy once each way on school days only.

Kenmore

The picturesque village of Kenmore lies at Loch Tay's eastern end, 6 miles west of Aberfeldy. Dominated by a striking archway leading to Taymouth Castle (not open to the public), it was built by the 3rd Earl of Breadalbane in 1760 to house his estate workers.

⭐**Scottish Crannog Centre**   MUSEUM

(📞 01887-830583; www.crannog.co.uk; tours adult/child £10/7; ⊙10am-5.30pm Apr-Oct; P 🚹) Less than a mile south of Kenmore on the banks of Loch Tay is the fascinating Scottish Crannog Centre, perched on stilts above the loch. Crannogs – effectively artificial islands – were a favoured form of defensive dwelling from the 3rd millennium BC onwards. This superb re-creation (based on studies of Oakbank crannog, one of 18 discovered in Loch Tay) offers a guided tour that includes an impressive demonstration of fire making and Iron Age crafts.

Taymouth Marina   SCOTTISH **££**

(📞01887-830450;http://taymouthmarinarestaurant.co.uk; mains £14-25; ⊙11am-9.30pm; P 🛜🚹) This appealing modern restaurant has a prime position on the banks of Loch Tay, with window tables making the most of the gorgeous views. Service is friendly and the menu runs from Scottish mussels and Cullen skink to seafood platters and sirloin steaks.

❶ Getting There & Away

Local buses run from Aberfeldy to Kenmore (£2.80, 15 minutes) twice a day on school days only.

Loch Tay & Ben Lawers

Loch Tay is the heart of the ancient region known as Breadalbane (from the Gaelic Bràghad Albainn, 'the heights of Scotland') – mighty Ben Lawers (1214m), looming over the loch, is the highest peak outside the Ben Nevis and Cairngorms regions. Much of the land to the north of Loch Tay falls within the Ben Lawers National Nature

Reserve (www.nnr.scot), known for its rare alpine flora.

The main access point for the ascent of Ben Lawers is the car park 1.5 miles north of the A827, on the minor road from Loch Tay to Bridge of Balgie. The climb is 6.5 miles and can take up to five hours (return): pack wet-weather gear, water and food, and a map and compass. There's also an easier nature trail here.

Loch Tay is famous for its fishing – salmon, trout and pike are all caught here. Fish 'n' Trips (p60) can kit you out for a day's fishing with boat, tackle and guide for £120 for two people, or rent you a boat for £60 a day.

The main road from Kenmore to Killin runs along the north shore of Loch Tay. The minor road along the south shore is narrow and twisting (unsuitable for large vehicles), but offers great views of the hills to the north.

Fortingall

Fortingall is one of the prettiest villages in Scotland, with 19th-century thatched cottages in a tranquil setting beside an ancient church with impressive wooden beams and a 7th-century monk's bell.

The famous Fortingall Yew Tree in the churchyard is estimated to be between 2000 and 3000 years old, one of the oldest living organisms in Europe. Its girth was measured at 16m in 1769, but since then souvenir hunters and natural decay have reduced it to a few gnarly but thriving boughs – in 2015 it produced berries for the first time on record. It was almost certainly around when the Romans camped in the meadows by the River Lyon in the 1st century AD; popular, if unlikely, tradition says that Pontius Pilate was born here.

Glen Lyon

The 'longest, loneliest and loveliest glen in Scotland', according to Sir Walter Scott, stretches for 32 unforgettable miles of rickety stone bridges, native woodland and heather-clad hills, becoming wilder and less populated as it snakes its way west. The ancients believed it to be a gateway to Faerieland, and even the most sceptical of visitors will be entranced by the valley's magic.

From Fortingall, a narrow road winds up the glen, while another steep and spectacular route from Loch Tay crosses the hills to meet it at Bridge of Balgie. The road continues west as far as the dam on Loch Lyon, passing a memorial to Robert Campbell (1808–94; a Canadian explorer and fur trader, born in the glen).

There are no villages in the glen – the majestic scenery is the main reason to be here – just a cluster of houses and a tearoom (☑ 01887-866221; Bridge of Balgie; snacks £3-6; ☉ 10am-5pm Apr-Oct; P 🛜 🏔) 🍴 at Bridge of Balgie.

There are several waymarked woodland walks beginning from a car park a short distance beyond Bridge of Balgie, and more challenging hill walks into the surrounding mountains (see www.walkhighlands.co.uk/perthshire). Cycling is an ideal way to explore the glen, and fit riders can complete a loop over to Glen Lochay via a potholed road (motor vehicles not permitted) leading south from the Loch Lyon dam.

★ Milton Eonan   B&B ££

(☑ 01887-866337; www.miltoneonan.com; Bridge of Balgie; per person £39-43; P 🛜 🏔) 🍴 Milton Eonan is a must for those seeking tranquillity. On a bubbling stream where a watermill once stood, it's a working rare-breed croft with a romantic one-bedroom cottage at the bottom of the garden (available as B&B or self-catering). It can sleep three at a pinch.

The helpful owners offer packed lunches and evening meals using local and home-grown produce. After crossing the bridge at Bridge of Balgie, you'll see Milton Eonan signposted to the right.

WEST HIGHLANDS

This region extends from the bleak blanket-bog of the Moor of Rannoch to the west coast beyond Glen Coe and Fort William, and includes the southern reaches of the Great Glen. The scenery is grand throughout, with high, rocky mountains rising above wild glens. Great expanses of moor alternate with lochs and patches of commercial forest. Fort William, at the inner end of Loch Linnhe, is the only sizeable town in the area.

Since 2007 the region has been promoted as Lochaber Geopark (www.lochaber geopark.org.uk), an area of outstanding geology and scenery.

Glen Coe

Scotland's most famous glen is also one of its grandest and – in bad weather – its grimmest. The approach to the glen from the east is guarded by the rocky pyramid of Buachaille Etive Mor – the Great Shepherd of Etive – and the lonely Kings House Hotel (closed for renovation until 2019). After the Battle of Culloden in 1745 it was used as a Hanoverian garrison – hence the name.

The A82 road leads over the Pass of Glencoe and into the narrow upper glen. The southern side is dominated by three massive, brooding spurs, known as the Three Sisters, while the northern side is enclosed by the continuous steep wall of the knife-edged Aonach Eagach ridge, a classic mountaineering challenge. The road threads its way past deep gorges and crashing waterfalls to the more pastoral lower reaches of the glen around Loch Achtriochtan and the only settlement here, Glencoe village.

◉ Sights

Glencoe Visitor Centre　　　　　MUSEUM
(NTS; ☑01855-811307; www.nts.org.uk; adult/child £6.50/5; ⊙9.30am-5.30pm Mar-Oct, 10am-4pm Nov-Feb; ℗) ✐ The centre provides comprehensive information on the geological, environmental and cultural history of Glen Coe via high-tech interactive and audiovisual displays, charts the history of mountaineering in the glen, and tells the story of the Glencoe Massacre in all its gory detail. It's 1.5 miles southeast of Glencoe village.

Glencoe Folk Museum　　　　　MUSEUM
(☑01855-811664; www.glencoemuseum.com; adult/child £3/free; ⊙10am-4.30pm Tue-Sat Easter-Oct) This small, thatched cottage houses a varied collection of farm equipment, tools of the woodworking, blacksmithing and slate-quarrying trades, and military memorabilia, including a riding boot that once belonged to Robert Campbell of Glenlyon, who took part in the Glencoe Massacre.

🏃 Activities

There are several short, pleasant walks around Glencoe Lochan, near the village. To get there, turn left off the minor road to the SYHA hostel, just beyond the bridge over the River Coe. There are three walks (40 minutes to an hour), all detailed on a signboard at the car park. The artificial lochan was created by Lord Strathcona in 1895 for his homesick Canadian wife, Isabella, and is surrounded by a North American–style forest.

A more strenuous hike, but well worth the effort on a fine day, is the climb to the Lost Valley, a magical mountain sanctuary still haunted by the ghosts of MacDonalds who died here while escaping the Glencoe Massacre in 1692 (only 2.5 miles round trip, but allow three hours). A rough path from the car park at Allt na Reigh (on the A82, 6 miles east of Glencoe village) bears left down to a footbridge over the river, then climbs up the wooded valley between Beinn Fhada and Gearr Aonach. The route leads steeply up through a maze of giant, jumbled, moss-coated boulders before emerging – quite unexpectedly – into a broad, open valley with a half-mile-long meadow as flat as a football pitch. Back in the days of clan warfare, the valley – invisible from below – was used for hiding stolen cattle; its Gaelic name, Coire Gabhail, means 'corrie of capture'.

The summits of Glen Coe's mountains are for experienced mountaineers only. The Cicerone guidebook *Ben Nevis & Glen Coe*, by Ronald Turnbull, available in most bookshops and outdoor equipment stores, details everything from short easy walks to challenging mountain climbs.

Steven Fallon Mountain Guides　　OUTDOORS
(☑0131-466 8152; www.stevenfallon.co.uk; per person from £69) If you lack the experience or confidence to tackle Scotland's challenging mountains alone, then you can join a guided hill walk or hire a private guide from this outfit.

Glencoe Mountain Resort　　　OUTDOORS
(☑01855-851226; www.glencoemountain.com; Kingshouse; chairlift adult/child £12/6; ⊙9am-4.30pm) Scotland's oldest ski area (eight lifts and 20 runs), established in the 1950s, is also one of the best, with grand views across the wild expanse of Rannoch Moor. The lower chairlift continues to operate in summer providing access to mountain-biking trails. In winter a lift pass costs £32 a day; equipment hire is £25.

The Lodge Café-Bar (open 9am to 8.30pm) at the base station has comfy sofas where you can soak up the view through floor-to-ceiling windows.

There are tent pitches (£6 per person), camping pods (£50 a night) and campervan hookups (£15 a night) beside the car park.

JOE CORNISH / GETTY IMAGES ©

1. Loch Awe (p102) 2. Caledonian Canal (p160) and Ben Nevis (p164) 3. Loch Ness (p130) 4. Schiehallion (p151)

GORDIE BROWN PHOTOGRAPHY / GETTY IMAGES ©

2

SIMON BUTTERWORTH / GETTY IMAGES ©

Lochs & Mountains

Since the 19th century, when the first tourists started to arrive, the Scottish Highlands have been famed for their wild nature and majestic scenery, and today the country's biggest draw remains its magnificent landscape. At almost every turn is a vista that will stop you in your tracks – keep your camera close at hand.

Ben Nevis

Scotland's highest peak is a perennial magnet for hillwalkers and ice climbers, but it's also one of the country's most photographed mountains. The classic viewpoints for the Ben include Corpach Basin at the entrance to the Caledonian Canal, and the B8004 road between Banavie and Gairlochy, from where you can see the precipitous north face.

Loch Ness

Scotland's largest loch by volume (it contains more water than all the lakes in England and Wales added together) may be most famous for its legendary monster, but it is also one of Scotland's most scenic. The minor road along the southeastern shore reveals a series of classic views.

Schiehallion

From the Gaelic *Sìdh Chailleann* (Fairy Hill of the Caledonians), this is one of Scotland's most distinctive mountains, its conical peak a prominent feature of views along Loch Tummel and Loch Rannoch. It's also one of the easier Munros, and a hike to the summit is rewarded with a superb panorama of hills and lochs.

4

Loch Awe

Loch Awe is a little off the beaten track, but is well worth seeking out for its gorgeous scenery. Dotted with islands and draped with native woodlands of oak, birch and alder, its northern end is dominated by the evocative ruins of Kilchurn Castle, with the pointed peaks of mighty Ben Cruachan reflected in its shifting waters.

🛏 Sleeping

There are several campsites, B&Bs and hotels in and around Glencoe village at the western end of the glen, plus camping at Glencoe Mountain Resort (p155) at the eastern end.

**Invercoe Caravan
& Camping Park** CAMPSITE **£**
(☎01855-811210; www.invercoe.co.uk; Invercoe; tent sites without car per person £11, campervan sites £25; 🐾) This place has great views of the surrounding mountains and is equipped with anti-midge machines. There's a covered cooking area for campers.

Glencoe Independent Hostel HOSTEL **£**
(☎01855-811906; www.glencoehostel.co.uk; farmhouse/bunkhouse dm £17/15; 🅿@🛜) This handily located hostel, just 1.5 miles southeast of Glencoe village, is set in an old farmhouse with six- and eight-bed dorms, and a bunkhouse with another 16 bed spaces in communal, alpine-style bunks. There's also a cute little wooden cabin that sleeps up to three (£80 per night).

Glencoe SYHA HOSTEL **£**
(☎08155-811219; www.syha.org.uk; dm/tr £19/83; 🅿@🛜🐾) Very popular with hikers, though the atmosphere can be a little institutional. It's a 1.5-mile walk from Glencoe village along the minor road on the northern side of the river.

Clachaig Inn HOTEL **££**
(☎01855-811252; www.clachaig.com; s/d £57/114; 🅿🛜) The Clachaig, 2 miles east of Glencoe village, has long been a favourite haunt of hill walkers and climbers. As well as comfortable en suite accommodation, there's a smart, modern lounge bar with snug booths and high refectory tables, mountaineering photos and bric-a-brac, and climbing magazines to leaf through.

Climbers usually head for the lively Boots Bar on the other side of the hotel – it has log fires, serves real ale and good pub grub (mains £10 to £21, served noon to 9pm), and has live Scottish music on Saturday nights.

Kings House Hotel HOTEL **£££**
(☎01855-851259; www.kingshousehotel.co.uk; Kingshouse; s/d £45/100; 🅿) This remote hotel claims to be one of Scotland's oldest licensed inns, dating from the 17th century. It has long been a favourite meeting place for climbers, skiers and walkers (it's on the West Highland Way). It closed in 2017 for a major redevelopment, which includes a hikers' bunkhouse, and is scheduled to reopen in January 2019.

🍴 Eating

⭐ **Glencoe Café** CAFE **£**
(☎01855-811168; www.glencoecafe.co.uk; Glencoe village; mains £4-8; ⏱10am-4pm, to 5pm May-Sep, closed Nov; 🅿🛜) This friendly cafe is the social hub of Glencoe village, serving breakfast fry-ups till 11.30am (including vegetarian versions), light lunches based on local produce (think Cullen skink, smoked salmon quiche, venison burgers), and the best cappuccino in the glen.

Crafts & Things CAFE **£**
(☎01855-811325; www.craftsandthings.co.uk; Annat; mains £4-8; ⏱9.30am-5pm Mon-Thu, to 5.30pm Fri-Sun Apr-Oct, shorter hours Nov-Mar; 🅿🛜♿) Just off the main road between Glencoe village and Ballachulish, the tearoom in this craft shop is a good spot for a lunch of homemade lentil soup with crusty rolls, ciabatta sandwiches, or just coffee and carrot cake. There are tables outdoors and a box of toys to keep little ones occupied.

ℹ Getting There & Away

Scottish Citylink (www.citylink.co.uk) buses run between Fort William and Glencoe (£8.50, 30 minutes, four to eight daily) and from Glencoe to Glasgow (£22.70, 2¾ hours, four to eight daily). Buses stop at Glencoe village, Glencoe Visitor Centre and Glencoe Mountain Resort.

Stagecoach (www.stagecoachbus.com) bus 44 links Glencoe village with Fort William (£4.10, 40 minutes, hourly Monday to Saturday, three on Sunday) and Kinlochleven (£2.20, 15 minutes).

Kinlochleven

POP 900

Kinlochleven is hemmed in by high mountains at the head of beautiful Loch Leven, about 7 miles east of Glencoe village. The aluminium smelter that led to the town's development in the early 20th century has long since closed, and the opening of the Ballachulish Bridge in the 1970s allowed the main road to bypass it completely. Decline was halted by the opening of the West Highland Way, which now brings a steady stream of hikers through the village.

The final section of the West Highland Way stretches for 14 miles from Kinlochleven to Fort William. The village is also the starting point for easier walks up the glen of the River Leven, through pleasant woods to the Grey Mare's Tail waterfall, and harder mountain hikes into the Mamores.

🏃 Activities

Via Ferrata
ADVENTURE SPORTS

(☏ 01397-747111; http://verticaldescents.com/via-ferrata/via-ferrata.html; Unit 3, Kinlochleven Business Park; per person/family £65/240) Scotland's first via ferrata – a 500m climbing route equipped with steel ladders, cables and bridges – snakes through the crags around the Grey Mare's Tail waterfall, allowing non-climbers to experience the thrill of climbing (you'll need a head for heights, though!).

Ice Factor
ADVENTURE SPORTS

(☏ 01855-831100; www.ice-factor.co.uk; Leven Rd; ⏰ 9am-10pm Tue & Thu, to 6pm Mon, Wed & Fri-Sun; 🚻) If you fancy trying your hand at ice-climbing, even in the middle of summer, the world's biggest indoor ice-climbing wall offers a one-hour beginner's 'taster' session for £30. You'll also find a rock-climbing wall, an aerial adventure course, a soft-play area for kids, and a cafe (open 9am to 5pm) and bar-bistro (food served 6pm to 9pm).

🛌 Sleeping & Eating

Blackwater Hostel
& Campsite
HOSTEL, CAMPSITE £

(☏ 01855-831253; www.blackwaterhostel.co.uk; Lab Rd; tr/q from £63/84, tent sites per person £10, pods from £45; 🅿 🛜) This 39-bed hostel (preference given to groups – individual travellers should check availability in advance) has spotless dorms with en suite bathrooms and TV, and a well-sheltered campsite with the option of wooden 'glamping' pods for two or four persons.

★ Lochleven Seafood Cafe
SEAFOOD ££

(☏ 01855-821048; www.lochlevenseafoodcafe.co.uk; meals £11-23, whole lobster £40; ⏰ meals noon-3pm & 6-9pm, coffee & cake 10am-noon & 3-5pm mid-Mar–Oct; 🅿🚻) This outstanding place serves superb shellfish freshly plucked from live tanks – oysters, razor clams, scallops, lobster and crab – plus a daily fish special and some non-seafood dishes. For warm days, there's an outdoor terrace with a view across the loch to the Pap of Glencoe. The cafe is 5 miles west of Kinlochleven, on the north shore of the loch.

ℹ️ Getting There & Away

Stagecoach bus 44 runs from Fort William to Kinlochleven (£5.30, one hour, hourly Monday to Saturday, three on Sunday) via Ballachulish and Glencoe village.

Fort William

POP 9910

Basking on Loch Linnhe's shores amid magnificent mountain scenery, Fort William has one of the most enviable settings in all of Scotland. If it weren't for the busy dual carriageway crammed between the less-than-attractive town centre and the loch, and one of the highest rainfall records in the country, it would be almost idyllic. Even so, the Fort has carved out a reputation as the 'Outdoor Capital of the UK' (www.outdoorcapital.co.uk), and easy access by rail and bus makes it a good base for exploring the surrounding mountains and glens.

Magical Glen Nevis begins near the northern end of the town and wraps itself around the southern flanks of Ben Nevis (1345m) – Britain's highest mountain and a magnet for hikers and climbers. The glen is also popular with movie makers – parts of *Braveheart* (1995), *Pokemon: Detective Pikachu* (2018), the Harry Potter movies and the *Outlander* TV series were filmed here.

👁️ Sights

★ Jacobite Steam Train
HERITAGE RAILWAY

(☏ 0844 850 4685; www.westcoastrailways.co.uk; day return adult/child from £35/20; ⏰ daily mid-Jun–Aug, Mon-Fri mid-May–mid-Jun, Sep & Oct) The Jacobite Steam Train, hauled by a former LNER K1 or LMS Class 5MT locomotive, travels the scenic two-hour run between Fort William and Mallaig. Classed as one of the great railway journeys of the world, the route crosses the historic Glenfinnan Viaduct, made famous by the Harry Potter films – the Jacobite's owners supplied steam locomotive and rolling stock used in the film.

Trains depart from Fort William train station in the morning and return from Mallaig in the afternoon. There's a brief stop at Glenfinnan station, and you get 1½ hours in Mallaig.

West Highland Museum
MUSEUM

(☏ 01397-702169; www.westhighlandmuseum.org.uk; Cameron Sq; ⏰ 10am-5pm Mon-Sat May-Sep, to 4pm Oct-Apr, 11am-3pm Sun Jul & Aug)

FREE This small but fascinating museum is packed with all manner of Highland memorabilia. Look out for the secret portrait of Bonnie Prince Charlie – after the Jacobite rebellions, all things Highland were banned, including pictures of the exiled leader, and this tiny painting looks like nothing more than a smear of paint until viewed in a cylindrical mirror, which reflects a credible likeness of the prince.

Activities

3 Wise Monkeys Climbing   CLIMBING
(☏01397-600200; www.threewisemonkeysclimbing. com; Fassifern Rd; adult/child £9/6; ⊙10am-10pm Mon-Fri, to 8pm Sat & Sun; ☝) When the weather on the mountains keeps you off the crags, you can keep your fingers in trim at this popular indoor climbing wall. There's a cafe too, and you can book a sports massage. Hire of rock shoes and harness is £5, and instruction is available.

Crannog Cruises   WILDLIFE
(☏01397-700714; www.crannog.net/cruises; adult/child £15/7.50; ⊙11am, 1pm & 3pm Easter-Oct) Operates 1½-hour wildlife cruises on Loch Linnhe, visiting a seal colony and a salmon farm.

 Festivals & Events

UCI Mountain Bike World Cup   SPORTS
(www.fortwilliamworldcup.co.uk) In June, Fort William pulls in crowds of more than 18,000 spectators for this World Cup downhill mountain-biking event. The gruelling downhill course is at nearby Nevis Range ski area.

Sleeping

It's best to book well ahead in summer, especially for hostels.

Calluna   APARTMENT £
(☏01397-700451; www.fortwilliamholiday.co.uk; Heathercroft, Connochie Rd; dm/tw £20/44, 6-person apt per 3 nights £124; P @) Run by well-known mountain guide Alan Kimber and wife Sue, the Calluna offers self-catering apartments geared to groups of hikers and climbers, but also takes individual travellers prepared to share. There's a fully equipped kitchen and an excellent drying room for your soggy hiking gear.

Fort William Backpackers   HOSTEL £
(☏01397-700711; www.scotlands-top-hostels.com; Alma Rd; dm/tw £21/50; P @) A 10-minute walk from the bus and train stations, this lively and welcoming hostel is set in a grand

---

THE CALEDONIAN CANAL

Running for 59 miles from Corpach, near Fort William, to Inverness via lochs Lochy, Oich and Ness, the Caledonian Canal (www.scottishcanals.co.uk) links the east and west coasts of Scotland, avoiding the long and dangerous sea passage around Cape Wrath and through the turbulent Pentland Firth. Designed by Thomas Telford and completed in 1822 at a cost of £900,000 – a staggering sum then – the canal took 20 years to build, including 29 locks, four aqueducts and 10 bridges.

Conceived as a project to ease unemployment and bring prosperity to the Highlands in the aftermath of the Jacobite rebellions and the Clearances, the canal proved to be a commercial failure – the locks were too small for the new breed of steamships that came into use soon after its completion. But it proved to be a success in terms of tourism, especially after it was popularised by Queen Victoria's cruise along the canal in 1873. Today the canal is used mainly by yachts and pleasure cruisers, though since 2010 it has also been used to transport timber from west-coast forestry plantations to Inverness.

Much of the Great Glen Way follows the line of the canal; it can be followed on foot, by mountain bike or on horseback, and 80% of the route has even been done on mobility scooters. An easy half-day hike or bike ride is to follow the canal towpath from Corpach to Gairlochy (10 miles), which takes you past the impressive flight of eight locks known as Neptune's Staircase, and through beautiful countryside with grand views to the north face of Ben Nevis.

If you're cycling the length of the Great Glen Way, you can hire mountain bikes from Nevis Cycles (p162) in Fort William and drop them off at Ticket to Ride (p122) in Inverness, or vice versa.

The glen can also be explored by water, by following the Great Glen Canoe Trail (www.greatglencanoetrail.info).

Victorian villa, perched on a hillside with great views over Loch Linnhe.

6 Caberfeidh
B&B ££

(☑ 01397-703756; www.6caberfeidh.com; 6 Caberfeidh, Fassifern Rd; d/f £78/108; 🐾) Friendly owners and comfortable accommodation make a great combination; add a good central location and you're all set. Choose from one of two family rooms (one double and one single bed) or a romantic double with four-poster. Freshly prepared breakfasts include scrambled eggs with smoked salmon.

St Andrew's Guest House
B&B ££

(☑ 01397-703038; www.standrewsguesthouse. co.uk; Fassifern Rd; s/d £75/85; ⊙ Mar-Oct; P 🐾) Set in a lovely 19th-century building that was once a rectory and choir school, St Andrew's retains period features such as carved masonry, wood panelling and stained-glass windows. It has six spacious bedrooms; those at the front have stunning views.

★ Grange
B&B £££

(☑ 01397-705516; www.grangefortwilliam.com; Grange Rd; d from £180; P 🐾) An exceptional 19th-century villa set in its own landscaped grounds, the Grange is crammed with antiques and warmed by log fires, and has two luxury suites fitted with leather sofas, handcrafted furniture and rolltop baths, one situated in a charming self-contained cottage in the sprawling gardens, all with a view over Loch Linnhe. No children.

Lime Tree
HOTEL £££

(☑ 01397-701806; www.limetreefortwilliam.co.uk; Achintore Rd; r from £140; P 🐾🍽) Much more interesting than your average guesthouse, this former Victorian manse overlooking Loch Linnhe is an 'art gallery with rooms', decorated throughout with the artist-owner's atmospheric Highland landscapes. Foodies rave about the restaurant, and the gallery space – a triumph of sensitive design – stages everything from serious exhibitions (works by David Hockney and Andy Goldsworthy have appeared) to folk concerts.

🍴 Eating & Drinking

DeliCraft
DELI £

(☑ 01397-698100; www.delicraft.co.uk; 61 High St; mains £3-10; ⊙ 8am-6.30pm Mon-Sat, 10am-4pm Sun; 🥢) This deli serves great coffee, excellent pizza and delicious sandwiches, including deli classics such as pastrami on rye, to eat in or take away, as well as a range of Scottish cheeses, craft beers and gins.

★ Lime Tree
SCOTTISH ££

(☑ 01397-701806; www.limetreefortwilliam.co.uk; Achintore Rd; mains £16-20; ⊙ 6.30-9.30pm; P 🐾) 🌿 Fort William is not over-endowed with great places to eat, but the restaurant at this small hotel and art gallery has put the UK's Outdoor Capital on the gastronomic map. The chef turns out delicious dishes built around fresh Scottish produce, ranging from Loch Fyne oysters to Loch Awe trout and Ardnamurchan venison.

★ Crannog Seafood Restaurant
SEAFOOD ££

(☑ 01397-705589; www.crannog.net; Town Pier; mains £15-24; ⊙ noon-2.30pm & 6-9pm) 🌿 The Crannog wins the prize for the best location in town – perched on the Town Pier, giving window-table diners an uninterrupted view down Loch Linnhe. Informal and unfussy, it specialises in fresh local fish – there are three or four daily fish specials plus the main menu – though there are lamb, venison and vegetarian dishes, too. Two-/three-course lunch costs £16/19.

Geographer
INTERNATIONAL ££

(☑ 01397-705011; www.geographerrestaurant. co.uk; 88 High St; mains £10-15; ⊙ noon-2pm & 5-9.30pm; 🐾🥢🔊) Bright and modern in atmosphere, this restaurant takes its inspiration from the owner's travels with a menu that mixes standards, such as burgers and fish and chips, with a selection of dishes from around the globe, including Middle Eastern falafel and flatbread, Mexican vegetable chilli and Burmese lamb curry. There's also a selection of Scottish gins and bottled craft beers.

Grog & Gruel
PUB

(☑ 01397-705078; www.grogandgruel.co.uk; 66 High St; ⊙ noon-midnight; 🐾) The Grog & Gruel is a traditional-style, wood-panelled pub with an excellent range of cask ales from regional Scottish and English microbreweries.

🛍 Shopping

★ Highland Bookshop
BOOKS

(www.highlandbookshop.com; 60 High St; ⊙ 9.30am-6pm Mon-Sat, 11am-4pm Sun) As well as a good selection of fiction and children's books, this shop stocks a superb range of outdoor-related books and maps covering climbing, walking, cycling, canoeing and other subjects. The upstairs lounge offers coffee and tea, and hosts regular literary events.

DON'T MISS

COMMANDO MEMORIAL

Near Spean Bridge, at the junction of the B8004 and A82, 2.5 miles east of Gairlochy, stands the Commando Memorial, which commemorates the WWII special forces soldiers who trained in this area.

The Commandos were an elite unit of the British armed forces, formed in 1940 to carry out raids behind enemy lines in German-occupied Europe. In 1942, a centre was set up at Achnacarry, 6 miles west of Spean Bridge, where Commando units were trained in secrecy. This memorial was erected in 1952, in a glorious setting with superb views of Ben Nevis and its neighbouring mountains.

ⓘ Information

Fort William Tourist Office (☑ 01397-701801; www.visithighlands.com; 15 High St; internet per 20min £1; ⊙ 9am-5pm Mon-Sat, 10am-3pm Sun, longer hours Jun-Aug; ⏏)

ⓘ Getting There & Away

BUS

Scottish Citylink (www.citylink.co.uk) buses link Fort William with other major towns and cities.

Edinburgh £37, 5¼ hours, four daily with a change at Glasgow; via Glencoe and Crianlarich

Glasgow £25, three hours, four daily

Inverness £12.20, two hours, six daily

Oban £9.40, 1½ hours, two daily

Portree £32.20, three hours, three daily

Shiel Buses (☑ 01397-700700; www.shielbuses.co.uk) service 500 runs to Mallaig (£6.10, 1½ hours, four daily Monday to Friday, plus one daily Saturday and Sunday) via Glenfinnan and Arisaig (£5.60, one hour).

TRAIN

The spectacular West Highland line runs from Glasgow to Mallaig via Fort William. The overnight **Caledonian Sleeper** (www.sleeper.scot) service connects Fort William and London Euston (from £135 sharing a twin-berth cabin, 13 hours).

There's no direct rail connection between Oban and Fort William – you have to change at Crianlarich, so it's faster to use the bus.

Edinburgh £40, five hours; change at Glasgow's Queen St station, three daily, two on Sunday

Glasgow £30, 3¾ hours, three daily, two on Sunday

Mallaig £13, 1½ hours, four daily, three on Sunday

ⓘ Getting Around

BICYCLE

Nevis Cycles (☑ 01397-705555; www.neviscycles.com; cnr Montrose Ave & Locheil Rd, Inverlochy; per day from £25; ⊙ 9am-5.30pm) Located a half-mile northeast of the town centre, this place rents everything from hybrid bikes and mountain bikes to full-suspension downhill racers. Bikes can be hired here and dropped off in Inverness.

BUS

A Zone 2 Dayrider ticket (£9.10) gives unlimited travel for one day on Stagecoach bus services in the Fort William area, as far as Glencoe and Fort Augustus. Buy from the bus driver.

CAR

Fort William is 146 miles from Edinburgh, 104 miles from Glasgow and 66 miles from Inverness. The tourist office (p162) has listings of car-hire companies.

Easydrive Car Hire (☑ 01397-701616; www.easydrivescotland.co.uk; North Rd; ⊙ 8am-5.30pm Mon-Fri, to 5pm Sat, to 4pm Sun) Hires out small cars from £40/175 a day/week, including tax and unlimited mileage, but not Collision Damage Waiver (CDW).

TAXI

There's a taxi rank on the corner of High St and the Parade.

Around Fort William

Glen Nevis

Scenic Glen Nevis – used as a filming location for *Braveheart* and the Harry Potter movies – lies just an hour's walk from Fort William town centre. The **Glen Nevis Visitor Centre** (☑ 01397-705922; www.bennevisweather.co.uk; ⊙ 8.30am-6pm Jul & Aug, 9am-5pm Apr-Jun, Sep & Oct, 9am-3pm Nov-Mar) is situated 1.5 miles up the glen, and provides information on hiking, weather forecasts, and specific advice on climbing Ben Nevis.

From the car park at the far end of the road along Glen Nevis, there is an excellent 1.5-mile walk through the spectacular Nevis Gorge to Steall Meadows, a verdant valley dominated by a 100m-high bridal-veil waterfall. You can reach the foot of the falls by crossing the river on a wobbly, three-cable wire bridge – one cable for your feet and one for each hand – which is a real test of balance!

🛏 Sleeping & Eating

Glen Nevis SYHA HOSTEL £
(SYHA; ☎ 01397-702336; www.syha.org.uk; dm £24; P @ 🛜) Benefitting from a complete overhaul in early 2018, this hostel is 3 miles from Fort William, right beside one of the starting points for the tourist track up Ben Nevis. Cooked breakfasts (£7) and packed lunches (£6) are available.

Glen Nevis Caravan & Camping Park CAMPSITE £
(☎ 01397-702191; www.glen-nevis.co.uk; tent sites per person £9.50, campervan £26; ⊙ mid-Mar–early Nov; 🛜) This big, well-equipped site is a popular base camp for Ben Nevis and the surrounding mountains. The site is 2.5 miles from Fort William, along the Glen Nevis road.

Achintee Farm B&B, HOSTEL ££
(☎ 01397-702240; www.achinteefarm.com; Achintee; B&B d £110, hostel tw/tr £54/81; ⊙ B&B May-Sep, hostel year-round; P 🛜) This attractive farmhouse offers excellent B&B accommodation and also has a small hostel attached. It's at the start of the path up Ben Nevis.

★ Ben Nevis Inn SCOTTISH ££
(☎ 01397-701227; www.ben-nevis-inn.co.uk; Achintee; mains £10-15; ⊙ noon-11pm Apr-Oct, Thu-Sun Dec-Mar, closed Nov; P) This great barn of a pub serves real ale and tasty bar meals (till 9pm), and has a comfy 24-bed bunkhouse downstairs (beds £17 per person). It's at the start of the path from Achintee up Ben Nevis, and only a mile from the end of the West Highland Way.

ⓘ Getting There & Away

Bus 41 runs from Fort William bus station to the Glen Nevis SYHA (p163) hostel (£2.30, 15 or 20 minutes, two daily year-round, five daily Monday to Saturday June to September). Check at the tourist office for the latest timetable, which is liable to alteration.

Nevis Range

Six miles to the north of Fort William lies Nevis Range ski area, where a gondola gives access to the upper part of Aonach Mor mountain. The facility operates year-round, allowing visitors to access mountain paths and downhill mountain-biking trails outside of the ski season.

🏃 Activities

Nevis Range Downhill & Witch's Trails MOUNTAIN BIKING
(☎ 01397-705825; www.nevisrange.co.uk/bike; single/multitrip ticket £18.50/34.50; ⊙ downhill course 10.15am-3.45pm Apr-Oct, forest trails 24hr year-round) Nevis Range ski area has a world championship downhill mountain-bike trail – for experienced riders only; bikes are carried up on the gondola cabin. There's also a 4-mile XC red trail that begins at the ski area's Snowgoose restaurant, and the Witch's Trails – 25 miles of waymarked forest road and singletrack in the nearby forest, including a 5-mile world championship loop.

A multitrip ticket gives unlimited uplift for a day; full-suspension bike hire costs from £65 per day.

Nevis Range OUTDOORS
(☎ 01397-705825; www.nevisrange.co.uk; day ticket per adult/child £21/12; ⊙ 10am-6pm Jul & Aug, to 5pm Apr-Jun, Sep & Oct, 9.30am-dusk Nov-Mar) The Nevis Range ski area, 6 miles north of Fort William, spreads across the northern slopes of Aonach Mor (1221m). The gondola that gives access to the bottom of the ski area at 655m operates year-round. At the top there's a restaurant and a couple of hiking trails through nearby Leanachan Forest, as well as excellent mountain-biking trails.

The gondola takes 15 minutes each way; tickets are valid for multiple trips.

During the ski season a one-day lift pass costs £34.50/22.50 per adult/child; a one-day package, including equipment hire, lift pass and two hours' instruction, costs £78.50.

NEPTUNE'S STAIRCASE

Three miles north of Fort William, at Banavie, is **Neptune's Staircase**, an impressive flight of eight locks that allows boats to climb 20m to the main reach of the **Caledonian Canal**. The B8004 road runs along the west side of the canal to Gairlochy at the south end of Loch Lochy, offering superb views of Ben Nevis; the **canal towpath** on the east side makes a great walk or bike ride (6.5 miles).

CLIMBING BEN NEVIS

As the highest peak in the British Isles, Ben Nevis (1345m) attracts many would-be ascensionists who would not normally think of climbing a Scottish mountain – a staggering (often literally) 100,000 people reach the summit each year.

Although anyone who is reasonably fit should have no problem climbing Ben Nevis on a fine summer's day, an ascent should not be undertaken lightly; every year people have to be rescued from the mountain. You will need proper walking boots (the path is rough and stony, and there may be snow on the summit), warm clothing, waterproofs, a map and compass, and plenty of food and water. And don't forget to check the weather forecast (www.bennevisweather.co.uk).

Here are a few facts to mull over before you go racing up the tourist track: the summit plateau is bounded by 700m-high cliffs and has a sub-Arctic climate; at the summit it can snow on any day of the year; the summit is wrapped in cloud nine days out of 10; in thick cloud, visibility at the summit can be 10m or less; and in such conditions the only safe way off the mountain requires careful use of a map and compass to avoid walking over those 700m cliffs.

The tourist track (the easiest route to the top) was originally called the Pony Track. It was built in the 19th century for the pack ponies that carried supplies to a meteorological observatory on the summit (now in ruins), which was in use continuously from 1883 to 1904.

There are three possible starting points for the tourist track ascent – Achintee Farm (p163); the footbridge at Glen Nevis SYHA (p163) hostel; and, if you have a car, the car park at Glen Nevis Visitor Centre (p162). The path climbs gradually to the shoulder at Lochan Meall an t-Suidhe (known as the Halfway Lochan), then zigzags steeply up beside the Red Burn to the summit plateau. The highest point is marked by a trig point on top of a huge cairn beside the ruins of the old observatory; the plateau is scattered with countless smaller cairns, stones arranged in the shape of people's names and, sadly, a fair bit of litter.

The total distance to the summit and back is 8 miles; allow at least four or five hours to reach the top, and another 2½ to three hours for the descent. Afterwards, as you celebrate in the pub with a pint, consider the fact that the record time for the annual Ben Nevis Hill Race is just under 1½ hours – up and down. Then have another pint.

❶ Getting There & Away

Bus 41 runs from Fort William bus station to Nevis Range (£2.30, 25 minutes, three daily Monday to Saturday, limited service October to April). Check at Fort William's tourist office (p162) for the latest timetable, which is liable to alteration.

Ardnamurchan

Ten miles south of Fort William, a car ferry makes the short crossing to Corran Ferry. The drive from here to Ardnamurchan Point (www.ardnamurchan.com), the most westerly point on the British mainland, is one of the most beautiful in the western Highlands, especially in late spring and early summer when much of the narrow, twisting road is lined with the bright pink and purple blooms of rhododendrons.

The road clings to the northern shore of Loch Sunart, going through the pretty villages of Strontian – which gave its name to the element strontium, first discovered in ore from nearby lead mines in 1790 – and Salen.

The mostly single-track road from Salen to Ardnamurchan Point is only 25 miles long, but it'll take you 1½ hours each way. It's a dipping, twisting, low-speed roller coaster of a ride through sun-dappled native woodlands draped with lichen and fern. Just when you're getting used to the views of Morvern and Mull to the south, it makes a quick detour to the north for a panorama over the islands of Rum and Eigg.

◉ Sights

Ardnamurchan Lighthouse LIGHTHOUSE
(☑01972-510210; www.ardnamurchanlighthouse.com; Ardnamurchan Point; visitor centre adult/child £3/2, guided tour £6/4; ⏰10am-5pm Apr-

Oct; (P)(⊕)) The final 6 miles of road from Kilchoan to Ardnamurchan Point end at this 36m-high, grey granite tower, built in 1849 by the 'Lighthouse Stevensons' – family of Robert Louis – on the westernmost point of the British mainland. There's a tearoom, and the visitor centre will tell you more than you'll ever need to know about lighthouses, with lots of hands-on stuff for kids.

The guided tour (every half-hour 11am to 4pm) includes a trip to the top of the lighthouse. But the main attraction here is the expansive view over the ocean – this is a superb sunset viewpoint, provided you don't mind driving back in the dark.

Ardnamurchan Natural History & Visitor Centre
MUSEUM

(☑ 01972-500209; www.ardnamurchannatural historycentre.com; Glenmore; ⊗ 8.30am-5pm Sun-Fri; (⊕)) **FREE** This fascinating centre – midway between Salen and Kilchoan – was originally devised by a wildlife photographer and tries to bring you face to face with the flora and fauna of the Ardnamurchan peninsula. The Living Building exhibit is designed to attract local wildlife, with a mammal den that is occasionally occupied by hedgehogs or pine martens, an owl nest-box, a mouse nest and a pond.

If the beasties are not in residence, you can watch recorded video footage of the animals. There's also seasonal live CCTV coverage of local wildlife, ranging from nesting herons to a golden eagle feeding site.

Ardnamurchan Distillery
DISTILLERY

(Map p93; ☑ 01972-500285; www.adelphi distillery.com; Glenbeg; tours per person from £7; ⊗ 10am-6pm Mon-Fri, 11am-5pm Sun Easter-Oct, phone for winter hours) This whisky distillery went into production in 2014, complete with visitor centre and tasting room. Although you will be able to see the whisky-making process, the finished product will be matured in casks until 2022 before being bottled as a single malt.

🛏 Sleeping & Eating

Ardnamurchan Campsite
CAMPSITE £

(☑ 01972-510766; www.ardnamurchanstudycentre. co.uk; Kilchoan; sites per adult/child £9/4; ⊗ May-Sep; (🛜)) Basic but beautifully situated campsite, with the chance of seeing otters from your tent. It's along the Ormsaig road, 2 miles west of Kilchoan village.

★ Ard Daraich
COTTAGE ££

(☑ 01855-841384; www.ardgour-selfcatering. co.uk; Sallachan, Ardgour; studio per week from £645; (P)(🛜)(🐾)) 🍴 About 3 miles southwest of Corran Ferry, this handsome West Highland house once belonged to florist Constance Spry (who arranged flowers for Queen Elizabeth II's coronation), and is set in beautiful gardens filled with rhododendrons, azaleas and heathers; there's a chance of seeing otters and pine martens nearby. Let as a two-person garden studio, and five-person cottage.

Salen Hotel
INN ££

(☑ 01967-431661; www.salenhotel.co.uk; Salen; r £100-120; (P)(🛜)(🐾)) A traditional Highland inn with views over Loch Sunart, the Salen Hotel has three rooms in the pub (two with sea views) and another three rooms (all en suite) in a modern chalet out the back. The cosy lounge has a roaring fire and comfy sofa, and the bar meals, including seafood, venison and other game dishes, are very good.

Lochview Tearoom
CAFE £

(Ardnamurchan Natural History & Visitor Centre, Glenmore; mains £5-8; ⊗ 8.30am-4.30pm Sun-Fri; (P)(🛜)(⊕)) The cafe at the wildlife centre (p165) serves coffee, home-baked goods and lunch dishes, including fresh salads and homemade soup.

ℹ Information

Kilchoan Village Hall (☑ 01972-510222; Pier Rd, Kilchoan; ⊗ 9am-5pm Mon-Sat Easter-Nov), on the road to the pier, has information and leaflets on walking and wildlife.

ℹ Getting There & Away

Shiel Buses (www.shielbuses.co.uk) service 506 runs from Fort William to Acharacle, Salen and Kilchoan (£9.90, 2½ hours, one daily Monday to Saturday) via **Corran Ferry** (car £8.20, bicycle & foot passenger free; ⊗ every 30min). There's a car ferry between Kilchoan and Tobermory on the Isle of Mull.

Road to the Isles

The 46-mile A830 road from Fort William to Mallaig is traditionally known as the Road to the Isles, as it leads to the jumping-off point for ferries to the Small Isles and Skye, itself a stepping stone to the Outer Hebrides. This is a region steeped in Jacobite history, having witnessed both the beginning and the end of Bonnie Prince Charlie's doomed attempt to regain the British throne in 1745–46.

The final section of this scenic route, between Arisaig and Mallaig, has been upgraded to a fast straight road. Unless you're in a hurry, opt instead for the more scenic old road (signposted Alternative Coastal Route).

Between the A830 and the A87 far to the north lie Knoydart and Glenelg – Scotland's 'Empty Quarter'.

❶ Getting There & Around

Shiel Buses service 500 runs from Fort William to Mallaig (£6.10, 1½ hours, four daily Monday to Friday, one on Saturday and Sunday) via Glenfinnan (30 minutes), Arisaig (one hour) and Morar (1¼ hours).

The Fort William–Mallaig railway line has four trains a day (three on Sunday), with stops at many points along the way, including Corpach, Glenfinnan, Lochailort, Arisaig and Morar.

Glenfinnan

POP 100

Glenfinnan is hallowed ground for fans of Bonnie Prince Charlie; the monument here marks where he raised his Highland army. It is also a place of pilgrimage for steam train enthusiasts and Harry Potter fans – the famous railway viaduct features in the Potter films, and is regularly traversed by the Jacobite Steam Train (p159).

◉ Sights & Activities

Glenfinnan Monument MONUMENT

FREE This tall column, topped by a statue of a kilted Highlander, was erected in 1815 on the spot where Bonnie Prince Charlie first raised his standard and rallied the Jacobite clans on 19 August 1745, marking the start of his ill-fated campaign, which would end in disaster at Culloden 14 months later. The setting, at the north end of Loch Shiel, is hauntingly beautiful.

Glenfinnan Visitor Centre MUSEUM

(NTS; www.nts.org.uk; adult/child £3.50/2.50; ⊙9am-7pm Jul & Aug, to 6pm Mar-Jun, Sep & Oct, 10am-4pm Nov-Feb; P) This centre recounts the story of the '45, as the Jacobite rebellion of 1745 is known, when Bonnie Prince Charlie's loyal clansmen marched and fought their way from Glenfinnan south via Edinburgh to Derby, then back north to final defeat at Culloden.

Glenfinnan Station Museum MUSEUM

(www.glenfinnanstationmuseum.co.uk; admission by donation, suggested £1; ⊙9am-5pm Easter-Oct; P) This fascinating little museum records the epic tale of building the West Highland railway line. The famous 21-arch Glenfinnan viaduct, just east of the station, was built in 1901, and featured in several Harry Potter movies. A pleasant walk of around 0.75 miles east from the station (signposted) leads to a viewpoint for the viaduct and for Loch Shiel.

Loch Shiel Cruises CRUISE

(☑07801 537617; www.highlandcruises.co.uk; per person £12-22; ⊙Apr-Sep) Boat trips along Loch Shiel, with the opportunity of spotting golden eagles and other wildlife. There are one- to 2½-hour cruises on Tuesday and Thursday. On Wednesday the boat goes the full length of the loch to Acharacle (one way/return £20/30), calling at Polloch and Dalilea, allowing for walks and bike rides using the forestry track on the eastern shore.

The boat departs from a jetty near Glenfinnan House Hotel.

🛏 Sleeping & Eating

Sleeping Car Bunkhouse HOSTEL £

(☑01397-722295; www.glenfinnanstationmuseum. co.uk; Glenfinnan Station; per person £15, entire coach £130; ⊙May-Oct; P) Two converted railway carriages at Glenfinnan Station house this unusual 10-berth bunkhouse and the atmospheric **Dining Car Tearoom** (☑01397-722300; mains £6-10; ⊙9am-4.30pm; P).

★**Prince's House Hotel** INN £££

(☑01397-722246; www.glenfinnan.co.uk; s/d from £95/160; P) A delightful old coaching inn dating from 1658, the Prince's House is a great place to pamper yourself – ask for the spacious, tartan-draped Stuart Room (£225), complete with four-poster bed, if you want to stay in the oldest part of the hotel. The relaxed but well-regarded restaurant specialises in Scottish produce (four-course dinner £46).

There's no documented evidence that Bonnie Prince Charlie actually stayed here in 1745, but it was the only sizeable house in Glenfinnan at that time, so...

Arisaig & Morar

The 5 miles of coast between the tiny villages of Arisaig and Morar is a fretwork of rocky islets, inlets and gorgeous silver-sand beaches backed by dunes and machair, with stunning sunset views across the sea to the silhouetted peaks of Eigg and Rum. The **Silver Sands of Morar**, as they are known, draw crowds of bucket-and-spade holiday-makers in July and August, when the many campsites scattered along the coast are filled to overflowing.

Sights & Activities

Camusdarach Beach BEACH
(P) Fans of the movie *Local Hero* still make pilgrimages to Camusdarach Beach, just south of Morar, which starred in the film as Ben's beach. To find it, look for the car park half a mile north of Camusdarach Campsite (p167); from here, a wooden footbridge and a quarter-mile walk through the dunes lead to the beach. (The village that featured in the film is on the other side of the country, at Pennan.)

Land, Sea & Islands Visitor Centre MUSEUM
(www.arisaigcommunitytrust.org.uk; Arisaig; ⊙10am-6pm Mon-Sat, noon-5pm Sun Apr-Oct, shorter hours Sat-Mon Nov-Mar; P) FREE This centre in Arisaig village houses exhibits on the cultural and natural history of the region. A small but fascinating exhibition explains the part played by the local area as a base for training spies for the Special Operations Executive (SOE, forerunner of MI6) during WWII, including famous names such as Violette Szabo (made famous by the 1958 film *Carve Her Name with Pride*) and the Czech paratroopers who assassinated Nazi leader Reinhard Heydrich in Prague in 1942.

Arisaig Marine WILDLIFE WATCHING
(01687-450224; www.arisaig.co.uk; Arisaig Harbour; ⊙late Apr-Sep) In summer Arisaig Marine operates wildlife-watching cruises (minke whales, basking sharks, porpoises, dolphins) from Arisaig harbour to Eigg (£18 return, one hour, six weekly), Rum (£25 return, 2½ hours, two or three weekly) and Muck (£20 return, two hours, three weekly). Sailing times allow four or five hours ashore on Eigg, and two or three hours on Muck or Rum.

Sleeping & Eating

There are at least a half-dozen campsites between Arisaig and Morar; all are open in summer only, and are often full in July and August, so book ahead.

WORTH A TRIP

GLENUIG INN

Set on a peaceful bay, halfway between Lochailort and Acharacle on the A830, the **Glenuig Inn** (01687-470219; www. glenuig.com; Glenuig; B&B s/d/q from £80/120/170, bunkhouse per person £35; P🐾) is a great place to get away from it all. As well as offering comfortable accommodation, good food (mains £10 to £25, served noon to 9pm) and real ale on tap, it's a great base for exploring Arisaig, Morar and the Loch Shiel area.

Rockhopper Sea Kayaking (07739 837344; www.rockhopperscotland.co.uk; half-/full day £50/80) can take you on a guided kayak tour along the wild and beautiful coastline, starting and finishing at the inn.

Camusdarach Campsite CAMPSITE £
(01687-450221; www.camusdarach.co.uk; Arisaig; tent/campervan sites £10/17.50, plus per person £5; ⊙Apr-Sep; 🐾🌳) 🌿 A small and nicely landscaped site with good facilities, only three minutes' walk from the *Local Hero* beach via a gate in the northwest corner.

Leven House B&B £
(01687-450238; www.thelevenhouse.co.uk; Arisaig; s/d from £45/60; P🐾) Set back from the main road, three miles east of Arisaig village, this peaceful farmhouse offers a warm welcome and gorgeous views over the sea towards the Small Isles. Breakfasts include homemade bread and marmalade, and the friendly host is a mine of information about local history and wildlife. There's also a lovely two-bedroom, self-catering cottage (£400 a week).

Old Library Lodge & Restaurant SCOTTISH ££
(01687-450651; www.oldlibrary.co.uk; Arisaig; mains £10-21; ⊙noon-2pm & 6-8.30pm; P🐾) 🌿 The Old Library is a charming restaurant with rooms (singles/doubles £75/120) set in converted 200-year-old stables overlooking the waterfront in Arisaig village. The lunch menu concentrates on soups, burgers and smoked fish or meat platters, while dinner is a more sophisticated affair offering local seafood, beef and lamb.

Mallaig

POP 800

If you're travelling between Fort William and Skye, you may find yourself overnighting in the bustling fishing and ferry port of Mallaig (*mahl*-ig). Indeed, it makes a good base for a series of day trips by ferry to the Small Isles and Knoydart.

Mallaig has a post office, a bank with ATM and a co-op supermarket.

◎ Sights & Activities

Mallaig Heritage Centre   MUSEUM
(☑01687-462085;   www.mallaigheritage.org.uk; Station Rd; adult/child £2.50/free; ⊙11am-4pm Mon-Sat Apr-Oct, longer hours Jul & Aug, shorter hours Nov-Mar) The village's rainy-day attractions are limited to this heritage centre, which covers the archaeology and history of the region, including the heart-rending tale of the Highland Clearances in Knoydart.

Seafari Adventures Skye   BOATING
(☑01471-833316;   Harbour Pontoons; adult/child £42/34; ⊙Easter-Sep) Seafari runs three-hour whale-watching cruises around Skye and the Small Isles aboard the single-hulled *Amelia* and the 36-seat catamaran *Orion*. These trips have a high success rate for spotting minke whales in summer (an average of 180 sightings a year), with rarer sightings of bottlenose dolphins and basking sharks.

⊨ Sleeping & Eating

Springbank Guest House   B&B **££**
(☑01687-462459;   www.springbank-mallaig.co.uk; East Bay; s/d from £45/75; ⊛) The Springbank is a traditional West Highland house with six homely guest bedrooms, with superb views across the harbour to the Cuillin of Skye.

Seaview Guest House   B&B **££**
(☑01687-462059; www.seaviewguesthousemallaig. com; Main St; s/d £65/90, cottage per week £600; P ⊛) This comfortable B&B has grand views over the harbour, not only from the upstairs bedrooms but from the breakfast room too. There's also a cute little cottage next door that offers self-catering accommodation (www.selfcateringmallaig.com; one double and one twin room).

Jaffy's   FISH & CHIPS **£**
(www.jaffys.co.uk; Station Rd; mains £4-7; ⊙noon-3pm & 5-8pm Mon-Sat Apr-Nov, 5-8pm Thu-Sat Dec-Mar) ✐ Owned by a third-generation fish merchant's family, Mallaig's chippy serves superbly fresh fish and chips, as well as kippers, prawns and other seafood.

Fish Market Restaurant   SEAFOOD **££**
(☑01687-462299;   www.thefishmarketrestaurant. co.uk; Station Rd; mains £12-28; ⊙noon-3pm & 6-9pm) ✐ At least half-a-dozen signs in Mallaig advertise 'seafood restaurant', but this bright, modern, bistro-style place next to the harbour is our favourite, serving simply prepared scallops, smoked salmon, mussels, and fresh Mallaig haddock fried in breadcrumbs, as well as the tastiest Cullen skink on the west coast.

Upstairs is a coffee shop (Station Rd; mains £4-8; ⊙11am-4pm, to 6pm Jun-Aug).

❶ Getting There & Away

BOAT

A passenger ferry operated by Western Isles Cruises (p169) links Mallaig to Inverie on the Knoydart Peninsula (25 to 40 minutes) four times daily Monday to Saturday (three on Sunday) from April to October.

CalMac (☑0800 066 5000; www.calmac. co.uk) operates the passenger-only ferry from Mallaig to the following destinations in the Small Isles:

Canna £10.90 return, two hours, six weekly

Eigg £8 return, 1¼ hours, five weekly

Muck £9.20 return, 1½ hours, five weekly

Rum £8.60 return, 1¼ hours, five weekly

There are CalMac car ferry services to Armadale in Skye (car/passenger £9.70/2.90, 30 minutes, eight daily Monday to Saturday, five to seven on Sunday), and Lochboisdale in South Uist (car/passenger £57.65/10.45, 3½ hours, one daily).

BUS

Shiel Buses (www.shielbuses.co.uk) service 500 runs from Fort William to Mallaig (£6.10, 1½ hours, four daily Monday to Friday, plus one daily Saturday and Sunday) via Glenfinnan (£3.30, 30 minutes) and Arisaig (£5.60, one hour).

TRAIN

The West Highland line runs between Fort William and Mallaig (£13, 1½ hours, four daily, three on Sunday).

Knoydart

POP 180

The Knoydart peninsula – a rugged landscape of wild mountains and lonely sea lochs – is the only sizeable area in Britain that remains inaccessible to the motor car, cut off by miles of rough country and the embracing arms of Lochs Nevis and Hourn (Gaelic for the lochs of Heaven and Hell). The main reasons for visiting are to climb the 1020m peak of Ladhar Bheinn (laar-ven), or just to enjoy the feeling of remoteness. There's no TV and no mobile-phone reception; electricity is provided by a private hydroelectric scheme.

No road penetrates this wilderness of rugged hills – Inverie, its sole village, can only be reached by ferry from Mallaig, or on foot from the remote road's end at Kinloch Hourn (a tough 16-mile hike). A 4WD track leads northwest from Inverie for 7 miles to the outposts of Doune and Airor, which offer even more remote accommodation options.

🛏 Sleeping & Eating

Inverie has a pub and tearoom, and there's a small community shop (www.knoydartshop. org) stocked with canned and dry goods.

Knoydart Foundation Bunkhouse HOSTEL £ (☎ 01687-462163; www.knoydart-foundation. com; Inverie; dm adult/child £18/10; @ 🛜) ⏀ A 15-minute walk east of Inverie ferry pier, this is a cosy hostel with wood-burning stove, kitchen and drying room.

Long Beach Campsite CAMPSITE £ (☎ 01687-462242; www.knoydart-foundation.com; Inverie; per tent & 1 person £4, per extra person £3) A basic but beautiful campsite, a 10-minute walk east of the ferry; there's a water supply, fire pits and composting toilet, but no showers. The ranger comes around to collect fees; firewood available for £4.50 a bundle.

Knoydart Lodge HOSTEL ££ (☎ 01687-460129; www.knoydartlodge.co.uk; Inverie; r per person from £30; 🛜🐾) ⏀ This must be some of the most spacious and luxurious accommodation on the whole west coast, let alone in Knoydart. The fantastic, modern timber-built lodge – reminiscent of an Alpine chalet – has large, stylish two- to six-person bedrooms just a short stroll from the beach. You can order breakfast packs (from £5 per person) in advance.

⭐ **Old Forge** PUB FOOD ££ (☎ 01687-462267; www.theoldforge.co.uk; Inverie; mains £16-24; ⊗ 12.30-11.30pm Thu-Tue mid-Mar–Oct, 4-11pm Thu-Tue Nov–mid-Mar; 🛜🍴) ⏀ The Old Forge is listed in the *Guinness Book of Records* as Britain's most remote pub. It's

surprisingly sophisticated – as well as having real ale on tap, there's an Italian coffee machine. Food is served 12.30pm to 2.30pm and 6.30pm to 9.30pm; the house special is a seafood platter (£38); all ingredients are sourced within 7 miles of the pub.

In the evening you can sit by the fire, pint of beer in hand and join the impromptu *ceilidh* (an evening of traditional Scottish entertainment including music, song and dance) that seems to take place just about nightly.

ℹ Getting There & Away

Western Isles Cruises (☎ 01687-462233; https://westernislescruises.co.uk; one-way/day return £10/20, bike £3) Passenger ferry linking Mallaig to Inverie (25 to 40 minutes) four times daily Monday to Saturday and three on Sunday from April to October. Taking the morning boat gives you up to 10 hours ashore in Knoydart before the return trip (first and last boats of the day should be booked in advance). There's also an afternoon sailing between Inverie and Tarbet on the south side of Loch Nevis, allowing walkers to hike along the northern shore of Loch Morar to Tarbet and return by boat (£15 Tarbet–Inverie–Mallaig).

It's also possible to join the boat just for the cruise, without going ashore (£22 for Mallaig–Inverie–Tarbet–Inverie–Mallaig).

SMALL ISLES

The scattered jewels of the Small Isles – Rum, Eigg, Muck and Canna – lie strewn across the silvery-blue Cuillin Sound to the south of Skye. Their distinctive outlines enliven the glorious views from the beaches of Arisaig and Morar.

Rum is the biggest and boldest of the four, a miniature Skye of pointed peaks and dramatic sunset silhouettes. Eigg is the most pastoral and populous, dominated by the miniature sugarloaf mountain of the Sgurr. Muck is a botanist's delight with its wildflowers and unusual alpine plants, and Canna is a craggy bird sanctuary made of magnetic rocks.

If your time is limited and you can only visit one island, choose Eigg or Rum; they have the most to offer on a day trip.

ℹ Getting There & Away

The main ferry operator is **CalMac** (www.calmac. co.uk), which runs the passenger-only ferry from Mallaig.

Canna £10.90 return, two hours, six weekly

Eigg £8 return, 1¼ hours, five weekly

Muck £9.20 return, 1½ hours, five weekly

Rum £8.60 return, 1¼ hours, five weekly

You can also hop between the islands without returning to Mallaig, but the timetable is complicated and it requires a bit of planning – you would need at least five days to visit all four islands. Bicycles are carried for free.

Rum

POP 22

The Isle of Rum (www.isleofrum.com) – the biggest and most spectacular of the Small Isles – was once known as the Forbidden Island. Cleared of its crofters in the early 19th century to make way for sheep, from 1888 to 1957 it was the private sporting estate of the Bulloughs, a Lancashire family who made their fortune in the textile industry. Curious outsiders who ventured too close were liable to find themselves staring down the wrong end of a gamekeeper's shotgun.

The island was sold to the Nature Conservancy in 1957 and has since been a wildlife reserve with deer, wild goats, ponies, golden and white-tailed eagles, and a 120,000-strong colony of Manx shearwaters. Its dramatic, rocky mountains, known as the Rum Cuillin for their similarity to the peaks on neighbouring Skye, draw hill walkers and climbers.

Kinloch, with ferry landing, shop, post office and public telephone, is the island's only settlement.

◎ Sights & Activities

There's some great coastal and mountain walking on the island, including a couple of easy, waymarked nature trails in the woods around Kinloch. The first path on the left after leaving the pier leads to an otter hide (signposted).

The climb to the island's highest point, Askival (812m), is a strenuous hike and involves a bit of rock scrambling (allow six hours for the round trip from Kinloch).

Glen Harris is a 10-mile round trip from Kinloch, on a rough 4WD track – allow four to five hours' walking, or two hours by bike. You can hire bikes from Rum Bike Hire (☑ 01687-462744; fliss@isleofrum.com; Rum Crafts; per day £15; ☉ 10am-6pm) at the craft shop near Kinloch Castle.

★ **Kinloch Castle**   CASTLE

(☑ 01687-462037; www.isleofrum.com; adult/child £9/4.50; ☉ guided tours Mon-Sat Apr-Oct, to coincide with ferry times) When George Bullough, a dashing, Harrow-educated cavalry officer, inherited Rum along with half his father's fortune in 1891, he became one of the wealthiest bachelors in Britain. Bullough blew half his inheritance on building his dream bachelor pad – the ostentatious Kinloch Castle. Since the Bulloughs left, the castle has survived as a perfect time capsule of upper-class Edwardian eccentricity – the guided tour should not be missed.

Bullough shipped in pink sandstone from Dumfriesshire and 250,000 tonnes of Ayrshire topsoil for the gardens, and paid his workers a shilling extra a day to wear tweed kilts – just so they'd look more picturesque. Hummingbirds were kept in the greenhouses and alligators in the garden, and guests were entertained with an orchestrion, the Edwardian equivalent of a Bose hi-fi system (one of only six that were ever made).

⫸ Sleeping & Eating

Bring plenty of food supplies, as there is only one tearoom (www.isleofrumteashop.co.uk; Kinloch; mains £3-6; ☉ 10am-4pm Mon-Fri, to 3pm Sat Apr-Sep; 🛜), and the grocery shop (☑ 01687-460328; ☉ 5-8pm, also 10am-noon on ferry days) opening times are limited.

Kinloch Village Campsite   CAMPSITE £

(www.isleofrum.com; sites per adult/child £6/3, cabins £35; 🐾) Situated between the pier and Kinloch Castle (p170), this basic campsite has toilets, a water supply and hot showers. There are also two wooden camping cabins (sleeping two persons), which must be booked in advance at rumkabins@gmail.com.

Rum Bunkhouse   HOSTEL £

(☑ 01687-460318; www.isleofrum.com; Kinloch; dm/tw £23/50; 🛜) This beautiful, Scandinavian-style timber building was purpose-built as a hostel in 2014, and now provides the island's main accommodation, complete with hot showers, a wood-burning stove and picture windows overlooking the sea.

ⓘ Information

Kinloch has a visitor centre (☉ 8.30am-5pm Apr-Oct) near the pier where you can get information and leaflets on walking and wildlife. For more information see www.isleofrum.com.

Eigg

POP 90

The island of Eigg (www.isleofeigg.org) made history in 1997 when it became the first Highland estate to be bought out by its inhabitants. The island is now owned and managed by the Isle of Eigg Heritage Trust, a partnership among the islanders, Highland Council and the Scottish Wildlife Trust.

It takes its name from the Old Norse *egg* (meaning 'edge'), a reference to the Sgurr of Eigg (393m), an impressive mini-mountain that towers over Galmisdale, the main settlement. Ringed by vertical cliffs on three sides, it's composed of pitchstone lava with columnar jointing similar to that seen on the Isle of Staffa and at the Giant's Causeway in Northern Ireland.

🏃 Activities

The climb to the summit of the Sgurr of Eigg (4.5 miles round trip; allow three to four hours) begins on the road that leads steeply uphill from the pier, which continues through the woods to a red-roofed cottage. Go through the gate to the right of the cottage and turn left; just 20m along the road a cairn on the right marks the start of a boggy footpath that leads over the eastern shoulder of the Sgurr, then traverses beneath the northern cliffs until it makes its way up onto the summit ridge.

On a fine day the views from the top are magnificent – Rum and Skye to the north, Muck and Coll to the south, Ardnamurchan Lighthouse to the southeast and Ben Nevis shouldering above the eastern horizon. Take binoculars – on a calm summer's day there's a good chance of seeing minke whales feeding down below in the Sound of Muck.

A shorter walk (2 miles; allow 1½ hours round trip, and bring a torch) leads west from the pier to the spooky and claustrophobic Uamh Fraing (Massacre Cave). Start as for the Sgurr but 800m from the pier turn left through a gate and into a field. Follow the 4WD track and fork left before a white cottage to pass below it. A footpath continues across the fields to reach a small gate in a fence; go through it and descend a ridge towards the shore.

The cave entrance is tucked inconspicuously down to the left of the ridge. The entrance is tiny – almost a hands-and-knees job – but the cave opens out inside and runs a long way back. Go right to the back, turn off your torch, and imagine the cave packed shoulder to shoulder with terrified men, women and children. Then imagine the panic as your enemies start piling firewood into the entrance. Almost the entire population of Eigg – around 400 people – sought refuge in this cave when the MacLeods of Skye raided the island in 1577. In an act of inhuman cruelty, the raiders lit a fire in the narrow entrance and everyone inside died of asphyxiation. There are more than a few ghosts floating around in here.

🛌 Sleeping & Eating

All accommodation should be booked in advance; wild camping is allowed. For a full listing of accommodation, see www.isleofeigg.org.

Eigg Organics   CAMPSITE **£**
(☎01687-482480; www.eiggorganics.co.uk; Cleadale; tent sites per person £5, yurt £50-55; 🐾) This organic croft in the north of the island has a campsite with basic facilities, and also offers accommodation for two in a Mongolian yurt.

Glebe Barn   HOSTEL **£**
(☎01687-315099; www.glebebarn.co.uk; Galmisdale; dm/tw £20/45; 🐾) Excellent bunkhouse accommodation in the middle of the island, with a smart, maple-floored lounge with a central fireplace, a modern kitchen, a laundry, a drying room, and bright, clean dorms and bedrooms.

★ **Lageorna**   B&B **££**
(☎01687-460081; www.lageorna.com; Cleadale; s/d £85/110; 🐾) 🐾 This converted croft house and lodge in the island's northwest is Eigg's most luxurious accommodation. Rooms are fitted with beautiful, locally made, 'driftwood-style' timber beds, and even have iPod docks (but no mobile-phone reception). Evening meals are available (£25 a head), with the menu heavy on locally grown vegetables, seafood and venison.

Galmisdale Bay   CAFE **£**
(☎01687-482487; www.galmisdale-bay.com; The Pier, Galmisdale; mains £6-11; ⏰check website, closed Wed & Sun) 🐾 The cafe-bar above the ferry pier is the social hub of the community, and serves tasty, great-value soups, salads and sandwiches, plus hot lunch specials. Opening hours differ from day to day; in winter they coincide with ferry arrivals and departures.

ℹ️ Information

Above the pier, the **Isle of Eigg Shop** (☑ 01687-482432; https://isleofeiggshop.com; The Pier, Galmisdale; ⏰ 10am-5pm Mon, Wed & Fri, 11am-3pm Thu, noon-5pm Sat May–mid-Oct, shorter hours winter) serves as an information centre; it also has a post office, craft shop and cafe. You can hire **bikes** (☑ 01687-347007; www.eigg adventures.co.uk; The Pier, Galmisdale; per day £15) here, too.

Canna

POP 15

The island of Canna (www.theisleofcanna. com) is a moorland plateau of black basalt rock, just 5 miles long and 1.25 miles wide; it was gifted to the National Trust for Scotland in 1981 by its owner, the Gaelic scholar and author John Lorne Campbell.

The ferry arrives at the hamlet of A'Chill at the eastern end of the island, where visiting sailors have left extensive graffiti on the rock face south of the harbour. There's a tearoom and craft shop by the harbour, and a tiny post office in a hut. There is no mobile-phone reception.

You can walk to An Coroghon, just east of the ferry pier, a medieval stone tower perched atop a sea cliff, and continue to Compass Hill (143m), which contains enough magnetite (an iron oxide mineral) to deflect the navigation compasses in passing yachts, or take a longer hike along the southern shore past Canna House (the former home of John Lorne Campbell) and an ornately decorated early Christian stone cross. In 2012 a *bullaun* ('cursing stone'), with an inscribed cross was discovered nearby; these are common in Ireland, but this was the first to be found in Scotland.

Facilities are limited. Tighard (☑ 01687-462474; www.tighard.com; r £85-100; 📶 🐕) is the only B&B, while Canna Campsite (☑ 01687-462477; www.cannacampsite.com; tent sites £10, pods £25-30, caravans £45; 🐕) provides tent, caravan and glamping pod accommodation.

Cafe Canna   BISTRO, CAFE **££**

(☑ 01687-482488; www.cafecanna.co.uk; mains £10-20; ⏰ 11am-10pm Wed-Mon May-Aug, 1-9pm Wed-Mon early Sep; 📶) 🐕 The only eating place on the island, this cafe serves meals such as haddock and chips (fish freshly landed at Mallaig) and Canna rabbit stew, in a lovely setting beside the harbour. Best to book for evening meals.

Muck

POP 38

The tiny island of Muck (www.isleofmuck. com), measuring just 2 miles by 1 mile, has exceptionally fertile soil, and the island is carpeted with wildflowers in spring and early summer. It takes its name from the Gaelic *muc* (pig), and pigs are still raised here.

Ferries call at the southern settlement of Port Mor. There's a tearoom and craft shop above the pier, which also acts as a tourist office.

It's an easy 15-minute walk along the island's only road from the pier to the sandy beach at Gallanach on the northern side of the island. A longer and rougher hike (3.5 miles; 1½ hours round trip) goes to the top of Beinn Airein (137m) for the best views. Puffins nest on the cliffs at the western end of Camas Mor, the bay to the south of the hill.

Northern Highlands & Islands

Best Places to Eat

➜ Three Chimneys (p215)

➜ Côte du Nord (p189)

➜ Captain's Galley (p188)

➜ Waterside (p203)

➜ Langass Lodge Restaurant (p226)

Best Places to Stay

➜ Torridon (p200)

➜ Pennyland House (p183)

➜ Mey House (p183)

➜ Craigvar (p176)

➜ Hillstone Lodge (p215)

➜ Tigh an Dochais (p207)

Why Go?

Scotland's vast and melancholy soul is here: an epic land with a stark beauty that indelibly imprints the hearts of those who journey through the mist and mountains, rock and heather. Long, sun-blessed summer evenings are the pay-off for so many days of horizontal rain. It's simply magical.

Stone tells stories throughout. The chambered cairns of Caithness and structures of the Western Isles are testament to the skills of prehistoric builders; cragtop castles and broken walls of abandoned crofts tell of the Highlands' turbulent history.

Outdoors is the place to be, whatever the weather; there's nothing like comparing windburn or mud-ruined boots over a well-deserved dram by the crackling fire of a Highland pub. The landscape lends itself to activity, from woodland strolls to thrilling mountain-bike descents, from sea kayaking to Munro bagging, from beachcombing to birdwatching. Best are the locals, big-hearted and straight-talking; make it your business to get to know them.

When to Go
Portree

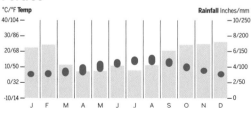

Jun Long evenings bathe achingly sublime landscapes in dreamy light.

Jul The Hebridean Celtic Festival is a top time to experience the culture of the Outer Hebrides.

Sep Less busy than summer, the midges have gone and temperatures are (maybe!) still OK.

Northern Highlands & Islands Highlights

1 North Coast 500 (p189) Driving one of Europe's most spectacularly scenic road trips.

2 Ullapool (p195) Gorging on fresh, succulent seafood in this delightful town with its picture-perfect harbour.

3 Harris (p221) Dipping your toes in the water at some of the world's most beautiful beaches in the Western Isles.

4 Cuillin Hills (p211) Shouldering the challenge of these hills, with their rugged silhouettes brooding over the skyscape of Skye.

5 Far Northwest (p191) Picking your jaw up off the ground as you marvel at the epic Highland scenery.

6 Cape Wrath (p193) Taking the trip out to Britain's gloriously remote northwestern shoulder.

7 Plockton (p201) Relaxing in a postcard-pretty village where the Highlands meet the Caribbean.

8 Skye (p206) Launching yourself in a sea kayak to explore the otter-rich waters around the Isle of Skye.

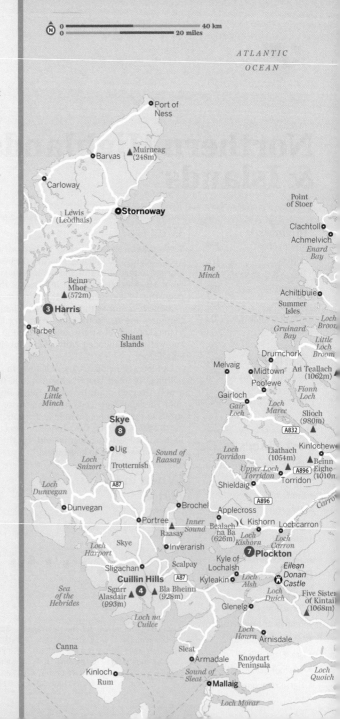

EAST COAST

In both landscape and character, the east coast is where the real barrenness of the Highlands begins to unfold. A gentle splendour and a sense of escapism mark the route along the twisting A9, as it heads north for the last of Scotland's far-flung, mainland population outposts. With only a few exceptions the tourism frenzy is left behind once the road traverses Cromarty Firth and snakes its way along wild and pristine coastline.

While the interior is dominated by the vast and mournful Sutherland mountain range, along the coast great heather-covered hills heave themselves out of the wild North Sea. Rolling farmland drops suddenly into the icy waters, and small, historic towns are moored precariously on the coast's edge.

Strathpeffer

POP 1100

Strathpeffer is a charming old Highland spa town, with creaking pavilions and grandiose hotels dripping with faded grandeur. It rose to prominence during Victorian times, when the fashionable flocked here in huge numbers to bathe in, wash with and drink the sulphurous waters. The tourist influx led to the construction of grand buildings and architectural follies.

◉ Sights & Activities

There are many good signposted walking trails around Strathpeffer.

Highland Museum of Childhood MUSEUM
(☑01997-421031; www.highlandmuseumofchildhood.org.uk; Old Train Station; adult/child £3/1.75; ⊙10am-5pm Mon-Sat Apr-Oct; ⛑) Strathpeffer's former train station houses a wide range of social-history displays about childhood and also has activities for children, including a dressing-up box and toy train. In the complex there's also a gift shop to buy presents for a little somebody and a peaceful cafe. Call for hours during winter, as it does open on some days.

Spa Pavilion & Upper Pump Room HISTORIC BUILDING
(☑01997-420124; www.strathpefferpavilion.org; Golf Course Rd; ⊙Pump Room 10am-5pm Jun-Aug, 10am-5pm Tue-Thu & Sat, 1-5pm Mon, Fri & Sun Sep-Dec & Mar-May) FREE In Strathpeffer's heyday, the Pavilion was the social centre and venue for dances, lectures and concerts. These days it's a renovated performing-arts venue. The neighbouring Upper Pump Room has some splendid displays showing the bizarre lengths Victorians went to for a healthy glow. There are also local art exhibitions, as well as artisanal sweets and tourist information in the friendly shop. Opening hours vary.

Eagle Stone ARCHAEOLOGICAL SITE
The Eagle Stone is well worth a look. It's a pre-7th-century Pictish stone connected to a figure from local history – the Brahan Seer, who predicted many future events. The impressive carved eagle is topped by an arc dotted with symbols. It's a short, well-signposted stroll from the centre of town.

🍴 Sleeping & Eating

★ Craigvar B&B ££
(☑01997-421622; www.craigvar.com; The Square; r £105; ℗🛜) Luxury living with a refined touch is what you'll find in this delightful Georgian house in Strathpeffer's heart. Classy little extras are all here, including a welcome drink, Highland-Belgian chocolates, bathrobes, mini-fridges and fresh fruit. The owners offer wonderfully genuine hospitality with guest comfort paramount. The two light, elegant rooms are great, with fabulous modern bathrooms and thoughtful extras.

Beds are extremely comfortable and the downstairs lounge area is very elegant and commodious. The gourmet breakfasts, with lots of fish options, are a real highlight. It's hard to conceive how this place could improve, yet every time we visit it has done just that. A standout.

Coul House Hotel HOTEL £££
(☑01997-421487; www.coulhousehotel.com; Contin; s £172-236, d £215-295; ℗@🛜🐾) 🐾 At Contin, south of Strathpeffer on the A835, Coul House dates from 1821 but has a light, airy feel in contrast to many country houses of this vintage. It's family run, and very cordial. Beautiful dining and lounge areas are complemented by elegant rooms with views over the lovely gardens; superiors look up the glen to the mountains beyond.

There's a fairy trail in the garden, forest paths for walking or mountain biking right on the doorstep, and a good restaurant. You can often find lower prices or multiday offers on the website.

Red Poppy
BISTRO ££

(☑ 01997-423332; www.redpoppyrestaurant.co.uk; Main Rd; mains £12-19; ⊙ 11.30am-9pm Tue-Sat, 12.30-4pm Sun; 🐾) On the main road opposite the spa buildings, this is comfortably Strathpeffer's best eating establishment. The casual modern interior with its bright red chairs is the venue for confident, well-presented dishes covering game and other classic British ingredients. It's a little cheaper at lunchtime, when set-price menus are available, and for traditional hot-meal high teas from 5pm.

❶ Getting There & Away

Stagecoach (☑ 01463-233371; www.stage coachbus.com) operates from Inverness to Strathpeffer (£5.45, 45 minutes, hourly Monday to Saturday, five on Sunday) via Dingwall (£2, 15 minutes). Services from Inverness to Gairloch and Durness, plus some buses from Inverness to Ullapool, also drop in.

Tain
POP 3700

Scotland's oldest royal burgh, Tain is a proud sandstone town that rose to prominence as pilgrims descended to venerate the relics of St Duthac, who is commemorated by the 12th-century ruins of St Duthac's Chapel, and St Duthus Church. It makes a fine stop on the way north.

Glenmorangie
DISTILLERY

(☑ 01862-892477; www.glenmorangie.com; tours £7.50; ⊙ tours 10am-4pm Jun-Aug, 10am-3pm Mon-Sat Apr-May & Sep-Oct, 10am & 2pm Mon-Fri Nov-Mar) Located on Tain's northern outskirts, Glenmorangie (emphasis on the second syllable) produces a fine lightish malt, subjected to a number of different cask finishes for variation. The tour is less in-depth than some but finishes with a free dram. There's a more comprehensive Signet tour (£35) and, for real whisky geeks, a full-day Heritage Tour (£130, April to October).

Tain Through Time
MUSEUM

(☑ 01862-894089; www.tainmuseum.org.uk; Tower St; adult/child £3.50/2.50, museum only £1.50/50p; ⊙ 10am-5pm Mon-Fri Apr-Oct, plus Sat Jun-Aug) Set in the grounds of St Duthus Church is Tain Through Time, an entertaining heritage centre with a colourful and educational display on St Duthac, King James IV and key moments in Scottish history. Another building focuses on the town's fine

THE RIGHT SIDE OF THE TRACKS

Sleeperzzz (☑ 01408-641343; www.sleeperzzz.com; Rogart; dm £18-20, s/tw £30/54, d with bathroom £69; ⊙ Mar-Oct; 🅿🐾) is an unusual hostel is set in three caringly converted railway carriages, an old bus and a beautiful wooden caravan parked in a siding by Rogart station. The carriages contain cute two-person bedrooms, kitchenettes and tiny lounges. There's also a B&B in the former waiting room, now an en suite chamber with kitchen; light breakfast is supplied. The hostel is run on sustainable lines.

It's on the A839, 11 miles east of Lairg, but is also easily reached by train on the Inverness–Wick line (£1 discount if you arrive this way or by bike). There's beautifully lonely Highland scenery in the vicinity and a local pub doing food (whose future was in some doubt at the time of research).

silversmithing tradition and this is also a centre for Clan Ross. Admission includes an audio-guided walk around town.

Platform 1864
BISTRO ££

(☑ 01862-894181; 1 Station Rd; mains £11-16; ⊙ food noon-3pm & 5-9.30pm, to 8pm Nov-Feb; 🐾👶) ✎ Real love has gone into this excellent restoration of Tain's train station building, which has become a handsome wood-clad bar and restaurant, open all day. The menu features hearty, bar-style fare with a few flourishes. The enthusiastic owner and a beer garden make it a fine place to drop by for a drink or coffee at any time, too.

Bonar Bridge & Around

While the main road north crosses Dornoch Firth near Tain, an alternative scenic route brings you to the almost-joined villages of Ardgay and Bonar Bridge. This is an area worth exploring, with reminders of the Clearances, fine old-growth forest and good scope for outdoor activities. The A836 to Lairg branches west at Bonar Bridge.

Croick
VILLAGE

From Ardgay, a single-track road leads 10 miles up Strathcarron to Croick, the scene of notorious evictions during the

1845 Clearances. You can still see the evocative messages scratched by refugee crofters from Glencalvie on the eastern windows of Croick Church.

Kyle of Sutherland Trails
MOUNTAIN BIKING

(☑0300-067-6850; www.scotland.forestry.gov.uk/visit/balblair) At Balblair, a mile from Bonar Bridge off the Lairg road, there are two mountain-biking trails. A two-mile blue trail winds through the forest, while a 4.5-mile black track will test expert bikers with a stiff climb and an adrenalin-surging rock-slab descent.

Alladale Wilderness Reserve
LODGE ££££

(☑01863-755338; www.alladale.com; Ardgay; self-catering per week from £1200, r with full board Oct-May £213-340; P ☎ ⊛) In deep wilderness near Croick, this lodge is part of a notable rewilding project. The main lodge (which includes meals) is, in summer, for entire hire only (it sleeps 12 to 14). Individual rooms are available in low season. Smaller buildings – a farmhouse and cottages – accommodate up to four on a self-catering basis. The scope for outdoor activity here is superb.

Crannag
BISTRO ££

(☑01863-766111; www.crannag.com; Bonar Bridge; mains £12-19; ⊙6-8.30pm Tue-Sat; ☑) This likeable Highland bistro in Bonar Bridge is our favourite eating establishment in the area.

Lairg & Around

POP 900

Lairg is an attractive village, although the tranquillity can be rudely interrupted by the sound of military jets roaring overhead (the valley is frequently used by the RAF for low-flying exercises). Located at the southern end of Loch Shin, it's a remote but important Highlands crossroad, gateway to central Sutherland's remote mountains and loch-speckled bogs.

Falls of Shin
WATERFALL

(www.facebook.com/fallsofshin; ⊙visitor centre approx 10am-3pm late Oct-Feb, 9am-8pm Mar-late Oct; ☑) FREE Four miles south of Lairg, the picturesque Falls of Shin provide one of the best places in the Highlands to see salmon leaping on their way upstream to spawn (June to September). A short, easy footpath leads to a viewing terrace overlooking the waterfall; there are waymarked forest trails here. There's also a gift shop and a pleasant community-run cafe in a salmon-shaped structure, with information panels on the fish.

★ Pier Café
CAFE, BISTRO £

(☑01549-402971; www.pier-cafe-co.uk; Lochside, Lairg; lunch mains £8-11; ⊙10am-4pm Mon-Sat, plus 5.30-9pm Fri & Sat, 10am-6pm Sun; ☎ ☑) A very worthwhile stop, this bustling cafe by the loch has pleasant views, art exhibitions on the walls and real flair. Great chalkboard specials augment a Mediterranean-influenced bistro menu that draws on local produce. The coffee is the best for some distance around and the cafe is licensed. There's a little craft shop too.

Dornoch

POP 1200

On the northern shore of Dornoch Firth, 2 miles off the A9, this attractive old market town, all elegant sandstone, is one of the east coast's most pleasant settlements. Dornoch is best known for its championship golf course, but there's a fine cathedral among other noble buildings. Other historical oddities: the last witch to be executed in Scotland was boiled alive in hot tar here in 1722 and Madonna married Guy Ritchie here in 2000.

◉ Sights & Activities

Have a walk along Dornoch's golden-sand beach, which stretches for miles. South of Dornoch, seals are often visible on the sandbars of Dornoch Firth.

Dornoch Cathedral
CHURCH

(www.dornoch-cathedral.com; St Gilbert St; ⊙9am-7pm or later) FREE Consecrated in the 13th century, beautiful Dornoch Cathedral, one of the Highlands' loveliest churches, is an elegant Gothic edifice with an interior softly illuminated through modern stained-glass windows. The controversial first Duke of Sutherland, whose wife restored the church in the 1830s, lies in a sealed burial vault beneath the chancel.

By the western door is the sarcophagus of Sir Richard de Moravia, who died fighting the Danes at the battle of Embo in the 1260s. Until then, the battle had been going rather well for him; he'd managed to slay the Danish commander with the unattached leg of a horse that was to hand.

Royal Dornoch GOLF
(☑ 01862-810219; www.royaldornoch.com; Golf Rd;
summer green fee £160) Royal Dornoch is one
of Scotland's most famous links, described
by Tom Watson as 'the most fun I ever had
playing golf'. It's public, and you can book a
slot online. Twilight rates are the most economical. A golf pass (www.dornochfirthgolf.
co.uk) lets you play several courses in the
area at a good discount.

🛏 Sleeping & Eating

⭐ **2 Quail** B&B **££**
(☑ 01862-811811; www.2quail.com; Castle St; r
£120-130; 🤶) Intimate and upmarket, 2 Quail
offers a warm main-street welcome. Tasteful,
spacious chambers are full of old-world comfort, with sturdy metal bed frames, plenty
of books and plump duvets. The downstairs guest lounge is an absolute delight,
while the guest dinners (two/three courses
£22/27) are a treat, as one of the owners is a
noted chef. It's best to book ahead.

Dornoch Castle Hotel HOTEL **£££**
(☑ 01862-810216; www.dornochcastlehotel.com;
Castle St; s/d £75/135, superior/deluxe d £185/260;
🅿 🤶) This 16th-century former bishop's palace makes a wonderful place to stay. Standard rooms are compact but comfortable,
although this is a spot to splash out on an
upgrade. Spacious castle rooms come with a
rustic Scottish feel, views, sherry and chocolates on the welcome tray; the two Deluxe
rooms are unforgettable: you'll feel like a
monarch in your own castle.
   Add to this the convivial bar and restaurant and helpful staff and you have a very
impressive package.

Courthouse Cafe CAFE **£**
(☑ 01862-811632; www.thecarnegiecourthouse.
co.uk; Castle St; mains £7-11; ⊙ 9am-5pm Apr-Oct,
10am-4pm Nov-Mar; 🤶) Beautifully set in the
former town courtroom, this is an atmospheric upstairs spot for a coffee or lunch,
with a range of attractive wooden tables,
comfortable armchairs and other places
to perch.

Luigi ITALIAN, CAFE **££**
(☑ 01862-810893; www.luigidornoch.com; Castle
St; lunch £7-12, dinner mains £16-21; ⊙ 10am-5pm
daily, plus 6.45-9pm Fri & Sat Mar-Oct, daily Jul &
Aug; 🤶) The clean lines of this contemporary
Italian-American cafe make a break from
the omnipresent heritage and history of the
coastline. Ciabattas and salads stuffed with

tasty deli ingredients make it a good lunch
stop; more elaborate dinners usually include
fine seafood choices. The coffee is the best
in town.

ℹ Information

Carnegie Courthouse (☑ 01862-811632;
www.thecarnegiecourthouse.co.uk; Castle St;
⊙ 9am-5pm) There's visitor information downstairs in the old courthouse. Winter opening
times are restricted.

ℹ Getting There & Away

There are buses roughly hourly from Inverness
(£12.05, 1¼ hours), with some services continuing north to Wick or Thurso.

Golspie
POP 1400

Golspie is a pretty little village most visited
for nearby Dunrobin Castle. It's a congenial
place to stop for a night or two, with good
facilities and a pleasant beach.
   There are several good local walks,
including the classic 3.75-mile (return) hike
that climbs steeply to the summit of **Ben
Bhraggie** (394m), crowned by a massive
monument to the Duke of Sutherland, notorious for his leading role in the Highland
Clearances.
   On the same slopes, **Highland Wildcat**
(www.highlandwildcat.com; per day £3; ⊙ dawn-
dusk) offers excellent mountain biking.

⭐ **Dunrobin Castle** CASTLE
(☑ 01408-633177; www.dunrobincastle.co.uk; A9;
adult/child £11.50/7; ⊙ 10.30am-4.30pm Apr,
May & Oct, 10am-5pm Jun-Sep) Magnificent
Dunrobin Castle, a mile past Golspie, is the
Highlands' largest house. Although it dates
to 1275, most of what you see was built in
French style between 1845 and 1850. The
home of the dukes of Sutherland, it's richly
furnished and offers an intriguing insight
into the aristocratic lifestyle. The beautiful
castle inspires mixed feelings locally; it was
once the seat of the first Duke of Sutherland,
notorious for some of the cruellest episodes
of the Highland Clearances.
   The duke's estate was, at over 6000 sq km,
the largest privately owned area of land in
Europe. He evicted around 15,000 people
from their homes to make way for sheep.
   The classic fairy-tale castle is adorned
with towers and turrets, but only 22 of its
187 rooms are on display, with hunting

trophies much to the fore. Beautiful formal gardens, where impressive falconry displays take place two or three times a day, extend down to the sea. In the gardens is a museum with an eclectic mix of archaeological finds, natural-history exhibits, more non-PC animal remains and an excellent collection of Pictish stones.

❶ Getting There & Away

Trains (£19.90, 2¼ hours) and buses (£12.05, 1½ hours) from Inverness towards Wick/Thurso stop in Golspie and at Dunrobin Castle.

Helmsdale

POP 700

Surrounded by hills whose gorse explodes mad yellow in springtime, this sheltered fishing town, like many spots on the east coast, was a major emigration point during the Clearances and also a booming herring port. It's surrounded by stunning, undulating coastline, and the River Helmsdale is one of the best salmon rivers in the Highlands.

Timespan   MUSEUM

(☑ 01431-821327; www.timespan.org.uk; Dunrobin St; adult/child £4/2; ⊘ 10am-5pm Easter-Oct, 2-4pm Tue, 10am-3pm Sat & Sun Nov-Easter) In the heart of Helmsdale, this heritage centre has an impressive display covering local history, including a Pictish stone, the Clearances, the fishing industry and the 1869 gold rush; look out also for the impressive audiovisual content. Up the back are recreations of a traditional croft house, smithy, shop and byre. There are also local art exhibitions upstairs, a geology garden and a cafe.

CAITHNESS

Once you pass Helmsdale, you are entering Caithness, a place of jagged gorse-and-grass-topped cliffs hiding tiny fishing harbours. Scotland's top corner was once Viking territory, historically more connected to Orkney and Shetland than the rest of the mainland. It's a mystical, ancient land dotted with old monuments and peopled by folk who are proud of their Norse heritage.

CROFTING & THE CLEARANCES

The wild empty spaces of the northern Highlands are among Europe's least populated regions, but this wasn't always so. Ruins of cottages in desolate areas are mute witnesses to one of the most heartless episodes of Scottish history: the Highland Clearances.

Until the 19th century the most common form of farming settlement here was the *baile*, a group of a dozen or so families who farmed the land granted to them by the local chieftain in return for military service and a portion of the harvest. The arable land was divided into strips called *rigs*, which were allocated to different families by annual ballot so that each took turns at getting the poorer soils; this system was known as *runrig*. The families worked the land communally and their cattle shared grazing land.

After the Battle of Culloden, however, the king banned private armies and new laws made the clan chiefs actual owners of their traditional lands, often vast tracts of territory. With the prospect of unimagined riches allied to a depressing failure of imagination, the lairds decided that sheep were more profitable than agriculture and proceeded to evict tens of thousands of farmers. These desperate folk were forced to head for the cities in the hope of finding work or to emigrate to the Americas or the southern hemisphere. Those who stayed were forced to eke out a living from narrow plots of marginal agricultural land, often close to the coast. This form of smallholding became known as crofting. The small patch of land barely provided a living and had to be supplemented by other work such as fishing and kelp-gathering. It was always precarious, as rights were granted on a year-by-year basis, so at any moment a crofter could lose not only the farm but also the house they'd built on it.

The late 19th-century economic depression meant many couldn't pay their rent. This time, however, they resisted expulsion, instead forming the Highland Land Reform Association and their own political party. Their resistance led the government to accede to several demands, including security of tenure, fair rents and eventually the supply of land for new crofts. Crofters now have the right to purchase their farmland and 2004 laws finally abolished the feudal system, which created so much misery.

Helmsdale to Lybster

This spectacular stretch of coast follows the folds of the undulating landscape through villages established on the shoreline when communities were evicted from the interior in the Highland Clearances in the early 19th century.

The village of Dunbeath is spectacularly set in a deep glen. Lybster is a purpose-built fishing village dating from 1810, with a stunning harbour area surrounded by grassy cliffs. In its heyday, it was Scotland's third-busiest port. Things have changed – now there are only a couple of boats – but there are several interesting prehistoric sites in the area.

Grey Cairns of Camster   ARCHAEOLOGICAL SITE
(⊘24hr) FREE Dating from between 4000 BC and 2500 BC, these burial chambers are hidden in long, low mounds rising from an evocatively lonely moor. The Long Cairn measures 60m by 21m. You can enter the main chamber, but must first crawl into the well-preserved Round Cairn, which has a corbelled ceiling. From a turn-off a mile east of Lybster on the A99, the cairns are 4 miles north. You can continue 7 further miles to approach Wick on the A882.

Whaligoe Steps   HISTORIC SITE
(⊘24hr) FREE At Ulbster, 5 miles north of Lybster, this staircase cut into the cliff provides access to a tiny natural harbour, with an ideal grassy picnic spot, ringed by vertical cliffs and echoing with the cackle of nesting fulmars. The path begins at the end of the minor road opposite the road signposted 'Cairn of Get'. There's a cafe (☑01955-651702; www.whaligoesteps.co.uk; Ulbster; light meals £6-12; ⊘10.30am-5.30pm Thu-Sun mid-Mar–Sep, 11am-5pm Sat & Sun Oct-Dec) at the top.

Wick

POP 7100

Wick is worth a visit, particularly for its excellent museum and attractive, spruced-up harbour area, and it has some very good places to stay. More gritty than pretty, however, it's been a little down on its luck since the collapse of the herring industry. It was once the world's largest fishing port for the 'silver darlings', but when the market dropped off after WWII, job losses were huge and the town hasn't ever totally recovered.

⦿ Sights & Activities

★**Wick Heritage Centre**   MUSEUM
(☑01955-605393; www.wickheritage.org; 20 Bank Row; adult/child £4/50p; ⊘10am-5pm Apr-Oct, last entry 3.45pm) Tracking the rise and fall of the herring industry, this great town museum displays everything from fishing equipment to complete herring boats. It's absolutely huge inside, and is crammed with memorabilia and extensive displays describing Wick's heyday in the mid-19th century. The Johnston collection is the star exhibit. From 1863 to 1977, three generations photographed everything that happened around Wick and the 70,000 photographs are an amazing record.

Old Pulteney   DISTILLERY
(☑01955-602371; www.oldpulteney.com; Huddart St; tours £10; ⊘10am-4pm Mon-Fri Oct-Apr, 10am-5pm Mon-Fri, 10am-4pm Sat May-Sep) Though it can no longer claim to be the most northerly whisky distillery on mainland Scotland (that goes to the upstart Wolfburn in Thurso), friendly Pulteney still runs excellent tours twice or more daily (normally at 11am and 2pm), with more expensive visits available for aficionados. Their Stroma whisky liqueur is dangerously more-ish.

Caithness Seacoast   BOATING
(☑01955-609200; www.caithness-seacoast.co.uk; South Quay; ⊘Apr-Oct) This outfit will take you out to sea to inspect the rugged coastline of the northeast. Various options include a half-hour jaunt (adult/child £19/12), a 1½-hour tour (£30/22) and a three-hour return trip down to Lybster (£50/39).

🛏 Sleeping & Eating

Bank Guesthouse   B&B ££
(☑01955-604001; www.guesthousewick.co.uk; 28 Bridge St; s £50-60, d £75-85; P 🛜) In the very centre of Wick, this striking Victorian building contains a warmly welcoming B&B run by a local family. Rooms have plenty of space and feature attractive carpets, wallpaper and fabrics along with modern bathrooms with great showers. Breakfast is well above average. Stairs might be a problem for the less mobile.

Mackays Hotel   HOTEL ££
(☑01955-602323; www.mackayshotel.co.uk; Union St; s/d £93/129; 🛜) Hospitable Mackays is Wick's best hotel by a long stretch. Attractive, mostly refurbished rooms vary in layout and size, so ask to see a few;

NORTHERN HIGHLANDS & ISLANDS HELMSDALE TO LYBSTER

prices are usually lower than the rack rates. On-site **No 1 Bistro** (mains £17-24; ⊙ noon-2pm & 5-9pm; 🐾) is a fine option for lunch or dinner. The world's shortest street, 2.06m-long Ebenezer Place, is one side of the hotel.

Guests get free use of a local gym and pool. The hotel also has some self-catering apartments and town houses nearby.

Bord de l'Eau ⁣ FRENCH ££
(🖉 01955-604400; 2 Market St; mains £16-24; ⊙ noon-2pm & 6-9pm Tue-Sat, 6-9pm Sun) This serene, relaxed French restaurant is Wick's best place to eat. It overlooks the river and serves a changing menu of mostly meat and game French classics, backed up by daily fish specials. Starters are great value, and mains include a huge assortment of vegetables. The conservatory dining room with water views is lovely on a sunny evening.

ℹ️ Information

Wick Tourist Office (🖉 01955-602547; 66 High St; ⊙ 9am-5.30pm Mon-Sat) Upstairs in McAllans Clothing Store. Has a good selection of information.

ℹ️ Getting There & Away

AIR
Wick is a Caithness transport gateway. Loganair flies to Edinburgh and Flybe/Eastern Airways to Aberdeen (three daily, Monday to Friday).

BUS
Stagecoach and Citylink operate to/from Inverness (£20.15, three hours, six daily) and Stagecoach to Thurso (£3.90, 40 minutes, hourly). There's also connecting service to John O'Groats and Gills Bay (£3.60, 30 minutes, four to five Monday to Saturday) for the passenger and car ferries to Orkney.

TRAIN
Trains service Wick from Inverness (£21.10, 4¼ hours, four daily Monday to Saturday, one on Sunday).

John O'Groats

POP 300

Though not the northernmost point of the British mainland (that's Dunnet Head), John O'Groats still serves as the end point of the 874-mile trek from Land's End in Cornwall, a popular if arduous route for cyclists and walkers, many of whom raise money for charitable causes. Most of the settlement is taken up by a stylish modern self-catering

complex. There's a passenger ferry from here to Orkney.

Duncansby Head ⁣ VIEWPOINT
Two miles east of John O'Groats, Duncansby Head has a small lighthouse and 60m-high cliffs sheltering nesting fulmars. A 15-minute walk through a sheep paddock yields spectacular views of the sea-surrounded monoliths known as Duncansby Stacks.

Wildlife Cruises ⁣ BOATING
(🖉 01955-611353; www.jogferry.co.uk; adult/child £18/9; ⊙ mid-Jun–Aug) The friendly folk who run the Orkney ferry also have 1½-hour wildlife cruises to the island of Stroma or Duncansby Head. There are also **day tours** (⊙ May-Sep) of Orkney available.

ℹ️ Information

John O'Groats Tourist Office (🖉 01955-611373; joginfor@btconnect.com; ⊙ 10am-4pm Nov-Apr, to 5pm May & Sep-Oct, 9am-6pm Jun-Aug) This locally run tourist office at the John O'Groats car park is helpful and, as well as information and souvenirs, has a fine selection of local novels and nonfiction titles.

ℹ️ Getting There & Away

Stagecoach (www.stagecoachbus.com) runs between John O'Groats and Wick (£3.60, 30 minutes, four to five Monday to Saturday) or Thurso (£4.25, 40 minutes, five to eight Monday to Saturday).

From May to September, a passenger ferry (p232) shuttles across to Burwick in Orkney. Three miles west, a car ferry (p232) runs all year from Gills Bay to St Margaret's Hope in Orkney.

Mey

POP 200

West of John O'Groats, the small village of Mey has a major drawcard for lovers of the Royal Family in its pretty castle, formerly a residence of the Queen Mother.

Castle of Mey ⁣ CASTLE
(🖉 01847-851473; www.castleofmey.org.uk; adult/child £11.75/6.50; ⊙ 10.20am-5pm May-Sep, last entry 4pm) The Castle of Mey, a big crowd-puller for its Queen Mother connections, is 6 miles west of John O'Groats. The exterior is grand but inside it feels domestic and everything is imbued with the Queen Mum's character. The highlight is the genteel guided tour, with various anecdotes recounted by staff who once worked for her. In the grounds there's a farm zoo, an unu-

sual walled garden that's worth a stroll and lovely views over the Pentland Firth.

The castle normally closes for a couple of weeks at the end of July for royal visits; Prince Charles often comes here in summer. There may also be limited April openings; check the website.

★**Mey House** B&B **£££**
(☑ 01847-851852; www.meyhouse.co.uk; East Mey; r £139; ⊙ Easter–mid-Oct; P 🛜) Beautifully situated among green fields running down to water and with majestic views of Orkney, Dunnet Head and the nearby Castle of Mey, this modern top-drawer sleep is a welcoming, sumptuous place to stay. They've thought it all through: the huge, luxurious rooms have arty designer decor, excellent custom-made beds, Nespresso machines, flatscreen TVs, sound bar and stunning modern bathrooms.

Breakfast comes with a view. The friendly owners offer free transfers to the Gills Bay ferry and can set you up with tours on Orkney. No toddlers are allowed, as there's an interior balcony. There's a minimum two-night stay.

Thurso & Scrabster

POP 7600

Britain's most northerly mainland town, Thurso makes a handy overnight stop if you're heading west or across to Orkney. There's a pretty town beach, riverside strolls and a good museum. Ferries for Orkney leave from Scrabster, 2.5 miles away.

◉ Sights & Activities

Thurso is an unlikely surfing centre but the nearby coast has arguably the best and most regular surf on mainland Britain. There's an excellent right-hand reef break on the eastern side of town, directly in front of the castle (closed to the public), and another shallow reef break 5 miles west at Brimms Ness. You'll want to wear 6mm cover outside the summer season. Conditions are best in autumn.

Caithness Horizons MUSEUM
(☑ 01847-896508; www.caithnesshorizons.co.uk; High St; adult/child £4/2; ⊙ 10am-4pm Tue-Sat Nov-Mar, 10am-5pm Tue-Sat Apr-Oct) This museum brings Caithness history and lore to life through excellent displays. Fine Pictish cross-slabs greet visitors downstairs; the main exhibition is a wide-ranging look

DUNNET HEAD

Eight miles east of Thurso a minor road leads to dramatic **Dunnet Head**, the most northerly point on the British mainland. There are majestic cliffs dropping into the turbulent Pentland Firth, inspiring views of Orkney, basking seals and nesting seabirds below (it's an RSPB reserve), and a lighthouse built by Robert Louis Stevenson's grandad. Two cottages are available for rent (see www.dunnetheadlighthouse.com).

at local history using plenty of audiovisuals. There's also a gallery space, an exhibition on the Dounreay nuclear reactor, tourist information and a cafe.

🛏 Sleeping & Eating

Sandra's Backpackers HOSTEL **£**
(☑ 01847-894575; www.sandras-backpackers.co.uk; 24 Princes St; dm/d/f £18/42/65; P @ 🛜) In the heart of town, this budget backpacker option has en suite dorms, mostly four-berthers with aged mattresses, a spacious kitchen and traveller-friendly facilities such as help-yourself cereals and toast. It's not luxurious but it's a reliable cheap sleep.

★**Pennyland House** B&B **££**
(☑ 01847-891194; www.pennylandhouse.co.uk; A9; s £80, d £90-100; P 🛜 🐾) A super conversion of a historic house, this is a standout B&B choice. It offers phenomenal value for this level of accommodation, with huge oak-furnished rooms named after golf courses: we especially loved St Andrews – super-spacious, with a great chessboard-tiled bathroom. Hospitality is enthusiastic and helpful, and there's an inviting breakfast space, garden and terraced area with views across to Hoy.

Two-night minimum stay in summer.

Camfield House B&B **££**
(☑ 01847-891118; www.riversideaccommodation.co.uk; Janet St; r £125-145; P 🛜) A Narnia-style portal leads from central Thurso through a gate and you're suddenly in what feels like an opulent rural estate. The garden is sumptuous and extravagantly features a manicured par-3 golf hole, complete with bunker and water hazard. The interior lacks nothing by comparison, with spacious rooms with huge TVs, quality linen and excellent bathrooms. There's even a full-sized billiard table.

RPHSTOCK/SHUTTERSTOCK ©

1. North Coast 500 (p189)
The drive along Scotland's far northern coastline is one of Europe's finest road trips.

2. Tain (p177)
Scotland's oldest royal burgh is home to the world-famous Glenmorangie distillery (pictured; p177)

3. Lewis (p218)
This isle is home to the Callanish Standing Stones (pictured; p220), one of the Outer Hebrides' most evocative historic sites.

4. Eilean Donan Castle (p203)
This is one of Scotland's most iconic castles.

3

PHOTIMAGEON/ALAMY ©

3

1. Skye (p204)

The sheltered coves and sea lochs around the coast provide enthusiasts with magnificent sea-kayaking opportunities (p206).

2. Dunrobin Castle (p179)

This magnificent castle is the Highlands' largest house.

3. North & West Coast (p188)

This quintessential Highland country is breathtakingly empty, a rarity in modern, highly urbanised Britain.

4. Caithness (p180)

Scotland's top corner is filled with Viking heritage and tiny fishing harbours, such as Lybster (pictured).

Marine B&B ££
(☎ 01847-890676; www.themarinethurso.co.uk; 38 Shore St; s £75-90, d £85-100; P 🛜) Tucked away in Thurso's most appealing corner you'll find a top spot right by the pretty town beach, offering spectacular vistas over it and across to Orkney. Rooms are just fabulous, with a designer's touch and a subtle maritime feel, and surfers can study the breakers from the stunning conservatory lounge. Two rooms in the adjacent house make a great family option.

Forss House Hotel HOTEL £££
(☎ 01847-861201; www.forsshousehotel.co.uk; s/d £125/175; P 🛜🐕) Tucked into trees 5 miles west of Thurso is this Georgian mansion offering elegant accommodation with both character and style. Sumptuous upstairs rooms are preferable to basement rooms as they have lovely garden views. There are also beautifully appointed suites in the garden itself, providing both privacy and tranquillity. Thoughtful extras like CDs and books in every room add appeal.

It's right alongside a beautiful salmon river and if you've had a chilly day in the waders, some 300 malt whiskies await in the hotel bar. There are some cheaper rooms available (d £135) also.

★ Captain's Galley SEAFOOD £££
(☎ 01847-894999; www.captainsgalley.co.uk; Scrabster; 5-course dinner £53.50, with wine flight £77; ⏱ 6.30-9pm Thu-Sat) 🌿 Classy but friendly Captain's Galley, by the Scrabster ferry, offers a short, seafood-based menu featuring local and sustainably sourced produce prepared in delicious ways that let the natural flavours shine through. The chef picks the best fish off the local boats, and the menu describes exactly which fishing grounds your morsel came from. It's worth scheduling a night in Thurso to eat here.

ℹ️ Information
The Caithness Horizons museum (p183) provides helpful local tourist information.

ℹ️ Getting There & Away
BUS
Stagecoach/Citylink buses link Thurso/Scrabster with Inverness (£20.15, three hours, five daily). There are also buses roughly every hour to Wick (£3.90, 40 minutes), as well as every couple of hours to John O'Groats (£4.25, 40 minutes, five to eight Monday to Saturday).

TRAIN
There are four daily trains (one on Sunday) from Inverness (£21.10, 3¾ hours), with a connecting bus to Scrabster.

It's a 2-mile walk from Thurso train station to the ferry at Scrabster; there are buses from Olrig St.

NORTH & WEST COAST
Quintessential Highland country such as this, with breathtaking emptiness, a wild, fragile beauty and single-track roads, is a rarity on the modern, crowded, highly urbanised island of Britain. You could get lost up here for weeks – and that still wouldn't be enough time.

Carving its way from Thurso to Glencoul, the north and northwest coastline is a feast of deep inlets, forgotten beaches and surging peninsulas. Within the rugged confines, the interior is home to vast, empty spaces, enormous lochs and some of Scotland's highest peaks.

Whether in blazing sunshine or murky greyness, the character of the land is totally unique and constantly changing – for that window of time in which you can glimpse it, you'll capture an exclusive snapshot of this ancient area in your mind. Park the car and gaze. This northernmost slab of the Highlands is the stuff of coastal-drive dreams.

Thurso to Durness
It's 80 winding – and utterly spectacular – coastal miles from Thurso to Durness.

Ten miles west of Thurso, the Dounreay nuclear power station was the first in the world to supply mains electricity; it's currently being decommissioned. The clean-up is planned to be finished by 2025; it's still a major source of employment for the region.

Beyond, Melvich overlooks a fine beach and there are great views from Strathy Point (a 2-mile drive from the coast road, then a 15-minute walk).

Bettyhill is a pretty village that overlooks a magnificent stretch of coastline, and the scenery just improves as you head west through Coldbackie and Tongue, with a succession of gorgeous sea lochs, stunning beaches and striking rock formations backed by imposing hills and mountains.

Bettyhill

POP 500

Bettyhill is a crofting community of resettled tenant farmers kicked off their land during the Clearances. The spectacular panorama of a sweeping, sandy beach backed by velvety green hills with rocky outcrops makes a sharp contrast to that sad history.

Strathnaver Museum   MUSEUM
(☑01641-521418; www.strathnavermuseum.org.uk; adult/child £2/1; ☺10am-5pm Mon-Sat Apr-Oct) Housed in an old church, this museum tells the sad story of the Strathnaver Clearances through posters created by local kids. The museum contains memorabilia of Clan Mackay, various items of crofting equipment and a 'St Kilda mailboat', a small wooden boat-shaped container bearing a letter that was used by St Kildans to send messages to the mainland.

Outside the back door of the church is the **Farr Stone**, a fine carved Pictish cross-slab.

Bettyhill Hotel   INN ££
(☑01641-521202; www.bettyhillhotel.com; s/d without bathroom £60/90, d with bathroom £140; ☺Apr-Oct, check for winter opening; P🛜🐾)

This historic hotel has a fabulous position overlooking the marvellous perspective of the sandy beach fringing Torrisdale Bay. The owners have been doing a great renovation and the excellent updated rooms are bright, with top-grade mattresses. Rooms come in many different types (some have super views), with lots of singles as well as a cottage. Bar and restaurant meals are available.

★Côte du Nord   MODERN SCOTTISH £££
(☑01641-521773; www.cotedunord.co.uk; The School House, Kirtomy; degustation £35-45; ☺7.30pm Wed, Fri & Sat Apr-Sep; 🚗) 🍴 Brilliantly innovative cuisine, wonderfully whimsical presentation and an emphasis on local ingredients are the highlights of the excellent gastronomic degustation menu here. It's an unlikely spot to find such a gourmet experience; the chef is none other than the local GP who forages for wild herbs and flavours in between surgery hours. Top value. It's tiny, so reserve well ahead.

Kirtomy is signposted off the main road about 2.5 miles east of Bettyhill; the restaurant is about a mile down this road.

NORTH COAST 500

The drive along Scotland's far northern coastline is one of Europe's finest road trips. Words fail to describe the sheer variety of the scenic splendour, which unfolds before you as you cross this empty landscape that combines desolate moorlands, brooding mountains, fertile coastal meadows and stunning white-sand beaches.

In a clever piece of recent marketing, it's been dubbed the North Coast 500, as the round-trip from Inverness is roughly that many miles, though you'll surely clock up a few more if you follow your heart down narrow byroads and seek perfect coastal vistas at the end of dead-end tracks.

In our opinion, the scenery is best viewed by taking the route anticlockwise, heading north from Inverness up the east coast to Caithness, then turning west across the top of Scotland before descending down the west coast. This way, you'll make the most of the coastal vistas, the light and the awesome backdrop of the Assynt mountains.

Much of the drive is along single-track road, so it's important to pull over to let both oncoming vehicles and faster traffic behind you pass. Though Inverness companies hire out prestige sports cars for the journey, these really aren't roads where you want to open the throttle; a lazy pace with plenty of photo stops makes for the best journey. It's worth taking several days to do it; in fact you could easily spend a week between Inverness and Ullapool, stopping off for leisurely seafood lunches, tackling some emblematic hills, detouring down valleys to explore the legacy of the Clearances or daring a dip in the North Sea.

While the drive hasn't actually changed, the new name has caught the imagination of tourists, so visitor numbers are well up. The villages along the way aren't overstocked with accommodation, so it's well worth reserving everything in advance if you're travelling the route in the spring or summer months. In winter lots of accommodation is closed so it's a good idea to book then too.

FORSINARD & STRATHNAVER

Though it's tough to tear yourself away from the coast, we recommend plunging down the A897 just east of Melvich. After 14 miles you reach the railway at **Forsinard**. On the platform is **Forsinard Flows Visitor Centre** (☑01641-571225; www.rspb.org.uk; Forsinard; ⊙ visitor centre 9am-5pm Apr-Oct, trails open all year) FREE, a small nature exhibition. There's a live hen-harrier cam, plus guided walks and 4WD excursions available – phone for dates. A 1-mile trail and an impressive viewing tower introduce you to the Flows peatland; 4 miles north is a 4-mile trail crossing golden plover and dunlin nesting grounds. The deep peat blanket bog is a rare and important habitat, at risk from climate change.

Past here, the epic peaty moorscapes stir the heart with their desolate beauty. Take a right at Kinbrace onto the B871, which covers more jaw-dropping scenery before arriving at Syre. Turn right to follow the Strathnaver (valley) back to the coast near Bettyhill. **Strathnaver** saw some of the worst of the Clearances; the **Strathnaver Trail** is a series of numbered points of interest along the valley relating to both this and various prehistoric sites.

Accommodation options on this lonely detour include **Cornmill Bunkhouse** (☑01641-571219; www.achumore.co.uk; A897; dm £15; ℗), a comfortable, modern hostel occupying a picturesque old mill on a working croft in the middle of nowhere; it's on the A897 4 miles south of the coast road. Turning left instead of right at Syre, you'll eventually reach the remote **Altnaharra Hotel** (☑01549-411222; www.altnaharra.com; Altnaharra; s £70, d £109-120, superior d £140-160; ⊙ Mar-Dec; ℗ 🐝 🐾).

ℹ Getting There & Away

From Monday to Friday, there's one daily bus from Bettyhill to Dounreay, which feeds services to Thurso (£3.40, 1¼ hours total). You can also get to Wick.

There are also one to two services with Far North Bus (p191) from Monday to Saturday to Tongue (£3.30, 35 minutes).

Durness

POP 400

Scattered Durness (www.durness.org) is wonderfully located, strung out along cliffs rising from a series of pristine beaches. When the sun shines, the effects of blinding white sand, the cry of seabirds and the spring-green-coloured seas combine in a magical way.

◉ Sights & Activities

Walking the sensational sandy coastline is a highlight, as is a visit to **Cape Wrath**. Durness' beautiful beaches include **Rispond** to the east, **Sango Sands** below town and **Balnakeil** to the west. At Balnakeil, a craft village occupies a one-time early-warning radar station. A northerly beach walk leads to **Faraid Head**, where there are puffins in early summer.

Bikes can be hired from a shed on the square.

Smoo Cave   CAVE

(www.smoocave.org) FREE A mile east of the centre of Durness is a path down to Smoo Cave. From the vast main chamber, you can head through to a smaller flooded cavern where a waterfall sometimes cascades from the roof. There's evidence the cave was inhabited about 6000 years ago. You can take a **tour** (☑01971-511704; www.smoocavetours.weebly.com; adult/child £5/2; ⊙ 11am-4pm Apr-May & Sep, 10am-5pm Jun-Aug) to explore a little further into the interior.

🛏 Sleeping

Sango Sands Oasis   CAMPSITE £

(☑07838 381065; www.sangosands.com; sites per adult/child £9/6, second child £3, others free; ℗ 🐝 🐾) You couldn't imagine a better location for a campsite: great grassy areas on the edge of cliffs, descending to two lovely sandy beaches. Facilities are good and very clean and there's a pub next door. Electric hook-up is an extra £4. You can camp for £9 per site from November to March, but don't complain about the cold.

Lazy Crofter Bunkhouse   HOSTEL £

(☑01971-511202; www.visitdurness.com/bunkhouse; dm £20; 🐝) Durness' best budget accommodation is here, opposite the supermarket. A bothy vibe gives it a very Highland feel. Inviting dorms have plenty of room and lockers, and there's also a sociable shared table for meals and board games, and a great wooden deck with sea views, perfect for midge-free evenings.

★ **Mackays Rooms** HOTEL **££**
(☑ 01971-511202; www.visitdurness.com; d standard £129, deluxe £149-159; ☺ May-Oct; P 🛜 🐾) You really feel you're at the furthest corner of Scotland here, where the road turns through 90 degrees. But whether heading south or east, you'll go far before you find a better place to stay than this haven of Highland hospitality. With its big beds, soft fabrics and contemporary colours, it's a romantic spot with top service and numerous boutique details.

There's also a self-contained cabin here, which can be rented on a self-catering or B&B basis. With two rooms, it sleeps up to four.

Morven B&B **££**
(☑ 01971-511252; morven69@hotmail.com; s/d £50/70; P 🛜 🐾) Cheery owners, a handy next-to-pub location and a serious border-collie theme are key features of this ultra-cosy place. Rooms, which are upstairs and share a downstairs bathroom, have been renovated and feel new and super-comfortable. One is especially spacious and has a top coastal vista.

Smoo Lodge B&B **£££**
(☑ 01971-511423; www.smoolodge.co.uk; r £135-155; P 🛜) A sizeable former shooting lodge on ample grounds has been lovingly restored to a very high standard. Excellent rooms feature high-quality mattresses and bedding as well as great modern bathrooms. Asian-inflected evening meals are available, and breakfast features an excellent Korean option – a nice change from bacon and eggs. No under-12s.

✖ **Eating**

★ **Cocoa Mountain** CAFE **£**
(☑ 01971-511233; www.cocoamountain.co.uk; Balnakeil; hot chocolate £4, 10 truffles £10; ☺ 9am-6pm Easter-Oct) 🍴 At the Balnakeil craft village, this upbeat cafe and chocolate maker offers handmade treats including a chilli, lemongrass and coconut white-chocolate truffle, plus many more unique flavours. Tasty espresso and hot chocolate warm the cockles on those blowy horizontal-drizzle days. It offers light lunches and home-baking too, plus chocolate-making workshops.

Smoo Cave Hotel PUB FOOD **££**
(☑ 01971-511227; www.smoocavehotel.co.uk; mains £9-15; ☺ kitchen 11.30am-9.30pm; 🛜) Signposted off the main road at the eastern end of Durness, this amiable local has quality bar food in hefty portions. Haddock or daily seafood specials – plump scallops are a highlight – are an obvious and worthwhile choice; there's also a restaurant area with clifftop views.

🛈 **Information**

Durness has full services, including an ATM, shops and petrol.

🛈 **Getting There & Away**

A year-round service with **Far North Bus** (☑ 07782 110007; www.thedurnessbus.com) heads to Lairg (£9, 2½ hours, Monday to Friday), where there is a train station. On Saturday buses head to Inverness (£13.40, three hours) and Thurso (£10.30, 2½ hours). In summer school holidays, there's also an Ullapool service (£10, 2½ hours). All these services should be booked; some have bicycle capacity.

There are also two Tuesday services with **Transport for Tongue** (☑ 01847-611766; www.transportfortongue.co.uk) between Tongue and Durness (£7, one hour).

Durness to Ullapool

Perhaps Scotland's most spectacular road, the 69 miles connecting Durness to Ullapool is a smorgasbord of dramatic scenery, almost too much to take in. From Durness you pass through a broad heathered valley with the looming grey bulk of Foinaven and Arkle to the southeast. Heather gives way to a rockier

WORTH A TRIP

SANDWOOD BAY

South of Cape Wrath, **Sandwood Bay** boasts one of Scotland's best and most isolated beaches, guarded at one end by the spectacular rock pinnacle Am Buachaille. Sandwood Bay is about 2 miles north of the end of a track from Blairmore (approach from Kinlochbervie), or you could walk south from the cape (allow eight hours) and on to Blairmore. Sandwood House is a creepy ruin reputedly haunted by the ghost of a 16th-century shipwrecked sailor from the Spanish Armada.

landscape of Lewisian gneiss pockmarked with hundreds of small lochans. This is the most interesting zone geologically in the UK, with Britain's oldest rock. Next come gorse-covered hills prefacing the magnificent Torridonian sandstone mountains of Assynt and Coigach, including Suilven's distinctive sugarloaf, ziggurat-like Quinag and pinnacled Stac Pollaidh. The area has been named as the Northwest Highlands Geopark (www.nwhgeopark.com).

Scourie & Handa Island

Scourie is a pretty crofting community with decent services, halfway between Durness and Ullapool. A few miles north lies Handa Island, a nature reserve run by the Scottish Wildlife Trust.

Handa Island
Nature Reserve   NATURE RESERVE
(www.scottishwildlifetrust.org.uk) A few miles north of Scourie Bay lies this nature reserve run by the Scottish Wildlife Trust. The island's western sea cliffs provide nesting sites for important breeding populations of great skuas, arctic skuas, puffins, kittiwakes, razorbills and guillemots. Reach the island from Tarbet, 6 miles north of Scourie, via the Handa Island Ferry (07780 967800; www. handa-ferry.com; Tarbet Pier; adult/child return £15/5; outbound 9am-2pm Mon-Sat Apr-Aug, last ferry back 5pm); call for times and to book your spot.

★ Shorehouse Seafood
Restaurant   SEAFOOD ££
(01971 502251; www.shorehousetarbet.co.uk; Tarbet Pier; mains £10-19; noon-/pm Mon-Sat Easter-Sep) By the ferry pier for Handa Island Nature Reserve, Shorehouse is a restaurant and cafe in a lovely setting, looking across the sound to the sandy beach on Handa Island. There's a conservatory and outdoor terrace that make the most of the view, and a menu that concentrates on local seafood including crab and prawn salads and Achiltibuie smoked salmon.

Kylesku & Loch Glencoul

Hidden away on the shores of Loch Glencoul, tiny Kylesku served as a ferry crossing on the route north until it was made redundant by beautiful Kylesku Bridge in 1984. It's a good base for walks; you can hire bikes too.

Eas a'Chual Aluinn   WATERFALL
Five miles southeast of Kylesku, in wild, remote country, lies 213m-high Eas a'Chual Aluinn, Britain's highest waterfall. You can hike to the top of the falls from a parking area at a sharp bend in the main road 3 miles south of Kylesku; allow five hours for the 6-mile return trip. It can also be seen on boat trips (01971-502231; www.kyleskuboattours.com; adult/child £30/20; Apr-Sep) from Kylesku.

★ Kylesku Hotel   SEAFOOD ££
(01971-502231; www.kyleskuhotel.co.uk; mains £12-23; noon-2.30pm & 6-9pm mid-Feb-Apr & Oct-Nov, noon-9pm May-Sep;) In this remote lochside location, it's a real pleasure to gorge yourself on delicious sustainable seafood. Local langoustines, squat lobsters and mussels are the specialties at this convivial restaurant, that has a new extension offering extra waterview seating. There's a good atmosphere of mingling locals and visitors at the bar.

Lochinver & Assynt

With its otherworldly scenery of isolated peaks rising above a sea of crumpled, lochan-spattered gneiss, Assynt epitomises the northwest's wild magnificence. Glaciers have sculpted the hills of Suilven (731m), Canisp (846m), Quinag (808m) and Ben More Assynt (998m) into strange, wonderful silhouettes.

Lochinver is the main settlement, a busy little fishing port that's a popular port of call with its laid-back atmosphere, good facilities and striking scenery. Just north of Lochinver (or if coming from the north, not far south of Kylesku), a 23-mile detour on the narrow B869 rewards with spectacular views and fine beaches. From the lighthouse at Point of Stoer, a one-hour cliff walk leads to the Old Man of Stoer, a spectacular sea stack.

🏃 Activities

The limestone hills around Inchnadamph are famous for their caves. There's some excellent walking in the area.

NorWest Sea Kayaking   KAYAKING
(07900 641860; www.norwestseakayaking.com; half-/full-day trip £55/85) This outfit offers introductory sea-kayaking courses and guided kayaking tours around the Summer Isles and in the Lochinver and Ullapool area. It also hires kayaks and will do pick-ups and drop-offs.

CAPE WRATH

Though its name actually comes from the Norse word *hvarf* ('turning point'), there is something daunting and primal about Cape Wrath, the remote northwesternmost point of the British mainland.

The danger of the hazardous, stormy seas led to the building of the lighthouse at the cape by Robert and Alan Stevenson in 1828. The last keepers had left by 1998, when people were replaced by automation. Three miles to the east are the seabird colonies of Clo Mor, the British mainland's highest vertical sea cliffs (195m).

Part of the moorland has served for decades as a bombing range. The island of An Garbh-Eilean, 5 miles from the cape, has the misfortune to be around the same size as an aircraft carrier and is regularly ripped up by RAF bombs and missiles. There is no public access when the range is in use; times are displayed on www.visitcapewrath.com.

A cafe at the lighthouse serves soup and sandwiches. It's open year-round and John, the owner, will never turn anyone away whatever the time of day.

Getting to Cape Wrath involves taking a **ferry** (📞07719 678729; www.capewrathferry. co.uk; single/return trip £5/7; ⊘Easter–mid-Oct) – passengers and bikes only – across the Kyle of Durness (10 minutes). It connects with the **Cape Wrath Minibus** (📞01971-511284; www.visitcapewrath.com; single/return trip £7/12; ⊘Easter–mid-Oct), which runs the very slow and bumpy 11 miles to the cape (50 minutes).

This combination is a friendly but eccentric and sometimes shambolic service with limited capacity, so plan on waiting in high season, and call ahead to make sure the ferry is running. The ferry leaves from 2 miles southwest of Durness, and runs twice or more daily from Easter to mid-October. If you eschew the minibus, it's a spectacular 11-mile ride or hike from boat to cape over bleak scenery.

An increasingly popular but challenging walking route, the **Cape Wrath Trail** (www. capewrathtrail.org.uk) runs from Fort William up to Cape Wrath (230 miles). It's unmarked so buy the *Cape Wrath Trail* guidebook (www.cicerone.co.uk) or go with a guide – **C-n-Do** (📞01786-445703; www.cndoscotland.com) is one operator.

🛏 Sleeping & Eating

Clachtoll Beach Campsite CAMPSITE £
(📞01571-855377; www.clachtollbeachcampsite. co.uk; B869, Clachtoll; site £6-12, plus per adult/child £5/2; ⊘Apr–mid-Oct; 🅿🔌🐕) Set among the machair beside a lovely white-sand beach and emerald seas, Clachtoll is a divine coastal camping spot, though somewhat overwhelmed by the adjacent self-catering development. It's 6 miles northwest of Lochinver by road.

Achmelvich Beach SYHA HOSTEL £
(📞01571-844480; www.syha.org.uk; dm/tw £21/53; ⊘Apr-Sep) Off the B869, this whitewashed cottage is set beside a great beach at the end of a side road. Dorms are simple, and there's a sociable common kitchen and eating area. Heat-up meals are available as is a basic shop in summer; otherwise, there's a chip van at the adjacent campsite, or you can take the 4-mile walk to Lochinver.

Davar B&B ££
(📞01571-844501; www.davar-lochinver.co.uk; Baddidarroch, Lochinver; s £60, d £90-100; 🅿🔌) Run

with a genuine welcome and enthusiasm, this is a beautiful house with a garden and a fabulous outlook across the bay to Suilven and the Assynt mountainscape. The four rooms are well appointed and have plenty of space; it's the ideal base for exploring the region. To find it, turn west at the northern end of Lochinver.

★**Albannach** HOTEL £££
(📞01571-844407; www.thealbannach.co.uk; Baddidarroch, Lochinver; s/d/ste £135/170/235; ⊘mid-Feb–mid-Dec; 🅿🔌) 🍴 The Albannach combines old-fashioned country-house elements – steep creaky stairs, stuffed animals, fireplaces and noble antique furniture – with strikingly handsome rooms that range from a sumptuous four-poster to more modern spaces with underfloor heating and, in one case, a private deck with outdoor spa. Glorious views, spacious grounds and great walks in easy striking distance make this a perfect place to base yourself.

The renowned restaurant is closed but the welcoming owners do food at the **Caberfeidh** (📞01571-844321; www.thecaberfeidh.co.uk;

Main St, Lochinver; tapas £5-8, mains £12-18; ⊗kitchen 6-9pm Tue-Sat, 12.30-8pm Sun East-er-Oct, plus noon-2.30pm Tue-Sat in summer, 6-8pm Thu-Sat, 12.30-8pm Sun Nov-Mar; ☎) ✎ in town. The Albannach was for sale at the time of research so things may change.

Lochinver Larder
& Riverside Bistro   CAFE, BISTRO ££
(☑01571-844356;   www.lochinverlarder.co.uk; 3 Main St, Lochinver; pies £5-6, mains £12-16; ⊗10am-7.45pm Mon-Sat, to 5.30pm Sun Apr-Oct, 10am-4pm Mon-Sat Nov-Mar; ☎) An outstand-ing menu of inventive food made with local produce is on offer here. The bistro turns out delicious seafood dishes in the evening, while the takeaway counter sells tasty pies with a wide range of gourmet fillings (try the wild boar and apricot). It also does quality meals to take away and heat up: great for hostellers and campers.

ⓘ Getting There & Away

There are buses from Ullapool to Lochinver (£5.10, one hour, two to three Monday to Satur-day) and a summer bus that goes on to Durness.

Coigach

The region south of Assynt, west of the main A835 road from Ullapool to Ledmore Junc-tion, is known as Coigach (www.coigach. com). A lone, single-track road penetrates this wilderness, leading through gloriously wild scenery to remote settlements. At the western end of Loch Lurgainn, a branch leads north to Lochinver, a scenic backroad so narrow and twisting that it's nicknamed the Wee Mad Road.

Coigach is a wonderland for walkers and wildlife enthusiasts, with a patchwork of sinuous silver lochs dominated by the iso-lated peaks of Cul Mor (849m), Cul Beag (769m), Ben More Coigach (743m) and Stac Pollaidh (613m). The main settlement is the straggling township of Achiltibuie, 15 miles from the main road, with the gorgeous Sum-mer Isles moored just off the coast, and sil-houettes of mountains skirting the bay.

Stac Pollaidh   HIKING
Despite its diminutive size, Stac Pollaidh (613m) provides one of the most exciting hill walks in the Highlands, with some good scrambling on its narrow sandstone crest.

Begin at the car park overlooking Loch Lurgainn, 5 miles west of the A835, and follow a clearly marked and well-made foot-path around the eastern end of the hill to ascend from the far side; return by the same route (3 miles return, two to four hours).

Summer Isles Seatours   CRUISE
(☑07927 920592; www.summerisles-seatours. co.uk; adult/child £30/15; ⊗Mon-Sat May-Sep) Cruises to the Summer Isles from Old Dornie pier, northwest of Achiltibuie. You get to spend some time ashore on Tanera Mòr.

Acheninver Hostel   HOSTEL £
(☑01854-622283; www.acheninverhostel.com; dm £20, d £50; ⊗Apr-Sep) A quarter-mile walk off the road a couple of miles southeast of Achiltibuie, this off-the-beaten-track hostel has a remote, serene location that's one of the country's best. It's a cosy spot, and has a female dorm with single beds, a male dorm with bunks and three en suite huts sleeping two to three. There's a kitchen, and some limited supplies are available.

★Summer Isles Hotel   HOTEL £££
(☑01854-622282; www.summerisleshotel.com; Achiltibuie; s £110-190, d £150-250; ⊗Easter-Oct; P☎🐾) This is a special place, with crack-ing views and wonderfully romantic rooms (one themed on Charlie Chaplin, who stayed here), plus other suites in separate cottages and a snug bar with outdoor seating. 'Court-yard view' rooms are darkish; it's worth up-grading to one with vistas. It's the perfect spot for a romantic getaway or some quality time off life's treadmill.

The restaurant (noon to 3pm and 6pm to 9pm; dinner £49) is of high quality, with local lobster usually featuring in addition to renowned cheese and dessert trolleys. There's also a great wine list considering you're in the middle of nowhere.

Salt Seafood Kitchen   SEAFOOD ££
(☑01854-622380; www.saltseafood.com; 140 Badenscaillie; mains £11-16; ⊗5-9.15pm Mon-Sat Apr-Oct) ✎ A mile south of Achiltibuie, this sweet chalet offers views to the Summer Isles and fresh local seafood served with a smile. What's on offer varies, but expect to find mussels, langoustines and squat lobster among other denizens of the sea, as well as burgers, sandwiches and soups. Prices are very reasonable, and the seafood platter is an absolute feast for two.

ⓘ Getting There & Away

There are buses from Ullapool to Achiltibuie (£6.20, 1¼ hours, one to three daily Monday to Saturday).

Ullapool

POP 1500

This pretty port on the shores of Loch Broom is the largest settlement in Wester Ross and one of the most alluring spots in the Highlands, a wonderful destination in itself as well as a gateway to the Western Isles. Offering a row of whitewashed cottages arrayed along the harbour and special views of the loch and its flanking hills, the town has a very distinctive appeal. The harbour served as an emigration point during the Clearances, with thousands of Scots watching Ullapool recede behind as they began a journey to a new continent.

◎ Sights & Activities

Ullapool is a great centre for hill walking. A good path up Gleann na Sguaib heads for the top of Beinn Dearg from Inverlael, at the inner end of Loch Broom. Ridge-walking on the Fannichs is relatively straightforward and many different routes are possible.

The Ullapool Tourist Office (p196) can supply you with all the information and maps you need. Good walking books are also sold there, and at Ullapool Bookshop (☑ 01854-612918; www.ullapoolbookshop.co.uk; Quay St; ☺ 9am-5.30pm Mon-Sat, 11am-5pm Sun Nov-Mar, to 9pm Mon-Sat Apr-Oct), or you can pick up a copy of the freebie guide to local woodland walks.

Ullapool Museum   MUSEUM
(☑ 01854-612987; www.ullapoolmuseum.co.uk; 7 West Argyle St; adult/child £4/free; ☺ 11am-4pm Mon-Sat Apr-Oct) Housed in a converted Telford church, this museum relates the prehistoric, natural and social history of the town and Lochbroom area, with a particular focus on the emigration to Nova Scotia and other places. There's also a genealogy section if you want to trace your Scottish roots.

Shearwater Cruises   BOATING
(☑ 01854-612472; www.summerqueen.co.uk; ☺ Mon-Sat May-Sep) Weather permitting, the catamaran *Shearwater* takes you out to the Summer Isles for a 2¼-hour cruise (adult/child £35/30). They leave twice a day.

⌂ Sleeping

There's a good selection of B&Bs, with some standout options. Note that during summer Ullapool is very busy and finding accommo-

THE SUMMER ISLES

The dozen islands scattered in the sea to the west of Achiltibuie are known as the Summer Isles. There's a superb view of the islands, with the hills of Wester Ross in the background, from the minor road between Altandhu and Achnahaird – look out for a layby with a bench and a signpost, where a short path leads to the viewpoint.

In the late 19th century the Summer Isles were home to 120 people working at the herring fishery, but now the permanent population is only half a dozen, augmented by holiday visitors. The largest island, Tanera Mòr, has self-catering cottages.

You can visit the Summer Isles on boat trips from Ullapool; tour operators include **Seascape** (☑ 07511 290081; www.sea-scape.co.uk; ☺ May-Sep) and Shearwater Cruises. Otherwise, there are cruises with Summer Isles Seatours (p194) and other boat transport from Old Dornie pier, northwest of Achiltibuie, available in summer by prior arrangement.

dation can be tricky – book ahead. Several places don't accept single-night stays.

Ullapool SYHA   HOSTEL £
(☑ 01854-612254; www.syha.org.uk; Shore St; dm/tw/q £21.50/55/96; ☺ Apr-Oct; ☎) You've got to hand it to the SYHA – it's chosen some very sweet locations for its hostels. This one is right in the heart of town on the pretty waterfront; some rooms have harbour views and the busy dining area and little lounge are also good spots for contemplating the water.

★ Tamarin Lodge   B&B ££
(☑ 01854-612667; www.tamarinullapool.com; 9 The Braes; s/d £45/90; P ☎ ☀) Effortlessly elegant modern architecture in this hilltop house is noteworthy in its own right, but the glorious vistas over the hills opposite and water far below are unforgettable. All rooms face the view; some have a balcony, and all are very spacious, quiet and utterly relaxing, with unexpected features and gadgets. The great lounge and benevolent hosts are a delight.

Follow signs for Braes from the Inverness road.

★ **West House** B&B ££

(☎01854-613126; www.westhousebandb.co.uk; West Argyle St; d without breakfast £75-85; ☺ May-Sep; P 🛜) 🖉 Slap bang in Ullapool's centre, this solid house, once a manse, has excellent rooms with contemporary style and great bathrooms. There's no breakfast, but you get a fridge, juice and decent coffee, plus there are two good cafes close by. Most rooms have great views, as well as lots of conveniences. The genial owners also have tempting self-catering options in the area.

There's a minimum two-night stay.

Waterside House B&B ££

(☎01854-612140; www.waterside.uk.net; 6 West Shore St; d £85-95; ☺Apr-Oct; P) This typical whitewashed home is right on the waterfront, so close to the ferry that you can watch it docking out of your window. Waterside House features three compact but beautifully appointed rooms with excellent modern bathrooms. The location and the friendly welcome are fabulous, and your hosts go the extra mile at breakfast time – delicious. Minimum two-night stay in summer.

★ **Ceilidh Place** HOTEL £££

(☎01854-612103; www.theceilidhplace.com; 14 West Argyle St; s £70-96, d £140-170; P 🛜 🐕) This hotel is a celebration of Scottish culture: we're talking literature and traditional music, not tartan and Nessie dolls. Rooms go for character over modernity; instead of TVs they come with a selection of books chosen by Scottish literati, plus eclectic artwork and cosy touches. The sumptuous lounge has sofas, chaise longues and an honesty bar. There's a bookshop here, too.

It's not luxurious but it's one of the Highlands' more unusual and delightful places to stay.

✗ Eating

West Coast Delicatessen CAFE £

(☎01854-613450; www.westcoastdeli.co.uk; 5 Argyle St; light meals £3-7; ☺9am-5pm Mon-Sat; 🛜) A likeable venue for a coffee or snack, this upbeat modern place has sub rolls, decent coffee and a variety of deli produce, including some very tasty cheeses. It also does a good soup, perfect for windier Ullapool days.

Seafood Shack SEAFOOD £

(☎07876 142623; www.seafoodshack.co.uk; West Argyle St; takeaways £4-9; ☺noon-6pm Apr-late Oct) High-quality fresh seafood is served out of a trailer in this vacant lot by two

cheery lasses. There's a wide range of tasty fare available, from hand-dived scallops to calamari to mussels, crab, oysters and fish.

Ceilidh Place SCOTTISH ££

(☎01854-612103; www.theceilidhplace.com; 14 West Argyle St; mains £10-18; ☺8am-9pm Feb-Dec; 🛜) The restaurant in this hub of culture and good cheer serves inventive dishes that focus on fresh local seafood backed up by stews, plus lighter meals like pies and burgers during the day. Quality depends a bit on staffing, but it's an atmospheric, cosy place with outdoor seating, good wines by the glass and regular live music and events.

ℹ Information

Ullapool Library (☎01854-612543; www.highlifehighland.com; Mill St; ☺9am-5pm Mon-Fri, plus 6-8pm Tue & Thu, shorter hours & closed Mon & Wed during public holidays; 🛜) Free internet access.

Ullapool Tourist Office (☎01854-612486; ullapool@visitscotland.com; 6 Argyle St; ☺9am-6pm Mon-Sat, 9.30am-4.30pm Sun Jul & Aug, 9.30am-5pm Mon-Sat, 10am-3pm Sun Jun & Sep, 9.30am-4.30pm Mon-Sat, 10am-3pm Sun Easter-May & Oct, 9am-2pm Mon, Fri & Sat, 10am-2pm Sun Nov-Easter) Can book ferries and buses.

ℹ Getting There & Away

Citylink has buses from Inverness to Ullapool (£14, 1½ hours, one to three daily), connecting with the Lewis ferry.

Two daily ferries (only one on winter Sundays) with **CalMac** (☎0800 066 5000; www.calmac.co.uk) run from Ullapool to Stornoway on Lewis in the Outer Hebrides (adult/car £9.50/50.95, 2½ hours).

Ullapool to Kyle of Lochalsh

Although it's less than 50 miles as the crow flies from Ullapool to Kyle of Lochalsh, it's more like 150 miles along the circuitous coastal road – but don't let that put you off. It's a deliciously remote region and there are fine views of beaches and bays backed by mountains all the way along.

Twelve miles southeast of Ullapool at Braemore, the A832 doubles back towards the coast as it heads for Gairloch (the A835 continues southeast across the wild, sometimes snowbound, Dirrie More pass to Garve and Inverness). If you're hurrying to Skye, use the A835 and catch up with the A832 further south, near Garve.

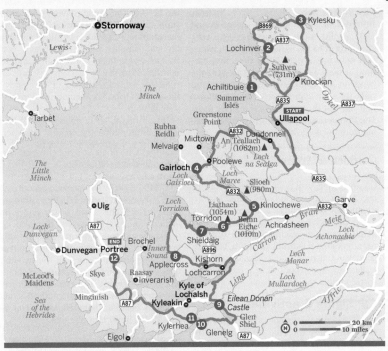

Driving Tour
Wee Roads & Mighty Mountains

START ULLAPOOL
END PORTREE
LENGTH 320 MILES; THREE TO FOUR DAYS

Starting in photogenic harbourside Ullapool, this drive takes in some of the lesser-known roads and the most majestic of Highland scenery, leaving you on the Isle of Skye.

Leave your bags in the hotel, because the first day is a long round trip from Ullapool. Head north on the A835, and turn left to ❶ **Achiltibuie** (p194), where, after gaping at impressive lochside Stac Pollaidh en route, you can admire the outlook over the Summer Isles. From here, backtrack 6 miles then turn left up the Wee Mad Road, a narrow, tortuous but scenic drive north to pretty ❷ **Lochinver** (p192). From here, the B869 winds north past spectacular beaches at Achmelvich and Clachtoll to ❸ **Kylesku** (p192), where the hotel makes a great lunch stop. Return south to Ullapool on the main road (A894–A837–A835), with classic northwestern scenery and things to see along the way, including the Inchnadamph Caves, Ardvreck Castle and Knockan Crag.

The next day head inland along the A835 before taking the A832 ❹ **Gairloch** (p198) turn-off, following the long, circuitous coast road with plenty of activity options, from whale-watching trips to a botanic garden and hill walking around scenic Loch Maree. At ❺ **Kinlochewe** (p199) turn back coastwards on the A896, descending a spectacular pass to ❻ **Torridon** (p200), where the rugged beauty is simply breathtaking. There are good overnight stops all along this route.

From ❼ **Shieldaig** (p200), take the coastal road to sublime little ❽ **Applecross** (p200), then brave the Bealach na Bà pass to get you back to the main road. A loop around Loch Carron will eventually bring you to the A87. Turn left, passing ❾ **Eilean Donan Castle** (p203) and, reaching Glen Shiel, take the right turn to ❿ **Glenelg** (p203), a scenic, out-of-the-way place with a wonderfully rustic summer ferry crossing to Skye. Disembark at ⓫ **Kylerhea** (p207) and enjoy the vistas on one of the island's least-trafficked roads before hitting the A87 again. From here, ⓬ **Portree** (p212) is an easy drive, but numerous picturesque detours – to Sleat or Elgol for example – mean you might take a while to reach it yet.

Falls of Measach
WATERFALL

Just west of the junction of the A835 and A832, 2 miles south of Braemore, a car park gives access to the Falls of Measach, which spill 45m into spectacularly deep and narrow Corrieshalloch Gorge. You can cross the gorge on a swaying suspension bridge, and walk west for 250m to a viewing platform that juts out dizzyingly above a sheer drop. The thundering falls and misty vapours rising from the gorge are very impressive.

Gairloch & Around

POP 1000

Gairloch is a group of villages (comprising Achtercairn, Strath and Charlestown) around the inner end of a loch of the same name. Gairloch is a good base for whale- and dolphin-watching excursions and the surrounding area has beautiful sandy beaches, good trout fishing and birdwatching. Hill walkers also use Gairloch as a base for the Torridon hills and An Teallach.

◉ Sights & Activities

The B8056 runs along Loch Gairloch's southern shore, past the cute little harbour of Badachro, to end at the gorgeous pink-sand beach of Red Point – a perfect picnic spot. Another coastal road leads north from Gairloch 11 miles to the settlement of Melvaig. From here a private road (open to walkers and cyclists) continues 3 miles to Rua Reidh Lighthouse (building and grounds off-limits to nonguests).

★ Inverewe Garden
GARDENS

(NTS; ☑01445-712952; www.nts.org.uk; adult/concession £11/9.50; ⊙9.30am-6pm Jun-Aug, to 5pm Mar, Apr & Sep, to 5.30pm May, to 4pm Oct, 10am-4pm Nov-Feb) Six miles north of Gairloch, this splendid place is a welcome splash of colour on this otherwise bleak coast. The climate here is warmed by the Gulf Stream, which allowed Osgood MacKenzie to create this exotic woodland garden in 1862. There are free guided tours on weekdays at 1.30pm from March to October. The licensed cafe-restaurant serves great cakes.

Parking for non-members is £2.

Russian Arctic Convoy
Exhibition Centre
MUSEUM

(☑01445-731137; www.russianarcticconvoymuseum. org; Birchburn, Aultbea; adult/child £3.50/free; ⊙10am-4pm Mon-Sat Apr–mid-Dec, 11am-3pm Fri-Sun Jan-Mar) The Arctic convoys were a vital supply line for Russia during WWII; these merchant ships escorted by Allied warships brought supplies into the northern ports through a gauntlet of German ships and submarines. Many left from Loch Ewe, and this volunteer project tells some of the stories of those tough trips. It's fascinating; there's also a small shop.

It's on the A832, 12 miles north of Gairloch. Winter opening hours may vary according to volunteer availability.

Gairloch Marine Wildlife
Centre & Cruises
WILDLIFE, CRUISE

(☑01445-712636; www.porpoise-gairloch.co.uk; Pier Rd; cruises adult/child £20/15; ⊙10am-4pm Easter-Oct) ✎ This small visitor centre has audiovisual and interactive displays, lots of charts, photos and knowledgable staff. From here, cruises run three times daily (weather permitting); during the two-hour trips you may see basking sharks, porpoises and minke whales. The crew collects data on water temperature and conditions, and monitors cetacean populations, so you are subsidising important research.

Hebridean Whale Cruises
WILDLIFE, CRUISE

(☑01445-712458; www.hebridean-whale-cruises. com; Pier Rd; cruises 2½/4hr £50/80; ⊙Apr-Oct) Based at Gairloch's harbour, this set-up runs three trips: a standard 2½-hour whale-watching excursion (from May), a three-hour visit to the seabird-rich Shiant Islands and a four-hour excursion to further-flung feeding grounds in search of orca. Other wildlife it's possible to see include otters, dolphins and seals. Trips are in a zippy rigid inflatable.

🛏 Sleeping & Eating

Gairloch Sands Youth Hostel
HOSTEL £

(☑01445-712219; www.hostellingscotland.org. uk; Carn Dearg; dm/tw/q £22/55/96; ⊙Apr-Sep; P 🗟 🐾) Located 2.5 miles west of Gairloch in a stunning coastal position, this hostel is close to beaches and well set up fo walkers. Wood-panelled rooms and a large dining room/lounge offer comfort, but the real star is that view...magic!

Rua Reidh Lighthouse
LODGE ££

(☑01445-771263; www.stayatalighthouse.co.uk; Melvaig; s £75-90, d £100-120; ⊙Easter-Oct; P 🐾) Three miles down a narrow private road beyond Melvaig (11 miles north of Gairloch), this simple yet excellent lodge gives a taste of a lighthouse keeper's life. It's a wild, lonely location great for walking and birdwatching. Breakfast is included and tasty evening meals are available. There's no mobile-phone signal or wi-fi and there's usually a two-night minimum stay: book well ahead.

There's a separate self-catering apartment that's available year-round.

Shieldaig Lodge HOTEL **£££**
(☑ 01445-741333; www.shieldaiglodge.com; Badachro; s £150, d £200-300; P ☎) This refurbished hunting lodge has a super waterside position on a sizeable estate offering good walking and fishing as well as falconry and archery. It's a cosy place – think drams and a log fire – with a good restaurant, a very well-stocked bar and tasteful rooms, the best of which have water views. There's also a snooker table and a lovely library.

Mountain Coffee Company CAFE **£**
(☑ 01445-712316; www.facebook.com/mountain coffee.gairloch; Strath Sq, Strath; light meals £4-7; ☺9am-5.30pm, shorter hours low season) 🍴 More the sort of place you'd expect to find on the gringo trail in the Andes, this offbeat and cosy (if brusque) spot is a shrine to mountaineering and travelling. It serves tasty savoury bagels, home baking and sustainably sourced coffees. The conservatory is the place to lap up the sun, while the attached Hillbillies Bookshop is well worth a browse.

There are rather sweet rooms available, too.

Isle of Ewe Smokehouse FOOD
(☑01445-731304; www.smokedbyewe.com; Ormiscaig, Aultbea; ☺9am-5.30pm Mon-Fri) This excellent spot 14 miles north of Gairloch does really delicious hot- and cold-smoked salmon as well as other seafoody delicacies and a range of deli products. Addicted after your visit? Don't worry, they deliver by mail.

ℹ Information

Gairloch Tourist Office (☑ 01445-712071; www.galeactionforum.co.uk; Achtercairn; ☺9.30am-5.30pm Mon-Sat, 10.30am-5pm Sun Jun-Sep, 10am-5.30pm Mon-Sat, 10.30am-4.30pm Sun Oct-May) Community-run information centre in the wooden Gale Centre, on the road through town. Has good walking pamphlets; there's also a cafe here.

ℹ Getting There & Away

Public transport to Gairloch is very limited. **Westerbus** (☑ 01445-712255) runs to/from Inverness (£10.30, 2¼ hours, Monday to Saturday) and Ullapool (£5.15, 1¾ hours, Thursday).

Loch Maree & Around

Stretching 12 miles between Poolewe and Kinlochewe, Loch Maree is considered one of Scotland's prettiest lochs, with the imposing bulk of Slioch on its northeastern side and Beinn Eighe on the southwestern. Look out for black-throated divers on the lake in summer. At its southern end, tiny Kinlochewe makes a good base for outdoor activities.

Beinn Eighe Mountain Trail WALKING
This waymarked 4-mile loop walk to a plateau and cairn on the side of Beinn Eighe has magnificent views over Loch Maree. It's quite exposed up here, so take some warm clothing. The walk starts from a car park on the A832 about 1.5 miles northwest of the Beinn Eighe Visitor Centre.

From the same trailhead there's a shorter 1-mile trail through Scots pine forest.

Kinlochewe Hotel INN, HOSTEL **££**
(☑ 01445-760253; www.kinlochewehotel.co.uk; Kinlochewe; dm £17.50, s £60, d £100-110; P ☎ ☺) 🍴 This is a welcoming hotel that's very walker-friendly, with features such as a handsome lounge well stocked with books, a great bar with several real ales on tap and a menu of locally sourced food. There are 'economy' rooms that share a bath-only bathroom (£90) and also a bunkhouse with one no-frills 12-bed dorm, plus a decent kitchen and clean bathrooms.

★ Whistle Stop Cafe CAFE, BISTRO **££**
(☑01445-760423; www.facebook.com/Whistle-Stop -Cafe-Kinlochewe-223096744444313; Kinlochewe; meals £8-16; ☺8am-8pm Mon-Sat, 10am-5pm Sun Apr-Sep, reduced hours mid-Feb–Mar & Oct–mid-Nov) A colourful presence in the former village hall, this is a tempting place to drop by for anything from a coffee to enticing bistro fare. There are great daily specials and delicious home baking, juices and smoothies. It's very friendly, and used to pumping life back into chilly walkers and cyclists. It's unlicensed, but you can take your own wine (£1 corkage).

Opening hours vary substantially season by season; check its Facebook page.

Torridon

The road southwest from Kinlochewe passes through Glen Torridon, amid some of Britain's most beautiful scenery. Carved by ice from massive layers of ancient sandstone that takes its name from the region, the mountains here are steep, shapely and imposing, whether flirting with autumn mists, draped in dazzling winter snows, or reflected in the calm blue waters of Loch Torridon on a summer day.

The road reaches the sea at spectacularly sited Torridon village, then continues westwards to lovely Shieldaig, which boasts an attractive main street of whitewashed houses right on the water.

🏃 Activities

The Torridon Munros – Liathach (1054m; pronounced 'lee-agakh', Gaelic for 'the Grey One'), Beinn Eighe (1010m; 'ben *ay*', 'the File') and Beinn Alligin (986m; 'the Jewelled Mountain') – are big, serious mountains for experienced hill walkers only. Though not technically difficult, their ascents are long and committing, often over rough and rocky terrain. Further information is available at the Torridon Countryside Centre (NTS; ☑ 01445-791221; www.nts.org.uk; ⊙ 10am-5pm Sun-Fri Easter-Sep).

Torridon Activities (☑ 01445-791242; www.thetorridon.com/activities; activities half/full day £40/60) runs a number of outdoor pursuits, including sea kayaking and mountain biking.

🛏 Sleeping & Eating

Torridon SYHA HOSTEL £
(☑ 01445-791284; www.syha.org.uk; Torridon; dm/tw £21.50/55; ⊙ daily Mar-Oct, Fri & Sat nights Nov-Feb; P @ 🛜 🛜) This spacious hostel has enthusiastic, can-do management and sits in a magnificent location, surrounded by spectacular mountains. Roomy dorms and privates (twins have single beds) are allied to a huge kitchen and convivial lounge area, with ales on sale. It's a very popular walking base, with great advice from the in-house mountain rescue team, so book ahead.

As well as breakfasts, there are packed lunches and heat-up dinners on offer.

Torridon Inn INN ££
(☑ 01445-791242; www.thetorridon.com; Torridon; s/d/q £110/140/215; ⊙ daily Easter-Oct, Thu-Sun Nov & mid-Feb–Easter, closed Dec–mid-Feb; P 🛜 🛜) This convivial but upmarket walkers hang-out has excellent modern rooms that vary substantially in size and layout. Rooms for groups (of up to six) offer more value than the commodious but overpriced doubles. The sociable bar serves all-day food and there are numerous activities on offer.

★ Torridon HOTEL £££
(☑ 01445-791242; www.thetorridon.com; Torridon; r standard/superior/deluxe/master £265/320/390/450; ⊙ closed Jan, plus Mon & Tue Nov, Dec, Feb & Mar; P @ 🛜 🛜) If you prefer the lap of luxury to the sound of rain beating on your tent, head for this lavish Victorian shooting lodge with a romantic lochside location. Sumptuous contemporary rooms with awe-inspiring views, top bathrooms and a cheery Highland cow atop the counterpane couldn't be more inviting. This is one of Scotland's top country hotels, always luxurious but never pretentious.

Tigh an Eilean HOTEL £££
(☑ 01520-755251; www.tighaneilean.co.uk; Shieldaig; s/d £72.50/145; ⊙ Feb-Dec; 🛜) With a lovely waterfront position in the pretty village of Shieldaig, this is an appealing destination for a relaxing stay, offering old-style rooms that are comfortable, not luxurious. Loch-view rooms – with gloriously soothing vistas – are allocated on a first-booked basis, so it's worth reserving ahead. Service is very helpful, and there's a cosy lounge with an honesty bar.

Prices drop for stays of three or more nights.

Shieldaig Bar & Coastal Kitchen SEAFOOD ££
(☑ 01520-755251; www.shieldaigbarandcoastalkitchen.co.uk; Shieldaig; mains £10-21; ⊙ food noon-2.30pm & 6-8.30pm or 9pm, closed some winter lunchtimes; 🛜) This attractive pub has real ales and waterside tables plus a great upstairs dining room and an outdoor deck. There's an emphasis on quality local seafood as well as wood-fired pizzas and bistro-style meat dishes such as steak-frites or sausages and mash. Blackboard specials feature the daily catch.

Applecross

POP 200

The delightfully remote seaside village of Applecross feels like an island retreat due to its isolation and the magnificent views of Raasay and the hills of Skye that set the pulse racing, particularly at sunset. On a clear day it's an unforgettable place. The campsite and pub fill to the brim in school holidays.

A road leads here 25 winding miles from Shieldaig, but more spectacular (accessed from further south on the A896) is the magnificent Bealach na Bà (626m; Pass of the Cattle), the third-highest motor road in the UK, and the longest continuous climb. Originally built in 1822, it climbs steeply and hair-raisingly via hairpin bends perched over sheer drops, with gradients of up to 25%, then drops dramatically to the village with views of Skye.

Hartfield House   HOSTEL £

(☑01520-744333; www.hartfieldhouse.org.uk; dm/s/tw/d £25/40/50/55; ☺Mar-Oct; P🏠) This former hunting lodge on the Applecross estate is about a mile off the road in a lovely rural location. With lots of beds across two separate buildings in both dorms and private rooms, plus good common areas, it offers plenty of space and comfort. Walkers and cyclists have decent facilities and a help-yourself continental breakfast is included.

Applecross Inn   INN £££

(☑01520-744262; www.applecross.uk.com; Shore St; s/d £90/140; P🏠🏠) The hub of the spread-out Applecross community, this inn is a great spot to hole up, but you'll need to book ahead. Seven snug bedrooms all have a view of the Skye hills and the sea. It's a magical spot and there's a cracking pub and restaurant (mains £10-18; ☺noon-9pm; 🏠) too. It also has some cottage accommodation along the waterfront.

🛈 Getting There & Away

There are two buses a week (Wednesday and Saturday) with **Lochcarron Garage** (☑01520-722997; www.facebook.com/BCSLochcarron Garage) from Inverness to Lochcarron that continue to Applecross (£11.10, 3½ hours) via Shieldaig on prior request.

Lochcarron

POP 900

Appealing, whitewashed Lochcarron is a veritable metropolis in this area of Scotland, with two supermarkets, a bank with an ATM and a petrol station. A long shoreline footpath at the loch's edge provides the perfect opportunity for a stroll to walk off breakfast.

Old Manse   B&B ££

(☑01520-722208; www.theoldmanselochcarron.com; Church St; s/d £45/75, tw with loch view £85; P🏠🏠) The Old Manse is a top-notch Scottish guesthouse, beautifully appointed and in a prime, quiet lochside position. Rooms are traditional in style and simply gorgeous, with elegant furniture. Those overlooking the water are larger and well worth the extra tenner. Follow signs for the West End.

Pathend B&B   B&B ££

(☑01520-722109; www.pathend-lochcarron.co.uk; Main St; s/d £60/80; 🏠🏠) This cottage on the waterfront road offers a genuine welcome and some charming features in its front-facing rooms, such as a heritage fireplace and great sunken bath. It's a lovely outlook, and patchwork quilts and plush red sofas add to the vintage appeal. Evening meals are available by prior arrangement.

★Kishorn Seafood Bar   SEAFOOD ££

(☑01520-733240; www.kishornseafoodbar.co.uk; A896, Kishorn; mains £8-18; ☺11am-5pm Mon-Sat, noon-4pm Sun, 6-9pm Thu-Sat Mar-Oct, plus 6-9pm Tue & Wed Jul-Aug, call for winter hours) 🍴 Four miles west of Lochcarron, the Kishorn Seafood Bar is a cute, pale blue bungalow that serves the freshest of local seafood simply and well, with very fair prices. The views are spectacular, and you've got the satisfaction of knowing that much of what you eat was caught in Loch Kishorn just below. Book for dinner.

Plockton

POP 400

Idyllic little Plockton, with its perfect cottages lining a perfect bay, looks like it was designed as a film set. And it has indeed served as just that – scenes from *The Wicker Man* (1973) were filmed here, and the village became famous as the location for the 1990s TV series *Hamish Macbeth*.

With all this picture-postcard perfection, it's hardly surprising that Plockton is a tourist hot spot, crammed with day trippers and holidaymakers in summer. But there's no denying its appeal, with 'palm trees' (actually hardy New Zealand cabbage palms) lining the waterfront, a thriving small-boat sailing scene and several good places to stay, eat and drink. The big event of the year is the **Plockton Regatta** (www.plockton-sailing.com; ☺Jul/Aug).

The website www.visitplockton.com is a useful source of local information.

🏃 Activities

Hire canoes and rowboats on the waterfront to explore the bay.

Calum's Seal Trips   BOATING
(☑ 01599-544306;   www.calums-sealtrips.com; adult/child £12/6; ⊙ Apr-Oct) Seal-watching cruises visit swarms of the slippery suckers just outside the harbour. There's excellent commentary and you may even spot otters as well. Trips leave several times daily. There's also a longer dolphin-watching trip available.

Sea Kayak Plockton   KAYAKING
(☑ 01599-544422;   www.seakayakplockton.co.uk; 1-day beginner course £85) Sea Kayak Plockton offers everything from beginner lessons to multiday trips around Skye and right out to St Kilda.

🛏 Sleeping

Plockton Station Bunkhouse   HOSTEL £
(☑ 01599-544235;   www.visitplockton.com/stay/ bunkhouse; dm £18; P 🛜) Airily set in the former train station (the new one is opposite), this hostel has cosy four-bed dorms, a garden and kitchen-lounge with plenty of light and good perspectives over the frenetic comings-and-goings (OK, that last bit's a lie) of the platforms below. The owners also have good-value B&B accommodation (single/ double £35/60) next door in the inaccurately named 'Nessun Dorma'.

★ Plockton Hotel   INN ££
(☑ 01599-544274;   www.plocktonhotel.co.uk; 41 Harbour St; s/d £100/150, cottage s/d £65/100; 🛜) ✔ Black-painted Plockton Hotel is one of those classic Highland spots that manages to make everyone happy, whether it's thirst, hunger or fatigue that brings people knocking. Assiduously tended rooms are a real delight, with excellent facilities and thoughtful touches. Those without a water view are consoled with more space and a balcony with rock-garden perspectives. The cottage nearby offers simpler comfort.

★ Tigh Arran   B&B ££
(☑ 01599-544307;   www.plocktonbedandbreakfast. com; Duirinish; s/d £70/80; P 🛜🐾) It's hard to decide which is better at this sweet spot 2 miles from the Plockton shorefront – the warm personal welcome or the absolutely stunning views across to Skye. All three of the en suite rooms – with appealing family

options – enjoy the views, as does the comfy lounge. A top spot, far from stress and noise, it's great value as well.

Seabank   B&B ££
(☑ 01599-544221;   www.seabank-plockton.co.uk; 6 Bank St; d £80-90; ⊙ Easter-early Oct; 🛜) On the water and centrally located, but still a little removed from the main-street bustle, this tranquil spot has two very sweet rooms with dormer windows overlooking the loch. There's a little garden by the water where you can sit and absorb the peace. The delightful host makes staying here a very pleasant experience. There's a separate self-catering apartment that's great, too.

One room has an en suite, the other a private bathroom outside the room.

🍴 Eating

★ Plockton Shores   SEAFOOD ££
(☑ 01599-544263; www.plocktonshoresrestaurant. com; 30 Harbour St; restaurant mains £14-19; ⊙ cafe 9am-5.30pm Mon-Sat, noon-4pm Sun, restaurant 5-9pm Tue-Sat; ✔) ✔ This restaurant attached to a shop has a tempting menu of local seafood, including good-value platters with langoustines, mussels, crab, squat lobster and more, and succulent hand-dived tempura scallops. There's also a very tasty line in venison, steaks and a small selection of good vegetarian dishes that are more than an afterthought. The licensed cafe does home baking and light lunches.

Hours are reduced in winter but it's open year-round.

Plockton Inn   SEAFOOD ££
(☑ 01599-544222;   www.plocktoninn.co.uk; Innes St; mains £10-18; ⊙ noon-2.15pm & 6-9pm; 🛜) Offering a wide range of anything from haggis to toothsome local langoustines (Plockton prawns) and daily seafood specials, Plockton Inn covers lots of bases and has genuinely welcoming service.

A range of rooms – some substantially more spacious than others, and some in an annexe – are also available at a decent price.

ℹ Getting There & Away

Trains running between Kyle of Lochalsh (£2.80, 15 minutes) and Inverness (£23.10, 2½ hours) stop in Plockton up to four times daily each way.

Kyle of Lochalsh

POP 700

Before the connecting bridge was opened in 1995, this was Skye's principal mainland ferry port. Visitors now tend to buzz through town, but Kyle has some good boat trips if you're interested in marine life, and there's some great seafood eating here. The railway trip from Inverness is spectacular.

Seaprobe Atlantis   BOATING
(☑0800 980 4846; www.seaprobeatlantis.com; adult/child from £14/8; ⊙Easter-Oct) A glass-hulled boat takes you on a spin around the kyle to spot seabirds, seals and maybe an otter. The basic trip includes entertaining commentary and plenty of beautiful jellyfish; longer trips also take in a WWII shipwreck. At the time of research pick-ups were from Kyleakin across on Skye but the ticket office was still in Kyle.

Buth Bheag   SEAFOOD £
(☑01599-534002; www.buthbheag.co.uk; Old Ferry Slip; salads £3-6; ⊙10am-5pm Tue-Fri, to 3pm Sat Easter-Oct, 10am-3pm Tue-Fri Nov-mid-Dec & mid-Jan-Easter) This tiny place by the water near the tourist office has great fresh seafood salads and rolls for a pittance. Get them to take away and munch on them while sitting by the harbour. They were hoping to move to slightly larger premises just across the road at our last visit.

★**Waterside**   SEAFOOD ££
(☑01599-534813;www.watersideseafoodrestaurant. co.uk; Train Station; mains £17-21; ⊙5.30-9pm mid-Mar-mid-Oct) 🖉 In a former waiting room on Kyle's train station platform, this quaint little spot serves reliably delicious fresh fish and shellfish. A big effort is made to source sustainably from local producers, and the quality is sky-high. A great list of specials is chalked up nightly on the blackboard. In summer you nearly always have to book ahead.

ℹ Information

Kyle of Lochalsh Tourist Office (☑01471-822716; ⊙9.30am-4.30pm Easter-Oct) Next to the main seafront car park, this tour booking office has tourist information on Skye and the Lochalsh region. Next to it is one of Scotland's most lavishly decorated public toilets.

ℹ Getting There & Away

Citylink runs two to three daily buses from Inverness (£21.70, two hours) and three from Glasgow (£41.20, five to six hours).

The train route between Kyle of Lochalsh and Inverness (£24.10, 2¾ hours, up to four daily) is marvellously scenic.

Kyle to the Great Glen

It's 55 miles southeast via the A87 from Kyle to Invergarry, which lies between Fort William and Fort Augustus, on Loch Oich. The road passes one of Scotland's most famous castles and through picturesque Glen Shiel, while a detour leads to the off-the-beaten-track Glenelg area.

Eilean Donan Castle

Photogenically sited at the entrance to Loch Duich, **Eilean Donan** (☑01599-555202; www.eileandonancastle.com; A87, Dornie; adult/child/family £7.50/4/20; ⊙10am-6pm Apr-May & Oct, 9.30am-6pm Jun & Sep, 9am-6pm Jul & Aug, 10am-4pm Nov-Dec & Feb-Mar, closed Jan) is one of Scotland's most evocative castles and must now be represented in millions of photo albums. It's on an offshore islet, elegantly linked to the mainland by a stone-arched bridge. It's very much a recreation inside, with an excellent introductory exhibition. Citylink buses from Fort William and Inverness to Portree stop opposite the castle. The last entry is strictly one hour before closing.

Keep an eye out for the photos of castle scenes from the movie *Highlander;* there's also a sword used at the battle of Culloden in 1746. The castle was bombarded into ruins by government ships in 1719 when Jacobite forces were defeated at the Battle of Glenshiel; it was rebuilt between 1912 and 1932.

Glen Shiel & Glenelg

From Eilean Donan Castle, the A87 follows Loch Duich into spectacular Glen Shiel, with 1000m-high peaks soaring on either side of the road. Here, in 1719, a Jacobite army was defeated by Hanoverian government forces. Among those fighting on the rebel side were clansmen led by famous outlaw Rob Roy MacGregor and 300 soldiers loaned by the king of Spain; the mountain above the battlefield is still called Sgurr nan Spainteach (Peak of the Spaniard).

At Shiel Bridge, home to a famous wild-goat colony, a narrow side road goes over the Bealach Ratagain (pass), with great views of the Five Sisters of Kintail peaks, to Glenelg, where there's a community-run ferry to Skye. From palindromic Glenelg round to the road-end at Arnisdale, the scenery becomes even more spectacular, with great views across Loch Hourn to the remote Knoydart peninsula. Along this road are two fine ruined Iron Age brochs.

There are several good walks in the area, including the two-day, cross-country hike from Morvich to Cannich via scenic Gleann Lichd and Glen Affric SYHA (35 miles). The Five Sisters of Kintail hill-walking expedition is a classic but seriously challenging.

Glenelg Inn GASTROPUB ££
(☏ 01599-522273; www.glenelg-inn.com; Glenelg; mains £10-18; ⊙ kitchen 12.30-3pm daily, plus 6.30-9pm Thu-Sun Easter-Oct; P 🛜 🐕) One of the Highlands' most picturesque places for a pint or a romantic away-from-it-all stay (doubles £120), the Glenelg Inn has tables in a lovely garden with cracking views of Skye. The elegant dining room and cosy bar area serve posh fare, with local langoustines, scallops and fish usually featuring. Winter opening is sporadic; check the website.

❶ Getting There & Away

BOAT

A picturesque community-owned **vehicle ferry** (www.facebook.com/glenelgskyeferry; foot passenger/bike/car with passengers £3/4/15; ⊙ 10am-6pm Easter–mid-Oct) runs from Glenelg across to Kylerhea on Skye. This highly recommended way of reaching the island runs every 20 minutes and doesn't need booking.

BUS

Citylink buses between Fort William/Inverness and Skye travel along the A87.

One bus runs Monday, Tuesday and Friday from Kyle of Lochalsh to Arnisdale, via Shiel Bridge, Ratagan and Glenelg (£8, 1¼ hours).

SKYE

POP 10,000

The Isle of Skye (an t-Eilean Sgiathanach in Gaelic) takes its name from the old Norse *sky-a,* meaning 'cloud island', a Viking reference to the often-mist-enshrouded Cuillin

Hills. It's the second-largest of Scotland's islands, a 50-mile-long patchwork of velvet moors, jagged mountains, sparkling lochs and towering sea cliffs.

The stunning scenery is the main attraction, but when the mist closes in there are plenty of castles, crofting museums and cosy pubs and restaurants; there are also dozens of art galleries and craft studios.

Along with Edinburgh and Loch Ness, Skye is one of Scotland's top-three tourist destinations. However, the crowds tend to stick to Portree, Dunvegan and Trotternish – it's almost always possible to find peace and quiet in the island's further-flung corners. Come prepared for changeable weather: when it's fine it's very fine indeed, but all too often it isn't.

🏃 Activities

Walking

Skye offers some of the finest – and in places, the roughest and most difficult – walking in Scotland. There are many detailed guidebooks available, including a series of four walking guides by Charles Rhodes, available from the Aros Centre (p212) and the tourist office (p213) in Portree. You'll need Ordnance Survey (OS) 1:50,000 maps 23 and 32, or Harvey's 1:25,000 *Superwalker – The Cuillin.* Don't attempt the longer walks in bad weather or in winter.

Easy, low-level routes include: through Strath Mor from Luib (on the Broadford–Sligachan road) and on to Torrin (on the Broadford–Elgol road; allow 1½ hours, 4 miles); from Sligachan to Kilmarie via Camasunary (four hours, 11 miles); and from Elgol to Kilmarie via Camasunary (2½ hours, 6.5 miles). The walk from Kilmarie to Coruisk and back via Camasunary and the 'Bad Step' is superb but slightly harder (11 miles round-trip; allow at least six hours). The Bad Step is a rocky slab poised above the sea that you have to scramble across; it's easy in fine, dry weather, but some walkers find it intimidating.

Skye Wilderness Safaris (p206) runs one-day guided hiking trips for small groups (four to six people) through the Cuillin Hills, into the Quiraing or along the Trotternish ridge; transport to/from Portree is included.

Climbing

The Cuillin Hills are a playground for rock climbers, and the two-day traverse of the

Skye & Outer Hebrides

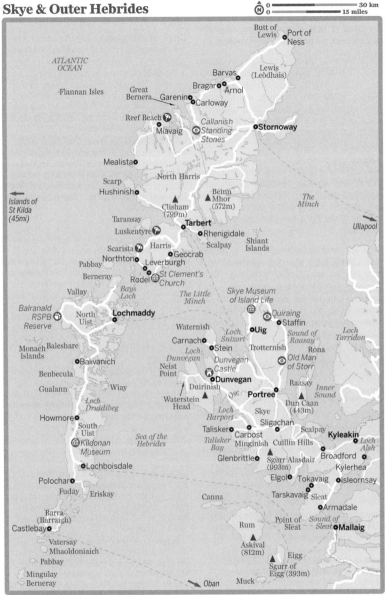

Cuillin Ridge is the finest mountaineering expedition in the British Isles. There are several mountain guides in the area who can provide instruction and safely introduce inexperienced climbers to the more difficult routes.

Skye Guides (p207) offers a one-day introduction-to-rock-climbing course for around £260; a private mountain guide can be hired for £280 a day (both rates are for two clients).

Sea Kayaking

The sheltered coves and sea lochs around the coast of Skye provide enthusiasts with magnificent sea-kayaking opportunities.

Whitewave Outdoor Centre KAYAKING
(☑ 01470-542414; www.white-wave.co.uk; 19 Linicro, Kilmuir; half-day kayak session per person £40-50; ☺ Mar-Oct) Provides sea kayaking instruction and guiding for both beginners and experts; prices include equipment hire. Other activities include mountain-boarding, bushcraft and rock climbing.

Tours

There are several operators who offer guided minibus tours of Skye, covering history, culture and wildlife. Rates are from £150 to £200 for a six-hour tour for up to six people.

Skye Wilderness Safaris WALKING
(☑ 01470-552292; www.skye-wilderness-safaris.com; per person £95-120; ☺ May-Sep) Runs one-day guided hiking trips for small groups (four to six people) through the Cuillin Hills, into the Quiraing or along the Trotternish ridge; transport to/from Portree included.

Skye Tours BUS
(☑ 01471-822716; www.skye-tours.co.uk; adult/child £40/30; ☺ Mon-Sat) Five-hour sightseeing tours of Skye in a minibus, taking in the Old Man of Storr (p215), Kilt Rock and Dunvegan Castle (p214). Tours depart from Kyle of Lochalsh train station at 11.30am (connects with 8.55am train from Inverness, returns to Kyle by 4.45pm in time to catch the return train at 5.13pm).

Information

Only Portree and Broadford have banks and ATMs.
Columba 1400 Community Centre (☑ 01478-611407; www.columba1400.com; Staffin; per hour £1; ☺ 10am-8pm Mon-Sat Apr-Oct; ☎) Internet access.

Portree Community Hospital (☑ 01478-613200; www.nhshighland.scot.nhs.uk; Fancyhill) There's a minor injury unit and dental surgery here.

Portree Tourist Office (☑ 01478-612992; www.visitscotland.com; Bayfield Rd; ☺ 9am-6pm Mon-Sat, 10am-4pm Sun Jun-Aug, shorter hours Sep-May; ☎) The only tourist office on the island; provides internet access and an accommodation booking service. Ask for the free *Art Skye – Gallery & Studio Trails* booklet.

Getting There & Away

BOAT

Despite the bridge, there are still a couple of ferry links between Skye and the mainland. Ferries also operate from Uig on Skye to the Outer Hebrides.

The **CalMac** (www.calmac.co.uk) ferry between Mallaig and Armadale (passenger/car £2.90/9.70, 30 minutes, eight daily Monday to Saturday, five to seven on Sunday) is very popular on weekends and in July and August. Book ahead if you're travelling by car.

The **Glenelg-Skye Ferry** (☑ 07881 634726; www.skyeferry.co.uk; car with up to 4 passengers £15; ☺ Easter-mid-Oct) runs a tiny vessel (six cars only) on the short Kylerhea to Glenelg crossing (five minutes, every 20 minutes). The ferry operates from 10am to 6pm daily (till 7pm June to August).

BUS

There are buses from Glasgow to Portree (£44, seven hours, three daily), and Uig (£44, 7½ hours, two daily) via Crianlarich, Fort William and Kyle of Lochalsh, plus a service from Inverness to Portree (£26.40, 3¼ hours, three daily).

CAR & MOTORCYCLE

The Isle of Skye became permanently tethered to the Scottish mainland when the Skye Bridge opened in 1995. The controversial bridge tolls were abolished in 2004 and the crossing is now free.

Much of the driving is on single-track roads – remember to use passing places to allow any traffic behind you to overtake. There are petrol stations at Broadford (open 24 hours), Armadale, Portree, Dunvegan and Uig.

Getting Around

BUS

Getting around the island by public transport can be a pain, especially if you want to explore away from the main Kyleakin–Portree–Uig road. Here, as in much of the Highlands, there are fewer buses on Saturday and only a handful of Sunday services.

Stagecoach (www.stagecoachbus.com) operates the main bus routes on the island, linking all the main villages and towns. Its Skye Dayrider/Megarider ticket gives unlimited bus travel for one/seven days for £9.20/34.60. For timetable info, call **Traveline** (☑ 0871 200 22 33; www.travelinescotland.com).

TAXI

You can order a taxi or hire a car (arrange for the car to be waiting at Kyle of Lochalsh train station) from **Kyle Taxi Company** (☑ 01599-534323; www.skyecarhire.co.uk; car hire per day/week from around £40/240).

Kyleakin (Caol Acain)

POP 100

Poor wee Kyleakin had the carpet pulled from under it when the Skye Bridge opened and it went from being the gateway to the island to a backwater bypassed by the main road. It's now a pleasant, peaceful little place, with a harbour used by yachts and fishing boats.

About 3 miles southwest of Kyleakin, a minor road leads southwards to **Kylerhea**, where there's a 1½-hour nature trail to a shore-front otter hide, where you stand a good chance of seeing these elusive creatures. A little further on is the jetty for the car ferry to Glenelg on the mainland.

Bright Water Visitor Centre   VISITOR CENTRE

(☑01599-530040; www.eileanban.org; The Pier; adult/child £1/free; ⊙10am-4pm Mon-Fri Easter-Sep) The community-run visitor centre serves as a base for tours of **Eilean Ban** – the island used as a stepping stone by the Skye Bridge – where Gavin Maxwell (author of *Ring of Bright Water*) spent the last 18 months of his life in 1968–69, living in the lighthouse keeper's cottage. The island is now a nature reserve, and tours (£7 per person, departing 2pm weekdays) are available in summer; bookings are a must.

The visitor centre also houses a child-friendly exhibition on Maxwell, the lighthouse and the island's wildlife.

Broadford (An T-Ath Leathann)

POP 750

The long, straggling village of Broadford is a service centre for the scattered communities of southern Skye. It has a 24-hour petrol station, a bank and a large Co-op supermarket with an ATM.

There are lots of B&Bs in and around Broadford and the village is well placed for exploring southern Skye by car.

🛌 Sleeping

Skye Basecamp   HOSTEL £

(☑01471-820044; www.skyebasecamp.co.uk; Lime Park; dm/q from £20/70; P🐕) Run by the mountaineers at **Skye Guides** (☑01471-822116; www.skyeguides.co.uk), this well-equipped hostel is set in a converted residential house with great views across the sea towards the Crowlin Islands. Maps, guidebooks, weather forecasts and walking advice are all to hand.

⭐ **Tigh an Dochais**   B&B ££

(☑01471-820022; www.skyebedbreakfast.co.uk; 13 Harrapool; d£105; P🐕) ✔ A cleverly designed modern building, Tigh an Dochais is one of Skye's best B&Bs – a little footbridge leads to the front door, which is on the 1st floor. Here you'll find the dining room (gorgeous breakfasts) and lounge offering a stunning view of sea and hills; the bedrooms (downstairs) open onto an outdoor deck with that same wonderful view.

Berabhaigh   B&B ££

(☑01471-822372; www.isleofskye.net/berabhaigh; 3 Lime Park; r per person £42.50; ⊙Mar-Oct; P🐕) This lovely old croft house with bay views is located just off the main road at the eastern end of the village, not far from Creelers (p207).

Skye Picture House   B&B ££

(☑01471-822531; www.skyepicturehouse.com; Ard Dorch; s/d from £40/80; P🐕) Perched just a stone's throw above the sea with a view across to the island of Scalpay, the setting of this welcoming B&B could hardly be better. No cooked breakfast, but the cold buffet is delicious.

🍴 Eating

⭐ **Creelers**   SEAFOOD ££

(☑01471-822281; www.skye-seafood-restaurant. co.uk; Lower Harrapool; mains £14-20; ⊙noon-8.30pm Tue-Sat Mar-Nov; 🚗) ✔ Broadford has several places to eat but one really stands out: Creelers is a small, bustling restaurant (refurbished in 2018) that serves some of the best seafood on Skye. The house speciality is traditional Marseille bouillabaisse (a rich, spicy seafood stew). Best to book ahead.

⭐ **Cafe Sia**   CAFE, PIZZERIA ££

(☑01471-822616; www.cafesia.co.uk; Rathad na h-Atha; mains £7-17; ⊙10am-9pm; 🐕🚗) ✔ Serving everything from eggs Benedict and cappuccino to cocktails and seafood specials, this appealing cafe specialises in wood-fired pizzas (also available to take away) and superb artisan coffee. There's also an outdoor deck with great views of the Red Cuillin. Takeaway coffee from 8am.

1. Puffin on Staffa (p99) 2. Glenbrittle (p211), Isle of Skye
3. Mainland cliffs, Shetland (p250) 4. Iona Abbey (p99)

Scotland's Islands

Scotland's sweeping array of islands – 790 at last count, around a hundred of which are inhabited – defines the country's complex coastline. Ruins, from prehistoric religious centres to staunch castles, overlook landscapes where sheep crop lush grass, the scant remaining fisherfolk take on powerful seas, and urban professionals looking for a quieter life battle with unreliable wi-fi.

Geography & History

Though in the modern world these islands might seem remote outposts, Scotland's complex geography has meant that, from Celts through to Vikings and the Lords of the Isles, transport, trade and power are intimately tied to the sea. Today's lonely island stronghold was yesteryear's hub of connections spreading right across western and northern Britain and beyond.

Sights & Activities

For the visitor, there's bewildering scope. The once-Norse islands of Orkney and Shetland are Britain's northernmost parts, while the Hebrides guard the west coast like a storm shield against the mighty Atlantic. The choice is yours: for scenic splendour with hills to climb and memorable walks you might choose spectacular Skye, diverse Mull, accessible Arran or lonely Jura. Neolithic villages, standing stones, evocative prehistoric monuments? Head to far-flung Orkney, Shetland or the Outer Hebrides. Abbeys, castles or stately homes? Magical Iona, Bute, Coll, Barra or Westray. Beaches? Pick Harris or Tiree. Birdlife? Unst, the Uists, Fair Isle, Noss, North Ronaldsay or Staffa. Whisky? It's got to be Islay. A convivial pub, local seafood and a warm welcome? Take your pick of any, then find yourself a snug cottage with a scent of the salty breeze and call it home for a day or three.

Armadale & Sleat

If you cross over the sea to Skye on the ferry from Mallaig you arrive in Armadale, at the southern end of the long, low-lying peninsula known as Sleat (pronounced 'slate'). The landscape of Sleat itself is not exceptional, but it provides a grandstand for ogling the magnificent scenery on either side – take the steep and twisting minor road that loops through Tarskavaig and Tokavaig for stunning views of the Isle of Rum, the Cuillin Hills and Bla Bheinn.

Armadale is little more than a store, a post office, a cluster of craft shops and a scattering of houses.

Museum of the Isles   MUSEUM
(☑ 01471-844305; www.clandonald.com; adult/child £8.50/7; ☉10am-5.30pm Apr-Oct, occasionally shorter hours Oct; ℙ🐾) Just along the road from Armadale pier is the part-ruined Armadale Castle, former seat of Lord MacDonald of Sleat. The neighbouring museum will tell you all you ever wanted to know about Clan Donald, and also provides an easily digestible history of the Lordship of the Isles. Prize exhibits include rare portraits of clan chiefs, and a wine glass that was once used by Bonnie Prince Charlie. The ticket also gives admission to the lovely castle gardens.

Shed   CAFE ££
(☑ 01471-844222; mains £6-15; ☉9am-6pm May-Sep, call to check Oct-Apr; ℙ) A cute little wooden shed at Armadale pier has some outdoor tables and serves good seafood salads, pizzas, fish and chips, and coffee. You can sit in or take away.

ⓘ Getting There & Away

From late May to August there are three to five buses a day Monday to Saturday (three on Sunday) from Armadale to Broadford (£4.10, 30 minutes) and Portree (£7.70, 1¼ hours), timed to meet the arrival of ferries from Mallaig. Outside the summer season, services are less frequent and may not coincide with ferry times.

Isleornsay

This pretty bay, 8 miles north of Armadale, lies opposite Sandaig Bay on the mainland, where Gavin Maxwell lived and wrote his much-loved memoir *Ring of Bright Water*. It's home to an atmospheric old hotel and bar, and an arts and crafts gallery.

Torabhaig Distillery   DISTILLERY
(☑ 01471-833447; www.torabhaig.com; Teangue; tours per person £10; ☉10am-5pm Mon-Fri) A converted farm steading overlooking the sea houses Skye's second distillery, opened in 2017. There's a visitor centre and cafe; tours are best booked in advance.

★**Toravaig House Hotel**   HOTEL ££
(☑ 01471-820200; www.toravaig.com; Toravaig; d £110-149; ℙ🐾) This hotel, 3 miles south of Isleornsay, is one of those places where the owners know a thing or two about hospitality – as soon as you arrive you'll feel right at home, whether relaxing on the sofas by the log fire in the lounge or admiring the view across the Sound of Sleat from the lawn chairs in the garden.

The spacious bedrooms – ask for room 1 (Eriskay), with its enormous sleigh bed – are luxuriously equipped, from the crisp bed linen to the huge, high-pressure shower heads. The elegant restaurant serves the best of local fish, game and lamb. After dinner you can retire to the lounge with a single malt and flick through the yachting and angling magazines.

Hotel Eilean Iarmain   HOTEL £££
(☑ 01471-833332; www.eilean-iarmain.co.uk; d from £200; ℙ🐾🐾) A charming old Victorian hotel with log fires, chintzy traditional decor, a candlelit restaurant and 12 luxurious rooms (plus another six in the Garden House), many with sea views. The hotel's cosy, wood-panelled **Praban Bar** (mains £11-16; ☉noon-2.30pm & 5.30-9pm) hosts live folk music and serves delicious, upmarket pub grub.

An Crùbh   CAFE £
(☑ 01471-833417; http://ancrubh.com; Dulsdale Beag; mains £4-10; ☉10am-4.30pm Wed-Sun Apr-Sep; ℙ🐾) This gorgeous modern community centre, opened in 2017, has a cafe with fantastic views over the sea to the mainland mountains, and sofas in front of a wood-burning stove. As well as coffee and cake, there are soups, salads and sandwiches that make the most of local produce.

Elgol (Ealaghol)

On a clear day, the journey along the road from Broadford to Elgol is one of the most scenic on Skye. It takes in two classic postcard panoramas – the view of Bla Bheinn across Loch Slapin (near Torrin), and the superb view of the entire Cuillin range from Elgol pier. Elgol itself is a tiny settlement at the end of a long, single-track road.

👁 Sights

Spar Cave CAVE
Just east of Elgol is the Spar Cave, famously visited by Sir Walter Scott in 1814 and mentioned in his poem 'Lord of the Isles'. The 80m-deep cave is wild, remote and filled with beautiful flowstone formations. It is a short walk from the village of Glasnakille, but the approach is over seaweed-covered boulders and is only accessible for one hour either side of low water. Check tide times and route information at the tearoom in Elgol.

🧭 Tours

Aquaxplore BOATING
(✆0800 731 3089; www.aquaxplore.co.uk; Elgol Pier; ☺Apr-Oct) Runs 1½-hour high-speed boat trips from Elgol to an abandoned shark-hunting station on the island of Soay (adult/child £30/22), once owned by *Ring of Bright Water* author Gavin Maxwell. There are longer trips (£60/48, four hours) to Rum, Canna and Sanday to visit breeding colonies of puffins, with the chance of seeing minke whales on the way.

Misty Isle BOATING
(✆01471-866288; www.mistyisleboattrips.co.uk; Elgol Pier; adult/child £25/12.50; ☺Apr-Oct) The pretty, traditional wooden launch *Misty Isle* offers cruises to Loch Coruisk with 1½ hours ashore (no Sunday service).

🛏 Sleeping & Eating

The only places to eat are the cafe above the car park halfway down the hill towards the pier, and the restaurant at **Coruisk House** (✆01471-866330; www.coruiskhouse.com; ☺Mar-Oct; P🐾). You can buy groceries and get takeaway soup and sandwiches at the **Elgol Shop** (www.elgolshop.com; ☺10am-5pm Mon-Sat; P) nearby.

⭐**Mary's Thatched Cottages** COTTAGE £££
(✆01471-866275; www.isleofskyecottages.com; 4/7 nights from £700/945; ☺Apr-Sep; P🐾🐶) These thatch-roofed dwellings (each sleeping two to four people) by the roadside as you arrive in Elgol from Broadford must be the island's cutest accommodation. Four beautifully reconstructed stone cottages have been designed with modern comforts

in mind – the stone slab floors have under-floor heating. Minimum stay is three nights, Friday to Monday; book as far in advance as possible.

ℹ Getting There & Away

Bus 55 runs from Broadford to Elgol (£4.30, 40 minutes, three daily Monday to Friday only).

Cuillin Hills

The Cuillin Hills are Britain's most spectacular mountain range (the name comes from the Old Norse *kjöllen,* meaning 'keel-shaped'). Though small in stature – Sgurr Alasdair, the highest summit, is only 993m – the peaks are near-alpine in character, with knife-edge ridges, jagged pinnacles, scree-filled gullies and hectares of naked rock.

While they are a paradise for experienced mountaineers, the higher reaches of the Cuillin are off limits to the majority of hikers. The good news is that there are also plenty of good low-level hikes within the ability of most walkers.

There are two main bases for exploring the Cuillin – Sligachan to the north (on the Kyle of Lochalsh–Portree bus route), and Glenbrittle to the south (no public transport).

One of the best hikes (on a fine day) is the steep climb from Glenbrittle campsite to Coire Lagan (6 miles round trip; allow at least three hours). The impressive upper corrie contains a lochan for bathing (for the hardy!), and the surrounding cliffs are a playground for rock climbers – bring your binoculars.

Even more spectacular, but much harder to reach on foot, is Loch Coruisk (from the Gaelic Coir'Uisg, the Water Corrie), a remote loch ringed by the highest peaks of the Cuillin. Accessible by boat trip (✆0800 731 3089; www.bellajane.co.uk; Elgol Pier; adult/child £28/16; ☺Apr-Oct) from Elgol, or via an arduous 5.5-mile hike from Kilmarie, Coruisk was popularised by Sir Walter Scott in his 1815 poem 'Lord of the Isles'. Crowds of Victorian tourists and landscape artists followed in Scott's footsteps, including JMW Turner, whose watercolours were used to illustrate Scott's works.

Glenbrittle Campsite CAMPSITE £
(✆01478-640404; www.dunvegancastle.com; Glenbrittle; sites per adult/child incl car £10/6; ☺Apr-Sep) Excellent site, close to mountains

and sea, with a shop selling food and outdoor kit. The midges can be diabolical, though.

Glenbrittle SYHA HOSTEL £
(☑01478-640278; www.syha.org.uk; Glenbrittle; dm/tw £20/59; ☺Apr-Sep; Ⓟ) Scandinavian-style timber hostel that quickly fills up with climbers on holiday weekends.

Sligachan Campsite CAMPSITE £
(www.sligachan.co.uk; Sligachan; sites per person £8; ☺Apr-Oct) This basic campsite is across the road from the Sligachan Hotel. Be warned – this spot is a midge magnet. No bookings.

Sligachan Hotel HOTEL £££
(☑01478-650204; www.sligachan.co.uk; Sligachan; r from £170; Ⓟ☏) The Slig, as it has been known to generations of climbers, is a near village in itself, encompassing a comfortable hotel, a microbrewery, self-catering cottages, a small mountaineering museum, a big barn of a pub – **Seamus Bar** (mains £9-18; ☺food served noon-9pm Apr-Oct, to 3pm Nov-Mar; ☏♿) – and an adventure playground.

Minginish

Loch Harport, to the north of the Cuillin, divides the Minginish peninsula from the rest of Skye. On its southern shore lies the village of **Carbost**, home to Talisker malt whisky, produced at Talisker Distillery.

Magnificent **Talisker Bay**, 5 miles west of Carbost, is framed by a sea stack and a waterfall.

As well as the excellent **Skyewalker** (☑01478-640250; www.skyewalkerhostel.com; Fiskavaig Rd, Portnalong; dm £20-22; Ⓟ) hostel and the **Old Inn** (☑01478-640205; www.theoldinnskye.co.uk; Carbost; bunkhouse per person from £23, B&B s/d £75/100; Ⓟ), there are several B&Bs and self-catering cottages. As ever, book ahead to avoid being caught without a bed.

Talisker Distillery DISTILLERY
(☑01478-614308; www.malts.com; tours from £10; ☺9am-5.30pm Mon-Sat, 10am-5.30pm Sun Apr-Oct, shorter hours Nov-Mar; Ⓟ) Skye's oldest distillery (established 1830) produces smooth, sweet and smoky Talisker single malt whisky. The guided tour includes a free dram.

Oyster Shed SEAFOOD £
(www.facebook.com/oystershedskye; Carbost; mains £4-20; ☺noon-5pm Mon-Fri Apr-Oct, shorter hours Nov-Mar) ✒ A farm shop selling fresh local seafood to take away, including oysters (£1.25 each), cooked mussels and scallops, lobster and chips, and seafood platters.

❶ Getting There & Away

There are two buses a day (school days only) from Portree to Carbost and Portnalong (£5.65, 55 minutes) via Sligachan.

Portree (Port Righ)

POP 2320

Portree is Skye's largest and liveliest town. It has a pretty harbour lined with brightly painted houses, and there are great views of the surrounding hills. Its name (from the Gaelic for King's Harbour) commemorates James V, who came here in 1540 to pacify the local clans.

◉ Sights & Activities

Aros Centre CULTURAL CENTRE
(☑01478-613750; www.aros.co.uk; Viewfield Rd; exhibition £5; ☺9am-5pm; Ⓟ♿) 🅵🆁🅴🅴 On the southern edge of Portree, the Aros Centre is a combined visitor centre, book and gift shop, restaurant, theatre and cinema. The St Kilda Exhibition details the history and culture of these remote rocky outcrops, and Xbox technology allows you to take a virtual tour of the islands.

The centre is a useful rainy-day retreat, with an indoor soft play area for children.

MV Stardust BOATING
(☑07798 743858; www.skyeboat-trips.co.uk; Portree Harbour; adult/child £20/10) MV *Stardust* offers 1½-hour boat trips around Portree Bay, with the chance to see seals, porpoises and – if you're lucky – white-tailed sea eagles. There are longer two-hour cruises to the Sound of Raasay (£25/15). You can also arrange fishing trips, or to be dropped off for a hike on the Isle of Raasay and picked up again later.

🛏 Sleeping

Portree is well supplied with B&Bs, but accommodation fills up fast from April to October, so be sure to book ahead.

Portree SYHA HOSTEL £
(☑01478-612231; www.syha.org.uk; Bayfield Rd; dm/tw £26/78; Ⓟ☏) This SYHA hostel (formerly Bayfield Backpackers) was completely renovated in 2015 and offers

brightly decorated dorms and private rooms, a stylish lounge with views over the bay, and outdoor seating areas. Its location in the town centre just 100m from the bus stop is ideal.

Torvaig Campsite CAMPSITE £
(☑ 01478-611849; www.portreecampsite.co.uk; Torvaig; tent sites per person £9, campervan £21; ☺ Apr-Oct; 🛜) An attractive, family-run campsite located 1.5 miles north of Portree, on the road to Staffin.

Ben Tianavaig B&B B&B ££
(☑ 01478-612152; www.ben-tianavaig.co.uk; 5 Bosville Tce; r £80-98; P 🛜) 🍴 A warm welcome awaits from the Irish-Welsh couple who run this appealing B&B bang in the centre of town. All four bedrooms have a view across the harbour to the hill that gives the house its name, and breakfasts include free-range eggs and vegetables grown in the garden. Two-night minimum stay April to October; no credit cards.

Woodlands B&B ££
(☑ 01478-612980; www.woodlands-portree.co.uk; Viewfield Rd; r £80; ☺ Mar-Oct; P 🛜) A great location, with views across the bay, and unstinting hospitality make this modern B&B, a half-mile south of the town centre, an excellent choice.

Cuillin Hills Hotel HOTEL £££
(☑ 01478-612003; www.cuillinhills-hotel-skye. co.uk; Scorrybreac Rd; r from £295; P 🛜) Located on the eastern fringes of Portree, this luxury hotel enjoys a superb outlook across the harbour towards the Cuillin mountains. The more expensive rooms cosset guests with four-poster beds and panoramic views, but everyone can enjoy the scenery from the glass-fronted restaurant and well-stocked whisky bar.

✕ Eating

Café Arriba CAFE £
(☑ 01478-611830; www.cafearriba.co.uk; Quay Brae; mains £6-12; ☺ 7am-6pm May-Sep, 8am-5pm Tue-Sat Oct-Apr; 🍴) 🍴 Arriba is a funky little cafe, brightly decked out in primary colours and offering delicious flatbread melts (bacon, leek and cheese is a favourite), as well as the best choice of vegetarian grub on the island, ranging from a veggie breakfast fry-up to felafel wraps with hummus and chilli sauce. Also serves excellent coffee.

Isle of Skye Baking Co CAFE £
(www.isleofskyebakingco.co.uk; Old Woollen Mill, Dunvegan Rd; mains £4-9; ☺ 10am-5pm Mon-Sat; P 🍴) 🍴 Famous for its 'lunch bread' – a small loaf baked with a filling inside, like cheese and leek, or beef stew – and platters of Scottish cheese and charcuterie, this cafe is also an art gallery and craft shop.

★ Scorrybreac MODERN SCOTTISH ££
(☑ 01478-612069; www.scorrybreac.com; 7 Bosville Tce; 3-course dinner £42; ☺ 5-9pm Wed-Sun year-round, noon-2pm mid-May–mid-Sep) 🍴 Set in the front rooms of what was once a private house, and with just eight tables, Scorrybreac is snug and intimate, offering fine dining without the faff. Chef Calum Munro (son of Donnie Munro, of Gaelic rock band Runrig fame) sources as much produce as possible from Skye, including foraged herbs and mushrooms, and creates the most exquisite concoctions.

Dulse & Brose MODERN SCOTTISH ££
(☑ 01478-612846; www.bosvillehotel.co.uk; Bosville Hotel, 7 Bosville Tce; mains £17-23; ☺ noon-3pm & 6-10pm May-Sep, 6-8.15pm Oct-Apr; 🛜) 🍴 This hotel restaurant sports a relaxed atmosphere, an award-winning chef and a menu that makes the most of Skye produce – including lamb, game, seafood, cheese, organic vegetables and berries – and adds a French twist to traditional dishes. The neighbouring Merchant Bar (food served noon to 5pm), also part of the Bosville Hotel, serves tapas-style bar snacks through the afternoon.

ℹ Information

Portree Tourist Office (p206).

ℹ Getting There & Around

BUS

The main bus stop is at Somerled Sq. There are five or six Scottish Citylink buses every day from Kyle of Lochalsh to Portree (£7.10, one hour) continuing to Uig.

Local buses (mostly six to eight Monday to Saturday, three on Sunday) run from Portree to:

Armadale (£7.70, 1¼ hours) Connecting with the ferry to Mallaig late May to August.

Broadford (£6, 45 minutes) Four or five daily.

Dunvegan Castle (£5.35, 50 minutes) Four daily on Saturday year-round; also four daily Monday to Friday from May to September.

There are also three buses a day on a circular route around Trotternish (in both directions), taking in Flodigarry (£4.10, 35 minutes), Kilmuir (£4.80, 45 minutes) and Uig (£3.60, 30 minutes).

BICYCLE
Island Cycles (☑ 01478-613121; www.island cycles-skye.co.uk; The Green; bike hire per 24hr £20; ☺9am-5pm Mon-Sat) You can hire bikes here.

Dunvegan (Dun Bheagain)
Dunvegan, an unremarkable village on the western side of Skye, is famous for its historic namesake castle which has links to Sir Walter Scott and Bonnie Prince Charlie.

Dunvegan Castle   CASTLE
(☑ 01470-521206;   www.dunvegancastle.com; adult/child £14/9;   ☺10am-5.30pm Easter–mid-Oct; P) Skye's most famous historic building, and one of its most popular tourist attractions, Dunvegan Castle is the seat of the chief of Clan MacLeod. In addition to the usual castle stuff – swords, silver and family portraits – there are some interesting artefacts, including the Fairy Flag, a diaphanous silk banner that dates from some time between the 4th and 7th centuries, and Bonnie Prince Charlie's waistcoat and a lock of his hair, donated by Flora MacDonald's granddaughter.

Coral Beaches   BEACH
From the end of the minor road beyond Dunvegan Castle (p214) entrance, an easy 1-mile walk leads to the Coral Beaches – a pair of blindingly white beaches composed of the bleached exoskeletons of coralline algae known as *maerl*.

Edinbane Pottery   ARTS & CRAFTS
(☑ 01470-582234;   www.edinbane-pottery.co.uk; Edinbane;   ☺9am-6pm Easter-Oct, Mon-Fri Nov-Easter) On the way to Dunvegan from Portree you'll pass Edinbane Pottery, one of the island's original craft workshops, established in 1971, where you can watch potters at work creating beautiful and colourful stoneware.

❶ Getting There & Away
Stagecoach bus 56 runs from Portree to Dunvegan (£5.35, 50 minutes), four times on Saturday year-round, and also Monday to Friday from May to September.

Duirinish & Waternish
The Duirinish peninsula to the west of Dunvegan, and Waternish to the north, boast some of Skye's most atmospheric hotels and restaurants, plus an eclectic range of artists' studios and crafts workshops.

The sparsely populated Duirinish peninsula is dominated by the distinctive flat-topped peaks of Helabhal Mhor (469m) and Helabhal Bheag (488m), known locally as **MacLeod's Tables**. There are some fine walks from Orbost, including the summit of **Helabhal Bheag** (allow 3½ hours return) and the 5-mile trail from Orbost to **MacLeod's Maidens**, a series of pointed sea stacks at the southern tip of the peninsula.

It's worth making the long drive beyond Dunvegan to the western side of the Duirinish peninsula to see the spectacular sea cliffs of **Waterstein Head** and to walk down to **Neist Point lighthouse** with its views to the Outer Hebrides.

🛏 Sleeping
Eco Bells Glamping   CAMPSITE £
(☑ 01470-521461; www.facebook.com/skyeecobells; Orbost, Duirinish; per tent £86; ☺Apr-Sep; P) Tucked away in a remote corner, on a minor road about 3 miles south of Dunvegan, this place offers accommodation in three large bell tents in a rural setting. Each tent sleeps up to three adults (or two adults and two children) and has beds, heating, a fire pit and barbecue. There's also a smaller tent and two wooden cabins.

⭐**Hillstone Lodge**   B&B £££
(☑ 01470-511434;   www.hillstonelodge.com;   12 Colbost; r from £140; P) You can't help notice the many new houses on Skye that bear the hallmarks of award-winning local architects Rural Design – weathered timber walls and modern materials used with traditional shapes and forms. Hillstone is one of the best, with tasteful modern styling and stunning views across Loch Dunvegan. It's about 1km north of the Three Chimneys (p215), above the pier.

🍴 Eating
Cafe Lephin   CAFE £
(☑ 01470-511465;   www.cafelephin.co.uk;   2 Lephin, Glendale;   ☺11am-4.30pm Tue-Sat;) A mixture of modern and rustic with touches of tweed and sheepskin, this wee cafe cap-

tures the spirit of enterprise that's bringing life back to areas of Skye that were deserted during the Highland Clearances. Great coffee, comfy sofas and a menu of cake and quiche.

Stein Inn   PUB FOOD **££**
(☑ 01470-592362; www.stein-inn.co.uk; Stein, Waternish; mains £8-16; ⊗ kitchen noon-4pm & 6.30-9pm Easter-Oct, 12.30-2.30pm & 5.30-8pm Nov-Easter; ℗) This old country inn dates from 1790 and has a lively little bar and a delightful beer garden beside the loch – a real suntrap on summer afternoons. The bar serves real ales from the Isle of Skye Brewery and excellent bar meals. Food is served in winter too, but call ahead to confirm hours.

There's also a handful of bedrooms here (£83 to £125 per room), all with sea views.

★ Loch Bay   SEAFOOD **£££**
(☑ 01470-592235; www.lochbay-restaurant.co.uk; Stein, Waternish; 3-course dinner £43.50; ⊗ 12.15-1.45pm Wed-Sun, 6.15-9pm Tue-Sat Apr-early Oct; ℗) ✐ One of Skye's most romantic restaurants, a cosy farmhouse kitchen of a place with terracotta tiles and a wood-burning stove, Loch Bay was awarded a Michelin star in 2018. The menu includes most things that swim in the sea or live in a shell, but there are non-seafood choices too. Best to book ahead.

★ Three Chimneys   MODERN SCOTTISH **£££**
(☑ 01470-511258; www.threechimneys.co.uk; Colbost; 3-course lunch/dinner £40/68; ⊗ 12.15-1.45pm Mon-Sat mid-Mar–Oct, plus Sun Easter-Sep, 6.30-9.15pm daily year-round; ℗ 🔊) ✐ Halfway between Dunvegan and Waterstein, the Three Chimneys is a superb romantic retreat combining a gourmet restaurant in a candlelit crofter's cottage with sumptuous five-star rooms (double £345) in the modern house next door. Book well in advance, and note that children are not welcome in the restaurant in the evenings.

Red Roof   SCOTTISH **£££**
(☑ 01470-511766; www.redroofskye.co.uk; Glendale, Duirinish; 3-course dinner £35; ⊗ 7-9pm Tue-Thu Apr-Oct; ℗ 🔊 👪 🎵) ✐ Tucked away up a glen, a mile off the main road, this restored 250-year-old byre is a wee haven of home-grown grub. The dinner-only menu, served at 7.30pm, specialises in Skye seafood, game and cheeses served with salad leaves and edible flowers grown just along the road. Must be booked in advance.

Trotternish

The Trotternish peninsula to the north of Portree has some of Skye's most beautiful – and bizarre – scenery. A loop road allows a circular driving tour of the peninsula from Portree, passing through the village of Uig, where the ferry to the Outer Hebrides departs.

⊙ Sights

★ Quiraing   NATURAL FEATURE
Staffin Bay is dominated by the dramatic basalt escarpment of the Quiraing: its impressive land-slipped cliffs and pinnacles constitute one of Skye's most remarkable landscapes. From a parking area at the highest point of the minor road between Staffin and Uig you can walk north to the Quiraing in half an hour.

Old Man of Storr   NATURAL FEATURE
(℗) The 50m-high, pot-bellied pinnacle of crumbling basalt known as the Old Man of Storr is prominent above the road 6 miles north of Portree. Walk up to its foot from the car park at the northern end of Loch Leathan (2-mile round trip). This seemingly unclimbable pinnacle was first scaled in 1955 by English mountaineer Don Whillans, a feat that has been repeated only a handful of times since.

Fairy Glen   AREA
Just south of Uig, a minor road (signposted 'Sheader and Balnaknock') leads a mile or so to the Fairy Glen, a strange and enchanting natural landscape of miniature conical hills, rocky towers, ruined cottages and a tiny roadside lochan.

Skye Museum of Island Life   MUSEUM
(☑ 01470-552206; www.skyemuseum.co.uk; Kilmuir; adult/child £2.50/50p; ⊗ 9.30am-5pm Mon-Sat Easter-late Sep; ℗) The peat-reek of crofting life in the 18th and 19th centuries is preserved in the thatched cottages, croft houses, barns and farm implements of the Skye Museum of Island Life. Behind the museum is Kilmuir Cemetery, where a tall Celtic cross marks the grave of Flora MacDonald; the cross was erected in 1955 to replace the original monument, of which 'every fragment was removed by tourists'.

Isle of Skye Brewery   FOOD & DRINKS
(☑ 01470-542477; www.skyeale.com; The Pier, Uig; ⊗ 10am-6pm Mon-Fri, to 4pm Sat, noon-4pm Sun

DINOSAUR FOOTPRINTS ON SKYE

The occasional dinosaur bone has been turning up in the Jurassic rocks of the Trotternish peninsula since 1982 – intriguing, but nothing very exciting. Then, following a storm in 2002, a set of fossilised dinosaur footprints was exposed at An Corran in Staffin Bay. Their interest piqued, geologists began taking a closer interest in the Trotternish rocks and, in 2015, a major discovery was made near Duntulm Castle – a 170-million-year-old trackway of footprints left by a group of sauropods. Skye is now a major focus for research into dinosaur evolution.

A collection of Jurassic fossils and further information on dinosaur sites in Skye can be found at the Staffin Dinosaur Museum (www.staffindinosaur museum.com; 3 Ellishadder, Staffin; adult/child £2/1; ⊙9.30am-5pm; P).

Apr-Oct) If you've time to kill while waiting for a ferry at Uig, the Isle of Skye Brewery shop sells locally brewed ales by the bottle, as well as gifts and souvenirs.

🛏 Sleeping & Eating

★ Cowshed Boutique Bunkhouse   HOSTEL £
(07917 536820; www.skyecowshed.co.uk; Uig; dm/tw £20/80, pod £70; P🐾🐕) This hostel enjoys a glorious setting overlooking Uig Bay, with superb views from its ultra-stylish lounge. The dorms have custom-built wooden bunks that offer comfort and privacy, while the camping pods (sleeping up to four, but more comfortable with two) have heating and en suite shower rooms; there are even mini 'dog pods' for your canine companions.

Shulista Croft   CAMPSITE £
(01470-552314; www.shulistacroft.co.uk; North Duntulm, Shulista; 2-/4-person pod per night £50/90; ⊙Mar-Nov) Set on a working croft amid sheep, lambs and chickens, Shulista has luxury timber camping pods with great views (two-night minimum stay; sleeps up to four, kids stay free). Each one is heated and insulated, and has an en suite shower room, basic kitchenette and even a TV. There are also more basic, two-person pods.

Dun Flodigarry Hostel & Camping   HOSTEL, CAMPSITE £
(01470-552212; www.hostelflodigarry.co.uk; Flodigarry; dm/tw £20/47, tent sites per person £10; P@🐾) A bright and welcoming hostel that enjoys a stunning location overlooking the sea, with views across Raasay to the mainland mountains. A nearby hiking trail leads to the Quiraing (p215) rock formation (2.5 miles away), and there's a hotel bar barely 100m from the door. You can also camp nearby and use all the hostel facilities.

Single Track   CAFE £
(www.facebook.com/singletrackskye; Kilmaluag; snacks £3-4; ⊙10.30am-5pm Sun-Thu mid-May-late Oct; P🐾) This turf-roofed, timber-clad art gallery and espresso bar will be familiar to fans of British TV's *Grand Designs* – it was featured on the Channel 4 series in 2012. The owners are serious about their coffee, and it's seriously good, as are the accompanying cakes and scones. Art by the owners and other Skye artists is on display, and for sale.

Raasay
POP 160
Raasay is the rugged, 10-mile-long island that lies off Skye's east coast. The island's fascinating history is recounted in the book *Calum's Road* by Roger Hutchinson.

There are several good walks here, including one to the flat-topped conical hill of Dun Caan (443m), and another to the extraordinary ruin of Brochel Castle, perched on a pinnacle at the northern end of Raasay. The Forestry Commission publishes a free leaflet (available in the ferry waiting room) with suggested walking trails.

Accommodation is very limited – don't turn up without a reservation unless you are planning to wild camp (there are plenty of places to do so in the east and north of the island).

Raasay Distillery   DISTILLERY
(01478-470178; https://raasaydistillery.com; Borodale House; tours £10; ⊙9.30am-5.30pm Mon-Sat; P) Raasay's first ever (legal!) distillery opened in 2017, and comes with a twist – you can stay the night here, in one of the six designer bedrooms in the Victorian hotel that has been incorporated into the modern building.

★ **Raasay House**   HOSTEL, B&B **£££**
(☑01478-660266; www.raasay-house.co.uk; dm £25, d £175; P🔊) 🍴 Beautifully renovated Raasay House (originally the laird's residence), just a short walk from the ferry pier, provides outdoor activity courses and accommodation ranging from hostel bunks to luxury B&B. The bar and restaurant (mains £10 to £23) serves good-quality seafood, beef and game, and locally brewed beers.

❶ Getting There & Away

CalMac (www.calmac.co.uk; return passenger/car £3.90/12.60) ferries run from Sconser, on the road from Portree to Broadford, to Raasay (25 minutes, nine daily Monday to Saturday, twice daily Sunday). There are no petrol stations on the island, nor is there any public transport.

OUTER HEBRIDES

POP 27,670

The Western Isles, or Na h-Eileanan an Iar in Gaelic – also known as the Outer Hebrides – are a 130-mile-long string of islands lying off the northwest coast of Scotland. There are 119 islands in total, of which the five main inhabited islands are Lewis and Harris (two parts of a single island, although often described as if they are separate islands), North Uist, Benbecula, South Uist and Barra. The middle three (often referred to simply as 'the Uists') are connected by road-bearing causeways.

The ferry crossing from Ullapool or Uig to the Western Isles marks an important cultural divide – more than a third of Scotland's registered crofts are in the Outer Hebrides, and no less than 60% of the population are Gaelic speakers.

If your time is limited, head straight for the west coast of Lewis with its prehistoric sites, preserved blackhouses and beautiful beaches.

❶ Information

The only tourist offices are in Stornoway and Tarbert. See www.visitouterhebrides.co.uk for tourist information.

❶ Getting There & Away

AIR

There are airports at Stornoway (Lewis), Benbecula and Barra. Flights operate to Stornoway from Edinburgh, Inverness, Glasgow, Aberdeen and Manchester. There are also two flights a day

(Tuesday to Thursday only) between Stornoway and Benbecula.

There are daily flights from Glasgow to Barra, and from Tuesday to Thursday to Benbecula. At Barra, the planes land on the hard-sand beach at low tide, so the schedule depends on the tides.

Eastern Airways (☑0870 366 9100; www.easternairways.com)

Loganair (☑0344 800 2855; www.loganair.co.uk)

BOAT

Standard one-way fares on CalMac ferries:

Crossing	Duration (hours)	Car (£)	Driver/ Passenger (£)
Ullapool–Stornoway	2¾	51	9.50
Uig–Lochmaddy	1¾	31	6.30
Uig–Tarbert	1½	31	6.30
Oban–Castlebay	4¾	68	14.75
Mallaig–Lochboisdale	3½	58	10.45

There are two or three ferries a day to Stornoway, one or two a day to Tarbert and Lochmaddy, and one a day to Castlebay and Lochboisdale. See www.calmac.co.uk for ferry timetables.

Advance booking for cars is recommended (essential in July and August); foot and bicycle passengers should have no problems. Bicycles are carried free.

❶ Getting Around

Despite their separate names, Lewis and Harris are actually one island. Berneray, North Uist, Benbecula, South Uist and Eriskay are all linked by road bridges and causeways. There are car ferries between Leverburgh (Harris) and Berneray and between Eriskay and Castlebay (Barra).

The local council publishes timetables of all bus and ferry services within the Outer Hebrides, which are available at tourist offices. Timetables can also be found online at www.cne-siar.gov.uk.

BICYCLE

Bikes can be hired for around £10 to £20 a day in Stornoway (Lewis), Leverburgh (Harris), Howmore (South Uist) and Castlebay (Barra).

BUS

The bus network covers almost every village in the islands, with around four to six buses a day on all the main routes; however, there are no buses at all on Sunday. You can pick up timetables from Stornoway tourist office (p219), or call Stornoway bus station (p219) for information.

NORTHERN HIGHLANDS & ISLANDS OUTER HEBRIDES

CAR & MOTORCYCLE

Apart from the fast, two-lane road between Tarbert and Stornoway, most roads are single track (p308). The main hazard is posed by sheep wandering about or sleeping on the road. Petrol stations are far apart (almost all of those on Lewis and Harris are closed on Sunday), and fuel is about 10% more expensive than on the mainland.

There are petrol stations at Stornoway, Barvas, Borve, Uig, Breacleit (Great Bernera), Ness, Barvas and Leverburgh on Lewis and Harris; Lochmaddy and Cladach on North Uist; Balivanich on Benbecula; Howmore, Lochboisdale and Daliburgh on South Uist; and Castlebay on Barra.

Cars can be hired from around £35/170 per day/week from **Car Hire Hebrides** (☑ 01851-706500; www.carhire-hebrides.co.uk; Ferry Terminal, Shell St).

Lewis (Leodhais)

POP 21,000 (INCLUDING HARRIS)

The northern part of Lewis is dominated by the desolate expanse of the Black Moor, a vast, undulating peat bog dimpled with glittering lochans, seen clearly from the Stornoway–Barvas road. But Lewis' finest scenery is on the west coast, from Barvas southwest to Mealista, where the rugged landscape of hill, loch and sandy strand is reminiscent of the northwestern Highlands. The Outer Hebrides' most evocative historic sites – Callanish Standing Stones (p220), **Dun Carloway** and Arnol Blackhouse (p220) – are also to be found here.

Stornoway (Steornabhagh)

POP 5715

Stornoway is the bustling 'capital' of the Outer Hebrides and the only real town in the whole archipelago. It's a surprisingly busy little place, with cars and people swamping the centre on weekdays. Though set on a beautiful natural harbour, the town isn't going to win any prizes for beauty or atmosphere, but it's a pleasant enough introduction to this remote corner of the country.

◉ Sights & Activities

Museum nan Eilean   MUSEUM

(www.lews-castle.co.uk; Lews Castle; ⊙10am-5pm Mon-Wed, Fri & Sat Apr-Sep, 1-4pm same days Oct-Mar; P) FREE The 'Museum of the Isles' opened in 2017, occupying a modern extension built onto the side of Lews Castle.

Artefacts, photos and videos celebrate the culture and history of the Outer Hebrides and explore traditional island life. The highlights of the collection are six of the famous **Lewis chess pieces**, discovered at Uig in west Lewis in 1831. Carved from whale and walrus ivory, they are thought to have been made in Norway more than 800 years ago.

Lews Castle   CASTLE

(☑ 01851-822750; www.lews-castle.co.uk; ⊙8am-5pm; P) FREE The Baronial mansion across the harbour from Stornoway town centre was built in the 1840s for the Matheson family, then owners of Lewis; it was gifted to the community by Lord Leverhulme in 1923. A major redevelopment completed in 2017 saw it converted to luxury self-catering accommodation, but the grand public rooms on the ground floor are free to visit when not in use. There's also an excellent **cafe** (mains £7-15; ⊙8am-4pm; 🛜♿), one of the few local eateries to open on Sundays.

The beautiful wooded grounds, crisscrossed with walking trails, are open to the public and host the Hebridean Celtic Festival (p218) in July.

An Lanntair Arts Centre   ARTS CENTRE

(☑ 01851-708480; www.lanntair.com; Kenneth St; ⊙10am-9pm Mon-Wed, to midnight Thu-Sat) FREE The modern, purpose-built An Lanntair (Gaelic for 'lighthouse'), complete with art gallery, theatre, cinema and restaurant, is the centre of the town's cultural life. It hosts changing exhibitions of contemporary art and is a good source of information on cultural events.

Hebridean Adventures   WILDLIFE WATCHING

(☑ 07871 463755; www.hebrideanadventures.co.uk; Stornoway Harbour; per person £95; ⊙Apr-Sep) Seven-hour whale-watching trips (Wednesdays only) out of Stornoway harbour in a converted fishing boat with a cosy saloon to shelter from any wild weather.

✦⚑ Festivals & Events

Hebridean Celtic Festival   MUSIC

(www.hebceltfest.com; ⊙Jul) A four-day extravaganza of folk, rock and Celtic music held in the second half of July.

🛏 Sleeping

★**Heb Hostel**   HOSTEL £

(☑ 01851-709889; www.hebhostel.com; 25 Kenneth St; dm/f £19/75; @🛜) The Heb is an easy-going hostel close to the ferry, with comfy wooden bunks, a convivial living room with peat fire and a welcoming owner who can provide all kinds of advice on what to do and where to go.

29 Kenneth St   B&B **££**
(☑ 07917 035295; www.stornowaybedandbreakfast. co.uk; 29 Kenneth St; s/d £65/105; ☎) Nine smartly fitted out bedrooms spread between two houses (the other is across the street at No 32) offer great-value accommodation, just five minutes' walk from the ferry terminal.

Hal o' the Wynd   B&B **££**
(☑ 01851-706073; www.halothewynd.com; 2 Newton St; r from £108; ☎) Touches of tartan and Harris Tweed lend a traditional air to this welcoming B&B, conveniently located directly opposite the ferry pier. Most rooms have views over the harbour to Lews Castle (p218).

Park Guest House   B&B **££**
(☑ 01851-702485; www.the-parkguesthouse.com; 30 James St; s/d from £79/110; ☎) A charming Victorian villa with a conservatory and six luxurious rooms (mostly en suite), the Park Guest House is comfortable and central and has the advantage of an excellent restaurant specialising in Scottish seafood, beef and game plus one or two vegetarian dishes (three-course dinner £38). Rooms overlooking the main road can be noisy on weekday mornings.

✖ Eating

Artizan Cafe   CAFE **£**
(☑ 01851-706538;   www.facebook.com/artizan stornoway; 12-14 Church St; mains £4-7; ⊙10am-6pm Mon-Fri, 9am-6pm Sat; ☎✚) Recycled timber and cool colours mark out this cafe-gallery as one of Stornoway's hip hang-outs, serving great coffee and cake and tapas-style lunches (noon to 2.30pm). Hosts cultural events, including poetry nights on Saturday.

An Lanntair Arts Centre   BISTRO **££**
(www.lanntair.com;   Kenneth St;   mains £11-17; ⊙kitchen 10am-8pm Mon-Sat; ☎✎✚) The stylish and family-friendly cafe-bar at the arts centre (p218) serves a broad range of freshly prepared dishes, from tasty bacon rolls at breakfast to burgers, salads or fish and chips for lunch and chargrilled steaks or local scallops for dinner.

OFF THE BEATEN TRACK

BUTT OF LEWIS

The **Butt of Lewis** (**P**) – the extreme northern tip of the Hebrides – is windswept and rugged, with a very imposing lighthouse, pounding surf and large colonies of nesting fulmars on the high cliffs. There's a bleak sense of isolation here, with nothing but the grey Atlantic between you and Canada. The main settlement is **Port of Ness** (Port Nis), which has an attractive harbour. To the west is the sandy beach of **Traigh**, which is popular with surfers.

Lido   INTERNATIONAL **££**
(☑ 01851-703354; 5 Cromwell St; mains £8-13; ⊙noon-3pm & 5-9pm Mon-Sat; ☎✚) Black-and-chrome decor and grey-granite table-tops lend an art-deco air to this busy diner, whose menu covers all bases from gourmet burgers to smoked-salmon salads to Italian meatballs. Speciality of the house is pizza, though, and these are excellent – thin, crispy and well-fired.

★**Digby Chick**   BISTRO **£££**
(☑ 01851-700026; www.digbychick.co.uk; 5 Bank St; mains £19-26, 2-course lunch £15; ⊙noon-2pm & 5.30-9pm Mon-Sat; ✚) ✎ A modern restaurant that dishes up bistro cuisine such as haddock and chips, slow-roast pork belly or roast vegetable panini at lunchtime, the Digby Chick metamorphoses into a candlelit gourmet restaurant in the evening, serving dishes such as grilled langoustines, seared scallops, venison and steak. Three-course early bird menu (5.30pm to 6.30pm) for £24.

ⓘ Information

Sandwick Rd Petrol Station (Engebret Ltd; ☑ 01851-702304; www.engebret.co.uk; Sandwick Rd; ⊙6am-11pm Mon-Sat, 10am-4pm Sun) The only shop in town that's open on a Sunday, selling groceries, alcohol, hardware, fishing tackle and outdoor kits. The Sunday papers arrive around 2pm.

Stornoway Tourist Office (☑ 01851-703088; www.visitouterhebrides.co.uk; 26 Cromwell St; ⊙9am-6pm Mon-Sat Apr-Oct, to 5pm Mon-Fri Nov-Mar)

ⓘ Getting There & Away

The **bus station** (☑ 01851-704327; South Beach) is on the waterfront next to the ferry terminal (left luggage 25p to £1.30 per piece).

Bus W10 runs from Stornoway to Tarbert (£4.80, one hour, four or five daily Monday to Saturday) and Leverburgh (£6.80, two hours).

The Westside Circular bus W2 runs a circular route from Stornoway through Callanish (£2.70, 30 minutes), Carloway, Garenin and Arnol; the timetable allows you to visit one or two of the sites in a day.

The bus network covers almost every village in the islands, with around four to six buses a day on all the main routes; however, there are no buses at all on Sunday. You can pick up timetables from the tourist offices, or call Stornoway bus station for information.

Arnol

One of Scotland's most evocative historic buildings, the Arnol Blackhouse (HES; ☑ 01851-710395; www.historicenvironment.scot; adult/child £5/3; ⊘ 9.30am-5.30pm Mon-Sat Apr-Sep, 10am-4pm Mon, Tue & Thu-Sat Oct-Mar; P) is not so much a museum as a perfectly preserved fragment of a lost world. Built in 1885, this traditional blackhouse – a combined byre, barn and home – was inhabited until 1964 and has not been changed since the last inhabitant moved out. The museum is about 3 miles west of Barvas.

The staff faithfully rekindle the central peat fire every morning so you can experience the distinctive peat-reek; there's no chimney, and the smoke finds its own way out through the turf roof, windows and door – spend too long inside and you might feel like you've been kippered!

At nearby Bragar, a pair of whalebones forms an arch by the road, with the rusting harpoon that killed the whale dangling from the centre.

Garenin (Na Gearrannan)

The picturesque and fascinating Gearrannan Blackhouse Village is a cluster of nine restored thatch-roofed blackhouses perched above the exposed Atlantic coast. One of the cottages is home to the Blackhouse Museum (☑ 01851-643416; www.gearrannan. com; adult/child £3.60/1.20; ⊘ 9.30am-5.30pm Mon-Sat Apr-Sep; P), a traditional 1955 blackhouse with displays on the village's history, while another houses a cafe (mains £3-6; ⊘ 9.30am-5.30pm Mon-Sat).

Some of the blackhouses in the village are let out as self-catering holiday cottages (☑ 01851-643416; www.gearrannan.com; 2-person cottage for 3 nights £275; P).

Callanish (Calanais)

Callanish, on the western side of Lewis, is famous for its prehistoric standing stones. One of the most atmospheric prehistoric sites in the whole of Scotland, its ageless mystery, impressive scale and undeniable beauty leave a lasting impression.

Callanish Standing Stones   HISTORIC SITE

(HES; www.historicenvironment.scot; ⊘ 24hr) FREE The Callanish Standing Stones, 15 miles west of Stornoway on the A858 road, form one of the most complete stone circles in Britain. It is one of the most atmospheric prehistoric sites anywhere. Sited on a wild and secluded promontory overlooking Loch Roag, 13 large stones of beautifully banded gneiss are arranged, as if in worship, around a 4.5m-tall central monolith.

Some 40 smaller stones radiate from the circle in the shape of a cross, with the remains of a chambered tomb at the centre. Dating from 3800 to 5000 years ago, the stones are roughly contemporary with the pyramids of Egypt.

Calanais Visitor Centre   MUSEUM

(☑ 01851-621422; www.callanishvisitorcentre. co.uk; admission free, exhibition £2.50; ⊘ 9.30am-8pm Mon-Sat Jun-Aug, 10am-6pm Mon-Sat Apr, May, Sep & Oct, 10am-4pm Tue-Sat Nov-Mar; P) This visitor centre near the Callanish Standing Stones is a tour de force of discreet design. Inside is a small exhibition that speculates on the origins and purpose of the stones, and an excellent cafe (mains £4-7).

Great Bernera

This rocky island is connected to Lewis by a bridge built by the local council in 1953 – the islanders had originally planned to blow up a small hill with explosives and use the material to build their own causeway. Great Bernera's attractions include fine coastal walks, a remote sandy beach, and a fascinating reconstruction of an Iron Age house.

Bosta   BEACH

(Bostadh) On a sunny day, it's worth making the long detour to Great Bernera's northern tip for a picnic at the perfect little sandy beach of Bosta. As an alternative to driving, there's a signposted 5-mile coastal walk from Breacleit, the island's only village, to Bosta.

Iron Age House   HISTORIC SITE
(☑01851-612314; Bosta; adult/child £3/1; ☺noon-4pm Mon-Fri May–mid-Sep; ⓟ) In 1996 archaeologists excavated an entire Iron Age village at the head of Bosta (p220) beach. Afterwards, the village was reburied for protection, but a reconstruction of an Iron Age house now stands nearby. Gather round the peat fire, above which strips of mutton are being smoked, while the custodian explains the domestic arrangements – fascinating, and well worth the trip. Opening hours are provisional, so call ahead to check.

Western Lewis

The B8011 road (signposted Uig, on the A858 Stornoway–Callanish road) from Garrynahine to Timsgarry (Timsgearraidh) meanders through scenic wilderness to some of Scotland's most stunning beaches. At Miavaig, a loop road detours north through the Bhaltos Estate to the pretty, mile-long white strand of Reef Beach; there's a basic but spectacular campsite (Cnip; Traigh na Beirigh; tent sites £10; ☺May-Sep) in the machair behind the beach.

From Miavaig, the road continues west through a rocky defile to Timsgarry and the vast, sandy expanse of Traigh Uige (Uig Sands). The famous 12th-century Lewis chess pieces, made of walrus ivory, were discovered in the sand dunes here in 1831.

The minor road that continues south from Timsgarry to Mealista passes a few smaller, but still spectacular, white-sand and boulder beaches on the way to a remote dead end; on a clear day you can see St Kilda on the horizon.

◉ Sights & Activities

Uig Museum   MUSEUM
(www.ceuig.co.uk; Timsgarry; adult/child £2/free; ☺noon-5pm Mon-Sat May–mid-Sep) This small community museum, housed in the local school, has lots of info on the Lewis chess pieces (discovered nearby in 1831) and on other historic sites in western Lewis.

Gallan Head   LANDMARK
(www.gallanhead.org.uk) Gallan Head, 3 miles north of Uig, was once an RAF radar station and surveillance post until it was abandoned in the 1960s. The old military camp, ringed by spectacular sea cliffs, has undergone several incarnations as a hotel and restaurant, but was finally taken over in 2016 by a local community trust that plans to clean up the site and create a visitor centre, cafe, wildlife-watching viewpoint and all-abilities hiking trail.

Meanwhile, the headland remains a strange hybrid of alternative community and ugly dereliction. You can drive through the gate beyond the settlement to reach the former radar base; there are views west to the Flannan Isles in clear weather.

SeaTrek   BOATING
(☑01851-672469; www.seatrek.co.uk; Miavaig Pier) From April to September, SeaTrek runs two-hour boat trips (adult/child £38/28, Monday to Saturday) in a high-speed RIB to spot seals and nesting seabirds. There are also three-hour trips (£48/38) to deserted islands in Loch Roag, with time ashore to go exploring.

🍴 Sleeping & Eating

There are precious few places to eat out here, so check that your accommodation offers evening meals if you don't want to go hungry.

★Port Carnish   COTTAGE £££
(☑07855 843375; www.portcarnishlewis.co.uk; Carnais, Uig; per week £995) A beautifully designed timber building set on an old croft with a stunning outlook across the sands of Uig Bay, this romantic cottage offers luxury self-catering accommodation for two people.

Baile-na-Cille   B&B £££
(☑01851-672242; www.bailenacille.co.uk; Timsgarry; per person £75; ⓟ🗢) This lovely old house hidden away at the northern end of Uig Bay is well worth seeking out for its friendly, old-fashioned hospitality, comfortable rooms and stunning location; there's even a tennis court and croquet lawn. Evening meals are available most nights (book in advance) for £35 per person.

Harris (Na Hearadh)

POP 2000

Harris, to the south of Lewis, is the scenic jewel in the necklace of islands that comprise the Outer Hebrides. It has a spectacular blend of rugged mountains, pristine beaches, flower-speckled machair and barren rocky landscapes. The isthmus at Tarbert splits Harris neatly in two: North Harris is dominated by mountains that rise forbiddingly above the peat moors to the south of Stornoway – Clisham (799m) is the highest point. South Harris is lower-lying, fringed by beautiful white-sand beaches in the west and a convoluted rocky coastline to the east.

Harris is famous for Harris Tweed, a high-quality woollen cloth still hand-woven in islanders' homes. The industry employs around 400 weavers; staff at Tarbert tourist office can tell you about weavers and workshops you can visit.

Tarbert (An Tairbeart)

POP 480

Tarbert is a harbour village with a spectacular location, tucked into the narrow neck of land that links North and South Harris. It is one of the main ferry ports for the Outer Hebrides, and home to the Isle of Harris Distillery.

Village facilities include two petrol stations, a bank, an ATM, two general stores and a tourist office.

Isle of Harris Distillery   DISTILLERY
(☑ 01859-502212; www.harrisdistillery.com; Main St; tours £10; ☉ 10am-5pm Mon-Sat; P) This distillery started production in 2015, so its first batch of single malt whisky will be ready in 2019; meanwhile, it's producing Isle of Harris gin too. The modern building is very stylish – the lobby feels like a luxury hotel – and 75-minute tours depart two or three times daily (weekdays only) in summer; they're popular, so book in advance. There's a cafe here too.

🛏 Sleeping & Eating

Tigh na Mara   B&B £
(☑ 01859-502270; flora@tigh-na-mara.co.uk; East Tarbert; per person £30-35; P) Excellent-value B&B (though the single room is a bit cramped) just five minutes' walk from the ferry – head up the hill above the tourist office and turn right. The owner bakes fresh cakes every day, which you can enjoy in the conservatory with a view over the bay.

Harris Hotel   HOTEL ££
(☑ 01859-502154; www.harrishotel.com; s/d from £90/115; P ☎) Run since 1903 by four generations of the Cameron family, Harris Hotel is a 19th-century sporting hotel, built in 1865 for visiting anglers and deer stalkers, and retains a distinctly old-fashioned atmosphere. It has spacious, comfy rooms and a decent restaurant; look out for JM Barrie's initials on the dining-room window (the author of *Peter Pan* visited in the 1920s).

Hotel Hebrides   HOTEL £££
(☑ 01859-502364; www.hotel-hebrides.com; Pier Rd; s/d/f £80/160/190; ☎) The location and setting don't look promising – a nondescript building squeezed between the ferry pier and car park – but this modern establishment brings a dash of urban glamour to Harris, with flashy fabrics and wall coverings, luxurious towels and toiletries, and a stylish restaurant and lounge bar. There are also luxury suites (from £215 per night) in a separate building.

Distillery Canteen   CAFE £
(Harris Distillery, Main St; mains £6-9; ☉ 10am-4pm Mon-Sat) The cafe at the Isle of Harris Distillery, with its communal, scrubbed-timber tables and chunky benches, is bright and convivial. The menu is not extensive – a choice of soups, cakes, home-baked bread, smoked salmon and crowdie (Scottish cream cheese) – but the quality of the food shines brightly, most of it sourced directly from Harris.

Hebscape   CAFE £
(www.hebscapegallery.co.uk; Ardhasaig; mains £3-7; ☉ 10.30am-4.30pm Tue-Sat Apr-Oct; P ☎) 🖉 This stylish cafe and art gallery, a couple of miles outside Tarbert on the road north towards Stornoway, occupies a hilltop site with breathtaking views over Loch A Siar. Enjoy home-baked cakes or scones with Suki tea or freshly brewed espresso, or a hearty bowl of homemade soup, while admiring the gorgeous landscape photography of co-owner Darren Cole.

ℹ Information

Tarbert Tourist Office (☑ 01859-502011; www.visithebrides.com; Pier Rd; ☉ 9am-5pm Mon-Sat Apr-Oct)

ℹ Getting There & Away

There are four or five daily buses, Monday to Saturday, from Tarbert to Stornoway (£4.80, one hour) and Leverburgh (£3.20, 50 minutes) via the west coast road.

Tarbert also has ferry connections to Uig (car/pedestrian £31/6.30, 1½ hours, one or two daily) on Skye.

North Harris

Magnificent North Harris is the most mountainous region of the Outer Hebrides. There are few roads here, but many opportunities for climbing, walking and birdwatching.

The B887 leads west, from a point 3 miles north of Tarbert, to Hushinish, where there's a lovely silver-sand beach. Along the way the road passes an old whaling station, one of Lord Leverhulme's failed development schemes, and the impressive shooting lodge of Amhuinnsuidhe Castle (www.amhuinnsuidhe.com), now exclusive holiday accommodation.

Golden Eagle Observatory BIRDWATCHING
Between the old whaling station and Amhuinnsuidhe Castle, at Miavaig, a parking area and gated track gives hikers access to a golden eagle observatory, a 1.3-mile walk north from the road. On Wednesday from April to September, local rangers lead a 3½-hour guided walk (£5 per person) in search of eagles; details from Tarbert tourist office (p222) or www.north-harris.org.

South Harris

South Harris' west coast has some of the most beautiful beaches in Scotland. The blinding white sands and turquoise waters of Luskentyre and Scarasta would be major holiday resorts if they were transported to somewhere with a warm climate; as it is, they're usually deserted.

The east coast is a complete contrast to the west – a strange, rocky moonscape of naked gneiss pocked with tiny lochans, the bleakness lightened by the occasional splash of green around the few crofting communities. Film buffs will know that the psychedelic sequences depicting an alien landscape in *2001: A Space Odyssey* were shot from an aircraft flying over Harris' east coast.

The narrow, twisting road that winds along this coast is known locally as the Golden Road because of the vast amount of money it cost per mile. It was built in the 1930s to link all the tiny communities known as 'The Bays'.

Sights & Activities

★Luskentyre BEACH
(Losgaintir) Luskentyre is one of the biggest and most beautiful beaches in Scotland, famed for its acres of low-tide white sands and turquoise waters. A minor road leads along the northern side of the bay to a parking area beside an ancient graveyard; from here you can walk west along the beach or through the grassy dunes with gorgeous views across the sea to the island of Taransay.

Clò Mòr MUSEUM
(☑01859-502040; Old School, Drinishader; ☺9am-5.30pm Mon-Sat Mar-Oct; P) FREE The Campbell family has been making Harris tweed for 90 years, and this exhibition (behind the family shop) celebrates the history of the fabric known in Gaelic as *clò mòr* (the 'big cloth'); ask about live demonstrations of tweed weaving on the 70-year-old Hattersley loom. Drinishader is 5 miles south of Tarbert on the east coast road.

St Clement's Church HISTORIC BUILDING
(Rodel; ☺9am-5pm Mon-Sat) FREE At the southernmost tip of the east coast of Harris stands the impressive 16th-century St Clement's Church, built by Alexander MacLeod of Dunvegan between the 1520s and 1550s, only to be abandoned after the Reformation. There are several fine tombs inside, including the cenotaph of Alexander MacLeod, finely carved with hunting scenes, a castle, a *birlinn* (the traditional longboat of the islands) and various saints, including St Clement clutching a skull.

Talla na Mara ARTS CENTRE
(☑01859-503900; www.tallanamara.co.uk; Pairc Niseaboist; ☺9am-5pm Mon-Sat; P) FREE Opened in 2017 as a community enterprise, this beautiful modern building houses several artists' studios and an exhibition space that displays works celebrating the landscapes and culture of Scotland's Western Isles.

Sea Harris BOATING
(☑01859-502007; www.seaharris.com; Leverburgh Pier; ☺Apr-Sep) Operates private-hire boat trips to spot wildlife around the Sound of Harris (from £40 per person), and also runs 10-hour day trips to St Kilda (£185 per person) with four to five hours ashore.

Kilda Cruises BOATING
(☑01859-502060; www.kildacruises.co.uk; Leverburgh Pier; per person £215) Operates 12-hour day trips to the remote and spectacular island group of St Kilda. Daily from mid-April to mid-September.

Sleeping

Lickisto Blackhouse Camping CAMPSITE £
(☑01859-530485; www.freewebs.com/vanvon; Liceasto; tent sites per adult/child £12/6, yurt £70; ☻) ✿ Remote and rustic campsite on an old croft, with pitches set among heather and outcrops and chickens running wild. Campers can use a communal kitchen-lounge in a converted blackhouse,

NORTHERN HIGHLANDS & ISLANDS HARRIS (NA HEARADH)

and there are two yurts with wood-burning stove and gas cooker (no electricity). Bus W13 from Tarbert to Leverburgh stops at the entrance.

Am Bothan
HOSTEL £

(☎01859-520251; www.ambothan.com; Ferry Rd, Leverburgh; dm £25; P 🛜) An attractive, chalet-style hostel, Am Bothan has small, neat dorms and a great porch where you can enjoy morning coffee with views over the bay. The hostel has bike hire and can arrange wildlife-watching boat trips.

Carminish House
B&B ££

(☎01859-520400; www.carminish.com; 1a Strond, Leverburgh; s/d £75/95; ⊘Apr–Oct; P 🛜) The welcoming Carminish is a modern house with three comfy bedrooms. There's a view of the ferry from the dining room, and lots of nice little touches such as handmade soaps, a carafe of drinking water in the bedroom and tea and cake on arrival.

Sorrel Cottage
B&B ££

(☎01859-520319; www.sorrelcottage.co.uk; 2 Glen, Leverburgh; s/d from £70/90; P 🛜🐾) Sorrel Cottage is a pretty crofter's house with beautifully modernised rooms, about 1.5 miles west of the ferry at Leverburgh. Vegetarians and vegans are happily catered for. Bike hire available.

★ Borve Lodge Estate
COTTAGE £££

(☎01859-550358; www.borvelodge.com; per 3/7 nights £900/1850; P 🛜) This estate on the west side of South Harris has developed some of the most spectacular self-catering accommodation in the Outer Hebrides, including the Rock House, a turf-roofed nook built into the hillside with sweeping views over the sea, and the stunning Broch, a three-storey rock tower based on Iron Age designs (both sleep two persons).

✖ Eating

★ Skoon Art Café
CAFE £

(☎01859-530268; www.skoon.com; Geocrab; mains £5–9; ⊘10am–4.30pm Tue–Sat Apr–Sep, shorter hours Oct–Mar; P) 🐾 Set halfway along the Golden Road, this neat little art gallery doubles as an excellent cafe serving delicious homemade soups, sandwiches, cakes and desserts (try the gin-and-tonic cake).

Temple Cafe
CAFE £

(☎07876 340416; www.facebook.com/thetemple cafe; Northton; mains £5–12; ⊘10.30am–5pm Tue–

Sun Apr–Sep, shorter hours Oct–Mar; P 🌼) Set in a cute stone-and-timber 'hobbit house' that was originally a visitor centre, and strewn with cushions covered in Harris tweed, this rustic cafe serves homemade scones, soups, salads and hot lunch specials to a soundtrack of '70s tunes. Evening meals 6.30pm to 8pm Friday to Sunday in summer (must be booked in advance).

★ Machair Kitchen
SCOTTISH ££

(☎01859-550333; www.tallanamara.co.uk; Talla na Mara; mains £7–15; ⊘noon–4pm & 6–9pm) The restaurant in this community centre (p223) and art gallery enjoys a stunning location, with views across the sea to the island of Taransay, and an outdoor deck that makes the most of any sunny weather. The menu includes local mussels, crab and smoked salmon, plus sandwiches, fish and chips and burgers. Open for coffee and cake from 10am to 5pm.

❶ Getting There & Away

A **CalMac** (www.calmac.co.uk) car ferry zigzags through the reefs of the Sound of Harris from Leverburgh to Berneray (pedestrian/car £3.60/13.55, one hour, three or four daily Monday to Saturday, two or three Sunday).

There are two to four buses a day (except Sunday) from Tarbert to Leverburgh; W10 takes the main road along the west coast (£3.20, 40 minutes), while W13 winds along the Golden Road on the east coast (£3.20, one hour).

Berneray (Bearnaraigh)
POP 138

Berneray was linked to North Uist by a causeway in October 1998, but that hasn't altered the peace and beauty of the island. The beaches on its west coast are some of the most beautiful and unspoilt in Britain, and seals and otters can be seen in Bays Loch on the east coast.

Accommodation on the island is limited to the Gatliff Hostel (www.gatliff.org.uk; dm adult/child £16/8, camping per person £11), a bunkhouse, two B&Bs and half a dozen self-catering cottages (see the full listing at www.isleofberneray.com), so be sure to book ahead.

Bus W19 runs from Berneray (Gatliff Hostel and Harris ferry) to Lochmaddy (£2.30, 20 to 30 minutes, eight daily Monday to Saturday). There are daily ferries to Leverburgh (Harris).

North Uist
(Uibhist A Tuath)

POP 1255

North Uist, an island half-drowned by lochs, is famed for its trout fishing (www.nuac.co.uk) but also has some magnificent beaches on its north and west coasts. For birdwatchers this is an earthly paradise, with regular sightings of waders and wildfowl ranging from redshank to red-throated diver to red-necked phalarope. The landscape is less wild and mountainous than Harris but it has a sleepy, subtle appeal.

Little Lochmaddy is the first village you hit after arriving on the ferry from Skye. It has a couple of stores, a bank with an ATM, a petrol station, a post office and a pub.

◉ Sights

Balranald RSPB Reserve   WILDLIFE RESERVE
(www.rspb.org.uk; P) FREE Birdwatchers flock to this Royal Society for the Protection of Birds (RSPB) nature reserve, 18 miles west of Lochmaddy, in the hope of spotting the rare red-necked phalarope or hearing the distinctive call of the corncrake. There's a visitor centre with a resident warden who offers 1½-hour guided walks (£6), departing at 10am Tuesday from May to September.

St Kilda Viewpoint   VIEWPOINT
(P) From the westernmost point of the road that runs around North Uist, a minor, drivable track leads for 1.5 miles to the summit of Clettraval hill where a lookout point with telescope affords superb views west to the distant peaks of St Kilda and the Monach Isles.

Taigh Chearsabhagh   ARTS CENTRE, MUSEUM
(☎01870-603970; www.taigh-chearsabhagh.org; Lochmaddy; arts centre free, museum £3; ⊙10am-5pm Mon-Sat Apr-Oct, to 4pm Nov-Mar; P) Taigh Chearsabhagh is a museum and arts centre that preserves and displays the history and culture of the Uists, and is also a thriving community centre, post office and meeting place. The centre's cafe (mains £4 to £6, closes at 3pm) dishes up homemade soups, sandwiches and cakes.

🛏 Sleeping & Eating

Balranald Campsite   CAMPSITE £
(☎01876-510304; www.balranaldhebrideanholidays.com; Balranald Nature Reserve, Hougharry; tent sites £8-10, plus per person £2; 🛜) You can bird-watch from your tent at this lovely campsite set on the machair alongside the RSPB's Balranald nature reserve, and listen to rare corncrakes calling as the sun goes down beyond the neighbouring white-sand beach.

★Langass Lodge   HOTEL ££
(☎01876-580285; www.langasslodge.co.uk; Locheport; s/d from £95/115; P🛜) The delightful Langass Lodge hotel is a former shooting lodge set in splendid isolation overlooking Loch Langais. Refurbished and extended, it now offers a dozen appealing rooms, many with sea views, as well as one of the Hebrides' best restaurants (mains £15-25, 3-course dinner £38; ⊙6-8.30pm), noted for its fine seafood and game.

Rushlee House   B&B ££
(☎01876-500274; www.rushleehouse.co.uk; Lochmaddy; s/d £60/78; P🛜) A lovely modern bungalow with three luxuriously appointed bedrooms and great views of the hills to the south. No evening meals, but it's just a short walk to the restaurant at Hamersay House (p225). The B&B is 0.75 miles from the ferry pier; take the first road on the right, then first left.

Hamersay House   HOTEL £££
(☎01876-500700; www.hamersayhouse.co.uk; Lochmaddy; s/d £95/135; P🛜) Hamersay is Lochmaddy's most luxurious accommodation, with eight designer bedrooms, a lounge with leather sofas set around an open fire, and a good restaurant (mains £13 to £21, open 6pm to 8.30pm) with sea views from the terrace.

Hebridean Smokehouse   FOOD & DRINKS
(☎01876-580209; www.hebrideansmokehouse.com; Clachan; ⊙8am-5.30pm Mon-Fri, plus 9am-5pm Sat Easter-Oct) Smokehouse shop selling locally sourced, peat-smoked salmon, sea trout, scallops, lobster and mackerel.

Benbecula (Beinn
Na Faoghla)

POP 1305

Benbecula, which sits between North Uist and South Uist, and is connected to both by causeways, is a low-lying island with a flat, lochan-studded landscape that's best appreciated from the summit of Rueval (124m), the island's highest point. There's a path around the southern side of the hill (signposted from the main road; park beside the landfill site) that is said to be the route taken to the coast by Bonnie Prince Charlie and Flora MacDonald during the prince's escape in 1746.

The main village is **Balivanich**, which has a bank with an ATM, a post office, a couple of supermarkets and a petrol station (open on Sunday). It is also the location of Benbecula airport.

South Uist (Uibhist A Deas)

POP 1755

South Uist is the second-largest island in the Outer Hebrides and saves its choicest corners for those who explore away from the main north–south road. The low-lying west coast is an almost unbroken stretch of white-sand beach and flower-flecked machair – a waymarked hiking trail, the **Hebridean Way**, follows the coast – while the multitude of inland lochs provide excellent trout fishing (www.southuistfishing.com). The east coast, riven by four large sea lochs, is hilly and remote, with spectacular **Beinn Mhor** (620m) the highest point.

Driving south from Benbecula you cross from the predominantly Protestant northern half of the Outer Hebrides into the mostly Roman Catholic south, a religious transition marked by the granite statue of **Our Lady of the Isles** on the slopes of Rueval and the presence of many roadside shrines.

The ferry port of **Lochboisdale** is the island's largest settlement, with a bank, ATM, grocery store and petrol station.

Sights & Activities

Kildonan Museum
MUSEUM

(☏01878-710343; www.kildonanmuseum.co.uk; Kildonan; adult/child £3/free; ⊙10am-5pm Apr-Oct; P) Six miles north of Lochboisdale, Kildonan Museum explores the lives of local crofters through its collection of artefacts, an absorbing exhibition of B&W photography and firsthand accounts of harsh Hebridean conditions. There's also an excellent tearoom (mains £4 to £8, open 11am to 4pm) and craft shop.

Amid Milton's ruined blackhouses, half a mile south of the museum, a cairn marks the site of **Flora MacDonald's birthplace**.

Eriskay
ISLAND

There's not much to see on Eriskay, but you'll pass through it on the way to the car

ferry that crosses to Ardmhor at the northern end of Barra; Eriskay itself is connected to South Uist by a causeway that was constructed in 2001.

In 1745 Bonnie Prince Charlie first set foot in Scotland on the west coast of Eriskay, on the sandy beach (immediately north of the ferry terminal) still known as **Prince's Strand** (Coilleag a'Phrionnsa).

More recently the SS *Politician* sank just off the island in 1941. The islanders salvaged much of its cargo of around 250,000 bottles of whisky and, after a binge of dramatic proportions, the police intervened and a number of the islanders landed in jail. The story was immortalised by Sir Compton Mackenzie in his comic novel *Whisky Galore,* made into a famous film in 1949 and remade in 2016.

Uist Sea Tours
BOATING

(☏07810 238752; www.uistseatours.com; The Pier, Lochboisdale) From mid-April to mid-September this outfit runs two-hour boat trips (£40 per person) from Lochboisdale to spot bottlenose dolphins in the Sound of Barra (Monday, Wednesday and Friday evenings), and six-hour trips from Eriskay harbour (£85 per person) to see nesting puffins on the island of Mingulay (Friday). There are also seven-hour day trips to St Kilda (£175 per person).

Sleeping & Eating

Uist Storm Pods
CAMPSITE £

(☏01878-700845; www.uiststormpods.co.uk; Lochboisdale; per pod £70; P) This place has two Scandinavian-style timber camping pods set on a hillside on a working farm. Each has an outdoor deck and barbecue overlooking the sea; a mini-kitchen, fridge and chemical toilet; and can sleep up to four people. The pods are a short walk from the ferry; take the second road on the left, immediately before the RBS bank.

Tobha Mor Crofters' Hostel
HOSTEL £

(www.gatliff.org.uk; Howmore; dm adult/child £16/8, camping per person £10) An atmospheric hostel housed in a restored thatched blackhouse, about 12 miles north of Lochboisdale.

★ Polochar Inn
INN ££

(☏01878-700215; www.polocharinn.com; Polochar; s/d from £80/95; P) This 18th-century inn has been transformed into a stylish, welcoming hotel with a stunning location looking out across the sea to Barra. The excellent

ST KILDA

St Kilda is a collection of spectacular sea stacks and cliff-bound islands about 45 miles west of North Uist. The largest island, Hirta, measures only 2 miles by 1 mile, with huge cliffs along most of its coastline. Owned by the NTS, the islands are a Unesco World Heritage Site and are the biggest seabird nesting site in the North Atlantic, home to more than a million birds.

There is no accommodation on St Kilda other than a tiny campsite at Village Bay on Hirta (£12 per person, no more than six people) with toilets, showers and a drinking-water supply; the maximum permitted stay is five nights. Must be arranged in advance through the NTS (details at www.kilda.org.uk).

Boat tours to St Kilda are a major undertaking – day trips are at least seven-hour affairs, involving a minimum 2½-hour crossing each way, often in rough seas; all must be booked in advance and are weather-dependent (April to September only).

Tour operators include the following:

Go To St Kilda (☑ 07789 914144; www.gotostkilda.co.uk; Stein Jetty; per person £260)

Kilda Cruises (p223)

Uist Sea Tours (p226)

Sea Harris (p223)

restaurant and bar menu (mains £11 to £20; booking recommended) includes seafood chowder, venison casserole, local salmon and scallops, and Uist lamb. Polochar is 7 miles southwest of Lochboisdale, on the way to Eriskay.

Lochside Cottage　　　　　　　B&B **££**
(☑ 01878-700472; www.lochside-cottage.co.uk; Lochboisdale; s/d/f £50/70/90; P 🛜) Lochside Cottage is a friendly B&B, 1.5 miles west of the ferry, and has rooms with views and a sun lounge barely a fishing-rod's length from its own trout loch.

❶ Getting There & Around

Bus W17 runs about four times a day (except Sunday) between Berneray and Eriskay via Lochmaddy, Balivanich and Lochboisdale. The trip from Lochboisdale to Lochmaddy (£5.30) takes 1¾ hours.

CalMac (www.calmac.co.uk) ferries run between Lochboisdale and Mallaig.

Rothan Cycles (☑ 07740 364093; www.rothan. scot; Howmore; per day from £10; ⊙ 9am-5pm) offers bike hire, and a delivery and pick-up service (extra charge on top of rental) at various points between Eriskay and Stornoway.

Barra (Barraigh)

POP 1175

With its beautiful beaches, wildflower-clad dunes, rugged little hills and strong sense of community, diminutive Barra – just 14 miles

in circumference – is the Outer Hebrides in miniature. For a great view of the island, walk up to the top of Heaval (383m), a mile northeast of Castlebay (Bagh a'Chaisteil), the largest village.

You can hire bikes from Barra Bike Hire (☑ 07876 402842; www.barrabikehire.co.uk; Vatersay Rd, Castlebay; per half-/full day £10/16; ⊙ 9am-5pm Mon-Sat).

◉ Sights & Activities

The uninhabited islands of Pabbay, Mingulay and Berneray, gifted to the National Trust for Scotland (NTS) in 2000, are important breeding sites for seabird species such as fulmar, black guillemot, common and Arctic tern, great skua, puffin and storm petrel.

Uist Sea Tours (p226) runs boat trips to the islands from Lochboisdale in South Uist in settled weather. The puffin season lasts from June to early August.

Kisimul Castle　　　　　　　CASTLE
(HES; ☑ 01871-810313; www.historicenvironment. scot; Castlebay; adult/child incl ferry £6/3.60; ⊙ 9.30am-5.30pm Apr-Sep) Castlebay takes its name from the island fortress of Kisimul Castle, first built by the MacNeil clan in the 11th century. A short boat trip (weather permitting) takes you out to the island, where you can explore the fortifications and soak up the view from the battlements.

The castle was restored in the 20th century by American architect Robert MacNeil, who became the 45th clan chief; he gifted

NORTHERN HIGHLANDS & ISLANDS BARRA (BARRAIGH)

the castle to Historic Scotland in 2000 for an annual rent of £1 and a bottle of whisky (Talisker single malt, if you're interested).

Traigh Mor
BEACH

This vast expanse of firm golden sand (the name means 'Big Strand') serves as Barra's airport (a mile across at low tide, and big enough for three 'runways'), the only beach airport in the world that handles scheduled flights. Watching the little Twin Otter aircraft come and go is a popular spectator sport. In between flights, locals gather cockles, a local seafood speciality, from the sands.

Sleeping & Eating

Accommodation on Barra is limited, so make a reservation before committing to a night on the island. Wild camping (on foot or by bike) is allowed almost anywhere; campervans and car campers are restricted to official sites – check www.isleofbarra.com for details.

Dunard Hostel
HOSTEL £

(☑ 01871-810443; www.dunardhostel.co.uk; Castlebay, dm/tw from £20/48; P ☎) Dunard is a friendly, family-run hostel just a five-minute walk from the ferry terminal. The owners can help to organise sea-kayaking trips.

Tigh na Mara
B&B ££

(☑ 01871-810304; www.tighnamara-barra.co.uk; Castlebay; s/d £45/75; ☺ Apr-Oct; P ☎) A lovely cottage B&B with a brilliant location just above the ferry pier, looking out over the bay and Kisimul Castle (p227). Ask for the en suite double bedroom with bay view.

Castlebay Hotel
HOTEL ££

(☑ 01871-810223; www.castlebayhotel.com; Castlebay; s/d from £70/125; P ☎) The Castlebay Hotel has spacious bedrooms decorated with a subtle tartan motif – it's worth paying a bit extra for a sea view – and there's a comfy lounge and conservatory with grand views across the harbour to the islands south of Barra. The hotel bar is the hub of island social life, with regular sessions of traditional music.

The restaurant specialises in local seafood and game (often rabbit).

Deck
CAFE £

(www.hebrideantoffeecompany.com; Castlebay; mains £4-7; ☺ 9am-5pm Mon-Thu, to 7pm Fri & Sat, noon-4pm Sun Apr-Sep) There are only outdoor seats at this cafe (attached to the Hebridean Toffee factory), on a wooden deck overlooking the bay, but it's worth waiting for a fine day to sample the freshly baked scones and homemade cakes.

❶ Getting There & Away

There are two daily flights from Glasgow to Barra airport.

CalMac (www.calmac.co.uk) ferries link Eriskay with Ardmhor (pedestrian/car £3.05/10.55, 40 minutes, three to five daily) at the northern end of Barra. Ferries also run from Castlebay to Oban.

A bus service links ferry arrivals and departures at Ardmhor with Castlebay (£1.80, 20 minutes). Bus W32 makes a circuit of the island up to five times daily (except Sunday), and also connects with flights at the airport.

Orkney & Shetland

Best Places to Eat

➡ Scalloway Hotel (p257)

➡ Foveran (p236)

➡ Fjarå (p254)

➡ Hay's Dock (p255)

➡ Hamnavoe
Restaurant (p245)

Best Places to Stay

➡ Brinkies Guest
House (p244)

➡ Scalloway Hotel (p257)

➡ Almara (p259)

➡ West Manse (p247)

➡ Albert Hotel (p236)

➡ Busta House Hotel (p259)

Why Go?

Up here at Britain's top end it can feel more Scandinavian than Scottish, and no wonder. For the Vikings, the jaunt across the North Sea from Norway was as easy as a stroll down to the local mead hall and they soon controlled these windswept, treeless archipelagos, laying down longhouses alongside the stony remains of ancient prehistoric settlements.

An ancient magic hovers in the air above Orkney and Shetland, endowing them with an allure that lodges firmly in the soul. It's in the misty seas, where seals, whales and porpoises patrol lonely coastlines; it's in the air, where squadrons of seabirds wheel above huge nesting colonies; and it's on land, where standing stones catch late summer sunsets and strains of folk music disperse in the air before the wind gusts shut the pub door. These islands reward the journey.

When to Go
Lerwick

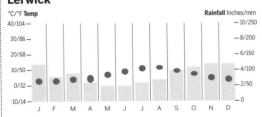

Jan Shetland's Up Helly Aa: horned helmets and burning Viking ships on the beach.

Jun Orkney rocks to the St Magnus Festival: book accommodation ahead.

Jul Summer sunlight and Scotland's longest daylight hours.

Orkney & Shetland Highlights

1 Skara Brae (p242) Shaking your head in astonishment at extraordinary prehistoric perfection that predates the pyramids.

2 Maeshowe (p241) Sensing the gulf of years in this ancient tomb enlivened by later Viking graffiti.

3 Hoy (p245) Soaking up the glorious scenery and making the hike to the spectacular Old Man of Hoy.

4 Northern Islands (p247) Island-hopping through Orkney, where crystal azure waters lap against glittering white-sand beaches.

5 Scapa Flow (p246) Submerging yourself among the sunken warships of Scapa Flow.

6 Lerwick (p245) Discovering your inner Viking at the Up Helly Aa festival.

7 Hermaness National Nature Reserve (p260) Capering with puffins and dodging dive-bombing skuas at Shetland's birdwatching centre.

8 Lighthouse Cottages (p256) Staying in one of Shetland's romantic lighthouse cottages; one of the best is at spectacular Sumburgh.

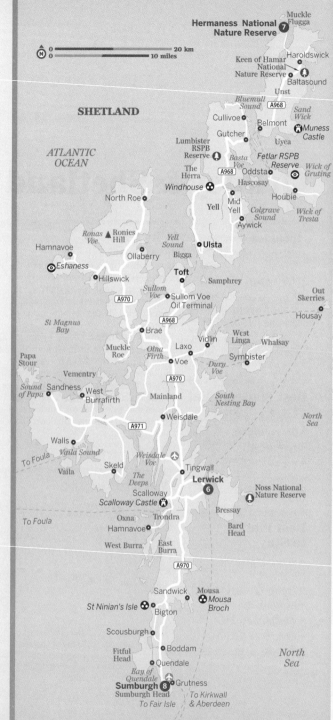

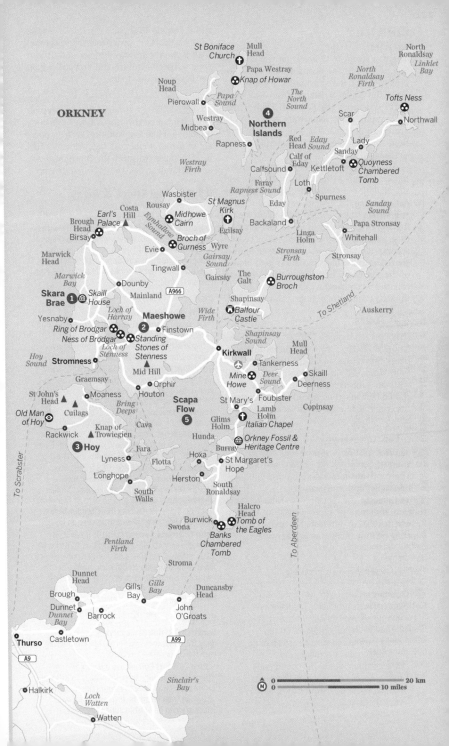

ORKNEY

North Ronaldsay
Linklet Bay

St Boniface
Church
Mull Head
Papa Westray
Knap of Howar

Noup
Head

Pierowall
*Papa
Sound*
*The
North
Sound*
*North
Ronaldsay
Firth*

Scar
Tofts Ness

Westray
Midbea
4
**Northern
Islands**
Northwall

Rapness
Red
Head
*Eday
Sound*
Sanday
Lady

Calfsound
Calf of
Eday
Kettletoft
Quoyness
Chambered
Tomb

*Westray
Firth*
Faray
Rapness Sound
Loth
Spurness
*Sanday
Sound*

Wasbister
St Magnus
Kirk
Eday
Papa Stronsay

Rousay
Midhowe
Cairn
Egilsay
Backaland
Linga
Holm
Whitehall

Brough
Head
Earl's
Palace
Costa
Hill
*Eynhallow
Sound*
Broch of
Gurness
Wyre
*Stronsay
Firth*
Stronsay

Birsay
Evie
*Gairsay
Sound*
Burroughston
Broch

Marwick
Head
Tingwall
Gairsay
The
Galt

To Shetland
Auskerry

*Marwick
Bay*
Dounby
Shapinsay

**Skara
Brae**
1
Skaill
House
Mainland
[A966]
*Wide
Firth*
Balfour
Castle

Yesnaby
*Loch of
Harray*
Maeshowe
Shapinsay

Ring of Brodgar
2
Finstown
*Shapinsay
Sound*

Ness of Brodgar
Standing
Stones of
Stenness
Kirkwall
Mull
Head

*Hoy
Sound*
Stromness
*Loch of
Stenness*
Tankerness
Skaill

Graemsay
Mid Hill
Mine
Howe
*Deer
Sound*
Deerness

St John's
Head
Moaness
Orphir
Houton
**Scapa
Flow**
St Mary's
Foubister
Copinsay

Old Man
of Hoy
Cuilags
*Bring
Deeps*
5
Lamb
Holm
Italian Chapel

Rackwick
Knap of
Trowieglen
Cava
Glims
Holm
Orkney Fossil &
Heritage Centre

3 Hoy
Fara
Hunda
Burray

Lyness
Flotta
Hoxa
St Margaret's
Hope

Longhope
Herston
South
Ronaldsay

South
Walls
Halcro
Head
Tomb of
the Eagles

Burwick
Swona
Banks
Chambered
Tomb

*Pentland
Firth*
Stroma

Dunnet
Head
Gills
Bay
*Gills
Bay*
Duncansby
Head

Brough
Dunnet
*Dunnet
Bay*
Barrock
John
O'Groats

Thurso
Castletown
[A99]

[A9]

Halkirk
*Sinclair's
Bay*

*Loch
Watten*
N
0
20 km

Watten
0
10 miles

To Scrabster

To Aberdeen

ORKNEY

POP 21,670

There's a magic to Orkney that you begin to feel as soon as the Scottish mainland slips astern. Only a few short miles of ocean separate the chain of islands from Scotland's north coast, but the Pentland Firth is one of Europe's most dangerous waterways, a graveyard of ships that adds an extra mystique to these islands shimmering in the sea mists.

An archipelago of mostly flat, green-topped islands stripped bare of trees and ringed with red sandstone cliffs, its heritage dates back to the Vikings, whose influence is still strong today. Famed for ancient standing stones and prehistoric villages, for sublime sandy beaches and spectacular coastal scenery, it's a region whose ports tell of lives shared with the blessings and rough moods of the sea, and a destination where seekers can find melancholy wrecks of warships and the salty clamour of remote seabird colonies.

☞ Tours

Orkney Archaeology Tours   TOURS
(☑ 01856-721450;   www.orkneyarchaeologytours.
co.uk) Specialises in all-inclusive multiday tours focusing on Orkney's ancient sites, with an archaeologist guide. These tours should be booked far ahead (a year or two). Also runs customisable private tours outside of the main season.

Orkney Uncovered   TOURS
(☑ 01856-878822;   www.orkneyuncovered.co.uk;
Viewfield, Sunnybank Rd; ☺ 8am-8pm Mon-Sat) These private minivan tours are fully customisable and run with real enthusiasm and insight by personable Kinlay. Tours can cover one or more aspects of Orkney, whether your interest be archaeological sites, wartime history or craft jewellery.

ORKNEY CRAFT TRAIL

Orkney is famous for its handicrafts, with makers producing fabulous jewellery, pottery, fabrics and chairs. The Orkney Craft Trail (www.orkney designercrafts.com) is an association of small producers, mostly based in little communities or the countryside, that produces a booklet you can use to navigate your way around their various workshops.

Great Orkney Tours   TOURS
(☑ 01856-861443;   www.greatorkneytours.co.uk)
Jean gets rave reviews for her enthusiasm about Orkney's culture and archaeology on her flexible private tours.

Wildabout Orkney   BUS
(☑ 01856-877737;   www.wildaboutorkney.com)
Operates tours covering Orkney's history, ecology, folklore and wildlife. Day trips operate year-round and cost £59, with pick-ups in Stromness (to meet the morning ferry) and Kirkwall.

❶ Getting There & Away

AIR

Loganair (☑ outside UK 0141-642 9407, within UK 0344 800 2855; www.loganair.co.uk) flies daily from Kirkwall to Aberdeen, Edinburgh, Glasgow, Inverness and Sumburgh (Shetland). There are summer services to Manchester, Fair Isle and Bergen (Norway).

BOAT

During summer, book car spaces ahead. Peak-season fares are quoted here. At the time of research, the road-equivalent tariff (RET) scheme was due to be rolled out on Orkney services, so prices should drop.

Northlink Ferries (☑ 0845 6000 449; www.northlinkferries.co.uk) Operates from Scrabster to Stromness (passenger/car £19.40/59, 1½ hours, two to three daily), from Aberdeen to Kirkwall (passenger/car £31.50/111, six hours, three or four weekly) and from Kirkwall to Lerwick (passenger/car £24.65/103, six to eight hours, three or four weekly) on Shetland. Fares are up to 35% cheaper in the low season.

Pentland Ferries (☑ 0800 688 8998; www.pentlandferries.co.uk; adult/child/car/bike £16/8/38/free) Leave from Gills Bay, 3 miles west of John O'Groats, and head to St Margaret's Hope on South Ronaldsay three to four times daily. The crossing takes a little over an hour.

John O'Groats Ferries (☑ 01955-611353; www.jogferry.co.uk; s £19, incl bus to Kirkwall £20; ☺ May-Sep) Has a passenger-only service from John O'Groats to Burwick, on the southern tip of South Ronaldsay, with connecting buses to Kirkwall. A 40-minute crossing, with two to three departures daily.

BUS

Scottish Citylink (www.citylink.co.uk) runs daily from Inverness to Scrabster, connecting with the Stromness ferries.

John O'Groats Ferries has a summer-only 'Orkney bus' service from Inverness to Kirkwall. Tickets (one way £25, five hours) include bus-ferry-bus travel from Inverness to Kirkwall. There are two daily from June to August.

ℹ️ Getting Around

The *Orkney Transport Guide* details all island transport and is free from tourist offices. There's a winter and summer version; ferry sailings, flights and some bus services are reduced from October to April.

The largest Orkney island, Mainland, is linked by causeways to four southern islands; others are reached by air and ferry.

AIR

Loganair Inter-Isles Air Service (☑ 01856-873457; www.loganair.co.uk) operates inter-island flights from Kirkwall to Eday, Stronsay, Sanday, Westray, Papa Westray and North Ronaldsay. Fares are reasonable, with some special discounted tickets if you stay a night on the outer islands. You have to book by email or phone.

BICYCLE

Various locations on Mainland hire out bikes, including **Cycle Orkney** (☑ 01856-875777; www.cycleorkney.com; Tankerness Lane, Kirkwall; per day/3 days/week £20/40/80; ⊗9am-5.30pm Mon-Sat) and **Orkney Cycle Hire** (p245). Both offer out-of-hours pick-ups and options for kids.

BOAT

Orkney Ferries (☑ 01856-872044; www.orkneyferries.co.uk) operates car ferries from Mainland to the islands. An Island Explorer pass costs £42 for a week's passenger travel in summer. Bikes are carried free.

BUS

Stagecoach (☑ 01856-870555; www.stagecoachbus.com) runs buses on Mainland and connecting islands. Most don't operate on Sunday. Dayrider (£8.65) and 7-Day Megarider (£19.25) tickets allow unlimited travel.

CAR

Small-car hire rates are around £45/240 per day/week, although there are sometimes specials for as low as £30 per day. **Orkney Car Hire** (James D Peace & Co; ☑ 01856-872866; www.orkneycarhire.co.uk; Junction Rd, Kirkwall; per day/week £45/240; ⊗8am-5pm Mon-Fri, 9am-1pm Sat) and **WR Tullock** (☑ 01856-875500; www.orkneycarrental.co.uk; Castle St; per day/week £45/240; ⊗8.30am-6pm Mon-Fri, to 5pm Sat) are both close to the bus station in Kirkwall.

Kirkwall

POP 7000

Orkney's main town is the islands' commercial centre and there's a comparatively busy feel to its main shopping street and ferry dock. It's set back from a wide bay, and its

---

ℹ️ EXPLORING ORKNEY

There's an excellent range of tourist information on Orkney, including a useful annual guide, as well as a separate guide to the smaller islands. The Kirkwall Tourist Office (p237) has a good range of info and very helpful staff.

The **Orkney Explorer Pass** (www.historicenvironment.scot; adult/child/family £19/11.40/38) covers all Historic Environment Scotland sites in Orkney, including Maeshowe, Skara Brae, the Broch of Gurness, the Brough of Birsay, the Bishop's Palace and Earl's Palace in Kirkwall and the Hackness Martello Tower on Hoy, as well as Jarlshof on Shetland. It lasts for 30 consecutive days and is only available from April to October.

---

vigour, combined with the atmospheric paved streets and twisting wynds (lanes), give Orkney's capital a distinctive character. Magnificent St Magnus Cathedral takes pride of place in the centre of town, and the nearby Earl's and Bishop's Palaces are also worth a ramble. Founded in the early 11th century, the original part of Kirkwall is one of the best examples of an ancient Norse town.

◉ Sights

★**St Magnus Cathedral**   CATHEDRAL
(☑ 01856-874894; www.stmagnus.org; Broad St; ⊗9am-6pm Mon-Sat, 1-6pm Sun Apr-Sep, 9am-1pm & 2-5pm Mon-Sat Oct-Mar) FREE Constructed from local red sandstone, Kirkwall's centrepiece, dating from the early 12th century, is among Scotland's most interesting cathedrals. The powerful atmosphere of an ancient faith pervades the impressive interior. Lyrical and melodramatic epitaphs of the dead line the walls and emphasise the serious business of 17th- and 18th-century bereavement. Tours of the upper level (£8) run on Tuesday and Thursday; phone to book.

Earl Rognvald Brusason commissioned the cathedral in 1137 in the name of his martyred uncle, Magnus Erlendsson, who was killed by Earl Hakon Paulsson on Egilsay in 1117. Magnus' remains are entombed in an interior pillar. Another notable interment is that of the Arctic explorer John Rae.

ORKNEY & SHETLAND KIRKWALL

Kirkwall

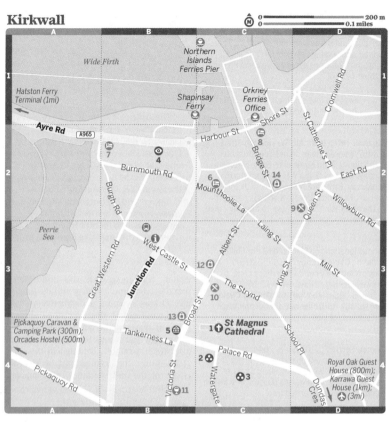

Kirkwall

★**Highland Park Distillery**   DISTILLERY
(☑01856-874619; www.highlandpark.co.uk; Holm Rd; tours adult/child £10/free; ⊙tours 10am-4pm Apr-Oct, 2pm & 3pm Mon-Fri Nov-Mar) South of Kirkwall's centre, this distillery is great to visit. Despite a dodgy Viking rebrand, it's a serious distillery that malts its own barley; see it and the peat kiln used to dry it on the excellent, well-informed hour-long tour (book ahead). The standard 12-year-old is a soft, balanced malt, great for novices and aficionados alike; the 18-year-old is among the

world's finest drams. This and older whiskies can be tasted on more specialised tours (£20 to £75), which you can prearrange.

Kirkjuvagr Orkney Gin DISTILLERY
(☑ 01856-875338; www.orkneydistilling.com; Ayre Rd; tours adult/child £15/8; ⊙ tours 11am & 2pm Mon-Sat) Opened in 2018, this distillery and visitor centre on the waterfront is a new showcase for this tasty Orkney spirit. Tours run for an hour and include an audiovisual display and a tasting; it's wise to prebook online. There's also a cafe-bar here. At the time of research, they were about to roll out an in-depth day-long tour that would let you create your own gin.

Earl's Palace RUINS
(☑ 01856-871918; www.historicenvironment.scot; Watergate; adult/child £5/3; ⊙ 9.30am-5.30pm Apr-Sep) The intriguing Earl's Palace was once known as the finest example of French Renaissance architecture in Scotland. One room features an interesting history of its builder, Earl Patrick Stewart, a bastard in every sense of the word, who was beheaded in Edinburgh for treason. He started construction in about 1600, but ran out of money and never completed it. When it's closed you can still get a good look at it from the garden. Admission includes the adjacent **Bishop's Palace**.

Orkney Museum MUSEUM
(☑ 01856-873191; www.orkney.gov.uk; Broad St; ⊙ 10.30am-5pm Mon-Sat year-round, closed 12.30-1.30pm Oct-Apr) **FREE** This labyrinthine display in a former merchant's house gives an overview of Orcadian history and prehistory, including Pictish carvings and a display on the ba' (p236). Most engaging are the last rooms, covering 19th- and 20th-century social history.

🎊 Festivals & Events

St Magnus Festival PERFORMING ARTS, MUSIC
(☑ 01856-871445; www.stmagnusfestival.com; ⊙ late Jun) Running for a week over midsummer, this festival is a colourful celebration of music and the arts, with high-quality orchestral performances at the heart of it. It's held in various venues around Kirkwall.

🛏 Sleeping

Orcades Hostel HOSTEL £
(☑ 01856-873745; www.orcadeshostel.com; Muddisdale Rd; dm/s/d £20/40/52; P@🌐) Book ahead to get a bed in this cracking hostel on the western edge of Kirkwall. It's a guesthouse conversion, so there's a very smart kitchen and lounge, and great-value doubles. Comfortable, spacious en suite dorms with just four bunks make for sound sleeping; enthusiastic owners give the place spark. There are lockers for valuables at reception.

Peedie Hostel HOSTEL £
(☑ 01856-877177; www.stayinkirkwall.co.uk; Ayre Rd; dm/s/tw £15/20/35; P🌐) Nestling into a corner at the end of the Kirkwall waterfront, this marvellously located hostel set in former fisherfolk's cottages has a cute, tiny downstairs section and a more sizeable upper area. Most of the dorms have just two beds, and there are three separate kitchen areas. It's normally unstaffed, but the keen new owner is giving it a gradual facelift.

Laundry facilities are available.

Pickaquoy Caravan & Camping Park CAMPSITE £
(Orkney Caravan Park; ☑ 01856-879900; www.orkneycaravanpark.co.uk; Muddisdale Rd; sites per adult/child £10/2.50, pod d £49; ⊙ Mar–mid-Dec; P🌐⚑🌐) There's no view, but plenty of grass and excellent modern facilities at this campsite, which is handily close to the centre of Kirkwall. There are also two camping pods sleeping up to six. If unattended, check in at the adjacent leisure centre.

Royal Oak Guest House B&B ££
(☑ 01856-877177; www.royaloakhouse.co.uk; Holm Rd; s £55-64, d £80; P🌐) This likeable spot south of Kirkwall's centre has eight bright rooms, all with modern en suite bathrooms. Photos of Orkney decorate the guesthouse, which features a luminous dining room and guest access to fridge, microwave and lounge. Best is having a great chat with owner Liz.

Shore HOTEL ££
(☑ 01856-872200; www.theshore.co.uk; Shore St; d £100-140; 🌐) Right on the harbour, the Shore has a can-do attitude and a friendly vibe. The rooms vary widely, from compact upstairs chambers to excellent, spacious premier doubles with water views (well worth the upgrade), but all are modern. Breakfast is also above average.

Karrawa Guest House GUESTHOUSE ££
(☑ 01856-871100; www.karrawaguesthouseorkney.co.uk; Inganess Rd; s £65-70, d £85-90; P🌐) In

a peaceful location on the southeastern edge of Kirkwall, this enthusiastically run guesthouse offers significant value for well-kept modern double rooms with comfortable mattresses. Breakfast is generously proportioned and bikes are available for hire.

★ **Albert Hotel** HOTEL **£££**
(☑01856-876000; www.alberthotel.co.uk; Mounthoolie Lane; s £97, d £146-181; ☎) Stylishly refurbished in plum and grey, this central but peaceful hotel is Kirkwall's finest address. Comfortable contemporary rooms in a variety of categories sport superinviting beds and smart bathrooms. Staff are helpful, and will pack you a breakfast box if you've got an early ferry. A great Orkney base, with the more-than-decent **Bothy Bar** (mains £7-12; ☉noon-2pm & 5-9pm; ☎) downstairs. Walk-in prices are often cheaper.

🍴 Eating & Drinking

Reel CAFE **£**
(www.facebook.com/thereelkirkwall; Albert St; sandwiches £3-6; ☉9am-6pm Mon-Sat; ☎) Part music shop, part cafe, the Reel is Kirkwall's best coffee stop and sits alongside St Magnus Cathedral (p233), bravely putting tables outside at the slightest threat of sunshine. It's a relaxed spot, good for a morning-after debriefing, a quiet Orkney ale, or lunchtime panini and musically named sandwiches (plus the cheese-and-mushroom Skara Brie).

It's a local folk-musicians' centre, with three evening sessions a week; check the Facebook page.

THE BA'

Every Christmas Day and New Year's Day, Kirkwall holds a staggering spectacle: a crazy ball game known as the ba'. Two enormous teams, the Uppies and the Doonies, fight their way, no holds barred, through the streets, trying to get a leather ball to the other end of town. The ball is thrown from the Mercat Cross to the waiting teams; the Uppies have to get the ba' to the corner of Main St and Junction Rd, the Doonies must get it to the water. Violence, skulduggery and other stunts are common, and the event, fuelled by plenty of strong drink, can last hours.

Judith Glue Real Food Cafe CAFE **£**
(☑01856-874225; www.judithglue.com; 25 Broad St; light meals £8-16; ☉9am-6pm Mon-Sat, 10am-6pm Sun mid-Sep–May, 9am-9pm Mon-Sat, 10am-6pm Sun Jun–mid-Sep; ☎) 🏃 At the back of a lively craft shop opposite St Magnus Cathedral, this licensed cafe-bistro serves tasty sandwiches and salads, as well as daily specials and succulent seafood platters. There's a strong emphasis on sustainable and organic ingredients, but put the feelgood factor aside for a moment when fighting for a table at lunchtime. Check Facebook for regular events.

★ **The Shore** SCOTTISH **££**
(☑01856-872200; www.theshore.co.uk; 6 Shore St; bar meals £9-11, restaurant mains £17-22; ☉food noon-2pm & 6-9pm Mon-Fri, 10am-9pm Sat & Sun, reduced hours winter; ☎) This popular harbourside place is a convivial spot with a helpful attitude. It offers high-standard bar meals and excellent evening meals in the restaurant section, which features local seafood and beautifully prepared meat dishes. Upstairs are some very decent rooms.

★ **Foveran** SCOTTISH **££**
(☑01856-872389; www.thefoveran.com; St Ola; mains £15-26; ☉6.30-8.30pm mid-May–mid-Sep, Fri & Sat only plus other days by arrangement low season; ☎) 🏃 Three miles down the Orphir road, one of Orkney's best dining options is surprisingly affordable for its quality. Tranquilly located, with a cosy eating area overlooking the sea, it shines with its classic Orcadian ingredients – the steak with haggis and whisky sauce is feted, while North Ronaldsay lamb comes in four different, deliciously tender cuts.

A medley of toothsome vegetables accompanies the mains, and interesting wines complement the dishes. If you like the spot – and why wouldn't you? – there are compact, comfortable, Laura Ashley-decorated rooms available (singles/doubles £85/125).

Old Storehouse SCOTTISH **££**
(☑01856-252250; www.thestorehouserestaurant withrooms.co.uk; Bridge St Wynd; mains lunch £9-12, dinner £14-22; ☉noon-11pm; ☎) This exciting project that was just about to open as we last passed by has seen a transformation of a listed 19th-century herring warehouse into an Orcadian restaurant. There are also eight luxurious, individu-

ally designed rooms upstairs (doubles £150 to £190).

Royal Cask PUB
(☑ 01856-873477; www.orkneyhotel.co.uk; 40 Victoria St; ☺ 11am-midnight Mon-Wed, to 1am Thu-Sat, noon-midnight Sun; ☎) Tucked away in the Orkney Hotel, this refurbished bar is best visited for its fabulous selection of single malt whisky, with over 800 different bottlings and lots of knowledge about them. There are also bar meals available to soak it all up.

🛍 Shopping

Kirkwall has some gorgeous jewellery and crafts along Albert St, as well as shops selling quality Orcadian food and drink.

Sheila Fleet JEWELLERY
(☑ 01856-861203; www.sheilafleet.com; 30 Bridge St; ☺ 9am-5pm Mon-Sat year-round, plus 11am-4pm Sun Jun-Aug) Orkney's best-known jewellery designer creates some exquisite pieces seemingly lit from within. She draws on local traditions and storytelling for her creations. If you want to see them being made you can visit her workshop, located past the airport in Tankerness.

Judith Glue ARTS & CRAFTS
(☑ 01856-874225; www.judithglue.com; 25 Broad St; ☺ 9am-6pm Mon-Sat, 10am-6pm Sun mid-Sep–May, 9am-9pm Mon-Sat, 10am-6pm Sun Jun–mid-Sep) This absorbing shop has some fine handmade knitwear as well as an eclectic range of Orkney crafts and souvenirs.

Aurora JEWELLERY
(☑ 01856-871521; www.aurora-jewellery.com; 69 Albert St; ☺ 9.30am-5.15pm Mon-Sat) This jewellery store features the work of three Orcadian designers, with their beautiful earrings, brooches and necklaces inspired by local landscapes and history.

ℹ Information

Balfour Hospital (☑ 01856-888000; www.ohb. scot.nhs.uk; New Scapa Rd) Follow Junction Rd south out of town and you'll see it on your right. It's scheduled to be replaced by **Orkney Hospital** (www.ohb.scot.nhs.uk; Foreland Rd) in 2019.
Kirkwall Tourist Office (☑ 01856-872856; www.visitorkney.com; West Castle St; ☺ 9am-5pm Mon-Sat Nov-Mar, to 6pm Mon-Sat Apr & Sep-Oct, to 6pm daily May-Aug) Has a good range of Orkney info and helpful staff. Shares a building with the bus station.

ℹ Getting There & Away

AIR
Kirkwall Airport (☑ 01856-872421; www.hial. co.uk) is located 2.5 miles southeast of town and is served regularly by bus 4 (15 minutes).

BOAT
Ferries to Orkney's northern islands depart from the **pier** (www.orkneyferries.co.uk; Shore St) in the centre of town. Here too is the **Orkney Ferries Office** (☑ 01856-872044; www.orkney ferries.co.uk; Shore St; ☺ 7am-5pm Mon-Fri, 7am-noon & 1-3pm Sat) for bookings. **Ferries to Shapinsay** (www.orkneyferries.co.uk; Shore St) depart from the next pier to the west.

Ferries to Aberdeen and Shetland use the **Hatston Ferry Terminal** (www.northlinkferries. co.uk; Grainshore Rd; ☎), 2 miles northwest. Bus X10 heads there to coincide with departures.

BUS
All services leave from the **bus station** (West Castle St):
Bus X1 Stromness (£3.20, 30 minutes, hourly Monday to Saturday, seven on Sunday); in the other direction to St Margaret's Hope (£3).
Bus 2 Orphir and Houton (£2.35, 20 minutes, four or five daily Monday to Saturday, five on Sunday from mid-June to mid-August).
Bus 6 Evie (£3.50, 30 minutes, three to five daily Monday to Saturday) and Tingwall (Rousay ferry). Runs Sunday in summer to Tingwall only.

East Mainland to South Ronaldsay

After a German U-boat sank battleship HMS *Royal Oak* in 1939, Winston Churchill had causeways of concrete blocks erected across the channels on the eastern side of Scapa Flow, linking Mainland to the islands of Lamb Holm, Glims Holm, Burray and South Ronaldsay. The Churchill Barriers, flanked by rusting wrecks of blockships, now support the main road from Kirkwall to Burwick.

East Mainland

On a farm at Tankerness, the mysterious Iron Age site of Mine Howe is an eerie underground chamber, about 1.5m in diameter and 4m high. Its function is unknown; archaeologists from the TV series *Time Team* carried out a dig here and concluded that it may have had some ritual significance, perhaps as an oracle or shrine. At the time of research it was closed to the public.

MARCIN KADZIOLKA/SHUTTERSTOCK ©

1. St Ninian's Isle (p258)
On the southern end of Shetland (p250), this isle is home to Britain's largest shell-and-sand tombolo (sand or gravel isthmus).

2. Lerwick (p252)
This Shetland town has a solidly maritime feel.

3. Old Man of Hoy (p245)
The 137m-high rock stack is situated on Orkney's second-largest island.

4. Skara Brae (p242)
Northern Europe's best preserved neolithic village is one of the world's most evocative prehistoric sites.

Lamb Holm

Italian Chapel CHURCH
(☑ 01865-781268; adult/child £3/free; ⊘ 9am-6.30pm Jun-Aug, to 5pm May & Sep, 10am-4pm Mon-Sat, to 3pm Sun Apr & Oct, 10am-1pm Nov-Mar) The Italian Chapel is all that remains of a POW camp that housed the Italian soldiers who worked on the Churchill Barriers. They built the chapel in their spare time, using two Nissen huts, scrap metal and their considerable artistic skills. It's quite extraordinary inside and the charming back story makes it an Orkney highlight. One of the artists returned in 1960 to restore the paintwork.

Orkney Wine Company DRINKS
(☑ 01856-781736; www.orkneywine.co.uk; ⊘ 10am-5pm Mon-Sat May-Sep, plus noon-4pm Sun Jul & Aug, reduced hours Mar-Apr & Oct-Dec) The Orkney Wine Company has handmade wines produced with berries, flowers and vegetables, all naturally fermented. Get stuck into some strawberry-rhubarb wine or blackcurrant port – unusual flavours but surprisingly delicious.

Burray

POP 400
This small island, a link in the chain joined by the Churchill Barriers, has a fine beach at Northtown on the east coast, where you may see seals. The village has a shop and places to stay, and there's a worthwhile museum on the island.

★ **Fossil & Heritage Centre** MUSEUM
(☑ 01865-731255; www.orkneyfossilcentre.co.uk; adult/child £4.50/3; ⊘ 10am-5pm mid-Apr–Sep) This eclectic museum is a great visit, combining some excellent 360-million-year-old Devonian fish fossils found locally with a well-designed exhibition on the World Wars and Churchill Barriers. Upstairs is a selection of household and farming implements. There's a good little gift shop and an enjoyable coffee shop. Coming from Kirkwall it's on the left half a mile after crossing onto Burray.

South Ronaldsay

POP 900
South Ronaldsay's main village, pristine St Margaret's Hope, was named after the Maid of Norway, who died here in 1290 on her way to marry Edward II of England (strictly a political affair: Margaret was only seven years old). The island has some intriguing prehistoric tombs and fine places to stay and eat, and is also the docking point of two of the three mainland ferries.

◉ Sights

★ **Tomb of the Eagles** ARCHAEOLOGICAL SITE
(☑ 01856-831339; www.tomboftheeagles.co.uk; Cleat; adult/child £7.50/3.50; ⊘ 9.30am-5.30pm Apr-Sep, 10am-noon Mar, 9.30am-12.30pm Oct) Two significant archaeological sites were found here by a farmer on his land. The first is a Bronze Age stone building with a firepit, indoor well and plenty of seating (a communal cooking site or the original Orkney pub?). Beyond, in a spectacular clifftop position, the neolithic tomb (wheel yourself in prone on a trolley) is an elaborate stone construction that held the remains of up to 340 people who died some five millennia ago.

An excellent personal explanation is given at the visitor centre; you meet a few spooky skulls and can handle some of the artefacts found, plus absorb information on the mesolithic period. It's about a mile's airy walk to the tomb from the centre, which is near Burwick.

Banks Chambered Tomb ARCHAEOLOGICAL SITE
(Tomb of the Otters; ☑ 01856-831605; www.bankschamberedtomb.co.uk; Cleat; adult/child £6/3; ⊘ 11am-5pm Apr-Sep) Discovered while digging was under way for a car park, this 5000-year-old chambered tomb has yielded a vast quantity of human bones, well preserved thanks to the saturation of the earth. The tomb, dug into bedrock, is an atmospheric if claustrophobic visit. The guided tour mixes homespun archaeological theories with astute observations. Within the adjacent bistro, you can handle discoveries of stones and bones, including the remains of otters, who presumably used this as a den. Follow signs for Tomb of the Eagles.

🛏 Sleeping & Eating

★ **Bankburn House** B&B ££
(☑ 01856-831310; www.bankburnhouse.co.uk; A961, St Margaret's Hope; s/d £60/90, without bathroom £47.50/75; ℗ @ 🛜 🐾) 🍴 This large rustic house does everything right, with smashing good-sized rooms and engaging owners who put on quality breakfasts and take pride in constantly innovating to improve guests' comfort levels. The huge lawn overlooks St Margaret's Hope and the

bay – perfect for sunbathing on shimmering Orkney summer days. Prices drop substantially for multinight stays. Evening meals are available by request.

They also have Tesla chargers and an electric car available for hire.

Robertsons · CAFE **£**
(☑ 01856-831889; www.facebook.com/coffee hoosebar; Church Rd, St Margaret's Hope; light meals £3-9; ☺ food 10am-9pm Mon-Sat, 11am-9pm Sun; ☏) Tastefully renovated, this characterful high-ceilinged former general store with chessboard tiles makes an atmospheric venue for a morning coffee and filled roll, or light meals such as soups and cheeseboards with local varieties (available for purchase). It also does cocktails and opens as a bar until midnight or later.

Skerries Bistro · SEAFOOD **££**
(☑ 01856-831605; www.skerriesbistro.co.uk; Cleat; lunch £6-10, dinner mains £14-18; ☺ noon-4pm & 6-9pm Mon, Wed, Fri & Sat, noon-4pm Tue, Thu & Sun Apr-Sep) This cafe-bistro occupies a spectacular setting at the southern end of South Ronaldsay. It's a smart, modern glass-walled building with a deck and great clifftop views. Meals range from soups and sandwiches to daily fish and shellfish specials. Dinner should be booked ahead. A romantic little separate pod is available for private dining.

West & North Mainland

This part of Mainland island is sprinkled with outstanding prehistoric monuments: the journey to Orkney is worth it for these alone and they stand proud as some of the world's most important neolithic sites. It would take a day to see all of them – if pushed for time, visit Skara Brae then Maeshowe, but book your visit to the latter in advance.

☉ Sights

The Heart of Neolithic Orkney is Unesco-listed and consists of four standout archaeological sites: Skara Brae (p242), Maeshowe, the Standing Stones of Stenness (p242) and the Ring of Brodgar (p242). These and other associated sites are not to be missed. It's important to prebook your entry slot to Maeshowe ahead of time.

★ **Maeshowe** · ARCHAEOLOGICAL SITE
(☑ 01856-761606; www.historicenvironment. scot; adult/child £5.50/3.30; ☺ 9.30am-5pm Apr-

Sep, 10am-4pm Oct-Mar, tours hourly 10am-4pm, plus 6pm & 7pm Jul & Aug) Constructed about 5000 years ago, Maeshowe is an extraordinary place, a Stone Age tomb built from enormous sandstone blocks, some of which weighed many tons and were brought from several miles away. Creeping down the long stone passageway to the central chamber, you feel the indescribable gulf of years that separate us from the architects of this mysterious tomb.

Entry is by 45-minute guided tours (prebooking online is strongly advised) that leave by bus from the visitor centre at nearby Stenness.

Though nothing is known about who and what was interred here, the scope of the project suggests it was a structure of great significance.

In the 12th century, the tomb was broken into by Vikings searching for treasure. A couple of years later, another group sought shelter in the chamber from a three-day blizzard. Waiting out the storm, they carved runic graffiti on the walls. As well as the some-things-never-change 'Olaf was 'ere' and 'Thorni bedded Helga', there are also more intricate carvings, including a particularly fine dragon and a knotted serpent.

Prebook tickets online as recommended, or buy them at the visitor centre in Stenness, from where the tour buses depart. Guides tend to only show a couple of the Viking inscriptions, but they'll happily show more if asked. Check out the virtual-reality tour in the visitor centre while you wait.

For a few weeks around the winter solstice the setting sun shafts up the entrance passage, and strikes the back wall of the tomb in

NESS OF BRODGAR

Ongoing excavations on the **Ness of Brodgar** (www.nessofbrodgar.co.uk; ☺ tours 2-3 times Mon-Fri early Jul-late Aug) **FREE**, between the Standing Stones of Stenness and the Ring of Brodgar, are rapidly revealing that this was a neolithic site of huge importance. Probably a major power and religious centre and used for over a millennium, the settlement had a mighty wall, a large building (a temple or palace?) and as many as 100 other structures, some painted. Each dig season reveals new, intriguing finds.

SKARA BRAE
••

Idyllically situated by a sandy bay 8 miles north of Stromness, and predating Stonehenge and the pyramids of Giza, extraordinary Skara Brae (www.historicenvironment.scot; Sandwick; adult/child Nov-Mar £6.50/3.90, Apr-Oct incl Skaill House £7.50/4.50; ⊘9.30am-5.30pm Apr-Sep, 10am-4pm Oct-Mar), one of the world's most evocative prehistoric sites, is northern Europe's best-preserved neolithic village. Even the stone furniture – beds, boxes and dressers – has survived the 5000 years since a community lived and breathed here. It was hidden until 1850, when waves whipped up by a severe storm eroded the sand and grass above the beach, exposing the houses underneath.

There's an excellent interactive exhibit and short video, arming visitors with facts and theory, which will enhance the impact of the site. You then enter a reconstructed house, giving the excavation (which you head to next) more meaning. The official guidebook, available from the visitor centre, includes a good self-guided tour.

In the summer months, your ticket also gets you into Skaill House (☑01856-841501; www.skaillhouse.co.uk; Sandwick; incl Skara Brae adult/child £7.50/4.50; ⊘9.30am-5.30pm Apr-Sep, 10am-4pm Oct), an important step-gabled Orcadian mansion built for the bishop in 1620. It may feel a bit anticlimactic catapulting straight from the neolithic to the 1950s decor, but it's an interesting sight in its own right. You can see a smart hidden compartment in the library as well as the bishop's original 17th-century four-poster bed.

At the time of research, a trial bus route (8S) was running to Skara Brae from Kirkwall and Stromness a few times weekly, but not all were useful to visit the site. It's possible to walk along the coast from Stromness to Skara Brae (9 miles), or it's an easy taxi (£15), hitch or cycle from Stromness. Mobility scooters are available at the visitor centre to cut out the walk to the site

spooky alignment. If you can't be here then, check the webcams on www.maeshowe.co.uk.

Ring of Brodgar
ARCHAEOLOGICAL SITE
(www.historicenvironment.scot; ⊘24hr) FREE A mile northwest of Stenness is this wide circle of standing stones, some over 5m tall. The last of the three Stenness monuments to be built (2500–2000 BC), it remains a most atmospheric location. Twenty-one of the original 60 stones still stand among the heather. On a grey day with dark clouds thudding low across the sky, the stones are a spine-tingling sight.

Standing Stones of Stenness
ARCHAEOLOGICAL SITE
(www.historicenvironment.scot; ⊘24hr) FREE Part of this Mainland area's concentration of neolithic monuments, four mighty stones remain of what was once a circle of 12. Recent research suggests they were perhaps erected as long ago as 3300 BC, and they impose by their sheer size; the tallest measures 5.7m in height. The narrow strip of land they're on, the Ness of Brodgar, separates the Harray and Stenness lochs and was the site of a large settlement inhabited throughout the neolithic period (3500–1800 BC).

Unstan Chambered Cairn
ARCHAEOLOGICAL SITE
(www.historicenvironment.scot; A965; ⊘24hr) FREE This atmospheric neolithic tomb, on a smaller scale than nearby Maeshowe, is a site that you may well get to yourself. It's a very tight squeeze down the entrance passage; once inside you can appreciate several different burial compartments divided by vertical stone slabs. The modern roof protects the structure.

Barnhouse Neolithic Village
ARCHAEOLOGICAL SITE
(www.historicenvironment.scot; ⊘24hr) FREE Alongside the Standing Stones of Stenness are the excavated remains of a village thought to have been inhabited by the builders of Maeshowe. Don't skip this: it brings the area to life. The houses are well preserved and similar to Skara Brae with their stone furnishings. One of the buildings was entered by crossing a fireplace: possibly an act of ritual significance.

Orkney Brewery
BREWERY
(☑01856-841777; www.orkneybrewery.co.uk; Quoyloo; tours adult/child £6.50/3.50; ⊘10am-4.30pm Mon-Sat, 11am-4.30pm Sun mid-Mar–Dec) The folk here have been producing their brilliant Orcadian beers – Dark Island is a standout, while Skullsplitter lives up to its

name – for years now, and this brewery's visitor centre is a great place to come and try them. Tours run regularly from noon to 3pm and explain the brewing process, while, fashionably decked out in local stone, the cafe-bar is atmospheric.

Birsay

The small village of Birsay is 6 miles north of Skara Brae, set amid peaceful countryside. It has some excellent attractions, including the Brough of Birsay, which makes a tempting picnic destination if you plan the tides right.

Brough of Birsay ARCHAEOLOGICAL SITE
(www.historicenvironment.scot; adult/child £5/3; ☺9.30am-5.30pm mid-Jun–Sep) At low tide – check tide times at any Historic Environment Scotland site – you can walk out to this windswept island, the site of extensive Norse ruins, including a number of longhouses and the 12th-century **St Peter's Church**. There's also a replica of a Pictish stone found here. This is where St Magnus was buried after his murder on Egilsay in 1117, and the island became a pilgrimage place. The attractive lighthouse has fantastic views. Take a picnic, but don't get stranded...

The Brough features heavily in George Mackay Brown's excellent novel, *Magnus*.

Earl's Palace RUINS
(☺24hr) FREE The ruins of this palace, built in the 16th century by the despotic Robert Stewart, Earl of Orkney, dominate the village of Birsay. Today it's a mass of half walls and crumbling columns; the size of the palace is impressive, matching the reputed ego and tyranny of its former inhabitant.

Birsay Hostel HOSTEL, CAMPSITE £
(☑after hours 01856-721470, office hours 01856-873535; https://orkney.campstead.com; junction of B9056 & A967; tent sites 1/2 people £8.25/12.70, dm/tw £19/37.90; ☺Apr-Sep; P☎) A former activity centre and school now has dorms that vary substantially in spaciousness – go for the two- or four-bedded ones. There's a big kitchen and a grassy camping area; kids and families sleep substantially cheaper. Book online to avoid an admin fee (private rooms only). It will open for bookings of four or more in the low season.

Birsay Bay Tearoom CAFE £
(☑01856-721399; www.birsaybaytearoom.co.uk; light meals £3-8; ☺11am-4.30pm Thu-Mon Apr, to 6pm Wed-Mon May-Sep, 10.30am-3.30pm Fri-Sun

Oct-Dec & Feb-Mar; ☎) A pleasant spot with sweeping views over green grass, black cows and blue-grey sea, this cafe serves tea, coffee, home baking and light meals. It's a good place to wait for the tide to go out before crossing to the Brough of Birsay (in plain sight). Check the website for latest winter opening times as these vary substantially.

Broch of Gurness

Broch of Gurness (www.historicenvironment. scot; Evie; adult/child £6/3.60; ☺9.30am-5.30pm Apr-Sep, 10am-4pm Oct) is a fine example of the drystone fortified towers that were both a status symbol for powerful farmers and useful protection from raiders some 2200 years ago. The imposing entranceway and sturdy stone walls – originally 10m high – are impressive; inside you can see the hearth and where a mezzanine floor would have fitted. Around the broch are a number of well-preserved outbuildings, including a curious shamrock-shaped house. The visitor centre has some interesting displays on the culture that built these remarkable fortifications.

The broch is on an exposed headland at Aikerness, a 1.5-mile walk northeast from the strung-out village of Evie.

Stromness

POP 1800
This appealing grey-stone port has a narrow, elongated, flagstone-paved main street and tiny alleys leading down to the waterfront between tall houses. It lacks the size of Kirkwall, Orkney's main town, but makes up for that with bucketloads of character, having changed little since its heyday in the 18th century, when it was a busy staging post for ships avoiding the troublesome English Channel during European wars. Stromness is ideally located for trips to Orkney's major prehistoric sites.

◉ Sights

Stromness, formerly a slightly rough-edged maritime town, has gone all arty, with a string of quirky craft shops, galleries and boutiques along the picturesque main shopping street. It's great for browsing.

★ **Stromness Museum** MUSEUM
(☑01856-850025; www.stromnessmuseum.co.uk; 52 Alfred St; adult/child £5/1; ☺10am-5pm daily Apr-Sep, 10am-5pm Mon-Sat Oct, 11am-3.30pm

Mon-Sat Nov-Mar) This superb museum, run with great passion, is full of knick-knacks from maritime and natural-history exhibitions covering whaling, the Hudson's Bay Company and the German fleet sunk after WWI. Recent finds from the jaw-dropping excavations at the Ness of Brodgar are on display and there's always an excellent summer exhibition, too. You can happily nose around for a couple of hours. Across the street is the house where local poet and novelist George Mackay Brown lived.

Pier Arts Centre   GALLERY
(☑01856-850209; www.pierartscentre.com; 30 Victoria St; ☺10.30am-5pm Tue-Sat year-round, plus Mon Jun-Sep) FREE This gallery has really rejuvenated the Orkney modern-art scene with its sleek lines and upbeat attitude. It's worth a look as much for the architecture as for its high-quality collection of 20th-century British art and changing exhibitions.

🎆 Festivals & Events

Orkney Folk Festival   MUSIC
(www.orkneyfolkfestival.com; ☺late May) A four-day event in late May, with folk concerts, *ceilidhs* (evenings of traditional Scottish entertainment) and casual pub sessions. Stromness packs out, and late-night buses from Kirkwall are laid on. Book tickets and accommodation ahead.

🛏 Sleeping

Hamnavoe Hostel   HOSTEL £
(☑01856-851202; www.hamnavoehostel.co.uk; 10a North End Rd; dm/s/tw £22/24/48; 🛜) This well-equipped hostel is efficiently run and has excellent facilities, including a fine kitchen and a lounge room with great perspectives over the water. The dorms are very spacious, with duvets, decent mattresses and reading lamps (bring a pound coin for the heating), and the showers are good. Ring ahead as the owner lives off-site.

Brown's Hostel   HOSTEL £
(☑01856-850661; www.brownsorkney.com; 45 Victoria St; s/d £22.50/40, d with bathroom £50; @🛜) On Stromness' main street, this handy, sociable place has cosy private rooms – no dorms, no bunks – at a good price. There's an inviting common area, where you can browse the free internet or swap pasta recipes in the open kitchen. There are en suite rooms in a house up the street, with self-catering options available.

Point of Ness Caravan
& Camping Park   CAMPSITE £
(☑office hours 01856-873535, site 01856-850532; https://orkney.campstead.com; Ness Rd; tent sites 1/2 people £8.25/12.70; ☺Apr-Sep; P🛜🐾) This breezy, fenced-in campsite has a super location overlooking the bay at the southern end of Stromness and is as neat as a pin.

★Brinkies Guest House   B&B ££
(☑01856-851881; www.brinkiesguesthouse.co.uk; Brownstown Rd; s £65, d £80-90; P🛜) Just a short walk from the centre of Stromness, but with a lonely, king-of-the-castle position overlooking the town and bay, this exceptional place offers five-star islander hospitality. Compact, modern rooms are handsome, stylish and comfortable, and the public areas are done out attractively in wood, but above all it's the charming owner's flexibility and can-do attitude that makes this place so special.

Breakfast is 'continental Orcadian' – a stupendous array of quality local cheese, smoked fish and homemade bere bannocks (a wheat-barley bread). Want a lie-in? No problem, saunter down at 10am. Don't want breakfast? How about a packed lunch instead? To get here, take Outertown Rd off Back Rd, turn right on to Brownstown Rd, and keep going.

Burnside Farm   B&B ££
(☑01856-850723; www.burnside-farm.com; North End Rd/A965; s £60, d £80-90; P🛜) On a working dairy farm on the edge of Stromness, this place has lovely views over green fields, town and harbour. Rooms are elegant and maintain the style from when the house was built in the late 1940s, with attractive period furnishings. The top-notch bathrooms, however, are sparklingly contemporary. Breakfast comes with views, and the kindly owner couldn't be more welcoming.

Anderson's Harbour Cottages   COTTAGE ££
(☑+27 79 492 9789; www.andersoncottage.co.uk; high season per week £595-995; P🛜) Within a few paces of the Stromness Museum are these five traditional stone cottages for rent, ranging from one to four bedrooms each. All are right on the water and some have a private jetty. They are well furnished with modern amenities, while still conserving the cosiness and romance of these former fishermen's dwellings.

✗ Eating

Bayleaf Delicatessen   DELI **£**
(☑ 01856-851605; www.bayleafdelicatessen.co.uk;
103 Victoria St; snacks £2-6; ⊗ 10am-5pm Mon-
Sat year-round, plus 10am-4pm Sun Jun-Aug) ✔
On the meandering main street through
Stromness you'll find this very likeable little deli. Local cheeses and yoghurts are a
highlight, alongside smoked fish, takeaway
seafood salads and other tasty Orkney produce. There's good coffee too and a friendly
attitude.

★ Hamnavoe Restaurant   SEAFOOD **££**
(☑ 01856-851226, 01856-850606; 35 Graham Pl;
mains £15-24; ⊗ 7-9pm Tue-Sun Jun-Aug) Tucked
away off the main street, this Stromness
favourite specialises in excellent local seafood in an intimate, cordial atmosphere.
There's always something good off the boats,
and the chef prides himself on his lobster.
Booking is a must. It opens some weekends in low season; it's worth calling ahead
to check.

Ferry Inn   PUB FOOD **££**
(☑ 01856-850280; www.ferryinn.com; 10 John
St; mains £10-19; ⊗ food 7am-9pm Apr-Oct; 🛜)
Every port has its pub, and in Stromness it's
the Ferry. Convivial and central, it warms
the cockles with folk music, local beers
and characters, and all-day food that offers
decent value in a dining area done out like
the deck of a ship. The fish and chips are
excellent, and a few blackboard specials fill
things out.

ⓘ Getting There & Around

BICYCLE

Orkney Cycle Hire (☑ 01856-850255; www.
orkneycyclehire.co.uk; 54 Dundas St; per day
£10-15; ⊗ 8am-5pm) Family options include
kids' bikes and child trailers.

BOAT

Northlink Ferries (www.northlinkferries.co.uk)
Runs services from Stromness to Scrabster
on the mainland (passenger/car £19.40/59,
1½ hours, two to three daily). At the time of
research, the road-equivalent tariff scheme
was due to be rolled out on Orkney services, so
prices should drop.

BUS

Bus X1 runs regularly to Kirkwall (£3.20, 30
minutes, hourly Monday to Saturday, seven
Sunday), with some going on to St Margaret's
Hope (£5.90, 1¼ hours).

Hoy
POP 400

Orkney's second-largest island, Hoy (meaning 'High Island'), got the lion's share of
the archipelago's scenic beauty. Shallow
turquoise bays lace the east coast and massive seacliffs guard the west, while peat
and moorland cover Orkney's highest hills.
Much of the north is a reserve for breeding
seabirds. The Scrabster–Stromness ferry
gives you a decent perspective of the island's
wild good looks.

◉ Sights

Old Man of Hoy   NATURAL FEATURE
Hoy's best-known sight is this 137m-high
rock stack jutting from the ocean off the tip
of an eroded headland. It's a tough ascent
and for experienced climbers only, but the
walk to see it is a Hoy highlight, revealing
much of the island's most spectacular scenery. You can also spot the Old Man from the
Scrabster–Stromness ferry.

The easiest approach to the Old Man is
from Rackwick Bay, a 5-mile walk by road
from Moaness Pier (in Hoy village on the
east coast, where the ferries dock) through
the beautiful Rackwick Glen. You'll pass
the 5000-year-old Dwarfie Stane, the
only example of a rock-cut tomb in Scotland. On your return you can take the path
via the Glens of Kinnaird and Berriedale
Wood, Scotland's most northerly tuft of
native forest.

From Rackwick Bay, where there's a
hostel, the most popular path climbs
steeply westwards then curves northwards,
descending gradually to the edge of the cliffs
opposite the Old Man of Hoy. Allow seven
hours for the return trip from Moaness Pier,
or three hours from Rackwick Bay.

**Scapa Flow Visitor
Centre & Museum**   MUSEUM
(☑ 01856-791300; www.orkney.gov.uk; Lyness;
⊗ 10am-4.30pm Mon-Sat Mar, Apr & Oct, 9am-
4.30pm Mon-Sat, 1st to last ferry Sun May-Sep)
FREE Lyness was an important naval base
during both World Wars, when the British
Grand Fleet was based in Scapa Flow. This
fascinating museum and photographic display, located in an old pumphouse that once
fed fuel to the ships, is a must-see for anyone interested in Orkney's military history.
Take your time to browse the exhibits and
have a look at the folders of supplementary

information: letters home from a seaman lost when the *Royal Oak* was torpedoed are particularly moving.

It's easily visited just by the ferry slip at Lyness, and there's a decent cafe here. The museum was being renovated at time of research and due to reopen in spring 2019.

Hackness Martello Tower & Battery FORT (www.historicenvironment.scot; Hackness; adult/child £5/3; ⏱9.30am-5.30pm Apr-Sep, 10am-4pm Mon-Sat Oct) Built during the Napoleonic Wars, when French ships passed through the Pentland Firth to prey on North Sea merchant vessels, this battery, accompanied by two towers (one across the water), never saw action but is an impressive piece of military architecture. The custodian gives an excellent tour of the barracks and tower – there's a lovely view from the gun platform on top – that really evokes the period.

🛏 Sleeping & Eating

Hoy Centre HOSTEL £ (☑office hours 01856-873535, warden 01856-791315; https://orkney.campstead.com; dm/tw £20/57.70; P⚟) This clean, bright, modern hostel has an enviable location, around 15 minutes' walk from Moaness Pier, at the base of the rugged Cuilags. Rooms are all en suite and include good-value family options; it also has a spacious kitchen and DVD lounge. It's open year-round: book via the website to avoid an admin fee (private rooms only).

Stromabank Hotel INN ££ (☑01856-701494; www.stromabank.co.uk; Longhope; s/d £55/90; P⚟) Perched on the hill above Longhope, the small atmospheric Stromabank Hotel has very acceptable, refurbished en suite rooms, as well as tasty home-cooked meals, including seafood and steaks (£8 to £14) using lots of local produce. (Served 6pm to 8pm Friday to Wednesday, plus noon to 2pm Sunday. They do meals for residents only on Thursday and takeaways on Saturday evenings.)

Beneth'ill Cafe CAFE £ (☑01856-791119; www.benethillcafe.co.uk; Hoy Village; light meals £7-9; ⏱10am-6pm Apr-Sep) Handy for the Moaness ferry, this cafe has a spectacular location by the water with great views of the brooding Hoy hills. It offers home baking and light meals such as salads and quiches. There's also a daily hot dish, often something hearty like stew, which is great after a walk. The food is pleasingly fresh, tasty and well presented.

ℹ Getting There & Away

Orkney Ferries (www.orkneyferries.co.uk) runs a passenger/bike ferry (adult £4.25, 30 minutes, two to six daily) between Stromness and Moa-

---

DIVING SCAPA FLOW

One of the world's largest natural harbours, Scapa Flow has been in near constant use by fleets from the time of the Vikings onwards. After WWI, 74 German ships were interned here; when the armistice dictated a severely reduced German navy, Admiral von Reuter, in charge of the fleet, took matters into his own hands. A secret signal was passed around and the British watched incredulously as every German ship began to sink. Fifty-two of them went to the bottom, with the rest left aground in shallow water.

Most were salvaged, but seven vessels remain to attract divers. There are three battleships – the *König*, the *Kronprinz Wilhelm* and the *Markgraf*. The first two were partially blasted for scrap, but the *Markgraf* is undamaged and considered one of Scotland's best dives.

Numerous other ships rest on the sea bed. HMS *Royal Oak*, sunk by a German U-boat in October 1939 with the loss of 833 crew, is a war grave and diving is prohibited.

It's worth prebooking diving excursions far in advance. **Scapa Scuba** (☑01856-851218; www.scapascuba.co.uk; Lifeboat House, Dundas St; beginner dive £85, 2 guided dives £160-185; ⏱noon-7pm Mon-Fri & 3-6pm Sat & Sun May-Sep) is an excellent operator that caters for both beginners – with 'try dives' around the Churchill barriers – and tried-and-tested divers. You'll need plenty of experience to dive the wrecks, some of which are 47m deep, plus have recent drysuit experience: this can be organised for you. Other boats that you can charter for dives include **MV Karin** (www.scapaflow.com) and **MV Jean Elaine** (www.jeanelaine.co.uk).

ness at Hoy's northern end, and a car ferry to Lyness (with one service to/from Longhope) from Houton on Mainland (passenger/car £4.25/ 13.60, 40 minutes, up to seven daily Monday to Friday, two or three Saturday and Sunday); book cars well in advance. Sunday service is from May to September only.

The Moaness ferry also stops at Graemsay. The Houton service also links to Flotta.

Northern Islands

The group of windswept islands north of Mainland is a haven for birds, rich in archaeological sites and blessed with wonderful white-sand beaches and azure seas. Though some are hillier than others, all offer a broadly similar landscape of flattish green farmland running down to scenic coastline. Some give a real sense of what Orkney was like before the modern world impinged upon island life.

Accessible by reasonably priced ferry or plane, the islands are well worth exploring. Though you can see 'the sights' in a matter of hours, the key is to stay a day or two and relax into the pace of island life.

Note that the 'ay' at the end of island names (from the Old Norse for 'island') is pronounced closer to 'ee'.

Orkney Ferries and Loganair Inter-Isles Air Service enable you to make day trips to many of the islands from Kirkwall.

Most islands offer a bus service that meets ferries: you may have to call to book this. The same operator often offers island tours.

Westray

POP 600

If you've time to visit only one of Orkney's Northern Islands, make Westray (www. westraypapawestray.co.uk) the one. The largest of the group, it has rolling farmland, handsome sandy beaches, great coastal walks and several appealing places to stay.

◉ Sights & Activities

★**Noltland Castle**   CASTLE
(www.historicenvironment.scot;   ⊙8am-8pm)
FREE A half-mile west of Pierowall stands this sturdy ruined towerhouse, built in the 16th century by Gilbert Balfour, aide to Mary, Queen of Scots. The castle is superatmospheric and bristles with shot holes, part of the defences of the deceitful Balfour, who plotted to murder Cardinal Beaton and,

after being exiled, the king of Sweden. Like a pantomime villain, he met a sticky end.

At the nearby Links of Noltland, archaeological investigation is regularly unearthing interesting neolithic finds. Most intriguing has been a chamber built over a spring, which was possibly used as a sauna.

Noup Head   NATURE RESERVE
FREE This bird reserve at Westray's northwestern tip is a dramatic area of sea cliffs, with vast numbers of breeding seabirds from April to July. You can walk here along the clifftops from a car park, passing the impressive chasm of Ramni Geo, and return via the lighthouse access road (4 miles).

Westray Heritage Centre   MUSEUM
(☎01857-677414;   www.westrayheritage.co.uk;
Pierowall; adult/child £3/50p;   ⊙11.30am-5pm
Mon, 9am-noon & 2-5pm Tue-Sat, 1.30-5pm Sun May-Sep, 2-4pm Wed or by arrangement Oct-Apr) This heritage centre has displays on local history, nature dioramas and archaeological finds, with some famous neolithic carvings (including the 5000-year-old 'Westray Wife'). These small sandstone figurines are the oldest known depictions of the human form so far found in the British Isles.

Westraak   TOURS
(☎01857-677777; www.westraak.co.uk; Pierowall; adult half-/full day £42/60) This husband-and-wife outfit runs informative and engaging trips around Westray, covering everything from Viking history to puffin mating habits. It also runs the island's taxi service.

🛏 Sleeping

★**West Manse**   B&B £
(☎01857-677482; www.westmanse.co.uk; Westside; r per person £25; P🖙📶🐾) 🐾 No timetables reign at this imposing house with arcing coastal vistas; make your own breakfast when you feel like it. Your welcoming hosts have introduced a raft of green solutions for heating, fuel and more. Kids will love this unconventional place, with its play nooks and hobbit house, while art exhibitions, eclectic workshops, venerably comfortable furniture and clean air are drawcards for parents.

There's also a self-catering apartment, Brotchie (£300 per week). The owners also let out a fabulous little waterside cottage in Pierowall that's totally designed for the needs of a visitor with a disability, accompanied by a carer.

ORKNEY & SHETLAND NORTHERN ISLANDS

Chalmersquoy & the Barn
B&B, HOSTEL £

(☑ 01857-677214; www.chalmersquoywestray.
co.uk; Pierowall; dm/s/q £24/32/72, B&B s/d
£58/80, apt for 4/6 £60/100, tent sites £9-12 plus
per adult/child £2/1; P 📶) This excellent, intimate, modern hostel is an Orcadian gem. It's
heated throughout and has pristine kitchen
facilities and an inviting lounge; rooms sleep
two or three in comfort. Out front, the lovely
owners have top self-catering apartments
with great views, and spacious en suite B&B
rooms. There's also a campsite and a fabulous byre that hosts atmospheric concerts. A
recommended all-round choice.

Bis Geos
COTTAGE ££

(☑ 01857-677420; www.bisgeos.com; per week from
£370; P) There are stunning views at this
spectacular, quirky and cosy self-catering
option between Pierowall and Noup Head.
There are three separate units here, with
the largest sleeping eight and offering the
finest vistas. Shorter stays are sometimes
available.

Braehead Manse
B&B ££

(Reid Hall; ☑ 01857-677861; www.braeheadmanse.
co.uk; Braehead; s/d £50/65; P 📶) 🧭 A top-
notch conversion of a former village hall
behind the church in the middle of Westray,
this place has two luminous, high-ceilinged
rooms with modern en suite bathrooms and
a swish open-plan kitchen/living/dining
area with excellent facilities. You can choose
either self-catering – perfect for a family of
four – or the B&B option, with your hosts
making breakfast.

Pierowall Hotel
PUB FOOD £

(☑ 01857-677472; www.pierowallhotel.co.uk; Pierowall; mains £9-14; ☺ food noon-2pm & 5-9pm May-
Sep, noon-1.30pm & 6-8pm Oct-Apr; 📶) The heart
of the Westray community, this refurbished
local pub is famous throughout Orkney for
its popular fish and chips – whatever has
turned up in the day's catch from the hotel's
boats is displayed on the blackboard. There
are also some curries available, but the sea
is the way to go here. It also has rooms, and
hires out bikes (£10 per day).

❶ Getting There & Away

There are daily flights with Loganair (p233) from
Kirkwall to Westray (one way £37, 20 minutes).

Orkney Ferries (www.orkneyferries.co.uk)
links Kirkwall with Rapness (passenger/car
£8.35/19.70, 1½ hours, daily). A bus to the main
town, Pierowall, meets the ferry.

Papa Westray

Known locally as Papay, this exquisitely
peaceful, tiny island (4 miles by 1 mile) is
home to possibly Europe's oldest domestic
building, the 5500-year-old **Knap of Howar**
(☺ 24hr) FREE, and largest Arctic tern colony.
Plus the two-minute hop from Westray is the
world's shortest scheduled air service. It's a
charming island with seals easily spotted
while walking its coast.

Papay Ranger
TOURS

(☑ 07931 235213; www.papawestray.co.uk) The
Papay ranger runs excellent day-long tours
of Papay in summer that include lunch
and afternoon tea (£50/25 per adult/child),
guided visits to **Holm of Papay** (£25/12.50),
bike hire on the island and bespoke tours.

Beltane House
GUESTHOUSE, HOSTEL £

(☑ 01857-644224; www.papawestray.co.uk; Bel-
tane; dm/s/d £20/28/44; P 📶 🐾) Owned by
the local community, this is Papa Westray's
hub. It has the only shop, and functions as
a makeshift pub on Saturday nights. One
wing is a hostel with bunks, the other a
guesthouse with immaculate rooms with
en suites. There are two kitchens, zippy
wi-fi (when it works), a big lounge/eating
area and views over grassy fields to the
sea beyond.

It's just over a mile north of the ferry.
You can also camp here (£8/4 per adult/
child) and there are camping pods available
that sleep two (£20 per person plus £5 for
bedding).

❶ Getting There & Away

AIR

There are two or three daily flights with Loganair
(p233) to Papa Westray (£18, 20 minutes) from
Kirkwall. The £21 return offer (you must stay
overnight) is great value. Some of the Kirkwall
flights go via Westray (£17, two minutes, the
world's shortest scheduled flight) or North
Ronaldsay (£17, 10 minutes).

BOAT

A passenger-only ferry with **Orkney Ferries**
(www.orkneyferries.co.uk) runs from Pierowall
on Westray to Papa Westray (£4.15, 25 minutes,
three to six daily in summer); the crossing is
free if you've come straight from the Kirkwall–
Westray ferry. From October to April the boat
sails by arrangement (call 01857-677216). On
Tuesday and Friday a car ferry from Kirkwall
makes the journey to Papa Westray.

Rousay

POP 200

Just off the north coast of Mainland, hilly Rousay merits exploration for its fine assembly of prehistoric sites, great views and relaxing away-from-it-all ambience. Connected by regular ferry from Tingwall, it makes a great little day trip, but you may well feel a pull to stay longer. A popular option is to hire a bike from Trumland Farm near the ferry and take on the 14-mile circuit of the island.

★ **Midhowe Cairn
& Broch** ARCHAEOLOGICAL SITE

(www.historicenvironment.scot; ⊙24hr) FREE Six miles from the ferry on Rousay, mighty Midhowe Cairn has been dubbed the 'Great Ship of Death'. Built around 3500 BC and enormous, it's divided into compartments, in which the remains of 25 people were found. Covered by a protective stone building, it's nevertheless memorable. Adjacent Midhowe Broch, whose sturdy stone lines echo the rocky shoreline's striations, is a muscular Iron Age fortified compound with a mezzanine floor. The sites are on the water, a 10-minute walk downhill from the main road.

Prehistoric Sites ARCHAEOLOGICAL SITE

(www.historicenvironment.scot; ⊙24hr) FREE Rousay's major archaeological sites are clearly labelled from the road ringing the island. Heading west from the ferry, you soon come to Taversoe Tuick, an intriguing burial cairn constructed on two levels, with separate entrances – perhaps a joint tomb for different families; a semidetached solution in posthumous housing. Not far beyond are two other significant cairns: Blackhammer, then Knowe of Yarso, the latter a fair walk up the hill but with majestic views.

Trumland Farm HOSTEL £

(☎01856-821252; trumland@btopenworld.com; sites £7, dm £15-16; P🐕) 🅿 An easy stroll from the ferry (turn left at the main road), this organic farm has a wee hostel with two dorms and a pretty little kitchen and common area. You can pitch tents and use the facilities; there's also well-equipped self-catering in a cottage and various farm buildings. Linen is £2 extra. Bikes can be hired here.

Taversoe INN ££

(☎01856-821325; www.taversoehotel.co.uk; s £40-50, d £80-95; P🕸) Two miles west from the ferry pier, Rousay's only hotel is an attrac-

> ### ORKNEYINGA SAGA
>
> Written around AD 1200, this saga is a rich tale of sorcery, political intrigue, and cunning and unscrupulous acts among the Viking earls of Orkney. Part myth and part historical fact, it begins with the capture of the islands by the king of Norway and recounts the tumultuous centuries until they became part of Scotland. It's a wonderful piece of medieval literature and well worth a read. Head to the Orkneyinga Saga Centre (⊙9am-6pm Apr-Oct) FREE in the south coast village of Orphir for more background.

tively low-key place, with renovated rooms offering excellent bathrooms – one suitable for people with disabilities – and beautiful water vistas. The best views are from the dining room, which serves good-value meals. The friendly owners will collect you from the ferry.

Food is served from noon to 5pm Monday, to 9pm Tuesday to Saturday and to 7.30pm Sunday from May to September, with shorter hours in winter.

❶ Getting There & Around

A small ferry connects Tingwall on Mainland with Rousay (passenger/bicycle/car £4.25/free/13.60, 30 minutes, up to six daily) and the nearby islands of Egilsay and Wyre.

Rousay Tours (☎01856-821234; www.rousaytours.co.uk; adult/child £35/12) offers taxi service and recommended guided tours of the island, including wildlife-spotting (seals and otters), visits to the prehistoric sites and an optional tasty packed lunch.

Sanday

POP 500

Aptly named, blissfully quiet and flat, Sanday is ringed by Orkney's best beaches – with dazzling-white sand of the sort you'd expect in the Caribbean. It's a peaceful, green, pastoral landscape with the sea revealed at every turn.

**Quoyness Chambered
Tomb** ARCHAEOLOGICAL SITE

(⊙24hr) FREE There are several archaeological sites on Sanday, the most impressive being this chambered tomb, similar to

Maeshowe and dating from the 3rd millennium BC. It has triple walls, a main chamber and six smaller cells.

Sanday Heritage Centre   MUSEUM
(www.sanday.co.uk; Lady; donations appreciated; ⊘9.30am-5pm May-Oct, weekends only Nov-Apr) FREE This museum in the former temperance hall has intriguing displays on various aspects of island history, including fishing, WWI, archaeology and shipwrecks. In an adjacent field a typical croft house is preserved.

Ayre's Rock Hostel
& Campsite   HOSTEL, CAMPSITE £
(☑01857-600410; www.ayres-rock-hostel-orkney. com; tent sites £8-10, pods £35, dm/s/tw £19.50/ 23.50/39; P🗢🐾) This super-friendly spot by a beach 6 miles north of the Sanday ferry offers a cosy three-room hostel sleeping two or four in beds, and a sweet, grassy campsite by the water. As well as tent pitches, there are heated two-person pods and a static caravan. Evening meals are available. It has a craft shop and Saturday chip shop; hosts are extremely helpful.

Backaskaill   B&B ££
(☑01857-600305; www.bedandbreakfastsanday orkney.com; s/d £50/80; P🗢) Set on a working cattle farm by the sea, this place offers comfortable accommodation in a noble stone farmhouse. The polished interior features an eclectic collection of art and curios. The hospitality is cordial and professional. Rooms feel light and modern, and there's a fabulous guest lounge. The island's best meals (mains £9 to £16) are here and can be booked by non-guests.

❶ Getting There & Away
There are flights with Loganair (p233) from Kirkwall to Sanday (one way £37, 20 minutes, once or twice daily).
 Orkney Ferries (www.orkneyferries.co.uk) runs from Kirkwall (passenger/car £8.35/19.70, 1½ hours), with a link to Eday. A bus meets the boat (book on 01857-600438).

North Ronaldsay
POP 70
North Ronaldsay is a real outpost surrounded by rolling seas and big skies. Delicious peace and quiet and the island's excellent birdwatching lure visitors. There are enough semi-feral sheep to seize power, but a 13-mile drystone wall running around

the island keeps them off the grass; they make do with seaweed, which gives their meat a distinctive flavour.

North Ronaldsay Lighthouse   LIGHTHOUSE
(www.northronaldsay.co.uk; ⊘10am-5pm May-Aug or by arrangement) At the northern end of the island, this lighthouse is over 100ft high and one of many built across Scotland by the Stevenson family. A visitor centre and licensed cafe are here, as are bikes for hire and a gift shop selling the woollens made from yarn supplied by the local seaweed-eating sheep. You can climb the lighthouse itself and/or visit the woollen mill on a tour (☑01857-633257, 07703-112224; www.north ronaldsay.co.uk; lighthouse or mill adult/child £6/4, combined £9/7).

On the shore to the south of the lighthouse is an earlier model, an 18th-century beacon tower some 70ft high.

Observatory Guest House   B&B, HOSTEL ££
(☑01857-633200; www.nrbo.co.uk; campsites £5, dm/s/d £18.50/42.50/85; P@🗢) ❃ Powered by wind and solar energy, this place offers first-rate accommodation and ornithological activities next to the ferry pier. There's a cafe-bar with lovely coastal views and convivial communal dinners (£15) in a (sometimes) sun-kissed conservatory; if you're lucky, local lamb might be on the menu. You can also camp here.

❶ Getting There & Away
There are two or three daily flights with Loganair (p233) to North Ronaldsay (£18, 20 minutes) from Kirkwall. The £21 return offer (you must stay overnight) is great value.
 Orkney Ferries runs from Kirkwall on Friday (passenger/car £8.35/19.70, 2½ hours), plus Tuesday in summer.

SHETLAND
Close enough to Norway geographically and historically to make nationality an ambiguous concept, the Shetland Islands are Britain's most northerly outpost. There's a Scandinavian lilt to the local accent, and streets named King Haakon or St Olaf are reminders that Shetland was under Norse rule until 1469, when it was gifted to Scotland in lieu of the dowry of a Danish princess.

The stirringly bleak setting – it's a Unesco geopark – still feels uniquely Scottish, though, with deep, naked glens flanked by steep hills, twinkling, sky-blue lochs and, of course, sheep on the roads.

Despite the famous ponies and woollens, it's no agricultural backwater. Offshore oil makes it quite a busy, comparatively well-heeled place, despite drops in barrel prices. Nevertheless nature still rules the seas and islands, and the birdlife (p262) is spectacular: pack binoculars.

🧭 Tours

Discover Shetland   TOURS
(☑ 07387-167205; www.discovershetland.net) Customisable tours of Shetland with a knowledgable guide, who's strong on the natural world and the ecology of the archipelago.

Shetland Nature   WILDLIFE
(☑ 01595-760333; www.shetlandnature.net) This operator specialises in otter-watching excursions but also runs birdwatching trips all around the archipelago as well as scenic tours.

ℹ Information

Visit www.shetland.org, an excellent website with good info on accommodation, activities and more.

The archipelago is replete with handicraft workshops, many working to produce artisanal jewellery and Shetland's famous woollens. The **Shetland Craft Trail** (☑ 07447-377856; www.shetlandartsandcrafts.co.uk) publishes a useful brochure of makers across the islands; the info is also available on their website.

Lerwick Tourist Office (p256) In the centre of the Shetland's main town, with comprehensive information on the islands.

Sumburgh Airport Tourist Office (☑ 01950-460905; www.shetland.org; Sumburgh Airport; ⊗8.45am-4.45pm Mon-Fri, 10.15am-4pm Sat, 10.30am-5.30pm Sun, closed Sat Nov-Mar) Brochures are available even when this office is shut.

ℹ Getting There & Away

AIR

Sumburgh Airport (☑ 01950-460905; www.hial.co.uk) is Shetland's main airport, 25 miles south of Lerwick. **Loganair** (☑ 0344 800 2855; www.loganair.co.uk) runs daily services to Aberdeen, Kirkwall, Inverness, Edinburgh and Glasgow, and summer services to Manchester and Bergen (Norway).

BOAT

Northlink Ferries (www.northlinkferries.co.uk) runs daily overnight car ferries between Aberdeen and Lerwick (high-season one way passenger/car £41/146, 12 to 15 hours), some stopping at Kirkwall, Orkney. With a basic ticket

you can sleep in recliner chairs or the bar area. It's £36.50 for a berth in a shared cabin and from £84 to £137 for a comparatively luxurious double cabin. Sleeping pods (£18) are comfortable, reclinable seats. Ferries have a cafe, bar, paid lounge and cinema on board, plus slow wi-fi. Road-equivalent tariffs were set to be rolled out on this route, so fares could drop.

ℹ Getting Around

Public transport within and between the islands of Shetland is managed by ZetTrans (www.zettrans.org.uk). Timetable information for all air, bus and ferry services can be obtained at http://travel.shetland.org, from the ZetTrans website and from Lerwick's Viking Bus Station (p256).

AIR

The **Shetland Inter-Island Air Service** (Airtask; ☑ 01595-840246; www.airtask.com) is operated by Airtask from Tingwall airport, 6.5 miles northwest of Lerwick. There are big discounts for under-25s. Flights run to Papa Stour, Foula and Fair Isle.

BICYCLE

If it's fine, cycling on the islands' excellent roads can be an exhilarating way to experience the stark beauty of Shetland. It can, however, be very windy and there are few spots to shelter. You can hire bikes from several places, including Grantfield Garage in Lerwick.

BOAT

Ferry services run by Shetland Islands Council (www.shetland.gov.uk/ferries) link Mainland to other islands from various points.

BUS

An extensive bus network, coordinated by **ZetTrans** (www.zettrans.org.uk), radiates from Lerwick to all corners of Mainland, with connecting services to the islands of Yell, Fetlar and Unst. The schedules aren't generally great for day tripping from Lerwick as they're suited to people coming in to the capital for the day.

CAR

Shetland has broad, well-made roads (due to oil money). Car hire is fuss-free, and vehicles can be delivered to transport terminals. Prices are usually around £40/200 for a day/week.

Bolts Car Hire (☑ 01595-693636; www.boltscarhire.co.uk; 26 North Rd; ⊗9am-5.30pm Mon-Fri year-round, plus to 1pm Sat Nov-Mar, to 4pm Sat Apr-Oct) Has an office in Lerwick and by the airport; delivers to Lerwick's ferry terminal.

Grantfield Garage (☑ 01595-692709; www.grantfieldgarage.co.uk; North Rd; ⊗9am-5.30pm Mon-Fri, to 5pm Sat) Generally the cheapest. A short walk towards Lerwick from the Northlink ferry terminal.

ORKNEY & SHETLAND SHETLAND

Star Rent-a-Car (☑ 01595-692075; www.star rentacar.co.uk; 22 Commercial Rd; ⊘ 8am-7pm Mon-Fri, to 6pm Sat, noon-5pm Sun) Opposite Lerwick's Viking Bus Station. Has an office at Sumburgh Airport as well.

Lerwick

POP 7000

Built on the herring trade and modernised by the oil trade, Lerwick is Shetland's only real town, home to a third of the islands' population. It has a solidly maritime feel, with aquiline oilboats competing for space in the superb natural harbour with the dwindling fishing fleet. Wandering along atmospheric Commercial St is a delight, and the excellent Shetland Museum provides cultural background.

◎ Sights & Activities

★ **Shetland Museum**   MUSEUM
(☑ 01595-695057; www.shetlandmuseumand archives.org.uk; Hay's Dock; ⊘ 10am-4pm Mon-Sat, noon-5pm Sun Sep-Apr) FREE This museum houses an impressive recollection of 5000 years' worth of culture, people and their interaction with this ancient landscape. Comprehensive but never dull, it covers everything from the archipelago's geology to its fishing industry, via local mythology – find out about scary *nyuggles* (ghostly horses), or detect *trows* (fairies). Pictish carvings and replica jewellery are among the finest pieces. The museum also includes a working lighthouse mechanism, a small gallery, a boat-building workshop and an archive for tracing Shetland ancestry.

Shetland Textile Museum   MUSEUM
(Böd of Gremista; ☑ 01595-694386; www.shetland textilemuseum.com; Gremista Rd; adult/child £3/free; ⊘ noon-5pm Tue-Sat, to 7pm Thu late-Apr–early Oct) A mile north of the centre of Lerwick, this four-square stone house, birthplace of P&O founder Arthur Anderson, was also once a fish-curing station. It now holds a good display on the knitted and woven textiles and patterns that Shetland is famous for.

Clickimin Broch   RUINS
(Clickimin Rd; ⊘ 24hr) FREE This fortified site, just under a mile southwest of Lerwick's town centre, was occupied from the 7th century BC to the 6th century AD. It's impressively large, and its setting on a tongue of land in a small loch gives it a feeling of being removed from the present day.

Knab   VIEWPOINT
(Knab Rd) This headland gives a marvellous perspective of the entrance to Lerwick's harbour, as well as Breiwick (bay) and Bressay. There's a golf course, parkland, a cemetery and fortifications to ramble around.

Shetland Wildlife Boat Tours   BOATING
(☑ 07876-522292; www.thule-charters.co.uk; adult/child £45/35; ⊘ Apr-Sep) This outfit runs two daily trips to Noss in summer in a small catamaran. An underwater camera offers glimpses of the birds diving in the depths.

Shetland Seabird Tours   BIRDWATCHING
(☑ 07767 872260; www.shetlandseabirdtours.com; adult/child £45/25; ⊘ Apr-Oct) With two daily departures, these three-hour cruises head out to watch gannets feeding, observe the raucous seabird colonies of Bressay and Noss, and do a bit of seal-spotting. You can book at the Lerwick Tourist Office (p256).

⚜ Festivals & Events

Shetland Folk Festival   MUSIC
(www.shetlandfolkfestival.com; ⊘ late Apr or early May) This four-day festival sees local and international folk musicians playing in various venues across Lerwick and beyond.

🛏 Sleeping

Lerwick has very average hotels but excellent B&Bs. Accommodation fills up year-round, so book ahead. There are no campsites within 15 miles.

Woosung   B&B £
(☑ 01595-693687; conroywoosung@hotmail.com; 43 St Olaf St; d £70, s/d without bathroom £40/65; 🛜📺) A budget gem in the heart of Lerwick B&B-land, this place has a wise and welcoming host, and comfortable, clean, good-value rooms with fridge and microwave. Two of them share a compact but spotless bathroom. The solid stone house dates from the 19th century, built by a clipper captain who traded tea out of the Chinese port it's named after.

Islesburgh House Hostel   HOSTEL £
(☑ 01595-745100; www.islesburgh.org.uk; King Harald St; dm/s/tw/q £21.50/39/43/61; 🅿@🛜) This typically grand Lerwick mansion houses an excellent hostel, with comfortable dorms, a shop, a laundry, a cafe and an industrial kitchen. Electronic keys offer reliable security and no curfew. It's wise to book ahead in summer. If nobody's about you can check in at the nearby community centre.

★**Fort Charlotte Guesthouse** B&B **££**
(🖉01595-692140; www.fortcharlotte.co.uk; 1 Charlotte St; s/d £40/80; 🛜🏠) Sheltering under Fort Charlotte's walls, this friendly place offers summery en suite rooms, including great singles. Views down the pedestrian street are on offer in some; sloping ceilings and Asian touches add charm to others. It has local salmon for breakfast and a bike shed. Very popular; book ahead. There's also a self-catering option available.

Aald Harbour B&B **££**
(🖉01595-840689; www.aaldharbourbedand breakfast.com; 7 Church Rd; s/d £55/80; 🛜) With a handy location just off the pedestrian street, this upbeat spot has four cute rooms decked out in IKEA furniture with Shetland fabrics and toiletries creating a cosy Nordic fusion. Rooms have fridges and good showers and wi-fi; there are good public areas downstairs. Breakfast includes fresh fruit and smoked fish options; an on-site tearoom operates some days.

Rockvilla Guest House B&B **££**
(🖉01595-695804; www.rockvillaguesthouse.com; 88 St Olaf St; s/d £65/90; 🛜🏠) Some of Shetland's B&Bs are aimed more at oil workers than visitors, but this is quite the reverse: a relaxing, welcoming spot in a fine house behind a pretty garden. The three rooms are colour themed: Blue is bright, with a front-and-back outlook, Red is sultry, with a sofa in the window, and smaller Green is shyer, under the eaves.

Your hosts are friendly, and Jeff runs airport transfers (£35) plus day tours to Sumburgh, Eshaness or Unst, among other places.

Breiview Guest House B&B **££**
(🖉01595-695956; www.breiviewguesthouse.co.uk; 43 Kantersted Rd; s/d £50/80; 🅿🛜) On a hill a little removed from Lerwick's centre, this is a fine option with some water views. Rooms – some in the house next door – are spacious, light and furnished with blonde wood and have good bathrooms. Dieter is a lifeboat volunteer but guarantees to get your morning eggs perfect before dashing off to rescue a stricken ship.

Coming from the centre, turn left after passing the big Tesco supermarket and follow the signs.

Alder Lodge Guesthouse B&B **££**
(🖉01595-695705; www.alderlodge-guesthouse.com; 6 Clairmont Pl; s/d £45/85; 🅿🛜) A friendly young family run this likeable place in a

---

UP HELLY AA

Shetland's long Viking history has rubbed off in more ways than just street names and square-shouldered locals. Most villages have a **fire festival** (www.uphellyaa.org; ⊘Jan), a continuation of Viking midwinter celebrations of the rebirth of the sun, with the most spectacular happening in Lerwick, on the last Tuesday in January.

Squads of *guizers* dress in Viking costume and march through the streets with blazing torches, dragging a replica longship, which they then surround and burn, bellowing out Viking songs from behind bushy beards.

---

former bank building handily located close to Lerwick's centre. Imbued with a sense of space and light, the rooms are large and very well furnished, with good en suites and fridges. The top-floor rooms are worth the climb with their cosy sloping ceilings. Breakfast is a filling affair.

Kveldsro House Hotel HOTEL **£££**
(🖉01595-692195; www.shetlandhotels.com; Greenfield Pl; s/d £118/145; 🅿🛜) Lerwick's best hotel overlooks the harbour and has a quiet but central setting. It's a dignified small set-up that will appeal to older visitors or couples. All doubles cost the same, but some are markedly better than others, with four-poster beds or water views. All boast new stylish bathrooms. The bar area is elegant and has fine perspectives.

✗ Eating

Mareel Cafe CAFE **£**
(🖉01595-745500; www.mareel.org; Hay's Dock; light meals £3-5; ⊘9am-11pm Sun-Thu, 9am-1am Fri & Sat, food to 9pm; 🛜) Buzzy, arty and colourful, this cheery venue in Mareel overlooks the water and does sandwiches and snacks by day, and shared platters, burgers and nachos in the evenings. The coffee is decent, too, and it's a nice place for a drink. Cocktail mixing at weekends, DJs and other events spice it up.

Peerie Shop Cafe CAFE **£**
(🖉01595-692816; www.peerieshop.co.uk; Esplanade; light meals £3-8; ⊘8am-6pm Mon-Sat; 🛜) If you've been craving proper espresso since leaving the mainland, head to this gem, with

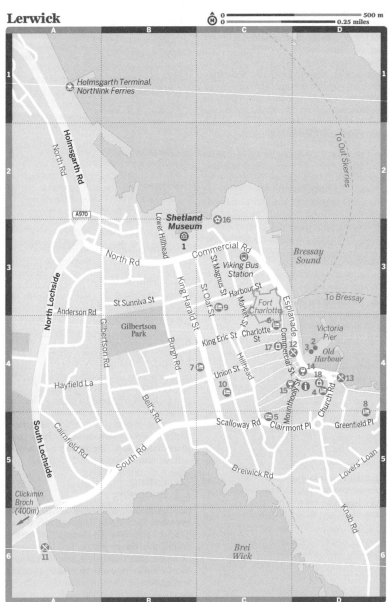

N
0 ————————— 500 m
0 ————————— 0.25 miles

Holmsgarth Terminal,
Northlink Ferries

Holmsgarth Rd

North Rd

A970

Shetland
Museum
1

16

Lower Hillhead

North Rd

Commercial Rd

St Magnus St

Viking Bus
Station

Bressay
Sound

To Out Skerries

North Lochside

St Sunniva St

Anderson Rd

Gilbertson Rd

Gilbertson
Park

King Harald St

St Olaf St

9

Harbour St

Market St

Fort
Charlotte

Esplanade

To Bressay

Victoria
Pier

King Eric St

Charlotte
St

6

17

12

Commercial St

2

3

Old
Harbour

Burgh Rd

7

Union St

Hillhead

10

14

18

13

Hayfield La

Bell's Rd

15

Mounthooly St

i

4

8

Cairnfield Rd

South Rd

Scalloway Rd

5

Clairmont Pl

Greenfield Pl

Church Rd

South Lochside

Breiwick Rd

Lovers' Loan

Clickimin
Broch
(400m)

Knab Rd

11

Brei
Wick

ORKNEY & SHETLAND LERWICK

art exhibitions, wire-mounted halogens and industrial-gantry chic. Newspapers, scrumptious cakes and sandwiches, hot chocolate that you deserve after that blasting wind outside, and – less often – outdoor seating give everyone a reason to be here.

★ Fjarå   CAFE, BISTRO ££
(☎ 01595-697388; www.fjaracoffee.com; Sea Rd; mains £8-22; ⊗ 8am-10pm Tue-Sat, 10am-6pm Sun, food until 8pm; 🅵) A cute wooden building in a super location, Fjarå is perched above a rocky shore and takes full advantage, with

Lerwick

big picture windows looking out over the water and occasionally some basking seals. It does a bit of everything, with breakfasts, sandwiches, salads and bagels, plus beers, cocktails and some excellent dinner offerings, including creative burgers, game and local seafood.

It's across the road from the Tesco supermarket at the southern entrance to town.

★ **Hay's Dock** SCOTTISH, CAFE ££
(☑01595-741569; www.haysdock.co.uk; Hay's Dock, Shetland Museum; mains lunch £8-13, dinner £17-24; ⊙10am-3pm Mon-Thu, 10am-3pm & 5-9pm Fri & Sat; 🕙🖥) 🌿 Upstairs in the Shetland Museum, this place sports a wall of picture windows and a fairweather balcony that overlooks the harbour. Clean lines and pale wood recall Scandinavia, but the menu relies on carefully selected local and Scottish produce, with a substantial dash of international influence. Lunch ranges from delicious fish and chips to chowder, while evening menus concentrate on seafood and steak.

Queen's Hotel SCOTTISH ££
(☑ 01595-692826; www.kgqhotels.co.uk; Commercial St; mains £11-22; ⊙ noon-2pm & 6-9.30pm; 🕙) The dining room in this slightly run-down hotel wins marks for its harbour views – book one of the window tables. It's best visited for beautifully presented, classy local seafood dishes.

Drinking & Entertainment

The Lounge PUB
(☑01595-692231; 4 Mounthooly St; ⊙11am-1am; 🕙) Tucked away behind Lerwick's tourist office, the Lounge features an earthy down-

stairs bar populated by friendly local characters. The attractive upstairs space features live music several times a week and informal jam sessions at other times. It's well worth checking out.

Captain Flint's PUB
(☑01595-692249; 2 Commercial St; ⊙11am-1am; 🕙) This upstairs port-side bar has a distinctly nautical, creaky-wooden feel. There's a cross-section of young 'uns, tourists, boat folk and older locals. It has live music some nights and a pool table tucked away on another level. Try a G&T with the seaweed-infused version of the local Reel gin.

Mareel ARTS CENTRE
(☑01595-745500; www.mareel.org; Hay's Dock) Modern Mareel is a thriving arts centre, with a cinema, concert hall and cafe in a great waterside location.

🛍 Shopping

Best buys are the woollen cardigans and sweaters for which Shetland is world-famous. For info on handicraft outlets around the islands grab the brochure for the Shetland Craft Trail (p251) from the Lerwick Tourist Office. It's also available from the trail website.

Shetland Times Bookshop BOOKS
(☑01595-695531; www.shetlandtimes.co.uk; 71 Commercial St; ⊙9am-5pm Mon-Sat) On Lerwick's picturesque main shopping street, this place has every book you could possibly want to read about Shetland, plus a good children's section.

ORKNEY & SHETLAND LERWICK

Mirrie Dancers
CHOCOLATE

(📞 01595-690592; www.mirriedancers.co.uk; 161 Commercial St; ⊙10am-5pm Mon, Tue & Thu-Sat) The amazing chocolate creations of this little high-street shop bring a touch of colour and sparkle to even the bleakest Shetland day. The name is a local term for the aurora borealis.

ℹ️ Information

There are several free wi-fi networks around the centre, and the **Shetland Library** (📞 01595-743868; www.shetland-library.gov.uk; Lower Hillhead; ⊙10am-8pm Mon & Thu, to 5pm Tue, Wed, Fri & Sat; 📶) has both terminals and wireless access.

Gilbert Bain Hospital (📞 01595-743000; www. shb.scot.nhs.uk; South Rd)

Lerwick Tourist Office (📞 01595-693434; www.shetland.org; cnr Commercial & Mounthooly Sts; ⊙9am-5pm Mon-Sat & 10am-4pm Sun Apr-Sep, 10am-4pm Mon-Sat Oct-Mar) Helpful, with a good range of books and maps.

ℹ️ Getting There & Away

Northlink Ferries (www.northlinkferries. co.uk; 📶) from Aberdeen and Kirkwall dock at **Holmsgarth Terminal** (Holmsgarth Rd), a 15-minute walk northwest from the town centre.

From **Viking Bus Station** (📞 01595-744868; Commercial Rd), buses service various corners of the archipelago, including regular services to/from Sumburgh Airport.

OFFBEAT ACCOMMODATION

Shetland offers intriguing options for getting off the beaten accommodation track. There's a great network of *böds* – simple rustic cottages or huts with peat fires. They cost £12 per person, or £10 for the ones without electricity, and are available March to October. Contact and book via Shetland Amenity Trust (📞 01595-694688; www.camping-bods. com; ⊙9am-5pm Mon-Thu, to 4pm Fri).

The same organisation runs three Shetland Lighthouse Cottages (📞 01595-694688; www.shetlandlight house.com; per 3 days high season £300-372, per week £700-868), all commanding dramatic views of rugged coastline: one, renovated and classy, at Sumburgh; one on the island of Bressay near Lerwick; and one at Eshaness. They sleep six to seven, and prices drop substantially in the low season.

Bressay & Noss

POP 400

These islands lie across Bressay Sound just east of Lerwick. Bressay (*bress*-ah) has interesting walks, especially along the cliffs and up **Ward Hill** (226m), which has good views of the islands. Much smaller Noss is a nature reserve, notable for its seabird life. As well as the crossing to Noss from Bressay, there are boat trips around the island from Lerwick.

⭐ Isle of Noss
NATURE RESERVE

(📞 0800 107 7818; www.nnr-scotland.org.uk/noss; boat adult/child £3/1.50; ⊙10am-5pm Tue, Wed & Fri-Sun mid-Apr–Aug) Little Noss, 1.5 miles wide, lies just east of Bressay. High seacliffs harbour over 100,000 pairs of breeding seabirds, while inland heath supports hundreds of pairs of great skua. Access is by dinghy from Bressay; phone in advance to check that it's running. Walking anticlockwise around Noss is easier, with better cliff-viewing. There's a small visitor centre by the dock.

Maryfield House Hotel
INN ££

(📞 01595-820203; www.maryfieldhousehotel. co.uk; Maryfield, Bressay; r £120; 🅿️📶) By the Bressay ferry slip, this solid old hotel has reopened and makes a fine alternative to staying in Lerwick. Comfortable rooms with good, large beds and refurbished bathrooms are complemented by friendly hosts. Decent bar meals are on offer, as well as items such as seafood platters, by preordering.

ℹ️ Getting There & Away

Ferries (passenger/car and driver return £5.50/13.60, seven minutes, frequent) link Lerwick and Bressay. The Noss crossing is 2.5 miles across the island.

Scalloway

POP 1200

Surrounded by bare, rolling hills, Scalloway (*scall*-o-wah) – Shetland's former capital – is a busy fishing and yachting harbour with a thriving seafood-processing industry. It's 6 miles from Lerwick.

There are pretty beaches and pleasant walks on the nearby islands (linked by bridges) of Trondra and East and West Burra.

Scalloway Museum
MUSEUM

(📞 01595-880734; www.scallowaymuseum.org; Castle St; adult/child £3/1; ⊙11am-4pm Mon-Sat,

2-4pm Sun mid-Apr–Sep; ♿) This enthusiastic modern museum by Scalloway Castle has an excellent display on Scalloway life and history, with prehistoric finds, witch-burnings and local lore all featuring. It has a detailed section on the Shetland Bus and a fun area for kids, as well as a cafe.

Shetland Bus Memorial   MONUMENT

(Main St) During WWII, the Norwegian resistance movement operated the 'Shetland Bus' from here. The trips were very successful, carrying agents, wireless operators and military supplies to Norway for the resistance movement and returning with refugees, recruits for the Free Norwegian Forces and, in December, Christmas trees for the treeless Shetlands. This is a moving tribute on the waterfront, built with stones from both countries. The Norwegian stones are from the home areas of 44 Norwegians who died running the gauntlet between Norway and Scalloway.

Scalloway Castle   CASTLE

(www.historicenvironment.scot; Castle St; ⊘24hr) FREE Scalloway's most prominent landmark is its castle, built around 1600 by Earl Patrick Stewart. The turreted and corbelled tower house is fairly well preserved. If you happen to find it locked, get keys from the Scalloway Museum (p256) or Scalloway Hotel.

★**Scalloway Hotel**   HOTEL £££

(☎01595-880444; www.scallowayhotel.com; Main St; s/d £100/140; P🛜) One of Shetland's best hotels, this energetically run waterfront place has very stylish rooms featuring sheepskins, local tweeds and other fabrics, and views over the harbour. Some rooms are larger than others; the best is the fabulous superior, with handmade furniture, artworks and a top-of-the-line mattress on a four-poster bed. The restaurant (restaurant mains £18-25; ⊘restaurant 5-9pm Mon-Sat, noon-9pm Sun, bar food also noon-3pm Mon-Sat; 🛜) is also excellent.

Da Haaf   SEAFOOD ££

(☎01595-772480; www.nafc.uhi.ac.uk; NAFC Marine Centre; lunches £6-10, dinner mains £12-20; ⊘8.30am-4pm Mon-Thu, 8.30am-4pm & 5.30-9pm Fri, 5.30-9pm Sat; 🛜) In a fisheries college, this place has a slightly canteeny feel but great water views out of big windows. It does simple but tasty snacks all day and lunches from noon to 2.30pm. The kitchen comes into its own at weekend dinnertime (must be booked), when haddock, monkfish and other seafood specials are served.

❶ Getting There & Away

Buses run from Lerwick (£1.80, 25 minutes, roughly hourly Monday to Saturday, four Sunday) to Scalloway.

South Mainland

From Lerwick, it's 25 miles down this narrow, hilly tail of land to Sumburgh Head. Important prehistoric sights, fabulous birdwatching and glorious white-sand beaches make it one of Shetland's most interesting areas. The lapping waters are an inviting turquoise – if it weren't for the raging Arctic gales, you'd be tempted to have a dip.

Sandwick & Mousa

Opposite the scattered village of Sandwick, where you pass the 60-degree latitude line, is the small isle of Mousa, an RSPB reserve protecting some 7000 breeding pairs of nocturnal storm petrels. Mousa is also home to rock-basking seals as well as impressive Mousa Broch, the best preserved of these northern Iron Age fortifications.

Mousa Broch   HISTORIC BUILDING

(⊘24hr) FREE On the island of Mousa, off Sandwick, this prehistoric fortified house, dating from some 2000 years ago, is an impressive sight. Rising to 13m, it's an imposing double-walled structure with a spiral staircase to access a 2nd floor. It has featured in Viking sagas as a hideout for eloping couples. In its walls nest hundreds of storm petrels, whose return to the nest at dusk is a stirring sight.

Mousa Boat   BOATING

(☎07901-872339; www.mousa.co.uk; Sandwick; ⊘Apr-Sep) This operator runs boat trips to Mousa (adult/child return £16/7, cash only, 15 minutes, daily except Saturday) from Sandwick, allowing three hours ashore on the island. It also offers night petrel-viewing trips (£25/10, dates on website) and short cruises. There's a small interpretation centre at the dock.

Mackenzies Farm Shop & Café   CAFE £

(☎01950-477790; www.mackenziesfarmshop.co.uk; A970, Cunningsburgh; mains £6-15; ⊘8.30am-6pm Mon-Thu, 7am-6pm Fri, 9am-5pm Sat, 11am-5pm

Sun, extended hours summer; ☎) / Local farmers supply the produce for this excellent shop and cafe, which stocks cheeses, quality meats and more, and presents dishes that range from quiches and sandwiches to fuller offerings with Shetland lamb.

Bigton & Boddam

On the western side of the narrow southern end of Mainland, Bigton sits near the largest shell-and-sand tombolo (sand or gravel isthmus) in Britain, St Ninian's Isle.

South of here, Shetland's best beach is gloriously white Scousburgh Sands (Spiggie Beach). Back on the main road, from small Boddam a side road leads to the Shetland Crofthouse Museum (🖉 01950-460557; www.shetlandmuseumandarchives.org.uk/crofthouse-museum; ⊙ 10am-1pm & 2-4pm May-Sep) FREE.

South of Boddam, a minor road runs southwest to Quendale. Here you'll find the small but excellent, restored and fully operational 19th-century Quendale Water Mill (🖉 01950-460969; www.quendalemill.co.uk; adult/child £4/1; ⊙ 10am-5pm mid-Apr–mid-Oct). The village overlooks a long, sandy beach to the south in the Bay of Quendale. West of the bay there's dramatic cliff scenery and diving in the waters between Garth's Ness and Fitful Head, and to the wreck of the oil tanker *Braer* off Garth's Ness.

Spiggie   INN ££

(🖉 01950-460409; www.spiggie.co.uk; s/d/superior d £70/120/140; 🅿 ☎ 🐾) An enthusiastic family has taken over this old Shetland stalwart near Scousburgh and guarantee a warm welcome. The Spiggie has compact, pretty rooms as well as larger chambers that can fit a family; there's also a self-catering lodge. Good dinners are available and the whole place boasts great views down over the local loch, a birdwatching haven.

Sumburgh

With sea cliffs, and grassy headlands jutting out into sparkling blue waters, Sumburgh is one of the most scenic places on Mainland, with a far greener landscape than the peaty north. It has a handful of excellent attractions clustered near Shetland's major airport.

★ Sumburgh Head   BIRDWATCHING

(www.rspb.org.uk) At Mainland's southern tip, these spectacular cliffs offer a good chance to get up close to puffins, and huge nesting colonies of fulmars, guillemots and razorbills. If you're lucky, you might spot dolphins, minke whales or orcas. Also here is the excellent Sumburgh Head Visitor Centre, in the lighthouse buildings.

★ Sumburgh Head
Visitor Centre   LIGHTHOUSE, MUSEUM

(🖉 01595-694688; www.sumburghhead.com; adult/child £6/2; ⊙ 11am-5.30pm Apr-Sep) High on the cliffs at Sumburgh Head, this excellent attraction is set across several buildings. Displays explain about the lighthouse, foghorn and radar station that operated here, and there's a good exhibition on the local marine creatures and birds. You can visit the lighthouse itself on a guided tour for an extra charge.

Jarlshof   ARCHAEOLOGICAL SITE

(🖉 01950-460112; www.historicenvironment.scot; adult/child £6/3.60; ⊙ 9.30am-5.30pm Apr-Sep, to 4.30pm Oct-Mar) Old and new collide here, with Sumburgh airport right by this picturesque, instructive archaeological site. Various periods of occupation from 2500 BC to AD 1500 can be seen; the complete change upon the Vikings' arrival is obvious· their rectangular longhouses present a marked contrast to the preceding brochs, roundhouses and wheelhouses. Atop the site is 16th-century Old House, named 'Jarlshof' in a novel by Sir Walter Scott. There's an informative audio tour included with admission.

Old Scatness   ARCHAEOLOGICAL SITE

(🖉 01595-694688; www.shetland-heritage.co.uk/old-scatness; adult/child £5/4; ⊙ 10.15am-4.30pm Fri mid-May–Aug; 👶) This dig brings Shetland's prehistory vividly to life; it's a must-see for archaeology buffs, but fun for kids, too. Clued-up guides in Iron Age clothes show you the site, which has provided important clues on the Viking takeover and dating of Shetland material. It has an impressive broch from around 300 BC, roundhouses and later wheelhouses. Best of all is the reconstruction with peat fire and working loom. At the time of research, a lack of funding had badly restricted the opening hours.

❶ Getting There & Away

Bus 6 runs to Sumburgh and Sumburgh Airport from Lerwick (£2.90 to Sumburgh, £3.30 to the airport; one hour, five to seven daily).

North Mainland

The north of Mainland is very photogenic – jumbles of cracked, peaty, brown hills blend with grassy pastureland and extend like bony fingers into numerous lochs and out into the wider, icy, grey waters of the North Sea. Different shades of light give it a variety of characters.

Around Hillswick, there's stunning scenery and several good places to stay; this makes it one of the best places to base yourself in the Shetland Islands.

Brae

The crossroads settlement of Brae has several accommodation options and is an important service centre for the whole of northern Shetland. It's no beauty, despite its bayside location, but there's fine walking on the peninsula west of Brae and to the south on the red-granite island of Muckle Roe, which is connected to the peninsula by a bridge. Muckle Roe also offers good diving off its west and north coasts.

South of Brae, Voe (Lower) is a pretty collection of buildings beside a tranquil bay on Olna Firth. With a cheap sleep and pub meals opposite, it can make a good stop.

★ **Busta House Hotel**   HOTEL **££**
(☑01806-522506; www.bustahouse.co.uk; Busta; s/d £99/125; P@🛜🐾) 🐾 This genteel, characterful hotel near Brae has a long, sad history and inevitable rumours of a (friendly) ghost. Built in the late 18th century (though the oldest part dates from 1588), it has creaks and quirks and likeable rooms that are compact and retain a cosy charm. Sea views and/or a four-poster bed cost a bit more.

There's also a fine restaurant, a lovely guest lounge and very helpful staff.

Frankie's Fish & Chips   FISH & CHIPS **£**
(☑01806-522700; www.frankiesfishandchips.com; Brae; mains £6-12; ⊙9.30am-8pm Mon-Sat, noon-8pm Sun; 🛜) 🐾 This famous Shetland chippie uses only locally sourced and sustainable seafood. As well as chip-shop standards, the menu runs to tasty Shetland mussels in garlicky sauces and, when available, plump juicy scallops. It also does breakfast rolls, baked potatoes and fry-ups. Eat in, out on the deck with views over the bay, or take away.

SEA KAYAKING

Paddling is a great way to explore Shetland's tortuous coastline, and allows you to get up close to seals and bird life. **Sea Kayak Shetland** (☑01595-840272; www.seakayakshetland.co.uk; beginner session £27, half-/full day £45/80) is a reliable operator catering for beginners and experts alike, and offering various guided trips.

❶ Getting There & Away

Buses from Lerwick to Brae (£2.90, 45 minutes, eight daily Monday to Saturday) run via Tingwall and Voe. Some continue to Hillswick.

Eshaness & Hillswick

Eleven miles northwest of Brae the road ends at the red basalt cliffs of Eshaness, site of some of Shetland's most impressive coastal scenery. When the wind subsides there's superb walking and panoramic views from the headland lighthouse. On the way, the village of Hillswick is set on a pretty bay.

Tangwick Haa Museum   MUSEUM
(☑01806-503389; ⊙11am-5pm mid-Apr–Sep) **FREE** A mile east of Eshaness, a side road leads south to the Tangwick Haa Museum, housed in a restored 17th-century house. The wonderful collection of old B&W photos captures the sense of community in this area.

★ **Almara**   B&B **££**
(☑01806-503261; www.almara.shetland.co.uk; s/d £40/80; ⊙Apr-Oct; P🛜) 🐾 Follow the puffin signpost a mile short of Hillswick to find Shetland's finest welcome. With sweeping views over the bay, this house has a great lounge, unusual features in the excellent rooms and bathrooms (including thoughtful extras such as USB chargers), and a good eye on the environment. You'll feel completely at home and appreciated; this is a B&B at its best.

St Magnus Bay Hotel   HOTEL **££**
(☑01806-503372; www.stmagnusbayhotel.co.uk; Hillswick; d £95, superior d £120; P🛜) This wonderful wooden mansion was built in 1896. The owners are involved in an ongoing renovation – a major project – to return it to former glories, and are doing a great

job. Try for a renovated room, but all are winningly wood-clad, and half also boast big windows taking full advantage of the fine water views. The bar serves food all day until 9pm.

❶ Getting There & Away

Three buses from Lerwick run to Hillswick (£3.50, 1¼ hours, Monday to Saturday), with a feeder bus on to Eshaness. Two buses run the return route. There are other connections at Brae.

The North Isles

Yell, Unst and Fetlar make up the North Isles of the Shetlands, which are connected to each other by ferry, as is Yell to Mainland. All are great for nature-watching; Unst has the most to offer overall.

Yell

POP 1000

Yell if you like but nobody will hear; the desolate peat moors here are typical Shetland scenery. The bleak landscape has an appeal though. Yell is all about colours: the browns and vivid, lush greens of the bogland, grey clouds thudding through the skies and the steely blue waters of the North Atlantic, which are never far away. The peat makes the ground look cracked and parched, although it's swimming most of the year. Though many folk fire on through to Unst, Yell offers several good hill walks, especially around the Herra peninsula, about halfway up the west coast.

Old Haa Museum MUSEUM
(☑01957-722339; www.shetlandheritageassociation. com; Burravoe; ⊙10am-4pm Mon-Thu & Sat, 2-5pm Sun mid-Apr–Sep) **FREE** This museum has a medley of curious objects (pipes, piano, a doll in cradle, tiny bibles, ships in bottles and a sperm-whale jaw), as well as an archive of local history and a tearoom. It's in Burravoe, 4 miles east of the southern ferry terminal in Ulsta.

Lumbister BIRDWATCHING
Red-throated divers, merlins, skuas and other bird species breed at this birdwatching hot spot on the Shetland moorland. The area is home to a large otter population, too, best viewed around Whale Firth, where you may also spot common and grey seals.

Quam B&B B&B **££**
(☑01957-766256; www.quambandbyellshetland. co.uk; Westsandwick; d £80; 🅿🛜) Just off the main road through Yell island, this farm B&B has friendly owners and three good rooms. Breakfast features eggs from the farm, which also has cute ponies that you can meet. Dinners (£15 per person) can be arranged.

❶ Getting There & Away

Yell is connected with Mainland by **ferries** (☑01595-745804; www.shetland.gov.uk/ ferries) between Toft and Ulsta (adult/car and driver return £5.50/13.60, 20 minutes, frequent). It's wise to book car space in summer.

An integrated bus and ferry connection runs once daily Monday to Saturday from Lerwick to Yell (£3.80, 1¼ hours), connecting with ferries to Fetlar and Unst; connecting services cover other parts of the island.

Unst

POP 600

You're fast running out of Scotland once you cross to rugged Unst (www.unst.org). Scotland's most northerly inhabited island is prettier than nearby Yell, with bare, velvety-smooth hills and settlements clinging to waterside locations, fiercely resisting the buffeting winds.

◉ Sights

★**Hermaness National Nature Reserve** NATURE RESERVE
(www.nnr-scotland.org.uk) At marvellous Hermaness headland, a 4.5-mile round walk takes you to cliffs where gannets, fulmars and guillemots nest, and numerous puffins frolic. You can also see Scotland's most northerly point, the rocks of **Out Stack**, and **Muckle Flugga**, with its lighthouse built by Robert Louis Stevenson's uncle. Duck into the **Hermaness Visitor Centre** (☑01595-711278; ⊙9am-5pm Apr-early Sep) **FREE**, with its poignant story about one-time resident Albert Ross.

The path to the cliffs is guarded by a squadron of great skuas who nest in the nearby heather, and dive-bomb at will if they feel threatened. They're damn solid birds too, but don't usually make contact.

★**Unst Bus Shelter** LANDMARK
(Bobby's Bus Shelter; www.unstbusshelter.shetland. co.uk; Baltasound) At the turn-off to Little-hamar, just past Baltasound, is Britain's most impressive bus stop. Enterprising locals,

FAIR ISLE

Fair Isle has stunning cliff scenery, isolation and squadrons of winged creatures. It's worth making the stomach-churning ferry ride here, to one of Scotland's most remote inhabited islands. About halfway to Orkney, it's only 3 miles by 1.5 miles in size and is probably best known for its patterned knitwear, still produced in three workshops on the island.

It's also a paradise for birdwatchers, who form the bulk of the island's visitors. Fair Isle is in the flight path of migrating birds, and thousands breed here. They're monitored by the bird observatory (p261), which collects and analyses information year-round; visitors are more than welcome to participate.

Fair Isle Lodge & Bird Observatory (☑01595-760258; www.fairislebirdobs.co.uk; s/d incl full board £80/150; ☺Apr-Oct; ℗@☂) The smart bird observatory offers good accommodation in en suite rooms. Rates include full board, and there are free guided walks and other bird-related displays and activities. Under-25s get a big discount, paying £40 per person.

From Tingwall, Shetland Inter-Island Air Service (p251) operates flights to Fair Isle (£84 return, 25 minutes). There's also a weekly service from Sumburgh in summer.

Ferries sail from Grutness (near Sumburgh) and some from Lerwick (one way passenger/car and driver £5.50/7.20, three hours) two to three times weekly.

tired of waiting in discomfort, decided to do a job on it, and it now boasts posh seating, novels, numerous decorative features and a visitors' book to sign. The theme and colour scheme changes yearly.

Unst Boat Haven MUSEUM
(☑01957-711809; Haroldswick; adult/child £3/free, combined ticket with Unst Heritage Centre £5; ☺11am-4pm Mon-Sat, 2-4pm Sun May-Sep) This large shed is a boatie's delight, packed with a beautifully cared for collection of Shetland rowing and sailing boats, all with a backstory. Old photos and maritime artefacts speak of the glory days of Unst fishing. There's a seasonal tearoom out front.

Unst Heritage Centre MUSEUM
(☑01957-711528; www.unstheritage.com; Haroldswick; adult/child £3/free, combined ticket with Unst Boat Haven £5; ☺11am-4pm Mon-Sat, 2-4pm Sun May-Sep) This heritage centre houses a modern museum with a history of the Shetland pony and a recreation of a croft house.

🛏 Sleeping & Eating

The only restaurants are at the Baltasound Hotel and Saxa Vord, though there are several cafes.

Self-caterers can stock up at Baltasound's Skibhoul Stores, which has a bakery and cafe, and the Final Checkout, between Baltasound and Haroldswick. Known locally as 'the garage', the Final Checkout has an ATM, and sells petrol and diesel.

★ **Gardiesfauld Hostel** HOSTEL, CAMPSITE £
(☑01957-755279; www.gardiesfauld.shetland.co.uk; 2 East Rd, Uyeasound; per adult/child tent sites £8/4, dm £16/9; ☺Apr-Sep; ℗☂) This spotless hostel has very spacious dorms with lockers, family rooms, a garden, an elegant lounge and a wee conservatory dining area with great bay views. You can camp here, too; there are separate areas for tents and vans. The bus stops right outside. Bring 20p coins for the showers. They'll open in winter if you prebook.

Saxa Vord HOSTEL £
(☑01957-711711; www.saxavord.com; Haroldswick; s/d £22.50/45; ☺mid-May–mid-Sep; ℗☂☃) This old RAF base (though the radar station it served reopened in 2018) is not the most atmospheric lodging, though the tired barracks-style rooms offer great value for singles, and there's something nice about watching the weather through the skylight-style windows. The restaurant dishes out surprisingly decent food, and there's a cafe, a bar – Britain's northernmost, by our reckoning – and a friendly, helpful atmosphere.

Wi-fi is only in public areas. Part of the same complex, self-catering houses (£788 per week) are good for families and are available year-round.

Baltasound Hotel HOTEL ££
(☑01957-711334; www.baltasoundhotel.co.uk; Baltasound; s £68-75, d £125-135; ☺Apr–mid-Oct; ℗☂) Brightly decorated rooms – some bigger than others – are complemented by wooden

ORKNEY & SHETLAND THE NORTH ISLES

WILDLIFE WATCHING IN SHETLAND

For birdwatchers, Shetland is paradise – a stopover for migrating Arctic species and host to vast seabird breeding colonies. June is the height of the season.

Every bird has its own name here: rain geese are red-throated divers, bonxies are great skuas, and alamooties are storm petrels. Clownish puffin antics are a highlight. The Royal Society for the Protection of Birds (RSPB; www.rspb.org.uk) maintains several reserves, plus there are National Nature Reserves at Hermaness, Keen of Hamar and Noss. Foula and Fair Isle also support large seabird populations.

Keep an eye on the sea: sea otters, orcas and other cetaceans are regularly sighted. Latest sightings are logged at useful www.nature-shetland.co.uk.

Shetland Nature Festival (www.shetlandnaturefestival.co.uk; ⊙ early Jul) has guided walks, talks, boat trips, open days and workshops.

chalets arrayed around the lawn here. Rooms feel a little overpriced so it's worth the small upgrade to the 'large doubles', which sport modern bathrooms. There's a lovely country outlook, and evening bar meals in a dining room dappled by the setting sun. Contact them for winter opening details.

ⓘ Getting There & Around

Unst is connected with Yell and Fetlar by ferries (p260) between Gutcher and Belmont (free if coming from Mainland that day, otherwise adult/car and driver £5.50/13.60 return, 10 minutes, frequent).

An integrated bus and ferry connection runs once daily Monday to Saturday from Lerwick to Baltasound and other Unst villages (£4.40, 2¼ hours). There are connecting services around Unst itself.

Unst Cycle Hire (☑ 01957-711254; www.unst cyclehire.co.uk; Saxa Vord, Haroldswick; per day/week £10/50; ⊙ 11am-5pm) at the Saxa Vord complex in Haroldswick has bikes for hire.

Fetlar
POP 60

Fetlar, a notable birdwatching destination, is the smallest but most fertile of the North Isles. Its name is derived from the Viking term for 'fat land'.

Fetlar Interpretive Centre   VISITOR CENTRE
(☑ 01957-733206; www.fetlar.com; Houbie; adult/ child £3/free; ⊙ 11am-4pm Mon-Sat, 12.30-4pm Sun May-Sep) The excellent Fetlar Interpretive Centre has photos, audio recordings and videos on the island and its history. You'll find it 4.5 miles from the ferry, by the water in the hamlet of Houbie.

ⓘ Getting There & Away

Four to nine daily ferries (p260; free if coming from Mainland that day, otherwise adult/car and driver £5.50/13.60 return, 25 minutes) connect Fetlar with Gutcher on Yell and Belmont on Unst.

Understand Scotland's Highlands & Islands

Scotland's Highlands & Islands Today

Although Scotland's Highlands and islands account for around 58% of Scotland's land area, the region is home to a mere 500,000 people, less than 10% of the country's total population. The region's mountainous terrain, scattered islands and low population density mean that it faces a very different set of challenges – and political imperatives – than its lowland neighbour. Industries such as tourism, energy, forestry, fishing, salmon farming and whisky distilling are important sources of employment.

Best in Print

Raw Spirit (Iain Banks; 2003) An enjoyable jaunt around the Highlands and islands in search of the perfect whisky.
Mountaineering in Scotland (WH Murray; 1947) Classic account of climbing in the Highlands in the 1930s, when just getting to Glen Coe was an adventure in itself.
The Poor Had No Lawyers (Andy Wightman; 2010) A penetrating, and fascinating, analysis of who owns the land in the Highlands, and how they got it.
The Scottish Islands (Hamish Haswell-Smith; 1996) A comprehensive and beautifully illustrated guide to the geography and history of 162 Scottish islands.

Best in Music

Letter from America (The Proclaimers; 1987) A modern lament for the Highland Clearances.
Hùg Air A' Bhonaid Mhòir (Julie Fowlis; 2007) Award-winning Gaelic folk singer from North Uist.
Loch Lomond (Runrig; 1979) Classic hit from the masters of Gaelic rock.
Oran Do'n Mhorairne (Griogair Labhruidh; 2007) Poet and musician working on the world's first Gaelic hip-hop album.
Caledonia (Dougie Maclean; 1983) A love song to Scotland.
Skea Brae (The Wrigley Sisters; 2011) Orkney sisters and champions of traditional fiddle music.

Renewable Energy

One of the central planks of the Scottish government's vision for the future of Scotland is its energy policy. The *Scottish Energy Strategy*, published in December 2017, sets an objective of 50% of the country's total energy consumption to be supplied from renewable sources by 2030. A target to produce 100% of electricity consumption from renewables by 2020 is well on track, with a figure of 68% achieved in 2017, making Scotland a world leader in ecofriendly electricity.

Of course, all this has an effect on the landscape, and on the Highlands and islands in particular, as the region is rich in wind, wave, tidal and hydro power resources. There has been a proliferation of wind turbines, even in some of the wilder parts of the country, and new hydroelectric power plants are being built, ranging in size from small local projects to the massive pumped-storage scheme (with new dam and reservoir) planned for Coire Glas in the Great Glen. Most visually intrusive is the controversial 137-mile-long, high-voltage overhead power line from Beauly (near Inverness) to Denny in Stirlingshire, which was completed in 2016 with 615 giant pylons marching through some of the Highlands' most scenic areas (notably along the A9 Perth–Inverness road near Drumochter).

However, the future of Scotland's energy industry arguably lies not on land, but in the sea: Scotland has access to 25% of Europe's available tidal energy, and 10% of its wave power. The country is at the leading edge of developing wave, tidal and offshore wind power; in 2012 the waters around Orkney and the Pentland Firth were designated as a Marine Energy Park, with a second one planned for southwest Islay in 2018.

Whisky Galore!

Scotch whisky is having something of a moment. Ten new whisky distilleries opened in Scotland in 2017, with a further 10 opening in 2018, bringing the total up to almost 130 (from around 90 in 2010). And it's not over yet – there are plans for a further 20 or so distilleries in the pipeline.

Some are brand new, such as those at Ardnamurchan and Raasay, while others are old distilleries that are being brought back to life, such as Brora in Sutherland and Port Ellen on the island of Islay. Most have visitor centres, which welcomed record numbers of tourists in 2017, with distillery tours (in total) approaching the popularity of major attractions such as Edinburgh Castle and even St Paul's Cathedral in London.

Another whisky record was set in 2017 – exports of Scotch whisky amounted to a total of £4.36 billion, the equivalent of 1.23 billion bottles, and accounting for over 20% of all UK food and drink exports.

Scottish Salmon – Farming Versus Fishing

You can't travel far along Scotland's western seaboard without noticing the circular net cages of a fish farm. Raising salmon for food took off in Scotland in the 1970s, and by 2017 the number of marine farms had risen to more than 250, producing around 170,000 tonnes of salmon. The industry sustains around 2000 jobs and accounts for £600 million in export income.

However, salmon farming has its downside. A report published in 2018 by the Scottish Parliament's Environment, Climate Change and Land Reform Committee *(Report on the Environmental Impacts of Salmon Farming)* claimed that fish farms have had a negative impact on the environment – uneaten fish food, waste products, pesticides and chemical treatments end up in the surrounding waters, causing an artificial 'desert' on the sea bed. In addition, salmon farms act as a breeding ground and 'sink' for sea lice, naturally occurring parasites that then infect and kill wild salmon and sea trout.

Rivers on the west coast of Scotland that were once famous for their salmon and sea trout fishing are now a shadow of their former selves, with anglers reporting a complete collapse in wild populations. Angling, of course, is an important source of income and employment in remote areas of the Highlands and islands, just as fish farming is. How the tension between the two will resolve itself, only time will tell.

POPULATION:
APPROXIMATELY 500,000

AREA: **APPROXIMATELY 17,550 SQ MILES**

ANNUAL WHISKY EXPORT:
1.23 BILLION BOTTLES (2017)

if Scotland were 100 people

96 would be white
3 would be Asian
1 would be African, Afro Caribbean or other

belief systems
(% of population)

44 no religion or not stated | Church of Scotland | Roman Catholic

6 Other Christian | 1 Muslim | 1 Other

population per sq mile

SCOTLAND'S HIGHLANDS & ISLANDS | SCOTLAND | ENGLAND

= 30 people

History

From the decline of the Vikings onwards, Scottish history has been predictably and often violently bound to that of its southern neighbour. Battles and border raids were commonplace until shared kingship, then political union, drew the two together. However, there has often been as much – if not more – of a cultural divide between Highland and Lowland Scotland than ever between Lowland Scotland and England.

Stories in Stone

Scotland's Neolithic period (3200 BC to 2200 BC) has left behind an astonishing record of human development, most impressively at Skara Brae in Orkney and Jarlshof in Shetland – some of the world's best-preserved prehistoric villages – but also in the cairns and stone circles of Lewis, Caithness and Kilmartin. All aspects of early life are represented, from primitive field systems and houses to ceremonial structures such as standing stones, tombs and tribal halls.

Crannogs (artificial islands built on stilts or heaped stones) were a favoured form of defensible dwelling through the Bronze Age (2200 BC to 750 BC), while the Iron Age (750 BC to AD 500) saw the construction of a remarkable series of defence-minded structures of a different sort: the drystone defensive towers known as brochs, which are unique to Scotland. The best preserved examples are Mousa in Shetland, Dun Carloway in Lewis and Dun Telve in Glenelg.

Romans & Picts

The origins of the people known as the Picts is a mystery, but they may have emerged as a confederation of northern Celtic tribes in reaction to the Roman invasion of Scotland in AD 80. Their territory (Pictland, also known as Pictavia) extended north through the Highlands from the Forth and Clyde estuaries to Orkney and the Western Isles.

Much of what we know about the Picts comes from the Romans, who attempted to conquer northern Scotland but failed to occupy any territory north of the Antonine Wall. This includes their name (from the Latin pictus, meaning 'painted', or possibly 'tattooed'). The main material

Top Prehistoric Sites

Jarlshof (Shetland)

Skara Brae (Orkney)

Maeshowe (Orkney)

Kilmartin Glen (Argyll)

Callanish (Lewis)

Tomb of the Eagles (Orkney)

Scottish Crannog Centre (Kenmore)

TIMELINE	4000–2200 BC	2200–500 BC	AD 43
	Neolithic farmers move to Scotland from mainland Europe. Stone circles and tombs from these ancient times dot the Highlands and islands; the best are concentrated in Orkney.	The Bronze Age produces swords and shields, and the construction of hill forts, crannogs and burnt mounds. Impressive stone towers known as brochs are built during the Iron Age.	Claudius begins the Roman conquest of Britain, almost a century after Julius Caesar first invaded. By AD 80 a string of forts is built from the Clyde to the Forth.

evidence of Pictish culture is their fabulous carved symbol stones, found in many parts of northern and eastern Scotland.

The Kingdom of Dalriada

By AD 500 another Celtic tribe, the Scots (from Scotti, a derogatory name given to them by the Romans), had begun to colonise western Scotland from northern Ireland, establishing a kingdom called Dalriada. From their ceremonial headquarters at the hill fort of Dunadd, these seafaring Celts conquered a territory that stretched from Kintyre and the Antrim coast of Ireland to the Isle of Skye and Wester Ross.

Their influence lives on in the districts of Lorn and Cowal, which take their names from Dalriadan chiefs, and the county name of Argyll (from *earra gael,* meaning 'the seaboard of the Gael') – and, of course, they eventually gave their name to the kingdom of Scotland. But perhaps their most important legacy is that they brought Christianity and the Gaelic language to the western Highlands and islands of Scotland.

In the 6th century, St Columba, Scotland's most famous missionary, arrived in the west. Columba was an Irish scholar and monk exiled, tradition has it, after involvement in a bloody battle. After fleeing Ireland in 563 he established a monastery on Iona and also travelled northeast to take his message to the Picts. By the late 8th century most of Scotland had converted.

In 843 the Dalriadan king Kenneth MacAlpin, who was the son of a Pictish princess, used the Pictish custom of matrilineal succession to take over the Pictish throne, uniting Scotland north of the Firth of Forth into a single kingdom. Thereafter the Scots gained complete cultural and political ascendancy.

Viking Invaders

The first Viking longboats were spotted off the shores of Orkney in the 780s, and must have inspired terror in those who saw them. The marauders struck without warning, ransacking entire villages, butchering the occupants and carting anything of value back to Norway. For the next 500 years the Norsemen pillaged the Scottish coast and islands, eventually taking control of Orkney, Shetland, the Outer Hebrides and all the islands off the west coast of Scotland from Skye to Arran, plus the mainland districts of Cowal and Kintyre.

Eventually the Viking colonies returned to Scottish rule, but they always retained a distinctively Scandinavian-tinged culture, especially Orkney and Shetland, which – unlike the Western Isles – were taken over by nobles from the Lowlands and ended up speaking a mixture of Scots and Norn (an ancient Viking dialect), rather than Gaelic.

Adomnan (627–704) succeeded St Columba as the abbot of Iona. His book, *Vita Columbae* (Life of Columba), is one of our most important sources of information on the Picts and the kingdom of Dalriada.

A well-presented and easily absorbed introduction to Scottish history is at www.bbc.co.uk/scotland/history. The accompanying videos help to bring the past to life.

HISTORY THE KINGDOM OF DALRIADA

Early 500s	6th century	780	848
A Celtic tribe, known as the Scots, cross the sea from northern Ireland and establish a kingdom in Argyll called Dalriada.	St Columba establishes a Christian mission on Iona. By the late 8th century the mission is responsible for the conversion of most of pagan Scotland.	Norsemen in longboats from Scandinavia begin to pillage the Scottish coast and islands, eventually taking control of Orkney, Shetland and the Western Isles.	Kenneth MacAlpin unites the Scottish and Pictish thrones, thus uniting Scotland north of the Firth of Forth into a single kingdom.

The west coast was returned to the Scottish king Alexander III after the Battle of Largs in 1263. Three years later the Western Isles were ceded to Scotland by the Treaty of Perth, in exchange for an annual rent to the King of Norway. Orkney and Shetland remained Norwegian possessions until 1468 and 1469 respectively, when they were mortgaged to King James III of Scotland in lieu of a dowry for his bride, Margaret, daughter of the king of Denmark.

Clan Versus Crown

Jacobite, a term derived from the Latin for 'James', is used to describe the political movement committed to the return of the Stuart kings to the thrones of England and Scotland.

The dynasty founded by Kenneth MacAlpin tightened its grip on the Highland mainland during the 10th century, but it wasn't until the reign of Malcolm II (1005–18) that the Scots extended their control south of the Forth–Clyde line, creating a single Scottish kingdom extending as far as the River Tweed. This was the beginning of a drift that saw the centre of royal power move southward from Scone to Stirling and Dunfermline, and then to Edinburgh, which eventually emerged as the capital of Scotland by the early 16th century.

However, the cultural and linguistic divide between Highlands and Lowlands had its origins at the other end of Britain, in the Norman invasion of 1066. Malcolm II's great-grandson Malcolm Canmore (1058–93) took a Saxon queen. His youngest son David I (1124–53) had been raised in England, and introduced the Anglo-Norman feudal system to Scotland, granting lands and titles (mostly in the south and east) to English-speaking Norman noblemen.

But in the remote Highland glens the Gaelic language and the clan system still held sway: loyalty and military service were based on ties of blood rather than feudal superiority. The clan was led by a chief who was granted his position through the ancient Dalriadan system of tanistry, in which the heir to the chief was nominated from a pool of eligible candidates whose great-grandfathers had been chiefs before them. This ensured that a chief never died without a potential heir, but resulted in many bloody feuds and murders instigated by those who felt their claim to the title had been denied.

The history of the Highlands from the 12th to the 16th centuries was volatile and violent. Robert the Bruce's struggle to win the Scottish crown involved not only fighting the English, but also vanquishing his foes in the Highlands. In 1306 Bruce famously murdered John Comyn, his main rival as king, making Bruce a blood enemy of the powerful Macdougalls of Lorne, whose chief Alexander was related to Comyn by marriage. The Macdougalls harried Bruce mercilessly until the king-to-be finally routed them at the Battle of the Pass of Brander in 1309.

Even after Bruce had defeated the English at Bannockburn in 1314 and guaranteed Scottish independence, the wrangling for power between

872	1040	1263	1314
The King of Norway creates an earldom in Orkney, also governing Shetland; these island groups become a vital Viking base for raids and colonisation down the west of Scotland.	Macbeth takes the Scottish throne after defeating Duncan. This, and the fact that he was later killed by Duncan's son Malcolm, are the only parallels with the Shakespeare version.	Norse power controls the entire western seaboard but is broken at the Battle of Largs, marking the retreat of Viking influence and eventual handing back of the western isles to Scotland.	Robert the Bruce wins a famous victory over the English at the Battle of Bannockburn, turning the tide in favour of the Scots for the next 400 years.

(and among) the Highland clans and the Scottish crown raged on for several centuries. Clan Campbell, supporters of Bruce, were rewarded for their continuing loyalty to the king with grants of land and titles, earning the bitter enmity of their rivals the Macdougalls and the Macdonalds. By the beginning of the 18th century, the chief of Clan Campbell had become the Duke of Argyll, owning most of the southwestern Highlands and capable of putting 5000 men into battle.

Much of the fighting that disrupted the Highlands during this period was between rival clans. The longest-running feud was between the Camerons and the Mackintoshs: following a battle over disputed land in 1337, the two clans remained sworn enemies for more than 300 years. The Battle of Mulroy (near Roy Bridge) in 1688, between Camerons and Macdonalds on one side and Mackintoshs on the other, turned out to be the last inter-clan battle before the Jacobite rebellions changed the Highlands forever.

The Jacobite Rebellions

The 'Glorious Revolution' of 1688 saw the Catholic king James II of England (VII of Scotland) deposed from the British throne, and replaced by his Protestant son-in-law William of Orange. From then until 1746 much of Highland history was dominated by the Jacobite rebellions that sought to restore a Catholic Stuart king to the British throne. Indeed, one of England's motivations for union with Scotland was fear of Jacobite sympathies in the Highlands being exploited by its enemy, the French.

A major manifestation of this fear was the building of government garrisons throughout the Highlands, notably Fort William, Fort Augustus and Fort George, and the driving of new military roads through the glens by General Wade and his successors. This wariness was well justified – there were Jacobite uprisings in 1689, 1708 and 1715.

By no means all of the Highland clans were Jacobite supporters, though. From his seat at Inveraray Castle, the Duke of Argyll, chief of Clan Campbell, served as the British government's political manager in Scotland for the first half of the 18th century. In fact, many of the clans that joined in the rebellions did so more out of hatred towards the Campbells than support for the exiled Stuart king. Following the 1689 uprising, King William demanded that all Highland chieftains swear an oath of allegiance or suffer violent reprisals; it was Campbell soldiers who were charged with making an example of the Macdonalds with the infamous Massacre of Glencoe.

In 1745 Charles Edward Stuart (better known as Bonnie Prince Charlie) landed in Scotland to claim the British crown for his father. Supported by an army of Highlanders, he marched southwards and captured Edinburgh in September 1745. He got as far south as Derby in England, but success was short-lived; a Hanoverian army led by the Duke of Cumberland pushed him all the way back to the Highlands, where Jacobite dreams

Bonnie Prince Charlie's flight after Culloden is legendary. He lived in hiding in the remote Highlands and islands for months before being rescued by a French frigate. His narrow escape from Uist to Skye, dressed as Flora MacDonald's maid, is the subject of the 'Skye Boat Song'.

1320	1328	1468–69	1560
The Declaration of Arbroath asserts Scotland's status as an independent kingdom in submission to the pope.	Continuing raids on northern England force Edward II to sue for peace; the Treaty of Northampton gives Scotland its independence, with Robert I, the Bruce, as king.	Orkney and then Shetland are mortgaged to Scotland as part of a dowry from Danish King Christian I, whose daughter is to marry the future King James III of Scotland.	As a result of the Reformation, the Scottish parliament creates a Protestant Church independent of Rome and the monarchy. The Latin Mass is abolished and the pope's authority denied.

were finally extinguished at the Battle of Culloden in 1746. Many wounded Highlanders were executed by 'Butcher' Cumberland following the battle, but Charles escaped and fled to France via Skye, aided by Flora MacDonald; he later died in exile.

The Highland Clearances

In the aftermath of the Jacobite rebellions, the government outlawed the wearing of Highland dress and the playing of the bagpipes. The Highlands were put under military control and private armies were banned. The ties of kinship and duty that once marked the relationship between Highland laird and clansman gradually transformed into the merely economic relationship of landlord and tenant. Lands that had been confiscated after 1745 were returned to their owners in the 1780s, but by then the chiefs had tasted the aristocratic high life and were tempted by the easy profits to be made from sheep farming.

John Prebble's classic *The Highland Clearances* (1963) is an emotive account of this controversial period of history. Eric Richards' book of the same name from 2007 takes a more balanced look at the factual events.

So began the Highland Clearances, one of the most shameful episodes in Scottish history. By no means all of the people who left their homes in the late 18th and 19th centuries were forcibly evicted; in the Hebridean islands, for example, a combination of poverty, overcrowding and lack of suitable land led many to choose emigration. But some of the forced clearances, especially in Sutherland, were so brutal that newspaper reporting of the events caused a national scandal.

Under the pretext of agricultural 'improvement', the peasant farmers, no longer of any use as soldiers and uneconomical as tenants, were evicted from their homes and farms to make way for flocks of hardy Cheviot sheep – in the Highlands the year 1792 (when Cheviots were first introduced) was known for decades afterwards as *Bliadhna nan Caorach* (the Year of the Sheep). The most notorious events took place in Strathnaver, where Patrick Sellar – the factor (land agent) of the Duke of Sutherland – cleared people from their homes using dogs, and set fire to cottages while possessions were still inside. He was later charged with arson and culpable homicide, but was acquitted.

After the evictions a few cottars stayed behind to work the sheep farms, but most were relocated to desperate crofts on poor coastal land or fled to the cities in search of work. Many thousands emigrated – some willingly, some under duress – to the developing colonies of North America, Australia and New Zealand. All over the Highlands today, only a ruckle of stones among the bracken remains where once there were whole villages. The Mull of Oa on Islay, for example, once supported a population of 4000 – today there are barely 40 people there.

Although the Clearances took place two centuries ago, they remain an emotive subject in the Highlands today. They marked the final nail in the coffin of the old clan system, and the beginning of the depopulation of

1603	1689	1692	1707
James VI of Scotland inherits the English throne in the so-called Union of the Crowns, becoming James I of Great Britain.	First Jacobite uprising, led by John Graham of Claverhouse ('Bonnie Dundee'); a rebel victory at Killiecrankie is soon followed by defeat, but rebellion prompts building of a government garrison at Fort William.	The Massacre of Glencoe causes further rifts between those clans loyal to the Crown and those loyal to the old ways.	Despite popular opposition, the Act of Union, which brings England and Scotland under one parliament, one sovereign and one flag, takes effect on 1 May.

POWER FROM THE GLENS

The high rainfall and rushing rivers of the Scottish Highlands led to the region being a world pioneer in the development of hydroelectric power. In 1896 the Foyers generating station on Loch Ness was the first large-scale hydroelectric scheme in Britain, powering one of the world's first electric aluminium smelters. Its success led the British Aluminium Company to build a much larger scheme based on the Blackwater Dam north of Glen Coe – in fact, it built a whole town at Kinlochleven to house workers from the smelter and the power station. By 1911 the Highlands of Scotland were producing one-third of the world's aluminium.

A vision of bringing investment, employment and electricity to the economically depressed Highlands spurred the government into creating the North of Scotland Hydro-Electric Board (motto: 'Power from the Glens'). Over the next few decades the board masterminded a series of vast civil engineering projects from Loch Awe to Glen Affric: by 1965, 78 dams had been built, with 54 power stations providing a total generating capacity of over 1000 megawatts.

Conscious of criticism that these developments would be detrimental to areas of great scenic beauty, the board decreed that the power stations be designed by architects in modernist and international styles using local stone, and some were concealed underground. Many sites are now tourist attractions, including the Cruachan power station at Loch Awe, and the salmon ladder beside the dam at Pitlochry power station.

With today's emphasis on renewable energy sources, hydroelectric power is back in fashion, and has the potential to supply up to one quarter of Scotland's homes. The country's biggest contemporary civil engineering project is the planned Coire Glas pumped-storage scheme at the north end of Loch Lochy in the Great Glen, which could be completed by 2022.

the Highlands, a process that is still going on. But it was rarely a straightforward story, and recent scholarship has challenged the popular image of poor tenants versus greedy landlords, claiming that in many cases the population pressure on marginal land had become unsustainable – something had to give. In bookshops from Oban to Inverness you'll find plenty of accounts of the Highland Clearances that offer food for thought.

Tartanry, Tourism & Deer-Stalking

The pacification of the Highlands in the wake of the Jacobite rebellions led to a wave of adventurous travellers venturing north in search of the wild and the picturesque. The most famous of these were Samuel Johnson (compiler of the first *Dictionary of the English Language*) and his biographer James Boswell, who travelled to Inverness, Skye, Mull and Oban in 1773 and wrote separate accounts of their journey – both were bestsellers.

Tales of this 'primitive' and 'unspoilt' region proved irresistible to the emerging Romantic movement in art and literature. Poets and

1745–46	Late 1700s–early 1800s	1848	1850–1900
The culmination of the Jacobite rebellions: Bonnie Prince Charlie lands in Scotland, gathers an army and marches south. He gains English territory but is eventually defeated at the Battle of Culloden.	Lowland Scotland flourishes during the Industrial Revolution, but the Highlands suffer the misery of the Clearances and mass emigration.	Queen Victoria buys Balmoral Estate in Aberdeenshire as a holiday home, and begins a trend for royal visits to the Scottish Highlands.	The spread of the railways opens up the Highlands to tourism; wealthy southerners buy up huge tracts of land as sporting estates.

artists toured the Highlands in search of the sublime, including William Wordsworth and Samuel Taylor Coleridge in 1803, and artist JMW Turner in 1831, the latter in the company of Sir Walter Scott. Scott himself penned a series of hugely popular historical novels – notably *Waverley*, *Rob Roy* and *The Pirate* – and the epic poems *The Lady of the Lake* and *The Lord of the Isles,* all of which were set in the Highlands.

In fact, it was Scott who pretty much single-handedly invented the romantic, tartan-clad image of the Highlands. In 1822, Scott engineered a state visit to Edinburgh by King George IV – the first time a reigning British monarch had been to Scotland since 1650 – where the king was greeted by a stage-managed parade of Highlanders in traditional tartan costume. The king himself was persuaded to wear a kilt for the occasion, triggering a wave of tartan-mania among the fashionable classes of England.

George's successor, Queen Victoria, fell utterly in love with the Highlands. Her consort Prince Albert purchased the Balmoral estate in 1852, and the royal couple spent their summer holidays there (a tradition maintained by the royal family to this day). After Albert's death in 1861, Victoria spent up to four months a year at Balmoral, often sneaking around the Highlands incognito in the company of her Scottish ghillie (attendant), John Brown. All this provoked enormous interest in the Highlands among the British upper and middle classes, sparking a wave of tourism assisted by the spread of the railways.

In the second half of the 19th century a decline in the profitability of sheep farming combined with the emergence of a wealthy nouveau-riche class in England led to a new phenomenon: the rise of the Highland sporting estate. Struggling Highland chiefs sold off their ancient lands to rich merchants from the south, who ran them as private fiefdoms of salmon fishing, grouse shooting and deer stalking. Today, more than 50% of the land area of the Highlands and islands is occupied by around 340 private sporting estates, two-thirds of them owned by absentee landlords.

Best Local History Museums

....

Stromness Museum (Stromness)

....

Shetland Museum (Lerwick)

....

Strathnaver Museum (Strathnaver)

....

Museum of Island Life (Skye)

....

Arnol Blackhouse (Lewis)

....

Museum of the Isles (Skye)

Crofting

During the mass upheaval of the Highland Clearances, those who chose not to emigrate or move to the cities were forced to eke a living from narrow plots of marginal agricultural land, often close to the coast. This was a form of smallholding that became known as crofting. The small patch of land was not enough to produce a living on its own, and had to be supplemented by other work such as fishing and kelp gathering. Tenure was always precarious, as tenancies were granted on a year-by-year basis, and there was no guarantee of benefiting from any improvements made – on a whim of the landlord, a crofter could be evicted and lose not only the farm but also the house they'd built on it.

1886	1914–1932	1939–45	1950s
Rent strikes and land raids lead to the Crofters Holdings (Scotland) Act, which grants security of tenure to crofters for the first time.	Scottish industry slumps during WWI and collapses in its aftermath in the face of new Eastern production and the Great Depression. About 400,000 Scots emigrate between 1921 and 1931.	WWII sees the sea lochs of the Highlands used as marshalling areas for Arctic and Atlantic convoys. In Shetland, the Shetland Bus operation ferries agents and supplies to occupied Norway.	The development of hydroelectric power sees many Highland rivers and lochs dammed to generate electricity.

The economic depression of the late 19th century meant that many crofters couldn't pay their rent. This time, however, the people resisted eviction, creating instead the Highland Land League and their own political movement, the Crofters Party. Several of their demands were met by the government in the Crofters' Holdings Act of 1886, including security of tenure and fair rents.

But it failed to address the issue of the lack of land for new crofts. More rent strikes and land raids (occupations) followed, most famously in the Isle of Lewis, where a monument recalls the Pairc Deer Raid of 1887, when several hundred crofters killed a large number of deer in protest at their landlord's clearing of crofts to make way for deer stalking. Police and troops were sent to quell this 'riot', an over-reaction that only generated more public sympathy for the crofters.

Further legislation improved the situation, but it wasn't until 1976 that crofters won the right to purchase their own land and become owner-occupiers. Today in the Highlands and islands there are around 20,000 crofts (smallholdings) averaging 5 hectares in area, supporting a crofting population of more than 33,000 people.

Scottish Devolution

In 1979 a referendum was held on whether to set up a directly elected Scottish Assembly. Fifty-two per cent of those who voted said yes to devolution, but Labour prime minister James Callaghan decided that everyone who didn't vote should be counted as a no, so the Scottish Assembly was rejected.

From 1979 to 1997 Scotland was ruled by a Conservative government in London, for which the majority of Scots hadn't voted. Separatist feelings, always present, grew stronger. Following the landslide victory of the Labour Party in 1997, another referendum was held on the creation of a Scottish parliament. This time the result was overwhelmingly and unambiguously in favour.

Elections were held and the Scottish parliament convened for the first time in 1999 in Edinburgh, with Labour's Donald Dewar, who died in office the very next year, becoming first minister. Labour held power until 2007, when the pro-independence Scottish National Party formed government. It was overwhelmingly re-elected in 2011 and pushed for a referendum on independence. The campaign engaged the nation and resulted in a huge turnout, and in September 2014 the Scots voted against becoming an independent nation by 55% to 45%.

One of the major factors for many Scots who voted to remain part of the UK was the guarantee of continued EU membership, so when in June 2016 the UK population narrowly voted to leave the EU, this again brought the issue of Scottish independence into the spotlight.

The effects of the Clearances were exacerbated by the potato famine of the 1840s. Between 1841 and 1861 the western Highlands and islands lost one-third of its population, mostly through emigration.

1970s	1999–2005	2003	2014
The discovery of oil and gas in the North Sea brings new prosperity to Aberdeen and the surrounding area, and also to the Orkney and Shetland Islands.	Scottish parliament is convened for the first time on 12 May 1999. Among the first policies to be enacted are the reform of land laws, and the recognition of Gaelic as an official language.	The Land Reform Act establishes the right of responsible access to private land, and the right of communities to buy the land they live on.	Around 340 sporting estates occupy more than 50% of the Scottish Highlands and islands, many owned by absentee landlords.

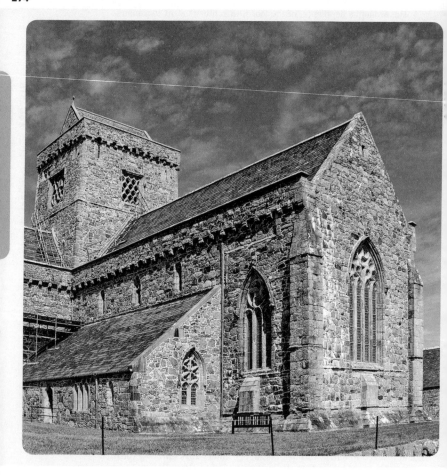

Highland Culture

The notion of 'Scottish culture' often conjures up clichéd images of bagpipe music, incomprehensible poetry and romanticised paintings of Highland landscapes. But the native culture of Scotland's Highlands and islands – strongly influenced by clan history and the Gaelic language – is distinctive and colourful, ranging from evocative Gaelic poetry and foot-tapping fiddle music to graceful Highland dancing and the fast and furious sport of shinty.

Literature

Above Iona Abbey (p99)

The Highlands and islands have a long and distinguished literary history, from the medieval monks of Iona to 20th-century writers such as George Mackay Brown, Neil Munro and Iain Crichton Smith, not forgetting the Lewis-based crime novels of Peter May.

Gaelic Poetry

Little has survived of early Gaelic literature, although the monks of Iona and other Scottish monasteries are known to have written in their native language as well as in Latin. But as descendants of the Celts, the Gaels had a strong bardic tradition, with songs, poems, stories and stirring tales of historic events passed down from generation to generation by word of mouth.

Alexander Macdonald (Alasdair Mac Mhaighstir Alasdair; 1695–1770), a schoolmaster from Moidart, is widely regarded as one of the finest of Gaelic poets, and was a genuine bard of the Clanranald Macdonalds. An ardent Jacobite, he gathered with the clans at Glenfinnan in 1745, and fought at Culloden the following year. His poetry ranged from minute descriptions of nature and wildlife to satirical and political verse, as well as songs in praise of Bonnie Prince Charlie.

Another bard who fought in the Jacobite wars was Duncan Ban MacIntyre (Donnchadh Bàn Mac an t-Saoir; 1724–1812) of Glen Orchy. But 'Fair Duncan', as he was known, fought on the Hanoverian side under the Duke of Argyll. He was also illiterate, and his beautiful nature poems were composed and stored in his memory before being dictated for someone else to write down. A prominent monument to him stands on a hilltop above Dalmally.

The greatest Gaelic poet of modern times was Sorley MacLean (Somhairle MacGill-Eain; 1911–96) from the Isle of Raasay. He was a teacher who wrote powerfully about the Highland Clearances, the Spanish Civil War and WWII, but who also produced some of the 20th century's most moving and delicate love poetry.

MacLean's contemporary, Lewis-born Iain Crichton Smith (1928–98), was one of the most prolific writers of Gaelic poetry (though he also wrote widely in English). Notable collections include *Burn is Aran* (Water and Bread) and *Na Guthan* (Voices); his *Towards the Human* is a fine collection of essays and poems on Gaelic life.

No mention of Gaelic literature would be complete without a word about the poet and politician James Macpherson (1736–96), from Ruthven (near Kingussie), who caused a huge stir in 1761 with the publication of *Fingal, an Ancient Epic Poem in Six Books*. An avid collector of Gaelic poetry, Macpherson claimed to have discovered the works of Ossian, a 3rd-century Gaelic bard. *Fingal* and two subsequent volumes of Ossian's poetry were denounced as fake – Macpherson never produced the original Gaelic manuscripts – but nevertheless proved enormously popular. The epic poems were translated into several European languages, and strongly influenced the emerging Romantic movement. (The poems were also responsible for the naming of Fingal's Cave on the Isle of Staffa.)

An Leabhar Mor: The Great Book of Gaelic is a collection of 100 Gaelic poems (with English translations) dating from AD 600 to the present day, accompanied by specially commissioned artworks. Described as a '21st-century Book of Kells', it can be viewed online at www.leabharmor.net.

20th-Century Highland Writers

The poet and storyteller George Mackay Brown (1921–96) was born in Stromness (in the Orkney Islands), and lived there almost all his life. Although his poems and novels are rooted in Orkney, his work transcends local and national boundaries. His novel *Greenvoe* (1972) is a warm, witty and poetic evocation of life in an Orkney community; his last novel, *Beside the Ocean of Time* (1994), is a wonderfully elegiac account of remote island life. His poetry has been published in collections such as *Travellers* (2001) and *Collected Poems: 1954–1992* (2005).

Another Orcadian worth looking out for is poet Edwin Muir (1887–1959), who wrote longingly about Orkney from his later life in Glasgow, and published the interesting travelogue *Highland Journey* in 1935.

Norman McCaig (1910–96) was born in Edinburgh but came from a Harris family and is widely regarded as the finest Scottish poet of his generation. He wrote eloquently about the Highlands and islands – his

THE GAELIC LANGUAGE

Scottish Gaelic (*Gàidhlig* – pronounced '*gah*-lic' in Scotland) is spoken by about 80,000 people in Scotland, mainly in the Highlands and islands. It is a member of the Celtic branch of the Indo-European family of languages, which has given us Gaelic, Irish, Manx, Welsh, Cornish and Breton.

Although Scottish Gaelic is the Celtic language most closely associated with Scotland, it was quite a latecomer to these shores. Other Celtic languages, namely Pictish and Brittonic, had existed prior to the arrival of Gaelic-speaking Celts from Ireland around the 5th century AD. These Irish settlers, known to the Romans as Scotti, were eventually to give their name to the entire country. As their territorial influence extended so did their language, and from the 9th to the 11th centuries Gaelic was spoken throughout the country. For many centuries the language was the same as the language of Ireland; there is little evidence of much divergence before the 13th century. Even up to the 18th century the bards adhered to the strict literary standards of Old Irish.

Gaelic culture flourished in the Highlands until the Jacobite rebellions of the 18th century. After the Battle of Culloden in 1746 many Gaelic speakers were forced from their ancestral lands, and the use of Gaelic was discouraged in favour of English. Although still studied at academic level, the spoken language declined, being regarded as little more than a mere 'peasant' language of no modern significance.

It was only in the 1970s that Gaelic began to make a comeback with a new generation of young enthusiasts who were determined that it should not be allowed to die. After two centuries of decline, the language is now being encouraged through financial help from government agencies and the EU. Gaelic education is flourishing from playgroups to tertiary levels, flowing on into the fields of music, literature, cultural events and broadcasting; now people from all over Scotland, and even worldwide, are beginning to appreciate their Gaelic heritage.

poem 'Climbing Suilven' is a superb description of what it feels like to climb a mountain, its images instantly recognisable to any hill walker. *Selected Poems* is probably the best collection of his work.

The hugely popular writer Neil Munro (1863–1930), born in Inverarary (in Argyll), is responsible for some of the best-loved books about the region, including the humorous *Tales of Para Handy,* featuring a rascally skipper and his boat the *Vital Spark,* which have been repeatedly dramatised on television, radio and the stage.

Caithness writer Neil M Gunn (1891–1973), born in Dunbeath, is celebrated as the best Scottish novelist of the 20th century, penning such evocative tales as *Morning Tide* and *The Silver Darlings,* a book about the herring industry. Sir Compton MacKenzie (1883–1972) spent much of his life on the island of Barra, where he is buried; his famous comedy *Whisky Galore* (made into a successful film in 1949) is based on the true story of islanders rescuing a cargo of whisky from the wreck of a ship off the island of Eriskay.

Essential Highland Novels

The Silver Darlings (Neil M Gunn; 1941)

Whisky Galore (Compton MacKenzie; 1947)

Consider the Lilies (Iain Crichton Smith; 1968)

Greenvoe (George Mackay Brown; 1972)

His Bloody Project (Graeme Macrae Burnet; 2016)

Scott & Stevenson

Sir Walter Scott (1771–1832) was Scotland's greatest and most prolific novelist. Although he was the son of an Edinburgh lawyer, and very much a Lowlander, Scott was a student of Highland history and legend, and many of his works are set north of the Highland line.

Scott's early works were rhyming ballads, such as 'The Lady of the Lake' (set in the Trossachs, about a medieval war between Highland clans and Lowland nobles) and 'The Lord of the Isles' (about Robert the Bruce), both of which created a surge of tourism to their Highland settings.

His first historical novel – Scott effectively invented the genre – was *Waverley,* which recounted the adventures of Edward Waverley, a young English soldier who is sent north in 1745 to fight with the Hanoverian

Top Inveraray Castle (p63)

Bottom Gaelic cross, Fort William (p159)

Pipe band performing at a Highland Games (p280)

army against the Jacobites. It was published anonymously (in those days novels were considered a poor relation to poetry, and Scott wanted to be taken seriously as a poet), but was so successful that he could not refuse the demand for more. The so-called Waverley novels included more on a Highland theme, including *Rob Roy,* about the notorious MacGregor outlaw, and *The Pirate,* based on the life of John Gow, an Orkney adventurer.

Along with Scott, Robert Louis Stevenson (1850–94) ranks among Scotland's best-known novelists. Born in Edinburgh into a family of famous lighthouse engineers, Stevenson is known and loved around the world for his classic tales, including *Kidnapped,* set in the Highlands in the aftermath of Culloden, and *The Master of Ballantrae,* about a family torn in two by the Jacobite wars.

Music & Dance

The website www. scottish-folk-music.com is a useful source for listings of folk sessions, gigs, venues and bands, as well as providing the lyrics for popular Scottish folk songs.

Music and dance have been at the centre of Highland life for centuries – the *ceilidh* (a traditional gathering, or party) revolves around live folk music and dancing.

Traditional Music

The Highlands and islands have always had a strong folk tradition, and in the 1960s the roots revival provided a forum for the Gaelic songs of Cathy-Ann MacPhee from Barra and Margaret Stewart from Lewis. Initially, most of the performers came from outside the region, but the arrival of the Boys of the Lough, headed by Shetland fiddler Aly Bain, introduced the world to authentic Highland folk music. Aly was probably the most influential folk musician Scotland has seen. He brought pipes, concertina, mandolins and other traditional instruments to a wide audience, recording with performers such as Tom Anderson and Phil Cunningham (see www.philandaly.com). Other much-admired fiddlers include Scott Skinner, Willie Hunter and Catriona MacDonald, who studied under the same master fiddler as Aly Bain.

The traditional melodies of the Highlands and islands reached a broader audience through the Gaelic compositions of Skye band Runrig, who transformed *ceilidh* music into stadium rock in the two decades following their formation in 1973. Other powerful ambassadors for Gaelic music included Capercaillie, Ossian and the Battlefield Band, which have all seen plenty of musicians from the Highlands and islands in their line-ups.

In recent years there has been a revival in traditional music, often adapted and updated for the modern age. Bands such as Shooglenifty blend Scottish folk music with anything from indie rock to electronica, producing a hybrid that has been called 'acid croft'.

The Scots folk songs that you will often hear sung in pubs and at *ceilidhs* draw on Scotland's rich history. A huge number of them relate to the Jacobite rebellions in the 18th century and, in particular, to Bonnie Prince Charlie – 'Hey Johnnie Cope', the 'Skye Boat Song' and 'Will Ye No Come Back Again', for example – while others relate to themes of working the land, emigration and the Highland Clearances.

Bagpipes

Although no piece of film footage about Scotland is complete without the drone of the pipes, this curious instrument actually originated in ancient Egypt and was brought to Scotland by the Romans.

The bagpipe consists of a leather bag held under the arm, kept inflated by blowing through the blowstick; the piper forces air through the pipes by squeezing the bag with the forearm. Three of the pipes, known as drones, play a constant note (one bass, two tenor) in the background. The fourth pipe, the chanter, plays the melody.

In 1747 the playing of the pipes was banned – under pain of death – by the British government as part of a scheme to suppress Highland culture after the Jacobite uprising of 1745, but the pipes were revived when Highland regiments were drafted into the British army towards the end of the 18th century. Highland soldiers were traditionally accompanied into battle by the skirl of the pipes, and the Scottish Highland bagpipe is unique in being the only musical instrument ever to be classified as a weapon.

Queen Victoria did much to repopularise the bagpipes with her patronage of all things Scottish. When staying at Balmoral she liked to be wakened by a piper playing outside her window. Competitive piping is still a popular pastime in the Highlands and islands – the sound of duelling bagpipes is quite an experience.

Scotland's most famous instrument has been reinvented by bands such as the Red Hot Chilli Pipers (www.redhotchillipipers.co.uk), who use pipes, drums, guitars and keyboards to create rock versions of traditional tunes that have been christened (tongue firmly in cheek) as 'Jock 'n' Roll'. They feature regularly at festivals throughout the country.

A *ceilidh* is an evening of traditional Scottish entertainment including music, song and dance. To find one, check the village noticeboard, or just ask at the local pub; visitors are always welcome.

Highland Dancing

Another homespun art form that the Scots have made their own is dance. The most famous routines are the formal Highland Dances performed at Highland games, which date back to the foundation of Scotland. There are four official dance disciplines: the Sword Dance, Seann Triubhas, the Reel of Tulloch and the Highland fling.

The Sword Dance *(gillie callum)* dates back to the legend that Malcolm Canmore celebrated his victory over a Macbeth chieftain by dancing over a crucifix made from his own claymore (sword) and the sword of his rival. The Seann Triubhas is attributed to the desire of Highlanders to shake off the hated *triubhas* (trousers) they were forced to wear instead of kilts after the 1745 rebellion.

A chilly congregation who danced to keep warm are credited with inventing the Reel of Tulloch, while the famous Highland fling was invented in the 1790s to mimic the movements of a stag; clansmen reputedly danced the steps on their targes (leather-covered shields).

Sport

Many Scots are sports-mad and follow football or rugby with a fierce dedication, identifying closely with local teams and individuals. The most popular games are football (soccer), rugby union, shinty, curling and golf, the last two of which the Scots claim to have invented.

Highland Games

According to oral tradition, Highland games date back to the kingdom of Dalriada and were essentially war games, allowing clan leaders to select their most skilled warriors for battle. In the 11th century King Malcolm Canmore is believed to have staged a royal contest to find the fastest runners in the kingdom to carry his messages across the Highlands.

Historical evidence for a tradition of annual clan games is patchy but the games certainly took off in the 19th century with the creation of the first Highland Societies. In 1848 Queen Victoria patronised the Braemar Highland Games and the tradition was incorporated into Highland legend.

Most of the activities in the games are based on equipment readily available to the average Highlander in ages past. The hammer throw was derived from the traditional mell used to drive fence-posts, while steelyard weights were thrown for distance and height. The caber (from the Gaelic for 'tree') was simply a tree trunk, and rounded river stones were used for weightlifting and putting the stone.

These days the traditional sporting events are accompanied by piping and dancing competitions, and attract locals and tourists alike. Games are held all over Scotland from May to September, with the biggest

THE TARTAN

This distinctive checked pattern, traditionally associated with the kilt, has become the definitive symbol of Scotland and the Highlands, inspiring skirts, scarves, blankets, ties, key-fobs and a thousand other souvenirs. The pattern is thought to date back to at least the Roman period, though it has become romantically associated with the Gaels, who arrived from Ireland in the 6th century. What is certain is that a tartan plaid had become the standard uniform of Highlanders by the start of the 18th century. Following the Battle of Culloden in 1746, the Disarming Act banned the wearing of Highland dress in an attempt to undermine the solidarity of the clans.

However, the ban was enforced only in the Highlands (it was repealed in 1782) and did not apply to the armed services, which in the second half of the 18th century included a large number of Highland regiments. The weaver William Wilson established a factory at Bannockburn to supply the army with tartan, experimenting with a wide range of new designs and colours. In 1778 the London Highland Society requested that clan chiefs submit a piece of their clan tartan to preserve the traditional designs, but most of the tartans recorded by the society were actually designed and woven by the Wilsons.

In the 19th century, tartan got caught up in the cult of so-called 'Balmorality' – Queen Victoria's patronage of Scottish culture – and many of the setts (tartan patterns) now associated with particular clans were created out of thin air by a pair of brothers known as the Sobieski Stuarts, who claimed descent from Bonnie Prince Charlie. The brothers' setts were based on a 'lost' document dating back to the 15th century and they published a hugely successful book of invented tartans, *The Costume of the Clans,* which became established as the genuine tartans of many Highland clans before their elaborate fraud was exposed. Today every clan, and indeed every football team, has one or more distinctive tartans, though few date back more than 150 years.

Highland dancing (p279)

HIGHLAND CULTURE SPORT

events staged at Dunoon, Oban and Braemar. You can find dates and details of Highland games at the Scottish Highland Games Association website (www.shga.co.uk).

Shinty

Shinty (*camanachd* in Gaelic) is a fast and physical ball-and-stick sport similar to Ireland's hurling, with more than a little resemblance to clan warfare. It's an indigenous Scottish game played mainly in the Highlands, and the most prized trophy is the Camanachd Cup. The cup final, held in September, is a great Gaelic get-together. The sport has long been dominated by a rivalry between the Kingussie and Newtonmore teams that stretches back more than a century, though Fort William and Kyles Athletic have come to the fore in recent years. The venue for the final is announced annually in February (see www.shinty.com).

Each year in October there's an international match between Scotland and Ireland, played under composite shinty/hurling rules, and held alternately in Ireland and Scotland.

Curling

Curling, a winter sport that involves propelling a granite stone weighing 42lb (19kg) along the ice towards a target, was probably invented in Scotland in medieval times. Though traditionally Scottish, it was very much a minority sport until it got an enormous publicity boost when the British women's team (all Scots) won the gold medal in the 2002 Winter Olympics, and a bronze in 2014.

Scottish teams took gold in the men's world championship in 2006 and 2009; in the women's world championship in 2013; and in the mixed world championship in 2017. For more information, see www.scottish curling.org.

Landscapes & Wildlife

Scotland's wildlife is one of its big attractions, and the best way to see it is to get out there: pull on the boots, sling on the binoculars, go quietly and see what you can spot. Many species that have disappeared from or are rare in the rest of Britain survive here, from the emblematic osprey and white-tailed eagle, to otter and red deer.

Geography & Geology

Scotland covers 30,414 sq miles, about half the size of England. It can be divided into three areas: Southern Uplands, Central Lowlands, and the Highlands and islands.

Above Red deer stag

South of a line joining Dunbar to Girvan lie the Southern Uplands, a range of rounded, heathery hills bordering England. The Central Lowlands comprise a broad slice from Edinburgh and Dundee in the east to Glasgow and Ayr in the west, home to the industrial belt and 80% of Scotland's population.

The Highland Boundary Fault, a geological feature, runs northeast from Helensburgh (west of Glasgow) to Stonehaven (south of Aberdeen) on the east coast. North of it lie the Highlands and islands, a mountainous area that makes up roughly two-thirds of the country. However, the low-lying, fertile agricultural belt that runs along the northeast coast from Aberdeen to Fraserburgh is usually lumped together, geographically and culturally, with the Lowlands.

The Highland hills – most of their summits reach the 900m to 1000m mark – were deeply dissected by glaciers during the last ice age, creating a series of deep, U-shaped valleys. The long, narrow sea lochs that today are such a feature of Highland scenery are, like Norway's fjords, glacial valleys that have been flooded by rising sea levels. Despite their pristine beauty, the wild, empty landscapes of the western and northern Highlands are artificial wilderness. Before the Highland Clearances many of these empty corners of Scotland supported sizeable rural populations.

Of Scotland's 790 islands, 94 are inhabited. To the west are the Inner Hebrides (from Islay to Skye) and the Outer Hebrides (Barra to Lewis). To the north are two other island groups, Orkney and Shetland, the northernmost outposts of the British Isles.

Moor & Mountain

Most of the Highland landscape consists of uncultivated heather moorland, peat bog and steep rocky mountains. Heather, whose tiny pink and purple flowers emerge on moor and mountain in August, is one of the symbols of Scotland, and also an excellent food source for the red grouse, an important game bird.

Peat bog – an endangered environment – covers large areas of the Highlands and islands, most notably in the Flow Country of Caithness and Sutherland, where it provides a haven for unusual plant species, such as the insect-eating sundew, and a nesting ground for birds that include golden plover, hen harrier and red-throated diver.

Britain's largest land animal, the red deer, is present in large numbers, managed as a sporting asset for hunting estates. You're bound to see them if you spend any time in the Highlands; in winter especially, harsh weather will force them down into the glens to crop the roadside verges.

On the high mountain tops, and especially in the subarctic climate of the Cairngorm plateau, alpine plants thrive alongside bird species such as the snow bunting and the ptarmigan (a type of grouse). Seldom seen below 700m, the ptarmigan has feathered feet and is the only British bird that plays the Arctic trick of changing its plumage from mottled brown in summer to dazzling white in winter, the better to blend in with the snowfields. Another mountain resident that displays this feature is the blue mountain hare.

Perhaps the most majestic wildlife sight on moor and mountain is the golden eagle, which uses its 2m wingspan to soar on rising thermals. Almost all of the 400 or so pairs known to nest in the UK are to be found in the Scottish Highlands and islands, preferring remote glens and open moorland well away from human habitation.

The grassland habitat of the once-common corncrake (a summer visitor from Africa) was almost completely wiped out by modern farming methods, but it still breeds in pockets of sedge and iris in the Hebrides, including nature reserves in Islay, Coll and the Uists. Listen for their distinctive *krek-krek-krek* call – like a thumbnail drawn along the teeth of a comb.

West Highland Way (p104)

Forest & Woodland

Although much of the Highlands was originally covered by the Caledonian forest – vast swathes of Scots pine in the inland glens, with coastal woods of oak, silver birch, alder and rowan – deforestation has reduced this to a few small pockets of native woodland; barely 1% remains. Important remnants of native Scots pine can be found at Rothiemurchus, Glen Affric and Beinn Eighe.

Managed regeneration forests are slowly covering more of the landscape, especially in the Highlands. Some 5000 sq miles (1.3 million hectares) of tree cover – 17% of the land area – now exists: not a huge figure, but an improvement on what it was (a mere 5% in 1900). About a third of this is controlled by the government's Forestry Commission, which, as well as conducting managed logging, dedicates large areas to sustainable recreational use. The vast majority of this tree cover is coniferous, and there's a plan to increase it to 25% of land area by 2050.

Scotland's woods are home to 75% of Britain's red squirrel population; they've been pushed out in most of the rest of the country by the domi-

Seventeen per cent of Scotland is forested, compared with England's 7%, Finland's 74% and a worldwide average of 30%.

BRINGING BACK LOST SPECIES

The European beaver was reintroduced to Knapdale, Argyllshire, in 2009 for a five-year trial period, a move opposed by some campaigners who felt beavers might negatively impact on forests or water quality. After a broadly successful trial, the Scottish government decided in 2016 that the project should continue.

But the mildly controversial beaver project pales beside events at the Alladale Wilderness Reserve (p178) in Sutherland, where the owner has already shipped in elk (moose), and plans to reintroduce wolves and bears.

Beinn Eighe Mountain Trail (p199)

nant greys, introduced from North America. The greys often carry a virus that's lethal to the reds, so measures are in place to try to prevent their further encroachment.

Other forest mammals that were slaughtered to the point of extermination in the 19th century include pine martens, polecats and wildcats. Populations of these are small and remote, but are slowly recovering thanks to their protected status and greater awareness.

The capercaillie, a black, turkeylike member of the grouse family, and the largest native British bird, was hunted to extinction in 1785 – then reintroduced from Sweden in 1837. Though still rare, it still inhabits forests of native Scots pine, notably in Rothiemurchus.

River & Loch

It rains a lot in Scotland – some parts of the western Highlands get over 4500mm of rain a year, making it the wettest place in Europe – so it's not surprising there's plenty of water about. Around 90% by volume of Britain's fresh water is in Scotland; Loch Ness alone contains more than twice the volume of water in all of the lakes in England and Wales combined.

The most iconic of Scottish fish is the Atlantic salmon, which fights its way up Highland rivers to spawn. Salmon arrive in different rivers at different times of year between March and October, and are usually seen leaping waterfalls; good places to spot them include Pitlochry fish ladder and the Falls of Shin.

The majestic osprey (a fish-eating bird of prey absent from Scotland for most of the 20th century) nests in Scotland from mid-March through to September, after migrating from West Africa. There are around 200 breeding pairs and you can see nesting sites throughout the country, notably at Loch Garten in the Cairngorms and Loch of the Lowes near Dunkeld.

Although the thistle is commonly used as a Scottish emblem, the national flower is the Scottish bluebell (*Campanula rotundifolia;* known in England as the harebell), which carpets the floor of native woodlands in spring. Loch Lomond is a good place to see them.

One of the best-loved pieces of Scottish wildlife writing is *Ring of Bright Water*, by Gavin Maxwell, in which the author describes life on the remote Glenelg peninsula with his pet otters in the 1960s.

Coast & Islands

The waters off Scotland's north and west coasts are rich in marine mammals. Harbour porpoises are the most common sighting, though common and bottle-nosed dolphins are also seen. Minke whales are regular summer visitors, and orcas (killer whales) are regularly sighted around Shetland and Orkney.

Seals are widespread. Both the Atlantic grey seal (identified by its Roman nose) and the common seal (with a face shaped more like a dog's) are easily spotted along the coasts, especially in the islands.

Otters are widespread in the Highlands and islands. They frequent both fresh and salt water, but are easiest to spot along the coast, where they time their foraging to coincide with an ebbing tide (river otters tend to be nocturnal). The best places to spot them are in the north and west, especially in Orkney, Shetland, Skye and the Outer Hebrides. The piers at Kyle of Lochalsh and Portree are otter 'hot spots', as the animals have learned to scavenge from fishing boats.

From May to August the sea cliffs of Orkney and Shetland and the north and west coasts of Scotland support some of the largest breeding colonies of seabirds in Europe, including 60% of the world's population of gannets and great skuas. Twenty-one of the British Isles' 24 breeding seabird species can be seen in Shetland, nesting in huge colonies: being entertained by the clownish antics of the puffins is a highlight for many visitors.

National Parks & Nature Reserves

Scotland has two national parks – Loch Lomond & the Trossachs National Park and the Cairngorms National Park. But national parks are only part of the story. There's a huge range of protected areas with a bewildering array of 25 distinct classifications. Forty-three National Nature Reserves (www.nnr.scot) span the country, and there are also marine areas under various levels of protection.

News on endangered Scottish birds has generally been positive in the last couple of decades. The Royal Society for the Protection of Birds (www.rspb.org.uk) is active here, with 34 reserves in the Highlands and islands, and has overseen several success stories, including the reintroduction of the white-tailed eagle and the red kite.

Environmental Issues

Scotland's abundance of wind and water means the government hasn't had to look far for sources of renewable energy. The grand plan is to generate half of the country's energy needs from renewable sources by 2020,

JOURNEY OF THE SALMON

One of Scotland's most thrilling sights is the salmon's leap up a fast-flowing cascade, resolutely returning to the river of its birth several years before. The salmon's life begins in early spring, hatching in the gravel bed of a stream in some Scottish glen. Called 'fry' at this stage and barely an inch long, they stay for a couple of years, growing through the 'parr' stage to become 'smolt' when they turn silver, swim downstream and head out to sea.

Their destination could be anywhere in the North Atlantic, from the Faeroes to southern Greenland, but eventually, after one to three winters at sea, they return home to reproduce. Arriving all through the year, but most commonly in late spring and autumn, they enter the river of their birth (identified by its scent) and run up to the headwaters to spawn in November and December. Having spawned, most of the adult fish die and the cycle begins anew.

Top Dunnet Head Lighthouse (p183)

Bottom White-tailed sea eagle

Butterfish

and things look to be on track. Scotland has been a European leader in the development of wind technology; wind farms now dot the hills and firths (estuaries), and the near-constant breeze in some areas means record-breaking output from some turbines.

The problem is that although everyone agrees that wind power is clean and economical, there's a powerful Nimby (not in my back yard) element who don't want the windmills spoiling their view. And it's not just the whirring blades, of course. A remote Highland wind farm is one thing, but the power lines trailing all the way down to the south have a significant visual and environmental impact.

Scotland accounts for one-third of the British mainland's surface area, but it has a massive 80% of Britain's coastline and only 10% of its population.

One of Scotland's major goals over the last decade or so has been to halt a worrying decline in biodiversity on land, in the air and in the sea. You can see progress reports on the Scottish Natural Heritage website (www.nature.scot), but a huge threat to existing species is, of course, climate change. A rise of a few degrees across the north would leave plenty of mountain plants and creatures with no place to go; it's already been speculated that the steady decline in Scotland's seabird population since the early '90s is partly caused by a temperature-induced decrease in certain plankton species.

The main cause of the worrying level of some fish stocks is clear: we've eaten them all. In 2010 the Marine (Scotland) Act was passed – it's a compromise solution that tries to both protect vulnerable marine areas and stocks and sustain the flagging fishing industry. But it may well be too little, too late.

Food & Drink

Traditional Scottish cookery is all about basic comfort food: solid, nourishing fare, often high in fat, that would keep you warm on a winter's day spent in the fields or out fishing. But a new culinary style known as Modern Scottish has emerged over the last two decades. Scotland's traditional drinks have also found a new lease of life in recent years, with single malts being marketed like fine wines, and a new breed of microbreweries springing up all over the country.

Scottish Specialities

Scotland is famous for top-quality produce such as smoked salmon and Aberdeen Angus beef, but there's also a range of lesser known specialities to try out.

Above Traditional Scottish breakfast, including haggis

Haggis

Scotland's national dish is often ridiculed because of its ingredients, which admittedly don't sound promising – the finely chopped lungs, heart and liver of a sheep, mixed with oatmeal and onion and stuffed into a sheep's stomach bag. However, it actually tastes surprisingly good.

Haggis should be served with champit tatties and bashed neeps (mashed potatoes and turnips), with a generous dollop of butter and a good sprinkling of black pepper.

Although it's eaten year-round, haggis is central to the celebrations of 25 January, which honour Scotland's national poet, Robert Burns. Scots worldwide unite on Burns Night to revel in their Scottishness. A piper announces the arrival of the haggis and Burns' poem *Address to a Haggis* is recited to this 'Great chieftan o' the puddin-race'. The bulging haggis is then lanced with a dirk (dagger) to reveal the steaming offal within: 'warm, reekin, rich'.

Vegetarians (and quite a few carnivores, no doubt) will be relieved to know that veggie haggis is available in some restaurants.

A Caledonian Feast, by Annette Hope, is a fascinating and readable history of Scottish cuisine, providing a wealth of historical and sociological background.

The Full Scottish

Surprisingly few Scots eat porridge for breakfast – these days a cappuccino and a croissant is just as likely – and even fewer eat it in the traditional way: with salt to taste, but no sugar. The breakfast offered in a B&B or hotel usually consists of fruit juice and cereal or muesli, followed by a choice of bacon, sausage, black pudding (a type of sausage made from dried blood), grilled tomato, mushrooms and a fried egg or two. If you're lucky, there'll be tattie scones (fried potato bread) as well.

Fish for breakfast may sound strange, but was not unusual in crofting (smallholding) and fishing communities, where seafood was a staple; many hotels still offer grilled kippers (smoked herrings) for breakfast, or smoked haddock poached in milk and served with a poached egg – delicious with lots of buttered toast.

It has been illegal to import haggis into the USA since 1971, because the US government declared that sheep lungs are unfit for human consumption.

Traditional Soups

Scotch broth, made with mutton stock, barley, lentils and peas, is nutritious and tasty, while cock-a-leekie is a hearty soup made with chicken and leeks. Warming vegetable soups include leek and potato soup, and lentil soup (vegetarians beware: it's traditionally made using ham stock).

Seafood soups include the delicious Cullen skink, made with smoked haddock, potato, onion and milk, and *partan bree* (crab soup).

Surf & Turf

Steak eaters will enjoy a thick fillet of world-famous Aberdeen Angus beef, and beef from Highland cattle is also much sought after. Venison from red deer is leaner and appears on many menus. Both may be served with a wine-based or creamy whisky sauce. And of course there's haggis, Scotland's much-maligned national dish.

Scottish salmon is famous worldwide, but there's a big difference between the now-ubiquitous farmed salmon (even the certified organic

---

EATING PRICE RANGES

The following price ranges refer to an average main course. Note, though, that lunch mains are often cheaper than dinner mains, and many places offer an 'early bird' special with lower prices (usually available between 5pm and 7pm).

£ less than £10

££ £10–£20

£££ more than £20

Haggis served with neeps and tatties

farmed salmon) and the leaner, tastier and considerably more expensive wild fish. Also, there are concerns over the environmental impact of salmon farms on the marine environment.

Smoked salmon is traditionally dressed with a squeeze of lemon juice and eaten with fresh brown bread and butter. Trout, the salmon's smaller cousin – whether wild, rod-caught brown trout or farmed rainbow trout – is delicious fried in oatmeal.

As an alternative to kippers you may be offered Arbroath smokies (lightly smoked fresh haddock), traditionally eaten cold. Herring fillets fried in oatmeal are good, if you don't mind picking out a few bones. Mackerel pâté and smoked or peppered mackerel (both served cold) are also popular.

Juicy langoustines (also known as Dublin Bay prawns), crabs, lobsters, oysters, mussels and scallops are also widely available.

Smoked Fish

Scotland is famous for its smoked salmon, but there are many other varieties of smoked fish – plus smoked meats and cheeses – to enjoy. Smoking food to preserve it is an ancient art that has recently undergone a revival, but this time it's more about flavour than preservation.

There are two parts to the process: first the cure, which involves covering the fish in a mixture of salt and molasses sugar, or soaking it in brine; and then the smoke, which can be either cold smoking (at less than 34°C), which results in a raw product, or hot smoking (at more than 60°C), which cooks it. Cold-smoked products include traditional smoked salmon and kippers. Hot-smoked products include *bradan rost* ('flaky' smoked salmon) and Arbroath smokies (haddock).

Kippers (smoked herring) were invented in Northumberland, in northern England, in the mid-19th century, but Scotland soon picked up the technique, and both Loch Fyne and Mallaig were famous for their kippers.

Clootie dumpling is a rich pudding made with currants, raisins and other dried fruits; it is wrapped in a linen cloth (or *cloot*, in old Scots) and steamed. It can be served freshly cooked with custard, or sliced cold the day after and fried in butter.

Haddock

There are dozens of modern smokehouses scattered all over Scotland, many of which offer a mail-order service as well as an on-site shop. We recommend the following:

➡ Inverawe Smokehouse & Fishery (p103) Delicate smoked salmon, plump juicy kippers.

➡ Hebridean Smokehouse (p225) Peat-smoked salmon and sea trout.

➡ Isle of Ewe Smokehouse (p199) Delicious hot- and cold-smoked salmon.

➡ Skipness Smokehouse (p67) Famous for its flaky hot-smoked salmon.

Best Seafood Restaurants

....

Café Fish (Tobermory)

....

Waterfront Fishouse Restaurant (Oban)

....

Lochleven Seafood Cafe (Kinlochleven)

....

Badachro Inn (Badachro)

....

Summer Isles Hotel (Achiltibuie)

....

Captain's Galley (Scrabster)

....

Loch Bay (Stein, Skye)

Vegetarians & Vegans

Scotland has the same proportion of vegetarians as the rest of the UK – around 8% to 10% of the population. Vegetarianism has moved away from the hippie-student image of a few decades ago and is now firmly in the mainstream. Even the most remote Highland pub usually has at least one vegetarian dish on the menu, and there are many dedicated vegetarian restaurants in towns and cities. If you get stuck, there's almost always an Italian or Indian restaurant where you can get meat-free pizza, pasta or curry. Vegans, though, may find their options a bit limited outside of Edinburgh and Glasgow.

Cookery Courses

More than a dozen places in Scotland offer courses in Scottish cookery. Two of the most famous:

Kinloch Lodge Hotel (☎01471-833333; www.kinloch-lodge.co.uk; Kinloch, Sleat) Courses in Scottish cookery and demonstrations using fresh, seasonal Scottish produce by Lady Claire Macdonald, author of *Scottish Highland Hospitality* and *Celebrations*. Fees range from £25 per person for a 45-minute express class, to £149 for a full-day workshop including breakfast and lunch.

Nick Nairn Cook School (☏01877-389900; www.nicknairncookschool.
com; 15 Back Wynd; 1-day course per person £149) One-day courses in modern
Scottish cooking at the school owned by Scotland's top TV chef, Nick Nairn, author
of *Wild Harvest* and *Island Harvest*.

Beer

Scottish breweries produce a wide range of beers. The market is dominated by multinational brewers such as Scottish & Newcastle, but
smaller local breweries generally create tastier brews, some of them very
strong. The aptly named Skull Splitter from Orkney is a good example, at
8.5% alcohol by volume.

Many Scottish beers use old-fashioned shilling categories to indicate
strength (the number of shillings was originally the price per barrel; the
stronger the beer, the higher the price). The usual range is from 60 to 80
shillings (written 80/-). You'll also see IPA, which stands for India Pale Ale,
a strong, hoppy beer first brewed in the early 19th century for export to
India (the extra alcohol meant that it kept better on the long sea voyage).

Draught beer is served in pints (usually costing from £2.60 to £4) or
half-pints; alcoholic content generally ranges from 3% to 6%. What the
English call bitter, Scots call heavy, or export.

Scottish Craft Beers

The increasing popularity of real ales and a backlash against the bland
conformity of globalised multinational brewing conglomerates has seen
a huge rise in the number of specialist brewers and microbreweries
springing up all over Scotland. They take pride in using only natural
ingredients, and many try to revive ancient recipes, such as heather- and
seaweed-flavoured ales.

The website
http://glasgow
camra.org.uk/
breweries.php
has a compre-
hensive list of
Scottish brew-
eries, both large
and small.

FOOD & DRINK BEER

OAT CUISINE

'Oats: a grain, which in England is generally given to horses, but in Scotland appears to support the people.' From *A Dictionary of the English Language* by Samuel Johnson (1709–84).

The most distinctive feature of traditional Scottish cookery is the abundant use of oatmeal. Oats grow well in the cool, wet climate of Scotland and have been cultivated here
for at least 2000 years. Up to the 19th century, oatmeal was the main source of calories
for the rural Scottish population. The crofter in his field, the cattle drover on the road to
market, the soldier on the march – all would carry with them a bag of meal that could be
mixed with water and baked on a girdle (a flat metal plate) or on hot stones beside a fire.

Long despised as an inferior foodstuff (see Johnson's sneering description above),
oatmeal is enjoying a return to popularity as research has proved it to be highly nutritious
(high in iron, calcium and B vitamins) and healthy (rich in soluble fibre, which helps to
reduce cholesterol).

The best-known Scottish oatmeal dish is, of course, porridge, which is simply rolled
oatmeal boiled with water. A lot of nonsense has been written about porridge and
whether it should be eaten with salt or with sugar. It should be eaten however you like it –
as a child in the 1850s, author Robert Louis Stevenson had his with golden syrup.

Oatcakes are another traditional dish that you'll certainly come across during a visit to
Scotland, usually as an accompaniment to cheese at the end of a meal. A mealie pudding
is a sausage-skin stuffed with oatmeal and onion and boiled for an hour or so. Add blood
to the mixture and you have a black pudding.

Skirlie is chopped onions and oatmeal fried in beef dripping and seasoned with salt
and pepper; it's usually served as a side dish. Trout and herring can be dipped in oatmeal
before frying, and oats can be added to soups and stews as a thickening agent. It's even
used in desserts: toasted oatmeal is a vital flavouring in cranachan, a delicious mixture of
whipped cream, whisky and raspberries.

Top Skull Splitter beer from Orkney Brewery (p242)

Bottom Macallan Distillery (p296)

These beers are sold in pubs, off-licences and delicatessens. Here are a few of our favourites to look out for:

➡ Black Isle Brewery (p129) Has a range of organic beers.

➡ Cairngorm Brewery (p136) Creator of multi-award-winning Trade Winds ale.

➡ Colonsay Brewery (p80) Produces lager, 80/- and IPA.

➡ **Islay Ales** (☏01496-810014; www.islayales.co.uk; Islay House Square, Bridgend; ◷10.30am-5pm Mon-Sat Apr-Sep, to 4pm Oct-Mar) Refreshing and citrusy Saligo Ale.

➡ Isle of Skye Brewery (p215) Distinctive Hebridean Gold ale, brewed with porridge oats.

➡ Orkney Brewery (p242) Famous for its rich, chocolatey Dark Island ale, and the dangerously strong Skull Splitter.

➡ Isle of Arran Brewery (p82) Produces light and hoppy Arran Blonde, and the highly addictive Arran Dark.

➡ Fyne Ales (p64) Great range of craft beers and a lovely bar-cafe.

The most expensive bottle of whisky ever sold? A Lalique crystal decanter holding 6L of a unique blend of Macallan single malts sold for $628,205 at auction in Hong Kong in 2014...

FOOD & DRINK WHISKY

Whisky

Scotch whisky (always spelt without an 'e' – 'whiskey' is Irish or American) is Scotland's best-known product and biggest export. The spirit has been distilled in Scotland at least since the 15th century.

As well as whiskies, there are whisky-based liqueurs, such as Drambuie. If you must mix your whisky with anything other than water, try a whisky-mac (whisky with ginger wine). After a long walk in the rain there's nothing better to put a warm glow in your belly.

At a bar, older Scots may order a 'half' or 'nip' of whisky as a chaser to a pint or half-pint of beer: a 'hauf and a hauf'. (Only tourists ask for 'Scotch' – what else would you be served in Scotland?) The standard measure in pubs is either 25mL or 35mL.

HOW TO BE A MALT WHISKY EXPERT

'Love makes the world go round? Not at all! Whisky makes it go round twice as fast.' From *Whisky Galore* by Compton MacKenzie (1883–1972).

Whisky-tasting today is almost as popular as wine-tasting was in the yuppie heyday of the late 1980s. Being able to tell your Ardbeg from your Edradour is de rigueur among the whisky-nosing set, so here are some pointers to help you impress your friends.

What's the difference between malt and grain whiskies? Malts are distilled from malted barley – that is, barley that has been soaked in water, then allowed to germinate for around 10 days until the starch has turned into sugar – while grain whiskies are distilled from other cereals, usually wheat, corn or unmalted barley.

So what is a single malt? A single malt is a whisky that has been distilled from malted barley and is the product of a single distillery. A pure (vatted) malt is a mixture of single malts from several distilleries, and a blended whisky is a mixture of various grain whiskies (about 60%) and malt whiskies (about 40%) from many different distilleries.

Why are single malts more desirable than blends? A single malt, like a fine wine's terroir, somehow captures the essence of the place where it was made and matured – a combination of the water, the barley, the peat smoke, the oak barrels in which it was aged, and (in the case of certain coastal distilleries) the sea air and salt spray. Each distillation varies from the one before, like different vintages from the same vineyard.

How should a single malt be drunk? Either neat, or preferably with a little water added. To appreciate the aroma and flavour to the utmost, a measure of malt whisky should be cut (diluted) with one-third to two-thirds as much spring water (bottled, still spring water will do). Ice, tap water and – heaven forbid – mixers are for philistines. Would you add lemonade or ice to a glass of Chablis?

Whiskies from Talisker Distillery (p212)

Top 10 Single Malts – Our Choice

After a great deal of diligent research (and not a few sore heads), Lonely Planet's various Scotland authors have selected their 10 favourite single malts from across the country:

Ardbeg (Islay) The 10-year-old from this noble Islay distillery is a byword for excellence. Peaty but well balanced. Hits the spot after a hill walk.

Bowmore (Islay) Smoke, peat and salty sea air – a classic Islay malt. One of the few distilleries that still malts its own barley.

Bruichladdich (Islay) A visitor-friendly distillery with a quirky, innovative approach – famous for very peaty special releases such as Moine Mhor.

Glendronach (Speyside) Only sherry casks are used here, so the creamy, spicy result tastes like Grandma's Christmas trifle.

Highland Park (Island) Full and rounded, with heather, honey, malt and peat. Has an award-winning distillery tour.

Isle of Arran (Island) One of the newest of Scotland's distilleries, offering a light-ish, flavoursome malt with flowery, fruity notes.

Macallan (Speyside) The king of Speyside malts, with sherry and bourbon finishes. The distillery is set amid waving fields of Golden Promise barley.

Springbank (Campbeltown) Complex flavours – sherry, citrus, pear-drops, peat – with a salty tang. Entire production process from malting to bottling takes place on site.

Talisker (Island) Brooding, heavily peaty nose balanced by a satisfying sweetness from this lord of the isles. Great post-dinner dram.

The Balvenie (Speyside) Rich and honeyed, this Speysider is liquid gold for those with a sweet tooth.

Survival Guide

Directory A-Z

Accessible Travel

Travellers with disabilities will find Scotland a strange mix of accessibility and inaccessibility. Most new buildings are accessible to wheelchair users, so modern hotels and tourist attractions are fine. However, most B&Bs and guesthouses are in hard-to-adapt older buildings, which means that travellers with mobility requirements may pay more for accommodation. Things are constantly improving, though.

It's a similar story with public transport. Newer buses have steps that lower for easier access, as do trains, but it's wise to check before setting out. Tourist attractions usually reserve parking spaces near the entrance for drivers with disabilities.

Many places such as ticket offices and banks are fitted with hearing loops to assist the hearing-impaired; look for a posted symbol of a large ear.

An increasing number of tourist attractions have audioguides. Some have Braille guides or scented gardens for the visually impaired.

VisitScotland produces the guide *Accessible Scotland* for wheelchair-bound travellers; its website (www.visitscotland.com/accommodation) details accessible accommodation and many tourist offices have leaflets with accessibility details for their area.

Many regions have organisations that hire wheelchairs; contact the local tourist office for details. Many nature trails have been adapted for wheelchair use.

Download Lonely Planet's free Accessible Travel guides from http://lptravel.to/AccessibleTravel.

Tourism for All (☑0845 124 9971; www.tourismforall.org.uk) Publishes regional information guides for travellers with disabilities and can offer general advice.

Accommodation

For budget travel, the options are campsites, hostels and cheap B&Bs. Above this price level is a plethora of comfortable B&Bs, pubs and guesthouses (£35 to £60 per person per night). Midrange hotels are present in most places, while in the higher price bracket (£65-plus per person per night) there are some superb hotels, the most interesting being converted castles and country houses, or chic designer options in the larger towns.

If you're travelling solo, expect to pay a supplement in hotels and B&Bs, meaning you'll often be forking out over 75% of the price of a double for your single room.

Almost all B&Bs, guesthouses and hotels (and even some hostels) include breakfast – either full Scottish or a continental style – in the room price. If you don't want it, you may be able to negotiate a lower price, but this is rare.

Prices increase over the peak tourist season (June to September) and are at their highest in July and August. Outside of these months, and particularly in winter, special deals are often available at guesthouses and hotels.

Booking Services

VisitScotland tourist offices provide an accommodation booking service, which can be handy, but note that they can only book places that are registered with VisitScotland. There are many other fine accommodation options that, mostly due to the hefty registration fee, choose not to register with the tourist board.

BOOK YOUR STAY ONLINE

For more accommodation reviews by Lonely Planet authors, check out http://lonelyplanet.com/scotland/hotels/. You'll find independent reviews, as well as recommendations on the best places to stay. Best of all, you can book online.

VisitScotland (www.visitscotland.com/accommodation) Book accommodation approved by the official tourist board.

Scottish Cottages (www.scottish-cottages.co.uk) Booking service for self-catering cottages.

Lonely Planet (www.lonelyplanet.com/scotland/hotels) Recommendations and bookings.

B&Bs & Guesthouses

B&Bs (bed and breakfasts) are an institution in Scotland. At the bottom end you get a bedroom in a private house, a shared bathroom and the 'full Scottish' (juice, coffee or tea, cereal and cooked breakfast – bacon, eggs, sausage, baked beans and toast). Midrange B&Bs have en suites, TVs in each room and more variety (and healthier options) for breakfast. Almost all B&Bs provide hospitality trays (tea- and coffee-making facilities) in bedrooms. Common B&B options range from urban houses to pubs and farms.

Guesthouses, often large converted private houses, are an extension of the B&B concept. They are normally larger and less personal than B&Bs.

Bothies, Barns & Bunkhouses

Bothies are simple shelters, often in remote places; many are maintained by the Mountain Bothies Association (www.mountainbothies.org.uk). They're not locked, there's no charge – usually no toilet – and you can't book. Take your own cooking equipment, sleeping bag and mat. Users should stay one night only, and leave it as they find it.

Walkers can stay in camping barns – usually converted farm buildings – for around £5 to £10 per night. Take your own cooking equipment, sleeping bag and mat.

Bunkhouses, a grade or two up from camping barns, have stoves for heating and cooking and may supply utensils. They may have mattresses but you'll still

need a sleeping bag. There will be toilets but probably no showers. Most charge from £10 to £15.

The **Shetland Amenity Trust** (☎01595-694688; www.camping-bods.com; ⊙9am-5pm Mon-Thu, to 4pm Fri) has created a number of *bòds* – converted croft houses or fishing huts with bunks and washing and cooking facilities, but often no electricity or heating – many in remote and dramatic locations. Beds cost £10 to £12 but you will need to book through the trust in Lerwick, where you'll be given the keys.

Camping & Caravan Sites

Free 'wild' camping became a legal right under the Land Reform Bill. However, campers are obliged to camp on unenclosed land, in small numbers and away from buildings and roads.

Commercial camping grounds are often geared to caravans and vary widely in quality. There are numerous campsites across Scotland; VisitScotland (www.visitscotland.com/accommodation) lists a good selection of them on its website and on a free map, available at tourist offices.

Homestays & House Exchange

A convenient and increasingly popular holiday option is to join an international house-exchange organisation. You sign up for a year and place your home on a website giving details of what you're looking for, where and

for how long. You organise the house swap yourself with people in other countries and arrange to swap homes, rent free, for an agreed period. Shop around, as registration costs vary between organisations. Check out Home Link International (www.homelink.org.uk) and Home Base Holidays (www.homebase-hols.com) for starters.

Hostels

Numerous hostels offer cheap, sociable accommodation and in Scotland the standard of facilities is generally very good. The more upmarket hostels have en suites in their dorms, and all manner of luxuries that give them the feel of hotels, if it weren't for the bunk beds.

Hostels nearly always have facilities for self-catering, and, apart from very remote ones, internet access of some kind. Many can arrange activities and tours.

In Highland areas you'll find bothies – simple walkers' hostels and shelters – and in the Shetlands there are *bòds* (characterful but basic shared accommodation).

INDEPENDENT HOSTELS

There are a large number of independent hostels, most with prices around £16 to £25 per person. Facilities vary considerably. Scottish Independent Hostels (www.hostel-scotland.co.uk) is an affiliation of over 100 hostels in Scotland, mostly in the north. You can browse them online or pick up the free *Scottish Independent Hostels* map-guide from tourist offices.

PRACTICALITIES

Newspapers The Aberdeen-based daily newspaper *Press & Journal* covers the Highlands and islands, as does the weekly *Oban Times*. The *Daily Record* is a popular tabloid, while the *Sunday Post* offers up rose-tinted nostalgia.

Radio BBC Radio Scotland (AM 810kHz, FM 92.4-94.7MHz) provides a Scottish point of view.

TV Watch BBC1 Scotland, BBC2 Scotland and STV for Scottish-specific programming. BBC Alba provides Gaelic-language TV.

Smoking In Scotland you can't smoke in any public place with a roof that's at least half enclosed, which means pubs, bus shelters, restaurants and hotels (basically, anywhere you might want to).

Weights & Measures Use the metric system for weights and measures, with the exception of road distances (in miles) and beer (in pints). The pint is 568mL, more than the US version.

SYHA HOSTELS

The **SYHA** (SYHA; ☏01786-891400, www.syha.org.uk; annual membership 26yr & over/25yr & under £15/6, life membership £150) has a network of decent, reasonably priced hostels and produces a free booklet available from SYHA hostels and tourist offices. There are dozens to choose from around the country, ranging from basic walkers' digs to mansions and castles. You've got to be a HI member to stay, but nonmembers can pay a £3 supplement per night that goes towards the £10 membership fee. Prices vary according to the month, but average around £18 to £25 per adult in high season.

Most SYHA hostels close from around mid-October to early March but can be rented out by groups.

Hotels

There are some wonderfully luxurious places, including elegant country-house hotels in fabulous settings, and castles complete with crenellated battlements, grand staircases and the obligatory rows of stag heads. Expect all the perks at these places, often including a gym, a sauna, a pool and first-class service. Even if you're on a budget, it's worth splashing out for a night at one of the classic Highland hotels.

Increasingly hotels use an airline-style pricing system, so it's worth booking well ahead to take advantage of the cheapest rates.

Rental Accommodation

The best place to start looking for this kind of accommodation is the website of VisitScotland (www.visitscotland.com/accommodation), which lists numerous self-catering options all over Scotland. These options also appear in the regional accommodation guides available from tourist offices.

Cottage Guide (www.cottageguide.co.uk) has lots of Scottish cottages to browse online.

Children

Scotland offers a range of child-friendly accommodation and activities suitable for families.

It's worth asking in tourist offices for local family-focused publications. The *List* magazine (available at newsagents and bookshops) has a section on children's activities and events in and around Glasgow and Edinburgh.

The **National Trust for Scotland** (☏0131-458 0200; www.nts.org.uk; annual membership adult/family £57/102) and **Historic Environment Scotland** (HES; ☏0131-668 8999; www.historicenvironment.scot; annual membership adult/family £55/101) organise family-friendly activities at their properties throughout the summer.

Children are generally well received around Scotland, and every area has some child-friendly attractions and B&Bs. Even dryish local museums usually make an effort with an activity sheet or child-focused information panels.

See also Lonely Planet's *Travel with Children*.

Customs Regulations

The UK's withdrawal from the EU on 29 March 2019 renders information in this section liable to change; it's important to check the current regulations before travel.

Travellers arriving in the UK from EU countries don't have to pay tax or duty on goods for personal use, and can bring in as much EU duty-paid alcohol and tobacco as they like. However, if you bring in more than the following, you'll probably be asked some questions:

➡ 800 cigarettes
➡ 1kg of tobacco
➡ 10L of spirits
➡ 90L of wine
➡ 110L of beer

Travellers from outside the EU can bring in the following, duty-free:

→ 200 cigarettes *or* 100 cigarillos *or* 50 cigars *or* 250g of tobacco

→ 16L of beer

→ 4L of non-sparkling wine

→ 1L of spirits *or* 2L of fortified wine or sparkling wine

→ £390 worth of all other goods, including perfume, gifts and souvenirs
Anything over this limit must be declared to customs officers on arrival. Check www.gov.uk/duty-free-goods for further details, and for information on reclaiming VAT on items purchased in the UK by non-EU residents.

Discount Cards

Historic Sites

Membership of Historic Environment Scotland (HES) and/or the National Trust for Scotland (NTS) is worth considering, especially if you're going to be in Scotland for a while. Both are organisations dedicated to the preservation of the environment, and both care for hundreds of spectacular sites. You can join up at any of their properties.

Historic Environment Scotland (HES; ☎0131-668 8999; www. historicenvironment.scot; annual membership adult/ family £55/101) This organisation cares for hundreds of sites of historical importance. An annual membership costs £55/101 per adult/family, and gives free entry to HES sites (half-price entry to sites in England and Wales). Also offers a short-term Explorer Pass – three days out of five for £31, or seven days out of 14 for £42. It can be great value, particularly if you visit both Edinburgh and Stirling castles.

National Trust for Scotland (☎0131-458 0200; www.nts. org.uk; annual membership adult/family £57/102) Looks after hundreds of sites of historical, architectural or environmental importance. An annual membership, costing £57/102 for an adult/family, offers free

access to all NTS and National Trust properties (in the rest of the UK). If you're 25 or under, it's a great deal at only £26.

Hostel Cards

If travelling on a budget, membership of the **Scottish Youth Hostels Association** (SYHA; ☎01786-891400; www. syha.org.uk; annual membership 26yr & over/25yr & under £15/6, life membership £150) is a must.

Senior Cards

Discount cards for those over 60 years are available for **train travel** (www.senior -railcard.co.uk; per year £30).

Student Cards

The most useful card is the International Student Identity Card (www.isic.org), which displays your photo. This gives you discounted entry to many attractions and on many forms of transport.

Electricity

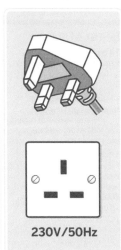

230V/50Hz

Food

For an overview of Scottish cuisine, see the Food & Drink chapter (p289).

Health

→ If you're an EU citizen, a European Health Insurance Card (EHIC) – available from health centres or, in the UK, post offices – covers you for most medical care. An EHIC will not cover you for nonemergencies, or emergency repatriation. The status of EHIC after Brexit (March 2019) is uncertain.

→ Citizens from non-EU countries should find out if there is a reciprocal arrangement for free medical care between their country and the UK.

→ If you do need health insurance, make sure you get a policy that covers you for the worst possible case, such as an accident requiring an emergency flight home.

→ The most painful problems facing visitors to the Highlands and islands are midges.

Ticks & Lyme Disease

Ticks are tiny invertebrates (barely 1mm or 2mm across) that feed on the blood of sheep, deer and, occasionally, humans. They lurk amid vegetation and clamber on as you brush past; then they find a spot of bare flesh and tuck in. Their bites are painless and, for the most part, harmless (they will drop off once full). But a small percentage of ticks are known to transmit Lyme disease, a potentially serious infection.

Ticks occur all over Scotland in woodlands, moorlands and long grass, but mainly in the wetter areas of the western Highlands. They are active mainly between March and October. Tips for avoiding ticks include sticking to paths, wearing long trousers tucked into socks, and using insect repellent. Check yourself (and your children and pets) for ticks after hiking, especially around the hairline, in the navel, groin and armpits, and between the toes, behind the ears and behind the knees. Outdoor shops sell plastic tick-removal tools.

More information: https:// www.mountaineering.scot/ safety-and-skills/health-and -hygiene/ticks.

Insurance

Insurance covers you not only for medical expenses, theft or loss but also for cancellation of, or delays in, any of your travel arrangements.

Lots of bank accounts give their holders automatic travel insurance – check if this is the case for you.

Always read the small print carefully. Some policies specifically exclude 'dangerous activities', such as scuba diving, motorcycling, skiing, mountaineering and even trekking.

There's a variety of policies, and your travel agent can give recommendations. Make sure the policy includes healthcare and medication in the countries you may visit on your way to/from Scotland.

You may prefer a policy that pays doctors or hospitals directly rather than forcing you to pay on the spot and claim the money back later. If you have to claim later, make sure you keep all documentation. Some policies ask you to call back (reverse charges) to a centre in your home country, where an immediate assessment of your problem will be made.

Not all policies cover ambulances, helicopter rescue or emergency flights home. Most policies exclude cover for pre-existing illnesses.

Worldwide travel insurance is available at www. lonelyplanet.com/travel -insurance. You can buy, extend and claim online anytime – even if you're already on the road.

Internet Access

➡ If you're travelling with a laptop, you'll find a wide range of places offering a wi-fi connection. These range from cafes to B&Bs and public spaces.

➡ Wi-fi is often free, but some places (typically, upmarket hotels) charge.

➡ There are increasingly good deals on pay-as-you-go mobile internet from mobile network providers.

➡ If you don't have a laptop or smartphone, the best places to check email and surf the internet are public libraries – nearly all of which have at least a couple of computer terminals, and they are free to use, though there's often a time limit.

➡ Internet cafes also exist in the cities and larger towns and are generally good value, charging approximately £2 to £3 per hour.

➡ Many of the larger tourist offices across the country also have internet access.

Legal Matters

➡ The 1707 Act of Union preserved the Scottish legal system as separate from the law in England and Wales.

➡ Police have the power to detain, for up to six hours, anyone suspected of having committed an offence punishable by imprisonment (including drugs offences).

➡ If you need legal assistance, contact the **Scottish Legal Aid Board** (☑0131-226 7061; www.slab. org.uk; 91 Haymarket Tce).

➡ Possession of cannabis is illegal, with a spoken warning for first offenders with small amounts. Fines and prison sentences apply for repeat offences and larger quantities. Possession of harder drugs is much more serious. Police have the right to search anyone they suspect of possessing drugs.

LGBTIQ+ Travellers

Although many Scots are fairly tolerant of homosexuality, overt displays of affection aren't wise if conducted away from acknowledged 'gay' venues or districts – hostility may be encountered.

Edinburgh and Glasgow have small but flourishing gay scenes. The website www.gayscotland.com and the monthly magazine *Scotsgay* (www.facebook. com/ScotsGayMag) keep gays, lesbians and bisexuals informed about local scenes.

Maps

If you're about to tackle Munros, you'll require maps with far greater detail than the maps supplied by tourist offices. The Ordnance Survey (OS) caters to walkers, with a wide variety of maps at 1:50,000 and 1:25,000 scales. Alternatively, look out for the excellent walkers' maps published by Harveys; they're at scales of 1:40,000 and 1:25,000.

Money

ATMs

ATMs (called cashpoints in Scotland) are widespread and you'll usually find at least one in small towns and villages. You can use Visa, MasterCard, Amex, Cirrus, Plus and Maestro to withdraw cash from ATMs belonging to most banks and building societies in Scotland.

Cash withdrawals from some ATMs may be subject to a small charge, but most are free. If you're not from the UK, your home bank will likely charge you for withdrawing money overseas; it pays to be aware of how much, as it may be much better to withdraw larger amounts less often.

If there's no ATM, it's often possible to get 'cash back' at a hotel or shop in remote areas – ie make a payment by debit card and get some cash back (the cash amount is added to the transaction).

Credit & Debit Cards

Credit and debit cards can be used almost everywhere except for some B&Bs that only accept cash. Make sure bars or restaurants will accept cards before you order, as some don't. The most popular cards are Visa and MasterCard; American Express is only accepted by the major chains, and virtually no one will accept Diners or JCB. Chip-and-PIN is the norm for card transactions; only a few places will accept a signature. Contactless card payments (up to £30) are increasingly accepted.

Moneychangers

Be careful using bureaux de change; they may offer good exchange rates but frequently levy outrageous commissions and fees. The best-value places to change money in the UK tend to be travel agents. A handy tool for finding the best rates is the website http://travel money.moneysavingexpert. com/buy-back.

You'll normally find better rates in London than in Scotland, so do your changing there if you're visiting that city first.

Banks, post offices and some of the larger hotels will change cash and travellers cheques.

Opening Hours

Opening hours may vary throughout the year, especially in rural areas where many places have shorter hours, or close completely, from October or November to March or April.

Banks 9.30am–4pm or 5pm Monday to Friday; some open 9.30am–1pm Saturday

Pubs & Bars 11am–11pm Monday to Thursday, 11am–1am Friday and Saturday, 12.30–11pm Sunday

Shops 9am–5.30pm (or 6pm in larger towns) Monday to Saturday, and often 11am–5pm Sunday

Restaurants Lunch: noon–2.30pm; dinner 6–9pm or 10pm

Post

The UK Post Office (www. postoffice.co.uk) is a reliable service with a network of dedicated mail centres as well as shops with post office facilities. Mail sent within the UK can go either 1st or 2nd class. First-class mail is faster (normally next-day delivery) and slightly more expensive.

Public Holidays

Although bank holidays are general public holidays in the rest of the UK, in Scotland they only apply to banks and some other commercial offices.

Scottish towns normally have four days of public holiday, which they allocate themselves; dates vary from year to year and from town to town. Most places celebrate St Andrew's Day (30 November) as a public holiday.

General public holidays:

New Year 1 & 2 January

Good Friday March or April

Christmas Day 25 December

Boxing Day 26 December

Safe Travel

The Highlands and islands of Scotland is one of the lowest-crime regions in the whole of Europe. The main nuisances are to be found in the natural world – biting insects such as midges (p38), and bad weather.

Telephone

You'll mainly see two types of phone booth in Scotland: one takes money (and doesn't

give change), while the other uses prepaid phonecards and credit cards. Some phones accept both coins and cards. Payphone cards are widely available.

The cheapest way of calling internationally is via the internet, or by buying a discount-call card; you'll see these in newsagents, along with tables of countries and the number of minutes you'll get for your money.

Mobile Phones

The UK uses the GSM 900/1800 network, which covers the rest of Europe, Australia and New Zealand but isn't compatible with the North American GSM 1900 network. Most modern mobiles can function on both networks, but check before you leave home just in case.

Roaming charges within the EU have been eliminated (though charges may reappear when the UK leaves the EU in 2019). Other international roaming charges can be prohibitively high, and you'll probably find it cheaper to get a UK number. This is easily done by buying a SIM card (around £1) and sticking it into your phone. Your phone may be locked to your home network, however, so you'll have to either get it unlocked or buy a cheap phone to use.

Operators offer a variety of packages that include UK calls, messages and data; a month's worth will typically cost around £20.

Though things are improving, coverage in Highland and island areas can be sketchy; don't rely on mobile data.

Pay-as-you-go phones can be recharged online or by buying vouchers from shops.

Phone Codes & Useful Numbers

Dialling the UK Dial your country's international access code then 44 (the UK country code), then the area code (dropping the first 0) followed by the telephone number.

Dialling out of the UK The international access code is 00; dial this, then add the code of the country you wish to dial.

Making a reverse-charge (collect) international call Dial 155 for the operator. It's an expensive option, but not for the caller.

Area codes in Scotland Begin with 01, eg Edinburgh 0131, Wick 01955.

Directory Assistance There are several numbers; 118500 is one.

Mobile phones Codes usually begin with 07.

Free calls Numbers starting with 0800 are free; calls to 0845 numbers are charged at local rates.

Time

Scotland is on UTC/GMT +1 hour during summer daylight-saving time (late March to late October) and UTC/GMT +0 the rest of the year.

Toilets

Public toilets are increasingly uncommon, but you'll still find them in larger towns. They are usually free, but there are some private toilets that charge a small fee.

Tourist Information

The Scottish Tourist Board, known as **VisitScotland** (www.visitscotland.com), deals with enquiries made by post, email and telephone. You can request, online and by phone, for regional brochures to be posted to you, or download them from the website.

Most larger towns have tourist offices ('information centres') that open 9am or 10am to 5pm Monday to Friday, and on weekends in summer. In small places,

particularly in the Highlands, tourist offices only open from Easter to September.

If you want to email a tourist office, it's [insert name of town]@visitscotland.com.

Visas

➡ If you're a citizen of the EEA (European Economic Area) nations or Switzerland, you don't need a visa to enter or work in Britain – you can enter using your national identity card.

➡ Visa regulations are always subject to change, which is especially likely after Britain's exit from the EU on 29 March 2019, so it's essential to check before leaving home.

➡ Currently, if you're a citizen of Australia, Canada, New Zealand, Japan, Israel, the US and several other countries, you can stay for up to six months (no visa required) but are not allowed to work.

➡ Nationals of many countries, including South Africa, will need to obtain a visa: for more info, see www.gov.uk/browse/visas-immigration

➡ The Youth Mobility Scheme, for Australian, Canadian, Japanese, Hong Kong, Monégasque, New Zealand, South Korean and Taiwanese citizens aged 18 to 31, allows working visits of up to two years but must be applied for in advance.

➡ Commonwealth citizens with a UK-born parent may be eligible for a Certificate of Entitlement to the Right of Abode, which entitles them to live and work in the UK.

➡ Commonwealth citizens with a UK-born grandparent could qualify for a UK Ancestry Employment

Certificate, allowing them to work full time for up to five years in the UK.

➡ British immigration authorities have always been tough; dress neatly and carry proof that you have sufficient funds with which to support yourself. A credit card and/or an onward ticket will help.

Volunteering

Various organisations offer volunteering opportunities in Scotland, with conservation, organic-farming and animal-welfare projects to the fore.

Women Travellers

Solo women travellers are likely to feel safe in Scotland.

The contraceptive pill is available only on prescription; however, the 'morning-after' pill (effective against conception for up to 72 hours after unprotected sexual intercourse) is available over the counter at chemists.

Work

Whatever your skills, it's worth registering with a number of temporary employment agencies; there are plenty in the cities.

Low-paid seasonal work is available in the tourist industry, usually in restaurants and pubs.

At the time of research, EU citizens didn't need a work permit, but this may change as a result of Britain's planned exit from the EU on 29 March 2019.

The Youth Mobility scheme allows working visits for some foreign nationals.

Transport

GETTING THERE & AWAY

Flights, tours and rail tickets can be booked online at lonelyplanet.com/bookings.

Entering the Region

Entry to the UK is generally straightforward. However, the UK's withdrawal from the EU on 29 March 2019 means that information on entry and exit requirements is liable to change; it's important to check the current regulations before travel.

Air

There are direct flights to Scottish airports from elsewhere in Britain, lots of European countries, the Middle East, the US and Canada. From elsewhere, you'll probably have to fly into a European or Middle Eastern hub and get a connecting flight to a Scottish airport – London has the most connections. This will often be a cheaper option anyway if flying in from North America.

Airports & Airlines

Scotland has four main international airports: Aberdeen (www.aberdeenairport.com), Edinburgh (www.edinburgh airport.com), Glasgow (www.glasgowairport.com) and Glasgow Prestwick (www.glasgowprestwick.com), with a few short-haul international flights landing at Inverness. London is the main UK gateway for long-haul flights. Sumburgh on Shetland has summer service from Norway.

Land

Bus

Buses are usually the cheapest way to get to Scotland from other parts of the UK.

Megabus (☑0141-352 4444; www.megabus.com) One-way fares from London to Glasgow from as little as £1 if you book well in advance. Has some fully reclinable sleeper services.

National Express (☑0871 781 8181; www.nationalexpress. com) Regular services from London and other cities in England and Wales to Glasgow and Edinburgh.

Scottish Citylink (☑0871 266 3333; www.citylink.co.uk) Daily service between Belfast and Glasgow and Edinburgh via Cairnryan ferry.

Car & Motorcycle

Drivers of EU-registered vehicles will find bringing a car or motorcycle into Scotland fairly easy. Note: this may change following the UK's exit from the EU on 29 March 2019; check the latest situation before travelling.

The vehicle must have registration papers and a nationality plate, and you must have insurance. The

---

CLIMATE CHANGE & TRAVEL

Every form of transport that relies on carbon-based fuel generates CO_2, the main cause of human-induced climate change. Modern travel is dependent on aeroplanes, which might use less fuel per kilometre per person than most cars but travel much greater distances. The altitude at which aircraft emit gases (including CO_2) and particles also contributes to their climate change impact. Many websites offer 'carbon calculators' that allow people to estimate the carbon emissions generated by their journey and, for those who wish to do so, to offset the impact of the greenhouse gases emitted with contributions to portfolios of climate-friendly initiatives throughout the world. Lonely Planet offsets the carbon footprint of all staff and author travel.

DEPARTURE TAX

An Air Passenger Duty, essentially a departure tax, is payable for air travel originating in the UK. It's included in the ticket price. If you have to cancel a flight, you can reclaim it even if the rest of the ticket is nonrefundable.

International Insurance Certificate (Green Card) isn't compulsory, but it's excellent proof that you're covered.

If driving from mainland Europe via the Channel Tunnel or ferry ports, head for London and follow the M25 orbital road to the M1 motorway, then follow the M1 and M6 north.

Train

Travelling to Scotland by train is faster and usually more comfortable than the bus, but more expensive. Taking into account check-in and travel time between city centre and airport, the train is a competitive alternative to air travel from London.

Caledonian Sleeper (www. sleeper.scot) This is an overnight service connecting London Euston with Edinburgh, Glasgow, Stirling, Perth, Dundee, Aberdeen, Fort William and Inverness. There are two departures nightly from Sunday to Friday.

Eurostar (www.eurostar.com) You can travel from Paris or Brussels to London in around two hours on the Eurostar service. From St Pancras, it's a quick and easy change to Kings Cross or Euston for trains to Edinburgh or Glasgow and on to Inverness.

Sea

Car-ferry links between Northern Ireland and Scotland are operated by **Stena Line** (☎08447 70 70 70; www. stenaline.co.uk) and **P&O Ferries** (☎01304-448888; www. poferries.com). Stena Line travels the Belfast–Cairnryan route and P&O Irish Sea the Larne–Cairnryan route.

The prices in the table are a guide only; fares are often less than this.

GETTING AROUND

Air

Most domestic air services are geared to business needs, or are lifelines for remote island communities. Flying is a pricey way to cover relatively short distances, but certainly worth considering if you're short of time and want to visit the Outer Hebrides, Orkney or Shetland.

Bicycle

Scotland is a compact country, and travelling around by bicycle is a perfectly feasible proposition if you have the time. Indeed, for touring the islands a bicycle is both cheaper (for ferry fares) and more suited to their small sizes and leisurely pace of life. For more information, see www.visitscotland. com/see-do/active and the Sustrans pages about the National Cycle Network (www. sustrans.org.uk/scotland/national-cycle-network).

Boat

The Scottish government has introduced a scheme called the Road Equivalent Tariff (RET) on most ferry crossings. This reduces the price of ferry transport to what it would cost to drive the same distance by road, in the hope of attracting more tourists and reducing business costs on the islands. Fares on many crossings have been cut by as much as 60%, and signs are that the scheme has been successful, with visitor numbers well up.

Caledonian MacBrayne (www. calmac.co.uk) Serves the west coast and islands. A comprehensive timetable booklet is available from tourist offices and on the website. There's a summer timetable and one for winter, when services are somewhat reduced. CalMac provides 28 Island Hopscotch tickets giving reduced fares for various combinations of crossings; these are listed on the website and in the CalMac timetable booklet. Bicycles travel free with foot passenger tickets.

Northlink Ferries (www.north linkferries.co.uk) Ferries from Aberdeen and Scrabster (near Thurso) to Orkney; from Orkney to Shetland; and from Aberdeen to Shetland.

Bus

Scotland's Highlands and islands are served by an extensive bus network that covers most of the country. On islands and in remote rural areas, however, services are geared to the needs of locals (getting to school or the shops in the nearest large town) and may not be conveniently timed for visitors.

Scottish Citylink (www.citylink. co.uk) National network of comfy, reliable buses serving main towns. Away from main roads, you'll need to switch to local services.

Stagecoach (www.stagecoach bus.com) Operates local bus routes in many parts of the Highlands.

Shiel Buses (www.shielbuses. co.uk) Runs many services in the west Highlands.

Bus Passes

National Entitlement Card (www.entitlementcard.org.uk) Available to seniors and people with disabilities who are Scottish citizens; allows free bus travel throughout the country. The youth version, for 11- to 26-year-olds, gives discounted travel, and SYHA members receive a 20% discount on Scottish Citylink services. Students do, too, by registering online.

Scottish Citylink Explorer Pass (www.citylink.co.uk/explorerpass.php) Offers unlimited travel on Scottish Citylink (and selected other bus routes) services within Scotland for any three days out of five (£49), any five days out of 10 (£74) or any eight days out of 16 (£99). Also gives discounts on various regional bus services, on Northlink and CalMac ferries, and in SYHA hostels. Can be bought in the UK by both UK and overseas citizens.

Car & Motorcycle

Scotland's roads are generally good and far less busy than in England, making driving more enjoyable.

Motorways (designated 'M') are toll-free dual carriageways, limited mainly to central Scotland. Main roads ('A') are dual or single carriageways and are sometimes clogged with slow-moving trucks or caravans; the A9 from Perth to Inverness is notoriously busy.

Life on the road is more relaxed and interesting on the secondary roads (designated 'B') and minor roads (undesignated), although in the Highlands and islands there's the added hazard of suicidal sheep wandering onto the road (be particularly wary of lambs in spring).

Petrol is more expensive than in countries like America or Australia, but roughly in line with the rest of Western Europe. Prices tend to rise as you get further from the main centres and are more than 10% higher in the Outer Hebrides. In remote areas petrol stations are widely spaced and sometimes closed on Sunday.

Car Hire

Car hire in the UK is competitively priced by European standards, and shopping around online can unearth some great deals, which can drop to as low as £23 per day for an extended hire period. Hit comparison sites like

Kayak to find some of the best prices.

The minimum legal age for driving is 17, but to rent a car, drivers must usually be aged 23 to 65 – outside these limits special conditions or insurance requirements may apply.

If planning to visit the Outer Hebrides or Shetland, it'll often prove cheaper to hire a car on the islands, rather than pay to take a hire car across on the ferry.

Driving Licences

A non-EU licence is valid in the UK for up to 12 months from time of entry into the country. If bringing a car from Europe, make sure you're adequately insured.

Road Rules

The *Highway Code*, widely available in bookshops, and also online and downloadable at www.gov.uk/highway-code, details all UK road regulations. Vehicles drive on the left. Seatbelts are compulsory if fitted; this technically applies to buses too.

The speed limit is 30mph (48km/h) in built-up areas, 60mph (96km/h) on single carriageways and 70mph (112km/h) on dual carriageways.

Give way to your right at roundabouts (traffic already on the roundabout has right of way).

Motorcyclists must wear helmets. They are not compulsory for cyclists.

It is illegal to use a hand-held mobile phone or similar device while driving.

The maximum permitted blood-alcohol level when driving is 50mg/100mL (22mg per 100mL of breath); this is lower than in the rest

of the UK but equivalent to the limit in many other countries.

Tours

There are numerous companies in Scotland offering all kinds of tours, including historical, activity-based and backpacker tours. It's a question of picking the tour that suits your requirements and budget.

Discreet Scotland (☑07989 416990; www.discreetscotland.com) Luxurious private tours in an upmarket 4WD that range from day trips from Edinburgh to full weeks staying in some of Scotland's finest hotels.

Haggis Adventures (☑0131-557 9393; www.haggisadventures.com) Offers fun backpacker-oriented tours, with longer options taking in the Outer Hebrides or Orkney.

Heart of Scotland Tours (☑0131-228 2888; www.heartofscotlandtours.co.uk) Specialises in mini-coach day tours of central Scotland and the Highlands, departing from Edinburgh.

Hebridean Island Cruises (☑01756-704704; www.hebridean.co.uk) Luxury small-boat cruises around the west coast, Outer Hebrides and northern islands.

Rabbie's (☑0131-226 3133; www.rabbies.com) One- to five-day tours of the Highlands in 16-seat minibuses with professional driver/guide.

Timberbush Tours (☑0131-226 6066; www.timberbush-tours.co.uk) Comfortable small-group minibus tours around Scotland, with Glasgow and Edinburgh departures.

FERRIES TO/FROM NORTHERN IRELAND

CROSSING	DURATION	FREQUENCY	FARE PASSENGER/CAR (£)
Belfast–Cairnryan	2¼hr	5-6 daily	from 24/119
Larne–Cairnryan	2hr	6-8 daily	from 27/129

SINGLE TRACK ROADS

In many country areas, especially in the Highlands and islands, you will find single-track roads that are only wide enough for one vehicle. Passing places (usually marked with a white diamond sign, or a black-and-white striped pole) are used to allow oncoming traffic to get by. Remember that passing places are also for overtaking – you must pull over to let faster vehicles pass. It's illegal to park in passing places.

Wilderness Scotland
(☎01479-420020; www.
wildernessscotland.com)
Provides a range of outdoor
adventure holidays, including
guided walking, mountain biking
and canoeing trips.

Train

Scotland's train network
extends to all major cities
and towns, but the railway
map has a lot of large, blank
areas in the Highlands where
you'll need to switch to road
transport. The West Highland
line from Glasgow to Fort
William and Mallaig, and the
Inverness to Kyle of Lochalsh
line, offer two of the world's
most scenic rail journeys.

National Rail Enquiry Service
(www.nationalrail.co.uk) Lists
timetables and fares for all trains
in Britain.

ScotRail (www.scotrail.co.uk)
Operates most train services
in Scotland; its website has
downloadable timetables.

Costs & Reservations

Train travel is more expensive
than bus, but usually more
comfortable.

Reservations are recom-
mended for intercity trips,
especially on Fridays and
public holidays. For shorter
journeys, just buy a ticket at
the station before you go. On
certain routes, including the
Glasgow–Edinburgh express,
and in places where there's
no ticket office at the station, you can buy tickets on
the train.

Children under five travel
free; those five to 15 years
usually pay half-fare.

Bikes are carried free on
all ScotRail trains but space
is sometimes limited. Bike
reservations are compul-
sory on certain train routes,
including the Glasgow–
Oban–Fort William–Mallaig
line and the Inverness–Kyle
of Lochalsh line; they are
recommended on many
others. You can make reservations for your bicycle from
eight weeks to two hours in
advance at main train stations, or when booking tickets by phone or online.

There's a bewilderingly
complex labyrinth of ticket
types. In general, the further
ahead you can book, the
cheaper your ticket will be.

Advance Purchase Book by 6pm
on the day before travel; cheaper
than Anytime tickets.

Anytime Buy any time and travel
any time, with no restrictions.

Off Peak There are time restrictions (you're not usually allowed
to travel on a train that leaves
before 9.15am); relatively cheap.

It's always worth checking
the ScotRail website for current family or senior offers.

Discount Cards

Discount railcards are available for people aged 60 and
over, for people aged 16 to
25 (or mature full-time students), for two over-16s travelling together, and for those
with a disability.

The Senior Railcard, 16-25
Railcard, Two Together Railcard and Disabled Persons
Railcard are each valid for
one year and give one-third
off most train fares in Scotland, England and Wales.

You'll find they pay for
themselves pretty quickly
if you plan to take a couple
of long-distance journeys or
a handful of short-distance
ones. Fill in an application
at any major train station.
You'll need proof of age
(birth certificate, passport
or driving licence) for
the Young Persons and
Senior Railcards (proof of
enrolment for mature-age
students) and proof of
entitlement for the Disabled
Persons Railcard. You'll need
a passport photo for all of
them. You can also buy railcards online, but you'll need
a UK address to have them
sent to.

Train Passes

ScotRail (www.scotrail.
co.uk) has a range of
good-value passes for train
travel. You can buy them
online, by phone or at train
stations throughout Britain.
Note that Travelpass and
Rover tickets are not valid
for travel on certain (eg
commuter) services before
9.15am weekdays.

Spirit of Scotland Travelpass
Gives unlimited travel on all
Scottish train services (with
some restrictions), all CalMac
ferry services and on certain
Scottish Citylink coach services
(on routes not covered by rail).
It's available for four days travel
out of eight (£139) or eight days
out of 15 (£179).

Highland Rover Allows unlimited
train travel from Glasgow to
Oban, Fort William and Mallaig,
and from Inverness to Kyle of
Lochalsh, Aviemore, Aberdeen
and Thurso. It also gives free
travel on the Oban/Fort William–
Inverness bus, on the Oban–Mull
and Mallaig–Skye ferries, and
on buses on Mull and Skye. It's
valid for four days travel out of
eight (£85).

Glossary

bag – reach the top of (as in to 'bag a couple of peaks' or 'Munro bagging')

bailey – the space enclosed by castle walls

birlinn – Hebridean galley

blackhouse – low-walled stone cottage with thatch or turf roof and earth floors; shared by both humans and cattle and typical of the Outer Hebrides until the early 20th century

böd – once a simple trading booth used by fishing communities, today it refers to basic accommodation for walkers etc

bothy – hut or mountain shelter

brae – hill

broch – defensive tower

burgh – town

burn – stream

cairn – pile of stones to mark path or junction; also peak

camanachd – Gaelic for *shinty*

ceilidh (*kay*-li) – evening of traditional Scottish entertainment including music, song and dance

Celtic high cross – a large, elaborately carved stone cross decorated with biblical scenes and Celtic interlace designs dating from the 8th to 10th centuries

chippy – fish-and-chip shop

Clearances – eviction of Highland farmers from their land by *lairds* wanting to use it for grazing sheep

Clootie dumpling – rich steamed pudding filled with currants and raisins

close – entrance to an alley

corrie – circular hollow on a hillside

craic – lively conversation

craig – exposed rock

crannog – an artificial island in a *loch* built for defensive purposes

crofting – smallholding in marginal agricultural areas following the Clearances

Cullen skink – soup made with smoked haddock, potato, onion and milk

dene – valley

dirk – dagger

dram – a measure of whisky

firth – estuary

gloup – natural arch

Hogmanay – Scottish celebration of New Year's Eve

howff – pub or shelter

HS – Historic Scotland

kyle – narrow sea channel

laird – estate owner

linn – waterfall

loch – lake

lochan – small *loch*

machair – grass- and wildflower-covered dunes

makar – maker of verses

Mercat Cross – a symbol of the trading rights of a market town or village, usually found in the centre of town and usually a focal point for the community

motte – early Norman fortification consisting of a raised, flattened mound with a keep on top; when attached to a *bailey* it is known as a motte-and-bailey

Munro – mountain of 3000ft (914m) or higher

Munro bagger – a hill walker who tries to climb all the *Munros* in Scotland

NNR – National Nature Reserve, managed by the *SNH*

NTS – National Trust for Scotland

nyvaig – Hebridean galley

OS – Ordnance Survey

Picts – early inhabitants of north and east Scotland (from Latin *pictus*, or 'painted', after their body paint decorations)

provost – mayor

RIB – rigid inflatable boat

rood – an old Scots word for a cross

RSPB – Royal Society for the Protection of Birds

Sassenach – from Gaelic 'Sasannach': anyone who is not a Highlander (including Lowland Scots)

shinty – fast and physical ball-and-stick sport similar to Ireland's hurling

SMC – Scottish Mountaineering Club

SNH – Scottish Natural Heritage, a government organisation directly responsible for safeguarding and improving Scotland's natural heritage

sporran – purse worn around waist with the kilt

SSSI – Site of Special Scientific Interest

SYHA – Scottish Youth Hostel Association

wynd – lane

Behind the Scenes

SEND US YOUR FEEDBACK

We love to hear from travellers – your comments keep us on our toes and help make our books better. Our well-travelled team reads every word on what you loved or loathed about this book. Although we cannot reply individually to your submissions, we always guarantee that your feedback goes straight to the appropriate authors, in time for the next edition. Each person who sends us information is thanked in the next edition – the most useful submissions are rewarded with a selection of digital PDF chapters.

Visit **lonelyplanet.com/contact** to submit your updates and suggestions or to ask for help. Our award-winning website also features inspirational travel stories, news and discussions.

Note: We may edit, reproduce and incorporate your comments in Lonely Planet products such as guidebooks, websites and digital products, so let us know if you don't want your comments reproduced or your name acknowledged. For a copy of our privacy policy visit lonelyplanet.com/privacy.

WRITER THANKS

Neil Wilson

Thanks to the friendly and helpful tourist office staff all over the Highlands; to Steven Fallon, Keith Jeffrey, Fiona Garven, Derek McCrindle, Brendan Bolland, Jenny Neil, Tom and Christine Duffin, Steve Hall, Elaine Simpson, Peter Fallon and Duncan Pepper; and, as ever, to Carol Downie. Thanks also to James Smart and the editorial team at Lonely Planet.

Andy Symington

It's always a huge pleasure to enjoy the very generous hospitality of Jenny Neil and Brendan Bolland, and to work with Neil Wilson, Cliff Wilkinson and the excellent LP team. Numerous other people have been very generous with time and information. I'd particularly like to thank Robin Mitchell, Maggie Maguire, Graeme Campbell, Jen Stewart and the staff at many tourist information offices, especially Judith and Janice at Bowmore, Sheona at John O'Groats, Susan at Callander and Neil at Kirkwall.

ACKNOWLEDGEMENTS

Climate map data adapted from Peel MC, Finlayson BL & McMahon TA (2007) 'Updated World Map of the Köppen-Geiger Climate Classification', Hydrology and Earth System Sciences, 11, 163344.

Cover photograph: Tobermory, Mull; Kathy Collins/Getty ©

THIS BOOK

This 4th edition of Lonely Planet's *Scotland's Highlands & Islands* guidebook was curated by Neil Wilson, and was researched and written by Neil and Andy Symington. Neil and Andy also wrote the previous two editions. This guidebook was produced by the following:

Destination Editor Clifton Wilkinson

Senior Product Editor Genna Patterson

Product Editor Will Allen

Senior Cartographer Mark Griffiths

Book Designer Clara Monitto

Assisting Editors Michelle Bennett, Nigel Chin, Victoria Harrison, Gabrielle Stefanos

Cover Researcher Naomi Parker

Thanks to Sandrine Dugast, C Raitt, Lyahna Spencer, Paul G Stewart, Bob Sweet

Index

Map Legend

Sights
- Beach
- Bird Sanctuary
- Buddhist
- Castle/Palace
- Christian
- Confucian
- Hindu
- Islamic
- Jain
- Jewish
- Monument
- Museum/Gallery/Historic Building
- Ruin
- Shinto
- Sikh
- Taoist
- Winery/Vineyard
- Zoo/Wildlife Sanctuary
- Other Sight

Activities, Courses & Tours
- Bodysurfing
- Diving
- Canoeing/Kayaking
- Course/Tour
- Sento Hot Baths/Onsen
- Skiing
- Snorkelling
- Surfing
- Swimming/Pool
- Walking
- Windsurfing
- Other Activity

Sleeping
- Sleeping
- Camping
- Hut/Shelter

Eating
- Eating

Drinking & Nightlife
- Drinking & Nightlife
- Cafe

Entertainment
- Entertainment

Shopping
- Shopping

Information
- Bank
- Embassy/Consulate
- Hospital/Medical
- Internet
- Police
- Post Office
- Telephone
- Toilet
- Tourist Information
- Other Information

Geographic
- Beach
- Gate
- Hut/Shelter
- Lighthouse
- Lookout
- Mountain/Volcano
- Oasis
- Park
- Pass
- Picnic Area
- Waterfall

Population
- Capital (National)
- Capital (State/Province)
- City/Large Town
- Town/Village

Transport
- Airport
- Border crossing
- Bus
- Cable car/Funicular
- Cycling
- Ferry
- Metro station
- Monorail
- Parking
- Petrol station
- S-Bahn/Subway station
- Taxi
- T-bane/Tunnelbana station
- Train station/Railway
- Tram
- Tube station
- U-Bahn/Underground station
- Other Transport

Routes
- Tollway
- Freeway
- Primary
- Secondary
- Tertiary
- Lane
- Unsealed road
- Road under construction
- Plaza/Mall
- Steps
- Tunnel
- Pedestrian overpass
- Walking Tour
- Walking Tour detour
- Path/Walking Trail

Boundaries
- International
- State/Province
- Disputed
- Regional/Suburb
- Marine Park
- Cliff
- Wall

Hydrography
- River, Creek
- Intermittent River
- Canal
- Water
- Dry/Salt/Intermittent Lake
- Reef

Areas
- Airport/Runway
- Beach/Desert
- Cemetery (Christian)
- Cemetery (Other)
- Glacier
- Mudflat
- Park/Forest
- Sight (Building)
- Sportsground
- Swamp/Mangrove

Note: Not all symbols displayed above appear on the maps in this book

OUR STORY

A beat-up old car, a few dollars in the pocket and a sense of adventure. In 1972 that's all Tony and Maureen Wheeler needed for the trip of a lifetime – across Europe and Asia overland to Australia. It took several months, and at the end – broke but inspired – they sat at their kitchen table writing and stapling together their first travel guide, *Across Asia on the Cheap*. Within a week they'd sold 1500 copies. Lonely Planet was born.

Today, Lonely Planet has offices in Franklin, London, Melbourne, Oakland, Dublin, Beijing and Delhi, with more than 600 staff and writers. We share Tony's belief that 'a great guidebook should do three things: inform, educate and amuse'.

OUR WRITERS

Neil Wilson

Neil was born in Scotland and has lived there most of his life. Based in Perthshire, he has been a full-time writer since 1988, working on more than 80 guidebooks for various publishers, including the Lonely Planet guides to Scotland, England, Ireland and Prague. An outdoors enthusiast since childhood, Neil is an active hill-walker, mountain-biker, sailor, snowboarder, fly-fisher and rock-climber, and has climbed and tramped in four continents, including ascents of Jebel Toubkal in Morocco, Mount Kinabalu in Borneo, the Old Man of Hoy in Scotland's Orkney Islands and the Regular Northwest Face of Half Dome in California's Yosemite Valley.

Andy Symington

Andy has written or worked on over a hundred books and other updates for Lonely Planet (especially in Europe and Latin America) and other publishing companies, and has published articles on numerous subjects for a variety of newspapers, magazines, and websites. He part-owns and operates a rock bar, has written a novel and is currently working on several fiction and non-fiction writing projects. Originally from Australia, Andy moved to northern Spain many years ago.

31901064552005

Published by Lonely Planet Global Limited
CRN 554153
4th edition – February 2019
ISBN 978 1 78657 286 8
© Lonely Planet 2019   Photographs © as indicated 2019
10 9 8 7 6 5 4 3 2 1
Printed in China